MW01284866

God's Empire

In *God's Empire*, Hilary M. Carey charts Britain's nineteenth-century transformation from Protestant nation to free Christian empire through the history of the colonial missionary movement. This wide-ranging reassessment of the religious character of the second British empire provides a clear account of the promotional strategies of the major churches and church parties which worked to plant settler Christianity in British domains. Based on extensive use of original archival and rare published sources, the author explores major debates such as the relationship between religion and colonisation, Church–state relations, Irish Catholics in the empire, the impact of the Scottish Disruption on colonial Presbyterianism, and competition between Evangelicals and other Anglicans in the colonies, and between British and American strands of Methodism in British North America.

HILARY M. CAREY is a professor of History at the University of Newcastle, New South Wales, and Life Fellow of Clare College, University of Cambridge. Her most recent book is the edited collection, *Empires of Religion* (2008).

God's Empire

Religion and Colonialism in the
British World, c. 1801–1908

Hilary M. Carey

CAMBRIDGE
UNIVERSITY PRESS

CAMBRIDGE UNIVERSITY PRESS
Cambridge, New York, Melbourne, Madrid, Cape Town, Singapore,
São Paulo, Delhi, Dubai, Tokyo, Mexico City

Cambridge University Press
The Edinburgh Building, Cambridge CB2 8RU, UK

Published in the United States of America by Cambridge University Press,
New York

www.cambridge.org
Information on this title: www.cambridge.org/9780521194105

First published 2011

Printed in the United Kingdom at the University Press, Cambridge

A catalogue record for this publication is available from the British Library

Library of Congress Cataloguing in Publication data
Carey, Hilary M. (Hilary Mary), 1957–
  God's Empire : Religion and Colonialism in the British World,
  c. 1801–1908 / Hilary M. Carey.
    p.   cm
  Includes bibliographical references and index.
  ISBN 978-0-521-19410-5
  1. Great Britain – Church history – 19th century.   I. Title.
  BR759.C365 2010
  270.09171′24109034–dc22
  2010045718

ISBN 978-0-521-19410-5 Hardback

In loving memory of
Guy Alexander Beange 1923–2004

Contents

Figure

Maps

Tables

Preface and acknowledgments

While I was conducting research for this book, it was reported that students at one of the Cambridge colleges had been obliged to abandon the chosen theme for their May Ball, which was 'Empire'. Protestors who set up a Facebook site objected that the British empire continued to be a 'highly sensitive subject' for many people and that it was inappropriate to use it as the theme for a light-hearted event.

As heirs to the legacy of the British empire, British prime ministers have been divided on the need to give an account of their moral stewardship. In 2007, Tony Blair apologised on the 200th anniversary of the abolition of the Atlantic slave trade; others said the time for apologies was past.[1] In the former colonies, there is also a mixed picture. While former Prime Minister John Howard refused to make any apology to the Australian Aborigines on the ground that his administration had played no role in their original colonisation and dispossession, his successor made an official apology to the 'stolen generations' one of his first acts on coming to power. Along with church leaders of many denominations, Pope Benedict XVI would appear to side with the apologisers, and, in May 2007, reflecting on his visit to Brazil, he lamented the injustice that had often accompanied Christian missions.

So why does the mere idea of empire now attract division when, a little over a hundred years ago, imperial church gatherings, such as the Pan-Anglican Congress of 1908 (discussed in the final chapter) captivated the London metropole?

This book sets out to answer this question from a particular point of view – that of the colonial missionary movement. It examines a set of ideas that rose and fell with the mass flow of people from Great Britain and Ireland to colonies in British North America, Australia, New Zealand and southern Africa in the nineteenth century. It concerns the institutions which were created by the churches to support the diaspora, including the colonial committees, colonial missionary societies,

---

[1] P. Brendon, 'A Moral Audit of the British Empire', *History Today*, 57 (2007), p. 44.

missionary colleges, missionary periodicals, and memoirs published by colonial clergy in their retirement. It was a large movement, even if it was not so large as either the foreign missionary movement, or those moral and humanitarian campaigns, including anti-slavery, temperance and labour reform, which also engaged the British churches at about the same time. Colonial missions were conservative: they helped to sustain bonds of allegiance and unite them in what they perceived to be a great spiritual and moral enterprise. However, they also helped to perpetuate the old animosities between Protestant and Catholic, established and Free Church, liberal and conservative, that had characterised churches in Britain.

Colonial churches therefore laboured under a double burden. They were central signifiers of older religious nationalisms, sectarianism and ethnicities, even as these things were breaking down under the multiple impacts of constitutional reform, emigration, colonisation and nation-building. At the same time, they were required to nurture the more tolerant, liberal and democratic values, which included the absence of an established Church and hereditary privilege, which would eventually be seen as hallmarks of the new Britains of the second British empire. Indeed, if they were to survive and meet the needs of new nations, rather than their home congregations in England, Scotland, Ireland and Wales, colonial missions had to sow the seeds of national churches in Australia, Canada, New Zealand, South Africa and other former settler colonies.

Each church met this challenge within different spiritual and rhetorical strategies: some by strengthening the union of the British or Anglo-Saxon race, others by celebrating their escape from it, some by denouncing the colonial enterprise, others by colluding with it. Assisted by generous public and private funding, the solutions they devised gave the religious character to what some liked to call 'Greater Britain' and which these days we tend to call the 'British world'. By the end of the nineteenth century, with the critical exception of South Africa, the dominions that made up the British world formed the loyal, white, Christian counterpart to the former colonies of settlement that had once rejected the bond with Britain – the United States. The churches were essential to the creation of a Christian consensus which supported the expansion of the British world through the planting of religious institutions in every conceivable corner of the empire.

The structure of this book generally follows a chronological trajectory though there are many thematic meanderings along the way. The first section begins by defining some terms and providing a survey of the major events which impacted on the religious affairs of the colonies in the nineteenth century. The second section, on colonial missions, is divided between Anglicans, Catholics, Evangelical Anglicans, Nonconformists and Presbyterians, and gives an account of all the major colonial missionary societies: the (Anglican) Society for the Propagation of the Gospel (SPG), the (Catholic) Association for the Propagation of the Faith (APF), the (Evangelical Anglican) Colonial and Continental Missionary Society (CCMS), the Wesleyan Methodist Missionary Society (WMMS), the (Congregationalist) Colonial Church Society (CCS) and the Colonial Schemes of the Free and established Church of Scotland. Since, apart from the SPG, most of these societies have not had the benefit of their own individual scholarly histories, this has required quite a lot of narrative compression of the printed and archival sources. It also led to some chronological overlap, but it did seem to make the best sense to follow this arrangement so I stuck with it. The third section concerns the colonial clergy – or at least their training in the two colleges that were specifically set up for this purpose in Ireland and England. There were others in the colonies, as well as the Irish College in Rome, which performed similar work; however, I have had less to say about them. The final section takes the colonial missionary movement to the promised lands of colonial settlement and looks at religious schemes of colonisation, especially those to New Zealand, and the controversy aroused by Edward Gibbon Wakefield and his theory of systematic colonisation. It concludes with the Britannia or Barr colony, which was established in Saskatchewan during the last great imperial land boom in the Canadian wheat lands of the northwest.

I would like to acknowledge a number of intellectual and institutional debts that I have incurred while writing this book. The original idea for *God's Empire* germinated while I was writing a chapter for *Australia's Empire*, the companion volume to the *Oxford History of the British Empire*, edited by Deryck Schreuder and Stuart Ward. At this time, I was in Dublin where I was serving a term as Keith Cameron Professor of Australian History at University College Dublin. Some of the ideas which find their way expanded into this volume began with discussions at the conference I organised with Hugh McLeod in Dublin in 2006.[2] It is also a book written from the perspective of Newcastle, the second city of New South Wales, where I have worked since 1991. In a multicultural and post-colonial nation like Australia, Newcastle's Victorian city centre and the cultural resilience of its former settler churches has become something of a rarity. While successive waves of

[2] H. M. Carey, ed., *Empires of Religion*, Cambridge Imperial and Post-Colonial Studies Series (Basingstoke, 2008).

new arrivals from around the globe have changed other imperial cities beyond recognition, the overall religious mix in Newcastle continues to preserve something of the character of its founding British churches. I have found it a good place to reflect on the complexities of the post-colonial world, in which cities, nations, churches and their people have been energetic in reinventing themselves and turning their backs on the imperial past.

Research for this book was funded from 2005 to 2007 by a Discovery Project grant from the Australian Research Council and aided by research leave from the University of Newcastle. Dr Troy Duncan provided exemplary research assistance while busy with his own biography of the seventh Anglican bishop of Newcastle, Francis de Witt Batty. I am grateful to Clare Hall Cambridge and the York Centre for Medieval Studies for accommodating me at various stages during the writing of this book, and to librarians and archivists in the British Library, Cambridge University Library, the Royal Commonwealth Library, the Dublin Diocesan Archives, the National Library of Ireland, the National Library of Scotland, the National Archives of Scotland, Lambeth Palace Library, the London Guildhall Library, Rhodes House Library Oxford, the Borthwick Institute York, Auckland City Library, Canterbury City Library New Zealand, the State Library of New South Wales and the Tasmanian State Archives, for their assistance. While I claim responsibility for all blemishes that remain, I feel especially indebted to Colin Barr and David Hilliard for sharing their knowledge of imperial religious history with me and rescuing me from innumerable blunders of fact and interpretation. For reading drafts, answering queries and providing me with many insights that had escaped my attention, I also thank Bernard Carey, John Gascoigne, Edward James, Stuart Piggin and Deryck Schreuder.

My final debt, one I cannot repay, is to my father, Guy Alexander Beange, who passed away just when I was getting started on this book. Although he never showed the slightest interest in his family history, I like to think he would have enjoyed reading about the background to the decision by his ancestor, Alexander Beange, who chose to leave the family farm in Aberdeen in 1860 and try his luck in the province pioneered by Free Church settlers in the south island of New Zealand.

Hilary M. Carey
University of Newcastle, NSW

Abbreviations

Annals	*Annals of the Propagation of the Faith*
APF	Association for the Propagation of the Faith (Oeuvre de la propagation de la foi)
CCCS	Colonial and Continental Church Society
CCS	Colonial Church Society
CMS	Church Missionary Society
COS CC	Church of Scotland Colonial Committee
DDA	Dublin Diocesan Archives
FCOS CC	Free Church of Scotland Colonial Committee
LMS	London Missionary Society
NGK	Dutch Reformed Church
NSS	Newfoundland School Society
SPCK	Society for Promoting Christian Knowledge
SPG	Society for the Propagation of the Gospel
SSPCK	Society in Scotland for Propagating Christian Knowledge
WMMS	Wesleyan Methodist Missionary Society

Maps

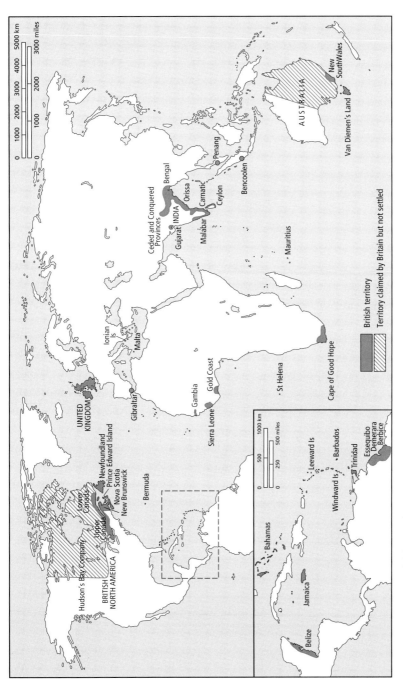

Map 1.1 British empire, 1815

5000 km
3000 miles

0 1000 2000 3000 4000

0 1000 2000 3000

British territory

Territory claimed by Britain but not settled

UNITED KINGDOM

Ionian Is

Malta

Gibraltar

Newfoundland
Prince Edward Island
Nova Scotia
New Brunswick

Lower Canada
Upper Canada

Hudson's Bay Company

BRITISH NORTH AMERICA

Bermuda

Gambia

Sierra Leone

Gold Coast

St Helena

Cape of Good Hope

Ceded and Conquered Provinces

Gujarat   INDIA

Bengal

Orissa

Carnatic

Malabar

Ceylon

Mauritius

Penang

Bencoolen

AUSTRALIA

New South Wales

Van Diemen's Land

1000 km

0 500

0 250 500 miles

Bahamas

Jamaica

Belize

Leeward Is

Windward Is   • Barbados

Trinidad

Essequibo
Demerara
Berbice

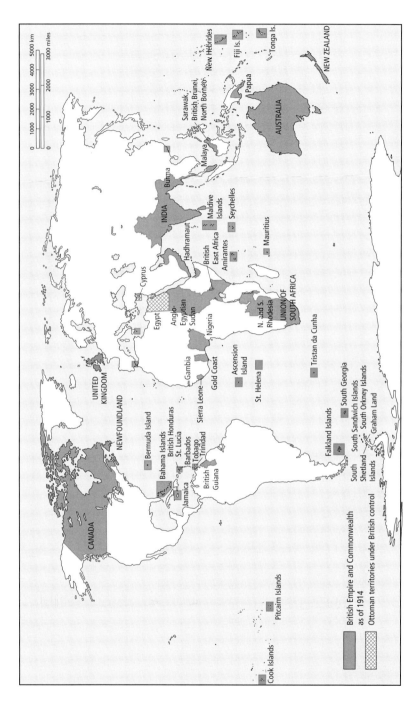

Map 1.2 British empire, 1914

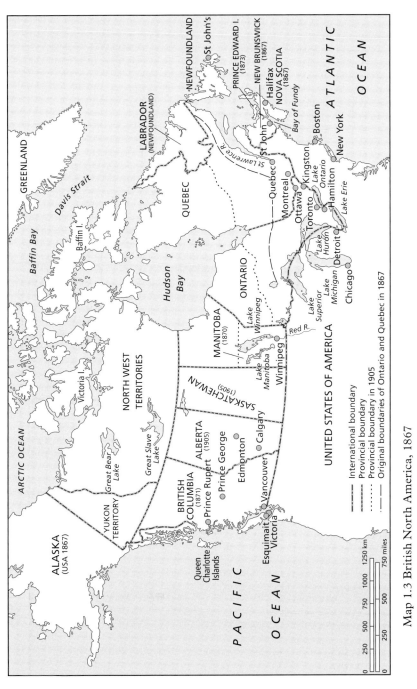

Map 1.3 British North America, 1867

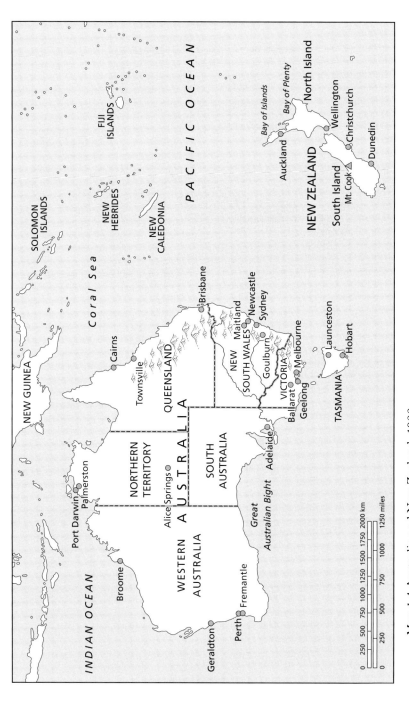

Map 1.4 Australia and New Zealand, 1900

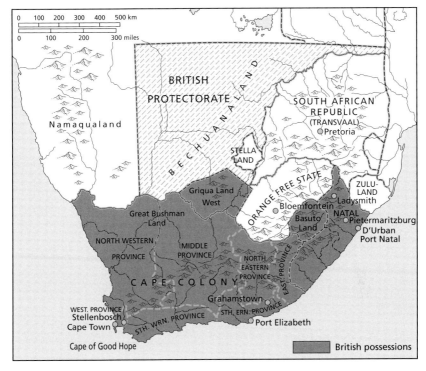

Map 1.5 South Africa, showing British possessions, July 1885

Part I

God's empire

1   Colonialism, colonisation and Greater Britain

Greater Britain – the English-speaking settler colonies of the British empire which we are more likely now to refer to as the British world – was an idea as much as a set of territories.[1] For the free Christian churches of the peoples of Great Britain and Ireland, it was also a mission field. This is a novel idea and one which I hope to argue throughout the course of this book. Chapter 1 begins by examining the idea of Greater Britain, first as a concept in the writing of Charles Wentworth Dilke (1843–1911), and then as it was taken up by the churches who adopted the term as their own in the last decades of the nineteenth century. It also introduces topics raised in subsequent chapters which examine the arrangements and organisations that were marshalled across the empire in order to provide religious services for colonists. In subsequent chapters, this book considers the development of missions to British settlers, including the colonial missionary societies (Chapters 3 to 7), missionary training colleges for colonial clergy (Chapters 8 to 10), church emigration societies (Chapter 10), and Christian colonisation (Chapters 11 and 12). Together, these provisions for the colonial churches helped shape the powerful, shared sense of British identity that suffused the British world and to which Dilke was able to give a name.

In 1897, the English Baptist pastor and writer, John Clifford (1836–1923), completed a tour of Australia, New Zealand and Canada, during which he was swept up in the elaborate colonial celebrations for the Queen's diamond jubilee.[2] Experiencing at close hand the wave of colonial devotion to the Queen, he confidently predicted a great coming federation of Greater Britain, which would be made up of the United Kingdom of Great Britain and Ireland, the Dominion of Canada and Newfoundland,

---

[1] For settler loyalism and the 'imagined British world', see C. Bridge and K. Fedorowich, eds., *The British World: Diaspora, Culture and Identity* (London, 2003); S. Ward, *Australia and the British Embrace: The Demise of the Imperial Ideal* (Melbourne, 2001); P. H. Buckner and R. D. Francis, eds., *Rediscovering the British World* (Calgary, Alberta, 2005).

[2] J. Clifford, *God's Greater Britain. Letters and Addresses* (London, 1899).

United Australasia, United South Africa and United Hindustan.[3] To his British Nonconformist readers, Clifford was delighted to report the extent to which the colonists had successfully cast off the burden of the 'Romanising Anglican Establishment', and had extended Christ's kingdom by democratic and social reforms.[4] An admirer of Kipling (whose verse he liked to quote), Clifford preached fervently about the prospects for even greater unity ahead: the whole world was becoming one through the redeeming power of Jesus Christ in the British empire. His published letters give us some idea of the power of his preaching on this theme:

> One insistent Voice reaches us at home; let us heed it! Go preach the Gospel to every Englander, and persuade him to accept it before he leaves for the new worlds of Africa, or India, of Canada or the Southern Seas, so that wherever he goes he may carry with him the saving energies of the Redeemer.[5]

At one level, Clifford's enraptured sermon offers transparent and enthusiastic endorsement for British, and indeed for specifically English, imperialism. However, religious rhetoric needs to be carefully deconstructed, and it must be emphasised that Clifford's enthusiasm was reserved for a religious rather than a political empire, though clearly he saw no real conflict between the two.

In the late nineteenth century, Nonconformists such as Clifford were among the many enthusiastic advocates of the cultural promise of the English-speaking lands of the British empire. For all the churches, the empire created opportunities for the construction of transnational spiritual networks that aimed to transcend the cultural constraints and legal proscriptions of the past. Like Clifford, Anglicans, Catholics and other Nonconformists were keen to take advantage of the empire to extend the geographical and spiritual boundaries of their churches. John Wolffe has suggested that religious leaders expressed this awareness of the British world through events such as the Lambeth Conferences, which called Anglican bishops from throughout the world to assemble in London every ten years beginning in 1867, as well as travel by church delegations.[6] At the close of the century, many Protestant churches held their own worldwide meetings in Britain, which drew delegates from Australasia, Canada, Asia, America and Africa, and encouraged similar aspirations.[7] For Catholics, the nineteenth International Eucharistic

---

[3] *Ibid.*, p. 22.   [4] *Ibid.*, p. 144.   [5] *Ibid.*, p. 167.

[6] J. Wolffe, *God and Greater Britain: Religion and National Life in Britain and Ireland, 1843–1945* (London, 1994), p. 220. For Nonconformist enthusiasm for empire, see J. Cox, 'Were Victorian Nonconformists the Worst Imperialists of All?', *Victorian Studies*, 46 (2004), pp. 243–55.

[7] E.g. the 'Pan-Presbyterian' Councils held in 1888, 1892, 1896 and 1901; Congregationalists met in London (1891), Boston (1899), Edinburgh (1908), Boston (1920)

Congress, held in London in 1908, was an opportunity to celebrate the imperial credentials of British Catholics.[8]

The common Christianity which suffused Greater Britain was, for the most part, assumed to be a 'generic' Protestantism, which encompassed imperial loyalty and the celebration of uniquely British (or Anglo-Saxon) virtues of freedom, tolerance, justice and civic duty.[9] In this modified form, it continued earlier visions of Britain as a Protestant nation heroically resisting the Catholic menace of Spain, France and Ireland, which Linda Colley, in an influential thesis, has suggested was integral to the British state forged in the eighteenth century.[10] The Evangelical Anglicans who founded the Colonial and Continental Church Society, considered in Chapter 5, were so entranced by the idea of Greater Britain that they incorporated the term in the title of their journal, the *Greater Britain Messenger*. In 1876, the following poem was recited at the close of a sermon delivered on behalf of the Colonial and Continental Church Society, in the hope that it would inspire listeners to respond to the religious needs of colonists:

> Rest not! but heed thy brother's cry of anguish
> For 'living bread' across the stormy sea.
> Shall famished souls in 'Greater Britain' languish
> When God has sent His messengers to thee?
>
> Haste! where as yet no heaven-pointing tower
> Reminds the settler of a better world;
> Go! teach his sons the source of England's power,
> The 'Spirit's sword', the Gospel-flag unfurl'd![11]

Though directed at an Evangelical Anglican rather than a Baptist audience, this poem sums up sentiments that are similar to those expressed

---

and Bournemouth (1930). The equivalent meetings of the Church of England included the Lambeth Conferences of bishops (from 1867), the Missionary Conferences of the Anglican Communion (1894) and, subsequently, the Pan-Anglican Conference (1908); the Methodists gathered in 1881 (London), 1891 (Washington) and 1901 (London); the first Baptist World Congress was held in London in 1905.

[8] *New York Times*, 6 September 1908.

[9] C. Hall, K. McClelland and J. Rendall, *Defining the Victorian Nation: Class, Race, Gender and the British Reform Act of 1867* (Cambridge, 2000), p. 47. See also H. McLeod, 'Protestantism and British National Identity, 1815–1945', in *Religion and Nationalism in Europe and Asia*, ed. P. Van Der Veer (Princeton, NJ, 1999), pp. 44–70.

[10] L. Colley, *Britons: Forging the Nation, 1770–1837* (New Haven, CT, 1992), p. 3. For discussion, see A. Hastings, *The Construction of Nationhood: Ethnicity, Religion and Nationalism* (Cambridge, 1992), p. 61; K. Kumar, *The Making of English National Identity* (Cambridge, 2003), p. 146; S. Pincus, '"To Protect English Liberties": The English Nationalist Revolution of 1688–1689', in *Protestantism and National Identity: Britain and Ireland, c.1650–c.1850*, ed. T. Claydon and I. McBride (Cambridge, 1998), p. 76; R. Strong, *Anglicanism and Empire* (Oxford, 2007), p. 20.

[11] *Greater Britain Messenger*, no. 1 (April 1876), p. 7.

by Clifford: the gospel was the source of England's power; British settlers had spread throughout the whole world; the Gospel flag, as much
as the British flag, should be their source of unity. Embedded in hymns,
sermons and tracts, texts such as these assumed that Britain's overseas settler colonies formed part of a wider Christian realm, a cultural
community that both transcended and reinforced other, more political
bonds.

As for 'God's Empire', preachers sometimes referred to this as well.
However, there was an important theological tradition that considered
all empires to be tainted with a burden of sin, if not actually evil.[12]
Christ had said, 'My kingdom is not of this world' (John 18: 36), and
this was generally taken to mean that Christians, especially professional
Christians such as missionaries, should stay out of politics. In a sermon
preached in 1866, the English Baptist, Octavius Winslow (1808–78),
a descendant of one of the Pilgrims who escaped the English yoke
by fleeing to America on the *Mayflower* in 1620, spoke of God's rule
extending over the four kingdoms of nature, providence, grace and
glory: 'These are not separate and independent sovereignties, but are
parts of one perfect whole – divisions of one great empire, God's sceptre
ruling alike over each and all. We may confirm and illustrate the unity
of God's empire, by the spiritual conversion of His people.'[13] In this
view, conversion, not conquest and colonisation, was the way to hasten
the coming of Christ's kingdom or perfect God's empire on earth.

These two alternative visions of empire, one more or less spiritual,
the other a vehicle for the expression of a British nationalism that transcended religious, political, racial and class difference, could hardly
be reconciled in a single ideology. However, for churchmen in the
imperial age, the ideal of 'Greater Britain' provided an opportunity
for doing so.

Greater Britain

The term Greater Britain is as old as the first British settlements of
America where it was used to refer to the combined territories of the
first British empire. However, according to Duncan Bell, the concept

---

[12] H. M. Carey, 'Religion and the "Evil Empire"', *Journal of Religious History*, 32 (2008),
pp. 179–92. For 'the Empire of Christ and the Empire of Britain' in relation to India,
see J. Cox, *Imperial Fault Lines: Christianity and Colonial Power in India, 1818–1940*
(Stanford, CA, 2002), pp. 23–51.

[13] O. Winslow, *The Lord's Prayer: Its Spirit and Its Teaching* (London, 1866), p. 206.
The term 'God's Empire' is used in a similar, purely religious sense by J. Vaughan,
Sermons Preached in Christ Church, Brighton (London, 1867), p. 3.

of Greater Britain (if not the term itself) was first formulated in the 1830s and 1840s in the wake of the Canadian rebellions (1837 and 1838). It was not until this time that it was felt necessary to articulate an ideology that favoured closer union between colonies and metropole since, before then, the colonies lacked a separate apparatus of government. Additional impetus for change came with the much-increased emigration to the British settler colonies that followed the end of the French wars. Between 1815 and 1840, about 1 million people left the British Isles; from 1847, the depopulation of Ireland (from 7.7 million in 1831 to 4.3 million in 1936) began, and, between 1850 and 1900, emigration from Britain to the colonies exceeded 7 million people. So immense was the impact of this global outpouring that James Belich has dubbed it the 'settler revolution', arguing that it was responsible for the creation of an Anglo-speaking, transnational superpower whose influence remains dominant in the world today.[14]

In the second half of the nineteenth century, the major colonies of settlement gradually became independent of British rule so that, by 1872, there were ten self-governing colonies: Newfoundland, Prince Edward Island, Canada (Ontario, Quebec, Nova Scotia and New Brunswick), New Zealand, New South Wales, Tasmania, South Australia, Victoria and Queensland and, most recently, Cape of Good Hope.[15] There were also important, if smaller, settler populations in Kenya and Southern Rhodesia as well as parts of India and South America. While rebellions in Canada and the Boer War (1899–1902) were challenges to the ideal, it could generally be assumed that British settlers overseas were loyal supporters of Britain – independent in many respects, but forming part of a common cultural sphere.

As a term in common use, 'Greater Britain' was popularised through the writing of Charles Wentworth Dilke (1843–1911) whose account of his youthful travels in 1866 and 1867 was a Victorian bestseller.[16] Dilke considered the preface to *Greater Britain* to be the best thing he ever wrote, largely because of its articulate defence of British colonisation, something he called 'the true as against the bastard Imperialism'.[17] While *Greater Britain* and its sequels are mostly unabashed apologies

---

[14] Figures from C. E. Carrington, *The British Overseas: Exploits of a Nation of Shopkeepers*, 2nd edn (Cambridge, 1968), pp. 501–11; J. Belich, *Replenishing the Earth: The Settler Revolution and the Rise of the Anglo-World* (Oxford, 2009).

[15] D. Bell, *The Idea of Greater Britain: Empire, Nation, and the Future of Global Order, 1860–1900* (Princeton, NJ, 2007), p. 3.

[16] C. W. Dilke, *Greater Britain: A Record of Travel in English Speaking Countries During 1866 and 1867*, 2 vols. (London, 1868).

[17] Cited by S. Gwynn and G. M. Tuckwell, *The Life of the Right Hon. Sir Charles W. Dilke*, 2 vols. (London, 1917), p. 96.

for British imperial expansion, Dilke was under no illusions about the moral cost of colonisation; he referred to the Anglo-Saxons as 'the only extirpating race' and subjected their treatment of native people in America and Australia to harsh criticism.[18] Dilke himself was not an advocate either of imperial federation or Anglo-Saxon supremacy; in *Problems of Greater Britain* (1890), he took pains to emphasise the differences as well as the common bonds which held the different parts or 'states of Greater Britain' together.[19] Indeed, Dilke regarded Greater Britain as a commodious term, and under that umbrella he included colonies and territories from both the older and the newer British empires: Newfoundland, Canada, the United States, the West Indies, Australia and New Zealand in the Pacific, South Africa and India – a much more heterogeneous group than simply the majority British settler colonies. What he admired was the energy, enthusiasm and possibility created by British influence over this swath of territory, not its uniformity or submission to British norms.

The notion that the Anglo-Saxon people formed a union that crossed political and national boundaries and included core cultural values was one that proved enormously fruitful in the decades that followed the publication of Dilke's book. Greater Britain was celebrated in songs and music, exhibitions and conferences, manuals for settlers and emigrants, and through publications which surveyed the history and expansion of the white, Christian, English-speaking British empire.[20] Perhaps because the term was later taken up by more radical enthusiasts for the imperial idea and, in the 1930s, by fascists such as Oswald Mosley,[21] 'Greater Britain' has come to be associated with the most strident excesses of Anglo-supremacy. However, this was not necessarily the case. For many religious and humanitarian thinkers and writers, Greater Britain was linked to the expansion of all that was best in British culture: its language, morality, system of law and constitution, the love of justice and religious and political liberty. Bell has argued that discussion of Greater Britain and especially the idea of a closer political and cultural union with settler Britons was an ideal that was discussed and embraced by public intellectuals across the political spectrum – from

---

[18] Dilke, *Greater Britain*, p. 561.
[19] C. W. Dilke, *Problems of Greater Britain*, 4th edn (London, 1890), p. 4.
[20] For songs and music, see Felix Burns, *Greater Britain Dance Album* (London: J. H. Larway, 1910); George R. Ceiley, *Greater Britain … War Song* (London: Weekes & Co., 1915); Clarence Collingwood Corri, *The Sons of Greater Britain … in Gay Piccadilly* (London: Hopwood & Crew, 1901); *The Greater Britain Exhibition, Earl's Court London* (London: Spottiswood & Co., 1899); G. Gordon Brown and G. Noel Brown, eds., *The Settlers' Guide: Greater Britain in 1914* (London, 1914).
[21] O. Mosley, *The Greater Britain* (London, 1932).

proto fascists who argued in favour of British world domination and political federation, to humanitarian idealists for whom imperial union was anathema.[22] What these thinkers had in common was the conviction that British or, more narrowly, English or 'Anglo-Saxon' values, might profitably be transported across the world. For some thinkers this vision was almost entirely secularised and rooted in racial and cultural hierarchies that bore little connection to religious ideals. For many others, religion provided significant props to the overall project.

Greater Britain was one solution to the problem created by British expansion in the second half of the nineteenth century – how to shape a national identity in the absence of a convincing internal or external Catholic threat. While 'Protestant Britain' had been an effective vehicle for a warrior island state, it was of less use in the changed conditions of the post-Napoleonic world in which religious divisions were an impediment to good order and government. In the British empire, multiple rather than unitary nationalism became the norm and Britishness supplied a new overarching identity that supplemented rather than supplanted older ethnic and religious loyalties. The Britishness encapsulated in the term 'Greater Britain' was all the more effective as a vehicle for colonial identity because it provided nationalism without government or religious establishment (though some people had aspirations in this direction).[23]

These ideas reflect the seminal influence of Benedict Anderson, who stressed the contingent character of the nation, which he defined as 'an imagined political community – and imagined as both inherently limited and sovereign'.[24] Anderson considered that nationalism was the most important modern heir to two earlier cultural systems, namely, the religious community, including the medieval notion of 'Christendom', and the dynastic realm.[25] In other words, nationalism was a kind of secular religion. Nevertheless, because he defined nationalism as the precursor rather than the collaborator to the creation of the nation state, Anderson's thesis about the cultural construction of national identity has some limitations as a tool for the religious historian. Even

---

[22] Bell, *Greater Britain*, p. 11.
[23] On the death of Queen Victoria, it was proposed that King Edward VII should take the title 'King … of Greater Britain beyond the seas'. For the defeat of this suggestion, see P. A. Buckner, *Canada and the British Empire* (Oxford, 2008), p. 89. For a scheme to create a governing structure for Greater Britain, see B. H. Thwaite, *The Electoral Government of Greater Britain* (London, 1895). On the history of a federated empire, see J. E. Kendle, *Federal Britain: A History* (London, 1997).
[24] B. Anderson, *Imagined Communities: Reflections on the Origin and Spread of Nationalism*, revised edn (London, 1991), pp. 5–6.
[25] *Ibid.*, p. 16.

in modern secular states, religion and nation are constantly interact-
ing with one another in multiple ways and should never be considered
isolated phenomena.[26] Adrian Hastings came closer to the mark when
he argued that religion, like language, was a component of all nationalisms.[27] This was true for Greater Britain as it was for earlier imagined
communities of the peoples of the Atlantic World. Throughout British
North America, Australia, New Zealand and southern Africa, the settler churches carried with them the burden and aspirations of the fused
ethnic and religious communities of their home societies. In these new
Britains, older religious ethnicities did not entirely disappear; rather,
under the imperial umbrella, the churches accommodated English
Anglicanism, Welsh Nonconformity, Irish Catholicism or Scottish and
Irish Presbyterianism, in modified forms.[28] In general, the sort of religious nationalism promoted through events such as the feasts of the
patron saints of England, Scotland or Ireland was thoroughly sanitised
before being endorsed by the churches for consumption by the faithful.
However, it was one of the mechanisms through which British imperialism continued to sustain a dialogue with its Christian and ethnic roots
in Great Britain and Ireland.

Defining the religious character of Greater Britain more precisely
than this is something of a challenge. However, unlike Britons in the
eighteenth century, Greater Britons in the new century tended to define
themselves less by their belligerent Protestantism than by their religious
toleration and love of liberty. Just as Great Britain had freed her slaves,
so she had granted full rights of citizenship to Catholics, Jews and
Nonconformists. The ending of war with France also defused tensions
which demonised the Catholic 'Other' and aggravated sectarian hostility at home. It was also significant that, as the British empire expanded,
it incorporated more and more non-Christians while providing ample
opportunities for Scots, Welsh and Anglo-Irish of all faiths to participate and prosper.[29] Even the despised colonial Irish could be redefined
as part of the white, Christian ruling class in opposition to the subject heathen races of India, Africa and Asia.[30] This involved significant

[26] For examples, see Michael Jeismann, 'Nation, Identity and Enmity', in *What Is a
Nation?: Europe 1789–1914*, ed. T. Baycroft and M. Hewitson (Oxford, 2006),
pp. 20–4.
[27] Hastings, *Construction of Nationhood*, p. 31.
[28] For comments on religious aspects of Irish, Scottish and Celtic nationalism, see the
essays in O. D. Edwards, *Celtic Nationalism* (London, 1968).
[29] C. Williams, 'The United Kingdom', in *What Is a Nation?: Europe 1789–1914*, ed.
T. Baycroft and M. Hewitson (Oxford, 2006), p. 278.
[30] For whiteness and the Irish in America, where they were defined against Afro-
Americans, see N. Ignatiev, *How the Irish Became White* (London, 1995). For the

realignment of earlier animosities, notably those between Catholics and conservative Protestants. However, in adjusting its religious character, Greater Britain followed the same trajectory as that of civil religion in America. In his witty and insightful essays on religious nationalism, Conor Cruise O'Brien suggested that American civil religion transmuted from 'pan-Protestant' to 'pan-Christian' in the interval between the American Civil War and the late twentieth century so that it eventually embraced Catholics such as Senator Joseph McCarthy.[31] Wryly, he observed that in the 1950s Americans 'discovered that the Antichrist had changed his address, moving from the Vatican to the Kremlin'.[32]

While the generation of a powerful common enemy was essential to the reorientation of religious nationalism in America, in the United Kingdom political change paved the way much earlier. Following the constitutional revolution, which included the passage of the Test and Corporation Acts (1828), Catholic Emancipation (1829) and the Reform Act (1832) at home, and the passage of the New South Wales Church Act (1836) and the secularisation of the Canadian clergy reserves (1854) in the colonies, there was a radical change to the standing of the Church of England and the Church of Scotland, which had previously dominated the political and religious union of Great Britain and Ireland. Mandler argues that a new understanding of the English national character emerged in the 1830s, one which reflected a religious consensus which was not linked to a specific church and was more tolerant, earnest and pluralist than any in the old regime.[33] In 1851, the death knell of Britain as a Protestant nation was popularly believed to have been tolled with the erection of an English Catholic hierarchy. The ensuing moral panic reflected a seismic shift in the standing of the Catholic Church in Britain. The shift was even more marked overseas. In Greater Britain, there would be neither official Protestantism nor Church establishment, but neither would there be, as in the American republic, a free marketplace for all denominations.

Dilke himself provided an interesting commentary on religion in Greater Britain, although he was far from conventionally pious. By the time he headed off to 'follow England around the world', he was

---

nineteenth-century invention of whiteness as a 'new religion' transcending ethnicity, race and religion, see M. Lake and H. Reynolds, *Drawing the Global Colour Line: White Men's Countries and the International Challenge of Racial Equality* (Cambridge, 2008), p. 247, quoting W. E. B. DuBois.

[31] C. C. O'Brien, *God Land: Reflections on Religion and Nationalism* (Cambridge, MA, 1988), p. 38.

[32] *Ibid.*, p. 36.

[33] P. Mandler, *The English National Character: The History of an Idea from Edmund Burke to Tony Blair* (New Haven, CT, 2006), p. 67.

already expressing serious reservations about the divinity of Christ and he was never a believer in British engagement in missionary work.[34] Yet, despite his personal religious reservations, he did not question the centrality of the churches to the cultural fabric of the empire, and he commented on religious matters shrewdly and thoroughly. Issues which concerned him included the status of Catholicism in regions with high Catholic emigration from Ireland, the influence of missionaries on native populations, and the colonial standing of the Church of England in the wake of the removal of the props provided by establishment. In Canada, he expressed anxiety about the rapid increase of the Irish Catholic population and the threat this posed to British Protestantism. Without stating his sources, he stated that the 'Fenians' (radical Irish republicans) were 'strong' in Toronto and 'not unknown' even in Montreal. However, he confidently predicted that the Dominion would be saved from a Catholic established church because of the lack of union between French and Irish Catholics.[35] In New Zealand, he reflected settler hostility to the influence of missionaries and declared that the 'Maori Church of Englandism', introduced by the CMS, was a failure.[36] In Australia, he noted the strength of Nonconformity, observing that the Wesleyans, Catholics and Presbyterians were stronger than other denominations (presumably he was thinking especially of the Church of England). Greater Britain was also more religiously diverse than he seems to have anticipated. In Melbourne he noted the incongruity, to his eyes, of the jostling together of religious buildings, where the Wesleyan church, the Chinese joss house and the Catholic cathedral stood in close proximity.[37]

Dilke tackled the thorny issue of colonial church establishment in the book that he produced as a sequel to his original survey.[38] He pointed out that many colonies had either never had an established Church, or had chosen to abolish it together with any ongoing financial assistance for religious purposes. Overall, he was fascinated by what the potential consequences of this might be.[39] The impact of colonial disestablishment was also of interest to the novelist Anthony Trollope (1815–82), who visited New Zealand and the Australian colonies from 1871 to 1872. With some amazement, Trollope observed: 'every branch of the Christian religion is now supposed to stand on equal footing, and to have an equal title to whatever support the State may be able and

---

[34] Gwynn and Tuckwell, *Charles W. Dilke*, vol. 1, p. 61. Dilke was pious as a young man, and, on at least one occasion (21 January 1883), he attended church with Gladstone. See Gwynn and Tuckwell, *Charles W. Dilke*, vol. 1, p. 514.
[35] Dilke, *Greater Britain*, p. 61.   [36] *Ibid.*, p. 321.   [37] *Ibid.*, p. 128.
[38] Dilke, *Problems of Greater Britain*.   [39] *Ibid.*, p. 581.

willing to give.'[40] Neither Dilke nor Trollope speculated on the political effects of Church disestablishment, though Dilke suggested that
it ensured that the colonies were less marked by sectarian divisions.[41]
At the same time, Dilke condemned colonial governors who stirred
up rivalries about ecclesiastical precedence and gave his approval to
Cardinal Moran, the Catholic archbishop of Sydney, for objecting to
the attempt to give precedence to the Anglican bishop of Sydney, Dr
Alfred Barry.[42] In his view, the privileges of the Church of England
were something which should be left behind once British settlers had
created their own societies beyond British shores.

Nonconformists were in no doubt that the lack of establishment
increased rather than decreased the loyalty of the British people in
the colonies. They were also aware that it opened up the field to other
churches. In 1913, when the theologian Walter Frederick Adeney
(1849–1920), former principal of Lancashire Independent College, led
a visit to Congregationalist churches in Canada, New South Wales,
New Zealand and southern Africa, his activities were promoted as 'the
day of opportunity for Colonial Missions'.[43] This optimistic view is in
marked contrast to those expressed by the first Congregationalist delegation to visit the colonies, which was undertaken by Daniel Tyerman
and George Bennet for the London Missionary Society. From 1821
to 1829, they toured the Society's stations in the South Pacific, Java,
China, India, Africa and Madagascar, suggesting plans for the future –
plans which did not include missions to colonists.[44] On Adeney's visit,
the Congregationalist magazine, *British Missionary*, called for generous
support for 'the cause of Christ in the British empire', reflecting that
'Christians in the Homeland … have no adequate conception of the
spiritual destitution of thousands of our fellow-countrymen scattered
throughout Greater Britain'.[45]

In ways such as this, Dilke's terminology was embraced by the colonial
missionary societies and used to extend their aspirations for a Christian
empire in which all the churches would have fair and equal representation. While class continued to divide Britons at home, across the seas

[40] A. Trollope, *Australia and New Zealand*, 2 vols. (London, 1873), vol. 1, p. 120.
[41] Dilke, *Greater Britain*, p. 599.
[42] *Ibid.* Moran's example was later recalled by the Lord Lieutenant of Ireland when he
gave ecclesiastical precedence to the Catholic archbishop of Dublin, Cardinal Paul
Cullen, at official events in Dublin Castle. I thank Dr Colin Barr for bringing this to
my attention.
[43] 'Tour of Church Leaders', *British Missionary* (April 1913), p. 31.
[44] D. Tyerman and G. Bennet, eds., *Journal of Voyages and Travels by the Reverend Daniel
Tyerman and George Bennet Esq.*, 2 vols. (London, 1831).
[45] 'The Editor's Corner', *British Missionary* (April 1913), p. 43.

they were united by a shared morality and religious commitment which was seen as a major advance on the divisions of earlier eras.[46]

Religion and imperialism

What was the nature of the relationship between the churches of Great Britain and Ireland and the British empire? There has been perennial debate about this question, both while the empire was expanding and now, when it has been mostly reduced to an uneasy memory. In discussing the rise and fall of the idea of the British empire, Thornton has argued that the connection between religion and imperialism was very indirect and bore only a modest connection to expansion of the British commercial empire.[47] He notes that the missionary David Livingstone advocated commerce in association with commerce for Africa, but not white settlement (though it is not clear how this was to be achieved). Andrew Porter, in a long series of pivotal empirical studies, has done much to demonstrate that missionaries in the field and their supporters at home, while they could hardly avoid implication in the great movement of the age, were among the most persistent and articulate critics of imperialism.[48]

Yet missionaries were only one aspect of the religious character of the empire. Besides giving support to missions and the moral uplift of native people, religious people with access to power promoted the idea that the British empire should itself be subject to moral governance. The churches provided important ideological support for imperial expansion. They generally regarded the empire as a force for good, and missionaries facilitated the extension of its boundaries even if they opposed colonial settlement in some circumstances, notably New Zealand.

To enter the debate about the nature of the relationship between religion and imperialism, we therefore need to define both terms with care. Imperialism is a notoriously slippery concept,[49] and increasingly it has

---

[46] Mandler, *English National Character*, p. 67.

[47] A. P. Thornton, *The Imperial Idea and Its Enemies: A Study in British Power* (London, 1959), p. 15. For commercial aspects of Christian expansion, see B. Stanley, 'Commerce and Christianity: Providence Theory, the Missionary Movement, and the Imperialism of Free Trade, 1842–1860', *Historical Journal*, 26 (1983), pp. 71–94.

[48] See especially A. N. Porter, *Religion Versus Empire?: British Protestant Missionaries and Overseas Expansion, 1700–1914* (Manchester, 2004), pp. 316–30.

[49] D. K. Fieldhouse, *Colonialism 1870–1945: An Introduction* (London, 1981), p. 1. For an attempt to track the meaning of this term historically, see R. Koebner and H. D. R. Schmidt, *Imperialism: The Story and Significance of a Political Word, 1840–1960* (Cambridge, 1964).

been replaced, as in the subtitle to this book, by colonialism.[50] Edward Said defined imperialism as 'the practice, the theory, and the attitudes of a dominating metropolitan center ruling a distant territory',[51] and argued that Christianity was essential to it. In a lecture delivered in Ireland in 1988, he argued that: 'At the heart of European culture during the many decades of imperial expansion lay what could be called an undeterred and unrelenting Eurocentrism. This accumulated experiences, territories, peoples, histories; it studied them, classified them, verified them; but above all, it subordinated them to the culture and indeed the very idea of white Christian Europe.'[52] For Said, colonialism was something that happened after imperial regimes were set in place: 'Colonialism', he states, 'which is almost always a consequence of imperialism, is the implanting of settlements on distant territory.'[53] It follows from this that anti-imperialism and anti-colonialism are distinct activities. Said regarded himself as an anti-imperialist, in that his resistance to the imperial condition was addressed to its core ideas, not just the creation of colonies which were accidental to the imperial condition. Nevertheless, he disagreed with the concept of Christian anti-imperialism. While there was a vigorous European debate, which might trace its origins to Bartolomé de las Casas (1484–1566), about the economic and moral dangers of planting colonies, for Said this internal criticism should not be equated with the anti-imperialism of resistance movements that defeated European colonisers in the modern age.[54] In this view, the British empire lacked an autonomous anti-imperial movement, despite the anti-colonialism espoused by humanitarians who lobbied for an end to the Atlantic slave trade, reforms to the conduct of British policy in India, or, as we will see in Chapter 11, the impact of colonial settlement on aboriginal people in British settler colonies.

Other theorists, writing after Said, have found it useful to draw distinctions between different kinds of colonialism in order to take into account the fact that imperial rule is not exerted in a simple way, but is nearly always complicated by factors such as resistance from those who are being colonised and by the rivalry of other potential colonisers. Nicholas Thomas has emphasised the need to analyse colonialism as a condition in its own right, with many local variables, not

---

[50] S. Neill, 'Colonialism and Missions', in *Concise Dictionary of the Christian World Mission*, ed. S. Neill, G. H. Anderson and J. Goodwin (London, 1970), p. 121.

[51] E. W. Said, *Culture and Imperialism* (New York, 1993), p. 8.

[52] E. W. Said, *Yeats and Decolonization: Nationalism, Colonialism and Literature* (Derry, 1988).

[53] Said, *Culture and Imperialism*, p. 9.   [54] *Ibid.*, p. 272.

simply as a response to the imposition of imperial rule.[55] Despite conceptual challenges, there has also been a concerted effort to try to recover the experience of imperialism from what Reynolds called 'the other side of the frontier'.[56] There is now a flourishing literature that considers colonialism from a 'subaltern' perspective, a term for a junior military officer originally adopted by the Italian socialist Antonio Gramsci (1891–1937) for those subordinated classes who have been excluded from history.[57] Generating a voice for the subaltern has been an important project for post-colonial critics whose main interest lies in the historiography of resistance to imperial rule from the point of view of indigenous and native subjects.[58] With its origins in Gramsci's theories of the need for resistance to the hegemonic power of the bourgeois culture and its religious norms, it is not surprising that subaltern theorists have generally seen Christianity as hopelessly mired in the expansion of imperialism and hardly worth studying. In another attempt to add complexity to these key terms, Fieldhouse distinguished between 'colonialism' as an ideology, especially when applied to territories where small numbers of Europeans exerted power over much larger populations of non-European people, and 'colonisation' in which there is substantial settlement which displaces or replaces the native population.[59]

Applying some of these conceptual tools to the analysis of the settler churches and their relationship with British colonialism, there are clear advantages in making use of Fieldhouse's colonialism/colonisation distinction. Colonisation is what happened in the first British empire when settlers first encountered indigenous people before rapidly overwhelming them and replacing them as the majority population. This occurred in the settler colonies of the second British empire, which are the subject of this book, in places such as Australia, New Zealand, Canada and, to some extent, southern Africa. Colonialism, on the other hand, is what happened to India, most of Africa, and Asia. Again, however, there are complications. The first is the tendency to reduce processes that in fact

[55] N. Thomas, *Colonialism's Culture: Anthropology, Travel and Government* (Cambridge, 1994).
[56] H. Reynolds, *The Other Side of the Frontier: Aboriginal Resistance to the European Invasion of Australia* (Ringwood, 1982).
[57] A. Gramsci, 'Notes on Italian History, 1934–5', in *Selections from the Prison Notebooks of Antonio Gramsci*, ed. Q. Hoare and G. Nowell-Smith (London, 1971), pp. 52–3.
[58] G. Prakash, 'Subaltern Studies as Postcolonial Criticism', *American Historical Review*, 99 (1994), pp. 1475–90; G. C. Spivak, 'Can the Subaltern Speak?', in *Marxism and the Interpretation of Culture*, ed. C. Nelson and L. Grossberg (Urbana, IL, 1988), pp. 271–313.
[59] Fieldhouse, *Colonialism*, pp. 4–6.

took place over a long time and went through many phases, into a single category. Another is the status of colonies such as New Zealand, Kenya and Southern Rhodesia, in which British settlers arrived in significant numbers but not so many as to completely overwhelm the native inhabitants. Does this constitute colonialism or colonisation?

Overall, it is probably better to consider colonisation as one phase in a series of imperial encounters which might begin with first contact, progress through engagement with temporary travellers, pioneers and beachcombers, and which might include colonial settlement as one stage of a broader imperial engagement. The churches were engaged with the progress of colonisation in all its phases. Chaplains, missionaries and bush parsons arrived as pioneers; bishops, and missionary and colonial church societies succeeded them and planted churches; they were often the first on new frontiers and the ones with the greatest call on resources from home to sustain their supply lines. While they never stopped complaining about the need for more money and personnel, the churches had distinct advantages over other imperial institutions. There was intense competition between them for colonial territory: Catholics competed with Protestants; Methodists competed with Anglicans and secured an effective alliance with Presbyterians and other Nonconformists; church parties and sects struggled with each other, and different ethnic churches had competing claims to the same people. Nevertheless, they could also draw on local sources of income and many clerical personnel, male and female, were prepared to work for very low wages. They rapidly adapted to new colonial conditions and became important players in colonial nationalist movements. They formed strategic alliances with the political parties that emerged in the fledgling colonial democracies: Anglicans with the conservatives, Nonconformists with liberals and Catholics in the labour movement. For the churches, moreover, colonialism continued well after the departure of more overt institutions of imperial power, such as the British army, navy and colonial administration.[60]

Contemporary theory turns out to be much better at explaining oppositional modes of colonialism, particularly opposition between people of different race and religion, than explaining the factors that allowed the colonisers to cohere in their new territories, or the colonised to embrace colonial values, including Christianity. As Dilke recognised, the settlers who came to occupy Greater Britain shared a high

---

[60] For this thesis, see especially Ward, *Australia and the British Embrace*. On settler colonialism, see Patrick Wolfe, 'Settler Colonialism and the Elimination of the Native', *Journal of Genocide Research*, 8 (2006), pp. 387–409.

degree of cultural cohesion to the extent that they thought of themselves as 'British subjects' long after their subjection to the British crown had become nominal at best. Despite significant differences in their class, ethnicity, religion and place of origin within Great Britain and Europe, Irish, English, Scottish and Welsh colonists happily embraced new identities as British Americans, Australians, New Zealanders and South Africans. Certainly, South Africa, with its large Dutch Calvinist population, would eventually rebel, but it is much more surprising that rebellion was averted everywhere else and British imperial patriotism flourished for so long. We need a theory that helps to explain this.

It is useful to begin by recognising the dimensions of the colonial missionary project. The physical scale of the religious colonisation of Greater Britain was vast, even if we need not go so far as Seeley who called the growth of Greater Britain 'the greatest English [*sic*] event of the eighteenth and nineteenth century'.[61] Church settlement began in earnest in the 1830s with the support of colonial missionary societies, which were created by almost all the churches and continued more or less unabated until the end of the century. Tables 1.1 to 1.6, mostly taken from colonial and imperial census data and from Carrington, provide data on the size of the British settler population and its religious settlement. In 1839, a reasonable estimate of the 'British Overseas' was calculated by R. M. Martin to be about 1.2 million people including 900,000 in British North America, 130,000 in Australia, 60,000 in the West Indies, and 56,000 garrisoned with the army.[62] By 1901, Carrington estimated that the British population had reached approximately 10 million shared among the two older dominions of Canada and Australia and the two newer ones of New Zealand and South Africa as well as smaller populations in Newfoundland, Southern Rhodesia, Kenya and India. This increase was achieved mostly by emigration, especially from Ireland and Scotland, whose population was transferred to Great Britain, America and the British settler colonies.[63]

The demographic effect of emigration from Ireland and Scotland was especially striking, giving the empire what Ferguson has called its 'enduringly Celtic tinge'.[64] In 1821, the population of Ireland was

[61] J. R. Seeley, *The Expansion of England* (London, 1883), p. 12.
[62] R. M. Martin, *Statistics of the Colonies of the British Empire* (London, 1839), abstracted by Carrington, *British Overseas*, p. 506.
[63] E. Richards, *Britannia's Children: Emigration from England, Scotland, Wales and Ireland since 1600* (London, 2004).
[64] N. Ferguson, *Empire: How Britain Made the Modern World* (London, 2004), p. 71. For detailed study of the demographic impact of settler emigration, see E. Richards, *Britannia's Children: Emigration from England, Scotland, Wales and Ireland since 1600* (London, 2004).

Table 1.1 *Populations of England, Scotland, Ireland and major settler colonies, 1801–1911 ('000s)*

	England and Wales	Scotland	Ireland (whole island)	Canada	Australia	New Zealand	Southern Africa[a] Cape Colony	Natal
1801	8,893	1,608						
1811	10,164	1,806						
1821	12,000	2,092	6,802					
1831	13,897	2,364	7,767					
1841	15,914	2,620	8,178					
1850							285	121
1851	17,928	2,889	6,554	2,436	405	22		
1856							267	
1860					1,146	80		
1861	20,066	3,062	5,799	3,230				153
1865							583	
1871	22,712	3,360	5,412	3,689	1,648	248		290
1875							721	
1880					2,232	528		
1881	25,974	3,736	5,175	4,325				403
1890					3,151	667		
1891	29,003	4,026	4,705	4,833			1,308	544
1901	32,528	4,472	4,459	5,371	3,765	808		
1904							5,175	
1910					4,425	1,050		
1911	36,070	4,761	4,390	7,207	4,455		5,973	

[a] The Union of South Africa was formed in 1910 through the merger of the colony of Cape of Good Hope and Natal, and the two Boer republics of the Transvaal and the Orange Free State.

Source: British and Colonial Censuses, 1801–1911 (B. R. Mitchell, *British Historical Statistics* (Cambridge, 1988)).

6.8 million, which was about one-third of the total population of Britain; by 1901, it had fallen to 1.45 million, which was only one-tenth. The impact of the departures in the overseas colonies was also remarkable. By 1911, the British and Irish population of Australia exceeded that of Ireland, and, in 1921, both Australia and Canada had larger British and Irish populations than either Scotland or Ireland.[65] It is estimated that total emigration from the British Isles to places outside Europe in the nineteenth century was between six and 7 million. There were particular peaks of output in the 1850s, when the

[65] Carrington, *British Overseas*, pp. 507–11. See Figure 1.1.

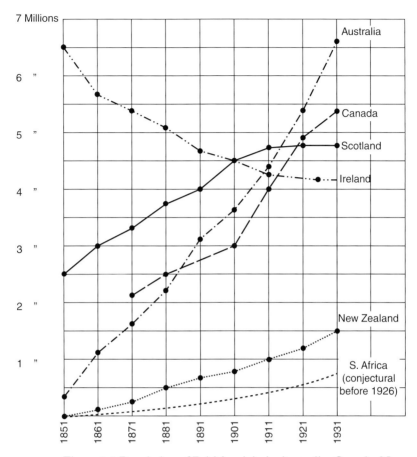

Figure 1.1 Population of British origin in Australia, Canada, New Zealand and South Africa compared with Ireland and Scotland. Source: C. E. Carrington, *British Overseas*, p. 507.

Irish abandoned Ireland and the Australian gold rushes drew emigrants south, and again in the 1890s, when the opening up of the Canadian wheat lands drew hundreds of thousands to Saskatchewan and the provinces of the northwest.

For the millions who participated in the great British *Völkerwanderung* of the Victorian era, the churches were among the most pervasive and enduring cultural institutions that the emigrant English, Irish and Scots chose to transplant and rear in colonial soil. To staff the new churches required a clerical army to be despatched by the various colonial missions set up by the churches for this purpose. Despite the scale of this project, the churches aimed to ensure that they left no frontier unattended by spiritual ministers; astonishingly, by the time of the imperial census in 1901, it was reported that the proportion of clergy to population throughout the settler colonies was more or less the same as it was in Britain itself.[66] In Chapters 3 to 7, I will try to make a direct calculation of the scale of investment that this represented for the different churches. However, by any measure it was a weighty and globally significant event.

There has been increasing interest in the role played by religion in different phases of British overseas expansion.[67] However, the bulk of published work has concentrated on the role of missionaries in those parts of the empire where British settlers remained in the minority.[68] As Porter notes, there are now three voluminous – but largely independent – bodies of historiography with which imperial religious historians must engage: the history of missions, the secular history of the British empire, and the autonomous histories of the national churches planted in the wake of missionary or colonial settlement.[69] There is also an ongoing debate about the relationship between religion and imperialism, especially the extent to which missionaries ought to carry responsibility for the ongoing impact of European empires in the developing world.[70] Yet, in all this, the settler churches have tended to disappear as an object of study.

We can try to measure this change in focus in imperial religious history in a simple way. In Porter's 2002 bibliography of imperial history,[71] the section on religion and belief has 1,490 items. Of these, there are 72 items that concern general imperial religious history, compared with 685 on religion and belief in particular colonial territories, 646 on missions and another 84 on education and primary sources. In other words, there are ten times as many works on missions or national religious

[66] *Census of the British Empire, 1901* (Westminster, 1906), p. xxxi.
[67] For reviews of recent work, see T. Ballantyne, 'Religion, Difference and the Limits of British Imperial History', *Victorian Studies*, 47 (2005), pp. 427–55; H. M. Carey, 'Introduction: Empires of Religion', in *Empires of Religion*, ed. H. M. Carey (Basingstoke, 2008), pp. 1–24; J. Gascoigne, 'Introduction: Religion and Empire, an Historiographical Perspective', *Journal of Religious History*, 32 (2008), pp. 159–78. Andrew Porter, 'Evangelical Visions and Colonial Realities', *Journal of Imperial and Commonwealth Histories*, 38 (2010), pp. 145–55.
[68] The literature on British missions is vast. Major surveys include J. Cox, *The British Missionary Enterprise since 1700* (New York, 2008); N. Etherington, ed., *Missions and Empire, Oxford Companion to the British Empire* (Oxford, 2005); Porter, *Religion Versus Empire*; A. N. Porter, 'Missions and Empire, c.1873–1914', in *World Christianities, c.1815–1914*, ed. S. Gilley and B. Stanley (Cambridge, 2006).
[69] Porter, *Religion Versus Empire?*, p. 7.
[70] N. Etherington, 'Missions and Empire', in *The Oxford History of the British Empire*, vol. 5, *Historiography*, ed. R. W. Winks and A. M. Low (Oxford, 1999), p. 304.
[71] A. N. Porter, *Bibliography of Imperial, Colonial, and Commonwealth History since 1600* (Oxford, 2002), pp. 479–533.

history as there are on colonial church history. Secular imperial history has also changed its emphasis. Older survey histories of British settlement such as Carrington's gave generous coverage to religious questions; Carrington also wrote a biography of John Robert Godley, the leader of the Canterbury settlement, which is considered in Chapter 11.[72] An appreciation of the relevance of ecclesiastical history to the study of the empire was also axiomatic for pro-imperialists such as Jose, even though he regarded the churches and their missionaries as an impediment to settler ambitions.[73] However, the new multi-volume histories of the British empire tend to leave it out almost entirely, something unthinkable to an earlier generation.

These historiographical changes reflect a tendency to associate the history of Christianity with the history of the white settler empire, a field which has in recent decades become marginalised within imperial history itself. This paradigm shift is very evident when contrasting the old *Cambridge History of the British Empire*, which appeared in thirteen volumes between 1929 and 1959, and its successors such as the five-volume *Oxford History of the British Empire*, edited by Roger Louis and published from 1999 to 2001, and the separately edited companion series which is still proceeding.[74] While the earlier project still assumed British beneficence and gave majority space to the settler dominions, they have been displaced in contemporary, revisionist histories of the British empire written since the 1960s. The new imperial history, this implies, is not about planting the Anglo-Saxon race in the Americas and the Antipodes, but about the British confrontation with other races in India, Africa and Asia. Reform and religious evangelisation were seen as either chimerical achievements or hypocritical and self-serving justifications for the advance of British power.[75] For Seeley and the generation which followed him, the central story concerned the expansion of 'England' and English institutions (including the churches) around the world.[76] By the 1990s, this had become so marginal that studies of Australia, Canada and Ireland all appeared as companion volumes to the main narrative history of the British empire. In some cases, the churches did not even appear in the margins. The Oxford companion

---

[72] C. E. Carrington, *John Robert Godley of Canterbury* (Christchurch, 1950); Carrington, *British Overseas*.

[73] A. W. Jose, *The Growth of the Empire: A Handbook to the History of Greater Britain*, 2nd edn (London, 1909).

[74] W. R. Louis, ed., *The Oxford History of the British Empire*, 5 vols. (Oxford, 1998–2000).

[75] C. A. Bayly, 'The Second British Empire', in *The Oxford History of the British Empire*, vol. 5, *Historiography*, ed. R. W. Winks and A. M. Low (Oxford, 1999), p. 63.

[76] Seeley, *Expansion of England*.

volume on Canada, for example, does not have a separate chapter on religion. While the work of Belich, Bell and the proceedings of the 'British World' conferences, first held in Cape Town in 2002, make it clear that revisionism is underway in relation to the settler contribution to empire, the churches – the most significant cultural face of the 'settler revolution' – have yet to be reintegrated into the imperial story.[77]

Religion and race

One consequence of this shift in the weight of scholarly preoccupation is that imperial religious history, and indeed imperial history in general, has become dominated by the discussion of race. Where they are not left out altogether, religious figures are generally identified with the forces of racist colonial oppression. Missionaries continue to be defined as agents for the 'colonisation of the mind' who institutionalised and legitimated Western cultural hegemony through their control of missions, schools, bible translation and publishing houses.[78] One study refers to missionaries as 'surrogate imperialists' whose writing was characterised by an obsession with gender, race and class, while they pursued opportunities for 'social advancement' and an 'exotic career' denied them at home.[79] Such interpretations reflect contemporary Western concerns about the colonial past and its legacy, but they provide no more than a partial view of the Victorian missionary movement.

While the debate about race is – quite properly – central to the study of foreign missions, it has a different significance in relation to the history of the settler churches. Because the British victory over native people in settler colonies was so overwhelming, once the frontier had passed and urbanisation began the vast majority of the 7 million British people who emigrated to Australia, New Zealand, Canada and South Africa rarely engaged spiritually with the indigenous inhabitants of the countries they had invaded. There are significant exceptions to this, especially in New Zealand and South Africa, where Christianity was

---

[77] Buckner, *Canada and the British Empire*; Belich, *Replenishing the Earth*; Bell, *Greater Britain*; Bridge and Fedorowich, eds., *British World*; Ward, *British Embrace*.

[78] For defences of missionaries from the charge of commercial and cultural imperialism, see A. N. Porter, '"Commerce and Christianity": The Rise and Fall of a Nineteenth-Century Missionary Slogan', *Historical Journal*, 28 (1985), pp. 597–621; A. N. Porter, '"Cultural Imperialism" and Protestant Missionary Enterprise, 1780–1914', *Journal of Imperial and Commonwealth History*, 25 (1997), pp. 367–91; Porter, *Religion Versus Empire*; D. L. Robert, ed., *Converting Colonialism: Visions and Realities in Mission History, 1706–1914* (2008), pp. 2–3; Stanley, 'Commerce and Christianity', pp. 71–94; B. Stanley, 'Conversion to Christianity: The Colonization of the Mind?', *International Review of Mission*, 92 (2003), pp. 315–31.

[79] A. Johnston, *Missionary Writing and Empire, 1800–1860* (Cambridge, 2003), pp. 6–8.

planted as much by missionaries as the colonial churches. However, whiteness was the majority condition of British settler societies and, as Patrick Wolfe has argued, since settlers 'came to stay' they tended inevitably – regardless of good intentions and Christian principles – to be both genocidal and monocultural.[80]

In these historical circumstances, it is problematic that some colonial theorists have only been able to imagine models of colonialism in which Europeans impact upon colonial subjects who are predominately non-European.[81] The anthropologist John Comaroff, for example, subdivides what Said called 'imperialism' into a number of different modes, including state colonialism, settler colonialism, and the civilising colonialism of the mission. However, he does not acknowledge that colonialism was a process that acted just as profoundly on settlers themselves as it did on the original inhabitants of colonised territories. The assumption that imperial religious exchanges were always conducted across – rather than within – racial categories needs to be interrogated. This does not mean that race is irrelevant to the history of the settler churches, or that colonial theory cannot provide us with tools to understand the way they acted cohesively to sustain the power of the British imperial project. The colonial churches and missions were imperial institutions and, as we will see, they rarely intervened to contest its power once colonisation was fully underway. This should not be lost from view, particularly by historians writing about Christian missions from a background within a particular confessional tradition, which probably still constitutes the majority of scholarly contributions to the field.

A sure remedy against the risk of confessional bias in imperial history is to engage with its non-European critics. In her foundational study of religious colonisation among Baptists in the West Indies, *Civilizing Subjects*, Catherine Hall acknowledged a debt to Frantz Fanon (1925–61).[82] Fanon was a physician and psychiatrist whose experiences with victims of French colonial oppression and torture in Algeria in the 1950s inspired some powerful writing on their behalf, including *Black*

---

[80] Patrick Wolfe, 'Settler Colonialism and the Elimination of the Native', *Journal of Genocide Research*, 8 (2006), pp. 387–409.

[81] J. L. Comaroff, 'Images of Empire, Contests of Conscience: Models of Colonial Domination in South Africa', in *Tensions of Empire: Colonial Cultures in a Bourgeois World*, ed. F. Cooper and A. L. Stoler (Berkeley, CA, 1997), pp. 179–81.

[82] C. Hall, *Civilising Subjects: Metropole and Colony in the English Imagination, 1830–1867* (Oxford, 2002); Hall, McClelland, and Rendall, *Defining the Victorian Nation*, p. 51. For additional discussion of Hall's use of Fanon, see Catherine Hall, Simon Gikandi, Thomas C. Holt and Philippa Levine, 'Discussion: Civilising Subjects: Metropole and Colony in the English Imagination, 1830–1867', *Journal of British Studies*, 42 (2003), pp. 505–29.

Skin, White Masks (*Peau noire, masques blancs*, 1952) and the posthumous *The Wretched of the Earth* (*Les Damnés de la terre*, 1961). In the earlier book, Fanon confronted the impasse created by the mutually constrained categories of black and white, each sealed in their own respective 'whiteness' and 'blackness' with no prospect, except possibly through psychoanalysis, of acknowledging a common humanity.[83] The apocalyptic language of the title of *The Wretched* (or 'damned') *of the Earth* is sustained by Fanon in his interpretation of the essentially dualistic and final nature of decolonisation which, he stated, is 'always a violent phenomenon', requiring the creation of a new order, with its own language, humanity and history to replace the old. Summing up what is required, he quotes from the parable of the labourers (Matthew 20: 1–16): '"The last shall be first and the first last": Decolonisation is the putting into practice of this sentence.'[84] In the exaggerated encounter that takes place across the frontier, Fanon has argued that there is only good and evil; it is a Manichaean world, in which the settler postulates the native as the source of all evil. The Manichaeism of the settler, in which all institutions share, generates in its turn a Manichaeism of the natives that leads inevitably to violence.

For Fanon, the Christian religion is deeply complicit with the colonising power: 'The Church in the colonies is the white people's Church, the foreigner's Church. She does not call the native to God's ways but to the ways of the white man, of the master, of the oppressor.'[85] Religion is always culpable for the creation of the burden of false national and other cultural identities, and divides those who might otherwise unite against a common oppressor: 'Inside a single nation, religion splits up the people into different spiritual communities, all of them kept up and stiffened by colonialism and its instruments.'[86] Paradoxical divisions between colonised peoples are created by the accidental rivalries of Catholicism and Protestantism, or the incursions of Islam and American Evangelicalism and the African responses to it – diversions, as Fanon sees it, from the anti-colonial struggle. The conclusion to this angry book is simultaneously a call to arms, but also a call to the Third World to create an alternative to the European stasis, something better than the achievement of the United States, a former European colony which had become a 'monster'.[87] Fanon has generally been followed by those who have attempted to discuss the religious constitution of whiteness and its association with racial prejudice in historical arenas such as

---

[83] F. Fanon, *Black Skin, White Masks* (London, 1986), pp. 10–12.
[84] F. Fanon, *The Wretched of the Earth* (London, 1967), pp. 28–29.
[85] *Ibid.*, p. 32.   [86] *Ibid.*, p. 129.   [87] *Ibid.*, p. 252.

post-bellum United States, and South Africa.[88] While Fanon's passion commands respect for his ideas, they were formed in a time of war, and challenges arise when attempting to translate them to other historical contexts.

The principal difficulty with adopting Fanon's uncompromising model of colonialism is that it assumes there was a binary relationship between colonisers and colonised, and between the metropole and periphery. This has considerable polemical force, but it rarely corresponds to the messy arrangements that characterised both the frontier and its aftermath. The difficulties increase in the case of cultural institutions such as the churches. While most churches employed rhetoric that boosted Anglo-Saxon and British virtues at the expense of heathens and pagans, the argument that all colonial religions were therefore vehicles for British cultural hegemony is not sustainable. A simple tool such as the census data on religion in the colonies of British settlement can illustrate the complexities of the interaction between race, mission and Church in colonies of British settlement.[89] In many colonies, including the West Indies, Cape Colony and New Zealand, church membership was strongly differentiated by race and, where this can be measured, class and occupation. In Cape Colony in 1898, for example, while no church was exclusively white or black, the majority Dutch Reformed Church (NGK), which made up 31.3 per cent of the total population, held over 60 per cent of the white population but less than 7 per cent of the 'coloured' (as this was defined by the census).[90] On the other hand, the Methodist Church, which was the NGK's main rival in terms of adherents, held the majority of the coloured population (52.8 per cent). There are also striking variables in the denominational adherence of the Dutch and the British settler people, reflecting profound cultural divisions between these colonial populations in the Cape. The churches, in other words, rapidly adjusted to the local conditions and became engaged on both sides of the frontier.

It is also important to avoid the assumption that white settlers formed a cohesive cultural bloc. This was rarely the case – to the perennial dismay of Christian leaders. Division took many forms, some imported from the old world, others manufactured in the crucible of the new. The longstanding struggle between 'imperial Anglicanism' and Nonconformity, which is so marked a feature of the religious politics of the American

---

[88] For whiteness and religion in associated with racial prejudice, see E. J. Blum, *Reforging the White Republic: Race, Religion, and American Nationalism, 1865–1898* (Baton Rouge, LA, 2005); M. F. Brewer, *Staging Whiteness* (Hanover, NH, 2005), p. 4.

[89] See Tables 1.1–1.6.   [90] For data from Cape Colony, see Table 1.4.

colonies in the eighteenth century, takes new forms in the nineteenth as state subsidies to the Church of England were reduced or abolished.[91] According to Vaudry, the character of Canadian Anglicanism was influenced by Irish Evangelicalism, especially in Quebec, as well as the numerical importance of both French and Irish Catholicism.[92] American and English rivalries played an important role in the development of Methodism in Canada, as we will see in Chapter 6. While Irish Catholicism was to triumph in much of the English-speaking empire, this was achieved at the expense of English Catholicism in Australia and New Zealand, and was limited by French Catholicism in British North America. In the latter, the separate spheres of Francophone and Anglophone Catholicism ensured that, even though in 1901 Catholics made up 41 per cent of the Canadian population, they were unable to translate this demographic into a united Catholic voice on political and social issues. For all the churches, factors such as their relationship to the state, the scale and ethnic character of emigration, the character of the resident European and native populations, and interaction with other churches, ensured that the culture and politics of the local churches differed both from each other and from the churches at home. In short, it was never a simple case of 'us' and 'them'.

While it is a term that is too convenient to discard, 'religion' is not an especially helpful category of historical analysis for British imperial history. We must talk instead about churches and their ethnic and political character as well as the way in which these porous and malleable institutions were adapted to their colonial setting. Colonial religious institutions also change over time. In the first British empire, the established churches were part of the imperial state, but this relationship was slowly dismantled in the course of the nineteenth century to be replaced with something quite different. As historians such as Robert Grant have stressed, the churches need to be considered along with writers, artists and cultural agents who played their parts in 'imagining the empire'.[93] The empire in these formulations had its political,

---

[91] For aspects of 'imperial' Anglicanism, see P. M. Doll, 'American High Churchmanship and the Establishment of the First Colonial Episcopate in the Church of England: Nova Scotia, 1787', *Journal of Ecclesiastical History*, 43 (1992), pp. 35–59; P. M. Doll, *Revolution, Religion and National Identity: Imperial Anglicanism in British North America* (2000); Strong, *Anglicanism and Empire*; J. F. Woolverton, *Colonial Anglicanism in North America* (Detroit, 1984).

[92] R. W. Vaudry, 'Evangelical Anglicans and the Atlantic World: Politics, Ideology, and the British North American Connection', in *Aspects of the Canadian Evangelical Experience*, ed. G. A. Rawlyk (Montreal 1997), p. 154.

[93] R. Grant, *Representations of British Emigration, Colonisation and Settlement: Imagining Empire, 1800–1860* (Basingstoke, 2005), pp. 27–58.

physical and material sides, but it was also a spiritual realm, God's empire, which requires detachment, nuance and sophistication if we hope to do its representation historical justice.

Religion and the settler empire

A disparate coalition of thinkers contributed to the creation of a religious model of the British settler empire.[94] In the early part of the nineteenth century, this included those radical conservatives who were sufficiently rattled by the French Revolution to propose a return to the verities of the old religion. Chief among these was Samuel Taylor Coleridge (1772–1834) who argued that a 'national Church' could provide an essential spiritual dimension to the state, an idea that was readily extended beyond Britain's island boundaries.[95] He also proposed that the 'Clerisy of the nation, or national Church' originally included 'the learned of all denominations'.[96] In the 1830s, Coleridge's ideas about the religious character of the British state and its intellectuals were taken up and developed by the educator Thomas Arnold (1795–1842), who promoted the idea of civil service at home and abroad as both mission and patriotic duty.[97] W. E. Gladstone and his circle did the most to advocate the idea of the national Church as an ideal for Britain and her colonies, a political vision we can trace through the creation of the Colonial Bishoprics' Fund (1841) and beyond. It permeates much of his thinking about the 'English-speaking people', which was for Gladstone as much a cultural and religious as a political ideal.[98]

Unsurprisingly, the Society for Propagation of the Gospel (SPG), the oldest missionary organisation of the Church of England, had the clearest idea of Greater Britain as a field of spiritual labour. This was expressed over many years in the annual sermons and publications of the societies and their benefactors,[99] but there were a number of more

[94] For the debate about the non-settler empire, see, for example, Wolffe, *God and Greater Britain*, ch. 8.

[95] S. T. Coleridge, *On the Idea of the Constitution of the Church and State, According to the Idea of Each* (London, 1830), in *Collected Works of S. T. Coleridge*, vol. 10, ed. J. Colmer (Princeton, NJ, 1976).

[96] *Ibid.*, pp. 46, 193.

[97] T. Arnold, 'The Church and the State', in *The Miscellaneous Works of Thomas Arnold*, ed. A. P. Stanley (London, 1845), pp. 466–75; T. Arnold, 'National Church Establishments', in *The Miscellaneous Works of Thomas Arnold*, ed. A. P. Stanley (London, 1845), pp. 486–92.

[98] F. H. Herrick, 'Gladstone and the Concept of the "English-Speaking Peoples"', *Journal of British Studies*, 12 (1972), pp. 150–6.

[99] For the Ramsden sermons, which have been delivered annually in Oxford or Cambridge since 1847 on the theme 'Church extension in the colonies and dependencies of

ambitious attempts to write the complete spiritual history of the empire. In 1900–1, G. Robert Wynne (1838–c.1906), archdeacon of Aghadoe and canon of St Patrick's cathedral, presented the Donnellan Lectures at Trinity College Dublin on the theme: 'The Church in Greater Britain'.[100] This was highly recommended to all 'Christian Imperialists' by the *Church of Ireland Gazette* which suggests something about its target audience.[101] The lectures themselves were not very distinguished; they consist mostly of potted summaries of the histories of the Church of England and the SPG, and Wynne does not bother to explain what he means by Greater Britain except that it refers to 'the subject of the planting and growth of the Colonial Church among our countrymen abroad, and among the various heathen tribes with which they are brought in contact'.[102] In the event, the lectures cover early missions from the British Isles, with subsequent chapters on the American colonies, Canada, Australia, New Zealand, the West Indies and South Africa, and 'lesser colonial possessions' including British Honduras, Bermuda, Fiji, British New Guinea, West Africa, the East and Central African Protectorate, Mauritius, Ascension, the Straits Settlement and Hong Kong, with a quick mention of the work of the bishop of Jerusalem who had oversight over Anglican clergy and missionary work in the Holy Land and Egypt, and, in South America, the bishop of the Falkland Islands and the bishop of Argentina. By a process of elimination, therefore, it would seem that, for Wynne at least, Greater Britain implied those parts of the empire where there were sufficient numbers of English settlers to provide a foothold for the English Church.

A more radical view of English Christianity linked symbiotically to the worldwide spread of the English race was promoted by the Reverend Henry William Tucker (1830–1902), prebendary of St Paul's cathedral, London, honorary secretary of the CMS and former secretary of the SPG.[103] His survey history of Anglicanism was entitled *The English Church in Other Lands* (1886). This covered, in eight chapters, missions to colonies where there had been significant English settlement: the United States; Newfoundland, Nova Scotia, Quebec and Ontario;

---

the British Empire', see R. Strong, 'The Church of England the British Imperial State: Anglican Metropolitan Sermons of the 1850s', in *Church and State in Old and New Worlds* ed. H. M. Carey and J. Gascoigne (Leiden, 2010) (in press).

[100] G. R. Wynne, *The Church in Greater Britain: The Donnellan Lectures Delivered before the University of Dublin, 1900–1901*, 3rd edn (London, 1911).

[101] *Church of Ireland Gazette*, 12 February 1904.

[102] Wynne, *Church in Greater Britain*, p. viii.

[103] Tucker also wrote memoirs of the lives of colonial bishops, including Edward Field (1877) and George Augustus Selwyn (1879), tracts for emigrants such as *A Word to Intending Colonists* (1897), and other missionary works.

northwest Canada; the West Indies; South America; Australia; New Zealand and the Pacific; and South Africa; with five more chapters on foreign missions on the east coast of Africa, the west coast of Africa, the East Indies and China, Japan and Borneo. The meaning of his subtitle ('The Spiritual Expansion of England') is developed in the conclusion. Here, Tucker links the outward spread of the English-speaking race and what he accepts as the inevitable triumph worldwide of their institutions, speech and thought, to the spread of English religion, which he conceived as not necessarily exclusively that of the Church of England: 'In all these lands, whither the Anglo-Saxon race drifts and settles, Christianity, imported, perhaps with all its differences and divisions, from Great Britain, will supply the people with spiritual life.'[104] Although it might be divided at home, diversity and adaptation to colonial conditions would be the greatest strength of the coming Catholic Church of England which, like Constantine, would bring Christian unity to the empire. He goes on to express a 'wild day-dream' that one day a great English Church, forged in the colonial furnace, might lead a new Reformation of the churches of the old world, conquering first the papacy, then Orthodoxy and the distinguished apostolic churches of the east, which he dismisses as 'corrupt churches which now cling with tenacity to their traditions, but show little zeal or other signs of life'.[105] It is notable that Tucker seems to intend to leave Protestant Europe to its own devices – but otherwise plans a spiritual assault, led by colonial shock troops, on the greater part of the landmass of Europe and the Middle East. Imperial ambitions for English religion probably never reached dizzier heights than this.

For more secular popularisers of colonisation, British religion – often expressed in somewhat vague terms it must be admitted – was appreciated as a unifying force that could assist in the dissemination of British social and ethical values. From about the 1860s, these ideas were affected by the impact of a wealth of new intellectual ideas, including German higher criticism and the rationalist rejection of what an articulate minority saw as superstitious elements within Christianity. In place of the national Church, which many saw as failing to provide moral and intellectual leadership to the world, progressive imperialists and broad churchmen within the Church of England advocated the transplantation of the national culture and British institutions.[106] At Oxford,

---

[104] H. W. Tucker, *The English Church in other Lands or the Spiritual Expansion of England* (London, 1886), p. 214.

[105] *Ibid.*, pp. 214–15.

[106] For Seeley's views of Coleridge, see J. R. Seeley, 'Ethics and Religion', *Fortnightly Review*, 45 (1889), pp. 501–14, discussed by D. S. A. Bell, 'Unity and Difference: John

the historian John Robert Seeley (1834–95) was one of those who saw the empire as a site for the spiritual advance of unity and righteousness under the British flag. Seeley was influenced by Coleridge, Arnold and Maurice and their aspirations for the Church of England to send the light of civilisation through the world, but he came to see the existing churches as inadequate to the task of serving the imperial state. While he continued to argue that religion had a vital role to play, Seeley advocated that it be served by a 'new clerisy', and updated Coleridge's original ideal to include bureaucrats and secular scholars like himself. He looked to a Universal Church of the future that would be defined not by national religion but rather by universal civilisation.[107] These ideas were also promoted by imperial organisations such as the Empire Day Movement, the League of Empire, and the Round Table, which aimed to facilitate the creation of an organic, moral union between Britain and her colonial offspring.[108] All of these organisations drew their strongest support from the white self-governing dominions of South Africa, Canada, Australia and New Zealand, with leadership in Britain itself coming from the press, the churches and the universities.

Like Greater Britain, the new clerisy imagined by Seeley was the lineal heir of an earlier religious ideal; its members were part priests and scholars, part public intellectuals.[109] Civic religion of the imperial age incorporated both historical events and secular and religious symbols into objects of veneration. To Frederick Alexander Kirkpatrick (1861–1953), for example, whose *Lectures on British Colonization and Empire* were published under the auspices of the League of the Empire, it was appropriate to end his survey with a reflection on two national monuments which he assumed were able to summarise the glory of the British nation: Nelson's flagship, *Victory*, anchored in Portsmouth Harbour, and Westminster Abbey, 'the ancient sanctuary which contains the tombs of many men who have done their part in the history of Great Britain and of the British empire'.[110] Westminster Abbey was of course a dedicated Christian church, but it was increasingly regarded as the central shrine to the British nation. In the nineteenth century, it came to hold the bodies of William Gladstone (1809–98), Charles Darwin (1809–82) and

Robert Seeley and the Political Theology of International Relations', *Review of International Studies*, 31 (2005), pp. 559–79. R. T. Shannon, 'John Robert Seeley and the Idea of a National Church', in *Ideas and Institutions of Victorian Britain*, ed. R. Robson (London, 1967), pp. 236–67.
[107] J. R. Seeley, *Natural Religion* (London, 1891), p. 191.
[108] D. Judd, *Balfour and the British Empire: A Study in Imperial Evolution, 1874–1932* (London, 1968), p. 321.
[109] B. Knights, *The Idea of the Clerisy in the Nineteenth Century* (Cambridge, 1978).
[110] F. A. Kirkpatrick, *Lectures on British Colonization and Empire* (London, 1906), p. 114.

Table 1.2 *Canada: principal religious denominations of the population, 1871–1901*

Denominations	1871 adherents	1881 adherents	1891 adherents	1901 adherents	1901 (%)
Catholic, Roman	1,492,029	1,791,982	1,992,617	2,229,600	41.51
Methodist	567,091	742,981	847,765	916,886	17.07
Presbyterian	544,998	676,165	755,326	842,442	15.68
Anglican	494,049	574,818	646,059	681,494	12.69
Baptist	227,898	275,291	302,565	316,477	5.89
Lutheran	37,935	46,350	63,982	92,524	1.72
Not specified	17,055	86,769	89,355	43,221	0.80
Other sects	37,949	26,018	46,009	33,023	0.61
Mennonite	—	21,234	—	31,797	0.59
Congregationalist	21,829	26,900	28,157	28,293	0.53
Jewish	1,115	2,393	6,414	16,401	0.31
Catholics, Greek	18	—	—	15,630	0.29
Pagan	1,886	4,478	—	15,107	0.28
Disciple	—	20,193	12,763	14,900	0.28
Brethren	15,375	8,831	12,911	12,316	0.23
Buddhists	—	—	—	10,407	0.19
Salvation Army	—	—	13,949	10,308	0.19
Evangelical	4,701	—	—	10,193	0.19
Doukhobor	—	—	—	8,775	0.16
Seventh-Day Adventist	6,179	7,211	6,354	8,058	0.15
Latter Day Saints (Mormon)	534	—	—	6,891	0.13
Confucian	—	—	—	5,115	0.10
United Brethren (Moravian)	694	—	—	4,701	0.09
Friends (Quaker)	7,345	6,553	4,650	4,100	0.08
Agnostic	—	—	—	3,613	0.07
Holiness (Hornerite)	—	—	—	2,775	0.05
Christian Scientist	—	—	—	2,619	0.05
Universalist	4,806	4,517	3,186	2,589	0.05
Unitarian	2,275	2,126	1,777	1,934	0.04

Source: Canadian census, 1871–1901. *The Canada Year Book 1911* (Ottawa, 1912). See also F. H. Leacy, ed., *Historical Statistics of Canada*, 2nd edn (Ottawa, 1983), Series A, pp. 164–84. Names of denominations follow those used in the Census.

David Livingstone (1813–73), along with its older complement of kings, queens and churchmen. In Edinburgh, the High Kirk of St Giles, with its memorials to churchmen, aristocrats and writers such as Robert Louis Stevenson (1850–94), was also a national church for Scots of all faiths.

Table 1.3 *Australia: principal religious denominations of the population, 1891, 1901*

Denominations	1891 adherents	1901 adherents	1901 (%)
Church of England	1,234,213	1,497,576	39.68
Catholic, Roman[a]	713,847	855,799	22.67
Methodist	397,366	504,101	13.36
Presbyterian	351,920	426,105	11.29
Baptist	72,278	89,838	2.38
Lutheran	70,826	75,021	1.99
Congregational	72,715	73,561	1.95
Indefinite[b]	54,036	45,071	1.19
Object to stating	39,400	42,131	1.12
Other non-Christian	43,138	38,132	1.01
Salvation Army	33,431	31,100	0.82
Churches of Christ	14,842	24,192	0.64
Other Christian	19,402	21,823	0.58
Protestant (undefined)	29,865	20,558	0.54
Hebrew	13,805	15,239	0.40
No religion[c]	8,084	6,779	0.18
Seventh-Day Adventist	713	3,332	0.09
Unitarian	3,889	2,629	0.07
Catholic, Greek	623	1,314	0.03
Totals	3,174,393	3,774,301	100

[a] Includes Catholic (undefined).
[b] Includes Freethinker, No denomination, Agnostic, Unspecified.
[c] Includes Atheist, Others.
Source: Australian census, 1891, 1901. *Official Year Book of the Commonwealth of Australia, 1901–1912* (Melbourne, 1913), p. 140.

At the height of the imperial age, these religious visions of empire, which were mostly Anglican or post-Anglican in origin, could and did mutate into something more menacing. Imperialism was no longer justified as a pragmatic political expansion for commercial gain, but as a spiritual enterprise through which the blessing of British rule would bring order and morality to the world. An enthusiasm for 'England's mission' united such disparate figures as the missionary David Livingstone, statesman W. E. Gladstone and the imperialist Cecil Rhodes, in a common creed.[111] This did not happen unobserved or unlamented. In 1936, Jawaharlal Nehru commented that the British assumption of racial destiny and contempt of those

[111] C. C. Eldridge, *England's Mission: The Imperial Idea in the Age of Gladstone and Disraeli 1868–1880* (London, 1973), p. 242.

Table 1.4 *Cape Colony: church membership and ethnicity, 1898*

Denominations	White adherents	%	Coloured adherents	%	Total	%
NGK	145,831	60.37	23,662	6.95	225,517	31.33
Methodist	23,189	9.60	179,878	52.80	203,067	28.21
Anglican	34,416	14.25	41,739	12.25	89,650	12.46
Presbyterian	9,055	3.75	13,526	3.97	30,679	4.26
Congregationalist/ LMS	3,749	1.55	38,539	11.31	41,409	5.75
Lutheran	5,108	2.11	40,428	11.87	44,111	6.13
Catholic, Roman	14,965	6.20	2,543	0.75	17,508	2.43
Baptist (German and English)	5,237	2.17	390	0.11	67,777	9.42
Totals	241,550	100	340,705	100	719,718	100

Source: Cape Colony census, 1898. R. Elphick and T. R. H. Davenport, *Christianity in South Africa: A Political, Social and Cultural History* (Oxford, 1997), p. 55. Colonial Secretary's Office, *Statistical Register of the Cape of Good Hope, 1898* (Cape Town, 1899).

who differed from them about Indian problems had 'something of the religious temper'.[112] At its most militaristic, Rudyard Kipling expressed the devotion inspired by the realm of Greater Britain in poems such as *The Young Queen* (1900), written to celebrate the birth of the Commonwealth of Australia in 1901. The refrain gives repeated homage to the 'five free nations' of Canada, Australia, New Zealand, South Africa and India. Kipling's *Song of the White Men* (1899) chillingly combined the white militarism and religious conviction in propaganda for the Boer War:

> Now is the faith that the White Men hold
> When they build their home afar –
> Freedom for ourselves and freedom for our sons
> And, failing freedom, War.[113]

The direct consequence of British patriotism in the colonies was to be the creation of a loyal imperial fighting force that could be marshalled

[112] Jawaharlal Nehru, *Autobiography* (London, 1936), p. 428, cited by Thornton, *Imperial Idea and Its Enemies*.
[113] F. V. Livingstone, *Bibliography of the Works of Rudyard Kipling* (New York, 1927), p. 238. The poem was a successful one for Kipling and was picked up by many journals in 1900 under the original title 'The Faith-Cup of the White Men': *The Friend*, 2 April; *New York Tribune*, 17 May; *Daily Mail*, 1 June 1; and in the *Cornhill Booklet*, August 1900 with the title 'The Song of the White Man'; 'The Young Queen' appeared in *The Times*, 4 October 1900 and in *Harper's Weekly*, 13 October 1900.

Table 1.5 *New Zealand: principal religious denominations of the population, 1891–1911*

Denominations	1891 (%)	1896 (%)	1901 (%)	1906 (%)	1911 (%)	1911 adherents
Church of England	40.51	40.27	40.84	41.51	41.14	413,842
Presbyterians	22.62	22.78	22.87	22.96	23.33	234,662
Methodists	10.14	10.45	10.86	10.06	9.43	94,827
Baptists	2.37	2.28	2.08	2	1.99	20,042
Congregationalists	1.07	0.97	0.87	0.83	0.87	8,756
Lutherans	0.9	0.79	0.63	0.55	0.44	4,477
Salvation Army	1.5	1.5	1.04	0.95	0.96	9,707
Society of Friends	0.05	0.05	0.04	0.04	0.04	412
Unitarians	0.05	0.05	0.06	0.09	0.13	1,316
Other Protestants	1.82	2.16	2.19	2.07	2.03	20,424
Roman Catholics	13.96	14.07	14.23	14.32	13.97	140,523
Greek Church	0.01	0.01	0.02	0.03	0.03	265
Hebrews	0.23	0.22	0.21	0.21	0.21	2,128
Buddhists, Confucians	0.63	0.48	0.3	0.17	0.15	1,501
Other [Christian] denominations	0.12	0.16	0.17	0.23	0.25	2,559
No denomination	1.32	1.22	1.07	1.04	0.9	9,177
No religion	0.25	0.27	0.14	0.19	0.55	5,529
Unspecified	—	—	—	—	—	2,416
Object to state	2.45	2.27	2.38	2.75	3.58	35,905
Totals	100	100	100	100	100	1,008,468

Source: New Zealand census, 1891–1911. M. Fraser, *Report on the Results of a Census of the Dominion of New Zealand … 2nd April, 1911* (John MacKay, Government Printer, 1913), p. 27. Names of denominations follow census categories.

for the killing fields of the first imperial war, which was enthusiastically endorsed by the majority of the churches.

While Kipling was publishing the first versions of *The Young Queen*, the duke and duchess of Cornwall were completing a tour of 'Greater Britain' that culminated in the official inauguration of the Commonwealth of Australia on 1 January 1901. On his return to the metropole from a journey of over 45,000 miles, the Duke could boast of never setting foot on land where the Union Jack did not fly. His journey had taken him to Gibraltar, Ceylon, Singapore, Australia, New Zealand, Mauritius, Natal and the Cape Colony, and Newfoundland and Canada; it was a tour of the whitest parts of the empire, which neatly bypassed imperial possessions in Borneo, New Guinea, India, Africa and British Guiana. Speaking in the London Guildhall on his return, the Duke declared that the strongest of all his impressions was

Table 1.6 *Australia and New Zealand: proportions of religious denominations in Australia and New Zealand according to census years 1871, 1881, 1901*

Year	State	Church of England (%)	Roman Catholics (%)	Presbyterians (%)	Wesleyan and other Methodists (%)	Congregationalists (%)	Baptists (%)	Jew, Hebrew (%)	All others (%)
1871	New South Wales	45.5	29.3	9.7	7.9	1.8	0.8	0.5	4.5
	Victoria	34.4	23.3	15.5	12.3	2.5	2.2	0.5	9.3
	Queensland	36.5	26.5	12.8	6.0	2.2	2.4	0.2	13.4
	South Australia	27.1	15.2	6.4	18.9	3.5	5.0	0.3	23.6
	Western Australia	59.0	28.7	2.1	5.6	3.6	0.2	0.2	0.6
	Tasmania	53.5	22.3	9.1	7.2	4.0	0.9	0.2	2.8
	New Zealand	41.8	13.9	24.8	8.6	1.3	1.9	0.5	7.0
	Australasia	39.1	23.1	13.6	10.5	2.4	2.0	0.4	8.9
1881	New South Wales	45.6	27.6	9.6	8.6	1.9	1.0	0.4	5.3
	Victoria	34.7	23.6	15.4	12.6	2.3	2.4	0.5	8.5
	Queensland	34.6	25.5	10.6	6.7	2.2	2.6	0.2	17.6
	South Australia	27.1	15.2	6.4	18.9	3.5	5.0	0.3	23.6
	Western Australia	54.7	28.3	3.4	7.0	4.3			2.3
	Tasmania	51.7	19.9	7.9	9.5	3.5	1.6		5.9
	New Zealand	41.5	14.1	23.1	9.4	1.4	2.3	0.3	7.9
	Australasia	39.1	22.2	13.4	10.9	2.2	2.2	0.4	9.6
1891	New South Wales	44.8	25.5	9.7	9.8	2.1	1.2	0.5	6.4

Victoria	35.2	21.8	14.7	13.0	1.9	2.5	0.6	10.3
Queensland	36.2	23.6	11.6	7.8	2.2	2.6	0.2	15.8
South Australia	27.9	14.7	5.7	19.0	3.7	5.5	0.3	23.2
Western Australia	49.7	25.3	4.0	9.2	3.2	0.6	0.3	7.7
Tasmania	49.9	17.6	6.6	11.7	3.1	2.2	8.9	
New Zealand	40.0	13.9	22.6	9.9	1.1	2.4	0.2	9.9
Australasia	39.1	21.1	13.0	11.4	2.1	2.3	0.4	10.6
1901 New South Wales	46.6	26.0	9.9	10.3	1.9	1.2	0.5	3.6
Victoria	35.8	22.3	16.2	15.2	1.5	2.8	0.5	5.7
Queensland	37.5	24.5	11.7	9.5	1.7	2.6	0.2	12.3
South Australia	30.3	14.8	5.2	25.5	3.8	6.2	0.2	14.0
Western Australia	42.0	23.3	8.2	13.6	2.5	1.7	0.7	8.0
Tasmania	49.6	17.9	6.8	14.8	3.3	2.8		4.8
New Zealand	41.7	14.6	23.4	11.1	0.9	2.1	0.2	6.0
Australasia	40.5	21.6	13.5	13.2	1.8	2.4	0.4	6.6

Source: Australian and New Zealand census. T. A. Coghlan, A Statistical Account of Australia and New Zealand 1902–3 (Sydney, 1904), p. 886.

that of colonial loyalty and devotion to the crown, 'a consciousness of a true and living membership in the Empire'.[114] He also spoke of a possible greater union, especially of military forces. The journalist with the *Morning Post* who accompanied the royal tour admired the imperial patriotism of Greater Britons: 'Australians as a body are more loyal to Great Britain than are the people of Great Britain themselves. Their patriotism is more fervent, and the Imperial sentiment is truer.'[115] By the time we get to Kipling at the height of the imperial age, it is evident that, for a certain audience, imperial nationalism was threatening to supplant church-based religious devotion to a worrying extent. Even though we can probably assume that the 'faith that the White Men hold' was deployed as a striking metaphor, there is still more than a hint of blasphemy in Kipling's use of religious language to refer to British patriotism for a secular and military cause. Not surprisingly, imperialist excesses of this kind were decried by many within the churches. Nevertheless, the fact that Kipling found it appropriate to use religious language in this way alerts us to the extent to which the empire had a religious as well as a secular character.

Conclusion

Greater Britain was far more than a travel route or a political subset of the British empire: for the churches it formed a religious field which was cultivated on an imperial scale. As a mission territory, Greater Britain was largely coterminous with the second British empire, or that collection of territories settled by people who were mostly happy to call themselves British and who participated in an extended series of relationships with the British metropole that were at their height in the first decade or so of the twentieth century and have still not entirely been extinguished.

There are several issues that we need to pursue from this point. In the first place, what meaning did religion have for those settlers who took their churches from Britain and planted them in the colonies? There has been fine work done by religious historians and sociologists in this field.[116] On the whole, they tend to argue that, apart from a few exceptional cases, emigrants and colonists were no more religious than the countrymen they left behind – but they were more enterprising and

---

[114] E. F. Knight, *With the Royal Tour* (London, 1902), p. 409.
[115] *Ibid.*, p. 132.
[116] H. R. Jackson, *Churches and People in Australia and New Zealand 1860–1930* (Sydney, 1987).

adaptable. In the new world, it was possible to let go of older allegiances, to change churches, to marry a partner who was not of the same church, or to abandon church-going altogether. Nevertheless, while secularisation was an option, most chose instead to adapt and nurture the religious traditions of their homelands. Church-going for colonists was one of the ways that they articulated a new identity, one that reminded them of home, demonstrated where they had come from, and what they aspired to achieve. We will find repeatedly that settlers were deeply interested in religious issues and went to extraordinary lengths to transplant their churches to the new settlements. Social historians have done much to establish the commercial and secular characteristics of the great British emigration of the second half of the nineteenth century. However, this is not the whole story. Emigration and colonisation had a religious dimension, which is why it was so energetically promoted by church agencies, including colonial missionary societies. I have suggested in this chapter that religion also played a significant role in shaping the idea of Greater Britain, a settler realm without an established Church, but with a Christian ethos shaped by the British churches. The next chapter will consider the religious history of the empire and the context for the colonial mission of the churches which followed. For those who went out into the British world in the nineteenth century, there were to be more religious options than there were for Britons in the Protestant nation which settled the Atlantic world in an earlier age.

2   Protestant nation to Christian empire, 1801–1908

The history of the planting of Christianity forms an essential part of the history of European empires.[1] Latourette, one of the few historians who has dared to write a complete, scholarly history of Christianity in all its branches, considered that it was not until 1944 (the year he completed his magisterial seven-volume survey) that Christianity began to be a world religion, rather than what he called a 'colonial or imperial extension, ecclesiastically speaking, of an Occidental faith'.[2] Nevertheless, the imperial phase of the planting of Christianity in the settler colonies of the British empire has tended to be forgotten in recent times. There are nationalist and post-colonial reasons for this. Where British settlers remained a majority force in the population, including Australia, British North America and New Zealand, the churches responded by generating national histories which emphasised autonomous developments and indigenous contributions to post-colonial churches; in regions where the settler population declined or disappeared in sites such as the British Raj, the plantation economies of the West Indies or the mobile occupying force of the British army in India, then the history of the settler churches has more or less been forgotten. However, the churches did not grow spontaneously in the native soil but were transported there with considerable deliberation and intent. This chapter provides a compressed narrative history of British religious settlement throughout the empire in order to provide a background to the particular studies of Christian emigration and the colonial missionary societies of Greater

---

[1] The fullest history of European settler Christianity remains that of K. S. Latourette, *A History of the Expansion of Christianity*, 7 vols. (London, 1938–45). For the territories considered in this book, Latourette may now be supplemented by the separate volumes of the *Oxford History of the Christian Church*, including I. Breward, *A History of the Churches in Australasia* (Oxford, 2001); R. E. Frykenberg, *Christianity in India: From Beginnings to the Present* (Oxford, 2008); and A. Hastings, *The Church in Africa, 1450–1950* (Oxford, 1994). See also S. Gilley and B. Stanley, eds., *World Christianities, c.1815–1914* (Cambridge, 2006).

[2] Latourette, *A History of the Expansion of Christianity*, vol. 7, p. 411.

Britain which follow. In the course of 200 years, it traces the revolution in religious aspirations for the British state, from Protestant nation to a free, moral and Christian settler empire.

Protestant nation, 1801

At the beginning of the nineteenth century, most European states – with the notable exception of post-revolutionary France – were locked into mutually hostile religious power blocs, the endgame which was the result of centuries of religiously fuelled ethno-political conflict. Following the Peace of Augsburg (1555), a kind of equilibrium had been achieved by bestowing constitutional endorsement on Catholicism or Protestantism depending on the religious persuasion of the reigning monarch according to the principle *cuius regno eius religio* ('whose realm, his religion'). While in practice few countries were able to secure a monopoly over people's private religious beliefs, it was widely accepted that a confessional state was essential on the grounds of national security, public morality and good order.

This was the religious background to the legal formation of the United Kingdom of Great Britain and Ireland at the beginning of the nineteenth century. Prompted by the Irish Rebellion of 1798, the Act of Union (1801) united the historic realms of England, Scotland, Ireland and Wales and Britain's overseas territories into a single state, ruled by a Protestant monarch, endowed with two established churches – the United Church of England and Ireland and the Church of Scotland – and governed by a single parliament in Westminster.[3] Britain's empire had been much reduced by the loss of most of her colonies in the American War of Independence, but in 1801 it incorporated islands in the West Indies such as St Kitts and Nevis (1625), Barbados (1662) and Jamaica (1655); chilly wilderness regions in North America including Newfoundland (1623) and the complex of territories which were divided into English-speaking Upper Canada and French-speaking Lower Canada (1791); the convict colonies of New South Wales and Van Diemen's Land in Australia (1788); inhospitable regions of eastern Africa; and military bases such as Gibraltar (1713).[4] Although it was occupied by the British in 1795, Cape Colony did not become a British colony until 1806.

[3] For the religious significance of the Acts of Union, see J. C. D. Clark, *English Society, 1660–1832: Religion, Ideology and Politics During the Ancien Régime*, 2nd edn (Cambridge, 2000); J. Smyth, *The Making of the United Kingdom, 1660–1800: State, Religion and Identity in Britain and Ireland* (London, 2001).
[4] Dates refer to the establishment of the colonies. See Maps 1.1 and 1.2.

Throughout these widely scattered domains there were significant
religious divisions which the government generally regarded as a threat
to national and imperial unity. In an attempt to subdue the voice of dissent, establishment Protestantism was therefore protected legally and
endowed financially. Only those who swore allegiance to the Protestant
monarch and publicly confessed to the Thirty-Nine Articles (the
sixteenth-century formulation of the doctrines of the Church of England)
were eligible to serve the British crown. Most of the professions – not just
the Anglican and Presbyterian ministry, but the judiciary, the universities, parliament, the colonies and commissioned ranks in the army and
navy – were closed to all but establishment Protestants. Among those
excluded were Nonconformists,[5] such as the old Baptists, Quakers,
Congregationalists and Unitarians, and the new Wesleyan Methodists,
as well as Catholics, Jews and adherents of all other religious faiths. Yet,
whatever their religious convictions, everyone was subject to church
taxes that contributed to the support of the two established churches
which were also richly supported from their historical endowments. In
Ireland, this meant that 3,150,000 Catholics and 900,000 Presbyterians
paid tithes in aid of 450,000 adherents of the established Church of
Ireland.[6] Like Irish Catholics, Welsh Nonconformists, who formed a
majority in much of the principality, were excluded from a say in the
governance of their own country. Laws that required them to pay taxes
to support a national Church to which they did not adhere also distressed
a significant number of Episcopalians in Scotland and Presbyterians in
England. Beyond British shores, the same inequitable system applied. In
Upper Canada, religious endowments were monopolised by an Anglican
and, from 1824, a Presbyterian minority. Religion was less of an issue in
colonies with a majority non-Christian population where the regimes of
the various charter companies kept missionaries – and other perceived
impediments to trade – firmly at bay.

Collectively, these constitutional arrangements ensured that state-
supported Protestantism was neither an accidental nor a marginal
characteristic of either the United Kingdom or her overseas colonies.
Indeed, as Linda Colley has argued in an influential thesis, it was vital

---

[5] 'Nonconformity' refers throughout this book to non-Anglican Protestantism. In the
nineteenth century, it incorporated the Unitarians, Congregationalists (or Puritans),
Baptists and Quakers, who had opposed the Act of Uniformity (1662), and newer
groups such as the Methodists, the Plymouth Brethren and the Salvation Army. The
Act of Toleration (1689) allowed Nonconformists to avoid penalties for non-attendance
at Anglican church services, but it was not until the repeal of the Test and Corporation
Acts (1828) and subsequent reforms that first Nonconformists, then Catholics (1829)
and Jews (1890), achieved full emancipation.
[6] C. Cook and J. Stevenson, *British Historical Facts 1760–1830* (London, 1980), p. 175.

in bringing together the various heterogeneous ethnic and religious components of the British nation.[7] Prior to the American Revolution, Protestantism had helped to define and shape the 'Atlantic World', a region of English-speaking cultural and economic dominion which stretched from the British Isles to the Americas, included the Caribbean, and followed the slave and sugar trades to Africa.[8] In the wake of the voyages of James Cook, the British Protestant state, with its enlightenment values, missionary enthusiasm and evangelical hopes, was also extended to the Pacific.[9] By 1851, the American writer Robert Baird celebrated the Christian advances of the Protestant powers of Holland, England and the United States in the following terms: 'Their colonies are numerous and important. England and Holland have all the great islands in the Indian and Pacific oceans. England, especially, is extending her influence and her Protestantism immensely, by means of her vast Colonial Possessions in the Old and New Worlds.'[10]

Other than the English Bible, the one thing British Protestants tended to have in common was opposition to Catholics – a not inconsiderable ideological force. As subjects of a Protestant monarch, most British citizens were ready and eager to defend and extend the faith of the realm both at home and abroad. Anti-Catholicism formed part of a nationalist discourse that decried Roman Catholicism as morally and politically tyrannical and celebrated Protestantism as the font of British liberty.[11] Nevertheless, the nationalist assertion of Protestant Britain smoothed over significant divisions between different kinds of British Protestantism, especially that which separated Nonconformity

[7] Colley, *Britons*. See also T. Claydon and I. McBride, eds., *Protestantism and National Identity: Britain and Ireland, c.1650–c.1850* (Cambridge, 1998). J. Black, 'Confessional State or Elect Nation?', in *Protestantism and National Identity: Britain and Ireland, c.1650–c.1850*, ed. T. Claydon and I. McBride (Cambridge, 1998). For the defence of the Anglican church-state by William Blackstone, see Clark, *English Society*, pp. 245–47.

[8] As argued by C. G. Pestana, *Protestant Empire: Religion and the Making of the British Atlantic World* (Philadelphia, 2009).

[9] K. Wilson, 'The Island Race: Captain Cook, Protestant Evangelicalism and the Construction of English National Identity, 1760–1800', in *Protestantism and National Identity*, ed. Claydon and McBride, pp. 265–90.

[10] R. Baird, *The Christian Retrospect and Register: A Summary of the Scientific, Moral and Religious Progress of the First Half of the Nineteenth Century* (New York, 1851), p. 199.

[11] J. Wolffe, 'Anti-Catholicism', in *Empires of Religion*, ed. H. M. Carey (Basingstoke, 2008), pp. 43–63. E. R. Norman, *Anti-Catholicism in Victorian England* (London, 1968); J. Wolffe, 'Anti-Catholicism and Evangelical Identity in Britain and the United States, 1830–1860', in *Evangelicalism: Comparative Studies of Popular Christianity in North America, the British Isles, and Beyond, 1700–1990*, ed. M. A. Noll, D. W. Bebbington and G. A. Rawlyk (New York, 1994), pp. 179–97.

and the two established churches of England and Scotland. Indeed, 'Protestant' should probably be seen as just as much of a flag of convenience as 'British', though none the less meaningful for all that. At the beginning of the century, when Catholics throughout Great Britain and Ireland began to press successfully for reform, they therefore faced strong opposition from all classes of society. Attempts by Westminster to ameliorate the worst of the disabilities affecting Catholics unleashed anti-Catholic riots in Edinburgh in 1779 and in London the following year when a Scottish peer, Lord George Gordon, incited the mob. Conservative Protestants never abandoned the aspiration to complete the Reformation by eradicating Catholicism from Britain entirely. For their part, Catholics defined England, Scotland and Ireland as mission fields and looked forward to the time when they would be restored to the one true Catholic and apostolic faith in communion with Rome.

The privileges of the established Church were supported by local colonial as well as imperial legislation. In the West Indies and in the Cape Colony, missionaries and other Nonconformist clergy were seen as a nuisance, and laws relating to their licence to preach were closely policed. In 1802, the Jamaican Assembly passed a law which gave magistrates the power to withdraw the licence to preach from anyone considered likely to incite the slave population to acts of rebellion: Baptists and Methodists were particularly suspect, and at least one licensed Methodist missionary was sent to jail for illegal preaching.[12] In New South Wales, Catholic priests associated with the convict uprising at Castle Hill in 1798, not long after the Irish Rebellion, had their permission to celebrate Catholic services removed. It is necessary to emphasise the legal nicety of all these arrangements. Public prayer and religious meetings could be – and occasionally were – regarded as seditious activities that attracted government sanction or proscription. Only members of the established Church or, after the abolition of the Test Acts, licensed dissenting ministers were able to pray in public – and even then only in properly established places of worship. Even where religious toleration was practised, the assumption of privilege by the Church of England and the subsidies provided to their clergy continued to be a major annoyance to colonists of other religious persuasion, or none.

While popular support for the established Church is difficult to judge and should not be underestimated,[13] the sectarianism that defined and divided the British Protestant nation in 1801 helped prop up an

---

[12] P. Wright, ed., *Knibb 'the Notorious': Slaves' Missionary, 1803–1845* (London, 1973), p. 25.

[13] R. Brown, *Church and State in Modern Britain 1700–1850* (London, 1991), p. 127.

unequal social and political order. The old religion sustained the power of the old regime, entrenching the advantages of a ruling elite that was defined narrowly by class, religion, gender and ethnicity. Aristocratic privilege, which was linked to the power of the established Church, was curtailed by the constitutional revolution, which ended what Brown calls the 'spiritual monopoly' of the Church of England.[14] Meanwhile, it fell as a particular burden on the lower orders, including the clergy of many churches who were constrained economically, socially and spiritually by conditions in Britain. Fortunately, one outlet for these poor, but rising and often highly ambitious and idealistic men, was provided by the colonies where there were opportunities to serve as chaplains or as agents of the missionary societies.

Chaplains

Chaplaincy was the system that evolved historically in the Church of England to provide religious services in free chapels, independent from the ordinary jurisdiction of the parish priest.[15] Traditionally, chaplains were appointed to royal and judicial courts, to wealthy private households or to dependencies of large ecclesiastical institutions. By the nineteenth century, chaplains had evolved into the mobile frontiersmen of the clerical profession. They could be found overseas in hardship posts or coping at home with the new social and political conditions sparked by the industrial revolution and the explosive growth of cities. From 1825, Church affairs in British colonies were regulated by an act of parliament.[16] This allowed British consuls to appoint chaplains 'at any foreign port or place', so long as they received a licence from the bishop of London, and government outlay was met with matching funds raised by local subscription. Since this was a relatively informal system – and the bishop of London was generally a long way away – complaints might arise if rival chaplains wished to serve the same community.[17]

Originally, as servants of the crown, chaplains were always ordained ministers of the two established churches. However, following the

---

[14] *Ibid.*, p. 203. See p. 11 above.
[15] T. Moore, *Dictionary of the English Church, Ancient and Modern* (London, 1881), pp. 98–102.
[16] Great Britain, Foreign Office, *Instructions to Her Majesty's Consuls Respecting Grants to British Church Establishments Abroad under the Act of Parliament 6 George IV, c. 87* (London, 1874).
[17] For an instance of this in Madeira, see R. T. Lowe, *Protest against the Ministration in Madeira of the Reverend T. K. Brown in Opposition to Episcopal Authority by the Reverend R. T. Lowe, the Chaplain Licensed by the Lord Bishop of London* (Funchal, 1848).

abolition of the Test and Corporation Acts and Catholic emancipation, Nonconformist and Catholic chaplains were given appointments, especially to jails, convict settlements and military settlements. Anglican, Presbyterian and Catholic chaplains were also employed by the East India Company to provide religious comforts to their troops in India and reform what they regarded as inhumane cultural practices. Charles Grant, Chairman of the East India Company, sponsored chaplains such as the Scottish theologian, Claudius Buchanan (1766–1815), in India, later an important advocate of the erection of a colonial Church establishment.[18]

Another group of clergy who served the British overseas were military and naval chaplains.[19] Both the Church of England and the Church of Scotland had been appointing military chaplains to regiments in the British Army since the sixteenth century. From 1796, army chaplains were coordinated under the Chaplain-General, who enjoyed a rank equivalent to that of a major general. There was also a long history of chaplains serving in the Royal Navy.[20] In 1812, the Lords Commissioner of the Admiralty put the organisation of naval chaplains on a much more formal basis and appointed a Chaplain-General to the Fleet. Naval chaplains received annual pay of £150, had their own servant and a pension, and in some places they took on surrogate duties as moral guardians and schoolmasters. Purchasing a commission to serve as a naval or regimental chaplain could be used as an easy way to earn a living since it was not difficult to pay someone else to take the services involved, though there were attempts to curb this vice.[21] As serving officers, army chaplains were expected to remain with their regiments when serving overseas and this seems to have been the beginning of an official religious presence, funded by the British government, in territories overseas. Chaplains might also be appointed to any expedition of an official character with the general idea that they represented the 'Defender of the Faith' and helped to elevate the tone. As Snape has shown, soldiers, sailors and their officers were often strongly religious and the army and navy served to promote British religious institutions

---

[18] For Buchanan, see p. 50 below.
[19] W. E. L. Smith, *The Navy and Its Chaplains in the Days of Sail* (Toronto, 1961); G. C. Taylor, *The Sea Chaplains: A History of the Chaplains of the Royal Navy* (Oxford, 1978). For the Church of Scotland, see I. C. Barclay, 'Chaplaincies, Military', in *Dictionary of Scottish Church History and Theology*, ed. N. M. D. S. Cameron (Edinburgh, 1993), pp. 162–63. and C. S. Dow, *Ministers to the Soldiers of Scotland: A History of the Military Chaplains of Scotland Prior to the War in the Crimea* (Edinburgh and London, 1962). See now M. F. Snape, *The Royal Army Chaplains' Department, 1796–1953: Clergy under Fire* (Woodbridge, Suffolk, 2007).
[20] Taylor, *Sea Chaplains*.   [21] Dow, *Ministers to the Soldiers of Scotland*, pp. 227–8.

in many remote places.[22] In Newfoundland, pious naval officers were among those who agitated for more regular religious services than those provided by the SPG and initiated subscriptions to repair its dilapidated churches.[23] If we look carefully, it is evident that the religious pluralism and toleration, which came eventually to be seen as characteristic of the British empire, was pioneered in the armed services from where it set the pace for later changes in religious arrangements in all British colonies.

Colonial chaplaincies were a natural extension of the provision of chaplains to military establishments, and first occur a little after the earliest military chaplains. We can see the blurring of the division between military and prison chaplains and the colonial clergy in relation to the chaplains appointed in the Australian colonies. Were men such as Richard Johnson and Samuel Marsden in New South Wales, or John Youl in Van Diemen's Land,[24] prison chaplains, or were they chaplains appointed as part of the colonial establishments? Johnson has been claimed as both a prison or convict chaplain and a colonial chaplain by historians, reflecting the dual nature of his role. The records of the SPCK show that, on 14 November 1786, before the First Fleet had left London, reference was made to the need to provide Johnson, 'who is going to Botany Bay as chaplain to the convicts, with some Bibles and other religious books for the use of this charge'.[25] While the SPCK seems to have considered Johnson to be a convict chaplain, his actual commission is more general, naming him 'Chaplain to the settlement within our territory called New South Wales'. It went on to state his duties in rather vague terms:

You are, therefore, carefully and diligently to discharge the duty of chaplain, by doing and performing all and all manner of things thereunto belonging; and you are to observe and follow such orders and directions, from time to time as you shall receive from our Governor of our said territory for the time being or any other your superior officers, according to the rules and discipline of war.[26]

Chaplains remained subject to such strict military rule until 1804, after which they were placed under the control of the 'principal

---

[22] M. F. Snape, *The Redcoat and Religion: The Forgotten History of the British Soldier from the Age of Marlborough to the Eve of the First World War* (London, 2005).

[23] Smith, *Navy and Its Chaplains*, pp. 184–7.

[24] P. C. Blake, *John Youl, the Forgotten Chaplain: A Biography of the Reverend John Youl (1773–1827) First Chaplain to Northern Tasmania* (Launceston, 1999).

[25] Minutes of the SPCK, 14 November 1786, cited by F. T. Whittington, *William Grant Broughton Bishop of Australia with Some Account of the Earliest Australian Clergy* (Sydney, 1936), pp. 3–4.

[26] Commission to Reverend Richard Johnson, 24 October 1786, cited by Whittington, *William Grant Broughton*, p. 5.

chaplain'. The state continued to interfere in the activities of chaplains in a way which was highly exacerbating, especially to colonial bishops, but was the logical result of their employment by the state.[27]

But apart from the appointment of chaplains, the British government really did little to promote religion in the colonies. In his monumental three-volume history of the Church of England in the colonies, James S. M. Anderson argued that there had never been a time in which England did not show an interest in the spiritual welfare of her foreign possessions.[28] However, even Anderson admitted that the main way in which this concern was expressed was through the provision of a thin stream of colonial chaplains under the auspices of the SPG.[29] What is more, colonial chaplains had a reputation for being second-raters who would not have been able to secure ordination in the ordinary way. This may just be the result of snobbishness, but it also reflected the conditions of their employment as lowly servants of what were often unpopular and distant colonial administrations. Writing in the middle of the nineteenth century, a low view of both the colonial chaplain as an institution, and the Anglican clergy in particular, is reflected by the English satirist William Makepeace Thackeray (1811–63) in the novel, *The Virginians* (serialised 1857–9). Virginia, he states, was an Anglican colony where the clergy were supported by the state. Without bishops of their own, they were brought over to America from Britain:

Such as came were not, naturally, of the best or most eloquent kind of pastors. Noblemen's hangers-on, insolvent parsons who had quarrelled with justice or the bailiff, brought their stained cassocks into the colony in hopes of finding a living there.[30]

Thackeray, who was born in Calcutta, may be reflecting here the common view of the day that a guaranteed income was a factor in the low moral and intellectual standing of clergy in colonies such as the West Indies. But his view of the low standards of the chaplains provided to British colonies was also common among American writers. According to Frank Samuel Child, writing in about 1896, the colonial parson of New England was 'no better than he should be',[31] and compared unfavourably with the eager Nonconformist Protestant clergy who dominated the American religious landscape. A commitment to raising the training and standing of chaplains appointed to the colonies

---

[27] The imperial grant for police, magistrates and chaplains to Western Australia ended in 1888.

[28] J. S. M. Anderson, *The History of the Church of England in the Colonies and Foreign Dependencies of the British Empire* 2nd edn, 3 vols. (London, 1856).

[29] *Ibid.*, vol. II, pp. 408–11 and 550–78.

[30] W. M. Thackeray, *The Virginians: A Tale of the Last Century* (New York, 1904), p. 59.

[31] F. S. Child, *The Colonial Parson of New England* (New York, 1896), p. 42.

was one consequence of the religious revival at the end of the eighteenth century. Through the activism of William Wilberforce (1759–1833) and the group of serious-minded Anglican Evangelicals known as the Clapham Sect, a number of poor men, many of them from Yorkshire, were supported through their studies at university and were then helped to colonial appointments.

From their posts in frontier settlements, colonial chaplains were sometimes lonely and isolated, both physically and culturally. From the convict colony in Botany Bay, Richard Johnson and Samuel Marsden wrote letters that are full of complaints about the trial of the voyage, the iniquity of their convict charges and, in Johnson's case, his long battle to recover from the authorities the cost of a temporary church which, after a wait of five years, he erected at his own expense.[32] Johnson was the only officer of the First Fleet who brought his family with him. When Marsden joined him some years later he also complained of the impact of his tour of duty on his wife. The Marsdens were six months at sea during which time Ann Marsden had her first child, completely unassisted except for her husband. According to Marsden, the only other woman on board was monopolised by the ship's captain as his mistress. Nevertheless, whereas Johnson begged to come home, Marsden flourished both physically and financially in the colony, informing bishop Moore that he had never once regretted accepting his appointment.[33] Johnson prayed God would open a way for him to return home: 'for at present my situation is truly uncomfortable, without any reasonable or apparent hope or Prospect of getting good to myself or doing good to others'.[34] Other chaplains, corresponding with Moore from their posts in other mission fields in India and North America, were also more cheerful than Johnson.[35]

At the beginning of the nineteenth century, it was widely recognised that these arrangements were inadequate to the needs of the settler colonies and reform was essential.[36] Nevertheless, bishops and ecclesiastical

---

[32] Johnson to Moore, 8 May 1793, Lambeth Palace Library, Moore Papers.

[33] Marsden to Moore, 4 May 1794; Johnson to Moore, 8 May 1793, Lambeth Palace Library, Moore Papers.

[34] Johnson Journal, 16 April 1794, fol. 29, Lambeth Palace Library, Moore Papers. Johnson addressed this volume of letters and reminiscences to William Wilberforce.

[35] See, for example, the cheerful letter by Mr Wilkinson from the island of St Helena where he had been appointed chaplain prior to taking up a post with the East India Company. Lambeth Palace Library, Moore Papers.

[36] R. Strong, 'A Vision of an Anglican Imperialism: The Annual Sermons of the Society for the Propagation of the Gospel in Foreign Parts 1701–1714', *Journal of Religious History*, 30 (2006), pp. 175–98; Strong, *Anglicanism and Empire*. For earlier studies, see E. Chilman, 'Bishops in the British Colonies: The Story of the Oversea

establishments were slow to appear in the colonies and initially their appointments arose in response to political crises into which a bishop was introduced as a pacifying gesture. The first Anglican colonial diocese to be erected was Nova Scotia (1787), the second was Quebec (1793), and, in 1836, the first outside the Americas was created for bishop Broughton of Australia.[37] In India, the Scottish theologian and educator, Claudius Buchanan (1766–1815) – described by Porter as an 'establishment propagandist'[38] – argued that Britain's geographical empire should correspond with its spiritual empire. At the invitation of Josiah Pratt, the Secretary of the CMS, Buchanan provided a rationale for the replacement of missionary and chaplaincy arrangements with an imperial Church establishment.[39] For Buchanan, the argument was simple: the 'law of God' was recognised by the British legislature. Just as Rome had for many years recognised a duty to extend Christianity throughout her empire, so, in the present age, that responsibility fell to Great Britain.[40] However, for this purpose, Buchanan felt the existing Church instruments, namely, the three missionary societies (the SPG, SPCK and CMS), were inadequate. He therefore proposed the creation of what he called a 'General Colonial Ecclesiastical Establishment for Great Britain', which would include at least seven dioceses: the West Indies, Bengal or North Hindostan, Madras or South and East Hindostan, Bombay or West Hindostan, Ceylon, South Africa and New South Wales, each with a bishop and clergy on the scale of the regular English dioceses.[41] While there were many reasons why in 1813 this proposal for the whole empire failed, it had the effect of keeping the cause of the English church and missions to India before the public eye, and securing funding from the East India Company for a bishopric and Anglican ecclesiastical establishments in India.

While some Anglicans called for an imperial expansion of the Church of England, religious reforms to the constitutional standing of Nonconformists and Catholics were soon reflected throughout the empire in many different ways. Anglicanism continued to enjoy priority, but, by the 1830s, religious provisions varied widely from colony to colony. As Blackstone had commented in the late eighteenth century,

Episcopate and the Colonial Bishoprics' Fund', *Crown Colonist*, 11 (1941), pp. 486–7; W. F. France, *The Oversea Episcopate: Centenary History of the Colonial Bishoprics' Fund, 1841–1941* (London, 1941).
[37] See Table 3.3, Anglican colonial and missionary bishoprics, 1900.
[38] Porter, *Religion Versus Empire?*, p. 71.
[39] C. Buchanan, *Colonial Ecclesiastical Establishment: Being a Brief View of the State of the Colonies of Great Britain, and of Her Asiatic Empire in Respect to Religious Instruction* (London, 1813).
[40] *Ibid.*, p. 14.   [41] *Ibid.*, p. 35.

there was no automatic transmission of Church establishment to British colonies.[42] However, in some places, including Barbados and Upper Canada, ecclesiastical establishments were created by special colonial legislation, as they had been in many (but not all) American colonies. In such places, the bishop could exert considerable political power. This was sometimes seen as aggressive imperial intrusion on the part of the Church of England and the SPG, especially by other Protestants.[43] In the absence of a presiding colonial bishop, the appointment of colonial clergy was carefully regulated by the bishop of London.[44] Before ordination, each candidate for colonial service was required to show testimonials from three or more clergymen, a certificate of birth or baptism, a document showing that their intention to seek ordination had been announced in their parish for three successive Sundays, a certificate of education as well as a 'firm promise' of an ecclesiastical appointment. The responsibilities of the bishop of London for colonial clergy ended with the appointment of colonial bishops, beginning with Nova Scotia in 1787. However, the licences of Anglican colonial clergy to practice in Britain continued to be controlled tightly under the Colonial Clergy Acts.[45]

Attempts to regulate the colonial churches by imperial legislation had mixed success but reveal a trend towards increasing religious toleration. Between 1634 and 1853, there were just eight orders-in-council and seven acts of parliament that related to the colonial Church.[46] These included arrangements for giving the bishop of London jurisdiction over plantations in the West Indies (1726), suppressing the number of Roman Catholic festivals in Trinidad (1822), ordaining clergy especially for the colonies (1819) and disposing of the clergy reserves in Canada (1827, 1840 and 1853). At a time of critical change in the constitutional position of the Church of England, W. E. Gladstone published *The State in Its Relations to the Church* (1838), which provided a comprehensive analysis of religious provisions for the military and the British colonies.[47] While personally supporting the ideal of a universal, or 'national

[42] See W. Blackstone, *Commentaries on the Laws of England [1765–1769]*, facsimile edn, 4 vols. (Chicago, 1979), vol. 4, pp. 106–8.

[43] B. S. Schlenther, 'Religious Faith and Commercial Empire', in *Oxford History of the British Empire*, vol. 2, *The Eighteenth Century*, ed. P. J. Marshall (Oxford, 1998), p. 132.

[44] For the Ordination Papers of Colonial Clergy, 1748–c.1824, see Fulham Papers (vols. XXI–XXXII), Lambeth Palace Library. See G. Yeo, 'A Case without Parallel: The Bishops of London and the Anglican Church Overseas, 1660–1748', *Journal of Ecclesiastical History*, 44 (1993), pp. 450–75.

[45] See the introduction to Part III below.

[46] A. Mills, *Colonial Constitutions: An Outline of the Constitutional History and Existing Government of the British Dependencies* (London, 1856), pp. 393–4.

[47] W. E. Gladstone, *The State in Its Relations with the Church* (London, 1838). A fourth edition, expanded to two volumes, appeared in 1841.

Church', Gladstone stressed that the Church of England had no automatic rights flowing from its establishment in England, even with serving members of the military. He noted that after Catholic emancipation Roman Catholic soldiers were exempted from attending 'Church' services, but that in Ireland their officers were obliged to attend Catholic religious services with them 'in order to prevent their being tampered with by political harangues' (a precaution which was subverted since the sermons were often given in Irish).[48] Nonconformists (referred to by Gladstone as Dissenters) were not exempted, but in every military station divine service was provided by local clergymen of the established churches of England and Scotland. For Gladstone, this demonstrated that full toleration was accorded to Catholics, recognition was given to the Church of Scotland in Scotland, and the Church of England was supported everywhere else.[49]

Indeed, for a brief period in the 1830s, the empire was a place of multiple establishments, or at least multiple churches, missions and chaplaincies supported by the imperial and colonial governments. The empire, it would seem, was Protestant and Anglican no longer. However, this new toleration came at a very significant financial cost. In 1839, James Stephen (1789–1859), British under-secretary for the colonies, prepared a return of the cost of colonial Church establishments for the House of Commons.[50] This revealed that this had risen to an impressive £168,242 per annum divided between the Church of England, which received £134,450 (80 per cent), the Church of Scotland £9,967 (5.9 per cent), the Dutch Reformed Church £6,886 (4.1 per cent), mostly in Cape of Good Hope, and the Roman Catholic Church (8.7 per cent), especially in Mauritius, Lower Canada, Trinidad, and New South Wales and Van Diemen's Land. The Wesleyan minister at the Cape of Good Hope received £75, and in Jamaica there was £500 for a Wesleyan chapel, £600 for a Baptist chapel, and £1,000 for a Jewish synagogue. While thirty-nine colonies benefited from this bounty, by far the largest sums were expended in maintaining Anglican ecclesiastical establishments in British North America and the West Indies, where the bishop of Jamaica and the bishop of Barbados both enjoyed salaries of £4,000. These were not large episcopal salaries by British standards, and were comparable to those of most bishops in Ireland.[51] Other

[48] W. E. Gladstone, *The State in Its Relations with the Church*, 2nd edn (London, 1839), p. 247.
[49] *Ibid.*, p. 248.
[50] 'Church Establishment (Colonies). Return of the Number of Persons on the Establishment of the Church of England, and other Religious Denominations, Maintained by Grant of Public Money, in Each of the Colonies', *House of Commons, British Parliamentary Papers*, 55 (1839).
[51] R. B. McDowell, *The Church of Ireland, 1869–1969* (London, 1975), p. 7.

colonial bishops received much less, particularly if they were dependent on the Colonial Bishoprics' Fund. Nevertheless, these expensive
arrangements were vulnerable to parliamentary economy drives, particularly under Whig reforming governments.[52] Always unpopular with
non-Anglicans, subsidies for ecclesiastical establishments, schools and
clergy in the colonies disappeared completely by the 1860s.

At about this time, Gladstone made repeated efforts to introduce
uniform imperial legislation that would create a more democratic and
independent form of synodal governance for the Church of England
across the empire, but was forced in the end to abandon the attempt.[53]
Following the Colenso case (1860), it was determined by the Privy
Council that the imperial government did not have the power to create territorial bishoprics in colonies with their own legislatures.[54]
After this date, the independent colonies, which had responsibility
for most other aspects of their own affairs, were given sole charge of
what remained of their ecclesiastical establishments. In some cases,
for example in Barbados, the colonial legislature re-established the
Church of England and continued to give grants to other churches.[55]
However, most governments embraced secularism and dispensed with
the financial and political burden of supporting religious institutions.
In the ensuing funding vacuum, church planting was taken over by
the colonial missionary societies or, where they could afford it, the
colonial churches.

Religious arrangements for settlers and travellers in the British empire
can thus be seen to have passed through a number of phases. In the first
place, chaplaincy services were supplied to military bases, hospitals and
penal establishments, and these were extended to colonial settlements
that served the same purposes. In the case of colonies, religious provisions varied according to the nature of the colony and whether it was
one intended predominately for British settlement or if missions to the
native population were also required; these were managed through

---

[52] Porter, *Religion Versus Empire?*, p. 158. In the 1860s, the archbishop of Armagh earned
£10,000 per annum while the nine less senior bishops earned on average £3,850 per
annum.

[53] H. M. Carey, 'Gladstone, the Colonial Church and Imperial State', in *Church and
State in Old and New Worlds*, ed. H. M. Carey and J. Gascoigne (Leiden, in press).

[54] P. Hinchliff, 'John William Colenso: A Fresh Appraisal', *Journal of Ecclesiastical
History*, 13 (1962); P. Hinchliff, 'Colonial Church Establishment in the Aftermath of
the Colenso Controversy', in *Religious Change in Europe, 1650–1914: Essays for John
McManners*, ed. N. Aston (Oxford, 1997), pp. 345–63.

[55] K. Hunte, 'Christianity and Slavery in the British Caribbean', in *Christianity in the
Caribbean: Essays on Church History*, ed. A. Lampe (Barbados, 2001), p. 117. The
grant to Anglican dioceses in the British West Indies ceased in 1868, and the Anglican
Church in the West Indies was disestablished in 1869.

the missionary societies. It was not until the 1840s that new arrangements, which asserted the central importance of resident, territorial bishops throughout the empire supplanted the old system of chaplains, societies and subsidies. Anglican colonial bishops were initially supported by government and later through the Colonial Bishoprics' Fund. Paradoxically, the arrival of these Anglican bishops occurred more or less at the same time as the collapse of state support for religious establishments anywhere except in Britain itself, and in some cases, not even there. At all times, it is important not to exaggerate the extent of state-supported religion in the British empire. Apart from the appointment of chaplains and ecclesiastical establishments in certain colonies, the government did little to promote the advancement of religion beyond Britain's shores. Even while Britons enthusiastically embraced its traditional identity as a Protestant kingdom, imperial religious provision was in reality left substantially in the hands of various voluntary societies.

Missions and societies

In contrast with the weak pulse of official religion, the voluntary missionary societies were quick to embrace the religious opportunities opened up by imperial expansion. Voluntarism was a broad ethos that embraced not only the older Anglican societies such as the Society for Promoting Christian Knowledge (SPCK), the Society for the Propagation of the Gospel (SPG) and the Society in Scotland for Propagating Christian Knowledge (SSPCK), but also the new missionary and benevolent societies.[56] While the larger societies soon extended their interests worldwide, there was an unspoken attempt to avoid too much duplication of Christian effort. The SPG retained responsibility for British colonists; the Baptist Missionary Society (BMS) was first in India, though soon the London Missionary Society (LMS), the Church Missionary Society (CMS) and the Wesleyan Methodist Missionary Society (WMMS) also had major missions there; the LMS had the Pacific; the CMS took on west Africa and the WMMS had a foothold in southern Africa. The importance of the voluntary principle to all these organisations does not mean they were entirely independent of either the government or the churches. Most were closely aligned with one or other of the churches

---

[56] The dates of the foundation of the major missionary societies is as follows: SPCK, 1698; SPG, 1701; SSPCK, 1709; Baptist Missionary Society, 1793; London Missionary Society, 1795; Church Missionary Society for Africa and the East, 1799; Sunday School Union, 1799; Religious Tract Society, 1799; Abolition of Slave Trade, 1807; British and Foreign Bible Society, 1804; and Wesleyan Methodist Missionary Society, 1813.

and, while they did not have an official character, they all accepted land grants and other government assistance to aid their work. One feature of the voluntary missionary societies was soon also to be reflected in the makeup of the colonial clergy, namely, the importance of personnel drawn, not just from outside the established Church but also from outside England, including Scottish, German, Danish, Dutch, Irish, Swiss and other trained missionaries from pietist societies and agencies in Europe.[57] For missionary work, the Catholic Church drew in the same way on its religious orders, which tended to field recruits from throughout the Catholic world where missionary feeling, and an excess of clergy to available opportunities for employment, ran high. These 'foreign' personnel helped to dispel the perception that the missionary societies acted as surrogates for British national interests.

Voluntary societies were also essential for the provision of religious literature and education, which was almost entirely a church-led operation. All the churches used schools as a means of supplying Christian education, which on some occasions meant students were supplied with religious indoctrination along with literacy and bible reading. In the colonies, the SPG supplied funds and trained staff for both churches and schools. The colonial mission of the SPG is discussed more fully in Chapter 3 and the SSPCK, its Scottish counterpart, in Chapter 7. The oldest of the religious publication societies was the SPCK, which was founded by Thomas Bray in 1698 and established with its own act of parliament in 1701. Bray's initiative was intended to provide pious reading matter for the poor and encourage the formation of parish libraries. Its publications were also the stock-in-trade of the itinerant preacher.[58] The objects of the SPCK included not only the publication and distribution of bibles and religious tracts, but the erection of charity schools in all parts of England and Wales. The extension of this work to British colonies was also encompassed by the final general object which was the promotion of Christian knowledge, both at home and 'in other parts of the world' by the best available means. This ensured that the publications of the SPCK, conveniently transportable to new worlds, were distributed rapidly throughout the British colonies.

[57] A. F. Walls, 'The Eighteenth-Century Protestant Missionary Awakening in Its European Context', in *Christian Missions and the Enlightenment*, ed. B. Stanley (Grand Rapids, MI, 2001), pp. 35–6.
[58] G. Best, 'Libraries in the Parish', in *The Cambridge History of Libraries in Britain and Ireland*, vol. 2, *1640–1850*, ed. G. Mandelbrote and K. A. Manley (Cambridge, 2006), p. 324.

In the course of the eighteenth century, the SPCK was joined in its work of establishing primary schools and publishing and distributing Christian reading material throughout the empire by societies whose members were affiliated with other churches and church parties. The Society for Promoting Christian Knowledge among the Poor (1750) was non-denominational and was intended to provide 'bibles, testaments and other good books' to those who could read, but could not afford their own books.[59] Two Scottish societies with the same purpose were formed in Edinburgh and Glasgow in 1756. However, the impetus for the establishment of an Anglican Evangelical rival to the SPCK was not effectively galvanised until after the French Revolution. The Religious Tract Society (1799) provided a vehicle to include the non-churched within the moral circle of a church increasingly anxious at the extent of working-class alienation from religion and susceptibility to a variety of evils ranging from Jacobism to Romanism. The philanthropist and writer Hannah More (1745–1833) was one of those who believed that the publication of pious tracts distributed to the poor would provide them with religious comforts, direct their attention to the coming kingdom of Christ, and incidentally dissuade them from revolution. At the very least she hoped, like her character Coelebs, to show how religion 'may be brought to mix with the concerns of ordinary life, without impairing its activity, lessening its cheerfulness, or diminishing its usefulness'.[60] On this principle, it was axiomatic that tracts would be distributed in enormous numbers to emigrants and colonists abroad as well as to the poor and disenfranchised at home. Other societies, especially the British and Foreign Bible Society (1804), the British and Foreign Schools Society (1807) and the societies which merged in 1851 to form what became the Colonial and Continental Church Society, were organised with the needs of the wider world opened up by the voyages of exploration of James Cook, and the advancing colonial settlements of the second British empire in Australia, southern Africa and the South Seas, specifically in mind.

The work of all the tract societies overseas was intended to provide a bridge between the well-resourced religious provision of the home society and the religious frontier.[61] At home, they supplied books to form pious libraries in parishes and Sunday schools and places without

---

[59] *An Account of the Society for Promoting Religious Knowledge among the Poor Begun 1750* (London, 1879), p. 5.
[60] H. More, *Coelebs in Search of a Wife: Comprehending Observations on Domestic Habits and Manners, Religion and Morals*, 6th edn, 2 vols. (London, 1809), p. xi.
[61] P. Fleming and Y. Lamonde, eds., *History of the Book in Canada*, 3 vols. (Toronto, 2004), p. 139.

other cultural resources. Abroad, there were grants to emigrant and convict vessels, workhouses, coastguard stations, poorhouses, Sunday schools, missionary family libraries, as well individual clergymen and schoolmasters – to anywhere and anyone, in short, who could find a use for them. In relation to British colonies in North America, the historian of the Religious Tract Society, William Jones, invokes the pity that was due to the poor emigrant and his lonely condition: 'the colonist of the interior, the fisherman in his lonely cabin by the wild shore, the settler who has raised his rude hovel on the borders of the primeval forest, or in the midst of some vast plain', who were all deprived of the means of grace.[62] There was considerable sympathy for these isolated settlers, and grants to colonists and missionary families were among the most financially significant of those made by the Society. By 1850, these amounted to £3,000, compared with £2,657 for Sunday and day schools.[63] Convicts were also the subject of popular appeal. In New South Wales, the Evangelical layman and former Arctic explorer, Sir W. Edward Parry (1790–1855), who took charge of the Australian Agricultural Company's operations at Port Stephens, received 3,000 tracts in 1831 and reported on the remarkable transformation of convict morals which resulted from access to good reading material.[64] According to Parry, conversion was the result of Christian contemplation of the exile's condition, a highly meritorious outcome. The Society's supporters were encouraged to see their activities as both a moral and patriotic duty. One correspondent wrote:

Will English Christians stand unconcerned, and see their exiled countrymen perishing in the dense woods and forests of these far-distant lands? Many of them deeply sigh for their home, their native land; their wives and blooming children, from whom, in the moment of folly they have banished themselves by their crimes.[65]

By 1849, when the Society commemorated its Jubilee by publishing a substantial history of its work to that date, its work was already being conceived in imperial terms, as the duty of the British people to evangelise the empire. For the supporters of the Religious Tract Society, such a role flowed naturally from the pre-eminence of Britain among the nations of the world and the acquisition of colonies, which could only be part of a divine plan:

Colonies established by other powers are now, by the providence of God, the dependants of our sea-girt island, and within the reach of our influence.

---

[62] W. Jones, *The Jubilee Memorial of the Religious Tract Society* (London, 1850), p. 572.
[63] *Ibid.*, p. 194.   [64] *Ibid.*, p. 530.   [65] *Ibid.*, pp. 539–40.

Our language and our religious literature will continue to follow our national course, and will become identified with a large portion of the world's population. Our commanding position, therefore, calls loudly on the churches of our country, by every practicable means, to 'hold forth the word of life' to all nations.[66]

These kinds of sentiments, in which there was a fusion of piety, nationalism and missionary commitment, were characteristic of the colonial missionary movement which flourished in all the major churches from the 1850s. In general, we will see that societies such as, in this case, the SPCK, which worked with emigrants – including convicts – was one of the first organisations to use this language in representations of emigration, convict exile and colonial settlement.

Through a combination of these forces – chaplains for colonists, missionaries for native people, school and publication societies to encourage Christian morality and education – the empire was well provided with religious services. However, there were some places they could not reach. The East India Company, the Africa Company and the Hudson's Bay Company, which were the trading companies that managed to survive into the post-Napoleonic era, generally opposed religious interference in their fields of operation. Nevertheless, the days of their exclusive control over their territories were numbered. The movement for reform came from within and without. Within, individuals such as Charles Grant (1746–1823), who was Chairman of the East India Company and a member of the Clapham Sect, advocated that the Company allow missionaries and chaplains to serve in India and improve the moral conditions of its people. Grant's efforts were just part of a great call for reform from all over the British world.

Reform and revival

There were a number of religious, political and social factors at work to bring about change to the religious condition of British people both at home and overseas. For all the British churches, the nineteenth century was a time of constitutional reform and religious enthusiasm. This encompassed the continuing impact of the evangelical revival, which had begun in the eighteenth century, the Oxford movement for the Church of England, and what Emmet Larkin called the Catholic 'devotional revolution'.[67] Evangelicalism also had a profound influence on

---

[66] *Ibid.*, p. 640.
[67] E. Larkin, 'The Devotional Revolution in Ireland, 1850–75', *American Historical Review*, 77 (1972), pp. 625–52.

the Church of Scotland where it gave rise to the Free Church movement. In Ireland, Evangelicals also prospered in greater numbers in
the former Church of Ireland than they did in the former Church of
England; both churches were of course merged by the Act of Union to
form the United Church of England and Ireland.

Evangelicalism was an international movement that extended to the
Americas and across Europe. In the American colonies, it was associated with the preaching of George Whitefield; in Europe, the Moravian
Brethren sparked a renewed enthusiasm for foreign missions, and in
Britain, the revival began in Wales where chapel culture would eventually supplant Anglicanism for most of the population. In whatever
denominational context they arose, religious revivals ensured that thousands of pious men and women who went out into the colonies burned
with the wish to reform the world for Christ under the commodious rule
of the British empire. Some chose to evangelise native people, others to
work among the poor and marginalised in cities, others to bring Jews,
or Roman Catholics in Ireland, Scotland and Europe, to Christ in the
belief that the final days were coming. Many saw the colonies as sites to
reforge their home churches and convert the whole British people to a
more perfect, Christian way of life.

The evangelical movement led to the creation of a number of new religious bodies, of which the most important for emigrants and settlers was
that founded by John Wesley (1703–91) and his brother Charles (1707–88).
Coming into being at much the same time as the rise in emigration,
Methodism was forged and tempered by the experience and opportunities
of British colonialism in America and the other settler colonies. Between
1801 and 1836, the total Methodist membership rose from only 1.65 per
cent to a modest 4 per cent of the adult population of England,[68] but its
growth in the new world was more vigorous. Before the arrival of the
Methodists, church planting in British North America had been strongly
influenced by the founding churches of the United States especially the
Congregationalists (or Independents), Presbyterians and Baptists. The
latter churches played the leading role in the American home missionary movement, which planted churches in the south and west where the
population was expanding throughout the nineteenth century.

With its flexible circuit structure, Methodism proved to be ideally
suited to the conditions on the frontier. Latourette called it 'an agency
for expanding Christianity'.[69] Wesleyans, as Koss has argued in the case

---

[68] Cook and Stevenson, *British Historical Facts 1760–1830*, p. 163.
[69] Latourette, *A History of the Expansion of Christianity*, vol. 4, p. 190.

of the Reverend Hugh Price Hughes (1847–1902), the founder of the *Methodist Times*, were conservative politically and saw the empire as a legitimate field for their aspirations to become a world church for the English-speaking peoples.[70] By the beginning of the next century, both Methodism and Presbyterianism would come to outstrip Anglicanism as the leading Protestant churches in British North America. In contrast, the balance of the churches in Australia and New Zealand was rather closer to that of the home society with Anglicanism making a strong showing in all colonies. However, even in the antipodes, Methodism was, by the end of the nineteenth century, the second largest Protestant denomination.[71] The evangelical revival also had a strong impact among a large number of serious Christians who chose to work for moral and spiritual reform within the Church of England, while forming a distinct 'low church' party within it.[72] Throughout this book, they are called Evangelicals (with a capital E) and, like the Methodists, they were one of the big success stories of colonial Christianity.

The colonies were important sites for religious reform because they were generally places of economic opportunity where social and cultural habits were more malleable than at home. In Britain itself, reform was initially more difficult to sustain. However, war with France, which continued until 1815, insurrection in Ireland and the colonies, and bouts of revolution in Europe, eroded traditional views of the relationship between Church and state. Rebellions in Canada (1837 and 1838) and the subsequent Durham Report sped up reforms to the system of Canadian clergy reserves and placed limits on the privileges of the Anglican minority.

Social changes were also important, especially the dramatic rise in emigration that followed the end of the Napoleonic Wars (1799–1815). After 1815, emigration from England rose from an average of more than 20–30,000 every five years until it reached more than 120,000 in the five years from 1851 to 1855, remaining at similarly high levels throughout the 1860s.[73] The flow from Ireland was astonishing.[74] Before the Great Famine (1845–9), up to 1 million people had already

---

[70] S. E. Koss, 'Wesleyanism and Empire', *Historical Journal*, 18 (1975), p. 110, citing *Methodist Times*, 6 January 1898.

[71] See Tables 1.1–1.6 for statistics on colonial denominational adherence.

[72] R. W. Vaudry, *Anglicans and the Atlantic World: High Churchmen, Evangelicals, and the Quebec Connection* (Toronto, 2003), p. 8, argues that 'Low Church' was used as a term of abuse by high churchmen against Anglican Evangelicals in British North America and that the two traditions were quite distinct.

[73] Mitchell, *British Historical Statistics*, p. 76. Mitchell notes that the real figure is likely to exceed these estimates.

[74] Estimates from D. Fitzpatrick, *Irish Emigration 1801–1921* (Dublin, 1984) pp. 1 *et seq.*

left Ireland for British North America, while about half that number had made the shorter trip to England, Scotland and Wales. After the famine, the flow became a flood with the most popular destinations being the United States and Great Britain. Irish emigrants of all denominations also made a substantial impact in the Australian colonies. Internal and external flows of emigrants from rural England and Scotland to overseas colonies were also very significant. Between 1815 and the First World War, it is estimated that more than 16 million people left the United Kingdom, up to half of them from Ireland.[75] As emigration rose, the churches responded by forming colonial missionary societies or colonial committees who managed the stream of applications for money and personnel for churches, missions and schools. From the 1880s, the churches also created emigration societies and committees which gave direct support for the emigration of socially deprived people, including children, to the colonies.

The colonial missionary movement was to the British empire what the home missionary movement was for the American West: a rapidly mobilised workforce deployed along a moving frontier for the planting of clergy, churches, schools and other religious institutions. In the United States, the 'home' missionary movement, which was restricted to the American continent, was dominated by women for whom it became an extension of the social gospel. According to one estimate of the Protestant home missionary movement in America, in the course of the nineteenth century over US$150 million was spent on planting churches. The estimate increases to US$360 million if the amounts spent on Sunday schools, Bible and tract printing, and Christian colleges are also taken into account.[76]

In contrast, the colonial missionary movement to Britain's overseas settler colonies was conducted on a more human, if still impressive, scale (though I do not know of any meaningful way to calculate the cost of it, since the work was divided between so many different organisations and places). Women participated in the British movement largely through the Catholic and Anglican female religious orders, most of whom worked as schoolteachers.[77] Otherwise, colonial missions were

---

[75] N. H. Carrier and J. R. Jeffery, *External Migration, a Study of the Available Statistics 1815–1950* (London, 1953), pp. 90–1, based on outward passenger figures from UK. The calculation of Irish emigration is complicated by high levels of internal migration to Great Britain prior, or in addition, to overseas.

[76] J. B. Clark, 'Home Missions', in *The New Schaff-Herzog Encyclopedia of Religious Knowledge*, ed. S. M. Jackson (New York and London, 1909), p. 345.

[77] On Irish Catholic nuns and education, see D. Murphy, *A History of Irish Emigrant and Missionary Education* (Dublin, 2000); C. Clear, *Nuns in Nineteenth Century Ireland* (Dublin, 1987); R. Fogarty, *Catholic Education in Australia, 1806–1950*, vol. 2,

led and organised almost entirely by men in work that was conceived as much in terms of empire building as the development of religious and social infrastructure. The outcome was that, by the end of the century, the number of clergy and churches in relation to the population of the settler colonies was close to that in Britain. The story of this movement is told in Chapters 3 to 7.

The empire of morality

Evangelicals from across the Protestant churches found that there were many issues on which they could agree. Together they formed a powerful lobby group whose reach extended well into the colonies ensuring that the 'call to seriousness', as it has been called by Ian Bradley,[78] had both an imperial as well as a domestic character. Of the many moral campaigns fought by the informal coalition of Anglican Evangelicals, Presbyterians and Nonconformists, the earliest and most successful was the movement to end the Atlantic slave trade and eliminate slavery throughout the empire. Since this was essentially an evil that had been created within Britain's settler colonies in the Americas, it can be seen as the first salvo in a campaign to moralise and cleanse the empire. In the late eighteenth century, agitation against the slave trade was initiated by Quakers who were instrumental in the founding of the Society for the Abolition of the Slave Trade (1787). In the same year, the impeachment of Warren Hastings (1732–1818), the first Governor-General of Bengal, brought to light what many felt were moral lapses in British rule in India, particularly the policy of leaving the work of colonisation entirely in the hands of commercial enterprises, such as the British East India Company. In his speeches against Hastings, Edmund Burke (1729–97) excoriated those 'who consider laws, religion, morality, and the principles of state policy of empires as mere questions of profit and loss'.[79] Although Hastings was acquitted in 1795, after the trial more consideration was given to the humane and religious administration of colonies. This need not imply that the later 'moral' British empire was any less destructive in its impact on native people than its earlier, more purely commercial, manifestation. Indeed, it may well have become more so, since missionaries generally assumed the right

---

Catholic Education under the Religious Orders, 2 vols. (Melbourne, 1959). For Protestant Home Missionaries in Australia, see A. P. O'Brien, *God's Willing Workers: Women and Religion in Australia* (Sydney, 2005) pp. 97–119.

[78] I. Bradley, *The Call to Seriousness: The Evangelical Impact on the Victorians* (London, 1976).

[79] E. Burke, *The Works of the Right Honourable Edmund Burke*, vol. VIII, *Speeches on the Impeachment of Warren Hastings*, 2 vols., vol. 2 (London, 1857), p. 50.

to make cultural demands, including conversion to Christianity, that were not expected by traders and planters.

Evangelicals also led the way in insisting that the commercial operations of Charter companies such as the East India Company, or the Hudson's Bay Company in Upper Canada, should acquire a moral character. The commercial nature of rule in India had not precluded all religious services, especially to other Europeans. Under its revised Charter (1698), the East India Company and other trading companies who conducted commercial enterprises in east Asia, Australia and America were required to appoint Anglican and Presbyterian chaplains whose teaching would reflect the orthodoxy of the established churches at home. Toleration of the religious representatives of other European colonial powers, such as the Catholic missionaries of formerly Portuguese Bombay, was also required as a consequence of the 1689 Toleration Act.[80] Nevertheless, the Charter gave the East India Company power to exclude disturbing influences, including missionaries, from territory under their control.[81] With the effective implementation of direct government rule of India by the India Office, the number of British administrators and their families resident in India expanded considerably. The passage of the Charter Renewing Act of 1813 marked the formal end to the policy that placed heavy restrictions on the activities of Christian missionaries. After 1814, the East India Company provided Anglican, Presbyterian, Methodist and Catholic chaplains to those serving in its military garrisons.[82]

The high water mark for the political influence of evangelicals was probably reached sometime before 1830 and declined thereafter. In contrast with their earlier triumphs in routing moral lapses in the West Indies (slavery) and India (Warren Hastings), humanitarians were unable to persuade the Colonial Office to support the findings of the 1835–6 Parliamentary Select Committee on Aborigines, which brought down a report which condemned settler brutality in Canada, southern Africa, Australia and New Zealand. Instead, the government moved to permit colonisation of New Zealand. Missionary influence over the New Zealand Treaty of Waitangi (1840) was supposed to lead to the moral management of the acquisition of land, but enraged the

---

[80] P. Carson, 'The British Raj and the Awakening of the Evangelical Conscience: The Ambiguities of Religious Establishment and Toleration, 1698–1833', in *Christian Missions and the Enlightenment*, ed. B. Stanley (Grand Rapids, MI, 2001), pp. 45–70, citing K. Ballhatchet, 'The East India Company and Roman Catholic Missionaries', *Journal of Ecclesiastical History*, 42 (1993), pp. 273–88.

[81] Carson, 'The British Raj and the Awakening of the Evangelical Conscience', p. 47.

[82] D. F. Wright, 'Chaplaincies, Colonial', in *Dictionary of Scottish Church History and Theology*, ed. N. M. D. S. Cameron (Edinburgh, 1993), p. 163.

pro-colonial lobby, led by Edward Gibbon Wakefield, who gave as his opinion that 'the origin of all the misery which has occurred in Tahiti and New Zealand is the missionaries not being confined to their calling'.[83] In fact, the Treaty failed to pacify the Maori who erupted in rebellion against British rule, following numerous local agendas, in the New Zealand Wars (1845–72).[84] At about the same time, the Jamaican Rebellion (1865) also discredited those who had predicted that the liberated slaves would evolve into grateful and passive British subjects – despite their exclusion from economic and political power in the West Indies. The *Anti-Slavery Reporter* might argue that the rebellion had its origin in the white community 'who seem actually to have driven the slaves into insubordination and resistance'.[85] Others were supportive of the settlers and, like Wakefield, regarded the Baptist and Methodist missionaries as fomenters of violence and native unrest.

Colonial churches

The planting of churches, rather than colonial chaplaincies and missions, began in the second quarter of the nineteenth century. At first, the most vigorous colonial churches tended to be those of people who had benefited from earlier political and religious reforms, including Catholics, Nonconformists, and evangelicals in both the Church of England and the Church of Scotland. While they were still subject to condescension by the established Church, there was considerable optimism that the free churches would liberate patterns of belief and worship, just as reform was liberating the legislature and widening the franchise.[86] In speaking in favour of the emancipation of Catholics, Thomas Chalmers, who would later become the leader of the Free Church of Scotland, argued that free religion would lead inevitably to the triumph of reformed Protestantism:

[G]ive the Catholics of Ireland their emancipation ... and give me the circulation of the bible, and with this mighty engine I will overthrow the tyranny of Antichrist, and establish the fair and original form of Christianity on its ruins.[87]

---

[83] E. G. Wakefield to Sir Robert Peel, 19 August 1844, British Library, Additional MS 40550, fols. 141–4.

[84] J. Belich, *The New Zealand Wars and the Victorian Interpretation of Racial Conflict* (Auckland, 1986).

[85] British and Foreign Anti-Slavery Society, 'Rebellion in Jamaica', *Anti-Slavery Reporter*, 5 (1833), p. 242.

[86] H. McLeod, *Religion and Society in England, 1850–1914* (Basingstoke, 1996), p. 110.

[87] Hanna, *Memoirs*, vol. III, pp. 235–42, cited by R. F. G. Holmes, *Thomas Chalmers and Ireland. Lecture Delivered at the Annual Meeting of the Presbyterian Historical Society of Ireland* (Belfast, 1979), p. 11.

Colonies and missions were seen as ideal workshops for this great spiritual experiment.

Surprisingly, the orthodox mainstream of the Church of England takes longer to move out to the colonies than Nonconformists or Evangelical Anglicans. In part, this was because the two oldest Anglican missionary organisations, the SPG and the SPCK, received some government funding for this purpose. In the 1830s, the reforming mood is reflected in a new, more vigorous spirit within the SPG under the leadership of Ernest Hawkins (1802–68), which is discussed in Chapter 3. At about the same time – and largely because of increased pressure on the existing mechanism of support for colonial churches provided by the diocese of London – Bishop Blomfield began agitating successfully for the creation of more colonial bishops. In relatively quick succession, moderate Anglicans consolidated their forces to launch the Colonial Bishoprics' Fund (1841), the colonial missionary college of St Augustine at Canterbury (1848), the Emigrants' Spiritual Aid Fund (1849) and the Anglican group settlement scheme for Canterbury in New Zealand (1850). These were promoted as works of the whole Church.

Anglican expansion was complicated by the divisions between different church parties which were redefined as a result of Tractarian controversies in the 1840s.[88] In places where high churchmen secured colonial dioceses, moderate Anglicans rallied behind the projects they created such as the Melanesian Mission, founded by bishop Selwyn of New Zealand.[89] Evangelicals continued to support the CMS; Anglo-Catholics preferred to channel funds towards their own missions such as the Universities' Mission to Central Africa, the Cambridge Mission to Delhi and the Oxford Mission to Calcutta, where missionaries would be free to establish what they saw as a more perfect form of the English church with full Catholic teaching and ritual, free from state intrusion.[90]

The creation of colonial bishoprics led in some instances to tense standoffs between different church parties in a number of Anglican dioceses. A comprehensive and unpopular attempt to install Anglican Christianity as part of the imperial occupation of India came with the consecration of Thomas Fanshaw Middleton (1769–1822) as bishop of

---

[88] P. B. Nockles, *The Oxford Movement in Context: Anglican High Churchmanship, 1760–1857* (Cambridge, 1997), p. 33.

[89] D. Hilliard, *God's Gentlemen: A History of the Melanesian Mission, 1849–1942* (Brisbane, 1978).

[90] *Ibid.*, p. 233; S. S. Maughan, 'Imperial Christianity? Bishop Montgomery and the Foreign Missions of the Church of England, 1895–1915', in *The Imperial Horizons of British Protestant Missions, 1880–1914*, ed. A. Porter (Grand Rapids, MI, 2003), p. 36.

Calcutta. His diocese embraced Ceylon, Malaya and New South Wales and attempted to impose a much stronger and more exclusive control over both missionaries and settlers in British India. This more imperial vision of Anglicanism was not successful and aroused the same kinds of resistance that had been common in the former American colonies. As the number of missionaries in India expanded dramatically in the second half of the nineteenth century, missionaries from other societies soon outnumbered those from the British societies.[91] High church ambitions to create an Anglican ascendancy in Australia, New Zealand and South Africa were also rebuffed.

The expansion of Catholicism in the British empire happened in two ways.[92] In the first place, Britain secured new territories through conquest and economic expansion in the nineteenth century, which for the first time included significant Catholic populations. The largest of these was in the former colony of New France or Quebec with its majority French population whose religious rights were protected under the Treaty of Paris (1763), the Quebec Act (1774) and the Constitutional Act of 1791, which created the Provinces of Upper and Lower Canada. After the war of 1812, during which the Catholic bishop of Quebec supported the British against the United States, the loyal status of French Catholics was no longer questioned and other Catholic disabilities were lifted.[93] By removing the privileges of the Church of England in Canada, the Act of Union (1840) effectively disestablished the Anglican Church and secured further gains for Catholics and other religious denominations in the new colony. More Catholics came under British rule with the absorption of Newfoundland, with a population that included large numbers of French and Irish Catholics, and even more with the capitulation of Mauritius, the former French colony of Île de France, on 3 December 1810. In India and Malaya, the British also encountered ecclesiastical arrangements inherited from former Catholic powers that included French, Portuguese and Italian bishops and missionaries as well as native Catholics whose faith had been planted centuries earlier.[94] Indeed, the Thomas Catholics in India claimed spiritual descent from the apostle Thomas in the earliest missionary days of the Church. In such cases, the Sacred Congregation for the Propagation of the Faith

---

[91] Frykenberg, *Christianity in India*, p. 265.
[92] W. T. Southerwood, *Catholics in British Colonies: Planting a Faith Where No Sun Sets – Islands and Dependencies of Britain Till 1900* (London, 1998).
[93] K. S. Latourette, *A History of the Expansion of Christianity*, vol. V, *The Great Century in the Americas, Australasia, and Africa AD 1800–AD 1914*, 7 vols. (London, 1943), pp. 10–11.
[94] The most ancient Catholic diocese on the subcontinent was Portuguese Goa, erected in 1533.

(Propaganda), the papal bureaucracy in charge of foreign missions, appointed vicars apostolic who were generally English Benedictines, or Irish or English Jesuits, who would be acceptable to the English government. The process of creating new missionary dioceses accelerated during the pontificates of Pius VII (1800–23) and Gregory XVI (1831–46), who had been prefect of Propaganda before his election. During the reigns of these two popes, twenty-nine vicariates and dioceses were established in British colonies in Australia, Canada, Oceania, Southern Africa, India, the West Indies and Madagascar.[95]

In the second place, there were Catholic emigrants from Britain to the colonies, which, even before Catholic emancipation in 1829, were provided with their own chaplains and bishops. Initially, poverty and cultural inhibitions ensured that Catholics made up a relatively small proportion of Britons overseas. However, from about 1850, the aftermath of famine in Ireland unleashed a flood of refugees and economic migrants who fled to England, Scotland, America and the British colonies. Between 1800 and 1880, the Catholic population in the United Kingdom rose from 90,000 to 1,300,000 in England and from 30,000 to 320,000 in Scotland, most of whom were concentrated in industrial cities such as Glasgow, Manchester and Liverpool. Millions more emigrated to the United States, British North America, Australia and New Zealand. These new Catholic populations were predominately Irish and they gave their allegiance and affection to Irish clergy and bishops. With the ascendancy of Paul Cullen (1803–78) as archbishop of Dublin, Propaganda increasingly bypassed both London and the English-born Catholics who had gone out to bishoprics in the colony of New South Wales and elsewhere and gave the nod to Hiberno-Romans selected by Cullen. As we will see in Chapter 4, below the bishops there was a clerical proletariat of parish priests and religious sisters and brothers, many of them belonging to religious orders in Ireland, who were sent in their thousands to Catholic dioceses throughout the empire.

Presbyterians also found opportunities in the empire, although, like mainstream Anglicans, they were not so quick to extend Reformed Protestantism overseas as those in other churches. In Scotland, the Episcopal Church had been disestablished since 1690 and the Presbyterian Church of Scotland given full benefit of establishment under the Act of Union (1707). Tensions continued between orthodox and evangelical Presbyterians, Episcopalians and Presbyterians, and between Protestants and minority Catholics in the Highlands and

---

[95] For a chronological list of the growth of the Catholic hierarchy in Britain and her colonies, see Table 4.2.

Islands. These long-running divisions may have contributed to the slow growth of interest by the Church of Scotland in the work of missions and colonial church extension. The Highland Clearances, which began in the 1760s, were responsible for the first significant departures to the colonies, with small groups heading for Nova Scotia and the Maritime Provinces, often accompanied by their own Gaelic-speaking Presbyterian and Catholic clergy. After the Peace of 1802 (which was supposed to secure peace between Britain and France), Scottish soldiers also turned settler in Upper Canada (Ontario). Alexander MacDonnell, who had led the Glengarry Fencibles to the region, went on to become its first Roman Catholic bishop (1826).[96] The Glasgow Colonial Society, discussed in Chapter 7, later incorporated into the Colonial Scheme of the Free Church of Scotland, supported Presbyterian Church extension in British North America. In New South Wales, the Presbyterian minister and emigration advocate, John Dunmore Lang (1799–1878), encouraged Scottish settlers to emigrate to Australia. Irish Presbyterians were critical to the expansion of the colonial church in British North America.

The imperial and global network of Presbyterianism was articulated not only through Scottish and Irish emigration throughout the British empire, but also through Presbyterian connections with other European reformed Protestants and their colonial empires and missionary movements. Hence, in southern Africa, Presbyterians forged bonds with the Calvinist adherents of the Dutch Reformed Church (NGK). Scottish and Irish Presbyterians were active in the non-denominational foreign and colonial missionary societies supported by the Congregationalists – the London Missionary Society and the Colonial Missionary Society. Finally, the Disruption of the Church of Scotland (1843) fired a much greater enthusiasm for all branches of mission, including foreign and colonial missions and missions to Jews, which were conducted by both the free and established Church of Scotland. British North America, Victoria in Australia and New Zealand attracted a particularly high proportion of Scottish settlers, many of them with Free Church affiliations. The most concrete example of Presbyterian aspirations in the colonies was the Free Church of Scotland's support for the colonisation of the province of Otago on the South Island of New Zealand, discussed in Chapter 11.

This little sketch, which covers just the major churches considered in this book, only scratches the surface of the dense imperial religious networks created by British churches and missionary societies in the

[96] Carrington, *British Overseas*, p. 131.

course of the nineteenth century. Almost every church – and every sect and church party within each church – attempted to negotiate a response to the British colonial empire in some way.[97] At the end of the nineteenth century, for example, the emergence of the Faith Mission movement, including the Scottish Faith Mission of John George Govan (1861–1927), was quickly extended to Canada and South Africa; Hudson Taylor's China Inland Mission, founded in 1865, was the model in Australia for the Aborigines Inland Mission founded by Retta Jane Long in 1905. Through groups such as Christian Missions in Many Lands, the Plymouth Brethren evangelised along the routes opened up by the British railway in Argentina. Pentecostalism, which began in 1906, spread like wildfire along imperial pathways. Because of the prestige attached to direct evangelism with non-Europeans, many societies chose to downplay the church planting and colonial institution building that underpinned foreign missionary efforts. Indeed, both the Faith Missions and Pentecostals tended to denounce earlier missionary efforts for their institutional encumbrances. They were too much concerned with God's Greater Britain, a political as well as a religious ideal, and not enough with the spiritual realm of God's empire. Nevertheless, in writing the history of the colonial missionary movement, a line must be drawn somewhere, and these themes will need to be pursued in other studies.

Conclusion

For the founding churches of the British empire, the nineteenth century ushered in a remarkable series of ecclesiastical changes both at home and in the colonies. The institutional and financial privileges of the Church of England and Ireland, which had been the base for most colonial missionary efforts in an earlier era, were dismantled in the colonies, as they would be later in Ireland (1871) and Wales (1920). This was only the precursor to the constitutional revolution which removed disabilities restraining Nonconformists and Catholics at home. While this was denounced by some religious conservatives, it led not to the collapse of religion but to a wave of reforming, colonising and missionary efforts in the empire at large. For reformed Protestants, missionary expansion was about the establishment of Christ's kingdom throughout the world. Initially, missionaries were successful in their proposal that

---

[97] For the examples which follow, see the notes in G. H. Anderson, *Biographical Dictionary of Christian Missions* (Grand Rapids, MI, 1999). For an authoritative survey of the British foreign missionary movement, see Cox, *British Missionary Enterprise*.

colonists should be restrained from occupying the lands of tribal peoples such as those who circled the Pacific world made known through the voyages of James Cook. However, by the 1860s, advocates of British colonial settlements rejected the idea that the colonies should be preserved for their original inhabitants and Christian missionaries.

This was a popular movement. However, Dilke spoke for colonists and settlers when he included the settler churches within the British cultural commonwealth that he promoted under the name of 'Greater Britain'. In the countries he traversed – British North America, Australia and New Zealand, southern Africa and other sites of significant white emigration and occupation throughout the empire such as the West Indies, India and South America – the colonising churches were moulded by the particular political and cultural settings of the settler states. This encompassed relationships with rival imperial powers and their churches: French Catholics and Protestant churches from the United States in the case of Canada, the Dutch Reformed Church in southern Africa, whereas the various British churches were virtually unencumbered by Christian rivals in their occupation of Australia and New Zealand apart from a small group of French Catholics. It also included encounters with native peoples, slaves and indentured labourers, who were imported to provide labour in the settler economies. In a wide range of debates – about slavery, convict transportation and the impact of colonisation on aborigines or tribal peoples in southern Africa, Australia, New Zealand and British North America – the settler churches were at the forefront of discussions about the morality of the empire. As the frontier passed westward and northward in both Australia and Canada, these moral anxieties receded. They would never really go away in both New Zealand and southern Africa. War in south Africa would demonstrate how fragile the consensus endorsing British cultural hegemony was, even in colonies of majority white settlement.

Over the course of a hundred years, what is perhaps the most distinctive change to the religious character of the empire was the loss of the dominant position enjoyed by the Church of England. This was accompanied by the disarticulation of the nexus between church and state that had given the first British empire – that which encompassed the Atlantic world – its Protestant identity. In the second English-speaking British empire, that of Greater Britain, the empire retained its Christian aspirations in informal ways. However, this was a voluntary movement made up of 'free' churches, which competed for resources from the state, rather than claiming them as a right.

The British empire was not planned as a Christian commonwealth. However, in the way of empires, the network of communication, affection and interest that bound peripheries to the metropole ensured that the drama of religious events in London, Dublin and Edinburgh was played out in the colonies. Despite their differing theological, ethnic and social origins, what the churches of Great Britain and Ireland had in common was the wish to extend their range and influence over the settler population and make the British a better, more Christian, people. In the next part of the book, we will look at the idea of 'colonial mission' and at the separate histories of the colonial missions of the major British churches, whose aim was to make God's empire contiguous with the British empire.

Before we go there, I should, perhaps, emphasise once again that this is not a history of religion in the British empire, nor even of all branches of Christianity in the British world, however defined. It merely concerns those Christian churches with the resources to create organisations which planted Christian seedlings in the majority settler colonies. Of course, this constitutes a good deal less than the total religious landscape of the empire. However, as Tables 1.1 to 1.6 demonstrate, by 1901 it includes religious adherents, as enumerated in the census, who made up over 95 per cent of the settler populations of Canada, Australia, Cape Colony and New Zealand, with smaller aggregations elsewhere. Together they formed an overseas British Christian world of around 10 million people. As we will see, this is more than enough for one book.

Part II

Colonial missionary societies

Introduction: colonial mission

In the course of the nineteenth century, the success of the foreign missionary movement led to a gradual shift in the meaning of the word 'mission', so that it came to refer exclusively to the evangelisation of non-European Muslims, Hindus, Buddhists, Jews and other non-Christian people. As a consequence, missions by British Christians to other British Christians appeared to be a contradiction in terms, even if it was sometimes argued that many so-called Christians were 'practically heathen' and in dire need of missionary aid. However, the earliest understanding of mission was simply the task of sending someone under properly delegated authority, to set up a branch of the Church in a new geographical area. A missionary (from the Latin *missio*, 'I send') was a messenger or diplomat. While a mission may have involved conversion if non-Christians were resident in the area, this was really incidental to the work he had been sent to perform. When Pope Gregory the Great sent Augustine as a missionary to the English in 597, his main responsibility was not to convert the Anglo-Saxons but rather to set up an English church, consecrate bishops (Bede says he was given orders for twenty-four: twelve bishops for London and twelve bishops for York) and create an administrative infrastructure so that the papacy had someone in charge whom they could deal with. In other words, mission was as much a bureaucratic as a spiritual charge. Having sent out a missionary, Christian conversion might then proceed, led by a bishop who would oversee the creation of the new church, which was bound administratively to the ruler who had sponsored it, and the religious authority, usually the pope, who had sent the missionary in the first place.

The religious revival of the eighteenth and nineteenth centuries changed the emphasis in British missions so that priority came to be given to the direct work of preaching the gospel to non-Christian people outside Europe. As we saw in Chapter 2, this work was led not by the institutional churches but by voluntary missionary societies, partly because of restrictions that had originally restricted the access of missionaries to British colonies.

Henry Venn (1796–1873), Secretary of the Church Missionary Society from 1841 to 1873, was chiefly responsible for advancing the ethos of foreign missions at the expense of the planting of churches in settler colonies, which in his view was tainted by its association with the state. On their point of departure for the field, Venn issued instructions to all CMS missionaries that defined their task in terms of the evangelisation of new recruits for the Church of England:

The one object of the Church Missionary Society is to provide for the preaching of the Gospel of Christ to those who have not yet received it; and to train up the Christian converts in the doctrine and discipline of the Church of England.[1]

This gave special emphasis to the conversion of the 'heathen', a work of such importance that all other missionary callings (including the colonial mission of the CMS's 'Church' rival, the SPG) should be made subordinate to it. For Venn, the final objective of missionaries was to create self-supporting, indigenous churches that would effectively make the original mission redundant.[2] He regarded all other work as a waste of resources, declaring in 1852 that the 'proper work of a Missionary Society is the evangelisation of the heathen, and not the perfecting of the Ecclesiastical framework of a Christian community'.[3] He was therefore not a supporter of the creation of bishoprics and ecclesiastical establishments which he considered a distraction from the work of building an indigenous church in colonies such as India.[4]

As the missionary movement in Great Britain and Ireland expanded and became more complex, it came to incorporate a host of activities, which ranged from the original tasks of church planting, conversion of the heathen and support for colonists, to include almost any work of Christian service, social welfare or evangelism. The two established churches had the most ambitious missionary programmes, as we can see from the activities outlined in sources such as the *Year Book of the Church of England*, first published in 1882.[5] Besides reports from

[1] W. Knight, *The Missionary Secretariat of Henry Venn* (London, 1880), p. 468, cited by W. R. Schenk, 'The Missionary and Politics: Henry Venn's Guidelines', *Journal of Church and State*, 24 (1982), p. 528.
[2] C. P. Williams, *The Ideal of the Self-Governing Church: A Study in Victorian Missionary Strategy* (Leiden, 1990).
[3] Venn and Snaith to the Reverend T. G. Ragland, 2 February 1852, cited by Williams, *The Ideal of the Self-Governing Church*, p. 4.
[4] Cox, *Imperial Fault Lines*, p. 43.
[5] C. Mackeson, *The Year-Book of the Church: A Record of Work and Progress in the Church of England, Compiled from Official Sources* (London, 1882); National Assembly of the Church of England, *The Official Year-Book of the Church of England* (London, 1883).

the colonial bishops (with frequent requests for men and money) the *Year Book* gave accounts of societies that catered for emigrants, colonists, seamen and soldiers, as well as missionary colleges that trained clergy for churches and missions overseas. The Church of Scotland also aimed to be comprehensive. Its 'schemes' included missions to the heathen, Jews, education, home and colonial missions, all of which provided detailed reports to the General Assembly. With so much going on, it was important to stress what distinguished colonial missions from other strands of missionary work. A report of the Colonial Scheme to the Church of Scotland's General Assembly in 1860 put this simply: 'The object of the Colonial Mission is to assist in providing a gospel ministry for the Presbyterian population scattered abroad in the different colonies of Great Britain.'[6] Other churches were also busy on many fronts. Colonial missions were just one part of a vast spiritual, social, educational and publication operation that provided services of one kind or another to virtually the entire British home and overseas population.

As colonial, foreign and other missions parted company, they acquired their own separate committees, organisations and journals. Sometimes it was necessary to explain that these varied activities were related phenomena. In an article for the *British Missionary*, the organ of the Congregational Colonial Missionary Society, S. W. Edwards stated: 'Colonial and Foreign Missions are two essentially related branches of one great enterprise.'[7] While most churches retained the old sense of mission as church extension under properly delegated authority, others saw missions as part of the core responsibilities of all Christians following Christ's injunction: 'As my Father hath sent me, so send I you' (John 20: 21). In other words, it was Christ, not the Church and certainly not the state, who sent the missionary. While this was the scriptural ideal, the practical need for missionaries to operate within the legal and financial constraints of colonial regimes ensured that missionaries were always supervised by missionary societies and they required support, especially in the form of land grants, from governments. Like colonial missions, in other words, they were dependent in many ways on the British government.

Emigration was the spur that led to the creation of many new colonial missionary societies, of which the Society for the Propagation

---

[6] *Home and Foreign Record of the Free Church of Scotland*, 15 June 1860, p. 272.
[7] S. W. Edwards, 'The Relation of Colonial to Foreign Missions', *The British Missionary*, October 1913, p. 107.

Table 3.1 *Colonial missionary societies and auxiliaries*

Denomination and party	Society and date of foundation	Date commenced colonial work
Baptist	Baptist Missionary Society (1792); in 1843, incorporated the Baptist Colonial Missionary Society in Upper Canada (1836)	1832
Catholic	Oeuvre de la Propagation de la Foi (Association for the Propagation of the Faith) (1822)	1822
Church of England (Evangelical)	South American Missionary Society (1854)	1854
Church of England	Society for the Propagation of the Gospel (1701)	1701
Church of England (Evangelical)	Newfoundland Church and School Society (1823) Colonial Church Society (1835) Amalgamated to form the Colonial Church and School Society (1851); renamed the Colonial and Continental Church Society (1861)	1823
Congregationalist	Colonial Missionary Society	1838
Methodist (Bible Christian)	Bible Christian Foreign Missionary Society	1821
Methodist (New Connexion)	Methodist New Connexion Missionary Society	1824
Methodist (Primitive)	Primitive Methodist Missionary Society	1843–44
Methodist	United Methodist Free Churches Foreign Missions (1857)	1857
Methodist	Wesleyan Methodist Missionary Society (1814)	1814
Presbyterian (pre-Disruption)	Glasgow Colonial Society (1825)	1825–36
Presbyterian (Established Church)	Church of Scotland Colonial Committee (1836)	1836
Presbyterian (Free Church)	Free Church of Scotland Colonial Committee (1843)	1843
Presbyterian	Presbyterian Church in Ireland Colonial Committee (1848)	1848

Source: Bliss, *Encyclopedia of Missions* (1891), pp. 307–8; Latourette, *History of the Expansion of Christianity*, vol. 5 (1943).

of the Gospel, founded in 1701, had been the earliest. By the 1840s, as Table 3.1 indicates, all the major churches – and some of the smaller ones – had created societies which had responsibility for raising funds, sending out trained clergy, catechists or school teachers, and encouraging the creation of independent colonial churches in their own image. Catholic missionary auxiliaries, notably the French Association for the Propagation of the Faith (APF), which is discussed in Chapter 4, raised funds to support similar work.

Venn's strategic dismissal of colonial missions continues to influence historical accounts of colonial missions. In the extensive entry on missions in the eleventh edition of the *Encyclopaedia Britannica*, Eugene Stock, the historian of the CMS, devoted no more than a single sentence to colonial missions in which he noted that missions to the British colonial population had been the priority of the Society for the Propagation of the Gospel, and to a lesser extent the Colonial Church [and School] Society (Church of England), and the Colonial Missionary Society (Congregational). However, he was not prepared to recognise that these societies did real missionary work: 'Those missions, however, are more properly an outlying branch of home missions, being to the professing Christian settlers or their descendants.'[8] These attitudes were entrenched in missionary discourse by the time of the Edinburgh World Missionary Conference (1910), from which colonial missions were excluded. In more recent times, the same attitude would seem to have informed the decision to exclude information relating to colonial missions from Mundus, the large, well-constructed internet gateway to British missionary collections.[9]

How significant were colonial missions in relation to missionary work as a whole? This question is difficult to answer because, unlike foreign missionary societies, colonial missionary societies have generally not had the benefit of recent scholarly histories making their statistics readily accessible to modern researchers.[10] Nevertheless, we can get some idea of the scale and significance of colonial missions from a number of different sources. In the first place, we can try to calculate the scale of funds supplied to support colonial as opposed to all other kinds of missionary work as this was reported in the *Missionary Register*. The *Missionary Register*, founded in 1813 by the Secretary of the CMS, Josiah Pratt, provided a digest of missionary

---

[8] E. Stock, H. T. Andrews and A. J. Grieve, 'Missions', in *The Encyclopaedia Britannica* (Cambridge, 1910–11), p. 589.

[9] Mundus, Gateway to missionary collections in the United Kingdom, www.mundus. ac.uk. This gateway does not include links to the extensive records of the Colonial and Continental Church Society in the London Guildhall, or the records of the Colonial Committee of the Free Church of Scotland.

[10] The data for colonial missions given here should be compared with the extensive data on foreign missions collected by Cox, *British Missionary Enterprise*, Appendix, Figure 2, British missionary income by denominational category, 1872.

work around the world, including brief notices about all Protestant missionary agencies with accounts of their Anniversary Sermons and meetings and resolutions.[11] The *Missionary Register* therefore also allows us to compare the earnings of the different streams of the missionary movement. In 1853–4, the annual income from all societies whose summary notices were included in the *Missionary Register* was £1,502,695. This was divided between societies classified as Anti-Slavery, Bible, Education, Jews, Missionary, Seamen, Tract and Book, Home, Colonial and other purposes.[12] Unsurprisingly, the largest incomes were earned by the societies with the largest church membership, namely, the CMS (£124,290), the WMMS (£111,048), the SPG (£104,521) and the LMS (£59,665). Of the Tract and Publication societies, the SPCK led the way (£85,436),[13] followed by the non-denominational Religious Tract Society (£74,144). We have already seen that the Tract and Bible societies were busy in the colonies and so these earnings are relevant to colonial missions.[14] As a group, the earnings of the specialist colonial missionary societies fell somewhere below the publication societies, with the Home and Colonial School Society (£6,939), Church of Scotland Colonial Mission (£3,420) and the Free Church of Scotland Colonial Mission (£5,884), all falling well below the £10,000 mark.[15]

If we were to sum up the overall financial picture, it would seem that colonial missions ranked at the lower end of missionary work in terms of both funding and prestige as these things were measured in the middle of the nineteenth century. Colonial missions lacked the appeal of the largest foreign mission societies, or the better known educational and home mission societies, but they nevertheless managed to do rather better than the specialised missions to Jews or Irish Roman Catholics or for ragged schools. Colonists, it would seem, were about on a par

---

[11] *The Missionary Register for the Year 1813(–55) Containing an Abstract of the Proceedings of the Principal Missionary and Bible Societies Throughout the World*, 43 vols. (London, 1813).

[12] 'Annual Receipts of Missionary, Bible, Education and Tract Societies', *Missionary Register* (1853–54), p. 493.

[13] The SPCK was responsible for administering a fund for emigrants, providing books and tracts for clergymen at Plymouth, Southampton and Liverpool, who visited emigrant ships (p. 494). In this year, 210,000 people sailed from the Mersey to the United States (194,922), the Australian colonies (20,000), British North America (about 20,000) and the rest to the East and West Indies. The SPCK also provided scholarships to St Augustine's College, Canterbury, and presented candidates for holy orders in the colonies with books for their use (p. 499).

[14] See Chapter 2.

[15] These receipts were similar to those of the following year (see *Missionary Register* (1854), p. 491): CMS, £123,915; Wesleyan, £114,498; SPG, £86,962; LMS, £7,678.

with British and foreign sailors, or the military (which also had their own missionary societies) in terms of their capacity to attract the beneficence of the British public to their cause.

Secondly, we can try to measure the circulation and ethos of colonial missionary periodicals, which – like those of all missionary societies – were produced in large numbers. The Missionary Periodicals Database hosted by the Yale University Divinity School Library attempts to provide an exhaustive coverage of the periodical literature generated by the foreign missionary movement. However, it does include colonial missionary periodicals in regional listings.[16] In relation to Australia and the Pacific, for example, there are 171 missionary periodicals listed from a total of 580, or just under 30 per cent of all those in the database. While some of these are concerned only with missions to Aborigines or to Pacific islanders, many also include accounts of colonial missions.

In his survey history of the British missionary movement, Cox argues that a central function of missionary periodicals was the defamation of the 'other' – the construction of the ignorant, black, benighted heathen whom the British missionary was sent to convert and uplift. He suggests that this propaganda function was much more important to the missionary societies than making money from what was, in effect, a vast publicity machine.[17] However, in colonial missionary writing, the definition of the 'other' turns out to be less significant than defining 'us', namely, the British and Irish people who supported colonial missionary societies. As we have already seen in relation to the publications of the Religious Tract Society, colonial missionary propaganda constructed a racialised narrative which emphasised the whiteness, homogeneity and community of colonists with their fellow British or 'Anglo-Saxon' compatriots at home. Catholic missions followed a similar rhetorical strategy by appealing sentimentally to the needs of poor Irish settlers exiled from home. Otherwise, the rationale provided to the public for supporting colonial missions was similar for all the churches.

So what attracted church-going people across the United Kingdom to give their financial and emotional support to colonial missions? In general, based on missionary publications, it would seem that support for colonial missions flowed to some degree from the same sources which generated enthusiasm for the British empire. These can be summarised under five headings. In the first place, there is what Niall Ferguson has

---

[16] Missionary Periodicals Database, http://research.yale.edu:8084/missionperiodicals/index.jsp. This site includes valuable annotations prepared by David Seton and Martha Smalley.

[17] Cox, *British Missionary Enterprise*, pp. 114–44.

called 'Anglobalization', namely, the combined effect of British economic power over commerce and labour and the cultural hegemony
of the English language and institutions, but with a special religious
twist.[18] The churches argued that, by building churches and extending
their ministry to the colonies, they were helping to spread the benefits
of British civilisation and make the world a better, freer and more moral
place. British imperial patriotism was the common coin of the publicity and fund-raising propaganda generated by the colonial missionary
societies as we will see in the case studies in the five chapters which
follow.

A second factor projected by the colonial missionary movement was
more specific to the churches, namely, sectarian rivalry. Protestantism,
as the constitutional and national face of the British nation, was integral to the colonisation of America and the extension of British rule in
areas of English-speaking settlement in the first imperial age, which
continued until the American revolutionary war.[19] In the second British
empire, religion does not wither away as a colonising force. However,
the established churches in Britain were challenged by legal reform at
home and the excitement of emigration and colonisation abroad. This
had the effect of placing the various British churches on a much more
equal pegging when it came to competing for the adherence of colonists. There was a sectarian element to the ensuing struggle. Although
the old language of Protestant freedoms and Catholic enslavement to
Rome appears with great regularity, particularly in the promotional
literature of the Church of Scotland and Evangelical Anglicans who
remained close to their Reformist roots, it lacked the coercive force of
earlier times. While the British nation was proudly Protestant, the colonial empire of the later nineteenth century was multi-denominational,
and the colonial missionary societies helped to make it so.

Thirdly, the churches were able to play an important role in perpetu-
ating the ethnicities that had once distinguished the separate national
institutions of England, Ireland, Wales and Scotland, and which had
been diluted in the constitutional merger of the Acts of Union. In
the colonies, the Church of England, the Church of Scotland, Irish
Catholicism and Welsh Nonconformity were given a vast new stage
on which to perform older national narratives and were determined to
make the most of it. The Church of England aspired to be the national
Church for the whole empire. Catholics promoted their settler missions
as a spiritual triumph for the Irish people. Since the Irish Catholic

---

[18] N. Ferguson, *Empire: How Britain Made the Modern World* (London, 2004), p. xxiv.
[19] Pestana, *Protestant Empire*, p. 6.

Church did not participate in the foreign missionary movement until the twentieth century, this ghostly achievement was entirely the production of the colonial missionary movement.

Fourthly, in all the colonies of British settlement, the churches were engaged as colonisers in the occupation and dispersal of indigenous peoples, as well as the conquest of earlier European colonisers. In colonies such as the Cape or New Zealand where the original population formed a significant, though minority, population, the Church originally planted separate missionary and colonial churches, which arguably facilitated the progress of colonisation and the institutional management of native people. I have little to say about this, but the successful creation of new British churches nearly always assumed the removal or neutralisation of the cultural institutions which preceded them.

Finally – and somewhat paradoxically given what I said above about the way in which the churches helped to preserve older ethnic religious allegiances – the churches assisted in the generation of new colonial nationalisms and, eventually, colonial democratic institutions. In all the territories to which the churches expanded, they found themselves in competition not only with the members of other British churches, but also with the adherents of the national churches of other European powers, including the Dutch Reformed Church in Cape Colony and the French Catholic Church in what became Canada. Because of the proximity of the United States, Canadian Protestantism was heavily influenced by its Protestant churches and their independence from those in the United Kingdom. While the churches were generally among the most conservative of forces, they also contributed to the creation of the distinctive religious development of the rising colonial nations.

To some extent, we will be able to trace these themes through the colonial missionary movement of the Anglican, Catholic, Anglican Evangelical, Methodist, Congregational and Presbyterian societies that are discussed in the next five chapters. Like Dilke, we will 'follow England round the world', telling the largely unknown history of the colonial missions which played an important role in shaping the cultural and religious identity of Greater Britain.

3   Anglicans

The first and oldest of the British missionary societies was the Society
for the Propagation of the Gospel (SPG). It has a major historiography,
which now extends over its full 300-year history to cover the entire
period of the rise and fall of the British empire.[1] This chapter examines
the way in which the Society moulded its original Charter in the nineteenth century to meet the changing tides of religious and imperial policy. It concentrates on two periods of reform when the SPG was forced to
redefine its role and the mission to British settlers that earlier had been
its most characteristic work. The first was in the 1840s when the launch
of the Colonial Bishoprics' Fund (1841) sparked renewed enthusiasm
for Anglican expansion into the settler colonies. The second occurred
at the end of the century under the leadership of Henry Hutchinson
Montgomery (1847–1932), formerly bishop of Tasmania, and Secretary
of the SPG from 1901 to 1918. As Secretary of the SPG in the heyday of
British imperial power, Montgomery was responsible more than anyone
for articulating a coherent ideology for the Anglican missionary movement that attempted to unite Christian idealism with British imperial
nationalism. That he failed to win majority support within the British
Anglican communion for this vision suggests that, even at the height of
the imperial age, colonial missions enjoyed only limited appeal.

The SPG was the major foreign missionary organisation for
high church Anglicans in the nineteenth century. However, unlike
Evangelicals who had one society for its foreign missions, the CMS, and
another for its colonial missions, the CCCS, discussed in Chapter 4, the
SPG was a hybrid. Two features of the SPG caused controversy in the
nineteenth century, and some confusion even today. In the first place,
there is the overall balance of the SPG's colonial mission to settlers as

---

[1] D. O'Connor, ed., *Three Centuries of Mission: The United Society for the Propagation of
the Gospel 1701–2000* (London, 2000); C. F. Pascoe, *Two Hundred Years of the SPG: An
Historical Account of the Propagation of the Gospel in Foreign Parts, 1701–1900* (London,
1901); H. P. Thompson, *Into All Lands: The History of the Society for the Propagation of
the Gospel in Foreign Parts, 1701–1950* (London, 1951).

opposed to – or rather in addition to – its foreign mission. Secondly, there is the Society's role as the overseas agency of the constitutionally fused English church and state. Both of these require some qualification. The charter of the Society gave it a dual character and the SPG was never exclusively a colonial missionary society. Nevertheless, before 1900, it was the SPG's missions to European colonists that absorbed a significant part of its resources and defined its character in relation to other missionary societies.

It is useful to try and calculate this more precisely in terms of personnel and funding expended by the SPG on the two branches of its mission work. The extent of the SPG's colonial, as opposed to foreign, mission work varied both from field to field and over time. However, the SPG missionary roll shows that, between 1701 and 1900, 2,607 or about 60 per cent of all the Society's ordained missionaries were sent to the older colonies of North America, as well as Newfoundland and Canada, Australasia and Europe – regions where they were largely occupied with missions to colonists. The West Indies was also a significant colonial mission for the SPG, especially prior to the end of slave transportation and the subsequent collapse of the planter economy. According to Pascoe, there were thirty-seven mission fields where the SPG's first-ranked mission work was to colonists as opposed to other races.[2] Missions to colonists engaged the majority of the 3,059 missionaries sent to these mission fields, which comprised about 70 per cent of the entire SPG missionary roll. While these figures do not include the substantial number of laymen and women agents sent, especially as schoolteachers, to British North America, these do not affect the overall picture. In terms of clerical personnel, it can therefore be concluded that colonial missions were central to the work of the SPG until at least 1900.

Another way to measure the scale of the SPG's investment in colonial missions is to calculate the funds spent on settler colonies as opposed to those conducted elsewhere in the empire.[3] Again, the evidence is rather mixed. In the eighteenth century, the SPG spent most of its budget in the American colonies. However, this changed in the nineteenth century so that an increasing proportion of the Society's work was redirected from colonial to foreign mission work. The shift was gradual. From 1814 to 1834, the SPG received a parliamentary grant totalling

[2] Pascoe, *Two Hundred Years of the SPG*, p. 847. See Table 3.2.
[3] See Table 3.3 and, for more detail, C. F. Pascoe and H. W. Tucker, eds., *Classified Digest of the Records of the Society for the Propagation of the Gospel in Foreign Parts, 1701–1892* (London, 1893).

Table 3.2 *SPG: summary of the missionary roll, 1701–1900*

Country	Number of ordained missionaries		Deaths in active service
	European and colonial	Native	
North America (older colonies now US), 1702–85	309	—	100
Newfoundland and Canada, 1703–1900	1,597	—	133
West Indies, Central and South America, 1712–1900	446	9	56
Africa, 1752–1900	505	93	48
Australasia, 1793–1900	530	6	13
Asia, 1820–1900	456	254	106
Europe, 1702–4, 1854–1900	171	—	9
Total for each category	4,014	362	
Total combined	4,376		465

Source: Pascoe, *Two Hundred Years*, p.847.

£241,850, which was mostly expended on clergy salaries in Upper Canada. After this grant was abolished, the SPG became much stricter with the disposal of funds raised by voluntary subscriptions, withdrawing grants when it was judged that the colonial churches were capable of becoming self-supporting. In 1853, however, almost twenty years after the ending of its parliamentary grant, 31 per cent of the SPG's income continued to be spent in British North America.[4] Africa (28.8 per cent) and India (25.5 per cent), where there were recently installed colonial bishops, were rising in importance and each received about a quarter of the SPG's total grant. Australasia (8.3 per cent) and the West Indies (4.8 per cent) received less, and the rest of the world very little (1.1 per cent). In his report, published in the *Missionary Register*, where it was widely read by supporters of other missionary societies, the SPG Secretary, Ernest Hawkins, stressed the Society's credentials in relation to 'strictly Missionary Work among the heathen'. He noted that wealthier colonies were expected to support themselves, and not draw on donations made by 'the working poor of this country'.[5] Nevertheless, he estimated that the total expenditure by the Society on 'Missions to the Heathen' was about £23,000; after accounting for administrative

---

[4] 'Gospel-Propagation Society: Report for the 153rd Year', *Missionary Register* (1854), p. 499.
[5] *Ibid.*

costs this amounted to less than a quarter (24 per cent) of total receipts for the year of £96,016. In other words, while the SPG was, indisputably, both a society for colonial and foreign missions, for much of the nineteenth century it continued to expend the lion's share of its income on settlers, just as it had done in the eighteenth.

A second controversial feature of the SPG has been the extent to which it could and should be identified with the imperial Protestantism of the British state. Confessional Protestantism was integral to the Society's founding principles. The SPG was set up by a layman, Thomas Bray (1656–1730), as a voluntary association. However its parliamentary Charter, issued on 16 June 1701, ensured that the Society was intimately connected to the English state and its established church. The Charter states that the original purpose of the Society was to protect the king's Protestant subjects from Romish priests and Jesuits and prevent popish superstition and idolatry from taking hold in the American colonies.[6] While this mission naturally evolved in the course of the eighteenth century, the SPG continued to operate to some extent as the colonial arm of the Church of England, rather than an independent foreign missionary society like the LMS or the CMS. Through its annual sermons, the SPG articulated what Rowan Strong has called a 'vision of Anglican imperialism' that promoted the Church of England as a church for the whole empire, not just Anglicans in England.[7] In order to support this nation-building work, the SPG raised funds in the United Kingdom with the authorisation of a letter from the king (which made donations to the Society appear both pious and patriotic). From 1814 to 1834, it also received a direct parliamentary grant for clergy salaries in North America. Nevertheless, the SPG's entanglement with the British state gradually unravelled in the course of the nineteenth century. After the loss of its direct grant, the SPG became heavily reliant on private fundraising so that it came to resemble more closely the other voluntary religious societies. And, while some American historians have stressed its ongoing imperial aspirations, historians from the other side of the Atlantic have been more sceptical of its influence with the British state. Porter notes how straitened the resources of the SPG were, and how unsympathetic the secular authorities were to any attempt to advance the cause of Anglicanism, which only stirred up resentment among the

[6] E. Hawkins, *Historical Notices of the Missions of the Church of England in the North American Colonies, Previous to the Independence of the United States; Chiefly from the MS Documents of the Society for the Propagation of the Gospel in Foreign Parts* (London, 1845), p. 415. The Charter is printed in full with commentary in Pascoe, *Two Hundred Years of the SPG*, pp. 932–42.
[7] Strong, 'Vision of an Anglican Imperialism', pp. 175–98.

non-episcopalian majority.[8] Indeed, these government constraints on the Society were one of the factors that encouraged laypeople to seek alternative ways to evangelise the empire that would enable it to escape the Erastian burden of government interference.

The beginning of a fundamental change in the *modus operandi* of the SPG occurred with the loss of the American colonies and its colonial churches, which led to a significant decline in its fortunes and prestige. While it was able to continue its pedestrian work of supporting colonial chaplains and providing for churches and schools in the settler colonies of British North America, the West Indies and Australia, the SPG was eclipsed by the glamour and enthusiasm of the second wave of missionary societies. Unlike the SPG, the new societies focused more or less exclusively on missions to native peoples in Africa, India and the Pacific. A further trial for the SPG began in the 1830s, during which the idea of the Church of England as a national Church both at home and in the colonies came under sustained attack. As liberal reformers succeeded in removing many of the traditional entitlements of the Church, conservative churchmen predicted revolution. In his account of the rise of the Oxford movement, the theologian William Palmer (1803–85) called the repeal of the Test and Corporation Acts (1828) 'a knife to the heart of the national church' and the emancipation of Roman Catholics which followed in 1829 'a measure which scattered to the winds public principle, public morality [and] public confidence'.[9] In 1833, a new low was reached when the Whig reform parliament pushed ahead with the rationalisation of the temporalities of the Church of Ireland, beginning with the extinction of ten bishoprics and two archbishoprics in Ireland.[10] In Ireland, tithes were mostly abolished in 1838, and later reforms included the civil registration of Protestant marriages (1845) and the abolition of the parish cess (1864). Overseas, the established church was also diminished by the removal of subsidies that had supported colonial clergy in the West Indies, where they were associated with the moral corruption of the slave trade and the decadence and immorality of plantation life. It could be pointed out that the SPG itself owned a number of slave plantations, which supported the Society's college in Barbados.

As the established church lost its institutional privileges, supporters of the SPG were forced to reassess its missionary role and reconsider

[8] Porter, *Religion Versus Empire?*, p. 21, arguing against the views of C. Bridenbaugh, *Mitre and Sceptre: Transatlantic Faiths, Ideas, Personalities and Politics* (New York, 1962), p. 57.
[9] Pascoe and Tucker, eds., *Classified Digest*, pp. 830–2.
[10] Brown, *Church and State*, p. 234.

the extent to which the Society should continue to act as the willing or unwilling agent for hereditary privilege and state power. Indeed, in the absence of government support for a national church in the colonies, it was difficult to see what the work of the SPG would be. The logical alternative, namely, the erection of independent Anglican dioceses in the colonies administered by local bishops, just like the Scottish Episcopal church, was slow to develop. In the American colonies, there was hostility to Anglican claims to be the official church. Later there were legal objections to the consecration of Anglican bishops who were not subjects of the British crown, but citizens of foreign powers, including the American republic.[11] There were also exaggerated concerns about the apostolic succession in cases where congregations elected their own bishops. Nevertheless, the American Revolution did clear the way for the creation of the first colonial bishopric in Nova Scotia, which was created by letters patent in 1787 in the wake of the formal separation of the Protestant Episcopal Church of the United States of America in 1785.[12] Bishops for Quebec (1793), Calcutta (1814), Jamaica (1824), Barbados (1824), Madras (1835), Australia (1836), Bombay (1837), Toronto (1839) and Newfoundland (1839) followed, most of which were funded directly by the government. The support of the SPG was always assumed to be an interim arrangement that would fade away when new, self-supporting episcopal churches emerged in the colonies. Would the SPG soon have no further work to do, other than provide chaplains for sailors, soldiers and convicts as it had done in the past?

This was the context for the remarkable revival of the spirituality and ethos of the colonial mission of the Church of England, which was reflected in the launch of the Colonial Bishoprics' Fund, and other Anglican institutions for the empire, as discussed in Chapter 2. Between 1841 and 1900, the Colonial Bishoprics Council secured £991,388, out of which it was able to provide part funding for sixty-seven new bishoprics. Suddenly it was possible to imagine the Church of England as the Church of the whole empire, led by bishops who were not dependent on the government for their authority and income. The Emigrants' Spiritual Aid Fund was established following reports of the horrific conditions endured by refugees from the Irish Famine at home ports and in North America, and provided an opportunity for the SPG to reassert its credentials as a missionary body with a duty of care to emigrants. In both the Colonial Bishoprics' Fund and the Emigrants' Spiritual Aid

[11] This difficulty was overcome by 26 George III, c. 84. For the constitutional reforms which led to the creation of the Colonial Church, see Pascoe, *Two Hundred Years of the SPG*, pp. 743–57.
[12] See Table 3.2 for a complete list of Anglican colonial and missionary bishoprics and the subsidy provided by the SPG.

Fund, the SPG and the SPCK took on the role of managing the funds of these projects and used their expertise and colonial networks to provide them with appropriate institutional support.

It may be significant that from this time the SPG began to change the way in which it presented itself to the world. From 1701, there was a standing order that a sermon was preached before the Society on the third Friday of every February by a preacher appointed by the President. Between 1702 and 1901, the sermon was preached by 142 English bishops, as well as twenty-nine Welsh, six Irish and five American (US) bishops and only once – in 1901 – by a colonial bishop, the bishop of Bombay.[13] Dr G. A. Selwyn, bishop of Lichfield and former bishop of New Zealand, preached in 1869. However, in general, the SPG did not look to the colonial episcopate for guidance, and a paternalistic conservatism was characteristic of most of its operations. Nevertheless, in 1853, it decided to cease printing the sermon as part of the report of the SPG. By this date, the winds of change had blown through the venerable society as resident bishops arrived in colonial dioceses. It seemed the SPG had new work to do after all and missions to British settlers were once again on the missionary agenda.

With the establishment of the Colonial Bishoprics' Fund, the relationship between metropole and colony changed significantly. However, it took some time before self-governing churches outside the British Isles emerged. The first step was to cut off, or at least slow down, the flow of funds as first Canada, and then the West Indies, were subjected to decisions to remove direct funding for SPG clergy. The SPG responded effectively by creating a voluntarist stream of funding independent of direct aid from the government.[14] The colonial churches also began to assume control of their own affairs. Provincial synods, which united the independent dioceses, were first held in British North America in 1861, but General Synods were long delayed by Evangelical fears that they would put too much power in the hands of colonial bishops, the majority of whom were unsympathetic to their aspirations. General Synods were first held in New Zealand (1859), with Australia and Tasmania (1872) and Canada (1893) following in due course. Provinces were also formed in South Africa (1870), the West Indies (1883) and Nippon Sei Ko Kai in Japan (1887). Unlike the clean cut created by the revolutionary breach with the Americas, the relationship between Canterbury and the colonies was to be marked by complex and interminable negotiations.[15]

---

[13] Pascoe, *Two Hundred Years of the SPG*, pp. 833–5.
[14] See Table 3.4, SPG: income from general and other sources, 1801–1910.
[15] For the constitutional complexities of the creation of colonial churches, see G. W. O. Addleshaw, 'The Law and Constitution of the Church Overseas', in *The Mission of the Anglican Communion*, ed. E. R. Morgan and R. Lloyd (London, 1948); and France,

Ernest Hawkins and the church in the colonies

One of the architects of a new, or at least renewed, mission for the SPG
was the Reverend Ernest Hawkins (1802–68), Fellow of Exeter College,
Oxford, Prebendary of St Paul's cathedral in London and, from 1843 to
1866, Secretary of the SPG.[16] Hawkins was actively involved in all the
colonial projects of the high church party. Until 1864, he was Secretary
of the Colonial Bishoprics' Fund;[17] he was also Secretary of the SPG's
Emigrants' Spiritual Aid Fund. He was a member of the committee
of management of the Canterbury Association, incorporated by Royal
Charter on 13 November 1849, which organised this Anglican colony
in the South Island of New Zealand, where a river now sustains his
memory.[18] In 1848, Hawkins became the first Secretary of the SPG
to undertake a tour of North America, the most populous of the settler colonies and the site of the SPG's busiest mission. Hawkins wrote
a detailed journal of his tour of duty, during which he visited the four
Canadian bishops of Quebec, Toronto, Fredericton and Nova Scotia.
He then went on to visit the United States and forge links with the
Domestic and Foreign Missionary Society of the Episcopal Church,
publishing a report in the *Missionary Register*.[19]

Hawkins was not alone in his plans for the SPG to take a more active
role in laying the foundations for new, more independent, colonial
churches. In 1849, George William Lyttelton (1817–76), one-time Under
Secretary of State for War and the Colonies in the Peel Conservative
government and later the major patron of the Canterbury Association,
wrote Hawkins a long letter.[20] Like his brother-in-law William
Gladstone, Lyttelton was fascinated by the prospects for the 'national'
(i.e. Anglican) church in the colonies, and did everything he could to
promote this cause.[21] On this occasion, Lyttelton's main aim was to

Oversea Episcopate. For the rise of synodalism in the colonies, see E. D. Daw, 'Church
and State in the Empire: The Conference of Australian Bishops 1850', *Journal of
Imperial and Commonwealth History*, 5 (1976), pp. 251–69.

[16] C. Brown, 'Hawkins, Ernest (1802–1868)', in *Oxford Dictionary of National Biography*
(Oxford, 2004).

[17] He was also its first historian: E. Hawkins, *Documents Relative to the Erection and
Endowment of Additional Bishoprics in the Colonies* (London, 1844). This pamphlet
includes an account of the origins of the fund.

[18] Appropriately enough, the Hawkins River is a major tributary of the Selwyn River in
the province of Canterbury.

[19] *Missionary Register* (1854), p. 495.

[20] L. Lyttelton, *A Letter to the Reverend Ernest Hawkins: Secretary to the Society for the
Propagation of the Gospel in Foreign Parts, on the Principles of the Operations of the Society*
(London, 1849).

[21] Lyttelton was not quite Gladstone's brother-in-law. His wife, Mary Glynne, was the
sister of Gladstone's wife, Catherine Glynne. The couples were married in the same
service.

encourage the SPG to provide better support to emigrants and withdraw its support from colonies where the churches should be encouraged to become independent. This was a radical proposition that changed fundamentally the nature of the relationship between the SPG and the settler colonies. In an earlier age, one of the SPG's primary functions was to support the state, which ensured that the largest supply funds were supplied to those colonies of greatest strategic significance to the British crown, in particular British North America. Now, Lyttelton urged that funding should be supplied according to financial need, and for as short a time as possible. It was the policy long adopted by the Methodists in their colonial arrangements, but it was a startling innovation for the SPG.

Prince Albert gave voice to the new, more expansive programme for the SPG in a speech given at the public meeting to celebrate the 150th Jubilee of the Society, an event that was held immediately after the Great Exhibition. This grand occasion occurred at the height of the Anglican controversy surrounding the bringing down of the judgment in the Gorham case in March 1850.[22] Keen to unite his audience behind a common cause, the Prince Consort praised the SPG as the bearer of civilisation to the British people, and deplored the internal dissension of the Church of England. His speech stressed the intimate connections that he perceived to characterise British civilisation and its Christian faith:

> This civilisation rests on Christianity, could only be raised on Christianity, can only be maintained by Christianity, the blessings of which are carried by this society to the vast territories of India and Australasia, which last are again to be peopled by the Anglo-Saxon race.[23]

This summarises effectively the ambitions of the Church of England to become the national Church in the colonies, a church which was fused ethnically and politically to the English-speaking people and which could and should be exported wherever the British empire spread its settlements.

Hawkins enhanced the public image of the SPG by launching a number of new periodicals, including *The Church in the Colonies* and *Missions to the Heathen*, later given the collective title of the Colonial

---

[22] S. J. Brown, *Providence and Empire: Religion, Politics and Society in the United Kingdom 1815–1914* (Edinburgh, 2008), pp. 176–8.

[23] T. Martin, *The Life of His Royal Highness the Prince Consort*, 3rd edn (n.p., 1875), Part ii, p. 63, cited by J. Stoughton, *Religion in England from 1800 to 1850: A History, with a Postscript on Subsequent Events*, 2 vols. (London, 1884), vol. 2, p. 372.

Church Library,[24] which popularised the two arms of the Society's work. While subsequently eclipsed by *The Mission Field*, which began in 1856 and went on to become the SPG's best-known periodical, in the 1840s they ensured that the colonial mission of the SPG received more effective publicity than it had ever done before. The colonial church series appears to have begun with a documentary history, edited by Hawkins, on the work of the SPG in the North American colonies. Much of this had already been published in the *British Magazine* and in several North American church periodicals. While in Boston in 1849, Hawkins personally donated a copy to Harvard University Library.[25] Setting the tone for the more assertive colonial ambitions of the SPG, Hawkins dedicated this to the American bishops, priests and deacons 'in the earnest desire that the mother and daughter churches may ever remain inseparably knit together in one communion and fellowship'.[26] The preface warns of the 'guilt and danger' of establishing colonies without appropriate religious provisions since 'the fellowship of the Church is the strongest tie between the Mother Country and her Colonies'.[27] He argued that new responsibilities had opened up with the expansion of the colonies, which were themselves becoming nations, and a Providential call was laid on both the Church and realm of England to provide the gospel in its most perfect form (which implies the presence of Anglican bishops) to both heathen lands and settler colonies.

There was something a little ingenuous about these claims. The episcopate of the American Episcopal Church was generated almost entirely after its break with the Church of England, and it had its own missions in the Americas to support. In due course, the American church created missionary bishops for its westward settlements and missionary dioceses (initially without bishops) in regions such as Alaska, Hawaii and the Philippines; American Episcopal bishops for 'foreign' churches within the American political sphere of influence first appeared in Haiti, Mexico and Spain.[28] While acknowledging historic ties to the English and Scottish episcopal churches, it did not relish claims for precedence by the Church in Britain. Perhaps reflecting some of these

---

[24] As advertised in the endpapers of R. W. Norris, *Annals of the Diocese of Adelaide* (London, 1852), by 1852 there were twenty-seven issues in the series.
[25] The dedication appears in the digitised copy made available by Harvard University Library through Google Books.
[26] Hawkins, *Historical Notices of the Missions of the Church of England*.
[27] *Ibid.*, p. vii.
[28] W. S. Perry, *The Episcopate in America* (New York, 1895), pp. lxiii–lxviii.

differences of opinion on mission policy, Hawkins' 1854 report of the SPG deputation to America is fulsome in its appreciation for American hospitality, but much lighter on actual outcomes of the visit.[29]

Hawkins also prepared *The Colonial Church Atlas*, which illustrated the worldwide spread of Anglican dioceses, supplemented with geographical and statistical tables. His stated aim was 'exhibiting, in a striking light, the utter inadequacy of her [the Church's] present operations in Foreign Parts, and the necessity of a more perfect organization'.[30] The *Atlas* was, in other words, the charter for a new, much expanded, role for the SPG and for the Church of England in the British world. In graphic form, it depicted all the missionary and colonial dioceses of the empire; British possessions were hand-coloured in red, with churches and missionary stations marked by crosses. Every map carried a printed stamp with the name of the diocese, the coat of arms of the bishop and the date of his consecration. Even bolder was the large-scale 'Colonial and Missionary Church Map of the World', which was coloured and varnished and showed all the Anglican dioceses and missionary stations. At six feet six inches by four feet five inches, this made a suitable purchase for a school-room or church hall, where it would allow the SPG's supporters to track where in the world their donations were being spent. Smaller scale versions were also available that could be folded up into a case. Neither of these items was cheap: the large map cost thirty-two shillings and the pocket ones two shillings apiece.

Journals of visitation made by the recently despatched colonial bishops on their first tours of duty were another voluminous source of information about the new colonial dioceses. The SPCK published these systematically throughout the 1840s.[31] Like the SPG's maps and atlases, despatches from the colonial bishops helped to delineate the territory over which the Society, or rather the Church of England, was making a spiritual claim. From New Zealand, George Augustus Selwyn wrote as though the entire country was vacant land on which he would be able to place the first Christian imprint:

---

[29] 'Deputation to America', *Missionary Register* (1854), p. 495.
[30] E. Hawkins, *The Colonial Church Atlas* (London, 1845).
[31] The series of twenty-eight bishops' visitation journals included: Toronto (1842), Quebec (1843, 1846), Nova Scotia, Cape Breton and New Brunswick (1843), New Zealand (Parts I–V, 1842–4), Australia (1843, 1845), Manéroo (i.e. Monero) and Moreton Bay, including a map of the Grazing Districts of New South Wales (1843), Quebec (1843–4), Newfoundland (1845), Fredericton (1845, 1846), Newfoundland (Parts I–II: 1845, 1846), Nova Scotia (1844, 1845), Labrador (1848), Cape Town (1848) and Tasmania.

I find myself placed in a position such as was never granted to any English Bishop before, with a power to mould the institutions of the Church from the beginning according to true principles.[32]

This was something of a slight to the Church Missionary Society, which had been planted in New Zealand by Samuel Marsden in 1814. In a dramatic series of voyages around his new domain, Selwyn records that he travelled 1,180 miles by sea, 762 on foot, 86 by horseback, and 249 by boat, making a total of 2,277 miles. He carefully noted the acceptance of his authority by both Europeans and natives, who assembled to receive the sacrament of confirmation at his hands: 'It was a most striking sight to see a church filled with native Christians, ready, at my first invitation to obey the ordinances of their religion.'[33] In fact, Selwyn was to lead the Anglican world in democratising the institutions of Anglican Church governance, but he chose to do so from an initial assumption of complete power. The sequence of bishops' visitation journals formed the foundation for cloth-bound volumes in the series entitled *Annals of the Colonial Church*, most of which were edited for publication by Hawkins.[34]

There appear to have been at least two intended audiences for the *Annals of the Colonial Church*, a series which functioned as a kind of encyclopaedic history of the SPG's renewed colonial mission. One was the traditional object of all missionary propaganda: the moral and financial supporters of missionary projects at home, people who enjoyed reading the lively travel narratives of the colonial bishops but who had no plans to head to the colonies themselves. It was these kinds of people who purchased the SPG's volume on New Zealand, which appeared in 1848.[35] This was a characteristic missionary publication, which drew heavily on correspondence from the field and included exotic details, such as a series of fine engravings of the Maori people. It provided recent news, such as the decision by Governor George Grey to increase the number of troops resident in New Zealand as a means to provide 'added security' to the colony.[36] There is also a final chapter and appendix, which gives an account of Bishop Selwyn's founding of the theological college of St John's to provide training of candidates for

---

[32] G. A. Selwyn, *New Zealand, Part I, Letters from the Bishop to the Society for the Propagation of the Gospel, Together with Extracts from the Visitation Journal from July 1842 to January 1843* (London, 1844), p. 102.

[33] *Ibid.*

[34] Hawkins edited the volumes on Fredericton, New Zealand, Toronto and Quebec.

[35] Society for Promoting Christian Knowledge, *Annals of the Diocese of New Zealand* (London, 1847).

[36] *Ibid.*, p. 211.

holy orders, as well as primary and secondary schooling for native and European Christians.[37] In all this, there is nothing that might be interpreted as an inducement to emigrants seeking a country of settlement. This accorded with the policy of the missionary societies, which were opposed to European colonisation in the interests of the Maori people, and resisted all attempts to cede, buy, or sell Maori land. Only after 1840 did the SPG take on a more active role in supporting the needs of the settler, as well as the Maori, church in New Zealand.[38]

The volumes for Canada and Australia are rather different. With their maps and reports of the visitation of the relevant bishop, always emphasising the need for greater efforts in both settlement and evangelisation, they have something of the character of handbooks for prospective emigrants, especially clerical emigrants. The bishop of Fredericton, New Brunswick, put the call for more men in dramatic italics: 'I could find immediate and full employment for twenty additional clergymen, without diminishing the labours of any one at present in Holy Orders.'[39] It was also a matter of church pride that the English church, which carried with it the authority of the state and sovereign at home, should be asserted more firmly than that of what are referred to as the 'noisy and importunate sects' who claimed equality with her in the colony.[40]

In Quebec, Hawkins was also inspired to a strong call for men and clergy to meet the challenge of emigration and the 'great destiny that seems assigned to them by the will of the Almighty – that of being the fathers and founders of great and populous empires beyond the seas'.[41] Hawkins wrote these books for the benefit of the people and churches of the expanding colonies. The final section of Hawkins' book on the Quebec diocese concerns the work of clerics ministering to sick, destitute and starving emigrants, mostly from Ireland, in the horrific conditions of the quarantine station. The cholera epidemics of 1832 devastated the people of Quebec, but worse was to come following the catastrophic failure of the potato crop in Ireland. Hawkins recognised what followed as one of the most searing tragedies in human memory. As the famine

---

[37] Recorded in the Appendix are the names of ten graduates of St John's who had been ordained by the bishop of New Zealand. One was the controversial William Colenso, ordained on Sunday, 22 September 1845 to be deacon for the district of Ahuriri. For the history of St John's, see A. K. Davidson, *Selwyn's Legacy: The College of St John the Evangelist Te Waimate and Auckland 1843–1992* (Auckland, 1993).

[38] A. Davidson, 'Colonial Christianity: The Contribution of the Society for the Propagation of the Gospel to the Anglican Church in New Zealand, 1840–80', *Journal of Religious History*, 16 (1990), pp. 173–84.

[39] E. Hawkins, *Annals of the Diocese of Fredericton* (London, 1847), p. 63.

[40] *Ibid.*, p. 66.

[41] E. Hawkins, *Annals of the Diocese of Quebec* (London, 1849), p. 70.

worsened, every port and every ship to America was crammed with paupers burning to escape what he calls the 'death-stricken' country of Ireland.[42] In the absence of government welfare services, the churches were burdened with the challenge of making some kind of Christian response to the emergency. George Jehoshaphat Mountain (1789–1863), the first Anglican bishop of Quebec to be raised in Canada, person-ally intervened. He went down to the quarantine station where he was overwhelmed by scenes of death and misery. He reported that about 1,700 ill and starving people were crammed onto the island and its two churches had been forced to become makeshift hospitals:

The daily amount of deaths was frightful. We had not, perhaps, above 300 Protestant sick out of this number, but so dispersed, ashore and afloat, and so intermingled with Romanists – sometimes two of different faiths in *one bed* – that the labour of attending to them ministerially was immense.[43]

In this account, it is difficult to tell if the bishop was more horrified at the unprecedented calamity of the famine and the unspeakable suffer-ing he witnessed, or the enforced mingling of Protestant and Catholic between the same sheets. Indeed, there was much to discourage those who sought to attend on the sick as many doctors, nurses and clergy of all religious persuasions fell victim to the epidemic. Of the fifteen Protestant clergy who served at the quarantine station, five had died by November of the first famine year. A more concerted programme of activity for emigrants was the direct consequence of these tragic events.

Despite hardships of this kind, the *Annals of the Colonial Church* shows the transformation of the churches under the impact of emigra-tion. They chronicle the new Anglican world arising in the colonies that the SPG was helping to create.

The SPG, 1850s–1880s

After the heroic expansion of the 1840s and 1850s, the later decades of the nineteenth century were a period of relative stagnation for the colo-nial mission of the SPG. The success of the appointment of colonial bishops to their dioceses in some respects removed its *raison d'être*. With bishops located in the colonies, they naturally became more directly responsible for the raising of funds for church work locally. With the loss of direct grants to both British North America, which had amounted to £16,000 in 1832, and the West Indies, the settler churches in both

---

[42] *Ibid.*, p. 263.   [43] *Ibid.*, p. 265.

the Society's major fields of operation had been pushed into independence.[44] The loss of funds created frank difficulties, and so it was possibly with some optimism that the bishops reassured each other that British loyalism – and willingness to support the Church of England – was undiminished. Most, whatever their original churchmanship, had to adjust.

Francis Fulford (1803–68), first bishop of Montreal, makes an interesting case study in the challenges facing colonial bishops in this generation.[45] Like the majority of Canadian bishops, Fulford was a high churchman. As a protégé of Ernest Hawkins, he had risen through the SPG in the 1830s. After the launch of the Colonial Bishoprics' Fund, he had become editor of the *Colonial Church Chronicle and Missionary Journal*, which provided an independent voice on colonial church matters. He expressed editorial disapproval, for example, of the high-handed action of Bishop Nixon of Tasmania, who used his episcopal authority to dismiss clergymen employed as convict chaplains against the wishes of the Lieutenant Governor.[46] Fulford was enthroned in Westminster Abbey on 25 July 1850 with all the dignity of a ducal coronation. (Bishops were not called 'My Lord' for nothing.) However, like Broughton in Sydney, Selwyn in New Zealand and other colonial bishops of this era, his pretensions to spiritual authority were tempered by the reality of colonial conditions. Fulford would declare his loyalty, but privately he surveyed his diocese of mixed Anglophone and French-speaking families and scattered Indian settlements and noted 'The people are disunited and few [are] in reality Church people.'[47]

As colonial governments systematically withdrew funding for all churches throughout much of North America, Australia and New Zealand, the Church of England was forced to adjust to a new voluntary regime in which it had to raise its own funding in order to survive. In these circumstances, some did better than others. In Canada and Australia, the most successful bishops created Church societies that took over the function of raising funds that had earlier been provided by the government and the SPG. The correspondence of the SPG continued to be full of begging letters from colonial bishops. However,

---

[44] The Anglican Church in Jamaica was disestablished in 1870; it continued in Barbados.

[45] John Irwin Cooper, 'Francis Fulford', *Dictionary of Canadian Biography*, vol. IX (1861–79). For an Evangelical critique of his career, see Vaudry, 'Evangelical Anglicans and the Atlantic World', p. 165.

[46] 'Church Legislation in the Colonies', *Colonial Church Chronicle*, 2 (1848), pp. 89–93.

[47] Fulford to Secretary of the SPG, 1850, cited by Cooper, 'Francis Fulford', *Dictionary of Canadian Biography Online*.

the Society showed increasing resolve to demand churches become self-supporting. Following gold discoveries in New South Wales and Victoria, no further funds were released to dioceses in these colonies, although the SPG continued to provide support for frontier regions in the north and west of Australia. An important effect of the drying up of funds from home was the impetus that it gave to cooperation with other dissenting Protestants. As Vaudry has argued, in British North America, Anglican Evangelicals cooperated earlier and more effectively with other Protestants in church extension work than was possible in Britain. He suggests that this was related to the Irish, rather than English, roots of many Anglican clergy in Quebec who were therefore more likely to support closer affiliation with other evangelical churches.[48] This takes us back to Fulford. In Montreal, Fulford discovered that the decline of the SPG had created opportunities for the Evangelical Colonial Church and School Society, who from 1851 began planting schools in his diocese. In Quebec, Mountain resolved against cooperation with the Colonial Church and School Society, which he saw as a source of disunity.[49] In contrast, given the shortage of personnel, Fulford found that his only option was collaboration. His sermons and addresses consistently stressed the complementary Catholic and Evangelical traditions of the Church of England and the practical reality that fund-raising and personnel would have to be raised locally if the church were to flourish in Canada.[50] This conclusion was reached by many of Fulford's contemporaries around the Anglican world.

In 1901, the SPG celebrated its bicentenary but was rather disappointed by the poor show at some of its events. It was showing its age and struggling to retain the support of all sections of the Church, which it needed to finance its work throughout the empire. The high church party, which was an important supporter of the venerable Society, had risen in importance to become the most influential group within the Church of England. However, the religious mainstream was wearied by decades of controversy about the revival of Catholic forms of ritual in Anglican churches and controversy generated by radical Evangelicals

---

[48] Vaudry, 'Evangelical Anglicans and the Atlantic World', p. 9. See also Vaudry, *Anglicans and the Atlantic World*.

[49] G. J. Mountain, *A Short Explanation of Circumstances Preventing Coalition with the Colonial Church and School Society* (Quebec, 1859); Pascoe, *Two Hundred Years of the SPG*, p. 403.

[50] F. Fulford, *Sermons, Addresses, and Statistics of the Diocese of Montreal* (Montreal, 1865). See, for example, his Primary Charge (1852), which stresses the need for financial independence from England (pp. 163–4), and the 'Lecture on Some of the Passing Events and Controversies of the Day', which discusses with some sympathy the views of John Henry Newman (pp. 281–308).

on one wing and radical Anglo-Catholics on the other. Mission priorities were changing and those high churchmen who felt enthusiasm for mission work could choose to channel their funds and energy into either the new Anglo-Catholic societies, which focused on native work in Africa and the Pacific, or the Evangelical CMS, which now had affiliated societies in many of the colonies as well. Many Evangelicals considered that the SPG was marginal to the real missionary work, which was aimed at non-British Christians, not British settlers who could look after themselves. Even the Colonial Bishoprics' Fund, once seen as the key to the full establishment of the Church of England throughout the world, was struggling. A sub-committee of the Colonial Bishoprics Council reported in 1895 that because of low interest it was proving impossible to avoid vacancies in a number of sees.[51]

It was proving equally difficult to raise financial support for colonial projects such as schools, once the mainstay of colonial missionary work. In 1898, the Reverend T. St John Perry Pughe wrote to archbishop Temple seeking his support for the establishment of an Anglican grammar school for boys in Brisbane, bemoaning that the 'average English Churchman seems callous to our needs. He has the idea we are a land of gold, not knowing that nearly all the wealth is owned by large English Companies, or has been taken out of the colony by successful colonists who in England ignore Colonial responsibilities.'[52] Temple responded that it seemed like a case that should be supported from the resources of the colony.[53] Instead of turning to Britain for financial aid, many argued that the colonial churches should be taking more responsibility not only for their own support but also for foreign missions in their regions. As the cause of foreign missions continued to rise, and that of colonial missions declined, Pughe was not alone in feeling abandoned by the empire. In 1896, in rural New South Wales, Bishop Anderson of Riverina complained that, with only fifteen clergy for a sparsely settle diocese as large as Great Britain, his people were lapsing into 'practical heathenism'. One of his people expressed his sense of grievance in terms of racial resentment:

---

[51] Brochure outlining accounts of the Colonial Bishoprics Council. Report of a Subcommittee Appointed May 17, 1895, in Lambeth Palace Library, Temple Papers, vol. 7, fol. 297.

[52] Pughe to Temple, 30 July; 2 September, 6 September; 29 September 1898, in Lambeth Palace Library, Temple Papers, vol. 18, fols. 118–20. Quotation comes from letter of 2 September 1898, in Lambeth Palace Library, Temple Papers, vol. 18, fol. 125.

[53] Pughe appears to have played no part in the establishment of the existing Brisbane Church of England Grammar School, which was founded in 1917 by Canon William Perry French Morris (1878–1960). See entry on Morris by John Cole, *Australian Dictionary of Biography*, vol. 15, pp. 415–17.

If we were negroes in south Africa or South Sea Islanders, if we were the vilest heathen races, then we might hope for some attention; but because we are white men, forced out into the wild bush, no one cares for us. We may lead the life of animals and die the death of dogs.[54]

White men were no longer a missionary cause. The SPG expected the colonial churches to manage independently, and lacked the will and the resources to do more.

Bishop Montgomery

The man who single-handedly did most to revive the fortunes of the SPG and the ideal of its colonial mission was Henry Hutchinson Montgomery, the former bishop of Tasmania.[55] In 1901, not without considerable heart-searching, Montgomery resigned his bishopric and accepted the position of Secretary of the SPG, a post he was to hold until 1918. Montgomery is an attractive figure whose letters and writing sparkle with a perpetual cheerfulness and enthusiasm for the causes dear to his heart: the Church, the empire, his family and cricket. He seems never to have doubted that imperialism and Anglicanism were natural and necessary partners in the spiritual reformation of the world. From Hobart, Montgomery wrote regularly to his former Harrow schoolmate, Randall Thomas Davidson (1848–1930), later archbishop of Canterbury (fl. 1903–28), about his aspirations for the mission field and for his own children in some field of empire: 'The Greatest Empire (that of Christ) was our hope for all of them if they heard calls; next to that the Queen's Empire.'[56] He was aware of the deficiencies of the SPG: 'I groan, I lament, I despair', he wrote, contrasting its dullness and lack of energy with the liveliness and sense of purpose of the CMS, which had just celebrated a spectacularly successful centennial. He passed on the succinct comment of one of his clergy, 'no CMS man' who summed up the general

---

[54] Cited by Pascoe, *Two Hundred Years of the SPG*, p. 403.
[55] On Montgomery, see R. S. M. Withycombe, *Montgomery of Tasmania: Henry and Maud Montgomery in Australasia* (Brunswick East, Victoria, 2009). The memoir edited by his wife, M. Montgomery, *Bishop Montgomery: A Memoir* (London, 1933) is based on Montgomery's unpublished manuscript in Lambeth Palace Library. S. S. Maughan, 'An Archbishop for Greater Britain: Bishop Montgomery, Missionary Imperialism and the SPG, 1897–1915', in *Three Centuries of Mission: The United Society for the Propagation of the Gospel 1701–2000*, ed. D. O'Connor (London, 2000), pp. 358–70; Maughan, 'Imperial Christianity?'; S. S. Maughan, 'Montgomery, Henry Hutchinson (1847–1932)', in *Oxford Dictionary of National Biography* (Oxford, 2004).
[56] Montgomery to Davidson, 28 May 1899, in Lambeth Palace Library, Davidson Papers, vol. 519, fol. 292v.

feeling of malaise with the pithy: 'Poor SPG'.[57] After he expressed his own dream that the Secretary of the SPG might be some 'really moving Mission leader – and the income will be £500,000', someone who would be an 'Empire man' and who would bring the SPG and CMS together,[58] it was probably not surprising that Davidson offered the position to Montgomery himself. Montgomery responded by speaking of his commitment to Australia and, quoting Dilke, his love of 'these problems in Greater Britain'.[59] Yet he did accept, with the proviso that the post carried with it the full episcopal dignity that he already enjoyed as bishop of Tasmania. In this way, as Vaughan has persuasively argued, Montgomery became a kind of 'archbishop for Greater Britain'.[60] Davidson agreed, and the Montgomerys packed up their beautiful house in Hobart and left for smoky London.

While everything Montgomery did appears to flow spontaneously from his own warm feelings, he was a successful and strategic publicist for the colonial mission of the SPG. Very early, he seems to have hit upon the idea that the best way to advance the colonial cause was to marry it to the ideology of British imperialism. In Australia, Montgomery was fired by the promise of Federation and the Jubilee of the Australasian Board of Mission (ABM), an organisation which grew out of the Australasian bishops' conference in 1850, but had remained more or less moribund for many years after that. Roused by federation and imperialism, he enthused: 'I do not know what we might not do.'[61] By promoting church work as part of an imperial mission, Montgomery sought to create a winning formula for raising funds, expanding the range of projects that the SPG might attempt, and re-staking the claim that the Church of England was the Church of the empire.

Montgomery was not alone in seeing imperial nationalism as an effective vehicle for rallying missionary enthusiasm, nor was the SPG entirely uncritical in its endorsement of the imperial cause. Other missionary societies, as we will see in later chapters, were attracted to the language and ideals of empire loyalty. In 1892, the Church Missionary Society decided to despatch a colonial deputation, led by Eugene Stock, the Editorial Secretary, and Reverend R. W. Stewart, in order to visit

[57] Montgomery to Davidson, 12 July 1899, in Lambeth Palace Library, Davidson Papers, vol. 519.
[58] Montgomery to Davidson, 12 July 1899 and 27 May 1901, in Lambeth Palace Library, Davidson Papers, vol. 519, fols. 246v and 283.
[59] Montgomery to Davidson, 7 June 1901, in Lambeth Palace Library, Davidson Papers, vol. 519, fol. 294.
[60] Maughan, 'Archbishop for Greater Britain'.
[61] Montgomery to Davidson, 24 May 1900, in Lambeth Palace Library, Davidson Papers, vol. 519, fol. 255v.

Australasia and Canada and promote the establishment of missionary auxiliaries who would raise funds and send out missionaries of their own, independently of the home society. Writing for the *Church Missionary Intelligencer*, George Ensor, later known as the first English missionary to Japan, described the work of the delegation as nothing less than a renewal of the bond that had drawn Australians to fight for Britain in the Sudan:

It was no mere vulgar hatred of the Arab race that unsheathed the Australian sword. It was not coarse love of gain, nor even craving for renown. It was to demonstrate the glorious principle of Imperial Unity. It was the love of the Motherland. It was for this idea that our colonial kinsmen died.[62]

As Stock and Stewart set sail, Ensor rejoiced that they would be calling Australians to serve a cause, which he described as nobler even than the unity of the Anglo-Saxon race or the imperial federation of Great Britain's colonies: the communication of the gospel to the whole world. Such calls to imperial unity helped to ease the difficulty that the new CMS auxiliaries would be setting themselves up as rivals to the Australasian Board of Missions and the work of the SPG.

SPG: *The East and the West*

The East and the West was a quarterly journal of the SPG, which, following Montgomery's plan, outlined issues arising in missions 'both in the colonies and amongst the heathen'.[63] For Montgomery, the empire provided the supporting frame for both aspects of the Society's signature dual mission. The colonial mission was showcased in two articles entitled, 'The Imperial Claims of the SPG'[64] and 'The Function of the Colonial Churches in Our Missionary Expansion', which were written by Alfred Barry (1826–1910), the former bishop of Sydney and Primate of Australia. Stuart A. Donaldson, brother of the high church bishop of Brisbane, contributed another on the colonial theme with a piece on education in South Africa. Barry provided a defence of the SPG's colonial mission, pointing out that according to the SPG charter the needs

---

[62] George Ensor, 'The Message of Australia to England', *Church Missionary Intelligencer* (April 1892), p. 248. For the later missions of the CMS in Australia, see A. Barry, 'The Function of the Colonial Churches in Our Missionary Expansion', *The East and the West: A Quarterly Review for the Study of Missions*, 1 (1903), p. 185; K. Cole, *A History of the Church Missionary Society of Australia* (Melbourne, 1971).

[63] S. A. Donaldson, 'Education in South Africa. Our Opportunity and Our Duty', *The East and the West: A Quarterly Review for the Study of Missions*, 1 (1903), p. 392.

[64] H. C. Richards, 'The Imperial Claims of the SPG', *The East and the West: A Quarterly Review for the Study of Missions*, 1 (1903), pp. 60–4.

of settlers within the Empire was 'the inspiring idea and the guiding principle of its first action'.[65] However, even he does not argue that the Society should continue to support work for the white populations in the self-governing dominions.

It was otherwise with Donaldson, who makes a bravura case for the SPG facilitating Anglo-supremacy in Africa.[66] Quoting Cecil Rhodes ('It takes a man five years to see South Africa, ten years to love it and fifteen years to know it'), Donaldson bemoaned the financial problems of South Africa, where 'The Church' was not a majority institution with substantial endowments but the sect of an ethnic enclave. He regretted that stipends for the clergy were pitifully low ('less than may be earned by a respectable butler'), and schools were especially under-resourced.[67] Donaldson's article was a more or less blatant pitch for funds to support Anglo-imperialism in South Africa by funding Anglican Church schools for boys, including the Diocesan College at Rondebosch in Cape Town, St Andrew's College at Grahamstown and Michaelhouse at Balgowan in Natal. From these schools, Donaldson, himself an old Etonian, boasted that boys went forth to rule the empire:

carrying with them all over the country the traditions and tone and characteristics of the English Public School, the joyousness of life, the love of sport, and above all that intense desire to see fair play and the 'run straight', which is so ingrained a feature in the English character, and to which England owes so much.[68]

Donaldson felt the issue was so important that he adds a few more lines in a footnote: 'Readers at home hardly realise the vastness of the issues at stake. In these schools are trained the pick of the future manhood of South Africa.' These calls were deaf to the needs of the people of very mixed racial character who made up the population and were unabashedly elitist. Nevertheless, the SPG agreed to set up a central fund to be initiated by grants from both the SPG and the SPCK in aid of education to middle-class white children in South Africa.[69]

There was also some execrable poetry in praise of the religious call of the colonies, which was contributed by George Alexander Chadwick, bishop of Derry and Raphoe (1896–1916). One verse (there are five more) is probably sufficient to demonstrate the bishop's gifts in this direction. Chadwick called it 'The Exiles':

---

[65] Barry, 'Function of the Colonial Churches', p. 185.
[66] Donaldson, 'Education in South Africa'.
[67] Ibid., p. 392.   [68] Ibid., p. 395.
[69] Pascoe, Two Hundred Years of the SPG, p. 774a, notes that the colleges mentioned by Donaldson had been funded by the SPG to provide pathways to the ministry for both native and colonial youth.

O children of a teeming race,
My realms have many an affluent place
Unpeopled: overthronged is home:
Your limbs, your hearts are strong to roam:

Go till the prairie, build the town,
Bring the tall forest crashing down,
And over ampler spaces spread
This fair flag gleaming overhead.[70]

This poem recalls earlier ventures in verse, such as the poetic greeting prepared by Barron Field (1786–1846), a judge in the New South Wales Supreme Court, for the LMS delegation of the Reverend Daniel Tyerman and George Bennet, who came to Sydney in 1825 after touring the Society's Pacific missions.[71] On that occasion, Field pleaded that the visitors consider the needs of colonists as much as those of heathen Pacific Islanders – lest the Tahitian should learn to know Christ better than the 'Austral Colonist'. Both poems lent a heroic glow to the pioneers who tamed the wilderness, ploughed the prairie, created settlements and civilisation and ensured that the British flag was flown whenever and wherever convenient. In all these contributions, the creation of a Christian church in the colonies was seen as synonymous with other empire-building work.

A more jingoistic interpretation of the work of the SPG was written by a layman, H. C. Richards, in an article that credited the SPG with both 'building up Imperial unity' and 'a greater Church of England in a Greater Britain'.[72] Richards begins by admitting that the missionary character of the SPG repelled many, without, he says, who did not understand what the SPG did. He went on to justify support for the Society on the ground that it alone had the capacity to unite the English race throughout the empire. Because it helped to lift up imperial patriotism, Richards argued that it was a vital work that should appeal to many who felt no sympathy for missions to the heathen. There was also a mystical side to the appeal to empire. In Richard's view, those who attended Anglican Church services formed a continuous chain: 'binding Englishmen all over the world to the Mother Land, and connecting them with the services of the old parish church in the villages and towns which they had left behind them.'[73] Such views, which

---

[70] G. A. Chadwick [Bishop of Derry and Raphoe], 'The Exiles', *The East and the West: A Quarterly Review for the Study of Missions*, 1 (1903), pp. 241–2.

[71] J. King, *Ten Decades: The Australian Centenary Story of the London Missionary Society* (London, 1894), p. 66.

[72] Richards, 'Imperial Claims', p. 64.   [73] *Ibid.*, p. 62.

emphasised the extent to which the Church of England was a vehicle for national and imperial pride as much if not more than Christian fellowship, were always more marked in the SPG than in the publications of any other colonial missionary society. While the movement to establish the Church of England as a national Church in the colonies ended in failure, it did live on in Anglican contexts such as this.

If we review the volume as a whole, it is clear that the contributions on settler religion and its mission opportunities were already becoming anachronistic. In the colonies themselves, the call of the empire was being transmuted into the call of the bush. The 'bush brotherhoods' were an initiative of Nathaniel Dawes, which were created after the 1897 Lambeth Conference.[74] Eventually, seven bush brotherhoods were established in Australia where they had an important impact on the colonial church; at least thirteen brothers went on to become bishops.[75] They were a practical and flexible response to the need for a committed and mobile clergy to work on the colonial frontier. There were other challenging calls for the indigenisation of the missionary and the colonial churches. Compared with Richards' sentimental jingoism about the empire, it is startling to read the critique of Herbert Hamilton Kelly (1860–1950), a young missionary who had only recently returned from South Africa and who would later go on to found the Society of the Sacred Mission.[76] Before there could be a self-supporting native church, Kelly argued, it was necessary for English workers to withdraw. Quoting from missionaries who expressed the lowest opinions of native industry, duty and morality, he argued that the major cause of the lingering dependence of missions in South Africa lay in an unwillingness to let go of English institutions and let things be done in a truly native fashion. Here Kelly appears to be reflecting Venn's view of the evolution of the self-governing church,[77] one in which English missionaries would be redundant. Nevertheless, it would be another generation or two before this radical proposal became a reality for any church outside Greater Britain. The outbreak of war in South Africa revealed how fragile the imperial consensus really was.

[74] R. Frappell, 'The Australian Bush Brotherhoods and Their English Origins', *Journal of Ecclesiastical History*, 47 (1996), pp. 82–97; R. Frappell, 'Imperial Fervour and Anglican Loyalty 1901–1929', in *Anglicanism in Australia: A History*, ed. B. Kaye (Melbourne, 2002), pp. 76–99; R. A. F. Webb, *Brothers in the Sun: A History of the Bush Brotherhood Movement in the Outback of Australia* (Sydney, 1978).

[75] J. W. S. Tomlin, *The Story of the Bush Brotherhoods* (London, 1949), p. 101.

[76] H. Kelly, 'Missionary Work in South Africa', *The East and the West: A Quarterly Review for the Study of Missions*, 1 (1903), p. 167.

[77] Williams, *Ideal of the Self-Governing Church*.

Enlistment to the colonial mission

Although it was becoming unfashionable, the colonial mission of the Church of England continued to attract new recruits. To enlist them, there was a need for promotional material. Bishop Montgomery produced this for the SPG in some quantity.[78] The SPCK also published colonial clergy memoirs which served the dual role of celebrating the achievements of colonial pioneers and providing information for those with a vocation for an overseas mission, whether to emigrants or to the heathen.[79] At the University of Cambridge, there was a series of lectures delivered by John Richardson Selwyn (1844–98), Master of Selwyn College, and a former bishop of Melanesia, at the request of the Theological Board as the Pastoral Lectures for 1896.[80] As Selwyn explained, these were intended for undergraduates, 'some of whom might possibly go out to the Colonies, or to the Mission Field', and to give them the benefit of his own experience. In fact, it was enthusiastic propaganda for the colonial mission. Selwyn was not a recruiting agent for the SPG's colonial mission, and yet he supported it as the natural, indeed morally imperative extension of British temporal rule overseas.

Selwyn began his lectures with an account of the origins of the colonial episcopate. For Selwyn, remembering the work of his father who had gone out to New Zealand in 1841 as its first Anglican bishop, the British church and people had been shamefully neglectful and ignorant of the needs of the colonial churches:

The Briton was very proud of himself. He liked to hear of the drum-beat which was heard round the world, of the flag on which the sun never set, &c., but as for knowing where the drum beat and why, or troubling himself over whose heads the Union Jack flew, that was quite another question. Every now and then a son went out to some remote region, and his family then found out where it was; and now and again a little war showed the Briton as he read his *Times* that the empire was extending.[81]

Nevertheless, Selwyn stated that public indifference was matched by an even greater indifference on the part of the Church, exacerbated by the reluctance of the British government to endow bishoprics. The answer to this problem was the Colonial Bishoprics' Fund that 'sowed

---

[78] H. H. Montgomery, *Handbook on Foreign Mission* (London, 1902); H. H. Montgomery, *Service Abroad* (New York, Bombay and Calcutta, 1910).
[79] J. J. Halcombe, ed., *The Emigrant and the Heathen, or, Sketches of Missionary Life* (London, 1870). For further discussion of clergy memoirs, see the Conclusion below.
[80] J. R. Selwyn, *Pastoral Work in the Colonies and the Mission Field* (London, 1902).
[81] *Ibid*., p. 6.

Bishops broadcast throughout the Colonies'.[82] In a few lines Selwyn sketched the factors that transformed the English-speaking colonies into fields for settlement. In brief, these were steam, gold and finally wool. Missionaries were needed to ensure that the British empire was a Christian empire, not simply a commercial and technological marvel.

In his subsequent lecture, Selwyn pointed out the important distinction between the English church and the Church in the colonies that arose because of the lack of any preference for the Anglican communion. Not only did the colonies lack an established church, Roman Catholicism and Nonconformity were strong rivals to the Church of England. Selwyn also highlighted the failure of the original system of appointing bishops by letters patent in the Church of England, drawing on the experience of his own father.[83] On the character of the colonists, Selwyn is warm, speaking of their materialism, but also their openness to new things, all experienced in the delightful climate. The other side to this was that the inducements to the external life made it less likely to find intellectualism and spiritual men out there. Selwyn used this as an argument in favour of continued recruiting from home: 'And therefore', Selwyn argues, 'it is that the supply of men from the old country, and especially from our Universities, becomes so important.'[84] Cambridge and Oxford might provide the leaven, while the colonist, who Selwyn calls 'essentially a man of sport and pleasure', would supply the physical and the material inducements to develop the colonial church.

Selwyn's third lecture was full of adventure stories and the allure of muscular Christianity in the style made popular by the writer and clergyman Charles Kingsley (1819–75). Although it was set in the time of Queen Elizabeth I, Kingsley had glamorised the opening up of the American frontier in his popular novel, *Westward Ho!* (1855). Back in Cambridge, Selwyn explained that only the strongest and bravest men were called to go out into the empire, where they might be asked to ford rivers, shoot elk and grizzlies, or amputate limbs, while always keeping their cool and behaving as English gentlemen:

They did this for sport; how many will do it for immortal souls? The souls of our own people, the children of our own race, that they may feel that their Mother does indeed care for them, since she puts such spirit into her servants that they do this thing for her, for them, and for her Lord. Can any work be more Apostolic?[85]

Having hit his rhetorical stride, Selwyn marched briskly on with tales of Christian warriors, who battled with the old religions among the

---

[82] *Ibid.*, p. 3.   [83] *Ibid.*, p. 37.   [84] *Ibid.*, p. 47.   [85] *Ibid.*, p. 77.

Hindus, Chinese and 'uncivilised races'. In such places, he advised his young audience, it was important not to feel too superior: 'You are teaching the brotherhood of men: be a brother and not a lord.'[86] There is something impossibly – and alarmingly – silly about all this. Did undergraduates ever accept this kind of talk seriously, even in 1902? However, the lectures were not quite over. There was a final benediction:

> Whether we go or whether we stay, we have one common duty, and that is to render this great English race, to which God has given such mighty privileges, and with them such awful responsibility, more true and pure, more God-fearing and God-loving in itself, and to render it a blessing, and not a curse, to the innumerable multitudes of every tongue and people, and race and nation, over which it rules, or with which it is brought in contact.[87]

Perhaps it *was* all a bit much. The volume now in the Cambridge University Library, which holds the library of the SPCK, has been firmly stamped: 'Not to be reprinted' and the date '19.10.10'.[88]

Selwyn's lectures belong to the age of the Edwardian imperial hero, a time when men might sacrifice themselves for a higher cause, for God, empire and their chums. The Religious Tract Society published a volume by the journalist and writer Henry Charles Moore (1862–1933) called *Brave Sons of the Empire* (he also published *Noble Deeds of the World's Heroines*) which expounded a genealogy of imperial heroics which extended from Oliver Cromwell, in the rather unlikely role as 'defender of the oppressed', and included soldier martyrs such as General Gordon and missionary martyrs such as James Chalmers of New Guinea.[89] There were heroes for the Arctic (Captain James and the Northwest Passage), the Antarctic (Sir James Ross) and the Australian desert (Burke and Wills). While some of these men were overt in their religious practices, for most, duty and empire were their major inspirations. The SPCK seems to have endorsed these patriotic ideals as the moral equivalent of a religious vocation. Less than eighteen months after it was decided not to reprint Selwyn's lectures, Captain Robert Falcon Scott (1868–1912) would lie dying in an Antarctic tent having travelled further, in the name of duty and empire, than any other southern missionary martyr. Nevertheless, as Selwyn's lectures indicate, he had inculcated the same heroic ethos as that which Selwyn purveyed to undergraduates considering a career of missionary service in the colonial empire.

---

[86] *Ibid.*, p. 135.   [87] *Ibid.*, p. 159.
[88] The call number of this volume in the Cambridge University Library is SPCK.1.1902.5
[89] H. C. Moore, *Brave Sons of the Empire* (London, 1910).

Table 3.3 *Anglican colonial and missionary bishoprics, 1900*

1787[a] Nova Scotia[b, c]	1867[a] Grafton and Armidale
1793[a] Quebec	1869[a] Maritzburg
1814[a] Calcutta	1869[a] Bathurst
1824[a] Jamaica	1870 Falkland Islands
1824[a] Barbados	1870[a] Zululand
1835[a] Madras	1872[a] Moosonee
1836[a] Australia (later Sydney)	1872[a] Trinidad
1837[a] Bombay	1872[a] Mid China
1839[a] Toronto	1873[a] Algoma
1839[a] Newfoundland	1873[a] St John's
1841[a] New Zealand (later Auckland)	1874[a] Mackenzie River
1842[a] Tasmania	1874[a] Saskatchewan
1842[a] Antigua	1874[a] Madagascar
1842[a] Guiana	1875[a] Ballarat
1842[a] Gibraltar	1875[a] Niagara
1845[a] Fredericton	1877[a] Lahore
1845[a] Colombo	1877[a] Rangoon
1846[a] Jerusalem	1878[a] Pretoria
1847[a] Cape Town	1878[a] North Queensland
1847[a] Newcastle	1878[a] Windward Islands
1847[a] Melbourne	1879[a] Caledonia
1847[a] Adelaide	1879[a] New Westminster
1849[a] Victoria (China)	1879[a] Travancore and Cochin
1849[a] Rupertsland	1880[a] North China
1850[a] Montreal	1883[a] South Tokyo
1850[a] Sierra Leone	1883[a] Honduras
1855[a] Grahamstown	1884[a] Riverina
1854[a] Mauritius	1884[a] Qu'Appelle
1855[a] Labuan	1884[a] Uganda
1856[a] Christchurch	1884[a] Athabasca
1857[a] Perth	1887[a] Calgary
1857[a] Huron	1889[a] Korea
1858[a] Wellington	1890[a] Chota Nagpur
1858[a] Nelson	1891 Selkirk
1858[a] Waiapu	1891[a] Mashonaland
1859[a] Brisbane	1891[a] Lebombo
1859[a] St Helena	1892[a] Rockhampton
1859[a] Columbia	1892 Likoma
1861[a] Ontario	1892[a] Lucknow
1861[a] Nassau	1894 Kiushu
1861[a] Zambesi (later Central Africa)	1895 Western China
1861[a] Honolulu	1896[a] Osaka
1861[a] Melanesia	1896[a] Ottawa
1862[a] Ontario	1896 Hokkaido
1863[a] Bloemfontein (Orange River)	

Table 3.3 (*cont.*)

1863[a] Goulburn	1898[a] Tinnevelly and Madura
1864[a] Western Equatorial Africa	1898[a] New Guinea
1866[a] Dunedin	1898 Mombasa

[a] This signifies that the Society has planted or supported Missions which now form a part of the diocese.
[b] This signifies that the Society has contributed to the support of the bishop by annual grants.
[c] This signifies that the Society has contributed to the permanent endowment of the see.
Source: H. W. Tucker, *The Spiritual Expansion of the Empire: A Sketch of Two Centuries of Work Done for the Church and Nation by the Society for the Propagation of the Gospel in Foreign Parts*, 4th edn (London, 1900), p. 124.

Conclusion

Although the SPG had sustained colonial missionary work as part of its mandate into the twentieth century, the needs of European settlers in colonies were hard to support in the face of the demands of the emerging national churches in Africa, India and Asia. Whether colonial and continental missions should be relegated with home missions rather than with the higher status work of direct evangelisation of the heathen in foreign lands had, by the first decade of the twentieth century, become irrelevant. Immigration was ensuring that home and foreign mission works were becoming increasingly entangled. Colonial Anglicans, who had once been the object of the missionary attentions of the SPG, had become missionaries in their own right. As Pascoe put it: 'Seed sown by the foreign missionary is bringing forth fruit in city and home mission fields, while the labours of those at home find their results in far distant lands.'[90] For the SPG, it was the end of a long run and an explanation for the demise of what had been an important part of its work for the best part of 200 years.

The colonial mission of the SPG was still active at the end of the nineteenth century, but it was increasingly being submerged beneath the more urgent claims of its missions to non-Europeans. The rise and fall of the SPG's work with settlers reflects in large measure the rise and fall of British colonisation. Its later influence was probably extended by the effectiveness of Montgomery in linking the work of the SPG, including its colonial mission, to imperialism. While other missionary societies also saw the benefit of banging the imperial drum in order to seek funds for their missionary operation, the SPG was probably more open to

[90] Pascoe, *Two Hundred Years of the SPG*, p. 368.

Table 3.4 *SPG: income from general and other sources, 1801–1910*

	General	Other funds	Total income		General	Other funds	Total income
1801	3,980	2,477	6,457	1851	45,504	55,582	101,086
1802	4,196	662	4,858	1852	51,834	31,501	83,335
1803	4,340	3,393	7,733	1853	59,374	27,520	86,894
1804	4,334	1,554	5,888	1854	50,590	23,429	74,019
1805	4,481	1,811	6,292	1855	66,093	16,117	82,210
1806	4,381	2,345	6,726	1856	69,572	34,895	104,467
1807	4,509	1,655	6,164	1857	79,249	13,239	92,488
1808	4,516	—	4,516	1858	90,071	12,521	102,592
1809	4,291	1,726	6,017	1859	90,443	25,986	116,429
1810	4,480	2,756	7,236	1860	78,213	13,023	91,236
1811	4,530	3,270	7,800	1861	84,269	5,043	89,312
1812	4,466	3,190	7,656	1862	86,748	6,577	93,325
1813	4,675	2,750	7,425	1863	82,257	5,575	87,832
1814	6,331	1,785	8,116	1864	95,330	7,666	102,996
1815	10,452	2,988	13,440	1865	86,972	7,285	94,257
1816	13,067	6,782	19,849	1866	84,723	6,461	91,184
1817	12,734	4,942	17,676	1867	94,327	20,219	114,546
1818	13,817	5,825	19,642	1868	88,893	14,239	103,132
1819	53,394	6,046	59,440	1869	90,464	15,970	106,434
1820	20,357	3,868	24,225	1870	79,509	12,954	92,463
1821	18,251	4,902	23,153	1871	85,843	11,761	97,604
1822	17,693	4,766	22,459	1872	101,031	12,093	113,124
1823	17,961	3,352	21,313	1873	97,018	13,241	110,259
1824	29,438	5,307	34,745	1874	103,910	30,928	134,838
1825	32,783	5,410	38,193	1875	99,103	26,191	125,294
1826	26,970	4,553	31,523	1876	101,035	35,871	136,906
1827	28,935	5,902	34,837	1877	119,109	29,329	148,438
1828	57,124	4,370	61,494	1878	113,230	32,007	145,237
1829	32,625	5,522	38,147	1879	86,788	34,943	131,674
1830	29,745	3,157	32,902	1880	85,277	42,569	138,289
1831	29,030	4,303	33,333	1881	84,709	39,643	134,978
1832	64,774	3,663	68,437	1882	90,846	33,571	142,612
1833	26,938	3,677	30,615	1883	90,976	18,596	109,572
1834	21,961	3,513	25,474	1884	90,656	19,383	110,039
1835	32,768	3,579	36,347	1885	101,825	16,146	117,971
1836	64,984	13,139	78,123	1886	86,969	18,743	105,712
1837	26,328	3,247	29,575	1887	92,003	17,762	109,765
1838	35,302	5,963	41,265	1888	117,385	20,982	138,367
1839	69,501	4,635	74,136	1889	101,398	23,641	125,039
1840	57,018	9,115	66,133	1890	116,076	48,307	164,383
1841	65,025	9,898	74,923	1891	97,529	18,991	116,520
1842	77,228	9,104	86,332	1892	100,031	27,118	127,149
1843	52,381	16,519	68,900	1893	94,471	18,608	113,079
1844	63,245	11,465	74,710	1894	104,553	17,774	122,327
1845	85,904	13,288	99,192	1895	97,508	20,750	118,258

Table 3.4 (*cont.*)

1846	56,755	12,206	68,961	1896	105,427	28,089	133,516
1847	45,572	40,253	85,825	1897	113,349	204,164	317,513
1848	81,804	14,203	96,007	1898	101,636	30,720	132,356
1849	67,489	19,149	86,638	1899	106,417	30,429	136,846
1850	62,365	27,068	89,433	1900	102,275	76,121	178,396
				Totals	6,108,046	1,689,326	7,846,579

Source: Pascoe, *Two Hundred Years of the SPG*, pp. 830–1901. 'General funds' were untied; 'Other funds' were committed for specific purposes.

the idea than others, if only because imperialism had been a part of the ideology of the Society from the time of its foundation. That being said, the SPG was not entirely bound by its history of engagement with the British state. As the Church of England was reformed in the course of the nineteenth century, it came increasingly to model the national Church that Coleridge had elevated to a cultural and spiritual ideal. More problematic for the Society was its identification with the most old-fashioned work of the Church, that to colonists, which restricted its appeal to Anglican donors and potential missionaries. In addition, from the 1830s, it had a rival for the provision of services to Anglican settlers, namely, the organisation that would eventually call itself the Colonial and Continental Church Society which will be considered in Chapter 5. Both of these Anglican societies were products of a Protestant nation that privileged the Church of England. In the colonies, there was little or no establishment and colonial missionary societies that supported the extension of Catholic and Nonconformist churches were a startling innovation without precedent in the United Kingdom. The SPG had been founded to defend the faith in the new world. Over the next four chapters, we will consider the spiritual empires that grew to rival the Church of England and the challenge these posed to the original mission of the SPG, beginning with the Catholic Church and its missionary auxiliary, the Association for the Propagation of the Faith.

4   Catholics

This chapter considers the paths by which the Catholic Church
was extended into British colonies in the nineteenth century and
the relationship between the settler churches and the various competing sources of clerical personnel and influence in England,
Ireland, France and Rome. Mostly, this involves explaining how
Irish Catholicism came to dominate the Catholic Church throughout much of the settler British world. Some of this covers familiar
territory: historians have long been aware of the role played by Paul
Cullen (1803–78), first as rector of the Irish College in Rome and
then in Ireland as archbishop of Armagh and subsequently of Dublin,
in stamping a 'Roman mould' on the Catholic Church in Australia
and New Zealand.[1] Other British colonies, particularly those in North
America, were more successful in defending themselves from falling
entirely within the Irish orbit.[2] However, both the Australasian case
and the American counter-examples need to be set within a global
context that was more extensive than the British empire. As we will
see, the ethnic and political profile of colonial Catholicism depended
on the interaction of three forces: the Sacred Congregation for the
Propagation of the Faith (Propaganda) – the bureaucracy within the
Roman Curia which appointed missionary bishops and had responsibility for the conduct of missions; the hierarchies of the resurgent

[1] For biographical accounts of Cullen, see D. Bowen, *Paul Cardinal Cullen and the
Shaping of Modern Irish Catholicism* (Dublin, 1983); E. Larkin, 'Cullen, Paul (1803–
1878)', in *Oxford Dictionary of National Biography* (Oxford, 2004); P. MacSuibhne, ed.,
Paul Cullen and His Contemporaries with Their Letters from 1820–1902, 5 vols. (Naas,
1965). For Cullen in Ireland, see C. Barr, *Paul Cullen, John Henry Newman and the
Catholic University of Ireland, 1845–65* (Leominster, 2003). For Rome and Australia,
the fullest account is now C. Dowd, *Rome in Australia: The Papacy and Conflict in the
Australian Catholic Missions, 1834–1884*, 2 vols. (Leiden, 2008). See also J. N. Molony,
The Roman Mould of the Australian Catholic Church (Melbourne, 1969).
[2] On resistance to Irish hegemony, see C. Barr, '"Imperium in Imperio": Irish Episcopal
Imperialism in the Nineteenth Century', *English Historical Review*, 123 (2008), pp.
611–50. For an earlier attempt at a synthesis, see Southerwood, *Catholics in British
Colonies*.

Catholic Church in England and Ireland who corresponded about the supply of colonial clergy; and the Association for the Propagation of the Faith (Oeuvre de la propagation de la foi) – the missionary auxiliary which coordinated fund-raising and publicity for Catholic overseas missions.[3] Other important figures were the rectors of the major seminaries in Rome and Ireland and the heads of the religious orders who recruited and trained personnel for the mission field.

Colonial missions to British colonies came to be an important source of Irish national pride, a means to build a spiritual empire that would form some compensation for Ireland's poverty and centuries of colonial subjection to Britain. In the face of ongoing Protestant hostility, they were also opportunities to demonstrate Catholic commitment to empire and nation-building in the colonies. While never pro-British, the Catholic colonial mission represented the most significant Irish investment in the empire that British enterprise opened up to Catholic settlement.

Catholics in Britain and Ireland

Looking at the conditions for Catholics in Britain at the beginning of the nineteenth century, few people could have predicted that they had the capacity to staff and resource a Catholic missionary movement in the British empire. Until the restoration of the Catholic hierarchy in England (1850), Catholics regarded England, Wales and Scotland as mission territories. Indeed, Scotland remained so until as late as 1878. Vicars apostolic not only managed local churches; they also worked and prayed for the reconversion of Protestant Britain to Roman Catholicism.[4] This was not a terribly realistic ambition given the small Catholic populations of England, Wales and Scotland and the numerical and cultural

---

[3] It is now one of four worldwide pontifical mission-aid societies. J. Waldersee, *A Grain of Mustard Seed: The Society for the Propagation of the Faith and Australia, 1837–1977* (Sydney, 1983) provides a history of the Society's activities in Australia. For the influence of the *Oeuvre* in defending missionaries in the French colonial empire, see J. P. Daughton, *An Empire Divided: Religion, Republicanism, and the Making of French Colonialism, 1880–1914* (Oxford, 2006), p. 256.

[4] A note on terminology: Catholics in Protestant countries as well as those in non-Christian territories were organised as 'missions' which were administered not by resident bishops but by ecclesiastical administrators with the rank, but not the local territorial title, of a bishop. Depending on the standing of the missionary territory, missions were organised as prefectures (headed by a 'Prefect Apostolic') or vicariates (headed by a 'Vicar Apostolic'). If appropriate, these might later advance to become dioceses (led by a bishop) and ultimately metropolitan archdioceses (led by an archbishop). See Table 4.2, Chronology of Catholic dioceses in Britain and settler colonies up to 1908.

supremacy of Protestantism at all levels of British society. At the time of the 1851 Census of Religious Worship, held after the impact of post-famine emigration from Ireland to mainland Britain had swelled their numbers, Catholics made 365,430 attendances at services in England and Wales, amounting to only 3.5 per cent of total attendances in all churches.[5] In Scotland, the relative proportion of Catholics in the population was a little higher, but Catholic attendances there were still only 4.6 per cent of the Scottish total.

It was reasonable to anticipate more from Ireland, where Catholics made up the majority of the population. But Ireland was a poor country and it made no significant investment in foreign missions until the twentieth century.[6] Nevertheless, unlike England, Scotland and Wales, Ireland had at least retained its Catholic hierarchy. The Irish Church was supplied with priests who were trained in seminaries in France, Belgium, Spain, Portugal and Rome, as well as members of the religious orders, including Jesuits, Dominicans and Franciscans, who also received their formation on the continent.[7] Emmet Larkin has suggested that, before the middle of the nineteenth century, the number of clergy in Ireland remained relatively small.[8] However, far from being cowed by the penal times, the Catholic Church in Ireland retained sufficient clerical and cultural resources to resist the 'Second Reformation' by zealous, well-funded English and Scottish Protestants in the 1820s.[9] Catholic emancipation in 1829 gave respectability to Catholic ambitions for a fuller role in British society at home, and sowed the seeds for imperial expansion based on the clerical resources of Ireland. At the same time, it fanned the flames of sectarianism, especially in western Scotland where it was linked to resentment of Irish emigrant labour.[10]

---

[5] 'Report on the 1851 Census of Religious Worship', *Parliamentary Papers* (1852–3), vol. LXXXIX, Table A, pp. clxxviii–clxxix, reprinted in Cook and Stevenson, *British Historical Facts 1760–1830*, p. 220.

[6] E. M. Hogan, *The Irish Missionary Movement: A Historical Survey 1830–1980* (Dublin, 1990); F. Bateman, 'Ireland's Spiritual Empire: Territory and Landscape in Irish Catholic Missionary Discourse', in *Empires of Religion*, ed. H. M. Carey (Basingstoke, 2008), pp. 267–87.

[7] T. J. Walsh, *The Irish Continental College Movement: The Colleges at Bordeaux, Toulouse, and Lille* (Dublin and Cork, 1973).

[8] E. J. Larkin, *The Pastoral Role of the Roman Catholic Church in Pre-Famine Ireland* (Dublin, 2006). I thank Dr Colin Barr for alerting me to this and other references in this chapter.

[9] B. McNamee, 'The "Second Reformation" in Ireland', *Irish Theological Quarterly*, 33 (1966), pp. 39–64; I. Whelan, *The Bible War in Ireland: The "Second Reformation" and the Polarization of Protestant–Catholic Relations, 1800–1840* (Dublin, 2005).

[10] Brown, *Church and State*, p. 467.

Catholics in the British empire

The outward movement of Catholics into the colonies of the British empire was a radical change for English and Irish Catholics, who played little part in earlier colonising movements to the Americas. There were one or two Catholic colonisation experiments in the British empire, of which the colony of Maryland, which was established by George Calvert (first Lord Baltimore) in 1634, is the best known. However, Maryland was not actually planted as a Catholic colony: it was simply the first English territory where Catholics enjoyed religious toleration.[11] A small population of Catholics continued to live in Maryland, which came to develop close links with the English Jesuits; there were more Catholics in Pennsylvania, Virginia and New Jersey. By the second half of the nineteenth century, when large-scale Irish emigration was encountering resistance in the United States, the example of Maryland was extolled by organisations such as the Irish Catholic Colonization Society. According to a promotional history written by John Lancaster Spalding, the first Catholic bishop of Peoria in Illinois, colonisation was a part of 'the spirit of every age' and religious colonisation, including the Catholic colonisation of Maryland, was integral to the development of the United States.[12] Nevertheless, the reality of religious animosity from mainstream Protestantism, coupled with low levels of Catholic emigration, ensured that Catholics were a minor force in English-speaking North America until the middle of the nineteenth century. Elsewhere in the empire, Catholics may have been proscribed commissions in the military and civil service, but this did not mean they were unable to work for the empire of British capitalism.[13] As we noted in Chapter 2, the East India Company engaged Catholic chaplains to cater for the religious needs of Irish who served in large numbers in India.[14]

Until the French Revolution interrupted its imperial expansion, it was not Irish but rather French Catholicism that left the largest imprint on colonial territories under British rule. Four British colonies had sizeable French-speaking Catholic populations, including Lower Canada (surrendered to the British under the Treaty of Paris (1763)), Newfoundland (whose status was left unresolved by the Treaty

---

[11] W. T. Russell, *Maryland: The Land of Sanctuary. A History of Religious Toleration in Maryland from the First Settlement until the American Revolution*, 2nd edn (Baltimore, 1908), p. 310.
[12] J. L. Spalding, *The Religious Mission of the Irish People and Catholic Colonization* (New York, 1978; first published by the Catholic Publication Society in 1880).
[13] Schlenther, 'Religious Faith', p. 128.
[14] Ballhatchet, 'East India Company'.

of Utrecht (1713)), Mauritius and Madagascar. In Canada, the history of the Catholic Church has been characterised as a bipolar tussle between Gallicanism and Romanism, which was not resolved until the end of the nineteenth century when the arrival of significant numbers of emigrants from Germany, Ukraine, Poland and Lithuania internationalised the Church.[15] From early in the nineteenth century, the Catholic Church was the most powerful institution in Lower Canada. It had its own metropolitan, full institutional church, including missionary orders who served both settlers and the native people, and a history of heroic missionary effort among the American Indians. Thus fortified, the Catholic Church was well placed to mount effective resistance to encroachment by both the French – and later the British – colonial governments. Although always divided between Francophones and Anglophones, the Catholic Church was by far the largest church in Canada by the time of the 1871 census, with almost three times the number of adherents of its closest Protestant rival, the Methodists.[16]

The Irish and Scottish Catholics who arrived in Upper Canada and the Maritime Provinces brought out their own clergy with their communities. Until 1840, Scottish Catholics in particular played an important role in church-building in both Prince Edward Island and Nova Scotia. However, French-speaking colonists were ministered to by the Oblates of Mary Immaculate, known as the Missionaries of Provence and, more romantically, as 'the Apostles of the North-West'.[17] The order was founded in France by St Eugene de Mazenod in 1816, and it played a key role in mission work among Europeans and native people in the North-Western Territory. It was the first religious order to arrive in Montreal after the British conquest of Quebec and fifteen of its members went on to become pioneer bishops.[18] French Catholicism also impinged on British interests in the Pacific. In New Zealand, both French and English missionaries preceded British colonisation (1840); until then, French Marist Fathers were authorised by Propaganda to establish their own vicariate focusing on the Maori and French colonists. Although eventually outnumbered by Irish Catholic settlers and Irish religious teaching orders such as the Marist and Christian Brothers, the French continued to play a role in both New Zealand and

[15] T. J. Fay, *A History of Canadian Catholics: Gallicanism, Romanism, and Canadianism* (Montreal, 2002).
[16] See Table 1.3 for precise figures.
[17] P. Duchaussois, *Mid Snow and Ice: The Apostles of the North-West* (London, 1923).
[18] *Ibid.*, p. 231.

neighbouring Australia, where the French Marist Fathers ran schools and trained missionaries for the Pacific Islands.[19] French missionaries justified their work in terms of a civilising mission, just like British Protestants, though naturally this was expressed in terms of the unique French, rather than British, cultural virtues. After the Revolution, they adapted to new political times and promoted republican colonialism along with the kingdom of God.[20]

Indirectly, the French Revolution may have been responsible for the reorientation of English Catholicism away from Europe and the old battle between Catholic and Protestant powers, and towards the fresh fields of the British empire. Before the Revolution, English Catholics were closely associated with the university at Douai in France which provided a steady stream of missioners whose goal was and remained the reconversion of the English people to the Roman Catholic faith. However, in 1793, during the Reign of Terror, most of the foreign clergy in France were imprisoned and their property confiscated. On their release and return to England as refugees in 1795, the plight of the English Benedictines attracted considerable sympathy and it was natural to turn to them for leadership of the English mission.[21] Possibly, the forced return of all the religious orders helped redirect the thoughts of Catholics in both England and Ireland beyond the missions in Britain and Ireland to the colonial diaspora.

A key figure in the creation of a new spirit of English Catholic mission overseas was the Benedictine William Poynter (1762–1827), who had been prefect of studies at the English College in Douai. As vicar apostolic of London District (1812–27), Poynter's responsibilities included the coordination of the appointment of Catholic chaplains working in Britain's colonies – an unofficial Catholic counterpart to the management of the Anglican 'oversea episcopate' by the bishop of London. Propaganda generally attempted to avoid antagonising colonial governments about ecclesiastical appointments, especially in cases where Catholics lived under Protestant regimes. Poynter's correspondence and diary show the important role he played in negotiating arrangements for Catholic overseas missions to British settlers in North

[19] J. Hosie, *Challenge: The Marists in Colonial Australia* (Sydney, 1987).

[20] Daughton, *Empire Divided*, p. 256.

[21] For the Benedictine colonial mission, see A. Bellenger, 'The English Benedictines and the British Empire', in *Victorian Churches and Churchmen: Essays Presented to Vincent Alan McClelland*, ed. S. Gilley (Woodbridge, Suffolk, 2005), pp. 94–109; P. Cunich, 'Archbishop Vaughan and the Empires of Religion in Colonial New South Wales', in *Empires of Religion*, ed. H. M. Carey (Houndmills, 2008), pp. 137–60.

America, India and the Mediterranean, the West Indies, Cape Colony
and Australasia.[22] These were important developments which the
English Benedictines anticipated would inaugurate a new Benedictine
missionary age.

At the beginning of the nineteenth century, there was no question of
Propaganda making appointments direct to British colonies and bypass-
ing either the colonial governors or the administration in Westminster.
In 1817, the Irish Cistercian, Jeremiah O'Flynn (1788–1831), arrived in
the colony of New South Wales claiming – possibly with justification –
to have been appointed prefect apostolic with authority from Rome
to begin a missionary apostolate among the Catholic convict population, and also – with no justification at all – to have obtained the
permission of the Colonial Secretary, Lord Bathurst, for this purpose.
Governor Lachlan Macquarie checked the facts and promptly had him
ejected.[23] Nevertheless, one of the first fruits of a new British spirit
of toleration towards Catholics in the empire was manifested in 1818
when Propaganda, following Poynter's suggestion, created a vicariate
apostolic which covered much of the British sphere of influence in the
southern hemisphere. The English Benedictine, Edward Bede Slater
(1774–1832), became vicar apostolic with responsibility for a daunting
expanse of territory which included Mauritius, Madagascar, the Cape
Colony and 'surrounding islands' (including the island continent of
Australia). Fortunately, he came to an agreement that allowed him to
reside in Mauritius though, like other bishops, he made efforts to tour
the bounds of his diocese. Propaganda may have assigned the vicariate to the English Benedictines partly because they could provide a
supply of English clergy whose earlier training in their motherhouse of
Douai gave them a good command of French.[24] Later in the century,
Mauritius was also significant for the role of Sir John Pope Hennessy
(1834–91), the first Catholic to be appointed as governor of a British

[22] Catholic Colonial Missions [Correspondence from Overseas Missions to Bishop
William Poynter, Westminster Cathedral Archives, 1803–1827] (East Ardsley,
Wakefield: Microform Academic Publishers, no date), www.microform.co.uk/aca-
demic/. For Poynter's diary, see P. Philips, ed., *The Diaries of Bishop William Poynter,
VA (1815–1824)*, *Catholic Record Society, Record Ser.*, 79 (London, 2006).

[23] The master of the ship in which he arrived was required to return him to England on
the same vessel but he was eventually deported in May 1818. See *Colonial Secretary
Index, 1788–1825*. State Records of New South Wales, re Reverend Jeremiah O'Flynn
28 November 1817–18 May 1818. In contrast to the official view, see the early char-
acterisation of him by W. Ullathorne, *The Catholic Mission in Australasia*, 3rd edn
(London, 1838), pp. 121–2, as a 'man of meek demeanour, who speedily won the deep
love of his people' and who left behind the Blessed Sacrament on his departure from
the colony.

[24] Bellenger, 'English Benedictines', p. 99.

colony. As Governor of Sierra Leone and Barbados, he went on to take responsibility for large populations of emancipated black slaves as well as Catholics. As Governor of Hong Kong, his liberal sympathies and abhorrence of slavery created conflict with settler elites.[25] The policy solution pursued by the Colonial Office in Mauritius, soon pursued effectively elsewhere in the empire, was to provide financial support for Catholic chaplains, tolerate a Catholic hierarchy that could demonstrate its loyalty, and appoint governors with the capacity for religious and racial toleration. Order – not Catholic advancement – was the object of this policy, but the expansion of British Catholic colonialism was one of its consequences.

From about 1820, the Catholic vicar general in London, like his Anglican counterpart, began to find it increasingly difficult to find sufficient Catholic clergy to serve the expanding Catholic populations in colonies and military bases overseas. If there were no English clergy available for colonial duties – which was often the case – the vicar apostolic wrote to his brother bishops in Ireland to try to secure the necessary appointments. This was the strategy taken by Poynter in response to a request from the Colonial Secretary, Lord Bathurst, to find two Roman Catholic clergymen for New South Wales to augment the two Irish priests already in place. On discovering that he could find no priest in England who was willing to go, Poynter wrote to James Doyle, bishop of Kildare and Leighlin, to see if there were any young men in the Carlow diocesan seminary who could take up the appointments. His letter conveyed the wish, firmly expressed to him by Lord Bathurst, 'that those who are to be sent should be men who would confine themselves solely to their religious duties'.[26] In 1826, having secured Roger Murphy and Daniel Power for the mission, Poynter wrote to them and stressed Bathurst's direction that colonial clergy behave with discretion and: 'merit the confidence and respect of the constituted authorities'.[27] In return for sticking to religion and not – by implication – straying into Irish activism, Catholic chaplains received a stipend of £100 per annum as well as free passage to the colony. All seemed set for the development of a low-key Catholic presence in the southern colonies, which would be

[25] D. Lambert and P. Howell, 'John Pope Hennessy and the Translation of "Slavery" between Late Nineteenth-Century Barbados and Hong Kong', *History Workshop Journal*, 55 (2003), pp. 1–24.
[26] 'William Poynter to Reverend Dr Doyle, Tullow, Co. Carlow, 13 October 1825', *Australasian Catholic Record*, 3 (1897), p. 134.
[27] Poynter to Revs. Roger Murphy and Daniel Power, 12 August 1826. Brian Condon: Letters and Documents in 19th Century Australian Catholic History. Source: Adelaide Archdiocesan Archives, www.unisanet.unisa.edu.au/research/condon/CatholicLetters/18260812.htm.

led by English Benedictines and staffed by an Irish clerical proletariat. This, at least, seems to have been the idea of the English Benedictines.

The situation in Cape Colony can illustrate the changing fortunes of the English Benedictine mission to Catholics in the southern colonies, the rise of Irish influence and the overall pattern of expanding toleration for colonial Catholicism.[28] From 1652 to 1795, the Dutch East India Company had maintained a complete prohibition on the presence of Catholic clergy in the Cape.[29] After 1804, the Batavian Republic allowed a number of priests to be sent from Holland to meet the needs of Catholic soldiers in the garrison. However, in 1806, the British insisted on their return under the terms of the surrender. Although there was an Irish priest in the colony when Edward Bede Slater OSB, vicar apostolic of Cape of Good Hope (1818–31), visited in 1819, he received no stipend from the government. The small size and the poverty of the Catholic community – who retained control of all church property – led the resident priest into dire financial straits, and, in 1824, he returned to Ireland in disgrace. Partly for this reason, but mostly because of the strength of both the Dutch Reformed and English Protestant churches in the Cape, the Catholic community remained small and vulnerable. The management of the Catholic community was only regularised with the arrival of the Irish Dominican, Patrick Raymond Griffith, who became the first resident Catholic bishop of the Cape vicariate.[30] It was an indication of changing times that the negotiations for Griffith's appointment as Catholic chaplain with a stipend of £200 were handled not by the London vicar apostolic but by Daniel Murray (1768–1852), archbishop of Dublin from 1825 until his death in 1852. Murray consecrated Griffith to his new office on 24 August 1837, one of many new bishops in British colonial territories that he helped to establish at the urging of Rome.

Murray's surviving correspondence reveals that he was the first Irish bishop to cultivate a Roman vision for the Catholic Church throughout the British empire. Working closely with Paul Cullen, who from 1830 to 1850 was rector of the Irish College in Rome and agent for Irish and colonial bishops, Murray's policy was to promote able men (including his own great-nephew) to the colonial episcopate. Like Cullen, he favoured those who had been educated at the Irish College in Rome over those who lacked experience outside Ireland.

[28] W. E. Brown, *The Catholic Church in South Africa from Its Origins to the Present Day* (London, 1960).

[29] J. B. Brain, 'The Irish Influence on the Roman Catholic Church', *Southern African–Irish Studies*, 2 (1992), pp. 121–2.

[30] P. Denis, *The Dominican Friars in Southern Africa: A Social History (1577–1990)* (Leiden, 1998), ch. 2.

Griffith was one of Murray's new men. His diary shows him to be an exceptionally energetic bishop, prepared to proselytise vigorously, mawkishly sentimental about Ireland, while sharing the international vision of his mentor.[31] On his arrival in the Cape, Griffith wrote to Murray that he had celebrated Easter in a room set aside for him by the Governor:

I spoke to them on the Resurrection and the necessity of Easter duty but said not a word of their dissensions which I regret to say are much more serious in a spiritual point of view than I could have imagined.[32]

To a friend he wrote that his congregation was wary of his claims to authority, and that only the Irish were inclined to attend to him. The others stayed away and seemed not to have understood what a bishop was for: 'I suspect many, if not most of them, would prefer a simple priest.'[33]

Like the majority of the Irish founder bishops of Catholic colonial churches, Griffith resorted to almost any means to fund and staff his diocese with clergy, from Ireland if possible, but from anywhere if necessary. He wrote repeatedly to All Hallows' Missionary College seeking priests, but his appeals were not answered, possibly because he did not accompany them with the necessary funds to pay for tuition or passage.[34] He was more successful in his requests to the Association for the Propagation of the Faith, which published his correspondence in the *Annals* and sent funds that he used to open at least one school. While Griffith slowly found his way, similar ventures in Catholic institution building, funded from Lyons and staffed from Ireland, were opened up throughout the British colonies.

The Irish spiritual empire

'The Irish do not colonise', according to Edward Gibbon Wakefield, 'they only emigrate miserably.'[35] In the face of competition from both English and other European, especially French, Catholic clergy, many

[31] J. B. Brain, ed., *The Cape Diary of Bishop Raymond Griffith for the Years 1837 to 1839* (Mariannhill, South Africa, 1988), p. 105; Denis, *Dominican Friars*, p. 76.
[32] Griffith to Murray, 22 April 1838, in Brain, ed., *Cape Diary*, p. 103, cited by Denis, *Dominican Friars*, p. 76.
[33] Griffith to a friend, Cape Town, 25 May 1838, reproduced in Brain, ed., *Cape Diary*, p. 105, cited by Denis, *Dominican Friars*, p. 76.
[34] Between 1844 and 1848, Griffith wrote fourteen letters to the presidents of All Hallows. See All Hallows College Drumcondra Archives; personal copies held by J. B. Brain, cited by Denis, *Dominican Friars*, p. 80.
[35] Cited by Carrington, *British Overseas*, p. 500. According to R. Garnett, *Edward Gibbon Wakefield: The Colonization of South Australia and New Zealand, Etc.* (New

with much wider experience of missionary work and without Ireland's
history of poverty, political isolation and educational deprivation, how
did Irish Catholics – in defiance of Wakefield – come to dominate the
settler dioceses of the Catholic British world? The simple answer to this
question is emigration and effective training programmes for priests,
religious teachers and nurses unmatched by Catholics, or indeed
Protestants, from any other community. The Irish spiritual empire was
not an accident but was the result of meticulous planning, building on
something that the Irish did very efficiently – professional education for
foreign service.

Until the early 1840s, the Irish diaspora was made up of mobile and
ambitious emigrants who were more likely than not to be Protestant.[36]
Given their poverty and lack of higher education, Catholics usually
paid for their ticket out of Ireland by service in the army and navy
or by training for one of the professions. Irish students for the priesthood had long been accustomed to seek training and employment in
Europe, where they formed an adaptable clerical underclass. After
Catholic emancipation, Irish soldiers and clergy, together with lawyers
and doctors, who braved clerical strictures against attendance at either
Trinity College or the Queen's University, found ready employment in
the service of the British empire.[37] Irish administrators flourished in
the Indian Civil Service; Irish lawyers brought English law to colonial
legislatures; Irish soldiers filled the ranks of the British army, marching
to defend the empire in campaigns from India to southern Africa. The
Irish also fought as mercenaries in foreign armies, liberating Spanish
South America, fighting for Napoleon and, with pleasing even-hand-
edness, for the pope.[38] They also fought for the Boers in southern
Africa.[39] Where colonial armies were succeeded or supplemented by
police, the Irish soon took up positions there as well. In short, the Irish
were practical imperialists – cheap, adaptable, willing to travel, hold a
gun, beat a drum, preach a sermon, and generally serve in many useful

York, 1898), p. 294, this comment is said to have come from a section on Irish emigration excluded from *The Art of Colonization*, which is now lost.

[36] S. Gilley, 'The Roman Catholic Church and the Nineteenth Century Irish Diaspora',
Journal of Ecclesiastical History, 35 (1984), pp. 188–207.

[37] For the examples cited, see S. B. Cook, 'The Irish Raj: Social Origins and Careers
of Irishmen in the Indian Civil Service, 1855–1914', *Journal of Social History*, 20
(1987), pp. 506–29; A. Daniel, 'Undermining British Australia: Irish Lawyers and
the Transformation of English Law in Australia', *Studies*, 84 (1995), pp. 61–70;
H. J. Hanham, 'Religion and Nationality in the Mid-Victorian Army', in *War and
Society: Historical Essays in Honour and Memory of J. R. Wester, 1928–1971*, ed. M. R. Foot
(London, 1973), pp. 57–69.

[38] G. F. Berkeley, *The Irish Battalion in the Papal Army of 1860* (Dublin, 1929).

[39] *Ibid.*

positions along the colonial frontier. There remains some reluctance to embrace this image of Irish Catholics as bearers of empire, as colonisers and collaborators rather than as victims of British imperialism.[40] Nevertheless, the new emphasis on the economic opportunities provided by the empire, and the willingness of Irish to take advantage of them, makes more sense than the one-sided victim histories of the past. The enormous growth of the Catholic Church in the British empire was an aspect of the global dispersal of Irish professional emigrants in the nineteenth century.

The Catholic Church in Ireland was remarkably swift to build up its capacity to supply priests for British colonial missions. In the decade following the lifting of the Irish penal laws (1782), diocesan seminaries such as Carlow College, founded in 1782 by James Keefe, bishop of Kildare and Leighlin, provided an education for priests of modest means and local connections. However, it was soon able to supply the needs of dioceses overseas. Between 1793 and 1993, Carlow trained over 300 priests for the Australian mission fields, including Fr John Joseph Therry (1790–1864), the first Catholic chaplain, and four Australian bishops.[41] In 1865, James Walshe, bishop of Kildare, stated that he had thirty-three seminarians studying for 'foreign' (i.e. non-Irish) missions, and that in the previous three years he had sent out sixteen missionary priests and deacons for dioceses including England (one), Scotland (one), the United States (six), Canada (one), Australia (two) and New Zealand (one).[42] Another diocesan seminary, St Peter's College, Wexford, was critical for the formation of the Catholic Church in the Cape Colony. Three of its early bishops and half a dozen pioneer clergy trained there for the priesthood.[43] St Patrick's College, Maynooth, founded as the National Seminary for Ireland, followed Carlow in 1795.

With the disruption of the continental colleges which followed the French Revolution, these Irish seminaries took on renewed importance, and most were able to survive the political backlash which followed the

[40] For debate about the Irish contribution to empire, see S. Howe, *Ireland and Empire: Colonial Legacies in Irish History and Culture* (Oxford, 2000); K. Jeffery, *An Irish Empire?: Aspects of Ireland and the British Empire* (Manchester, 1996); H. Morgan, 'An Unwelcome Heritage: Ireland's Role in British Empire Building', *History of European Ideas*, 19 (1994), pp. 619–25; R. Robinson, 'Non-European Foundation of European Imperialism: Sketch for a Theory of Collaboration', in *Studies in the Theory of Imperialism*, ed. R. Owen and B. Sutcliffe (London, 1972), pp. 117–42.

[41] J. McEvoy, *Carlow College 1793–1993: The Ordained Students and Teaching Staff of St Patrick's College, Carlow* (Carlow, 1993). See Table 10.3, Carlow College, destinations of alumni, below.

[42] 'Intelligence and Departures'. *Annals of the Propagation of the Faith*, 25 (March, 1865), p. 131. See note 51 below for this journal.

[43] Brain, 'Irish Influence', p. 126.

Irish Rising (1798), and the Act of Union (1800), which saw the transfer of the Irish parliament to Westminster. However, for the colonies the most important foundation was the Missionary College of All Hallows, Drumcondra, discussed more fully in Chapter 10. To a certain extent, every seminary and religious training house in Ireland was a provider of clergy for the colonies. Once bishops were in place, they began calling for new personnel, especially male and female teachers from the Irish religious orders, including the Sisters of Mercy, the Dominican Sisters of Cabra, Christian Brothers, Marist Brothers and many others. The flow of clerical personnel from Ireland to the empire was to continue undiminished for over 100 years.

Association for the Propagation of the Faith (1822)

Until the nineteenth century, Catholic missions were a three-fold operation, with responsibility for setting up new dioceses and appointing missionary bishops under the control of Propaganda in Rome, training and despatch of missionaries conducted by specialist missionary orders and seminaries, and missions backed by royal patronage in the major Catholic imperial powers. Missions and colonial churches had declined with the fading imperial fortunes of Spain and Portugal and the revolutionary implosion of France. The rise of Napoleon was an even more profound setback for the imperial aspirations of the Catholic Church with the Vatican battling for its survival and nearly losing control of its foreign office, the Congregation for the Propagation of the Faith. The great missionary orders, including the Jesuits and the Foreign Missionary Society of Paris, were not restored until 1814. Nevertheless, with the emperor's downfall, the Vatican busied itself with planning and implementing a massive global expansion that, for the first time in centuries, would be financially independent of the old regimes in Europe.[44]

The revival of the capacity of the Catholic Church to fund foreign missionary work was achieved largely through the Association for the Propagation of the Faith (APF), which was founded in 1822 in Lyons, the heart of Catholic France, by a laywoman, Pauline-Marie Jaricot (1799–1862). From Lyons it spread throughout Europe and the new world.[45] In 1840, pope Gregory XVI elevated the Association to that of

---

[44] For Catholic expansion in the nineteenth century, see R. Aubert, *The Church in a Secularized Society* (London, 1978), vol. 5; Latourette, *Expansion of Christianity*, vol. 4; S. Neill, *A History of Christian Missions* (New York, 1964).

[45] J. Fréri, *The Society for the Propagation of the Faith and the Catholic Missions, 1822–1900* (Baltimore, 1902), pp. 5–6.

a universal Catholic organisation, which helped extend its authority out-side France. At the same time, he imposed tight controls on those who damaged the 'general and Catholic' Association for the Propagation of the Faith by undertaking collection tours in Europe for the benefit of their own dioceses.[46] The Association was not under the control of the papacy or the French bishops. Instead, on the model of Protestant voluntary missionary societies, such as the LMS, it was a lay-led char-ity that publicised the missionary cause, collected funds and then dis-tributed them according to need. Generally, it negotiated a tightrope between the competing interests of the national Catholic churches by extolling the international missionary cause which properly recognised no boundaries. With papal 'encouragement', the real authority of the Association came from its endorsement and promotion by local bishops who were pressured by the Vatican to do the same.

Securing episcopal support for the Association in Ireland, where sup-port for papal policy was generally unquestioned, was easy. It proved more challenging to persuade the English vicars apostolic to do their duty and give up control of mission fund-raising to what they perceived as a French rival. The interval between Catholic emancipation (1829) and the re-erection of the English hierarchy by the papacy was a diffi-cult one for the Catholic Church in England. From at least 1837, the English vicars apostolic had been subjected to pressure from the Holy See and Propaganda for greater missionary efforts both in England and in British colonies, to which they were unable to respond effect-ively. In 1838, in an interview with Thomas Walsh, vicar apostolic of Midland District (1826–47) and Nicholas Wiseman, vice rector of the English College (1828–40), Pope Gregory XVI expressed the view that he did not wish to see the restoration of the English hierarchy because of the risk of the government interfering in episcopal appointments, as had previously been attempted in Ireland.[47] However, in every other respect, he was keen to see the English church expand and take up its missionary responsibilities. The same year, when it was proposed to increase the number of districts in the English mission, Propaganda responded by issuing *Statuta Proposita* (Proposed Statutes), drawn up under the supervision of Monsignor (later Cardinal) Charles Acton in Rome, with detailed provisions for regulating English colonial missions

---

[46] See the objections of the President of the Council of the Association for the Propagation of the Faith to the collections undertaken for the Detroit Mission, cited by R. F. Trisco, *The Holy See and the Nascent Church in the Middle Western United States, 1826–1850* (Rome, 1962), p. 352.

[47] B. Ward, *The Sequel to Catholic Emancipation*, 2 vols. (London, 1915), p. 127, citing a diary kept by Dr Griffiths, Westminster Archives.

overseas.[48] These included the establishment of the French Association for the Propagation of the Faith in England and Scotland, which had already occurred in Ireland. Secondly, they called for the foundation of a special missionary college exclusively for the colonies on the model of the foreign missionary seminary in Paris, the only question being whether it should be situated in England or in Ireland. Thirdly, they called for the creation of an Agent General for the Colonies in London, who would be given special responsibility for colonial business, and who would make it easier for communication to pass between the Holy See and British governors.

In response to all three of these proposals from Rome, the English vicars apostolic reacted with horror.[49] As one they replied that Catholics in the three realms of Britain lacked the means to provide for either a seminary for the colonies or to support a London Agent as requested. They were also unenthusiastic about admitting the Association for the Propagation of the Faith into their districts but would set up a committee of laymen to consider it. Rome was unimpressed, and it is noticeable that it was at this point that Propaganda turned resolutely to Dublin, which was already heavily engaged in colonial missions in the Cape and India, rather than to London for leadership in relation to the Catholic missionary effort in British imperial territories. As for the Association for the Propagation of the Faith, in May 1849 Thomas Griffiths, vicar apostolic of London District from 1833 to 1836, directed his brother bishops to step into line and establish regular collections for the French society.[50] In due course, funds began to flow from the Association to support Catholic missions in British colonies and they helped underpin the expansion of the Catholic Church in the British empire.

Under the title *Annals of the Propagation of the Faith* (*Annals*) an English translation of the Association's journal began in 1840.[51] *Annals* was the first modern Catholic missionary journal, and it set the model

---

[48] 'Statuta Proposita', Appendix E, in *ibid.*, pp. 244–51. The attribution to Acton is made by Ward. However, it seems just as likely that it was the result of consultation with Paul Cullen.

[49] Vicars apostolic P. A. Baines, T. Walsh, J. Briggs, T. Griffiths to Apostolic See, 30 November 1838, in Ward, *The Sequel to Catholic Emancipation*, p. 253.

[50] *Ibid.*, p. 153.

[51] *Annals of the Propagation of the Faith, a Periodical Collection of Letters from the Bishops and Missionaries Employed in the Missions of the Old and New World; and of All the Documents Relating to Those Missions, and the Institution for the Propagation of the Faith* (London: Institution for the Propagation of the Faith), vol. 1 (1839) to vol. 86 (1923) (hereinafter *Annals*). This is a translation of *Annales de la Propagation de la Foi (Receuil périodique des lettres des évêques et des missionaires des missions des deux mondes, et de tous les documents relatifs aux missions et à l'oeuvre de la propagation de la foi*), 72 vols. (Lyons and Paris, 1823–1900).

for the hundreds which succeeded it.[52] It provided a semi-official voice not just for the activities of the Association, but also for Propaganda and the missionary expansion of the Catholic Church in both the old and new worlds. The first English issue carried an encyclical letter from Pope Gregory XVI, in both Latin and English, which expressed his joy at the progress of the faith 'in America, the Indies and especially in other infidel countries' (*in America, in Indiis, atque in aliis Infidelium praesertim terris*).[53] Missions to 'America' included those in Canada, the United States and the British West Indies. From Oceania, there were also positive reports from New Zealand. As far as the pope was concerned, this suggests, progress in advancing the Catholic faith in the Protestant empires of the new world was only marginally less delightful than the conversion of Muslims and Buddhists in Asia. To advance either cause, those who took out a subscription and maintained daily prayers for the missions secured both a copy of the journal and also a range of plenary or partial indulgences, depending on the size of the donation.[54]

The reports of Catholic missions promoted in the *Annals* reflect the same range of themes, trials and adventures as those found in Protestant missionary journals. The model for both were the *Lettres édifiantes et curieuses, écrites des missions étrangères* ('Edifying and entertaining letters from the foreign missions'), which published reports by Jesuit missionaries in what had formerly been New France.[55] The *Annals* continued the practice of publishing letters from missionaries, which were mainly translations of those sent to the directors of the Propaganda College in Rome, or seminaries and other religious institutions that trained missionaries in France, Quebec and elsewhere. These were interspersed with appeals for missionary donations, which often compared Catholic efforts unfavourably with those achieved by Protestants in the same territories. Besides letters from bishops and missionaries, there were

---

[52] By 1918, a German Jesuit estimated that there were over 400 Catholic missionary magazines apart from formal reports and reference works. See A. Mattelart, *The Invention of Communication* (Minneapolis, 1996), p. 184.

[53] Pope Gregory XVI, 'Encyclical Letter of Our Holy Father Pope Gregory XVI, to All Patriarchs, Primates, Archbishops and Bishops', *Annals*, 1 (1840), p. 603.

[54] Fréri, *Society for the Propagation of the Faith*, pp. 17–18. In Catholic theology, an indulgence was a formal remission of the strict penances earlier required for admission of sin, which was generally assumed to extend to the punishment which otherwise awaited the sinner in the next life.

[55] For the English translation of this vast (seventy-three volume) corpus, see R. G. Thwaites, ed., *The Jesuit Relations and Allied Documents: Travels and Explorations of the Jesuit Missionaries in New France, 1610–1791*, 73 vols. (Cleveland, 1896–1900). Fréri, *Society for the Propagation of the Faith*, p. 15.

notices tracking the departure of missionaries to mission fields, and each year in May, 'Mary's month', there were financial summaries of funds raised by dioceses around the world. While the various missionary orders later acquired their own journals and fund-raising programmes, sales of the *Annals* and donations to the Association were one of the main fund-raising vehicles for Catholic missions and made an important contribution to the ongoing expansion of the Catholic Church in British territories. In 1840, total receipts by the Association amounted to 2,500,000 francs (£100,000) of which France contributed 54.8 per cent (£54,800).[56] In the British Isles, receipts were always a fraction of those for France and Italy, but Ireland led the way. Over the next twenty years, Irish donations declined in line with her loss of population while receipts from the British colonies rose. However, as Table 4.1 indicates, there was no steady progression and total collections would always suffer by comparison with those for missions in Protestant countries.

Religious rivalry was an important motivating factor for all fund-raising and missionary efforts. This increased with the publication of an English edition of the *Annals*, which was picked up by the Protestant missionary publications who compared Catholic efforts unfavourably with their own. The directors of the Association for the Propagation of the Faith were no less anxious to improve their efforts. They aspired to a day when the *Annals* was purchased by 100 million of the faithful throughout the civilised world who together would generate an income of £550,000 per annum for Catholic missions.[57] Nevertheless, they complained, although there were three times as many Catholics as Protestants, this would still fall short of the £1,500,000 allegedly squandered by Protestant sects on various enterprises:

This sum, however enormous, is not too much, when we recollect the extravagant salaries allowed the lordly missionaries of the Anglican Church in the East and West Indies, the immense sums swallowed up by the Methodist proconsuls, who rule it over the kings of the southern ocean, and the innumerable hawkers of the Bibles, whose prudent zeal extends no further than to introduce along the coasts of China, with smuggled opium, the sacred writings which they profane.[58]

Even hypothetically, these were vast sums. Using the retail price index, £550,000 in 1840 is the equivalent of over £39 million in 2008; as

---

[56] *Missionary Register*, 30 (1842), p. 11.
[57] Association for the Propagation of the Faith, 'Report for the Year 1839', *Annals*, 1 (1839–40), p. 334. These calculations were quoted in the *Missionary Register* (1842), p. 5.
[58] *Annals*, 1 (1839–40), p. 334.

Table 4.1 *British and world receipts (French francs) to the Society for the Propagation of the Faith, 1840, 1854–1860*

		1839	1840	1854	1856	1857	1858	1859
Great Britain and Ireland	England	33,549	32,595	34,656	40,825	37,979	NA	44,885
	Scotland	1,067	955	4,512	3,528	1,121	NA	932
	Ireland	58,553	163,741	120,018	132,446	130,843	NA	183,656
British colonies			5,341	11,230	10,858	16,099	NA	25,573
Totals		93,270	202,632	170,416	187,657	186,042	434,345	255,046

NA = Not Available.
Source: *Annals of the Propagation of the Faith* (May 1840, May 1860).

an equivalent share of the GDP of the UK it represents a staggering £1.45 billion in today's economy.[59] In response to Catholic slurs, the (Protestant) *Missionary Register* derided the 'eloquent but delusive and embittered statements', which were the mainstay of the *Annals*, while the *American Theological Review* sniffed that Catholic countries were hopelessly outclassed by Protestants as donors to the missionary cause.[60] Needless to say – given the competition – pious poverty was highly esteemed at all levels of the Catholic mission effort. The *Annals* commended the efforts of plucky Ireland to send out missionaries to British colonies, which were extolled as the bold resumption of the work of her medieval saints:

[W]ith what lively emotion have we received the contributions sent us from Ireland? Poor and venerable Church! she continues with us that mission which she never ceased to exercise from the time she sent St Gall and St Columban to preach the Gospel to barbarous Europe up to the present day, that she gives bishops and priests to the frozen regions of Newfoundland, and the savage shores of Australia.[61]

This acknowledged that Ireland may have been locked in the grip of the Great Famine (1845–52), but suggested that through mission work

---

[59] For these calculations, see Lawrence H. Officer, 'Five Ways to Compute the Relative Value of a UK Pound Amount, 1830 to Present', MeasuringWorth, 2008, www.measuringworth.com/ukcompare/.

[60] *Missionary Register* (1842), p. 5; *The American Theological Review*, 1 (1859), p. 778: '[A]mong all the Catholic countries only France rivals the missionary zeal of the Protestant Churches, though even she remains far behind England and America.'

[61] *Annals*, 1 (1839–40), p. 335.

her priests were staking out new claims for Catholic Ireland across territory that stretched from pole to pole.

The *Annals* catered to two audiences with this material. First, bishops and clergy might find the thrilling individual narratives useful both for their personal edification and to help preach the mission cause to their congregations. Secondly, lay Catholics, including people of very small means in Ireland, who could purchase copies of the *Annals* for sixpence an issue knowing that the profits benefited the foreign missions (as well as obtaining the papal indulgence). Initially, the English *Annals* was devoted exclusively to accounts of missions to the heathen by European missionary orders, which included the Jesuits in China, Korea and America, the Picpus Fathers in eastern Oceania, and the Marist Fathers in New Caledonia, Tonga and Samoa. From the 1840s, a new perspective was added when the first accounts of the arrival of English and Irish missionaries in British colonies in Australia, the Pacific and British North America began to appear. Until the establishment of the (English) Mill Hill Fathers, it is important to note that the 'missions' conducted by Catholics living in Britain and Ireland were almost entirely directed at Irish settlers in America and the British empire. Except through reading the *Annals* and making donations, Irish Catholics did not participate in the foreign missionary movement until the twentieth century.[62]

These points might be illustrated by looking at Catholic missionary efforts in British settler territories publicised in the *Annals* in two representative years, 1848 and 1874. In 1848, the *Annals* included accounts of missionary efforts among colonists in British North America and New South Wales. In British North America, French missionaries, including the Oblates of Mary Immaculate, dominated missionary work. Pierre Aubert (1814–90), the Oblate Superior, wrote about the history of the mission in the Red River Settlement (now Manitoba), where conditions for French Canadian trappers had originally differed little from those of the native Assiniboines (Sioux of the Rocks). They married Indian wives, lived by fishing and hunting, followed the buffalo to the prairies in winter and in spring returned to the rivers to fish.[63] In 1811, Thomas Douglas, earl of Selkirk, bought up stock in the Hudson's Bay Company that allowed him to set up a colony along the Red River. For Aubert, the consequent settlement of farmers from Scotland, as well as

[62] F. Bateman, 'Irish Missionary Movement', in *Empires of Religion*, ed. H. M. Carey (Basingstoke, 2008), pp. 260–87.
[63] 'Letter of the Reverend P. Aubert, Oblate of Immaculate Mary, to His Brother, Missioner of the Same Congregation, St Boniface of the Red River, June 29, 1846', *Annals*, 9 (1848), p. 56.

French Canadians seeking land, interrupted an idyllic existence as the new settlers brought vices previously unknown to the native people. It was in an attempt to counteract this that Selkirk chose to seek out Catholic missionaries from the bishop of Quebec; the missionaries set out from Montreal and arrived two months later: 'They found a population utterly demoralised, with but a shade of faith, but happily not of infidel notions.'[64] In 1837, they also erected a Catholic church that included accommodation for the vicar apostolic.

By 1848, when Aubert's account of the mission was published in the *Annals*, its character was already changing under the impact of Scottish settlement, and intermarriage by European settlers with the native people. The census of 1846 set the population at 6,000, of whom Aubert reckoned two thirds to be Catholics, the offspring of French Canadian fathers and Indian mothers, and the remaining third to be Presbyterians of Scottish origin.[65] Aubert also reported on the rapid decline in the native hunting and fishing resources that was likely to require both colonists and Indians to cultivate the soil. The climate was healthy, but extremely cold in winter: 'It will be also a subject of astonishment to you to hear that we travel in winter over great distances through the woods, or over the prairies, sleeping in the snow, and only sheltered by a tent – and all this without experiencing the slightest inconvenience.' With such compensation, Aubert professed that any missionary should be content: 'The Priest finds here, in his ministry, much more consolations than in the midst of the most civilised people, and if the study of savage languages is a repulsive avocation, you are well indemnified in many other respects.'[66] Typically, his romantic account of the mission glossed over its fragile state. In fact, the Red River mission was abandoned in 1847, and only resumed by Henri Joseph Faraud OMI, who managed alone until 1852.[67] In 1860, he was made bishop and stayed at his post until his death in 1890.

While the Oblates of Mary Immaculate were freezing in the North-West, the *Annals* reported on the expansion of the Catholic mission in New South Wales. It reported the departure on 17 October 1847 of a group of missionaries in the company of John Bede Polding, the Benedictine archbishop of Sydney, who was returning to his see after one of his many clerical recruiting drives in Europe. On this occasion,

[64] 'Letter of the Reverend P. Aubert', *Annals*, 9 (1848), p. 57.
[65] *Ibid.*, p. 59.   [66] *Ibid.*, p. 61.
[67] E. O. Drouin, 'Henri Faraud (1823–1890)', *Dictionary of Canadian Biography Online* (1881–90), vol. XI, citing Henri Faraud, *Dix-huit ans chez les sauvages: voyages et missions … dans l'extrême nord de l'Amérique britannique d'après les documents de Mgr l'évêque d'Anemour*, ed. F[rancois]-F[ortune] Fernand-Michel (Paris and Brussels, 1866).

his haul included the former Superior of the Passionists in Belgium, as well as English, French and Italian Benedictines from Monte Cassino, Solesmes, Douai, Downside near Bath, and two deacons and two students, probably from the new College of All Hallows near Dublin, as well as two nuns.[68] While this little band was unimpressive by the standards of the much larger parties of the various missionary orders, such as the Picpus Fathers, the Marist Fathers, the Oblates of Mary Immaculate, the Jesuits or the priests graduating from the Seminary of Foreign Missions in Paris, it was indicative of the evolution of the Catholic colonial mission in Australia and its attraction to mission-minded clergy.

Twenty-five years later, in 1874, the same mixture of contents, exciting tales from the field, calls for donations, and satisfying triumphs over Protestants, was still forming the bulk of the contents of the *Annals*. Sectarian tension was high in Newfoundland, which was a crucible for rival Protestant and Catholic settlers with a lamentable record of political tension fuelled by religion dating from the middle of the eighteenth century.[69] Thomas Sears, prefect apostolic of St George's Bay (1871–85) on the western French-speaking coast of the island, described his efforts to build a colonial mission among Catholics of French and Irish descent in a context of strong sectarian rivalry.[70] Irish Franciscan bishops, notably the controversial Michael Antony Fleming, bishop of St John's (fl. 1830–50), had been actively transforming the better settled eastern diocese along Irish ultramontane lines. However, in St George's, there were few resident Catholic clergy, and many fishermen relied on French priests travelling with the fleets to hear mass. According to Sears, there was a pressing need for more clergy: 'How often have I heard these poor people speak movingly of their moral isolation, of the hardships they had to undergo to procure religious assistance!'[71] Accounts of religious bigotry were recounted by Sears with surprising relish. A certain Father Hearn once came, exhausted, to the English village of Sandy Point; he knocked at the door only to be confronted by the angry Protestant owner:

At the sight of a Catholic Missioner, the wretched man, in place of being moved by compassion, burst out into a rage, loaded the pious traveller with curses, shut the door, and set his dogs at him – 'Unfortunate man!', said the Missioner, going off, 'you will be punished for your cruelty, and there will be more dogs

---

[68] 'Departure of Missionaries', *Annals*, 9 (1848), pp. 65–9.
[69] J. P. Greene, *Between Damnation and Starvation: Priests and Merchants in Newfoundland* (Quebec City, 1999).
[70] 'Report of the Reverend Thomas Sears', *Annals*, 9 (1848), pp. 177–8.
[71] *Ibid.*, p. 179.

than Christians at your death.' Sometime after, the wretched man committed suicide and his own dogs drank his blood.[72]

The bloodcurdling anecdote certainly indicates high levels of animosity between rivals for settler loyalties in Newfoundland.

There were also new missions to support in struggling British settlements such as Western Australia. Martin Griver, bishop of Perth (1873–86), wrote a pastoral letter pleading for donations to be made to the Association for the Propagation of the Faith to support 'our poor Mission'.[73] There was already a mission to the Aborigines, conducted by Spanish Benedictines under the inspiration of the remarkable Rosendo Salvado (1814–1900),[74] and Griver's call for alms was to assist poor Catholic settlers. By giving, his parishioners were invited to share in the wider Catholic world beyond their colony: 'The trifling alms you bestow on the Propagation of the Faith will entitle you to share in its many spiritual graces; you will thereby become auxiliary missioners, participating in the labours, the fruits, and the merits of all the Missioners throughout the world.'[75] The international formula for appealing for donations remained largely unchanged into the next century.

By the 1860s, the Oeuvre (as the APF was generally known in France) had become something of a victim of its own success and struggled to retain a monopoly over fund-raising for missions in the Catholic world. The diocese of Quebec, with its long history of mission work among native Americans and colonists in the North-West, as well as foreign missions in China, was one of the first to establish independence. With the permission of pope Gregory XVI, the diocese of Quebec had supported a branch of the Oeuvre since 1836.[76] In 1876, however, the president general of the Oeuvre advised the archbishop of Quebec that the central council in France wished to resume control of donations raised in the province. The archdiocese refused to cooperate, and from 1877 issued its own journal, the *Annales de la propagation de la foi pour la province de Quebec*, which reported on its missions at home and abroad without further reference to Lyons. The strategy for fund-raising in other English-speaking territories also changed. In the 1880s, the *Annals* was issued in an improved, monthly format, with striking illustrations on almost

[72] *Ibid.*, p. 180.
[73] 'Pastoral Letter of the Bishop of Perth', *Annals*, 9 (1874), pp. 240–6.
[74] E. J. Stormon, ed., *The Salvado Memoirs: Historical Memoirs of Australia and Particularly of the Benedictine Mission of New Norcia and of the Habits and Customs of the Australian Natives* (Nedlands, Western Australia, 1977).
[75] 'Pastoral Letter of the Bishop of Perth', *Annals*, 9 (1874), pp. 240–6.
[76] 'Aux associés de la propagation de la foi dans le diocèse de Quebec', *Annales de la Propagation de la Foi pour la province de Quebec*, 1 (1877), pp. 3–7.

every page. Instead of the old staples of missionary letters and pleas from bishops for funds, articles were selected to represent the picturesque and exotic people and settings of Catholic mission work around the world. There was a decisive shift away from Catholic missions in Protestant settler countries, to focus exclusively on foreign missions. In the revised format, Australia, Canada, New Zealand and southern Africa are mentioned, if at all, only in relation to missions to their native inhabitants. Mirroring the same pressures that caused a shift in the mission priorities of the SPG, the Society now demanded that wealthy Catholics in settler regions, including America, Canada and Australia, should improve their record of donations to those in greater need. In the English *Annals*, Catholics were shamed by comparison with the open-handedness of Germans: 'Imagine that with all our English-speaking readers in the United Kingdom, North America, India and Australia, we barely attain to as many sixpences as the German Catholics do pounds.'[77] Without the same ideological stress as that which divided the SPG and the Evangelical missionary societies over 'colonial' and 'foreign' missions, the Association reached the same practical outcome, which was the expansion of foreign missions at the expense of those to Europeans in either the old or new worlds.

Dublin and the colonies

While the Association for the Propagation of the Faith publicised and funded missions, it did not despatch missionaries or decide on the shape of new dioceses. This was the responsibility of Propaganda. In the case of English-speaking territories, many of the day-to-day decisions came to be coordinated through the office of the archbishop of Dublin and the rector of the two Roman seminaries that trained priests for postings in Britain and her colonies, the Irish College and the Propaganda College. This is the empire within an empire (*imperium in imperio*), which Barr connects with the rise of bishop Cullen.[78] Nevertheless, the engagement of Dublin in the extension of the Catholic spiritual did not begin with Cullen.

It is difficult to get a full picture of the contacts between Dublin and the colonies because of the ravages of time, politics and poverty on the archives. So long as the Irish bishops were living more or less on the run, they did not accumulate records that would allow us to trace their contacts with Irish clergy overseas; the Dublin Diocesan Archives hold

---

[77] *Illustrated Catholic Missions*, No. 36 (April 1889), p. 183.
[78] Barr, '"Imperium in Imperio"'.

only 150 items relating to the twelve archbishops from 1600 to 1770.[79] While the papers of Daniel Murray, the first bishop to be restored to the see of Dublin, are much fuller, the habit of record-keeping was not fully established in his reign and some of what remained was harvested by Patrick Frances Moran for his never-completed biography of his uncle, Paul Cullen.[80] Despite these depredations, enough remains to provide a picture of the growing interest of the Irish hierarchy in the needs and opportunities provided by the British colonial expansion. At the highest level, Murray and Cullen, his successor, sought to control the appointment of higher clergy in British settler colonies by using their influence with Propaganda in Rome. While certain dioceses were able to circumvent the wishes of Dublin, their victory was more or less complete in Australia and New Zealand. At the lower levels, the supply of both parochial and regular clergy for parishes and schools respectively were not so easy to control, if only because of the heroic scale of the emigration of priests, and religious sisters and brothers to be teachers and nurses in the colonies.[81] The Irish diaspora was initially served by priests trained on the continent; later, the Irish seminaries would take over. The single largest institution which trained priests for the Irish colonial mission was the College of All Hallows in Drumcondra near Dublin, which will be discussed in Chapter 10. The religious orders were also extremely important to the creation of a Catholic institutional infrastructure in the British colonies. Scores of male and female institutions were involved and while Irish orders were numerically important, they came from throughout Catholic Europe.[82]

Correspondence came to Murray in Dublin and to Cullen at the Irish College in Rome from all over the world pleading for Irish priests to serve emigrant communities. In the 1820s, the businessman John Oughanan wrote from Buenos Aires extolling the country which he describes as 'fertile and vast beyond limits'. He sent a cheque for £270 to cover the cost of sending out two clergymen from Ireland. Murray seems to have arranged for the Irish Jesuit, Patrick Moran, to be sent out as 'Chaplain to the Irish in Buenas Ayres [sic]' for in 1829 Moran was writing back to Murray stating: 'This My Lord is the Country for the Irish farmer to emigrate to ... the most productive soil in the world, the best harvests, and a people who will show themselves more friendly to Irishmen than

[79] D. Sheehy, 'Dublin Diocesan Archives – Pt 1 an Introduction; Pt 2 Murray Papers (7)', *Archivium Hibernicum: Irish Historical Records*, 40 (1987), p. 39.
[80] *Ibid.*, p. 41. These papers were only returned after Moran's death in 1911.
[81] Hogan, *Irish Missionary Movement*.
[82] For statistical surveys of the movement, see Fogarty, *Catholic Education in Australia*; Murphy, *History of Irish Emigrant and Missionary Education*.

to any other nation. They are partial to us.'[83] By the 1840s, such hopes had been dashed by the outbreak of civil war and Fr Anthony Fahey wrote to Murray asking him to use his influence with friends of the British government to prevent anarchy breaking out in Argentina. Fahey complained now about the bad impression of Argentina created by reports in the *Dublin Review*, which would discourage Irish migrants from making the trip to South America. He claimed the Irish mission was thriving but that he needed assistance from the Christian Brothers or the Sisters of Charity to begin a school.[84]

As the new missionary dioceses expanded, it is clear that neither the papacy nor European bishops such as Murray had the capacity to control clergy in distant colonies. In his detailed analysis of the relationship of the Australian church to Propaganda, Dowd is able to demonstrate how ineffectual was the Roman bureaucracy when dealing with recalcitrant prelates at the far reaches of the earth, when they decided to follow a particular line of action.[85] Only as time went on were bishops able to assert their authority and control the most problematic of their clergy. In Europe, a number of unscrupulous priests – how many we will never know – were also able to take advantage of the gullible Catholic public on the pretext of supporting the mission cause. As correspondence in the Dublin Diocesan Archives shows, John Coyle was one of them. From among his own parishioners, 'the poor and generous people of Bermondsey and Wapping', Coyle managed to raise funds which he immediately used to make his way to Rome, ostensibly to obtain a missionary appointment from Propaganda. In Rome, he met up with John Brady, the new bishop of Perth (1845–71), who offered him a position in Western Australia if he could obtain a free passage on a convict ship as a chaplain. When Lord Grey in the Colonial Office refused this request, Coyle resorted to printing the facts of his case complaining about his treatment by the secular and ecclesiastical authorities who thwarted his hopes for emigration. Indomitable, he later ended up in South Australia.

There must have been many clergy labouring under the same optimistic delusion that a colonial chaplaincy or missionary posting would be the solution to all their personal and career problems. Ignoring the poverty, monotony and challenge of frontier conditions in colonial parishes, they longed to escape from lapses of sobriety, chastity,

---

[83] Fr Patrick Moran SJ to Murray, 22 February 1829, Dublin Diocesan Archives, Murray Papers, File 33/13, no. 2.

[84] Fr Anthony Fahey to Murray, 12 September 1846, DDA, Murray Papers, File 33/13, nos. 6, 13.

[85] Dowd, *Rome in Australia*.

mental instability and financial embarrassment which burdened them at home. They rarely succeeded. Coyle may, nevertheless, have had a lucky escape as bishop Brady proved to be not without stratagems of his own. Brady had arrived in the struggling Swan River Colony as a chaplain to the Catholic community in 1843. In 1845, he had persuaded Propaganda to erect a diocese and send him back as bishop of Perth with no fewer than twenty-seven missionaries, based on his own testimony that Western Australia was home to millions of Aborigines hungry for salvation.[86] Although Coyle escaped his net, Brady gathered others from Spain, Italy, France, England and Ireland for this purpose. There was a viable mission for almost none of them and only the hardy Spanish Benedictines, Dom Rosendo Salvado and Dom Joseph Serra, survived. There was almost constant friction between the continental and Irish clergy of the diocese, with a stream of correspondence making its way to Dublin and Rome and to the Benedictine motherhouse in Norcia, Italy.[87]

In Dublin, Murray did what he could, but he lacked resources to meet the demands for personnel and crisis management that arrived with every post. While from Sydney Polding reported with great pleasure that the Sisters of Mercy had arrived and succeeded 'beyond his most sanguine expectation',[88] not every appointment was satisfactory. In New South Wales, there were Father Therry's financial problems – which had found their way into the papers.[89] Polding protested that a priest ordained for Sydney had left it against his own written instructions, and after having collected a generous subscription towards his travel expenses, 'to the great scandal of Religion'.[90] Murray also had more ambitious plans for Australia. An undated note which Colin Barr identifies as being in his hand is simply headed 'Divisions of Dioceses in NS Wales and Victoria'.[91] Victoria was not declared a colony until 1851 so the document cannot have been written any earlier than this.

---

[86] It is generally accepted that the total number of Aborigines in the entire continent of Australia at the time of first European settlement was no more than half a million or so.

[87] Correspondence with Brady and Serra in DDA, Cullen Papers. E. J. Stormon, ed., *The Salvado Memoirs: Historical Memoirs of Australia and Particularly of the Benedictine Mission of New Norcia by Dom Rosendo Salvado* (Perth, 1977). For the full story, see Dowd, *Rome in Australia*. For Brady's eventual demise, see Francis Murphy, bishop of Adelaide, to Tobias Kirby, 17 April 1852, Pontifical Irish College, Rome, KIR 1002.

[88] Polding to Murray, 5 March 1839, DDA, Murray Papers, File 33/12, no. 3.

[89] Polding to bishop of Hobarton, 15 February 1847 and 10 April 1847, DDA, Murray Papers, File 33/12, nos. 8, 9.

[90] Polding to Murray, 16 July 1852, DDA, Murray Papers, File 33/12, no. 16.

[91] [Murray], 'Divisions of Dioceses in New South Wales and Victoria', n.d., DDA, Murray Papers, File 33/12, no. 19.

In the last year of his life, therefore, Murray was thinking like the epis-copal general he had become, dividing his empire, like Napoleon, into new provinces. Possibly, the note was intended for discussion with Propaganda since the division of dioceses was strictly beyond his pow-ers, though not his imagination. He noted that New South Wales, with a Catholic population of 135,000, had four bishops, whereas Victoria had a Catholic population of about 140,000, 'in even better circumstances', and yet had only one bishop. Victoria, he mused, had three towns lar-ger than any in New South Wales, Ballarat, Geelong and Sandhurst: 'A parallel of Longitude from the Lachlan River to the point at which the Tarcutta Creek enters the Murray River, that creek and the mountains from which it comes might separate Goulburn from Albury.'[92] This was where the new dioceses were created.

After Murray, the architect of the colonial ascendancy of the Irish Catholic Church was his successor, the uncrowned pope of Greater Britain, Paul Cullen (1803–78), rector first of the Irish College in Rome from 1832 to 1850, then briefly pro-rector of Urban College, the mis-sionary seminary of Propaganda in Rome.[93] Cullen was made bishop of Armagh in 1849, transferred to the see of Dublin in 1852, and elevated to the cardinalate in 1866. He was Ireland's first cardinal, convened the country's national synod, secured the creation of a Catholic univer-sity for Ireland, and has been credited with a commanding influence, through his control of the Irish bishops and the many Irish appoint-ments to colonial sees in Australia, New Zealand, British Guyana and South America. His influence was rather less in British North America, New Zealand and southern Africa if only because, as a proportion of the total population, Irish emigrants were nowhere as significant as they were in Australia. In the United States and British North America, as in Scotland, there was more success in resisting the Cullenisation of the episcopate that occurred in the southern settler colonies.[94] Cullen was a methodical administrator whose mastery of detail and unswerv-ing devotion to Rome was expressed through his control of episco-pal appointments in British colonies. However, he was secretive and seems to have had no personal life, keeping a chilly distance from all his biographers, including his own nephew. Looking for some key to his

---

[92] *Ibid*. For minute analysis of the division of Victoria by Propaganda, see Dowd, *Rome in Australia*, pp. 375–92.

[93] Bowen, *Paul Cardinal Cullen*; MacSuibhne, ed., *Paul Cullen*; P. F. Moran, 'Paul Cullen', in *The Catholic Encyclopedia* (New York, 1908). See also Larkin, 'Cullen, Paul (1803–1878)' (though Larkin makes no mention of Cullen's role in the Irish Catholic Church overseas).

[94] Barr, '"Imperium in Imperio"'.

character, Bowen states: 'In Paul Cullen's total oblation to the militant missions of the popes that he served lies the secret to the mind and accomplishments of this most reserved and complex of men.'[95] Whether the popes alone – and Cullen knew five of them[96] – should be given responsibility for the almost obsessive attention that Cullen gave to the Catholic colonisation of the south is questionable. Cullen always had a bigger picture in mind, a vision of Ireland's destiny for the empire and the world. His close relatives were also beneficiaries of his work, with his own nephew and personal secretary, Patrick Francis Moran, securing the see of Sydney and a red hat of his own after Cullen's death. Nevertheless, we are unlikely to get any closer to Cullen than through an interrogation of the daily bloom of his endless correspondence.[97]

The gradual increase in importance of Australia can be measured in the Cullen correspondence, which begins in Rome and continues in an unbroken stream until his death. In Dublin, Cullen maintained what he had started at the Irish College in Rome, where he served as the agent for the Irish and Irish-Australian hierarchy in its dealings with Propaganda, writing to former students and missionary clergy and securing appointments which he adapted to his opinion of their capacity and loyalty to Rome. As archbishop of Dublin, his incoming letters were divided into three classes: those to Irish bishops, those to bishops outside Ireland, and those to the Holy See. In 1849, while he was still bishop of Armagh, Cullen received letters from the bishops of Halifax, Trinidad, the apostolic nuncio in Paris (five), the apostolic nuncio in Madrid, Philadelphia, cardinal Wiseman in London, York (two), Natchez (United States) and just one from Australia, from Patrick Boniface Geoghegan, the Irish Franciscan vicar general of the bishop of Melbourne, later bishop of Adelaide (1859–64). By 1866, the year he became a cardinal, Cullen was receiving dozens of letters concerning ecclesiastical appointments from bishops overseas while corresponding with Alessandro Barnabò, the prefect of Propaganda, at least two or three times a week. Dowd has argued that Cullen's intimacy with Barnabò and his lack of rapport with archbishop Polding of Sydney were the main reasons Polding's ambitions for the creation of a Benedictine province in Australia were so effectively subverted.[98]

Cullen achieved his ascendancy over colonial appointments largely because he had the confidence of Propaganda and was able to convince

[95] Bowen, *Paul Cardinal Cullen*, p. viii.
[96] Pius VII, Leo XII, Pius VIII, Gregory XVI and Pius IX.
[97] Colin Barr and a team are currently preparing a complete edition of the Cullen Correspondence.
[98] Dowd, *Rome in Australia*, vol. 1, p. 6.

them that it was appropriate to regard the dioceses of British settler colonies as effective dependencies of Dublin.

Cullen was a practical administrator. He sought to secure Irish control of Catholics in the British empire as a natural reflection of Ireland's position as the pre-eminent Catholic country in the British Isles. His influence in Australia is readily apparent by noting the expansion of Irish appointments in the *Catholic Registry*. First published in 1851, this periodical provided a list of Catholic clergy in English. It covered Rome, Ireland, England, Scotland, America and the Colonies – the last appearing for the first time in 1853. It also printed Catholic news and statistics, such as a list of Catholic converts, observations from the census demonstrating 'the decimation of unfortunate Ireland', and other historical annals. In 1853, the *Catholic Registry* described the 'Oceanican Register' as the fifth great division of the globe with the archdiocese of Sydney at its heart. The nationalities of its bishops and leading clerics were carefully delineated. John Bede Polding, 'native of England', was archbishop of Sydney. Other English natives held the sees of Hobart (Willson) and Maitland (Vaughan). A Spanish Benedictine, Rosendo Salvado, held Victoria (North Australia), and, with the forced retirement of John Brady in Western Australia, there were just two Irish bishops, Francis Murphy in Adelaide and the Augustinian, James Alipius Goold in Melbourne.[99] Nevertheless, in less than ten years, the much expanded Australian Register was dominated almost entirely by Irish appointments, many of them graduates of the Irish College in Rome where Cullen had served as rector. This gradual advance in the Irish episcopate was only part of the story, however, because, once a Cullenite bishop was in place, he then had the power to secure additional appointments to colonial seminaries, parishes, schools, hospitals and convents from among his own contacts. In this way, a single Irish bishop was likely to create a chain of additional appointments from Ireland that tended to accentuate and entrench the Irish character of the see.[100] The effect of this was to last well into the next century.

Given the depths of his power, just what was it that Cullen and his followers sought to achieve? He was not motivated by Irish nationalism in seeking to create an Irish ascendancy for the United Kingdom and Ireland and for the Catholic diaspora in the British empire. He was horrified at the prospect of Irish political radicalism and sought to suppress all moves

---

[99] *Catholic Directory, Almanac and Registry of Ireland, England and Scotland. Complete Ordo in English* (1851–), p. 468.
[100] Hogan, *Irish Missionary Movement*; Murphy, *History of Irish Emigrant and Missionary Education*.

to popular revolt that came within his aegis. He was repelled by excessive displays of Irish nationalism. In 1865, for example, Cullen wrote with concern about the scandalous behaviour of some alumni of All Hallows College, particularly on the matter of an overly close identification with their native country and its political problems.[101] In 1872, Cullen considered shutting it down.[102] Nevertheless, there would seem little doubt from his pattern of appointments and range of interests that Cullen wished to make Ireland and its Catholic Church central to the imperial expansion of Catholicism. Because of resistance to their policies in Ireland, Cullen was anxious to secure a power base for his own ultramontane Irish Catholic party among the English-speaking bishops overseas. However, even in the British empire, Cullen's season of influence was limited to the period of very rapid expansion of the colonial episcopate. Once the colonial churches secured their own metropolitan, Cullen's capacity to continue influencing the internal affairs of the national churches declined. When Patrick Francis Moran, Cullen's nephew, became archbishop of Sydney, the flow of correspondence from Australia to Dublin suddenly dried up. The one exception to this rule was the continuing significance, at the highest level of ecclesiastical appointment, of the Irish College in Rome where Tobias Kirby succeeded Cullen as rector in 1870, effectively extending his influence into the next generation.

The ultimate prize for Cullen's loyalty to Rome and control of the Irish episcopate in the British colonies was influence in the College of Cardinals (the body of leading clerics in the Catholic Church who elect the pope), and in church councils. In 1864, pope Pius IX announced the calling of the Vatican Council, the first ecumenical council of the Church to be held in 300 years. It opened in Rome in December 1869 and adjourned prematurely, but permanently, on 20 October 1870. The actual achievements of the Council, which ran from December 1869 to October 1870, were limited by the threatened invasion of the Papal States by the troops of the Risorgimento, the movement for Italian unification. However, in a climate of political crisis, they included the definition of 'papal infallibility' on questions of faith and morals, the culmination of an increasingly papal-centred and supernatural form of Catholicism which was especially challenging to both traditional Protestants and Gallican Catholics.[103] According to the journal of the

---

[101] Cullen Papers, DDA, Holy See, 1858–60, Letter no. 107.
[102] Moran to Murray, 21 July 1872, Maitland Diocesan Archives, cited by A. McLay, *James Quinn: First Catholic Bishop of Brisbane*, revised edn (Toowoomba, Queensland, 1989), p. 71.
[103] H. McLeod, *Religion and the People of Western Europe, 1789–1970* (1981), p. 47. The declaration on papal infallibility was preceded by the doctrine of the Immaculate Conception of the Blessed Virgin Mary (1854) and the Syllabus of Errors (1864).

English Benedictine William Ullathorne,[104] which is our major source of information about the inner workings of the Council, Cullen himself was responsible for the wording of the definition of papal infallibility. It was this formulation which managed to overcome the objections of many of the bishops at the Council who suspected it would give unprecedented power to the papacy and increase sectarian tensions throughout Europe. Cullen's major ally at the Council was Henry Manning, archbishop of Westminster (1865–92) and leader of the Catholic Church in England. Both Cullen and Manning, who came from outside the main group of European bishops in majority Catholic states, gave their unswerving support to the advance of papal power at the expense of national and imperial churches. In Cullen's case, his influence was strengthened psychologically by the Irish colonial bishops whose loyalty was also securely fastened on Rome, as meditated through Cullen, that Roman of the Romanists.[105] In this way, Cullen, and the colonial British bishops he appointed, helped reshape and reform the Catholic Church as a worldwide movement, breaking the dominance wielded by the Catholic states of the ancien regime.

Conclusion

In this chapter, we have seen that Irish ambitions for empire were created out of opportunities presented to them because of the emigration of Irish Catholics to British colonies and service in the armed forces. In contrast to the SPG, these prospects for the expansion of the Catholic Church were not articulated using the rhetoric of British imperialism, but that of the resurgent papal power under Pius IX in Rome, ably supported by Paul Cullen in Dublin. At their most ambitious, Irish bishops could be utterly ruthless in seeking to entrench their control over new mission territories. However, their power was neither absolute nor was it uncontested. Initially, it was English Benedictines who pioneered the expansion of the Catholic Church in the southern British colonies, and Scottish bishops in the Maritimes. At all times, European religious orders were significant providers of missionary clergy, especially in colonies such as Canada, Mauritius and Madagascar where France rather than Ireland provided leadership for the Church. Catholic power was also contested within the empire by the many rival Protestant churches of the British Isles which were striving, in the same period,

---

[104] Cited by Norman Tanner, 'Paul Cullen and the Declaration of the Papal Infallibility', unpublished conference paper, Paul Cullen and His World Conference, Pontificio Collegio Irlandese, Rome, 23–25 October 2009.
[105] MacSuibhne, ed., *Paul Cullen*.

Table 4.2 *Chronology of Catholic dioceses in Britain and settler colonies up to 1908*

Ireland
400–500 Early Irish monasteries and abbot bishops
1111 Armagh [Metr.], Cashel [Metr.]
1152 Dublin [Metr.], Tuam [Metr.] and 16 other dioceses

England and Wales
1622 England [AV], 1688 London, Northern, Midland & Western Districts [AV]
1840 Lancaster, Yorkshire, Wales and Central Districts [AV]
1850 Westminster [Metr.], and 12 other dioceses

Scotland
1653 Scotland [AP], 1694 [AV]
1727 Lowland, Highland, Eastern, Western & Northern Districts [AV]
1860 Arctic Pole [AP], 1869 Caithness, Orcades and Shetland [AP]
1878 Glasgow [AD], and 5 other dioceses

Australia
1818 Cape of Good Hope and Adjacent Territories [AV], 1819 Mauritius [AV] –
   Mauritius, South Africa, New Holland, etc.
1834 New Holland and Van Diemen's Land [AV], 1842 Sydney [D] and New Holland
   [AV], 1842 Sydney [Metr.] and Mission to the Aborigines [AP], 1847 Sydney [Metr.]
1842 Adelaide [D] and South Australia [AV], 1887 [Metr.]
1842 Hobartown [D] and Van Diemen's Land [AV], 1842 Hobart [D], 1888 Hobart [AD]
1845 Perth [D]
1845 King George Sound [AV]
1845 Essington [AV], 1847 Victoria [D]
1847 Maitland [D], 1995 Maitland-Newcastle
1847 Melbourne, 1874 [Metr.]
1847 Mission to the Aborigines [AP] abolished
1859 Brisbane, 1887 [Metr.]
1860 New Norcia [AP], 1867 New Norcia [Abb 'nullius']
1862 Armidale [D]
1862 Goulburn [D]
1865 Bathurst [D]
1874 Ballarat [D]
1874 Sandhurst [D]
1877 Queensland [AV], 1887 Cooktown
1882 Rockhampton
1887 Grafton, 1900 Lismore
1887 Kimberley [AV]
1887 Port Augusta [D]
1887 Queensland [AV for the Aborigines]
1887 Sale [D]
1887 Wilcannia [D]
1898 Geraldtown [D]
1906 Northern Territory [AP]

Canada
1622 England [AV], 1622 London District [AV]

Table 4.2 (*cont.*)

1658 New France [AV], 1674 Québec, 1819 [AD], 1844 [Metr.]
1784 United States of America [AP], 1789 Baltimore [D]
1784 Newfoundland [AP], 1856 Harbour Grace [D], 1858 Harbour Grace–Grand
 Falls
1795 Saint John's Newfoundland [AV], 1847 [D], 1904 [Metr.]
1817 Nova Scotia [AV], Halifax [D], 1852 [Metr.]
1819 Upper Canada [AV], 1826 Kingston [D], 1889 [Metr.]
1829 Charlottetown [D]
1836 Montréal [D], 1886 [Metr.]
1841 Toronto [D], 1870 [Metr.]
1842 Saint John in America [D]
1843 Oregon [AV], Victoria in Vancouver Island [AV], 1846 [D], 1903 [AD], 1908 [D]
1844 Arichat [D], Antigonish
1844 Nord-Ouest [AV], 1847 [D], Saint Boniface [D]
1852 Saint-Hyacinthe [D]
1852 Trois-Rivières [D]
1856 Hamilton [D]
1856 London [D]
1860 Chatham [D]
1860 Ottawa [D], 1886 [Metr.]
1862 Athabaska Mackenzie [AV], 1901 Athabaska [AV]
1863 British Columbia [AV], New Westminster [D], Vancouver [Metr.]
1867 Rimouski/ Saint-Germain de Rimouski [D]
1871 Saint Albert [D]
1871 Western Newfoundland [AP]
1882 Northern Canada [AV], 1882 Peterborough [D]
1874 Sherbrooke [D]
1878 Chicoutimi [D]
1882 Golfe Saint-Laurent [AP], 1905 [AV]
1882 Pontiac [AV], Pembroke [D]
1885 Nicolet [D]
1890 Alexandria in Ontario [D]
1891 Saskatchewan [AV], Prince-Albert et Saskatoon [D]
1892 Valleyfield
1892 Western Newfoundland [AV], 1904 Saint George's [D]
1901 Mackenzie [AV]
1904 Joliette [D]
1904 Sault Sainte Marie [D]
1908 Temiskamingue [AV]
1908 Yukon and Prince Rupert [AP]

New Zealand
1830 South Seas Islands [AP]
1836 Western Oceania [AV], 1848 Auckland [D]
1836 New Zealand and Oceania [D]
1848 Wellington [D], 1887 [Metr.]
1869 Dunedin
1887 Christchurch

Table 4.2 (*cont.*)

South Africa
1818 Cape of Good Hope and Adjacent Territories [AV]
1819 Mauritius [AV] – Mauritius, Madagascar, South Africa etc
1837 Cape of Good Hope [AV], 1847 Cape of Good Hope – Eastern District [AV]
1847 Cape of Good Hope – Western District [AV], 1939 Cape Town [AV], 1951 [Metr.]
1850 Natal [AV]
1874 Cape of Good Hope – Central District [AP]
1885 Orange River [AP]
1886 Kimberley in Orange [AP]
1886 Transvaal [AP
1898 Orange River [AV]
1904 Transvaal [AV]

Other British
1553 Goa [D], 1558 [AD]
1659 Great Mogul [AV], 1820 Bombay [AV], 1886 [Metr.]
1818 Trinidad [AV]
1820 Tibet-Hindustan [AV]
1832 Madras [AV], 1886 [Metr.]
1834 Bengal [AV], 1850 Western Bengal [AV], Calcutta [Metr.]
1834 Ceylon [AV]
1837 Jamaica [AV]
1841 Madagascar [AP], 1848 [AV], 1898 Central Madagascar [AV]
1850 Eastern Bengal [AV]
1880 Punjab [AV]
1886 20 dioceses renamed or established in India
1896 Southern Madagascar [AV]
1896 Northern Madagascar [AV]

Key: AD = Archdiocese, AP = Apostolic Prefecture, AV = Apostolic Vicariate, D = Diocese, Metr. = Metropolitan Archdiocese.
Source: Chronology of Erections of Catholic Dioceses, www.katolsk.no/utenriks/kronologi/. Another useful website is The Hierarchy of the Catholic Church, www.catholic-hierarchy.org.

to establish themselves. Overall, however, there was a symbiotic relationship between the British imperial need for personnel and the capacity of Ireland to export her people and cultural institutions, notably the Catholic Church, to the colonies. Catholic poverty and disability in the British Isles in the eighteenth century was the dramatic backdrop to the imperial expansion of Catholics in the nineteenth century. Catholic expansion was the hallmark of the nineteenth. However, all the churches, and their sects and church parties, found opportunities on the imperial stage. The next chapter considers the part played by Anglican Evangelicals in the Church of England beyond Great Britain.

5   Evangelical Anglicans

In 1883, the veteran missionary to the isolated settlement of Cardiff in the remote Canadian northwest wrote to the home committee of the Colonial and Continental Church Society (CCCS) pleading to be allowed to resign:

> The exposure of last winter has put me in such a state that I am not the man I was for this back-block mission. My dear wife and son are dead, my other two sons are obliged to leave me, so that my helpers are gone. I have never asked for a holiday, for my work here has been one great holiday to me; but it is now too hard for me. There is more suffering in the back bush of Canada than I ever saw in England. To see so much work before one, and not be able to get at it, is very trying.[1]

This letter was published in a short account of the work of the Society published in 1896, and it reflects the qualities that characterised the public face of the Society: seriousness about religion, a relish for the frontier and its human and spiritual demands, and a call to fellowship. Colonial missions, such testimonies demonstrate, required the same heroism and sacrifice as missions to heathen lands. Men and women like this were needed in the colonies, so why not come and join us?

   This chapter provides an account of the imperial work and ambitions of the CCCS, a colonial missionary society created to advance the cause of Christianity by ensuring as many Anglican Evangelical teachers and clergy as possible were able to find their way out to serve in colonial dioceses.[2] The colonial missionary ethos of the CCCS,

---

[1] Colonial and Continental Church Society, *Missions in Many Lands: The Work of the Colonial and Continental Church Society* (London, 1896).

[2] The CCCS has had many changes of name. According to the Intercontinental Church Society website, www.ics-uk.org/about/familytree.shtml, the Society was created in 1851 by the amalgamation of (1) the Newfoundland Society for the Education of the Poor (founded 1823), later called the Newfoundland and British North America Society for Educating the Poor (1829) and the Church of England Society for the Poor of Newfoundland and the Colonies (1846) and (2) the Western Australia Missionary Society (founded 1835), later called the Australian Church Missionary Society (1836)

like their poor missionary haunted by the deaths in his family in the backblocks of Canada, was frugal, pious and earnest. Perhaps, above all, it was resilient so that by the end of the twentieth century it was the only Society that survived with something like the old colonial mission spirit still intact. Overall, the CCCS was more Protestant and less overtly imperialistic than the SPG, but it was also more dogmatic, sectarian and proselytising. The CCCS was the vanguard of evangelicalism in the British world. Over the course of the nineteenth century, it adapted to colonial conditions, slowly discarding its old sectarian rhetoric and evolving to become one of the strongest supporters of the ideal of Greater Britain and its successor, the bush ethos, in the colonies.

Evangelicalism

Problems of definition have tended to dog historians of evangelicalism in both the British and the American traditions, but the term has three major meanings. At one level, the word 'evangelical' refers to the preaching of the Christian gospel. In a number of European languages, including German, it simply means 'Protestant'. Secondly, for example in the collection edited by Noll, Bebbington and Rawlyk, 'evangelicalism' refers to the network of Protestant movements which arose during the eighteenth century in the English-speaking world and has come to form one of the largest and most influential forces in world Christianity today.[3] Thirdly, 'Evangelicals' (distinguishable in this book by the use of a capital E) refers to a group of self-consciously serious Christians in the Church of England who originally came together in the eighteenth century and who sought to rejuvenate the religious foundations of their church. Bebbington suggests that, theologically, all evangelicals can be distinguished by commitment to the bible, a focus on the cross as a symbol of Christ's atonement, a conviction that conversion is possible and necessary for salvation, and active

and Colonial Church Society (1838). The amalgamated society was first called the Colonial Church and School Society (1851), then the Colonial and Continental Church Society (1861), then the Commonwealth and Continental Church Society (1958) and, since 1978, the Intercontinental Church Society (or 'Inter'). For simplicity, prior to 1851, the two societies will be referred to as the Newfoundland School Society (NSS) and Colonial Church Society (CCS) respectively, and, after 1851, as the Colonial and Continental Church Society (CCCS).

[3] M. A. Noll, D. A. Bebbington and G. A. Rawlyk, eds., *Evangelicalism: Comparative Studies of Popular Christianity in North America, the British Isles, and Beyond, 1700–1990* (New York, 1994). Alternatively, it is possible to speak of three denominational strands of evangelicalism: Anglican, Methodist and Nonconformist.

enthusiasm for spreading the gospel.[4] The most positive feature of the movement was its promotion of social and humanitarian projects such as elementary education and the reform or abolition of commercial and colonial institutions that were exploitative or immoral, notably the Atlantic slave trade. Less attractively, Evangelicals could be paternalistic, prudish and judgmental, and the conscience of its predominately middle-class adherents was much more alert to working-class vices such as gambling, sexual immorality, alcohol consumption and Sabbath-breaking than to political and social inequality. As their numbers grew in the course of the nineteenth century, Evangelicals and their Nonconformists allies came to exude a cheerful Protestantism in which anti-Catholicism and the defence of religious liberty were accepted as twin faces of the one cause.[5] Like other Victorians, they were also empire-minded.

Beginning in the 1820s, Evangelicals in the United Church of England and Ireland began to acquire something of the character of a church within a church. Under the leadership of Charles Simeon (1759–1836), they had already begun to buy up livings, which gave them the right to appoint to parishes, in prominent English towns and cities. Evangelical ordinands were supported financially by the Elland Society, which enabled many poor men to enter the clerical profession either at home or, as opportunities arose, for service as missionaries or colonial chaplains overseas.[6] In time, there were Evangelical bishops appointed to sees at home whose patronage in turn ensured that more Evangelical bishops were sent to the colonies.[7] There were Evangelicals who gave leadership in both Houses of Parliament and others in the bureaucracy, most

[4] D. W. Bebbington, *Evangelicalism in Modern Britain: A History from the 1730's to the 1980's* (London, 1989), pp. 2–17. Bebbington summarises these characteristics by the words: 'biblicism', 'crucicentrism', 'conversionism' and 'activism'.

[5] S. Thorne, '"The Conversion of Englishmen and the Conversion of the World Inseparable": Missionary Imperialism and the Language of Class in Early Industrial Britain', in *Tensions of Empire: Colonial Cultures in a Bourgeois World*, ed. F. Cooper and A. L. Stoler (Berkeley, CA, 1997); J. Wolffe, *The Expansion of Evangelicalism: The Age of Wilberforce, More, Chalmers and Finney* (Downers Grove, IL, 2007); J. Wolffe, ed., *Evangelical Faith and Public Zeal: Evangelicals and Society in Britain 1780–1980* (London, 1995).

[6] A. Yarwood, 'The Making of a Colonial Chaplain: Samuel Marsden and the Elland Society, 1765–93', *Historical Studies*, 16 (1975), pp. 362–80. See the edition of the records of the Society, ed. John Walsh and Stephen Taylor, *The Papers of the Elland Society, 1769–1828* (Boydell Press, 2009).

[7] Colonial Evangelical bishops were particularly important in Australia. Their number include Frederic Barker (1808–82) in Sydney, Charles Perry (1807–91) in Melbourne, Thomas Mesac (1816–92) in Goulburn; William Saumarez Smith (1836–1909) in Sydney, and, in the twentieth century, Howard West Kilvinton Mowll (1890–1958) in Sydney.

notably the Colonial Office. This cohesive and comprehensive imperial network created a secure funding base for Evangelical causes which were advanced by the innumerable Evangelical societies, many controlled by laymen and some women.[8]

The largest of these should be ranked among the most influential organisations in Victorian society: they had branches all over the country and auxiliaries in the colonies, their membership numbered in the thousands, they were patronised by royalty and they drew large audiences to regular meetings in their central meeting house at Exeter Hall in the Strand. Bradley, who monitors the meetings of Evangelical societies from the advertisements which were placed in the *Record*, the Evangelical magazine, notes that in the course of one week in May 1829 there were fifty meetings. These ranged from breakfast rallies for local causes to those supplying the resources of the vast international agencies.[9] An even longer list of societies was compiled by Ford K. Brown, suggesting that for every conceivable religious, moral, educational and philanthropic concern in Victorian England, there was a corresponding society to support it. While not all of these were dominated by Anglican Evangelicals, eight societies were foundational to the Evangelical network.[10] These were the Church Missionary Society (1799), the Religious Tract Society (1799), the British and Foreign Bible Society (1804), the London Society for Promoting Christianity Amongst the Jews (1808), the Prayer Book and Homily Society (1812), the British Newfoundland and North America Society for Educating the Poor (1823), the General Society for Promoting District Visiting (1828) and the Church Pastoral Aid Society (1836). Of these great societies, the Newfoundland Society, soon to be extended to include all settler colonies in the empire, became the vehicle for galvanising support for planting Evangelical churches, schools and ministers in the colonies.

Evangelicals had a striking impact on the colonial world because of the success of foreign and colonial missionary organisations, many of which they had helped to found, and the coherence of their vision of a world united by Christ and led by a devoted Protestant ministry at home and overseas. While this vision was and is fundamentally religious in nature, its proselytising characteristics made it the natural partner of other, expansive political and social movements. These included British imperialism.

---

[8] K. Heasman, *Evangelicals in the Church of England, 1734–1984* (London, 1962). For Evangelical societies, see also Bradley, *Call to Seriousness*, pp. 135–44.

[9] Bradley, *Call to Seriousness*, p. 137.

[10] F. K. Brown, *Fathers of the Victorians* (Cambridge, 1961), pp. 329–40.

Evangelicals and colonial missions

Missionary organisations would eventually become central to the self-image and success of Evangelical Anglicanism but until the early years of the nineteenth century they lacked an organisational base for extending their reach internationally in either the foreign or colonial mission fields. Missions only became a serious object of the Evangelical movement through the discussions of the Eclectic Society, whose key members included the former slave-ship captain and hymn-writer John Newton (1725–1807) and the politician William Wilberforce (1759–1833). Initially, like the SPG, the Eclectic Society made no particular distinction between missions to colonists and missions to the heathen. In fact, the first mission considered by the Society was that to the convict colony of Botany Bay (1786); a few years later missions to the East Indies (1789) and Africa (1791) were also discussed. Finally, on 18 February 1799, John Venn outlined the principles of a society that would conduct missions without the direct leadership of bishops. It would concentrate on Africa and the Far East, which were fields where no other English missionary society was active. This led to the foundation of the Church Missionary Society for Africa and the Far East (CMS), which was one of the major organisational achievements of the evangelical revival.[11] Before its attention was entirely directed away from the settler colonies, the CMS was responsible for the mission to the Maori in New Zealand, initiated by Samuel Marsden, as well as a short-lived mission to Aborigines in the interior of New South Wales.[12] From 1822, the CMS was also engaged in British North America and reports of these colonial missions were included in the Society's *Missionary Register*. After this time, the CMS remained focused on foreign missions to non-Christians and did not send missionaries to work among British settlers or the aborigines in British settlements.

Evangelicals also came out to the colonies to work as colonial chaplains drawing their stipend from the government purse. Indeed, the son of one of the first colonial chaplains in Australia, William Cowper, boasted that all four of the first chaplains sent to New South Wales were Evangelicals.[13] In 1787, John Newton despatched the Reverend

[11] E. Elbourne, 'The Foundation of the Church Missionary Society: The Anglican Missionary Impulse', in *The Church of England c. 1689–c. 1833*, ed. J. Walsh (Cambridge, 1993), pp. 247–64.
[12] Cole, *A History of the Church Missionary Society of Australia*. The CMS (Australia) resumed missions to the Australian Aborigines in the twentieth century.
[13] Namely, Richard Johnson, Samuel Marsden, Robert Cartwright and William Cooper. See W. M. Cowper, *The Autobiography and Reminiscences of William Macquarie Cowper, Dean of Sydney* (Sydney, 1902), p. 1.

Richard Johnson on his voyage with the First Fleet with a valedictory hymn which compared Johnson's spirituality favourably with the more material objectives of explorers such as James Cook.

> Go in the Saviour's name to lands unknown,
> Tell to the Southern Hemisphere His words of grace,
> An energy Divine thy words will own,
> And teach their untaught hearts to seek His face.
>
> Many in quest of gold or empty fame
> Would compass earth, or venture near the Poles;
> But how much nobler the reward and fame
> To spread His grace, and win immortal souls![14]

Despite such stirring sentiments, the funding of colonial mission work was initially felt by most Evangelicals to be the responsibility of the SPG and, as we will see in the next chapter, the occasional Wesleyan or Nonconformist chaplain.

Voluntary missionary societies formed by Anglican laymen had been common in the eighteenth century, but after Parliament granted a charter to the SPG this tended to suppress further efforts by individuals. Thereafter, most churches, not just the Church of England, committed mission work to the SPG and the SPCK. The new evangelical missionary societies founded later in the nineteenth century were controversial and different. Keen to do their bit to Christianise the empire in their own way, a number of pious laymen, including naval and military officers, commercial fishermen and colonial officials, helped to establish missionary societies which were in effect rivals to the efforts of the SPG.

The Newfoundland School Society (1823) and the Western Australia Missionary Society (1835, known by 1838 as the Colonial Church Society) had similar objects, summarised effectively by Underwood: 'to keep the white man Christian in whatever country he may settle.'[15] These two societies eventually merged to form the CCCS (now known as the Intercontinental Church Society), as we will see below. A third Evangelical colonial missionary society, the South American Missionary Society (SAMS),[16] was founded in 1843 by Allen Gardiner (1794–1851), a former captain in the Royal Navy, whose peripatetic evangelising over

---

[14] *Ibid.*, p. 3.

[15] B. Underwood, *Faith at the Frontiers: Anglican Evangelicals and Their Countrymen Overseas (150 Years of the Commonwealth and Continental Church Society)* (London, 1974), p. 20.

[16] The Society published an annual report (1863–1973), and later the *South American Missionary Society Magazine*, 1967–1963. For an institutional history, see P. Thompson, *An Unquenchable Flame: The Story of Captain Allen Gardiner, Founder of the South American Missionary Society* (London, 1983).

four continents eventually led him to attempt to convert the indigenous people of Tierra del Fuego. This mission had a more than usually disastrous inauguration when the first seven missionaries, including Gardiner himself, starved to death waiting for a ship to come and resupply them. The publication of Gardiner's journal provided a martyr for the cause, which helped fund-raising, and the Society was relaunched from a base in the Falkland Islands. Unfortunately, in November 1859, a second missionary team was wiped out by the Yaghan Indians with the loss of another eight lives. After this, the Society refocused on missions to colonists. Its work came to include evangelisation of Catholics in neighbouring Argentina, support for English, Welsh and Spanish-speaking settlers, and some work among native people in South America.[17]

Eventually, the CCCS would become the best known of all the organisations which served the needs of settler Christians in the British empire. Underwood has written an institutional history, originally published in 1974 and twice updated,[18] and the Society's records, which date back to 1823, are kept in excellent and accessible order in the London Guildhall Library. Like many societies, it also published an annual report with a copy of its annual sermon and other periodicals including the *Greater Britain Messenger*. It is unfortunate that some key records, including most of the early correspondence and all records relating to candidates applying to the Society appear to have been lost. Nevertheless, the surviving records of the CCCS and its predecessors provide one of the best sources of information about the spirit that generated and sustained the colonial missionary ideal within the broader Evangelical movement. Its story begins with two separate societies, both founded by laymen, and located at opposite ends of the earth.

Newfoundland School Society (1823–50)

Newfoundland was the oldest colony in the empire and it was the seat for the work of the colonial school society which grew into the CCCS. The island was named and added to European maps by John and Sebastian Cabot in 1497. It is the closest North American territory to Europe – tantalisingly close on current maps – and surrounded by what were then some of the richest fishing grounds on earth. It was

---

[17] By 1888, the Society had mission stations in Argentina, Chile, Panama, Paraguay, Peru, Uruguay and Brazil.

[18] Underwood, *Faith at the Frontiers*; B. Underwood, *Faith without Frontiers* (Cirencester, 1994); B. Underwood, *Faith and New Frontiers: A Story of Planting and Nurturing Churches, 1823–2003* (Warwick, 2004); J. D. Mullins, *Our Beginnings: Being a Short Sketch of the History of the Colonial and Continental Church Society* (London, 1923).

the latter which inspired a series of unsuccessful attempts to colonise the island in the sixteenth century, despite deeply inhospitable conditions, ultimately driving the indigenous Skraeling population to extinction. In the early seventeenth century, George Calvert (c. 1580–1632), later Lord Baltimore, obtained a land grant which he intended for a Catholic settlement. French, Irish and Scottish colonists arrived to fish the great herring banks over the next century. In 1713, following the Peace of Utrecht, France was forced to cede Newfoundland to Great Britain though retaining some fishing rights and two offshore islands. The population of tough fisher people was discouraged from settling permanently and the island had no resident clergy until a chaplain was supplied to Newfoundland by the SPG. The Reverend John Jackson survived there until 1705 though he was shipwrecked and nearly starved to death on his recall by the bishop of London.[19] His departure ensured that, for the 17,000 or so who swelled the island's population in summer, there were few religious services other than those provided by Catholic priests who visited the fleets at sea.[20]

The founder of the Newfoundland School Society (NSS) was a successful cod merchant and trader called, appropriately enough, Samuel Codner (1776–1858). The first meeting was in a London coffee house in 1823, during which Codner is said to observed: 'Britons had a special duty to perform arising out of their extensive colonies.' There is no record of this speech, as Underwood notes, in the accounts of the founding meeting.[21] However, such views mirrored the ambitions of leading Evangelical laymen and no doubt reflected those expressed by the Prime Minister, Lord Liverpool (1812–27), in a speech given to the British and Foreign Bible Society in 1822, which had been attended by Codner.[22] The distinguishing feature of the NSS was its commitment to the provision of evangelical teachers for a single colony rather than a more widespread charitable, educational or missionary purpose.[23] Its object was 'to teach the people the knowledge of the Holy Scriptures and the way of salvation in them'.[24] The first anniversary sermon, delivered

[19] Pascoe, *Two Hundred Years of the SPG*, p. 89.
[20] For Catholics on Newfoundland, see Greene, *Between Damnation and Starvation*; and Chapter 4 above.
[21] Underwood, *Faith at the Frontiers*. The main records of the Society are its *Annual Reports of the Committee of the Society for Educating the Poor of Newfoundland*, 1823–36, Centre for Newfoundland Studies, Memorial University, Microfilm 619, A-322, A323.
[22] W. Gordon Handcock, 'Samuel Codner, 1776–1858', *Dictionary of Canadian Biography Online*.
[23] Note the lower case for evangelical. The society was originally non-denominational.
[24] P. McCann, 'The Newfoundland School Society 1823–55: Missionary Enterprise or Cultural Imperialism?', in *'Benefits Bestowed?' Education and British Imperialism*, ed. J. A. Mangan (Manchester, 1988).

by the Reverend Edward Cooper, spoke of the Newfoundlanders as a people who 'speak our language and partake our civil and religious liberties', and who were crying out for a decent education for their children.[25] For such a small-scale project, the list of those who attached themselves to the cause is remarkable and included many of the leading figures in the Evangelical movement:[26] Lord Liverpool was Patron, and the first President was Lord Bathurst, Secretary of State for the Colonies (1808–28). Vice presidents included Henry Ryder, bishop of Lichfield, Lord Bexley, Chancellor of the Exchequer (1812–23) and William Wilberforce. According to Codner, it was Wilberforce who took the initiative, secured the appropriate level of patronage, and made the NSS a major Evangelical project. Codner was appointed Assistant Secretary and conducted its correspondence. His committee included Josiah Pratt and Edward Bickersteth (Joint Secretaries of the CMS), Henry Budd, Samuel Crowther and Daniel Wilson, vicar of Islington. There was an active women's auxiliary and the Laws and Regulations of the Society specified that 'the Schools shall be managed by Masters and Mistresses of the United Church of England and Ireland',[27] giving particular prominence to the lay teachers who would be the Society's mainstay in the colony. By the 1830s, the NSS had secured the patronage of Queen Victoria (reigned 1837–1901), the pinnacle of respectability for all religious organisations.

What was it that enabled a fish merchant – albeit one backed by Wilberforce – to persuade the Queen, the Prime Minister and many of London's most distinguished and active Evangelical clergy to take such a close interest in a colonial school society? There was certainly a need for basic education on Newfoundland, but the strength of support given to this project may be linked to Newfoundland's status as a colony with a near majority Catholic population on the Protestant frontier of Britain.[28] It was therefore the colonial equivalent of the Irish province of Ulster, or the Highlands and Western Islands of Scotland – regions of strongly contested religious rivalry, where it was useful to

---

[25] *Proceedings of the Society for Educating the Poor of Newfoundland: Third Year, 1825–26: Containing the Anniversary Sermon by Reverend Edward Cooper* (London, 1826), p. 19.

[26] Underwood, *Faith at the Frontiers*, p. 24.

[27] *Proceedings of the Society for Educating the Poor of Newfoundland: Third Year, 1825–26: Containing the Anniversary Sermon by Reverend Edward Cooper* (London, 1826), p. 5.

[28] According to the Returns of 1845, the number of Catholics and Protestants was more or less equal, i.e. 37,376 Roman Catholics and 37,376 Protestants. See *Population, Religion and Education* (1878), www.oldandsold.com/articles11/newfoundland-16.shtml.

assert Britain's reformed Protestant credentials. It was also a region where the SPG had failed to assert its earlier monopoly on the provision of a 'national' school system to people who were British subjects. Here was an opportunity for Evangelicals to show their effectiveness in an imperial, missionary, cause.

For its supporters, the NSS was an overwhelming success in meeting an educational need. As early as 1839, Martin gave warm endorsement to the work of the Newfoundland and British North American School Society in his great colonial digest.[29] More recently, historians have been more sceptical about both the benefits supplied and the motivation of those active in the Society. McCann queries whether the purpose of the NSS was ever more than nominally missionary in character and stresses what he interprets as the overt imperialist ideology of its traditions.[30] He argues that NSS schools tended to teach bible reading and little else and were narrowly focused on the promotion of an exclusive ideology at the expense of much of the population. In the 1820s, the supporters of the SPG were equally unhappy about the arrival of teachers supplied by a rival Anglican society. NSS teachers were generally fervent young Protestants and many proved to be a trial to the colonial governors and bishops, most of whom were Tory high churchmen with little sympathy for the Evangelical party in the Church of England. In 1823, the first year of its operation, Charles Hamilton, one of a succession of senior naval officers appointed as governors of Newfoundland, protested against the financial support given to the NSS by the Colonial Office. His own preference was to encourage the SPG and its diocesan schools.

Anglican bishops in North America were eventually forced to cooperate with whoever could provide staff and funding for their work. Others, notably John Inglis, third bishop of Nova Scotia (1825–50), were unwilling to compromise with what they perceived as an infringement on their episcopal jurisdiction.[31] Inglis insisted on control of all organisations within his diocese and refused to allow his clergy to attach themselves to Evangelical societies. Even-handedly, he also opposed extending the political rights of Roman Catholics.[32] He was strongly opposed by members of his own clergy, including the Evangelical

[29] Martin, *Statistics*, pp. 263–4.
[30] McCann, 'Newfoundland School Society'.
[31] This account draws on J. Fingard, 'Inglis, John', *Dictionary of Canadian Biography Online*, vol. VII, *1836–1850* (2000); J. Fingard, 'Uniacke, Robert Fitzgerald', *Dictionary of Canadian Biography Online*, vol. IX, *1861–1870* (2000).
[32] In 1822, Inglis opposed the election of Laurence Kavanagh, the first Anglophone Catholic to take a seat in a British colonial assembly, to the Nova Scotia House of Assembly.

Robert Fitzgerald Uniacke in Halifax. In New Brunswick, however, the NSS found unanticipated support from John Medley, bishop of Fredericton (1845–92), as well as the lieutenant governors. Medley was a Tractarian, indeed the first Tractarian bishop in the Church of England. However his outlook was not exclusive and he was prepared to work with the NSS and its successor, the Colonial Church Society. With this backing, the NSS was able to defy Inglis and other defenders of the SPG and its 'national' (i.e. orthodox Anglican) schools. Nevertheless, it was not until Edward Feild (1801–76) succeeded as the second bishop of Newfoundland (1844–76) that a rapprochement was reached. Although a definite high churchman himself, Feild ordained NSS schoolmasters as deacons and priests who subsequently played a major role as clergy in the fledging church. Inglis, in contrast, refused to ordain any missionaries other than those supported by the SPG or trained by his own King's College. Feild eventually supported proposals to widen the Society's franchise so that it might become 'the principal Colonial School Society in connection with the Established Church'.[33] This was effectively a capitulation to the Evangelical party, and recognition that the doughty Protestant agents of the NSS and the CCS had beaten the SPG at its own game – that of providing schools for British colonists.

Colonial Church Society (1835–50)

On the other side of the empire, in the remote reaches of the coast of Western Australia, another devout Evangelical layman was responsible for the establishment of the Western Australian Missionary Society, later the Colonial Church Society (CCS), which was initiated in 1825 by Captain Frederick Chidley Irwin (1788–1860).[34] Irwin, the son of a Church of Ireland clergyman, was a veteran of the Peninsular War who saw colonial service in Canada, Ceylon and the Swan River Colony in Western Australia, where he had command of the 63rd Regiment of Foot, and occasionally served as acting governor.[35] Irwin's original

---

[33] Underwood, *Faith at the Frontiers*, p. 27. Under Feild, the number of clergy who had earlier been supplied by the SPG but could now be sustained independently increased significantly.

[34] The First Report (no date but presumably 1837) calls the society the Australian Church Missionary Society; the Second Report (1838) renames it the Colonial Church Society and the Third Report (1839) the Colonial Church Society for Sending Out Clergymen, Catechists, and Schoolmasters to the Colonies of Great Britain, and to British Residents in Other Parts of the World.

[35] David Mossenson, 'Irwin, Frederick Chidley (1788–1860)', *Australian Dictionary of Biography*, vol. 2, pp. 5–6.

plan was to invite the Church Missionary Society to undertake a mission to the Aborigines in Western Australia along the same lines as their mission in New South Wales, with the cost to be met by private subscription in Glasgow and Dublin.[36] However, the CMS was unable to agree to Irwin's request for a mission, giving as their reason the wish to commence a mission in China. Faced with this disappointment, Irwin went ahead regardless.

While in London, where he had been recalled to give an account of the colony to the Colonial Office, Irwin enlisted the support of Baptist Noel, Minister of St John's Chapel, Bedford Row, the venue for the Eclectics who had given birth to the CMS. They convened a meeting in the vestry of St John's, which formed the Swan River Mission, 'having for its object the sending out of missionaries of the Church of England, and also schoolmasters, to the Aborigines and the colonists'; the Western Australian Missionary Society was founded shortly after, on 30 September 1835. Irwin then set up a Dublin committee, which included his father and some of the latter's clerical friends, such as the chaplains from the Molyneux Blind Asylum and the South Penitentiary, and a number of laymen. Together, they secured a missionary for Western Australia, the unfortunate Dr Louis Giustiniani, who arrived in the colony in 1836, but whose controversial mixed mission to Aborigines and colonists was terminated in 1838.

It is not difficult to suspect that neither the CMS nor the SPG were enthusiastic about what may have been perceived to be Irwin's lowbrow attempt to circumvent their jurisdiction, but we do not know the details. However, in a hasty postscript to his published account of the Swan River settlement, Irwin announced that 'unforeseen difficulties' had led to a change of plan for the mission.[37] The Dublin committee was downgraded to a fund-raising auxiliary and the 'parent Society' moved to London. Within a year, and without further consultation, the now London-based Society abandoned the idea of a mission to the Australian Aborigines (leaving Giustiniani to his fate), and expanded the objectives of the society to focus on missions to settlers across the empire. This time it carefully avoided any conflict of interest with the CMS.[38]

---

[36] F. C. Irwin, *The State and Position of Western Australia, Commonly Called the Swan-River Settlement* (London, 1835).

[37] *Ibid.*

[38] 'First Report of the Committee of the Western Australian Colonial Church Association', *Perth Gazette and Western Australian Journal*, 26 October 1839, pp. 171–2.

Irwin headed back to Western Australia in 1837, and the London committee secured an illustrious line-up of new patrons for the new Society. Lord Teignmouth, the former Governor General of India, agreed to be President, and Lord Glenelg, then Colonial Secretary, accepted a vice presidency. Both had Clapham connections.[39] Teignmouth had also been the first president of the Bible Society.[40] In Western Australia, Irwin was a member of the corresponding committee, but distance prevented him from taking a more active role in policy. The real work of the Society was conducted by a phalanx of London Evangelicals in Exeter Hall who had their fingers on the pulse of the imperial aspirations of the movement.

In its second year in London, the annual meeting of the CCS, presided over by Teignmouth and Captain Vernon Harcourt, announced ambitious plans to extend the sphere of its work 'to embrace all the Colonies of Great Britain'. Admiral Hawker, John Hutt, the recently appointed Governor of Western Australia, and Captain Sir Edward Parry (1790–1855), Arctic explorer and, from 1829 to 1834, Commissioner of the Australian Agricultural Company, passed motions. The Society had an office in the newly opened epicentre of Evangelical business in Exeter Hall. All seemed set for great things. The honour roll of vice presidents is especially impressive and included a number of serving or former colonial governors, naval officers or military men, including Sir John Franklin (1786–1847), Governor of Van Diemen's Land and, subsequently, hapless Arctic explorer, Sir Ralph Darling (1772–1858), former Governor of New South Wales, Sir Peregrine Maitland (1777–1854), formerly Lieutenant Governor of Upper Canada and former Governor of the Cape of Good Hope, as well as Parry. The President was Charles Middleton (First Baron Barham), the Lord of the Admiralty, a friend of Wilberforce and a notable figure in the anti-slavery campaign.[41] It is difficult to judge the extent of the interest of the great and the good in the work of the Society. Parry appears to have been the only one of the vice presidents to have attended an annual meeting. However, even he had other Evangelical interests and his time was not unlimited. Nevertheless, in his letters, he is said to have frequently mentioned the

---

[39] For the full committee, see *First Report of the Australian Church Missionary Society*, established 23 September 1835, Australian Joint Copying Project, p. 7; Underwood, *Faith at the Frontiers*, p. 29. For the Clapham links between Teignmouth and Wilberforce, see J. C. Colquhoun, *William Wilberforce: His Friends and His Times* (London, 1866), pp. 317–22.

[40] Colquhoun, *William Wilberforce*, p. 322.

[41] M. E. Moody, 'Religion in the Life of Charles Middleton, First Baron Barham', in *The Dissenting Tradition: Essays for Leland H. Carlson*, ed. C. R. Cole and M. E. Moody (Athens, OH, 1975).

CMS, along with the Society for Promoting Christianity Among the Jews, and the Naval and Military Bible Societies.[42]

As for ideology, the CCS was robustly patriotic and pro-colonial from its earliest days, which may be a reflection of the admirals and captains and military officers who were among its most important patrons. The tone was set in the opening sentence of the first CCS report: 'It is the glory of Great Britain, that by sending out her colonies to many lands, she extends through the earth the knowledge of her language, her manners, her laws, and her religion.'[43] But bringing Christianity to British settlers was not just a patriotic duty that appealed to pious elements in the navy, military and colonial service. It also made it possible for the CCS to secure investment in its particular work in the face of stiff competition from other missionary societies. The case for colonists is argued throughout the society's publications, which originally consisted of an annual report and 'Occasional Papers'. These stress the need for a particular Evangelical mission to colonists, pointing out the moral as well as the physical perils of the frontier, the Providential obligation placed on Englishmen to support colonists, and the danger of encroachment by Romanists and Tractarian crypto-Romanists in British territories overseas. In contrast to foreign missionary societies, such as the LMS and CMS, for whom settlers were perceived as an impediment to missionary progress, the CCS praised settlers, calling them the 'glory of Great Britain', and giving them credit for extending British power and commerce while they struggled against adversity. Although they had left Britain's shores, they were still connected by the closest ties; they retained 'English opinions, habits, and affections', and they deserved to be supported and remembered by their countrymen.[44] If earlier colonists had been guilty of moral lapses, particularly in relation to aboriginal people, then it was the task of the CCS to provide missionaries who would ensure that Christianity guided their future development.

The CCS was one of the first organisations (other than the SPG) to promote the cause of colonists, a group who had attracted few advocates in the era before Edward Gibbon Wakefield. Strategies to convince the British public included the provision of statistics, charts and tables which emphasised the scale of the work that needed to be done. In Upper Canada, for example, the 1838 report estimated that over the

[42] E. Parry, *Memoirs of Rear-Admiral Sir W. Edward Parry* (New York, 1857), p. 179.

[43] First Report [of the CCS] (1836), Australian Joint Copying Project, p. 3. This paragraph is a précis of the first editorial. The same sentiments and arguments are repeated in later reports and occasional papers.

[44] Second Report [of the CCS] (1838), Australian Joint Copying Project, p. 13.

next ten years 150,000 emigrants were likely to pour into the country where they would find what one writer described as a scene of spiritual destitution: 'no minister, no observance of the Sabbath, no Bible, no means of grace, no guide to glory.'[45] The need in the other colonies was equally striking. In addition, the CCS pointed out, unlike other mission causes, an investment in colonial missions would bring a speedy return. In time, like the northern states of the American Union, colonies such as Australia would not only become self-supporting but would be enabled to send out missionaries to the east.[46]

With plans to extend the work empire-wide, funding was always a critical problem and the Society followed a strategy of approaching the government and tapping the Evangelical network for support. At a meeting on 8 January 1839, the Secretary reported on his approach to Sir George Grey (1799–1882), who was then Under Secretary of State for War and the Colonies, seeking matching funding from the Foreign Office for churches and the stipends of ministers sent out by the CCS.[47] Over the next three months, letters were sent around the globe to the bishops of Nova Scotia, Calcutta, Bombay and Madras, seeking information about their dioceses. Not all were pleased to be approached. Bishop John Inglis of Nova Scotia, who had been similarly forthright concerning the Newfoundland School Society, replied that he saw no need for the formation of a new missionary society, and objected to a number of its rules.[48] The Clerical Secretary wore himself out on the home circuit, visiting Liverpool, Dublin, Glasgow, Edinburgh, Manchester and Birmingham. While he had a cordial reception in Dublin, where the collection raised £86, the situation in Liverpool, Glasgow, Manchester and Birmingham was not encouraging. On 19 February, a public meeting was held to set up a Ladies' Association, which was helpful, and on 5 March letters were sent directly to the lieutenant governors of the colonies of New Brunswick, Nova Scotia and Newfoundland with a tempting offer. The Society promised to send out a clergyman, with a salary of £150, to any settlement that was able to contribute an additional £50 a year, so long as the candidate had the sanction of the local bishop.[49] By this stage, the first offers were already

---

[45] *Ibid.*, p. 14.

[46] First Report [of the CCS] (1837), Australian Joint Copying Project, p. 4.

[47] CCS Committee Minutes, 8 January 1839, in London Guildhall Library, MS 15,673, vol. 1, p. 1.

[48] CCS Committee Minutes, 5 February 1839, London Guildhall Library, MS 15,673, vol. 1, p. 6.

[49] CCS Committee Minutes, 5 March 1839, London Guildhall Library, MS 15,673, vol. 1, p. 12

flowing in from clergy proposing themselves for mission postings in the colonies.

In another coup, the fledgling Society was delighted when a leader of the Evangelical party, Edward Bickersteth (1786–1850), agreed to preach the Society's annual sermon.[50] Bickersteth's sermon, printed with the report for 1839, was something of a spiritual call to arms.[51] In his thumbnail sketches of Exeter Hall speakers by 'one of the Protestant party',[52] there is this portrait of Bickersteth:

> Every Missionary Association throughout the country knows and loves Mr Bickersteth; and to the London audience the anniversary is incomplete, unless Mr Bickersteth be there. I have often thought that his is the *beau idéal* of the Society. The images he excites in the mind combine foreign service and home exertion, a perfect knowledge of all its doings abroad, and all its plans and wishes in committee. His dark, sallow countenance, hollow cheek and eye, emaciated figure, and sepulchral voice, give us as perfect a picture of the exhausted Missionary in person, as his benevolent smile, active carriage, and affectionate address present an excellent portraiture of the Missionary in spirit.[53]

We can easily picture him then, rising to preach on the text: 'But if any provide not for his own, and especially for those of his own house, he hath denied the faith, and is worse than an Infidel.' Bickersteth declaimed on the national duty to proclaim the Protestant Reformed religion established by law throughout the colonies and garrison them against the twin evils of heathenism and popery.[54] According to Bickersteth's correspondents, throughout the empire ships were arriving loaded with Roman Catholic bishops, priests and seminarians from Maynooth, and there was a desperate need for Evangelical clergy to defend the Reformation in Britain's expanding colonies. It was a theme he warmed to on other occasions,[55] and it lent a motivating zeal to the work of the Society as it did to some other Evangelical institution building and expansion at home.

Why was the Colonial Church Society expanding at just this time? As Bickersteth makes clear, Catholic emancipation, the Irish Tithe Act

---

[50] CCS Committee Minutes, 2 April 1839, London Guildhall Library, MS 15,673, vol. 1, p. 12.
[51] E. Bickersteth, *The Duty of Communicating the Gospel: A Sermon Preached before the Colonial Church Society on Monday, May 13, 1839 at St John's Chapel, Bedford Row* (London, 1839).
[52] *Random Recollections of Exeter Hall, in 1834–1837. By One of the Protestant Party*, (London, 1838).
[53] *Ibid.*
[54] Bickersteth, *Duty of Communicating the Gospel*.
[55] E. Bickersteth, *Popery in the Colonies: A Lecture Delivered before the Islington Protestant Institute* (London, 1847).

(1838) and the steady appointment of Catholic chaplains and bishops to the colonies, all aroused fears among conservative Protestants of a Catholic colonial threat.[56] This would be sufficient reason for organising an effective Evangelical response. However, another factor may have been the background to the launch of the Colonial Bishoprics' Fund which eventually occurred in 1841. The purpose of the Fund was to allow the expansion of the Church of England to cater for 'members of our National Church residing in the British colonies, and in distant parts of the world', as it was expressed in the original statement following the meeting of archbishops and bishops in Lambeth on Whit Tuesday (1 June) 1841.[57] By suggesting that there was a 'National Church' in the colonies, this excited tremendous interest in what was seen as the main body of the church taking up its pastoral responsibilities in the empire. However, Evangelicals also anticipated conflict between the colonial bishops and the Evangelical societies, including the CMS, who had up until then played a leading role in pioneering missions in colonial territories.[58]

The opposition of the bishop of Nova Scotia to the creation of the CCS was, therefore, no minor blip. Inglis wrote at length expressing his opposition to the new Society on the ground that it represented a direct rival to both the SPG and the newly created Colonial Bishoprics' Fund. He distributed his objections as widely as possible by means of a printed circular. Chairman T. Lewin and the Secretary E. A. Cotton replied with equal deliberation and elaborate formulations of respect.[59] They argued that the SPG was inadequate to the task of serving the colonial church and that the new society would not impact on its finances. The Colonial Bishoprics' Fund was in its infancy and the colonies needed all the support they could muster. Indeed, the statistics of the bishop's own diocese, despite his exertions over the previous fifteen years, demonstrated the need for a new missionary philosophy for the colonies:

The committee are happy to acknowledge the energy and activity which your lordship has displayed; but after all your lordship's exertions, aided by the funds

---

[56] J. Wolffe, 'Anti-Catholicism and the British Empire, 1815–1914', in *Empires of Religion*, ed. H. M. Carey (Basingstoke, 2008), pp. 44–9.

[57] The full text was extensively published, but see *Register of Ecclesiastical Intelligence* (July 1841), p. 8.

[58] H. Cnattingius, *Bishops and Societies: A Study of Anglican Colonial and Missionary Expansion, 1698–1850* (London, 1952).

[59] For the documents of the controversy, including the 'Circular Letter of the Lord Bishop of Nova Scotia', Halifax, 15 April 1841, and the 'Memorial of the Committee of the Colonial Church Society to the Right Reverend the Lord Bishop of Nova Scotia', with Inglis' reply, see *British Magazine and Monthly Register*, 20 (1841), pp. 200–11.

of the Propagation Society, what is the real state of the diocese? From a recent return, it would appear that there are only thirty working clergymen for a population of 250,000 souls, dispersed over an area of 15,000 square miles.[60]

Inglis' reply, which stressed the need to retain the unity of the Church, like the seamless garment of the crucified Redeemer, had dignity, but he could not really answer the weight of the CCS's arguments. The Society was plainly necessary. With its flawless Evangelical credentials, it had access to the serious-minded young men who would answer the call to go out and make careers in the colonies and make the 'National Church in the British Colonies' a working reality.

Tussles with the high church party, providentialism – the argument that God had ordained that the Society would succeed – and British patriotism, all helped to provide a rhetorical rationale for the work of the Society. However, the actual work of sending out missionaries and schoolteachers, and helping to build schools and churches, advanced rather more slowly than its committee would have liked. While deprecating the efforts of the SPG and the bishop of Nova Scotia, in truth the CCS struggled to do much better. Out in the colonies, throughout the 1830s and 1840s, the CCS gradually extended its work from its original base in Western Australia to the other Australian colonies and beyond them to the West Indies, British North America, and southern Africa. Publicity was provided by publishing a stream of letters from missionaries once they arrived in the field. These make for poignant reading as tentative beginnings are tempered by the challenge of the frontier conditions. In the remote Swan River Colony of Western Australia, where the number of colonists had just managed to exceed 2,000 in 1836, Giustiniani reported that the roof was rising on the first church in the colony and that he hoped to be able to open it on Christmas Day for divine service.[61] This was somewhat ingenuous since services were regularly performed in the Perth Court House by the colonial chaplain, and there was also a Wesleyan chapel elsewhere. Indeed, the colonial authorities seem to have imagined Giustiniani, who had erected a chapel and schoolhouse at Guildford, was planning a mission to the Aborigines rather than the settlers.[62] As in Newfoundland, it was by no means sure

---

[60] *British Magazine and Monthly Register*, 20 (1841), p. 329.
[61] According to the *First Report* [of the CCS] (1837), p. 3, Louis (or Luigi) Giustiniani was a convert and former Roman Catholic priest who had been the Roman Catholic chaplain to the Austrian embassy in Rome. I have not been able to confirm these details, nor that he was a 'Jesuit turned Protestant', a Lutheran, or 'probably of noble Venetian descent' as claimed in J. Jupp, *The Australian People: An Encyclopedia of the Nation, Its People and Their Origins* (Cambridge, 2001), p. 492.
[62] Martin, *Statistics*, p. 461.

that the local bishops would support a full-scale rival to the SPG. For all its impressive rhetoric, the expansion of the CCS was painfully slow.

Evangelicals and the colonies

A second phase in the development of the Evangelical mission to the colonies arose in the 1840s in the context of a widening rift between Evangelicals and other members of the Church of England. On the one hand, this was a time of extraordinary achievement for the Church, which was spiritually rejuvenated by the Oxford movement and the reforming zeal of Evangelicals in almost every sphere of social life. Overseas, the Colonial Bishoprics' Fund led to a rapid increase in the number of clergy and the Church gained prestige from the arrival of numerous ambitious and articulate leaders to assert local authority. On the other, there was continued anxiety about the loyalty and ortho-doxy of those within the Tractarian movement and the danger they were imagined to pose to the colonies. Conflicts about ritual and wor-ship threatened to derail the great revival of the Anglican Church and the special accommodation between its Catholic and Protestant tradi-tions which had been the hallmark of its success as a national institu-tion. While some breathed a sigh of relief when prominent Tractarians, including John Keble and Edward Pusey, departed for Rome in 1845–6, the real trouble was just beginning.

Disputes erupted in two fields. In the first place, there were direct concerns about increasing financial support by the state to Roman Catholics at what was perceived to be the expense of religious volun-tarists and Britain's own established Protestant churches. There were strenuous objections to the expansion of the grant to the national Irish seminary at Maynooth by the Peel government in 1845. Nevertheless, the uproar on this occasion was modest by comparison with the extraor-dinary reaction by British Protestants to the restoration of the Catholic hierarchy in England and Wales by Pius IX in 1850. Although there were already three Catholic hierarchies in the empire – in Ireland, Quebec and Australia – the ensuing moral panic over the alleged 'papal aggression' was one of the major events of the Victorian age.[63]

Secondly, there were bitter struggles within the Church of England about ecclesiastical appointments and the traditional authority of bishops to rule on the theological orthodoxy of clergy in their diocese. The most rancorous of these battles for theological precedence was the Gorham

---

[63] W. Ralls, 'The Papal Aggression of 1850: A Study in Victorian Anti-Catholicism', *Church History*, 43 (1974), p. 244.

case. George Cornelius Gorham (1787–1857) was an Evangelical minister whose views on baptism were declared to be 'unsound' by Henry Phillpotts, bishop of Exeter, who decided for this reason to refuse to institute him to a living in his diocese, thereby destroying his livelihood.[64] On appeal to the Judicial Committee of the Privy Council in March 1850, Phillpotts was ordered to reinstate Gorham, a judgment which Evangelicals saw as a triumph for the English constitution and the rule of law, and Anglo-Catholics as an appalling intrusion by the state in the proper jurisdiction of a bishop. The Gorham case cannot be extricated from the colonial church because, in a rash move, the bishops of Australia and New Zealand gathered for the 1850 Australasian bishops' conference had lent the weight of their assembly to a statement on baptism, the very issue that had been the focus of the Gorham dispute.[65] As one might expect, this divided along church party lines, with one statement signed by the bishops of Sydney, Adelaide, New Zealand, Newcastle and Tasmania, and another by the sole Evangelical, Charles Perry, bishop of Melbourne, who was a protégé of the CMS Secretary, Henry Venn.[66] From this time, colonial Evangelicals feared that high church bishops would use their majority influence in the colonies to proscribe Evangelicals, dominate colonial synods and block their access to appeal to the Privy Council.

As a major vehicle for the colonial work of the Evangelical party in the Church of England, the Newfoundland School Society and the Colonial Church Society had played an important part in these sectarian disputes. It was now time to unify their forces.

Colonial Church and School Society (1851)

Because of a gap in the surviving records of the Society's meetings,[67] it is no longer clear why or how the Newfoundland School Society and the Colonial Church Society were brought together. However, it was sufficiently urgent to interrupt the holiday season. Just two days before Christmas 1850, while Parliament rang with speeches declaiming the imminent collapse of Britain as a Protestant nation, representatives

---

[64] O. Chadwick, *The Victorian Church, Part One, 1829–1859* (London, 1966), pp. 250–2.

[65] For the minutes of the meeting, see R. A. Giles, *The Constitutional History of the Australian Church* (London, 1929), pp. 237–47.

[66] *Ibid.*, pp. 243–5; A. de Q. Robin, 'Perry, Charles (1807–1891)', *Australian Dictionary of Biography*, vol. 5 (1974), pp. 432–6.

[67] The Colonial Church Society Minute Book, London Guildhall Library, MS 15,673, covers the period from 1839 to 1842 and then ends. The CCCS Minute Book begins on 27 December 1850.

of the two societies met in London. The meeting decided that, from
1 January 1851, the NSS and the CCS should form a united society
to be called the 'Colonial Church and School Society for sending
Clergymen, Catechists, and Schoolmasters, to the Colonies of Great
Britain, and the British Residents in other parts of the world'.[68]
    In the 1850s and 1860s, the amalgamated society maintained the
hearty Evangelicalism of its two predecessors, but it had more ambitious plans. These included a takeover (from the bishop of London)
of responsibility for chaplaincies in continental Europe.[69] It also filled
the void left by battles between Tractarians and Evangelicals in the
diocese of Natal following the Colenso case (1863) – another dispute
involving the authority of a high church bishop.[70] As always, it was
lack of funds more than anything else which limited the expansion of
the Society. By October 1853, the state of the finances was sufficiently
grim that it was resolved to approach the bank to advance the sum of
£500 for six months at 5 per cent interest 'for which the Committee
hereby hold themselves personally responsible'.[71] The dire necessity
for this probably accounts for the lukewarm reception given to bishop
Perry of Melbourne, despite his strong Evangelical credentials, who
approached the committee with request for funds to appoint clergymen to the Victorian goldfields. At the same time, correspondence was
flowing in from Canada, the West Indies and Calcutta, which reported
on the work of agents who had already been despatched to their stations and who required ongoing support. Fund-raising remained very
much the business of the hour when Archdeacon Davies reported that
from 21 August to 17 October he had preached or held meetings in
aid of the Society at Chelsea, Tooting, Ashbourne, Guernsey, Jersey,
Birmingham, Cowes, Ryde, Southborough and Brighton, though he
does not say how much money he raised. The need for such exertions
is well demonstrated when weighed against the periodic appearances
of colonial bishops who came to plead their case to the committee, or in the flow of correspondence. Francis Fulford, first bishop
of Montreal (1850–68) and an Anglo-Catholic, paid the CCCS a

---

[68] CCCS Special General Meeting, 27 December 1850, London Guildhall Library, MS
15,674/1, p. 1.
[69] Underwood, *Faith at the Frontiers*, p. 45, describes 'many' earlier chaplains as 'debt-
ors, drunkards, bankrupts and adventurers who owed allegiance to no bishop and
accepted no ecclesiastical authority'. The Continental Committee began work in
1856.
[70] *Ibid*., pp. 53–4. For Colenso and the colonial church question, see Hinchliff, 'John
William Colenso'; and Hinchliff, 'Colonial Church Establishment'.
[71] CCCS Minute Book, 4 October 1853, London Guildhall Library, MS 15,674,
p. 592.

visit in December 1853 before departing to take up his post in Lower Canada.[72] He stressed the Roman Catholic influences which were 'paramount in the administration of affairs' and the need to match their efforts. Although sympathetic, the Society was unable to respond effectively and this seems to have had little or nothing to do with the churchmanship of the supplicant bishop. Faced with a small budget and multiple demands, they adopted the policy of part-funding all requests and requiring local people to make up the balance of the salaries of both clergy and schoolteachers despatched to the colonies. It seems to have created the breathing space that was needed.

Frontier

In the second half of the nineteenth century, the CCCS implemented a number of promotional strategies to sustain the urgency of colonial missions in the eyes of the Evangelical public. These might be summed up in the slogan (not one that was ever actually used by the Society): 'Frontier, Emigration and Empire'. In the chilly reaches of Upper Canada, tales of hardship on the colonial frontier were exploited to provide publicity for the cause in the tradition of other imperial adventure writing. A dramatic story was told by Dr Isaac Hellmuth (1817–1901), a Polish Jew who converted as a young man before emigrating to Canada.[73] Hellmuth was given charge of the Society's work in British North America in 1857, and became the second bishop of Huron in 1871. As he told his story, the party left Quebec at a time of bitter cold weather. It took all the energy of the party to cross the ice and reach their mission objectives. While crossing rapidly moving ice, all the men had to leap from their canoes and try to break through the ice so they could continue their journey. The rest of the time the passengers either sat still or kept the canoe rocking to prevent the craft freezing into the solid ice beneath.[74] In this icy world, every young missionary battled with the elements and became, for the period of his service, a hero of the Arctic. The pioneer saddlebag preacher, Joseph Gander (d. 1881), related the hazards of his occupation with phlegmatic resignation:

The Sunday before last, as I was going to morning church, my horse broke through the ice, and I was thrown into the water and obliged to ride nine miles in wet clothes. Last Sunday I could not go at all for the floods.[75]

[72] CCCS Minute Book, December 1853, London Guildhall Library, MS 15,674, p. 594.
[73] H. E. Turner, 'Isaac Helmuth', *Dictionary of Canadian Biography Online*, vol. 13 (1901–10).
[74] Colonial and Continental Church Society, *Missions in Many Lands*, p. 9.
[75] *Ibid.*

Gander was trained as a schoolteacher and was employed as a catechist by the Society on a salary of £100 per year, but he worked as much as a farmer, dentist and healer as a missionary before being ordained late in life. Gander's diary shows him to have a generous, hard-working temperament and gives us a glimpse into the heroism of the ordinary which made up the work of itinerant colonial missionaries. The final entry is dated 31 May 1876, at a time when he thought his wife of forty years was dying: 'At home feeling the effects of my tiresome journey yesterday … May all our fatiguing journeying in the wilderness help us to look more steadfastly to the Country where the wicked cease from rambling, and the weary are at rest.'[76]

The wilderness seems to have brought out fine qualities in some individuals and their families, while chilling others. In the 1890s, a German missionary described his work on the Ottawa River:

The country is the most desolate and the roughest part of the world that I have yet seen. From this house to the nearest village (and post-office) the distance is about 18 miles. If you travel along the road here in a northerly direction, through my mission, you see only a few clearances here and there, until at last you are lost in the solitude of the woods, and see nothing but large tracts covered with pine trees, long dreary roads, rugged rocks, and sometimes an old shanty.[77]

At the end of this series of bleak pictures comes the appeal: 'These tracts now fall into the hands of the Colonial Church, which, being unable to do the work alone, requires help from outside.' In the Americas, the CCCS committed itself to providing religious services to people for whom there was no other provision. These came to include missions to British sailors in colonial and foreign ports, to fugitive slaves on their arrival in Canada, and to Catholic populations in British colonies such as Malta. The Society was making a reputation as an organisation that would go to places neglected by every other missionary organisation.

Emigration

Emigration and the drama of colonisation also proved the basis for a reformed rhetoric for the combined society, one which gave it a wider appeal beyond the narrower band of conservative Protestants who had earlier been the mainstay of the Society. London Evangelicals, who led the way in many reforming movements in the nineteenth century, seem

---

[76] Cited by Bob Lyons, 'The Diary of a Saddlebag Preacher', *The Bancroft Times* (11 February 1987).
[77] Colonial and Continental Church Society, *Missions in Many Lands*, p. 11.

to have been among the first to recognise that there needed to be more organised and direct support for emigrants and settlers. The usual way this was done was by arranging speakers and collections for those in attendance. Visiting colonial bishops took advantage of the Evangelical network to preach on behalf of the colonial mission cause. Vincent Ryan, the first bishop of Mauritius (1854–88), delivered one such sermon on behalf of the Colonial Church and School Society in the Chapel of Ease, Islington, in 1855. His text was Galatians 6: 10: 'As we have therefore opportunity, let us do good unto all men, especially unto them who are of the household of faith.'[78] This makes an excellent text for a promotion of the colonial church and for the emigrants, settlers, sailors in foreign ports and fugitive slaves served by the CCCS. As usual, the bishop supplied figures to support his case and also drew on his own experience. In Mauritius, there was a large population of emancipated slaves among whom a single zealous layman was active. There were also over 100,000 Indian coolies, 'very accessible to Christian effort for their moral and spiritual improvement'.[79] Later in his episcopate, Ryan was inclined to be less optimistic about the character of the many former slaves and apprentices in his diocese.[80] The need of the diocese of Sydney, as reported in a recent appeal by the bishop, was also very pressing. In four years the population had risen from 35,000 to 60,000, but, of the five churches in Sydney open for public worship, only one was completed. And, finally, there was a plea for clergy to offer themselves for service to the isolated interior of Australia with a promise that they would be warmly received, and (despite the dire warning administered earlier about the heathen status of poor white emigrants) that the emigrants were not all without education or courtesy.[81]

Geography and statistics were tools deployed by the Society to press home its message. In the Society's annual report, one favoured method for dramatising the differences between the scale of the need and the available resources was to print maps of colonial territories overprinted with insert maps of the British homeland. On a map of the Dominion of Canada, for example, the whole of the British Isles was swallowed up in capacious reaches of Hudson's Bay;[82] England floated in the

[78] V. W. Ryan, *Christian Opportunity: A Sermon in Behalf of the Colonial Church and School Society* (London, 1855), p. 1.

[79] *Ibid.*, p. 19.

[80] R. B. Allen, *Slaves, Freedmen, and Indentured Laborers in Colonial Mauritius* (Cambridge, 1999), p. 130.

[81] Ryan, *Christian Opportunity*, p. 17.

[82] *Annual Report of the Colonial and Continental Church Society* (1901–2), p. 76.

deserts of Western Australia,[83] and the diocese of Honduras dwarfed the insert map of England.[84] With equal drama, the 'Ecclesiastical Map of Manitoba' featured some seventy-five districts which were home to scores of settler families and unnumbered populations of native people. However, many northern regions were reliant on a tiny number of resident clergymen provided by the CCCS, or the few Indian missions which were mostly clustered around Lake Winnipeg. Vast districts were labelled 'NO MISSION'.[85]

The new, broader and less sectarian appeal was effective, but only to a certain extent. There had been strong growth in the income of the CCCS following the merging of the Newfoundland School Society and the Colonial Church Society in 1851. Combined income trebled in the ten years to 1861. However, it did not really get much higher than this and stayed more or less stagnant for the next thirty years, despite a considerable increase in the population both at home and abroad. This is clear from Table 5.1.

How do we explain these lacklustre figures, especially when they are compared with receipts by the CMS and other foreign missionary societies for the middle decades of the nineteenth century? As for the SPG, this period was not a time of growth for the CCCS or the colonial missionary movement in general. Sectarian rivalry, which had been important to the society's formation and growth in the 1850s, was less effective in sustaining enthusiasm for the cause after the first great wave of settlement had flowed to the colonies. In addition, colonial disestablishment had removed the most significant organisational barrier which had stood between the Episcopal and Nonconformist churches, and encouraged their closer cooperation. The new voluntarist environment also put renewed emphasis on the personal qualities of the bishops who were forced to raise funds to support their own plans for expansion. In frontier regions, the most successful bishops were able to reconcile the warring church parties in the greater cause of church unity and development. Competition with other churches, notably the Methodists and Catholics, also had a sobering influence on those inclined to sustain old world party grievances in the Church of England. Representative of this spirit of colonial pragmatism is the response of William Wood (fl. 1834–78) who had emigrated from England to Canada in 1834. In 1848, he became the first agent of the Colonial Church Society in Ontario. His letters to his family, now in the Library of the University of Toronto, describe his experience working

[83] *Ibid.*, p. 165.   [84] *Ibid.*, p. 157.
[85] *Ibid.*, map between pp. 110 and 111.

Table 5.1 *Income of the Newfoundland School Society (NSS), Colonial Church Society (CCS), Colonial Church and School Society (CCSS), and Colonial and Continental Church Society (CCCS), 1831–1909*

Year	Society	Income (£)
1831	NSS	1,673
1841	NSS and CCS	5,015
1851	CCSS	5,717
1861	CCCS	16,316
1871	CCCS	18,563
1881	CCCS	18,401
1891	CCCS	18,092
1901	CCCS	24,196
1905–6	CCCS	21,002
1906–7	CCCS	32,271
1907–8	CCCS	35,741
1908–9	CCCS	42,426[a]

Note: The income figures differ in earlier summary statistics; for example, the *Annual Report of the CCCS* (1888–9), p. xxiv, has progressive income as £6,307 (1841), £6,979 (1851), £27,487 (1861), £32,183, £39,715 (1881), which shows steady growth.
[a] Includes £10,258 from the Pan-Anglican Thank Offering Fund.
Source: *Annual Report of the Colonial and Continental Church Society* (1908–9), pp. 36–7.

as an itinerant missionary on behalf of the Society. In 1857, he was delighted to report that the new bishop of Huron was an Evangelical, an excellent thing since 'these high church Puseyites ... drive members away to join other sects'.[86] In the long run, some colonial dioceses became Evangelical strongholds, others remained high church; most began eventually to train and recruit their own clergy who tended to reflect the churchmanship of the ruling bishop. These self-sustaining churches no longer needed to recruit all their clergy and teachers from home, thus removing the founding rationale for the CCCS.

A more telling factor may have been the success of the Colonial Bishoprics' Fund which, with careful nurturing by Gladstone, became a vehicle for the ambitions of gifted churchmen of all parties of the Church of England. Unlike the SPG or the CCCS, it was never dominated by one faction within the Church. However, the success of the Fund was a problem in that it funnelled the lion's share of private donations, which in earlier days might have flowed to the colonial

---

[86] William Wood to Emily Jane Wood, 10 August 1857, William Wood Papers, University of Toronto MS 225. Abstract online at www.library.utoronto.ca/fisher/collections/findaids/wood.pdf.

missionary societies, for the aid of the colonial churches. The pockets of the Anglican faithful were deep, but they were not limitless. Most preferred to send out a bishop who would then be responsible for generating a self-supporting church. In these circumstances, the SPG became increasingly restricted to aiding work on the frontiers of colonial settlement, and the CCCS did similar work, while continuing to assist those who shared its more Protestant vision of colonial development.

Greater Britain

The Society continued to publish its report in the 1860s, including a copy of the annual sermon. This was enlivened with occasional scenic views, but mostly it stuck to the old formula of narratives from missionaries in the field, and pleas for more workers in it. From the diocese of Melbourne came the request for 'clergymen of piety, missionary spirit, and pulpit power', or, failing this, 'young men of education, ability, and piety, having the qualifications requisite in candidates for the ministry'.[87] Those who responded to these calls were sent to places on the margins of the expanding colonial world – The Bend, Monckton in the diocese of Fredericton, Rum Cay and Fortune Island in the diocese of Jamaica, Emu Plains and Castlereagh in the diocese of Sydney, Yandilla in the diocese of Brisbane, or Middle Swan in the diocese of Perth. Like the Wesleyans, the CCCS recognised the thrifty virtue of an itinerant ministry. Mr R. Munden, a catechist from Yandilla, Darling Downs, wrote of his work in and around Tarawinaba in Queensland.[88] He held 'service as usual' on Sunday and read the Society's annual sermon out to the people. On Wednesday, he rode to Back Creek Station and conversed with a number of Chinese shepherds and left them some tracts in Chinese. On Friday, he walked to another shepherd's station, reading the scripture to the man and his family. On Saturday, he walked out to Head Station. This was the highlight of the week. His congregation was generally made up of shepherds on isolated stations. However, on this occasion he was pleased to be sustained by what he called a 'profitable conversation' with 'an intelligent Protestant Irishman'. In such accounts, it is difficult to say who is more to be pitied, the men and women on their isolated stations, slaves to the boss and their sheep, or the itinerant catechist who journeyed out to preach to them. Mr Munden concluded his report by stating that, in the course

---

[87] *Annual Report of the Colonial Church and School Society* (1860), p. 134.
[88] *Annual Report of the Colonial Church and School Society* (1861), p. 135.

of a year, he had travelled about two thousand miles, circulating copies of the scripture in English, German and Chinese. Munden had been working in this way since 1838, and states that, throughout this time, all his wants had been met. However, he was prepared to acknowledge that there were difficulties: 'it is a life which requires grace from above, to be enabled to live in the midst of so much worldliness, and hasting to be rich'.[89] He nevertheless kept to his original mission.

In order to sustain the work, a new defining ethos was needed, something which would bind colonists and their supporters at home together and would avoid the party bitterness which was a distraction from the spiritual and welfare objectives of the Society. The ethos of the empire provided the answer. By the 1870s, the rhetoric of the society shifted once more to take up this new strain and we can detect a much greater recourse to imperial nationalism to justify the expansion of the society. By his writing, Dilke provided a ready-made identity for the colonial missionary societies. In 1876, the Colonial and Continental Church Society incorporated his term 'Greater Britain' into the name of their journal: *The Greater Britain Messenger: Colonial and Continental Church Society Quarterly Paper*. The cover picture sums up a new, more upbeat strategy for the Society. It shows an emigrant vessel with flags flying 'Emigrants for Australia' at one end, and 'Emigrants for Canada' at the other. Below, a mountain scene shows churches amidst mountains with a sign 'To the English Service'. Above, missionaries are shown heading off by dog sled over snow, and by railway. There were advertisements for the services of visiting speakers, who would be happy to provide lectures on the following themes: 'Phases of colonial and continental life', 'Warm hearts in cold regions', 'Home from home – what it is and what I may be' and 'Emigrant and missionary life in the colonies'. Here was a new work for the Society, part religious travel service, part missionary adventure; it was an ideal that was more in tune with the more optimistic spirit of the later empire. The success of this new strategy is also reflected in the rising financial fortunes of the CCCS in the first decade of the twentieth century. In 1909, income reached an all-time high of £42,426 – swollen by a grant from the Pan-Anglican Thank Offering Fund. In addition, there were some 350 agents employed by the Society which now included about 200 stations in the colonies and 140 chaplaincies in Europe. There was also exciting news from the prairie churches which the Society was supporting in North-West Canada, discussed in more detail in connection with the Britannia Colony in Chapter 12. It was with quiet satisfaction that the annual report was

[89] *Ibid.*, p. 137.

headed with the text: 'The Lord hath been mindful of us: He will bless us' (Psalms cxv, 12).

Conclusion

By the end of the nineteenth century, the CCCS had passed through several stages that reflect the transformation in the Evangelical movement that sustained it. Both the Newfoundland School Society and the Western Australian Church Society were typical of the small, ardently Protestant ventures led by laymen which sprang up in vast numbers to support a host of causes in the early decades of the nineteenth century. That they survived at all is probably due to the need for a society that would act as a vehicle for Evangelical resistance to the perceived influence of the high church movement in the older colonial missionary societies, especially the SPG. But financial difficulties and the lack of dynamism in the Society's leadership (most of whom are non-entities) meant that it never really did become the empire-wide agency for the planting of Evangelicalism among the colonists to which it aspired. There was also the problem of the colonial bishops who were not, in the main, Evangelicals, and who preferred to appoint clergy who would avoid controversy. With funds perennially so short, even the most ultra-Protestant agent of the Society was forced in the end to deal with the bishop. In the wake of these clashes, the livelier ethos of the later decades of the century, which drew on imperialism rather than anti-Catholicism and anti-Tractarianism, is what came to characterise the Society's promotional literature. It embraced the ideal of Greater Britain and the principle of a wider Christian empire in which settlers were united by race and faith in the common cause. While never entirely abandoning the older sectarianism that had fuelled the Society's earlier activism, this new ethos also required greater cooperation with non-Anglican Protestants in their common efforts to Christianise the frontier. The next chapter looks at the colonial missions of the Nonconformists, including the Methodists, and the (Congregationalist) Colonial Missionary Society.

6   Nonconformists

This chapter considers the colonial missions of British Nonconformists, that is, Protestants outside the established churches. 'Nonconformity' was a term used in the nineteenth century to refer to the new Methodist churches as well as the older Baptists, Congregationalists and Quakers and a number of smaller groups including the Plymouth Brethren and the Salvation Army.[1] Following the Disruption, the Evangelical Presbyterians, who left the established Church of Scotland to form the Free Church, shared many theological and organisational features with Nonconformists (and Evangelical Anglicans) elsewhere in Britain. However, although it is convenient to consider them together, Nonconformists took pride in their independence, and it is important to pay as much heed to their distinctive cultural, theological and regional profiles[2] as to those things which they held in common. The character of the Nonconformist identity also tended to change over time. At the beginning of the nineteenth century, Wesleyan Methodists felt closer to the Church of England and it was only later that they came to feel part of the relatively cohesive Nonconformist 'chapel' culture.[3] The evangelical revival and, as we will argue in this chapter, the impact of emigration and imperial expansion, were critical in strengthening bonds between this diverse group of British Protestants.

Although they were a minority of the population, Nonconformists were some of Britain's most active Christians with a commitment to both empire and social and political reform and were open to the

---

[1] Nonconformity has been much better studied as a social and political movement than as an imperial network, though for important surveys see D. W. Bebbington, *The Nonconformist Conscience: Chapel and Politics, 1870–1914* (London, 1982); D. W. Lovegrove, *Established Church, Sectarian People: Itinerancy and the Transformation of English Dissent, 1780–1830* (Cambridge, 1988); I. Sellers, *Nineteenth-Century Nonconformity* (London, 1977).

[2] McLeod, *Religion and Society*, p. 34.

[3] R. J. Helmstadter, 'Orthodox Nonconformity', in *Nineteenth-Century English Religious Traditions: Retrospect and Prospect*, ed. D. G. Paz (Westport, CT, 1995), p. 57, suggests a four-fold division into Baptists and Congregationalists, Quakers and Unitarians, Methodists, and smaller sects including the Salvation Army.

potential of the colonial empire. In 1851, Nonconformists made up almost half the attendants at religious services reported in the census of religious worship in England and Wales; they also claimed to have more places of worship (though admittedly many were small) than the Church of England and Catholics combined.[4] Beyond their numerous churches and chapels, Nonconformists also held a strong grip on British cultural life through their involvement in school education. Between them, the non-denominational British and Foreign School Society and the various Nonconformist churches conducted over 1600 schools in England and Wales. Many more children received a regular injection of literacy, bible-reading and morality through the Sunday school movement. In alliance with Anglican Evangelicals, Congregationalists, Baptists and Methodists formed the core of the numerous evangelical societies which were considered at the beginning of the last chapter and which helped evangelicals maintain a stranglehold over Victorian public opinion on questions relating to morality, missions, education and what we would now call social welfare. Nonconformity had regional strengths; it was a particularly strong force in Wales where it gradually acquired something of the character of a national religion, an identification encouraged by the revival of the Welsh language which was promoted through Nonconformist chapels. Beyond Britain, Nonconformists who emigrated to the colonies were active in establishing auxiliary branches of evangelical societies, including the Religious Tract Society and the British and Foreign Bible Society, as well as lending their support to the colonial Sunday school and temperance movements, which together ensured that the Nonconformist conscience was as much an imperial as a national force.

Nonconformists held a distinctive view of their historical place in the nation and the British empire, past and present. Those who descended most directly from the seventeenth-century Puritans, notably the Baptists and Congregationalists, placed a premium on their status as 'free' churches, which had rejected state funding and, with

---

[4] For statistics on British church membership, see Latourette, *Expansion of Christianity*, vol. VII, pp. 175–223; Cook and Keith, *British Historical Facts*, p. 220, Table 3, citing 'Report on the 1851 Census of Religious Worship', Parliamentary Papers (1852–3), vol. LXXXIX, Table A, pp. clxxviii–clxxix. Out of a total 34,467 places of worship, Nonconformists (i.e. Presbyterians, Congregationalists, Baptists, Wesleyans, New Connexion Methodists, Primitive Methodists, Bible Christians, Wesleyan Methodist Association, Wesleyan Reformers, Calvinistic Methodists, Unitarians and Quakers) had 18,608 (54 per cent), Anglicans 14,077 (41 per cent) and Catholics 570 (1.6 per cent). The number of sittings by Nonconformists was 43 per cent, while Anglicans had 52 per cent and Catholics less than 2 per cent. According to the Minutes of the Wesleyan Methodist Conference, in 1850 there were 4,099 Wesleyan Methodists in Scotland and 21,107 in Ireland.

it, state interference in their spiritual affairs. Despite forming a power-ful and articulate religious minority in Britain, many Nonconformists had a shared history of persecution and marginalisation at the hands of the established Church of England. This played an important role in determining their views on colonial extension. They remembered that following the Act of Uniformity (1662) ministers who refused to con-form their liturgical practice to the Book of Common Prayer had been ejected from their churches: thousands were imprisoned; some were executed; and a whole generation chose to emigrate to the more tolerant shores of America.

While the repeal of the Test and Corporation Acts (1828) enabled Nonconformists to enter fully into British public life, many continued to nurture a tradition which cherished religious liberty, denounced bishops, church establishments and endowments as agents of tyranny, and celebrated the Protestant 'founding fathers' of the first American colonies as some of their greatest heroes. One practical effect of the seventeenth-century ejection of English Nonconformists was that non-episcopal Protestantism became the majority faith of the American colonists, who came to characterise themselves as the rightful heirs of the Reformation. Partly because of effective missionary exertions from the United States, Baptists, Congregationalists and Methodists were a stronger force in British North America than they were in the set-tler colonies of the southern hemisphere. In various ways, therefore, Protestant Nonconformity was central to the Christian settlement of the first British empire. An important corollary of this was that – just as they were on the foreign mission field – American Protestants were major rivals to British Nonconformists for control and influence over the frontier churches of British North America.

The pattern of Nonconformist extension into the British colonies in the nineteenth century differed from that in the first British empire. Methodists, who had fewer scruples about accepting state aid, were able to expand more rapidly in colonial territories than voluntarists such as the Congregationalists. Possibly for this reason, Methodists succeeded in supplanting other non-Anglican Protestants in the race to plant chapels in Canadian, Australian and New Zealand soil. Methodism seems to have been a creed which suited the young colonial democ-racies and, by the end of the nineteenth century, census returns show that it had become the largest Protestant denomination in Canada and the second largest (after the Church of England) in both Australia and New Zealand.[5] It was less significant in the Cape where competition

---

[5] See Tables 1.1–1.6 for detailed statistics.

from the combined forces of the Dutch Reformed Church and Scottish and Irish Presbyterianism pushed them into third position. However, Methodism was an important church for the coloured population, as we noted in the first chapter.

When emigration began to accelerate in the 1820s, some Non-conformists were unsure if the movement was Providential in origin. There were doubts about the moral dangers of the frontier with its promise of easy wealth, sexual laxity and impact on native people. Even emigration could be open to criticism if it was motivated by the lure of material, rather than spiritual, advancement. In 1844, almost sixty members of the congregation of two Strict Baptist chapels in Brighton emigrated to Australia. The impact of the loss of so many in a single journey probably influenced the views of the minister, J. C. Philpot, to oppose what he called 'the emigrating fever' which he viewed with alarm and was spreading daily:

> Those whose minds are teeming with schemes of emigration are not those who are enjoying the Lord's blessing in the house of prayer, and count a day in his courts better than a thousand; but either worldly professors, who know nothing of the sweetness and preciousness of the word of God's grace, or the backsliders in heart, who are filled with their own ways.[6]

Other Nonconformists disagreed, embraced the principles of Christian colonialism and created colonial missionary societies of their own.

The key to the shift in Nonconformist opinion was a redefinition of colonial settlement so that it was incorporated into the foreign missionary movement. Indeed, the Congregationalist supporters of the Colonial Missionary Society would eventually claim that colonial missions should take precedence over the cause of foreign missions: 'The MISSIONARY MOVEMENT of the last century was to Christianise the heathen; the Colonial Missionary Movement of to-day is largely an attempt to prevent the heathenising of Christians.'[7] While few would go this far, most Nonconformist churches duly incorporated colonial mission work into the range of their missionary activities. This required the rearrangement of some societies to meet the new need. The constitution of the Baptist Missionary Society (1817) originally stated that its object was 'the diffusion of knowledge of the religion of Jesus Christ throughout the heathen world', and this was generally assumed to exclude the British colonies. In 1843, however,

---

[6] 'A Strict Baptist View of Emigration, 1853', in D. Bebbington, K. Dix and A. Ruston, eds., *Protestant Nonconformist Texts*, vol. 3, *The Nineteenth Century*, 4 vols. (Aldershot, 2006), p. 183.
[7] *Evangelical British Missionary* [Colonial Missionary Society] (January 1905).

the Society decided to change the wording to refer to 'the whole world beyond the British Isles'.[8] This allowed it to incorporate the Baptist Colonial Missionary Society (1836) which worked in the province of Upper Canada. The Baptist Missionary Society also supported colonial missions to America and the Australian colonies from 1838 to 1850.[9]

Nonconformists were divided into a large number of separate churches, and this tended to limit what they were able to achieve through their voluntary missionary societies, even when they worked together, as they often did. As Jeffrey Cox notes, prior to the success of the Congregationalist and Baptist Unions, the missionary societies functioned to some degree as denominational surrogates for these groups.[10] Colonial missions were an important component of the work of the three largest Nonconformist denominations: Methodists, Congregationalists and Baptists. In this chapter, there is space to consider only the two largest of these: namely, the Wesleyan Methodist Missionary Society (formed between 1814 and 1818) and the Colonial Missionary Society (1836), both of which have extensive printed and archival sources relating to their work in the colonial field.[11]

Wesleyan Methodist Missionary Society (WMMS)

Missionary work was conducted by Methodists from the earliest days of the movement. However, it was not until 1817 that the Methodist Conference felt it was necessary to centralise this work which had earlier been conducted by locally based societies. From this time, the General Wesleyan Methodist Missionary Society coordinated the raising of funds for foreign missions, including the outfitting and despatch of missionaries, receiving accounts and journals of their work, and preparing and publishing a substantial report. Information about Wesleyan Methodist missionary work was published in the Society's most important periodical, *Missionary Notices*, first published in 1816;

---

[8] B. Stanley, *The History of the Baptist Missionary Society 1792–1992* (Edinburgh, 1992), p. 215.

[9] W. H. Brackney, *Historical Dictionary of the Baptists* (Lanham, MD, and London, 1999), pp. 31–2 and 97.

[10] Cox, *British Missionary Enterprise*, p. 102.

[11] Records of the Colonial (Commonwealth) Missionary Society, 1836–1966, form part of the archives of Council for World Mission (CWM), 1764–1977, held by the School of Oriental and African Studies, University of London. The CWM was formed in 1977 and incorporates the former Commonwealth Missionary Society which was merged with the London Missionary Society in 1966. For the antecedents to the current organisation, see the CWM website, www.cwmission.org/who-we-are.html.

they also appeared in the *Arminian Magazine*, first published 1778.[12] In its first report, the object of the WMMS was said to be no more than the better organisation of the work of Wesleyan Methodists and of others 'who are friends to the conversion of the Heathen World, and to the preaching of the Gospel, generally, in Foreign Lands'.[13] The effect of this was to ensure that Methodist missions were never really separated from the control of the Wesleyan Conference in the way of the voluntary associations such as the London Missionary Society, the Church Missionary Society or the Glasgow Missionary Society and Glasgow Colonial Society (though these societies were later brought under the direct control of the Assembly of the Church of Scotland). Nor were Methodist missions to the heathen abroad distinguished from those to Europeans, Jews or British colonists overseas. Until they established their own independent Conferences, calls for missionary assistance from British settlers in new countries of settlement were directly under the control of the British Conference and were highly regulated. Colonial missions to Methodist settlers in Canada began in the 1780s and continued until the establishment of an independent Canadian Conference in 1854; missions to Australasia began in 1818, to New Zealand and elsewhere in the Pacific in 1822 and continued until independence in 1855; missions to South Africa began in 1814 and closed with independence in 1882.[14]

From the beginning, Wesleyan Methodist missionary work was linked directly to the call of British patriotism. In their publications, Methodist missions were represented as a duty laid on the British nation by Christ that should therefore have no boundaries. In 1820, a meeting of the Liverpool auxiliary of the WMMS gave its support to missions in India, Africa, New South Wales, North America and Europe in the following way:[15]

Even one truly Christian nation, possessing the means and facilities of Britain, to send out its Missionaries ... might, in a very short time, produce the most

---

[12] The *Arminian Magazine* was renamed *Methodist Magazine* in 1798 and *Wesleyan Methodist Magazine* in 1822.

[13] *First Report of the General Wesleyan Methodist Missionary Society* (London, 1818), p. viii.

[14] [Wesleyan] Methodist Missionary Society/Methodist Church Overseas Division Archive, School of Oriental and African Studies Library, London. Notes to Archive in Mundus, Gateway to missionary collections in the United Kingdom, www.mundus.ac.uk.

[15] *Third Report of the Wesleyan Methodist Missionary Auxiliary Society, for the Liverpool District, for 1819*, Liverpool: Thomas Kaye, 1820 (*Reports of Missionary Societies* (a collection of tracts bound and enumerated by Mitchell Library, State Library of New South Wales), p. 7).

astonishing moral changes in the earth … Only let the whole nation be united by the spirit and roused by the energies of our holy religion, and soon all the strong holds of Satan must be overthrown, and the kingdom of our God and his Messiah established on their ruins.[16]

The colonies of British settlement were part of this mighty work of Providence. On reports from New South Wales, where three chapels had been erected and many new circuits established, it notes approvingly: 'We trust, by the blessing of God, that the foundations of an industrious and religious state of society will speedily be laid in a country which cannot fail ultimately to have an important influence in extending the kingdom of Christ in the Pacific and Indian Oceans.'[17] Not surprisingly, the practical difficulties of coordinating this worldwide effort were daunting. By 1824, the full report of the Wesleyan Methodist Missionary Society ran to 142 closely printed pages, with another 94 pages listing the names of contributors from auxiliaries and individuals all around the world.

The call of imperial patriotism is also evident in the reports from the WMMS auxiliaries in the colonies. Although the lion's share of contributions to the WMMS came from Britain itself, colonial auxiliaries assisted the Society at home by raising funds locally and sustaining enthusiasm for the cause among the Nonconformist colonial bourgeoisie who tended to make up their membership. We can examine one in detail. The Wesleyan Auxiliary Missionary Society for New South Wales met for the first time on 5 July 1820 with a committee made up of the various laymen and all the missionaries who were then in the colony, including the Reverend Walter Lawry and William Walker in Parramatta, the Reverend Benjamin Carvosso in Windsor, and the Reverend Ralph Mansfield, who acted as clerical secretary. The first Annual Meeting, held in Macquarie-street Chapel in Sydney on 1 October 1821, was chaired by the Reverend Samuel Leigh. This focused on work among the heathen, noting 'with lively interest' the projected missions to the South Seas and hailing 'with joy' the establishment of a mission to the Aborigines of New South Wales.[18] The New South Wales auxiliary saw its work as part of a great imperial enterprise, a 'holy cause' kindled throughout the British empire: 'A portion of that heavenly fervour has reached the southern world. The inhabitants of this remote region have not been deaf to the calls of suffering

---

[16] *Ibid.*, p. 2 (*Reports of Missionary Societies* (n. 15 above), p. 10).
[17] *Ibid.*, p. 11 (*Reports of Missionary Societies* (n. 15 above), p. 19).
[18] *First Report of the Wesleyan Auxiliary Missionary Society for New South Wales for 1821* (Sydney: Robert Howe, 1822), p. 9 [Reports of the Missionary Societies, p. 327].

humanity.'[19] Yet, it must be admitted, the report on the work in the colony itself was generally treated as if it were of lesser importance than work elsewhere, including France, where so many Protestant martyrs had suffered persecution, or even Ceylon, where Wesleyan missionaries were said to be halting the progress of paganism and Buddhism.[20] All of this seemed more exciting and rewarding than work among the local Aborigines which the Society quietly initiated at the same meeting. In 1821, the list of contributions to the mission to the Aborigines is headed by Governor Macquarie, who subscribed £5. The subsequent failure of this Aboriginal mission, which occupies some dismal lines in subsequent reports, is one of the less propitious omens of the Society.[21]

For colonial auxiliaries, foreign missions provided an opportunity to participate in a great overseas adventure, which, by definition, tended to happen somewhere else. By 1830, the New South Wales auxiliary was celebrating its tenth anniversary and reflecting on the previous decade's work, carried out against a background of imperial conflict, most notably involving Russia: 'The British Churches', it states, 'were not diverted by these political conflicts from their Master's work; their altars still smoked with the pure incense of prayer – their hearts still beat high with a holy ambition for the universal empire of the Prince of Peace – nor did they relax in their efforts to obey the call which reached them from heathen lands, "Men and brethren, come over and help us!"' It was hoped that this invitation would inspire a spirit of pious emulation and encourage Australian Methodists to replicate the work of the home societies. The report concludes: 'May Australia be as eminently the light of the South, as Great Britain incontestably is of the North; and may her sons and her daughters, by thus becoming the instruments of turning many to righteousness, shine as stars in the kingdom of heaven for ever and ever.'[22] The reality was rather more mundane, and, as might be expected, focused rather more on building churches at home and rather less on sending missionaries abroad than the rhetoric of its anniversary literature suggested. However, all colonial missions were girded about with the language of empire so that the most insignificant chapel could be seen, in a certain southern light,

[19] *Ibid.*, Report Read at the First Anniversary, 1 October 1821 (*Reports of Missionary Societies* (n. 15 above), p. 329).
[20] *Ibid.* [Reports of the Missionary Societies, p. 336].
[21] For the fate of this mission, see D. A. Roberts and H. M. Carey, '"Beong! Beong! (More! More!)": John Harper and the Wesleyan Mission to the Australian Aborigines', *Journal of Colonialism and Colonial History*, 10 (2009).
[22] *The Tenth Report of the Wesleyan Auxiliary Missionary Society of New South Wales, 1830* (Sydney: R. Mansfield, 1831), p. 13 [Reports of the Missionary Societies, p. 463].

as a monument to both Christ and the British patriots that had been responsible for building it.

Primitive Methodists

Among the Methodists, colonial mission work was not the prerogative of the Wesleyans alone. It also occupied a central place in the missionary work of the minor Methodist societies, particularly those whose membership was drawn from the aspiring working classes for whom emigration provided an opportunity for social betterment.[23] Both the 'Ranters' (Primitive Methodists) and the New Connexion Methodists provided news of colonists, emigration and colonial missions in their journals. Of the two groups, the Ranters threw themselves into church extension work with greater enthusiasm. By 1843, the Primitive Methodist Missionary Society was supporting forty-three stations in Great Britain as well as missions to North America, where the first missionary was sent in 1829, and Australia and New Zealand in 1844.[24] Mrs R. P. Hopper bases her history of the Primitive Methodists in Canada partly on her own memory of its pioneers. She characterises the origins of the Movement not as a schism but rather as 'a child of Providence' with a mission to bring vitality to all English Methodism. She calls it 'a gospel to the poor'.[25] The first Primitive Methodist to begin work in Canada, Robert Walker, emigrated to the city of Quebec with his wife and six children. On his arrival in 1829, he simply began preaching in a market square, gathering a group of Primitive Methodist emigrants from Yorkshire around him.[26]

Camp meetings, robust singing, an egalitarian ethos and a sense of joyful Christian community were characteristics of Primitive Methodist meetings. These qualities made them attractive to emigrants cut off from their home churches. The English Conference gave responsibility for the Canadian mission to the Hull circuit, which sustained the Canadian chapels with a stream of ministers and emigrants from

---

[23] In the 1830s, Wesleyan Methodism in England lost up to 100,000 members following a series of schisms. In order of their combined attendances at morning, afternoon and evening services, the most important groupings at the time of the 1851 religious census were: Wesleyans, 63.9 per cent (1,513,304); Primitive Methodists, 21.1 per cent (50,0331); New Connexion Methodists, 4.1 per cent (98,041); Wesleyan Methodist Association, 3.8 per cent (90,145); and Bible Christians, 3 per cent (72,695). Religious census data from C. Cook and B. Keith, *British Historical Facts, 1830–1900* (London, 1975), p. 220.

[24] The archives of the Society are now held in the School of Oriental and African Studies, London University, with other records of the WMMS.

[25] R. P. Hopper, *Old-Time Primitive Methodism in Canada, 1829–1884* (Toronto, 1904).

[26] *Ibid.*, p. 21.

northern England. More assistance from the English Conference came in 1844 with a visit from 'Venerable' Hugh Bourne (1772–1852), one of the two founders of Primitive Methodism. Bourne supported the extension of the sect by constant preaching and touring in Great Britain and Ireland as well as Canada and the United States.[27] In Canada, Methodist Union (1883) ended the separate identity of Primitive Methodism which retained to the end an English character and organisational structure.

Methodist New Connexion

The Methodist New Connexion was also keen to display their colonial credentials. The Connexion issued a brief (twelve to sixteen page) 'Missionary Chronicle' as part of the *Methodist New Connexion Magazine and Evangelical Repository*, which included extracts of letters from missionaries in Canada and Australia as well as China. This was replaced by *Gleanings in Harvest Fields* (1866–1907) which had the subtitle: 'Work in the Methodist New Connexion Missions at Home and Abroad'. The extension of the Connexion in Britain and abroad was seen as a vital sign of the life of the movement, and a recognition of the legitimacy of its secession from the Wesleyan mainstream. In 1847, the Liverpool meeting of the New Connexion Missionary Society reported on its missions in Ireland and Canada.[28] The report was made in a calamitous year in which the continuing effects of the famine in Ireland, and refugees in Canada, made a loud call on the members' charity. Missionary work was clearly envisioned as a three-pronged effort: to the society at home, to the 'perishing heathen', and to the mission in Canada, which is called 'that vast, and interesting portion of the British empire'.[29] In Ireland, however, there was terrible news. By the visitation of a mysterious Providence, at least two-thirds of the people, we were left with 'cleanness of teeth in all our cities' (Amos 4: 6). The passage from scripture described the conditions of purification and penance imposed by God prior to the final judgement. All the societies and congregations of the movement were affected by the eschatological mood.

Despite these traumas, the New Connexion Methodists reported sustained growth, supporting ten missionary stations in Ireland, and no less than thirty in Canada. The famine in Ireland may have helped

---

[27] H. B. Kendall, *The Origin and History of the Primitive Methodist Church*, 2 vols. (London, 1905), vol. 1, pp. 436–8, notes that the Canadian mission was more successful than that to the United States.

[28] Methodist New Connexion, *Report of the Methodist New Connexion Missionary Society, for Ireland, Canada, Etc.* (Liverpool, 1847).

[29] *Ibid.*, p. 15.

to inspire greater generosity for the migrant church: the amount raised in England was £1,847, in Ireland £429 and in Canada £248, making a total of £2,524, with an additional £800 from the Jubilee fund. From Canada, letters from missionaries gave a sense of the strenuous nature of their work. From Owen Sound in the 'back woods' of Canada, 'as far west almost as the enterprising colonist has fixed his habitation', came a report from Henry O. Crofts. Crofts was a minister of the English New Connexion Conference from 1840 to 1842 and came to Montreal in 1843. He was later Superintendent of Missions and four times President of the Canadian Conference before returning to England in 1852.[30] As a younger man, he gave an account of an arduous journey he undertook one Sabbath in August, from the log cabin that was the mission house to his congregations in the woods. He began the day in the house of Mr Blanchard where about thirty communicants crammed to attend the meeting; by four o'clock he was preaching in the house of Mr Gunn about four miles further away. On Monday, he travelled first to Mr Curey's, where he says he preached to a large congregation, before heading another six miles to a second appointment. This involved crossing a swamp and, although this was less than a mile wide, it took the missionary two hours to cross it because his horse kept falling repeatedly into the mud. At one point they both nearly drowned. Having achieved his destination, he cleaned his horse and saddle with grass, and proceeded to 'a delighted meeting' in the house of another friend. Two more meetings were held the next day. With the help of a friend (who this time guided him around the swamp), Crofts eventually returned the twenty-five miles to the mission house. 'The Lord has favoured us, in this place, with a gracious revival', he reported.[31]

Indeed, thanks in part to the exertions of men and women like Crofts, the Lord would seem to have favoured all branches of Methodism, for they all did well in the colonies, generally growing at a faster rate than the Anglican churches. Their expansion was helped by their flexible organisational structure, which deployed lay preachers on the frontiers of settlement, while maintaining a clear line of authority to the annual Conference. Methodists also knew how to encourage colonial independence. By the middle of the nineteenth century, the British Connexion of the largest, Wesleyan branch of Methodism was no longer willing or

---

[30] Ken Russell, 'Canadian Methodist Ministers, 1800–1925'. http://freepages.genealogy.rootsweb.ancestry.com/~methodists/.

[31] Methodist New Connexion, *Report of the Methodist New Connexion*. For recollections of Crofts' 'portly form, sonorous voice, ready quotations of scripture' and 'ready, racy wit', see William Williams, 'Historical Sketch of the Methodist New Connexion Church in Canada', in *Centennial of Canadian Methodism* (W. Briggs, 1891), p. 111.

able to continue its support for colonial missions. Instead, it was insisting that the colonies create their own separate Connexions that would take on the responsibility not only for their own clergy, chapel and circuits, but also for foreign mission work. Methodists in Australia and New Zealand were urged to adopt the Pacific as their special sphere of responsibility, just as those in North America were engaged in Africa and Asia. This was not achieved without some colonial disgruntlement. On the twentieth anniversary of the foundation of the Society in New South Wales, the annual report addresses for the first time the issue of the competing claims of heathen missions and missions to other Christians:

If the object of our missionary enterprise were only to spread nominal Christianity, our exclusive sphere would be amongst the heathen, and when the Christian name should be universally adopted, we might cherish the utmost complacency in the work of our own hands.[32]

Against such arguments, it is argued that the need for the gospel was universal, indeed: 'we regard every human being as morally diseased, guilty, and enslaved by sin, and the Gospel of Christ as the only suitable and sovereign remedy.'[33] In New Zealand, for example, work among the Maori was giving way to success in converting Europeans. But the tide, and the flow of funds, had turned. Colonial missions were seen as a temporary work which would wither away as the colonies became self-supporting. In 1850, the report to the annual meeting of the WMMS noted: 'To support prosperous existing Missions, until they may be able to sustain themselves, and extend and perpetuate Christianity in the countries where they have been respectively founded, is … the first care of a Missionary Society.'[34]

The creation of independent Wesleyan churches was touted as an ideal; however, this ignored the reality that British Wesleyans did not have the colonial field to themselves. Not only did they face rivalry from other British Nonconformists, but in North America there was vigorous competition from the American Methodist churches. While the WMMS was slowly extricating itself from colonial engagements in Australia and New Zealand, the home missionary movement in the United States was supplanting the influence of the British churches

[32] *The Twenty-Third Report of the Auxiliary Wesleyan Missionary Society of New South Wales, 1843–4* (Sydney: Kemp and Fairfax, 1841), p. 13 [Reports of the Missionary Societies, p. 669].

[33] *The Twentieth Report of the Auxiliary Wesleyan Missionary Society of New South Wales, 1840* (Sydney: Kemp and Fairfax, 1841), pp. 4–5 [Reports of the Missionary Societies, pp. 560 and 561].

[34] 'Missionary Notices', *Wesleyan-Methodist Magazine*, 53 (June 1850), p. 669.

among emigrants moving with the western frontier. It was also active in British North America. In the United States, the strongest churches in this internal settlement were those that had been planted most firmly in the older colonies: Congregationalists, Presbyterians and Baptists, as well as the more recently settled American Methodists.[35] Rivalry between the British and the American Wesleyan movement was intense. Indeed, it was war.

Missionary war

Wesleyan Methodism in Canada was subjected to particular strain as it addressed the competing claims of the American churches and those that remained connected with the British tradition.[36] The contestation between various branches of Nonconformity in Canada reflects much deeper tensions than mere sectarian rivalry. In determining whom they should give their loyalties to, Canadian Methodists were confronted with the same conflicts that had led to rebellion and republicanism south of the border. Indeed, as Colin Read has argued, clashes between Baptists and Methodists with opposing loyalties to the American and British Connexions were significant antecedents to the rising in western Upper Canada in 1837–8.[37]

This justifies a little excursion into the history of Methodism in the United States. In his lifetime, John Wesley had sent preachers to the American colonies but they had all been ordered to return when the American Revolution began. Although the Reverend Thomas Coke returned as Wesley's chosen supervisor of the American church, the subsequent expansion of Methodism was almost entirely initiated by native-born Americans. Americans were also active in extending the church on the western and northern frontiers of both the United States and Canada. The province of Upper Canada (now Ontario) was initially settled by United Empire Loyalists who began arriving after 1783. Despite their British loyalism, it was the New York Methodist Conference that sent ministers to the settlers along the St Lawrence River and later the Niagara circuit. These circuits were served by fit, active men (and sometimes their wives) working the itinerant system set up by John Wesley. As Henry Crofts could testify, they needed physical stamina for long journeys on horseback and psychological toughness

---

[35] Latourette, *Expansion of Christianity*, vol. 7, pp. 175–223. See also C. B. Goodykoontz, *Home Missions on the American Frontier* (Caldwell, ID, 1939).

[36] G. F. Playter, *The History of Methodism in Canada* (Toronto, 1862).

[37] C. Read, *The Rising in Western Upper Canada, 1837–8: The Duncombe Revolt and After* (Toronto, 1982), p. 185.

for the equally long absences from their families.[38] In the peace that followed the war of 1812 with France, British emigration to Lower Canada
was encouraged in order to secure British control of its new province,
bringing with it many new Methodists as settlers.[39] The newly formed
Wesleyan Methodist Missionary Society was also anxious to send missionaries to Canada along with their agents who were being despatched
to other mission fields. This soon led to conflict with the existing missionary arrangements of the American Church. In what has been called
the 'missionary war', American and British Methodists vied for control
of the rich pickings of the Canadian mission fields.[40] This was partly
resolved in 1820 when a compact was signed which ceded the occupation of Upper Canada to the Americans and Lower Canada to the
English Conference. This was a concession to the greater strength of
the American church, which at this stage had 3,000 members compared with some 744 controlled by the English. Further difficulties followed as the Methodists in both Canadas resisted their incorporation
by the British Conference.

The Union of the Methodist Episcopal Church and the Wesleyans,
and the subsequent formation of the Wesleyan Methodist Church of
Canada in 1833, led to closer ties with Britain and the arrival of a series
of English Presidents for the Canadian Conference. Unhappy with the
loss of the independence of local preachers, a group chose to reject the
Union and form a breakaway Methodist Episcopal Church in Canada;
they eventually rejoined the Wesleyan Methodist Church in 1847. A
more distinctive Canadian colonial nationalism was encouraged with
the unification of Upper and Lower Canada in 1841, though tensions
between English and American strands of Methodism continued to be
expressed. Branches of English Methodism, including the Primitive
Methodists and the Bible Christians, had missionary programmes in
Canada that ensured that controversies and excitement from English
Methodism were seeded in British North America. In 1884, these divisions were resolved in a Union of Canadian Methodism that incorporated all the strands of Methodism into a single church.

When the Methodist Church of Canada celebrated the centenary
of Canadian Methodism in 1884, it had become firmly established as
the largest Protestant Church in Canada. As the *Centennial History*
exulted: 'What hath God wrought? To Him let all praise be given! Who
could have predicted that in the ninetieth year of its age in Canada,

---

[38] K. A. Moyer, *My Saddle Was My Study: The Story of the Methodist Saddlebag Preachers
of Upper Canada* (Elmira, Ontario, 1974).
[39] *Centennial History of Canadian Methodism* (Toronto, 1891), p. 67.
[40] S. D. Clark, *Church and Sect in Canada* (Toronto, 1948), p. 199.

Methodism would occupy a position numerically in advance of all the Protestant Churches of the Dominion?'[41] From 1871 until 1884, while the population increased by 25 per cent, the number of Methodists had increased by 35 per cent. From this position of strength, the General Conference of Canadian Methodists began to take full responsibility for its own church extension work using the language of imperial expansion. An address to the General Conference in 1883 decried the waste created by Methodist division, and applauded efforts to direct church resources to the North-West and its swelling tides of emigrants from the older provinces and the Old World: 'It is an hour of highest privilege and duty. We are laying the foundations of empire in righteousness and truth. We are moulding the institutions of the future; we are shaping the destiny of the country. The heralds of the Cross must follow the adventurous pioneer to the remotest settlement of the Saskatchewan, the Qu'Appelle, and the Peace River, and the vast region beyond.'[42] By the time of the centenary of Canadian Methodist Missions (1924), there is a notable shift in self-perception of Canadian Methodists, which places them alongside central events in Canadian history – Methodist lay preachers, for example, are said to have come to Quebec in the army of General Wolfe and hence participated in the British conquest.[43] The formation of new Methodist communities is depicted by Stephenson not as the result of missionary overtures from Britain, but as the response to invitations from settlers.[44] Canada is no longer at the frontier of missionary efforts but (as in maps that feature as endpapers of the centenary history) is the centre for a thrusting outward missionary movement of her own.

Independent Wesleyan Methodist churches

Of all the major British churches, the British Methodist Conference was probably the most eager to ensure that its colonial missions were transformed into independent national churches. The elevation of the Australasian Wesleyan Methodist Conference in 1855, like the establishment of the Canadian Conference the year before (1854), and that of the Cape and Natal in 1882, put these churches on a footing of significantly greater independence from the metropole than the other large

---

[41] *Centennial History*, p. 301.

[42] J. Woodsworth, *Thirty Years in the Canadian North-West* (Toronto, 1917).

[43] F. C. Stephenson, *One Hundred Years of Canadian Methodist Missions, 1824–1924*, 2 vols. (Toronto, 1925), p. 39.

[44] For example, *ibid.*, pp. 20 and 34, notes appeals to the British Conference as the source of Methodist beginnings in New Brunswick, Montreal and elsewhere.

denominational presences in the Australian colonies, the Church of England and the Catholic Church. Reflecting this numerical success, in Australia, New Zealand and Canada, Wesleyans made claims to the colonial government for recognising them, rather than the Anglicans or Catholics, as the Church with the most flexible and thrifty organisation and hence the one best fitted to carry the aspirations of the emerging nations of Greater Britain. In 1846, William B. Boyce, Chairman of the Wesleyan Church in Australasia, wrote to the Colonial Secretary pointing out the Wesleyans had effectively covered not only the towns but also the rural districts of a vast territory. They understood how to create an effective colonial ministry which deployed lay agents, rather than an expensively educated professional ministry, and sustained a thrifty itinerant system instead of costly churches: 'To the Colonial Government, and to the colonists, the Wesleyan ministers feel that they have not been unprofitable servants.'[45] In their tussles with Anglicans in New Zealand, Wesleyans asserted the same view that theirs was the most effective church for the colonial world and that New Zealand had no need of an established church.

An important mark of independence of the colonial churches was their commitment to taking on responsibility for other foreign mission work, especially in their region. The motivation for this was both financial and practical. When the Australasian Conference took over the work, they reported at the first Conference that nearly £5,000 had been raised to support foreign missions with another £1,400 raised by children to equip the missionary brig, *John Wesley*.[46] The work of these missions was published in the newly independent Conference's *Missionary Notices*, and it is significant that these no longer contained news of the colonial work of setting up settler chapels and circuits.[47] Letters from missionaries in the field were now directed at potential labourers from the colonial churches: 'Are there not young men in all Australasia who will come to the help of the Lord against the mighty? *Others will fall unless aid is rendered*', pleaded the Reverend J. Waterhouse on behalf of the missionaries in Fiji.[48]

---

[45] Boyce to Colonial Secretary, 10 October 1846. Enclosure 3, in Despatch from Governor Sir C. Fitzroy to Earl Grey, in House of Commons, *Colonial Church Legislation. Part III, New South Wales*, 7 vols., vol. 3 (London, 1852), p. 18.

[46] J. E. Carruthers, *Lights in the Southern Sky: Pen Portraits of Australian Methodism with Some Sketches from Life of Humbler Workers* (Sydney, 1924), p. 31.

[47] *The Wesleyan Missionary Notices, Relating to the Missions under the Direction of the Australasian Wesleyan Methodist Conference* (Sydney: F. M. Stokes, 1857–78) [D. S. Mitchell Collection, DSM/279/W].

[48] 'Meeting of the Board of Missions, Pitt Street, Sydney, Oct. 12th, 1876', *The Wesleyan Missionary Notices … of the Australasian Wesleyan Methodist Conference*, 1 January 1877, p. 89. Letter of Reverend J. Waterhouse, dated Hobart Town, 8 June 1858, *The*

This was the ideal towards which the home society had aspired: the colonial church, established by missionaries in the 1820s and 1830s, was itself responsible for foreign missions. Australian Methodists were encouraged by news that their efforts, including the evangelisation of Chinese in Victoria and New South Wales, were 'favourably noticed' at the London Conference of British Methodists.[49] 'We would call upon our friends in the Southern hemisphere to emulate the Churches in our fatherland in the spirit of self-sacrifice with which they support and extend their Foreign missions at the time in which they are making vigorous efforts to consolidate and promote their Home work.'[50] Foreign missions, particularly among the startlingly different cannibals of Fiji and warriors of New Zealand, were one of the measures by which the Australasian Connexion demonstrated the distance it had travelled from its own missionary origins. If the colonial mission of the Wesleyan Methodists could be reduced to a single purpose, it was the creation of independent churches in the colonies that had the capacity to support foreign missions beyond their own shores. In WMMS missionary literature, this appeal was given additional weight by an appeal to patriotism and imperial duty. Nevertheless, as the clash between British and American Methodists for control of Lower Canada indicates, this led in some cases to conflicts more characteristic of tussles between colonists in more secular contexts.

Colonial Missionary Society

Such conflict between Christians, fuelled by competition for funding from the state, was anathema to Congregationalists. Their own colonial mission work followed quite a different path to that of the Methodists. The Colonial Missionary Society was established in 1836, partly at the instigation of Thomas Binney (1798–1834), in order to provide institutional support for Congregational clergy, churches and schools in British colonies. The formation of the Society arose in the context of the agitation against state endowments for churches, clergy and schools in Britain, part of what Stoughton calls the 'excitement of the age'.[51] This led ultimately to the disestablishment of the Church of England in Ireland and later in Wales. It also had the effect of encouraging religious emigration to colonies, which were free from what was perceived

Wesleyan Missionary Notices … of the Australasian Wesleyan Methodist Conference, July 1858, p. 79.

[49] Editorial, *Wesleyan Missionary Notices … of the Australasian Wesleyan Methodist Conference*, July 1859, p. 129.

[50] *Ibid.*, pp. 129–30.

[51] Stoughton, *Religion in England*, pp. 102 and 112–13.

to be the evil of church establishments. Unfortunately, little has survived of the Society's nineteenth-century archives, including almost all records relating to individual missionaries. This account is therefore based largely on published accounts of the society, and formal records of their meetings.[52]

Like the two Evangelical societies which came together to form the Colonial and Continental Church Society (CCCS), the Colonial Missionary Society was formed in response to the needs of a particular colony. Initially, this was French-dominated Lower Canada. On 20 December 1827, on the suggestion of the Reverend J. S. Christmas, the minister of the American Church in Montreal, a meeting was held to establish the Canada Education and Home Missionary Society. This was originally an interdenominational effort made up of Presbyterians, Baptists and Congregationalists in the manner of the interdenominational London Missionary Society. It was intended to support colonial missions in the same way that the LMS supported missions to the heathen.[53] By 1832, with the city of Montreal afflicted by a major outbreak of cholera and the Baptists and Presbyterians losing interest in its work, the Society was in difficulties. Action by the church in Britain was required. A series of deputations were sent to both Lower and Upper Canada in 1834 and there was also correspondence with churchmen in Van Diemen's Land in order to achieve a more coordinated international effort.

The creation of the Colonial Missionary Society was one of the first major successes of the Congregationalist Union. First proposed in 1811, the Union was only established in 1831 but took some years to be accepted. On Binney's initiative, a general meeting of the Union was held on 10 May 1836 which proposed the formation of 'a Colonial Missionary Society to establish Churches of our denomination in the British Colonies'.[54] The first secretary was Algernon Wells, the man to whom Richard Brown gives the credit for saving the Congregationalist Union and putting it on a sound economic basis.[55] One of his

---

[52] Commonwealth Missionary Society archive, London, School of Oriental and African Studies, London University. According to the CWM website, www.cwmission.org/history/overview-of-the-cwm-archive/page-5–2.html: 'Records include Board minutes (1836–1869 and 1899–1967), committee minutes (from early 20th century), home correspondence and subject files, and regional correspondence and subject files. Regional materials relate to Australia, Canada, Guyana, Jamaica, New Zealand, South Africa and the USA (all 20th century).'

[53] J. Brown, *The Colonial Missions of Congregationalism: The Story of Seventy Years* (London, 1908), p. 15. See also G. Walker, *Our Sons Far Away: A Century of Colonial Missions* (London, 1936).

[54] Brown, *Colonial Missions of Congregationalism*, p. 21.

[55] Brown, *Church and State*, p. 447.

contemporaries sniffs that Wells was rather inclined to weep on public occasions when carried away with the emotion of some cause, or if his plans were frustrated.[56] But he was a good organiser who succeeded in bringing together the fissiparous Congregationalists to provide the necessary infrastructure to enable new Congregations to be planted in the colonies. Following the establishment of the society, work began almost immediately and the first ministers were despatched to Canada following a service in Poultry Chapel, London, on 7 April 1837. By degrees, the work was extended from British North America to include Canada, Guyana, Jamaica, New Zealand, South Africa and the United States. Like the LMS, the Colonial Missionary Society operated according to the sacred 'voluntary principle' under which missionary work, and indeed any church work, was to be conducted free of government financial assistance. As Donaldson demonstrates in the case of the Reverend Richard Birt, LMS missionary in South Africa from 1838 to 1892, these principles could make it virtually impossible to establish a mission in the colonial frontier, especially when it was necessary to try to build a financial support base and educational infrastructure and sustain a mission on the basis of an impoverished and vacillating native population.[57] In colonies of British settlement, it was rather easier to get things going. But, in the absence of a culture of voluntary contributions, colonial Congregationalism proved to be a rather fragile plant which sought to advance the evangelical cause by cooperation with like-minded Protestants in other churches.

Binney's role is significant both for the establishment of the Colonial Missionary Society and for the imperial expansion of Congregationalism. The great work of Binney's life was that of unifying the Protestant churches and challenging what he saw as the evil of church establishment. In his lifetime he was regarded as a kind of archbishop of Nonconformity, 'the most honestly popular of any metropolitan preacher', as he is called by his biographer, Edwin Paxton Hood.[58] Binney saw a special role for Congregationalists in bringing Christians together for vital projects, such as the British and Foreign Anti-Slavery Society;[59] he was deeply interested in emigration and the mission of

[56] Stoughton, *Religion in England*, p. 113.
[57] M. Donaldson, 'The Voluntary Principle in the Colonial Situation: Theory and Practice', in *Studies in Church History*, ed. W. J. Sheils and D. Wood (Oxford, 1986), p. 381.
[58] E. P. Hood, *The Lamps of the Temple: Shadows from the Lights of the Modern Pulpit* (1852), p. 52; E. P. Hood, *Thomas Binney: His Mind, Life and Opinions* (London, 1874).
[59] C. Binfield, 'Thomas Binney and Congregationalism's "Special Mission"', *Transactions of the Congregational Historical Society*, 21 (1971), pp. 1–10.

Congregationalism in the English-speaking world, visiting Canada and the United States in 1845 and Australia in 1857–9, and, as we have seen, fostering the establishment of the Colonial Missionary Society. Two of his sons emigrated to Victoria and his former assistant, the celebrated preacher Llewelyn D. Bevan, came to Melbourne to serve as the minister of its central Congregationalist church.[60] Binney travelled to Australia to convalesce after an illness, and, though he did not intend to write a book about his travels there, he did publish a record of his correspondence with Augustus Short, the Anglican bishop of Adelaide, and his hopes for what he calls the 'church of the future'.[61]

Binney's debate with Short can be read as something of a charter of principles for a post-establishment Protestant faith to be raised up in the colonies. Above all, Binney preached a church that would be united and not divided by petty religious differences: 'Anything that leads to united religious action – to co-operative effort, aggressive, missionary, or whatever form it may take – anything that leads to this, among men who, while adhering to different forms of Church organisation, are one in faith, must be good.'[62] For Binney, the colonies provided a vision of what such a united church of the future might be – one in which the Church of England was 'one denomination among many', stripped of all pretensions to being a national Church which served – or rather dominated – the nation at large.[63] Binney poured considerable scorn on the idea of a national church for the colonies, pointing out that there was little indication that the Presbyterians, Wesleyans, Independents and other churches would ever abandon their independence and submit to English bishops.[64] The colonial mind, Binney declared, was naturally democratic and would reject any such arrangement.[65] Short, in his reply to Binney, was inclined to demur that the leadership of bishops was not incompatible with wise, consultative leadership, as the thirty colonial dioceses, and the standing of the Episcopal church in the United States, could testify. In relation to colonial missionary societies, Binney argued that they should be supported on two grounds: as a service to emigrants who wished to continue to know the Church of their fathers, but also as part of what he calls 'the great Christian Household, with a Gospel

[60] 'Binney, Thomas (1798–1874)', *Australian Dictionary of Biography*, pp. 164–5. See also R. Tudur Jones, 'Binney, Thomas (1798–1874)', *Oxford Dictionary of National Biography*.

[61] T. Binney, *Lights and Shadows of Church-Life in Australia*, 2nd edn (London, 1860). For an account of Binney in Australia, see B. Dickey, 'Thomas Binney in South Australia, 1858–1859', *Lucas: An Evangelical History Review* (1991).

[62] Binney, *Lights and Shadows*, pp. xxii–xxiii.

[63] *Ibid.*, p. xxx.   [64] *Ibid.*, p. xxxv.   [65] *Ibid.*, p. 146.

to preach, and a mission to fulfil … that, with our land's language, laws, literature, institutions, might be propagated and preserved her Evangelical Protestant Christianity'.[66] For Binney, the work of 'evangelising Australia' was a sacred task which was necessarily a shared duty.[67]

South Australia

Congregationalists and other Nonconformists played a central role in South Australia, a colony which fulfilled a number of their conditions for an ideal settlement. Unlike the other Australian colonies (with the original exception of Western Australia), South Australia was seen to be uniquely blessed because it had never been burdened with convict labour. There was no established church; all religions were tolerated there, and all its settlers were free.[68] While it was probably going too far to call it a 'paradise of dissent' (the title of the major history of the colony), Nonconformity flourished there better than anywhere else in Australia. This was due in part to the work of the Colonial Missionary Society, but mostly to the efforts of George Fife Angas (1789–1879), the Baptist merchant and philanthropist who played a leading role in the settlement of the colony.[69]

The first official agent of the Colonial Missionary Society, the Reverend Thomas Quinton Stow, was despatched to South Australia at Angas' expense. While not a colonial chaplain – like all Congregationalists he refused to accept government funding for religious services – Stow was intended to be the official face of Nonconformity in the settlement. He was also expected to set up a financially independent church, what Binney called 'the dependence of religion on Christian willinghood'.[70] Nine vessels departed for South Australia in 1836 with about 500 emigrants on board. Mr Stow and his party arrived in October 1837. Making use of a field-officer's marquee provided by the Colonial Missionary Society, Stow held his first service on the river bank.[71] His initial reports were rapturous: 'What a land is this to which you have sent me! The loveliness and glory of its plains and woods, its glens and hills! – its climate also, which is salubrious and delightful!' Other emigrants arrived from Britain, and more from New South Wales, Van Diemen's

---

[66] *Ibid.*, p. 116.   [67] *Ibid.*, p. 118.
[68] D. Pike, *Paradise of Dissent: South Australia, 1829–1857* (Melbourne, 1967).
[69] Brown, *Colonial Missions of Congregationalism*, p. 64.
[70] Binney quoted by Pike, *Paradise of Dissent*, p. 144.
[71] King, *Ten Decades*.

Land and the Swan River Colony.[72] From South Australia, a deacon of Mr Stowe's church in Adelaide advised that stations could be found at once for half a dozen ministers in South Australia, and 'an unlimited number' for the other colonies. The prospects were unlimited too, especially now that convictism, 'that fatal blight on the fairest prospects, that plague-spot on colonial society', was to cease.[73] Although the impact of religious dissent in South Australia was ultimately relatively small,[74] the scheme has considerable importance as a model for later plans for the more ambitious religious settlements in New Zealand based on the principles of Edward Gibbon Wakefield.

Funding for the dissenting settlers in South Australia and the other work of the Colonial Missionary Society was supported from 1840 by means of joint collections in all Congregationalist churches in the month of October. The proceeds from this collection were divided between the Home Missionary Society, the Colonial Missionary Society and the Irish Evangelical Society. From 1840 to 1878, the amount collected in this way was £40,000, although takings in any one year varied considerably.[75] This was roughly two-thirds of the amount that was raised by the CCCS in the same period and reflects the small scale of Congregationalist-led settlements in the colonies. Not surprisingly, in 1878, when the sum collected dropped to less than £700, arrangements for an annual collection ceased altogether. In the second half of the nineteenth century, rather more direct methods were adopted to bring out the trained clergy and schoolteachers required by particular congregations.

John Legg Poore

For the Australian colonies, the chief recruiting agent was John Legg Poore (1816–67).[76] Described by Gunson as the 'John Wesley of Congregationalism' in Australia, he took as his life's work the development of the colonial church.[77] Poore was ordained in 1839 after studying

---

[72] Brown, *Colonial Missions of Congregationalism*, p. 69.
[73] King, *Ten Decades*.
[74] By 1900, Methodists made up a quarter of the population of South Australia, the highest proportion in the Empire outside of Wales. See R. B. Walker, 'Methodism in the "Paradise of Dissent", 1837–1900', *Journal of Religious History*, 5 (2007), pp. 331–47. For England and Wales, see R. B. Walker, 'The Growth of Wesleyan Methodism in Victorian England and Wales', *Journal of Ecclesiastical History*, 24 (1973), pp. 267–84.
[75] Brown, *Colonial Missions of Congregationalism*, p. 111.
[76] Niel Gunson, 'Poore, John Legg (1816–1867)', *Australian Dictionary of Biography*, vol. 5, pp. 450–1.
[77] *Ibid.*

for the Congregational ministry at Yeovil Academy and Highbury College. Binney had sparked off Poore's interest in the Colonial Missionary Society and it was this which brought him to Melbourne in 1854. According to a speech which he made to the annual meeting of the Congregational Home Missionary Society in Sydney in 1859, Poore had lectured in England to some 50,000 people, collecting funds and seeking ministers who might be willing to go out to the colonies. Following recruiting drives to England in 1857, 1858 and 1863, he was able to send out twenty-eight ministers, at a cost of £4,500, to serve Australian congregations. Referring to his own methods in securing suitable people for this work, he stated that:

They had had to be hunted up and influenced by various motives; some by earthly, some by heavenly; some yielded to appeals through their families or friends, others by a desire to assist in carrying out the eternal purpose that the world should be filled with an intelligent, civilized, and Christian race.[78]

Poore's estimate of the overall success rate of the ministers he had brought to the colonies is perhaps a fair reflection of the success of the project of clerical migration generally. Of the twenty-eight ministers who had come over, two had died, four had returned home for personal or domestic reasons, one had returned 'on account of his inaptness and unfitness for service in the colonies', and another seems to have simply chosen to do something else.[79] This gives a failure rate of eight out of twenty-eight or 28.5 per cent. Poore became secretary of the Colonial Missionary Society in 1864 and was in Canada in 1865. He may have had other imperial projects in mind because, at the time of his death in 1867, he was planning to return to England.

Reports of Congregational work were published from both the LMS and the Colonial Missionary Society in the non-denominational *Evangelical Magazine* as well as colonial journals and newspapers.[80] Married to the new pattern of direct recruitment, we can see a change in the main vehicle for publicising the work of the Society, namely, *British Missions*, one in which much greater stress was played on the notion of an imperial destiny for the colonies enriched by the blessing of evangelical religion. *British Missions* was the combined report of the three Congregationalist societies which dealt with missions to

---

[78] *The Tenth Annual Report of the Congregational Home Missionary Society, for New South Wales, 1859–60* (Sydney: Reading and Wellbank, 1860), p. 10 (*Reports of Missionary Societies* (n. 15 above), p. 878).

[79] *Ibid.*, p. 10 (*Reports of Missionary Societies* (n. 15 above), p. 878).

[80] The *Evangelical Magazine* was published by Chapman from 1793 to 1813; then as the *Evangelical Magazine and Missionary Chronicle* from 1813 to 1904; then as the *British Missionary* from 1917 to 1956.

Christians: the Home Missionary Society, the Irish Evangelical Society and the Colonial Missionary Society.[81] In 1853, the three societies, which shared a common board of directors, though with separate treasurers and secretaries, met together in Poultry and Finsbury Chapels on 9, 10 and 19 May for their annual meeting.[82]

The directors' report provides a powerful depiction of colonial missions, and the tragedy of depopulation in Ireland, as part of a great Providential engine of change. 'All the world is moving', it reported, and the great exodus of people, including the Irish peasantry, was but a means to an end. Even the gold rushes were seen as part of a divine plan in which the emigration of people of all classes (but especially the 'sober, industrious and religious') would be transformed from the dependent colonies into 'powerful empires and sister kingdoms' united by trade, language, law and religion with the mother country. This, it goes on to state, was an epoch unparalleled since the Reformation, when the Protestant Church and the Anglo-Saxon family were poised to excel the conquests and achievements of Alexander, Caesar and Napoleon. 'Let the missionary spirit awake to its exalted destiny!', it exults, before making a straightforward appeal to British patriotism:

> Englishmen everywhere, faithful and free,
> Lords of the land, and kings of the sea,
> Anglo-Saxons, honest and true,
> By hundreds of millions, my word is to you:
> Love one another, as brothers in grace,
> That the world may be bless'd in the Saxon race.[83]

Buoyed by such hopes, the Society could report on expansion and success.

The seventeenth annual meeting of the Colonial Missionary Society, held in the Poultry Chapel on 9 May 1852, was chaired by the Lord Mayor, and the list of directors was headed by the names of Reverend Thomas Binney and Reverend J. B. Brown. The report of the meeting is extremely optimistic. There was 'devout thankfulness' that, over the previous two years, some ten missionaries had been sent out. The appeals from Australia had been urgent: 'Send us', they say, 'able and energetic men – your best men, and they will soon gather around them numerous and interesting congregations.'[84] The Committee had

[81] Stoughton, *Religion in England*.

[82] *British Missions: Comprising the 34th Annual Report of the Home Missionary Society; the 39th Annual Report of the Irish Evangelical Society; and the 17th Annual Report of the Colonial Missionary Society* (London, 1853).

[83] *Ibid.*, p. 4.   [84] *Ibid.*, p. 145.

deputed J. C. Gallaway to pay a visit to the churches in British North America, the results of which were reported in an appendix: in summary, in the Canadas, Nova Scotia and New Brunswick, 90 Congregational churches, numbering between 3,000 and 4,000 members, 85 places of worship, besides over 3,000 children attending Sabbath-schools and between 300 and 400 teachers, all paid for on the voluntary principle. There were two colleges: one at Toronto exclusively for training for the ministry, the other at Liverpool, Nova Scotia. Besides the European settlers, in western Canada the society was undertaking work among refugees from the United States, many of them former slaves. The Society had existed for only seventeen years, but in that time had seen Congregationalism grow from six or seven churches in the whole of Canada to its current condition. Other parts of the British empire were also calling for support: Port Elizabeth in the Cape of Good Hope, and Durban, the seaport town in the infant colony of Port Natal, which was given some assistance. There was more work for the Society in Australia as a result of the gold discoveries.

Yet, despite Binney's stated horror of denominational division, it seems undeniable that the work of the Colonial Missionary Society was intended as much to plant and extend Congregationalism in the colonies as to support the work of the gospel. 'If suitable ministers of our own body are not sent, our brethren will either be absorbed by other denominations, or, which would be infinitely worse, be corrupted by the deteriorating influences of colonial life, and lose the power, and perhaps the very profession of religion altogether.'[85] In statements such as this it was openly suggested that the conditions of colonial life were in themselves corrupting. The Congregationalists considered that they had a special, Christian mission in relation to colonisation. The 'British Churches of our faith' had an enormous responsibility:

They can conceive of nothing of greater moment. The salvation of the world depends in no small degree on the evangelization of our colonies. To what are to be attributed the high character of the New England States of America, and the mighty efforts that noble country is putting forth for the well-being of the world, but to the piety, the learning, and the zeal of the 'Pilgrim Fathers'. Let such men be sent to our Australian colonies, and a mighty influence will be exerted over the heathen nations in their proximity. Polynesia, India, and China, are nearer to them than to Britain: and should that vast island-continent be peopled and Christianized, what an impetus will be given to the efforts put forth for the conversion of the teeming millions of those vast empires.

[85] *Ibid.*, p. 150.

These were seen as powerful arguments. The special Australian Fund was generously subscribed and secured £3,072, of which £300 had come from the churches of Sydney, 'thus giving demonstrative evidence that the colonists are prepared to help'.[86]

Perhaps the most striking feature of the Colonial Missionary Society mid-century is how grand is its rhetoric, and how substantial and well funded its operations, when compared to what, in colonies such as New South Wales, turns out to be quite a small legacy. The Congregationalists are much the smallest of the three evangelical churches that eventually formed the Uniting Church of Australia and its North American equivalent, the United Church of Canada. There seems a general disproportion between the ambitions of the Society as expressed in its annual reports, and the actual business of creating churches and communities in the colonies. From the 1860s, most of the missionary societies began to demand that the new, independent colonial churches should take on responsibility for the extension of work among British settlers and also missions in their region. For the Congregationalists, this included the work of inland missions to isolated rural settlers in Australia and foreign missions to the Society's missions in the Pacific. In 1861, the LMS's 'Juvenile Missionary Society' changed its name to the 'Bush Missionary Society' (and, in 1862, to the New South Wales Bush Missionary Society) and declared its object to be the extension of opportunities for Christian education.[87] This work included the establishment of Sabbath-schools and, if there were sufficient numbers, preaching stations in the interior of the colony. Following the model of travelling missionaries in the United States, the Society had engaged a missionary to sell or give away copies of the Bible and other books and tracts and to read the Scripture, 'to those who would permit him to do so'. The Congregational Church also supported a Home Missionary Society for New South Wales, whose original purpose was 'introducing from England men fitted for the ministerial work in this Colony, and also to assist in sustaining ministers after their arrival. A third object was to send the Gospel by the best means within their reach to the distant bush.'[88]

In the Edwardian twilight of the British empire, the same imperial enthusiasm apparent in the SPG under the leadership of bishop

---

[86] *Ibid.*, pp. 150–1.

[87] *The Fifth Annual Report of the Juvenile Missionary Society, Now Changed to the Bush Missionary Society, 1861* (Sydney: G. R. Addison, 1861), pp. 5–6 [Reports of the Missionary Societies, pp. 825–6].

[88] *The Tenth Annual Report of the Congregational Home Missionary Society for New South Wales, 1859–60* (Sydney: Reading and Wellbank, 1860), p. 7 [Reports of the Missionary Societies, p. 875].

Montgomery came to characterise the Colonial Missionary Society. Like all missionary societies, the CMS had publicised its activities in a series of journals from its foundation in 1858.[89] While never hostile to the general imperial cause, a new, more jingoist strand of Congregationalism comes to be reflected in the *British Missionary*, which was a continuation of the venerable non-denominational *Evangelical Magazine*, founded in 1792.[90] In 1913, correspondents affirmed the value of colonial missions, and decried the fashion for prioritising missions to non-Christians. A Canadian settler is said to have declared:

> Talk of 'missions to the heathen': why, right here, within our own Empire, there are people of all nationalities thrown together. Here is a nation in the making.[91]

The same correspondent called for ministers with the spirit of the frontiersman about them: 'We don't want your weak-kneed tea-drinking type of parson here. We want robust men, who, in greatness of heart, will compare favourably with the Lumber Jack of the logging camp, or the labourer in the construction gang.'[92] Stanley W. Edwards declared that the work conducted by the Colonial Missionary Society was the religious equivalent of Dr Barnardo's work for young children, which was encouraging the flow of 'young, vigorous life' into Greater Britain. Before such emigrants lost their enthusiasm for religion, he argued, the Society had to ensure that churches were already in place to capture their hearts and minds: 'The work of Colonial Missions is a factor in Empire-building. It is generating that force which will safeguard the vigorous, independent colonial life from decay by bringing to bear upon that life the spirit of Christ. It is an imperial task.'[93] As to the relation between foreign and colonial missions, there was no conflict: 'Colonial Missions are endeavouring to keep Christian those who have come under Christian influences, while Foreign Missions are seeking to win

---

[89] In addition to the annual reports of the Colonial Missionary Society (1837–1955), the Society produced the *Colonial [Missionary] Chronicle: A Quarterly Record of the Transactions of the Colonial Missionary Society* (1858–c.1872).

[90] Like other non-denominational journals, the *Evangelical Magazine* struggled to survive once the missionary societies began to produce their own journals and market them to members of their affiliated churches. It was renamed the *Evangelical British Missionary* (1905–1909), and from 1913 to 1956 was published as the *British Missionary*, with the subtitle 'A Continuation of the Evangelical Magazine Founded 1792'. However, the journal was now an exclusive vehicle for the British Congregationalist Colonial Missionary Society.

[91] 'A Bitter Cry from BC', *British Missionary* (January 1913), p. 16.

[92] *Ibid.*

[93] Stanley W. Edwards, 'An Imperial Task', *British Missionary* (January 1913), p. 9.

those to whom Christianity is something quite new. But ultimately the interests and aim are the same.[94]

As an imperial work, the promotion of colonial missions drew on the iconography of imperial propaganda: illustrations depict scenes of colonial enterprise (breaking up the prairie with a motor plough) and scenic grandeur (the Canadian Rockies), religious service on the *RMS Empress of Britain*, Sunday in the backblocks of New Zealand, and a logging camp congregation in British Columbia. Following his visit to Canada, Daniel Burford Hooke, later Chairman of the Congregational Union of England and Wales (1916–17), presented the colonists as heroes of a gallant enterprise: 'To preach the Gospel to these men is a privilege of which one may well be proud.'[95] In the wheat-belt of Western Australia, the settlers were said to be just as eager for the gospel as they were in Canada. From remote Nungarin in the Australian outback, a young minister reported that a settler had requested a minister and offered to provide the musical accompaniment: 'Is there any chance of a service up our way? You can have the wool-shed for the meeting, and one of the girls can play the piano.'[96]

With the outbreak of war in 1914, this missionary discourse also served to demonstrate imperial patriotism. In a New Year's Greeting, John Eames wrote: 'The sons of the Empire have proved that we have not exaggerated the national and spiritual ties which bind them to the Motherland. The spirit of unity and the sense of solidarity manifest in all the Dominions and Commonwealths of the Empire bring with them a new vision of spiritual possibilities.'[97] Congregationalists across the empire boasted of their readiness for war: 'No English General since Oliver Cromwell had better material', says the Reverend Dr Warriner from the College at Montreal: 'From our own church we have stripped our Christian Endeavour Society of leaders, and nearly every unmarried man of our choir has gone. Gone, as Cromwell said, with a conscience in him. No conscript army can face that kind of men.'[98] In this manner, Nonconformists freely gave their loyalty to both the Church and the state. In the colonies, that loyalty was given to the British empire, which

---

[94] Stanley W. Edwards, 'The Relation of Colonial to Foreign Missions', *British Missionary* (October 1913), p. 107.

[95] D. Burford Hooke, 'A Sunday Visit to a Logging Camp in British Columbia', *British Missionary* (July 1913), p. 58.

[96] 'Opening out the Wheat-Belt of Western Australia', *British Missionary* (October 1913), p. 91.

[97] John Eames, 'A New Year's Greeting', *British Missionary* (January 1916), p. 97.

[98] Letter from Reverend Dr Warriner, Acting Principal of the College at Montreal, *British Missionary* (April 1916), p. 133.

like their religion was a voluntary tie, but one which was all the more powerful for that reason.

Conclusion

It was logical that Nonconformity should be extended through colonial missionary societies into Greater Britain just as it had forged a path to America. However, unlike their predecessors in the New World, the Baptists, Methodists, Congregationalists and Quakers who headed to British colonies in the nineteenth century did so as emigrants rather than exiles. In both the Wesleyan Methodist Missionary Society and the Colonial Church Society, colonial missions were seen as patriotic and worthwhile. However, they also had to contend with the significant number who regarded colonisation as, to some extent, morally compromised because it was born out of an ambition for material prosperity and it was the cause of untold suffering for native people. As with the missions conducted by Evangelical Anglicans for the Colonial and Continental Church Society, the most successful rhetorical strategy for combating this burden was by linking colonial missions to the imperial cause. In Chapter 1, we considered the Anglo-Saxon vision of the Baptist leader, John Clifford. Nevertheless, it is important to recognise that Clifford's vision is a religious one; the Anglo-Saxon empire he sees being lifted up is the empire of Christ, not of man. Clifford's view might be contrasted with that of his fellow Nonconformist, Thomas Binney, for whom the colonies were also full of potential as the crucibles of the Church of the future, one in which the divisions between Christians, and certainly those dividing the established Church from Nonconformists, might wither away.

7   Presbyterians

This is the fifth and final chapter to discuss the workings of the colonial missions of the various Christian churches which operated throughout the British empire. In the course of this section, we have examined two rather different types of society. The first kind was the centrally managed church organisation, such as the Anglican SPG and the Methodist WMMS. Catholic missions were also centrally managed through the joint efforts of Propaganda in Rome, the Catholic hierarchy and the APF (the French-based missionary auxiliary). These organisations were closely associated with their respective churches; they were generally dominated by high-ranking clergy, submitted annual reports to a central organisation which managed the colonial mission as part of a coordinated programme of missionary, welfare, educational and other activities that defined the church. Secondly, there were the voluntary associations; these often included laypeople in their management; they were independent of the churches and sometimes they worked cooperatively to assist the activities of a number of closely related sects. The template for voluntary associations of this kind was the London Missionary Society, which was originally interdenominational though it later came to be dominated by the Congregationalists. In the course of the nineteenth century, those colonial missionary societies which survived tended to lose their independent character and be drawn into the central administrative structure of their associated churches. As we saw in Chapter 5, this was the fate of the two Evangelical societies which merged to form the Anglican Colonial and Continental Church Society (CCCS): the Newfoundland School Society and the Colonial Church Society, as well as the Congregationalist Colonial Missionary Society.

We now come to the colonial missions of the Church of Scotland and we find that they follow the pattern of English societies such as the LMS and the CMS, though with some critical Scottish complications.

Early in the nineteenth century, the largest Scottish colonial missionary society was the Glasgow Colonial Society, a voluntary association outside the central control of the Church of Scotland. This situation proved to be untenable, and tensions about the control of missions were one factor which contributed to the Disruption of 1843, during which two-fifths of the ministers of the Church of Scotland, including all its missionaries and most of those engaged in evangelical outreach in poor parishes, left the established church. After the Disruption, there were, therefore, not one, but two, 'schemes' (as the missionary committees of the Scottish churches were known) for colonial missionary work: one supported by the established, and another by the Free Church of Scotland, each reporting to its own General Assembly.[1] A third substantial colonial mission was conducted by the Presbyterian Church in Ireland. For the Free Church, colonial missions became an important measure of its success and growth as an independent church, justifying its decision to sunder the established church. As we will see in this chapter, the struggle between free and established colonial schemes formed part of a battle to be accepted as the legitimate spiritual vehicle for the Scottish Reformed church overseas. Part national assertion, part Christian mission, part aspiration for a better way of life than that afforded by the starving and decaying hamlets of rural Scotland, the history of the colonial mission of the Church of Scotland encapsulates the whole story of Scottish emigration to Greater Britain.

Antecedents

In the earliest Scottish efforts at colonisation, religion was no more significant than for the English colonists who preceded them to the New World by a century or so.[2] Religion has traditionally been seen as a primary motivation for many of the colonial settlements established by English Puritans in the seventeenth century, including those at New Plymouth, Salem, Connecticut and Rhode Island, and the island of Santa Katalina (Providence), off South America. But, prior to the British Union, Scottish Covenanters, though locked equally in religious antagonism with an established church, seem to have been less inclined to flee British shores in pursuit of religious freedom.[3]

---

[1] It is possible that colonial schemes were also supported by the smaller Scottish churches, for example Ebenezer Erskine's Secession Church (1733) or Thomas Gillespie's Relief Church (1761) and their later unions, but I have not found records relating to this. The Scottish Episcopal Church was originally included in the SSPCK; it was instrumental in the formation of the American Episcopal Church and occasionally cooperated with the SPG. See Pascoe, *Two Hundred Years of the SPG*, pp. 312–13 and 350–1.

[2] G. P. Insh, *Scottish Colonial Schemes 1620–1686* (Glasgow, 1922), pp. 2–3.

[3] *Ibid.*, pp. 22–3, attributes this to differences in the English (more prudent) and Scottish (more dogged) temperaments.

Nevertheless, there were a number of Scottish Quakers who went to the New World, where they settled in the English colony of East Jersey, as well as Scottish colonial schemes for Newfoundland, Nova Scotia and Stuart's Town, South Carolina. Religion was important to these Scottish exiles, who sometimes linked it to the promise of a better life. Letters from Scottish settlers in East Jersey included pleas that 'good and Faithful Ministers' might be encouraged to travel to join them: 'they can live as well, and have as much as in Scotland, and more than many get', wrote the Quaker Peter Watson to his cousin in 1684.[4] James Johnstone also urged his brother John, a druggist in Edinburgh, to send them some ministers, 'for the encouragement of this Plantation'.[5] While the colonists were primarily interested in securing those things which would ensure the financial viability of the colony, ministers were desirable as bearers of religion, civilisation and Scottish national heritage. They helped mark rites of passage which would otherwise receive no Christian blessing in the wilderness.

Never very large, this piecemeal emigration to America from Scotland came to an abrupt halt in about 1650 and did not resume for 100 years. By this time, massive problems of social unrest, poverty, class tension and rural decay had combined to destroy the old comforts of clan and covenant. For many Scottish church leaders, the best solution to this situation was escape from Scotland and her woes. Eric Richards notes that Scottish clergy were at the forefront of what he calls the 'orchestration of communal emigration'.[6] This emigration was mostly based in the countryside rather than the cities, with emigrants sourced from the north of England and Scotland. They proceeded to the New World in groups of up to 400 or so and were often connected by chains of family, locality and religious affiliation. Clergy promoted emigration from Scotland as a way to find a homeland where communities who had been displaced by industrialisation and rural dislocation might sustain their religious traditions. This type of emigration accelerated after the end of the Napoleonic wars and grew to become a mass movement.

It is worth pausing to say something more about the nature of the Scottish contribution to empire. Like Ireland, in the early modern era Scotland was perennially associated in the English imagination with rebellion and religious radicalism whether by Catholic Jacobites or Protestant Reformers. With the passage of the Act of Union in 1707, the invention of Britishness, as Linda Colley has argued, was achieved

---

[4] Peter Watson to John Watson, New Perth, 20 August 1684, in *ibid.*, p. 248.
[5] James Johnstone to John Johnstone, East Jersey, 12 December 1684, in *ibid.*, p. 244.
[6] Richards, *Britannia's Children*, p. 104.

partly by Scottish collusion in the 'British' overseas empire – an empire that they played a large part in creating.[7] Scottish identity was not extinguished by the creation of the United Kingdom, but continued as a national sub-theme, particularly through the ministry of the Church of Scotland. Nevertheless, there were limits to the expression of Scottish religious and civic nationalism. The Union recognised the Church of Scotland as the established religion in Scotland, but Westminster subsequently did little to ensure that the national religion of Scotland – along with that of England – was exported to places of British settlement overseas. In Scotland itself, traditional communities and their way of life were threatened by the remorseless forces of agrarian reform, the Anglicisation of schooling, and British commercial hegemony.

Yet the picture was not entirely without hope. Thanks to the Union, the empire provided many opportunities for British people of Scottish extraction, especially the urban middle classes. In Edinburgh and other Scottish university cities, an alliance of moderate clergy, the city and the academy fostered a more secular and intellectual national culture.[8] From the late eighteenth century, Scottish administrators, educators, navigators, engineers and clergy, generated by the schools and universities of the Scottish enlightenment, found much to occupy themselves in the great trading companies of India, North America and the West Indies. Scots made disciplined and effective troops, and many rose to form the elite of the army and navy.[9] Against the slur of poverty and marginality, Scottish investment in the empire was celebrated as a triumph of virtue, intelligence and energy in the face of local adversity.

Nevertheless, this triumphal narrative must be read against the Scottish record of social distress and population decline to which we have already referred which continued relentlessly until the 1920s. By the beginning of the First World War, up to 2 million people had abandoned Scotland for new Scottish realms such as Ontario (Upper Canada) or the Maritime Provinces of Nova Scotia, Prince Edward Island and Cape Breton Island in North America. In the Antipodes, there were other important Scottish communities in Victoria, New Zealand and, from the end of the nineteenth century, Cape Colony. The earliest departures from Scotland – those associated with the Highland clearances – were involuntary, though the majority went willingly and

[7] Colley, *Britons*, p. 136.
[8] D. Allan, 'Protestantism, Presbyterianism and National Identity in Eighteenth-Century Scottish History', in *Protestantism and National Identity: Britain and Ireland, c.1650–c.1850*, ed. T. Claydon and I. McBride (Cambridge, 1998), p. 190.
[9] K. McNeil, *Scotland, Britain, Empire: Writing the Highlands, 1760–1860* (Columbus, OH, 2007), p. 12.

hopefully. In either case, the effect was to ensure that the per capita loss of population from Scotland was only a little less than that from Ireland. From 1801 to 1901, it is estimated that Scotland lost over half of her natural increase of population through overseas emigration.[10] In brutal terms, the Scots were leading contributors to the external expansion of the empire because of their country's capacity to export its people. However, in contrast to Ireland, the religious narrative of this transfer of population was one of liberation and promise rather than exile and loss. The Presbyterian colonial missionary societies and committees considered in this chapter contributed to this positive narrative of empire. They celebrated Scottish (and Irish) success in securing Scotland and Ireland for the Protestant Reformation against the tyranny of Rome, and then exporting the Hanoverian settlement to the colonies. They promoted the Scots as the natural defenders of the Reformation, who bore the martial and moral characteristics of ideal colonists.

This cohesive ethno-religious narrative was possible partly because, as a religious community, the Scots were relatively homogeneous when compared with other peoples of Great Britain and Ireland. Indeed, following the parliamentary union of 1707, the established Church of Scotland was one of the few institutions that remained intact to carry the burden of Scottish national identity. According to the 1851 religious census, over 85 per cent of church attendees in Scotland were Presbyterians.[11] However, partly because it had been spared the divisions in the Church of England that gave rise to the separate Nonconformist and Methodist traditions, the Church of Scotland carried unresolved tensions, particularly over lay patronage, which would eventually break out at the time of the Disruption and make a major impact on Presbyterian churches in the colonies. In addition, when considering the Presbyterian tradition in the empire as a whole, it is important to recognise that Presbyterianism, like Episcopalianism, had adherents throughout the United Kingdom. While British Presbyterianism was heavily influenced by Scotland, Presbyterians who emigrated to Canada, Australia, New Zealand, and South Africa in the nineteenth century, included many 'Scotch Irish' (Irish of Scottish descent, especially from the Irish province of Ulster), as well as English Presbyterians

[10] T. M. Devine, *The Scottish Nation, 1700–2000* (London, 1999), p. 468.
[11] Cook and Keith, *British Historical Facts, 1830–1900*, p. 221, citing the 'Report on the 1851 Census of Religious Worship: Scotland'. *Parliamentary Papers* (1854), vol. LIX, pp. 301–46. Church of Scotland, 351,456 (37.2 per cent); Free Church of Scotland, 292,308 (30.9 per cent); United Presbyterian Church, 159,191 (16.8 per cent); Other Protestant, 97,120 (10.2 per cent); and Catholic, 43,878 (4.6 per cent).

among their number. The Irish Presbyterian General Assembly supported colonial missions in British North America, Australia, Van Diemen's Land and New Zealand, in addition to Protestant missions in Ireland, a foreign mission in western India and missions to Jews in Hamburg, Bonn and Damascus.[12] It is also worth recalling that the Calvinism of the Church of Scotland was brought to Scotland by John Knox (c. 1510–72) from Geneva and was part of an international movement. This gave the majority religion of the Scottish people a transnational character, which stretched beyond the bounds of Scotland and the British empire, extending and strengthening their vision of the Christian world. Like Roman Catholics, therefore, Presbyterians belonged to a religious empire which was not co-terminous with the British empire.

Society in Scotland for Propagating Christian Knowledge (SSPCK)

Scottish colonial missions began well before the tide of emigration began emptying the highlands and distressed rural regions of Scotland, and the evangelical revival inspired Thomas Chalmers to take up the mission cause.[13] Like the Church of England, the Presbyterian Church of Scotland has a venerable society that was established to conduct missionary work at the beginning of the eighteenth century. Like the SPG, it was linked closely to the Protestant state and was sustained by aristocratic patronage. This was the Society in Scotland for Propagating Christian Knowledge (SSPCK), which was incorporated by letters patent in 1709, augmented in 1738, to serve in regions 'where error idolatry superstition and ignorance most abound', a pointed reference to the Scottish Highlands and Islands, as well as to 'Popish and infidel parts of the world', which would cover everywhere else.[14] In practical terms, the SSPCK functioned along similar lines to the Anglican

---

[12] H. Newcomb, ed., *A Cyclopedia of Missions: Containing a Comprehensive View of Missionary Operations Throughout the World*, 2nd edn (New York, 1860), p. 488. See also J. Thompson, *Into All the World: A History of 150 Years of the Overseas Work of the Presbyterian Church in Ireland* (Belfast, 1990).

[13] J. Roxborogh, *Thomas Chalmers, Enthusiast for Mission: The Christian Good of Scotland and the Rise of the Missionary Movement* (Carlisle, 1999), ch. 9.

[14] The records of the SSPCK (c.1701–1956) are held by the National Archives of Scotland, Edinburgh. For the Society's charter, see 'Letters Patent, 1709', SSPCK Minutes of General Meetings, vol. 1 (1709–18), National Archives of Scotland, GD 95/1/1. The Society does not seem to have published a journal, and the annual sermons, although continuous, make surprisingly few references to missions. The main archival records of SSPCK activities are therefore minutes of the meetings of the Society's directors in Edinburgh and its annual report. According to F. V. Mills, 'The

SPG and SPCK and the colonial New England Company, all of which supplied funds for schools, teachers and religious literature to those beyond the reach of the regular ministry of the Church. However, as Mills points out, while the significance of the NEC and the SPG is well understood, the colonial mission of the SSPCK has been relatively neglected by scholars.[15]

The SSPCK was, initially at least, the joint creation of Scottish Presbyterians and Episcopalians though after the Disruption it would be associated exclusively with the established Church of Scotland.[16] It cooperated closely with the Church of England, especially in arrangements for collecting funds to support the Society's work, which were taken up in England as well as in Scotland. In 1725, George I instituted a royal bounty of £1,000, later increased to £2,000, which ensured that the SSPCK had relatively generous funding by the standards of the voluntary colonial societies considered elsewhere in this part of the book. By 1879, the Society enjoyed a substantial regular income, based largely on donations, bequests and investments in land, of over £5,500 per year.[17] Royal benevolence ensured the SSPCK was nourished with a continuous supply of aristocratic patronage, and the Society's reports tended to be divided equally between accounts of the Society's schools and missions and long lists of its noble and royal benefactors. From 1833, these were led by the young Queen Victoria, who committed herself to make regular donations to the SSPCK from that time.[18] Celebrating this magnanimity, the SSPCK's Secretary, John Tawse, enthused:

What, then, must the feelings of every Christian be? and how must the heart of the poor and distant Highlander beat with gratitude and loyalty when he knows that all ranks and orders of people, the nobles of the land, and even Majesty itself have stretched forth their hand to aid in pouring the light of true religion, and the blessings of education into their distant islands and sequestered glens.[19]

Society in Scotland for Propagating Christian Knowledge in British North America, 1730–1775', *Church History*, 63 (1994), p. 15, the records of the Colonial Boards of the SSPCK have not survived.

[15] *Ibid.* For background to the early history of the SSPCK, I am indebted to my postgraduate student, Justine Atkinson.

[16] *Ibid.*, p. 16.

[17] Report of the Society in Scotland for Propagating Christian Knowledge (1879), National Archives of Scotland, GD95/14/35, p. 9.

[18] J. Tawse, *Report on the Present State of the Society in Scotland for Propagating Christian Knowledge* (Edinburgh?, 1833), p. 27. For the Society's patrons, see Society in Scotland for Propagating Christian Knowledge, *Short Account of the Object, Progress, and Exertions of the Society in Scotland for Propagating Christian Knowledge* (Edinburgh, 1825).

[19] Tawse, *Report on the SSPCK*, p. 27.

The views of the Highlanders are not recorded, and indeed are more or less invisible in all the published and archival records of the SSPCK.

Although the SSPCK's charter gave it a mandate to conduct foreign and colonial missions overseas, its efforts in this direction were small and they were controversial. In the annual sermons preached in the eighteenth century, there are few references to mission work other than to apologise for the limited capacity of the Society to do much along these lines. In 1755, for example, Principal William Robertson (1721–93) of the University of Edinburgh stated that: 'the conversion of distant nations is not the chief care of the SSPCK.'[20] After 1732, the General Assembly authorised a collection to be taken up to support its Highland schools, or to help 'subsist missionary ministers or schoolmasters in foreign parts of the world', which made it possible to support a mission in North America.[21] Missionaries, including the famous David Brainerd (1718–47), were appointed by local committees to work among the native Americans and, occasionally, Highland emigrants. From 1736 to 1742, the Edinburgh directors of the Society supported a minister to Highlanders in the new colony of Georgia. Later, it also attempted a mission to the West Indies.[22]

Despite these occasional colonial adventures, the SSPCK appears to have taken no pains to assert the right of the Church of Scotland to represent the British Church and nation overseas. Hence, the SSPCK is remembered now for its schools and catechists in the Highlands and Islands, and its missions to Native Americans, one of many efforts to convert and civilise the 'poor Indians' displaced by European colonisation.[23] Poverty, as well as a fixation on the need to educate and civilise the Highlanders closer to home, seem to have led to an atrophication of its colonial activities. The Society's original policy of teaching English in its Highland schools alienated Gaelic speakers and ensured that the SSPCK came to be associated with Lowland attempts to Anglicise Highland society and exterminate its native language, culture and

[20] William Robertson, *The Situation of the World at the Time of Christ's Appearance and Its Connection with the Success of His Religion Considered*, SSPCK Sermon, 6th edn (1791), p. 53. Cited by Roxborogh, *Thomas Chalmers Enthusiast for Mission*, ch. 9.

[21] H. R. Sefton, 'The Scotch Society in the American Colonies in the Eighteenth Century', *Records of the Scottish Church History Society* (1971), pp. 169–84.

[22] Teachers were not sent to the colonies, though A. S. Cowper, *SSPCK Schoolmasters, 1709–1872* (Edinburgh, 1997), notes Braes of Glenelg, who left for Canada in 1793, and Findlay McRae, who also left for Canada with his daughter and family in 1847.

[23] For the role of the SSPCK in defining this popular missionary common trope, see *ibid.*, p. 26 *et passim*; and C. G. Calloway, *White People, Indians, and Highlanders* (Oxford, 1997), p. 75. For a fuller history of the origins of the SSPCK in America, see M. Szasz, *Scottish Highlanders and Native Americans: Indigenous Education in the Eighteenth-Century Atlantic World* (Norman, OK, 2007), ch. 3.

religion.[24] Possibly for this reason, but also because of its association with lairds and landlords, the SSPCK lacked the broad appeal needed to sustain foreign or colonial mission work for the Scottish church on the scale achieved by the SPG for the Church of England.

The SSPCK hit further problems at the time of the Disruption (1843), when almost the entire population of the Highlands and Islands went over to the Free Church and withdrew their children from the schools conducted by the SSPCK.[25] As the government gradually assumed responsibility for basic education, the Society acquired resources which allowed it to extend its foreign mission efforts. This proved controversial. In 1872, a public meeting chaired by the MP, Duncan McLaren, protested against what was called 'the systematic diverting of the funds from educational purposes to the support of missions connected with the Established Church'.[26] This meeting objected both to the expenditure on foreign missions at the expense of schools in Scotland, and the monopolisation of the SSPCK by the established Church, against the intention of its original letters patent. By this stage, as one correspondent to MacPhail notes, there was an expanding gap between the established and the Free Church of Scotland in relation to missions and other philanthropic work.[27]

At the end of the eighteenth century, the modern Scottish missionary movement was ignited, largely, as I have already mentioned, on the model of the lay-dominated London Missionary Society (1795). Besides enthusiastically supporting the LMS with men and funds, dozens of city-based mission societies sprang up in cities and towns throughout Scotland. Presbyterian efforts were encouraged after 1796 when the General Assembly gave its approval to their work.[28] While many of these Scottish societies were 'auxiliaries' – that is, their function was the

[24] For analysis of this debate, see Cowper, *SSPCK Schoolmasters*; L. Leneman, 'The SSPCK and the Question of Gaelic in Blair Atholl', *Scottish Studies*, 26 (1982), pp. 57–9; C. W. J. Withers, 'Education and Anglicisation: The Policy of the SSPCK Towards the Education of the Highlander 1709–1825', *Scottish Studies*, 26 (1982), pp. 37–56.

[25] J. Calder MacPhail, 'SPCK Narrative', Educational Endowments Scotland Bill, and the Society in Scotland for Propagating Christian Knowledge, June 1881, SSPCK, National Archives of Scotland, GD1/1338/6/14.

[26] 'The Highlands and Their Educational Endowments – The SPCK Public Meeting on 21st April 1880', SSPCK, National Archives of Scotland, GD1/1338/1.

[27] John Webster to Reverend MacPhail, 20 July 1882, SSPCK, National Archives of Scotland, GD1/1338/2/4.

[28] For Scottish foreign missions, see E. Breitenbach, *Empire and Scottish Society: The Impact of Foreign Missions at Home, c.1790 to c.1914* (Edinburgh, 2009); E. Breitenbach, 'Religious Literature and Discourses of Empire: The Scottish Presbyterian Foreign Mission Movement', in *Empires of Religion*, ed. H. M. Carey (Basingstoke, 2008), pp. 84–112; N. Erlank, '"Civilizing the African": The Scottish Mission to the Xhosa',

raising of funds rather than the training and despatch of missionaries on their own behalf – the larger societies, notably the Glasgow Missionary Society, and the Edinburgh Missionary Society (both formed in 1796), also sent out mission personnel and conducted independent missions.

As in England, evangelicals in Scotland were seized with a passion for missionary work and for the reform, civilisation, moral cleansing and conversion of the world. This involved much more than simply missions to the heathen. The *Scottish Missionary Register*, the organ of the Scottish Missionary Society (1818) and the Scottish equivalent to the *Missionary Register*, included notices on foreign and colonial missions from Persia to South Africa, as well as 'British missions', that is, missions within Britain rather than overseas. The latter included the Edinburgh Society for Promoting the Education of the Poor in Ireland, the Jews' Society, and the London City Mission, as well as the various colonial missionary societies considered in this book.[29] As in England, foreign missions, particularly to India, initially attracted the greatest support from the Scottish public. However, in the 1820s and 1830s, reversals by the LMS in the Pacific and the Glasgow Missionary Society in Africa for a time had a discouraging effect on Scottish support for foreign missions.

It is in this context that Thomas Chalmers (1780–1847), the charismatic minister who later became the first moderator of the Free Church of Scotland, came to articulate a wider vision that included home missions and missions to colonists as part of a total reawakening of Scottish society both at home and overseas.[30] As leader of the moderate evangelicals in the Church of Scotland, Chalmers sought to renew the mission of the Church of Scotland and uplift the Scottish people both physically and spiritually. Initially at least, Chalmers supported a renewal of the missionary call of the SSPCK. On 2 June 1814, he preached the SSPCK's annual sermon and he used the occasion to denounce the collapse of moral and financial support for Scottish missionary efforts. Preaching to the text: 'And Nathaniel said unto him, Can there be any good thing come out of Nazareth?' (John 1: 46), he referred to the

---

in *Christian Missions and the Enlightenment*, ed. B. Stanley (Grand Rapids, MI, 2001), pp. 146–7.

[29] *Scottish Missionary Register*, 1820–46. After 1823, the full title changed to the *Scottish Missionary and Philanthropic Register Containing the Proceedings of the Scottish Missionary Society, and of Other Societies for the Propagation of the Gospel at Home and Abroad*. There was also the *Missionary Magazine*, begun in 1796 by Greville Ewing (1767–1841), of the Edinburgh Society.

[30] S. J. Brown, *Thomas Chalmers and the Godly Commonwealth in Scotland* (Oxford, 1982); S. J. Brown, 'Reform, Reconstruction, Reaction: The Social Vision of Scottish Presbyterianism, c.1830–1930', *Scottish Journal of Theology*, 44 (1991), pp. 489–517.

contempt for missionaries which had become general in Scotland. The SSPCK, he suggested, was currently ranked 'among the vilest of the vile', so that 'the very name of Missionary excites the most nauseous antipathy'.[31] He went on to observe that more tolerant attitudes prevailed south of the border, a cause of national shame for Scotland: 'We have reason to believe that this opposition is not so extensive, nor so virulent in England … It is most a [sic] Scottish peculiarity.' Chalmers helped to coordinate the dynamic Scottish missionary movement, which included church building, Sabbath schools and religious tract and bible societies at home, as well as evangelism and education for the heathen, and support for colonists overseas. However, the latter work was not instigated by the SSPCK. In its place, the Society that emerged to lead Scottish colonial missionary efforts was the Glasgow Colonial Society. A study of this society and its successors provides important insight into Scottish strategies for religious settlement and the extent to which these supported and/or resisted Scottish nationalism.

Glasgow Colonial Society, 1825–41

The Society for Promoting the Religious Interests of Scottish Settlers in British North America, better known as the Glasgow Colonial Society, was formed in 1825.[32] It was a voluntary missionary society with the distinctive purpose of providing clergy for British colonies in North America; it had a lay and clerical committee, published an annual report and held an annual sermon that was its major vehicle for fundraising and publicity.[33] The Society was formed after a meeting held in Trades' Hall in Glasgow to consider what might be done to meet the needs of Scottish emigrants heading to North America. Despite heavy Scottish emigration, especially to Upper Canada, little had been done

---

[31] T. Chalmers, *Discourses on the Christian Revelation Viewed in Connection with the Modern Astronomy Together with Six Sermons* (Andover, 1818), p. 304.

[32] M. Harper, 'Glasgow Colonial Society', in *Dictionary of Scottish Church History and Theology*, ed. N. M. D. S. Cameron (Edinburgh, 1993), p. 365. See also E. A. K. McDougall and J. S. Moir, eds., *Selected Correspondence of the Glasgow Colonial Society 1825–1840* (Toronto, 1994); J. Moir, 'Through Missionary Eyes: The Glasgow Colonial Society and the Immigrant Experience in British North America', in *The Immigrant Experience*, ed. C. Kerrigan (Guelph, Ontario, 1992).

[33] Glasgow Colonial Society, *First Annual Report of the Glasgow Society (in Connection with the Established Church of Scotland) for Promoting the Religious Interests of the Scottish Settlers in North America* (Glasgow, 1826). This was the Society's annual report, which was published in Glasgow from 1826 to 1835, after which its work was taken over by the Colonial Scheme of the Church of Scotland. The work of the Glasgow Society was also publicised in the *Edinburgh Christian Instructor and Colonial Religious Register*, edited by Robert Burns from 1838 until its closure in 1840.

to try to supply ministers, schoolmasters and catechists who together
would make it possible for Scottish Presbyterianism to be seeded in the
colonies. The Society had powerful supporters: the first meeting was
chaired by George Ramsay, ninth earl of Dalhousie (1770–1838) and
Governor in Chief of Upper and Lower Canada (1820–8). A society for
promoting the more effective planting of the Presbyterian faith fitted
well with the dozens of other intellectual, cultural and religious causes
that Dalhousie came to support as governor. A soldier and aristocrat,
Dalhousie's outlook was authoritarian but not sectarian, and he shared
the distaste of most colonists for the exclusive claims to the support of
the state that were advanced by certain Anglicans, notably bishop John
Inglis (1777–1850) of Nova Scotia. Having endorsed the motion, 'that
this meeting contemplates with deep interest the moral wants of the
Scottish Settlers in many parts of British North America and resolves
that a Society shall be formed in this city and neighbourhood with a view
of promoting their improvement by means of Ministers, Catechists and
School Masters to be sent to them; and by such other means as many be
found most expedient', the Society was underway.[34]

Patronage at the right level was always important in the nineteenth
century, and missionary societies could not prosper without it. However,
the idea of creating a Scottish missionary society to work for emigrants
came not from Dalhousie but was largely the initiative of three Church
of Scotland ministers and academics: Stevenson MacGill, Professor of
Divinity at the University of Glasgow, Dr John Scott and the Reverend
Robert Burns (1789–1869) of Paisley.[35] Burns, who had an appetite for
controversy, was to be the Society's most vigorous champion. After
the Disruption, he toured the US and the North American colonies
in 1844 where he delighted in extending the Free Church schism to
the colonial presbyteries. As Secretary of the Glasgow Colonial Society
from 1825, Burns was eventually responsible for selecting and sending
out over forty missionaries to North America, as well as acting as an
advocate for the needs of the colonial church with governments and in
reports to the church's General Assembly. He encouraged the creation
of Presbyterian colleges which would enable the colonies to create a
home-grown ministry which was sympathetic to the Free Church. This
was critical for the growth of the movement because of the decision by

---

[34] McDougall and Moir, eds., *Selected Correspondence of the Glasgow Colonial Society*,
p. xiv.
[35] H. J. Brigman, 'Robert Burns (1789–1869)', *Dictionary of Canadian Biography Online*,
1861–70; R. F. Burns, *The Life and Times of the Reverend Robert Burns* (Toronto, 1872);
W. Ewing, ed., *Annals of the Free Church of Scotland 1843–1900*, 2 vols. (Edinburgh,
1914), vol. 1, p. 109.

most Scottish academics to remain loyal to the established Church. In 1845, on his return from an extended tour of Canada, Burns took up an invitation to become minister to Knox Church in Toronto. On his departure for Canada, Burns took the records of the Glasgow Colonial Society with him, including 1,300 letters, mostly from ministers who had been sent overseas by the Society.

As Scottish emigration continued to rise, the Glasgow Colonial Society met an immediate and important need and was soon inundated with requests from sites of significant Scottish settlement in North America seeking to secure clergy for their communities.[36] In both Nova Scotia and New Brunswick, the Glasgow Colonial Society was a primary agent in facilitating Scottish colonisation.[37] While the agents sent out by the Society in 1835 to Black River Settlement found that there were only twenty-eight Presbyterian families who were 'generally very indifferent about religion',[38] other settlers were more devout and embraced the opportunity to maintain the religious services which were an important component of their cultural identity. The pleas from the isolated Scottish communities in newly settled regions could be stark: 'In few words, our labour is immense, and we are starving and in debt',[39] wrote the Reverend John McLaurin on hearing the good news of the formation of a society to promote the religious needs of Scottish settlers in colonies. On giving thanks for the gift of Lord Dalhousie of a complete set of the *Encyclopaedia Britannica* (which had not arrived), John McIntyre stated that a thirst for knowledge was inherent in Scotsmen: 'And though we have expatriated ourselves, and are now obscured by the interminable forests of Canada, we are still anxious to keep the intellectual machinery in motion.'[40] The thirst was apparently just as keen for well-educated clergy from home: 'The want of a stated Clergyman causes the people to embrace the opportunity of every vagrant who chooses to address them, and they are not infrequently imposed upon', wrote the Reverend Duncan Macaulay when requesting clergy for the townships of Ireland and Inverness.

---

[36] T. MacCulloch and J. MacGregor, *A Memorial from the Committee of Missions of the Presbyterian Church of Nova Scotia, to the Glasgow Society for Promoting the Religious Interests of the Scottish Settlers in British North America; with Observations on the Constitution of That Society* (Edinburgh, 1826).

[37] L. H. Campey, *With Axe and Bible: The Scottish Pioneers of New Brunswick, 1784–1874* (Toronto, 2007).

[38] *Ibid.*, p. 82.

[39] Reverend John McLaurin, New Longueil, Ottawa District, to the Reverend John Scott, 5 July 1825, in McDougall and Moir, eds., *Selected Correspondence of the Glasgow Colonial Society*, p. 4.

[40] John McIntyre, Dalhousie, to the Reverend Robert Burns, 5 July 1825, in *ibid.*, p. 11.

As well as performing his essential religious functions, a minister from Scotland was a mark of prestige for new emigrants. He demonstrated that they could provide for their own cultural needs instead of having to seek assistance from those outside their traditions. A petition from the Toronto Township, Upper Canada, stated: 'Baptists and Methodists it is true have sometimes visited us for a few Sabbaths but even these have been the very refuse of their respective sects ... We beg leave to add respecting them, they are the best we have here.'[41] What all these petitioners to the Glasgow Colonial Society seem to have valued was the capacity of ministers from home to recreate the ritual and intellectual conditions that were the distinctive mark of Presbyterian religious practice in Scotland. Lapses of education and cultivation from this metropolitan benchmark were deeply felt as the badges of colonial deprivation which might be remedied by the arrival of a properly trained minister from Scotland. The Reverend Alexander MacNaughton wrote with pride of the advances of his congregation in Lancaster, Upper Canada, who had just made his appointment permanent: 'In point of knowledge – secular & religious, the majority of them are far below the average of the general run of congregations at home – the natural result of the privations which as first settlers in an unreclaimed wilderness, they had to endure.'[42]

Above all, what was prized was true, heartfelt religion in a minister, 'a Scottish Missionary, not in name only, but in deed', as one petitioner hoping for an itinerant minister to come and work among them put it.[43] Such clergy had the capacity to create the dense pious texture of the Presbyterian churches at home. They could deliver lengthy, well-prepared sermons full of moral fervour, intimate knowledge of scripture, and sophisticated expositions of Calvinist theology, which were the hallmark of the Presbyterian divine. They could supply the orderly parishes with well-run schools, and preside at the Presbyterian funeral with its dignified service and burial and its wild, whiskey-fuelled wake. Most importantly, they could prepare the whole community for the 'communion season' which was the crown of Presbyterian ritual life, during which all work was suspended for up to a week. Only in regions of dense Scottish settlement was it possible to generate the resources needed for this tradition. The communion season began on Thursday

---

[41] Alan Robinet, Joseph Silverthorn, Thomas Silverthorn and five other petitioners, to the Reverend Dr John Scott, Greenock, 16 March 1825, in *ibid.*, p. 1.
[42] Reverend Alexander MacNaughton to the Reverend Robert Burns, 12 July 1834, in *ibid.*, p. 73.
[43] Reverend Alexander MacLean to the Reverend John Geddes, 22 February 1833, in *ibid.*, p. 218.

when the congregation would prepare with fasting, rest and guest preachers, moving to 'Men's Day' on Friday with the 'Ceist', a period of intense self-examination. On Saturday, there was the distribution of special tokens by the elders to those whose moral standing was sufficient to allow them to attend the Sunday service of the Lord's Supper the following day. The Sabbath was a joyful occasion with the church decked out as if for a grand dinner. There would be psalms, hymn singing, dramatic sermons and the sensational 'fencing of the tables', during which the unworthy would be denounced. In the hands of a skilled and humane minister, this included not just the humiliation of recalcitrants, but also their mortification, repentance and reintegration into the community. Having survived this, Monday was set aside for thanksgiving and recovery. As Clarke has described, the celebration of the full Presbyterian communion season in the colonies was not restricted to North America but was also a major achievement by the Free Church settlers of the province of Otago on New Zealand's South Island.[44]

General Assembly Colonial Committee

Despite the success of the Glasgow Colonial Society in providing clergy to meet the religious needs of Scottish settlers, it did have some drawbacks. In the first place, its work was limited to British North America at a time when there was increasing Scottish emigration to other parts of the empire. In addition, within the General Assembly, orthodox Presbyterians were concerned that evangelicals were working too closely with other evangelical Protestants, notably the Methodists. They felt that more should be done to secure patronage for the Church of Scotland, which was felt to be its due as an established church. In 1824, concerns of this kind had already led to the formation of a committee of the General Assembly to undertake foreign missions independently of the work of voluntary societies such as the Edinburgh Missionary Society and the Glasgow Society for Foreign Missions. Missions were too important to be left entirely in the hands of voluntary evangelical societies.

Initially, the General Assembly responded to the rising volume of correspondence on colonial matters by establishing the 'Committee on the Canada Petitions'. This was chaired by John Lee (1779–1859), who was Principal of the Academic Senate of Edinburgh University (1840–58) and moderator of the General Assembly (1844). Although Lee is unlikely to have appreciated the analogy, his position bore some

[44] A. Clarke, 'Days of Heaven on Earth: Presbyterian Communion Seasons in 19th Century Otago', *Journal of Religious History*, 26 (2002), pp. 274–97.

parallels with that of his contemporary, Paul Cullen whom we discussed in Chapter 4. As rector of the Irish College in Rome from 1832 to 1849, Cullen also acquired considerable power over the appointment of clergy to the leading colonial churches of his faith as they were planted throughout the expanding empire. In the Church of Scotland, all ministers were required to have a university degree in theology, which could be acquired in Scotland from only four places: the universities of Aberdeen, St Andrews, Edinburgh and Glasgow. This ensured that senior academics were frequently consulted about colonial appointments by communities in America and elsewhere looking for ministers for their congregations.

Within Lee's academic and ecclesiastical circle, the colonial ministry opened a pathway by which Scottish enlightenment, education and moral uplift could be sent out to the empire. From Montreal, a correspondent wrote to Lee in 1827 expressing his regret that 'the moral and the Religious influence of the North part of Britain have not equal scope and facility for diffusion in the distant parts of the Empire as those of the Sister Country'. This, he argued, was a missed opportunity:

[T]here is an intellectual and moral life which Scotland might, if her power in that respect were duly exerted, infuse into every colony of Britain & it would be giving to them of her abundance & would greatly increase her own intellectual wealth & exalt her fame. If the Government would make a suitable provision for churches & schools in connection with the Church of Scotland, this Province would be completely regenerated & attached to the Parent Country by innumerable and powerful ties.[45]

In other words, the Church of Scotland had a patriotic duty to enhance the cohesion and loyalty of the colonies by working more effectively to establish the Church in the empire. This work should not be left to a voluntary association, however worthy. In the 1830s, therefore, Lee began to argue that the support of the Church of Scotland in the colonies was more than a religious and patriotic mission, it was a constitutional obligation. These views were also supported by colonists, such as the Montreal merchant Thomas Blackwood (1773–1842), who campaigned effectively for the Church of Scotland in Canada to share in the clergy reserves on the same basis as the Church of England.[46] In a letter to Lee, Blackwood noted that it was commonly said that '[t]he conquest of the Country carried the King's Religion with it'. On the

---

[45] Correspondent (no signature) to John Lee, 14 December 1827, Lee Papers, National Library of Scotland, MS 3436/270.
[46] Blackwood to Lee, 22 March 1830, National Library of Scotland, MS 3438 (5). For Blackwood, see *Dictionary of Canadian Biography Online* (1821–35), vol. 6.

contrary, Blackwood argued, there were no grounds for giving exclusive rights to the Church of England and strong legal arguments which supported the colonial rights of members of the Scottish church. He was happy to take up Lee's suggestions that colonists should 'besiege His Majesty's Ministers with Petitions, Memorial etc.'; however, he suggested that this work could best be done by those closer to the seat of Government.

This was effectively a call to the General Assembly to take more responsibility for the extension of the Church of Scotland in the empire. Throughout the 1830s, the Church responded by steadily taking charge of the missionary movement and relegating the voluntary missionary societies, including both the Glasgow Colonial Society and the Glasgow Missionary Society, to the sidelines. Those most affected by these moves were evangelicals who dominated the Scottish missionary movement, just as they did in England. In the ten years from 1833, there was increasing conflict between moderates and evangelicals in the Church of Scotland which threatened the ambitious missionary programme of the revitalised church. As tensions mounted, evangelical Presbyterians sought to secure control over the nomination of ministers in Scotland and eliminate interventions by lay patrons (who were generally unsupportive of evangelicals). By 1842, evangelicals had control of the General Assembly, building on the influence they already had in the Scottish missionary movement, and the stage was set for a dramatic denouement.

The Disruption forms the background to the dispersal of the voluntary societies and the incorporation of their activities by the General Assembly. These problems would later be glossed over and, even in 1889, it was simply stated that the Glasgow Colonial Society had been 'amalgamated' in 1836 with the Colonial Committee of the Church of Scotland.[47] However, in reality, it was more of a hostile takeover. Indeed, the Glasgow Colonial Society can count itself fortunate that the records of its correspondence were taken to Canada where they have been published as a significant record of the history of Scottish settlement in North America. Other voluntary missionary societies, such as the Glasgow Missionary Society, have been all but forgotten.[48] But we need to return to the colonial mission, while bearing in mind that the same issues were being debated across the whole sphere of Presbyterian

---

Presbyterians had received a share of the income from the reserves since 1824 but not in proportion to their population.

[47] Any disagreement at the time is smoothed over by A. Williamson, *What Has the Church of Scotland Done for Our Colonies?* (Edinburgh, 1889), p. 5.

[48] P. Hinchliff, 'Whatever Happened to the Glasgow Missionary Society?', *Historiae Studia Ecclesiasticae* [*Church History Society of Southern Africa*], 18 (1992), pp. 104–20.

church life.[49] On the colonial front, in 1836, Lee succeeded in securing the full backing of the General Assembly, which carried with it the dignity and authority of the established Church of Scotland, for the conduct of the Church's colonial mission. This had a number of weighty consequences.

Colonial Committee of the General Assembly

The Colonial Committee established by the General Assembly of the Church of Scotland was convened for the first time on 1 June 1836 and continued to meet without a pause, even for the Disruption, for the best part of 100 years.[50] The original committee included many of Scotland's leading churchmen and academics, together with Scottish peers and Members of Parliament. However, perhaps the most significant feature of the committee was that it was not controlled by evangelicals. The first convenor was Duncan MacFarlan (1771–1857), principal and vice chancellor of Glasgow University from 1823 until his death. MacFarlan was an orthodox Calvinist and, in 1843, directly after the Disruption, he would become moderator of the General Assembly. To support the main committee, large sub-committees were set up in Edinburgh, Glasgow, Aberdeen, Dundee, Dumfries and Kelso. The Edinburgh sub-committee, which was convened by Dr Welsh, included forty-four members who were headed by Dr Chalmers. The Glasgow Committee was led by the moderator, Dr Patrick, with MacFarlan as convenor.

The Colonial Committee immediately began operating at the highest level of government. It opened correspondence with the Colonial Secretary, Lord Glenelg, on the matter of Presbyterian entitlements relating to the Canadian clergy reserves. This was to include a testimonial which would assert the rights of all members of the Church of Scotland residing in the colonies 'to be placed on a footing of perfect equality in all privileges, immunities, and emoluments ecclesiastical as well as civil with the members of the Church of England and Ireland resident there'.[51] The Colonial Committee therefore argued for the support of the Church of Scotland on a different basis from that of other voluntary colonial missionary societies, with the exception of the SPG.

---

[49] For contemporary context, see S. J. Brown and M. Fry, eds., *Scotland in the Age of the Disruption* (Edinburgh, 1993).

[50] Church of Scotland Colonial Committee (COS CC), National Library of Scotland, Dep. 298/222–244. The Colonial Committee later chose to celebrate its centenary in 1934: see J. Buchan, *The Scottish Church and the Empire: Centenary Address* (n.p., 1934), p. 2.

[51] COS CC Minutes, 1 June 1836, National Library of Scotland, Dep. 1298/222.

They looked to the Act of Union to support the claim of the ministers and other members of the Church of Scotland in every colony conquered or settled since 1706, and to favourable consideration in those acquired before that time. It was especially galling that the proceeds of the clergy reserves in Canada were being diverted to support Roman Catholics as well as other Protestants. The latter are described in withering terms as 'other non-descript Bodies, who, however respectable they may be as Individuals, are not recognised by the authorities or incorporated with the Constitutions of the Empire'.[52] Meanwhile, the colonial Presbyterian clergy struggled on low incomes to retain their respectability and the people were left in 'ignorance and Heathenism or abandoned to the perilous Ministrations of vagrant and unqualified Teachers'.[53] In fact, the clergy reserve income proved to be a chimera. Never popular with other churches, after a long campaign the reserves were nationalised by the government in 1854.[54]

While the situation in Canada was uppermost in the attention of the committee, its remit was far more extensive than the clergy reserves. In collections throughout Scotland, its stated aim was to 'assist in relieving the spiritual destitution and promote the religious and moral improvement of their Countrymen and Brethren in all parts of the habitable world'.[55] This proposed nothing less than the creation of a world church, supported financially by the imperial government, but underpinned for the first time by the General Assembly as a work of the whole church. John Buchan, the conservative novelist and statesman who served as the fifteenth Governor-General of Canada (fl. 1935–40), would later see this as the greatest achievement of the Scottish church in relation to the empire.[56] The Colonial Scheme of the Church of Scotland should therefore be seen as the equivalent of the creation of the Colonial Bishoprics' Fund for the Church of England, and, initially, its aspirations were no less ambitious. One of its first steps was to constrain the activities of the Glasgow Colonial Society, which was continuing to operate independently through its own auxiliaries and contacts in the parishes and presbyteries. This was clearly awkward. On 15 November 1836, the Edinburgh sub-committee therefore

---

[52] COS CC Minutes, 28 February 1837, National Library of Scotland, Dep. 1298/222, pp. 30–1.

[53] COS CC Minutes, 21 April 1837, National Library of Scotland, Dep. 1298/222, p. 41.

[54] J. Moir, 'The Settlement of Clergy Reserves, 1840–1855', *Canadian Historical Review*, 37 (1956), pp. 46–62; A. Wilson, 'The Clergy Reserves: "Economic Mischiefs" Or Sectarian Issue', *Canadian Historical Review*, 42 (1961), pp. 265–90.

[55] COS CC Minutes, 1 June 1836, National Library of Scotland, Dep. 1298/222, p. 7.

[56] Buchan, *Scottish Church and the Empire*, p. 2.

submitted a report regarding a 'plan of correspondence and co-operation' with the Glasgow Colonial Society. Attempting to mitigate the blow, Dr Chalmers moved that the Glasgow Colonial Society 'is entitled to the entire confidence of this Committee as a most efficient and successful instrument for promoting the interests of religion and the Church of Scotland in the North American Colonies'.[57] However, this did not extend to allowing the Glasgow Society to continue appealing for funds. Now that the General Assembly had committed itself to central fund-raising and management of the colonial church, the days of the Glasgow Society were clearly numbered.

Over the next ten years, the Colonial Committee gradually took over responsibility for all matters relating to the colonial churches which were not already covered by the committee on foreign missions. Besides corresponding as necessary with the government and other churches, this included the examination and despatch of suitably qualified clergy and schoolteachers as requested by Presbyterian communities around the world, as well as the provision of religious instructors, either ministers or schoolmasters, on emigrant vessels.[58] In India, the General Assembly required the Colonial Committee to extend its operation to cover members of the Church of Scotland resident in India, a large population including the military, civil servants, and chaplains provided at the expense of the colonial administration.[59] Particular difficulties arose with requests for ministers who were able to preach in the Gaelic language. In such cases, for example in response to a request from Dalhousie in June 1830, the committee asked if they would accept a minister who could only preach in English.[60]

All of these activities were dealt a fatal blow by the Disruption and the tensions which preceded it. Symptomatic of the strife of these bitter times was the resignation of Principal MacFarlan as convenor of the Colonial Committee in 1841 following the refusal of his own Committee to approve a young evangelical schoolmaster called Robert Duff for a colonial ministry in British Guiana, a place where four ministers had already died and in which he had heroically volunteered to serve. Appalled at this descent into small-minded controversy, MacFarlan grandly tendered his resignation, stating: 'I cannot consent that any

---

[57] COS CC Minutes, 15 November 1836, National Library of Scotland, Dep. 1298/222, p. 20.
[58] COS CC, Edinburgh Sub-Committee, 17 April 1838, National Library of Scotland, Dep. 1298/225, p. 3.
[59] COS CC Minutes, 7 June 1830, National Library of Scotland, Dep. 1298/224 (no page numbers used).
[60] *Ibid.*

man, or any set of men, shall avail themselves of my name and my exertions, however insignificant these may be, to crush an individual who has become obnoxious to them, and thereby advance a system of policy which I believe to be in the extreme dangerous to the Church and mischievous to society.'[61] Worse was to follow. From the outbreak of the schism, the Colonial Committee was suspended and met as an 'Acting Committee'. The title reflected the hope that the schism would end and that it would be possible to continue colonial work on a united basis. For those who remained, the main issue ceased to be sustaining a civilising mission throughout the empire, but rather sorting out who had remained loyal to the established church and who would have to go.

While nearly the entire body of foreign missionaries, who were mostly evangelicals, departed to join the Free Church, the colonial presbyteries were more divided. Two years after the Disruption, the Acting Committee of the established Church reported that, despite constant requests for ministers, due to the state of its finances, it was able to do very little. Much committee business was expended in praising those who had sustained their connection with the established Church and reprimanding those who had left, particularly if they tried to continue receiving financial benefit from the established Church.[62] In order to try and resolve the crisis, the established Church despatched a delegation to North America who reported the good news that the colonial presbyteries had not all gone the way of the Church of Scotland's foreign missions and crossed to the Free Church.

Despite the difficulties, the committee continued to manage a complex correspondence with all parts of the empire. Few individuals caused them as much trouble as the Reverend John Dunmore Lang (1799–1878), the veteran Presbyterian clergyman in the colony of New South Wales.[63] Following the Disruption, Lang refused to go with either the established or the Free Church, in part because no ministers would remain in a church if this obliged them to work with him. Lang's refusal to accept the verdict of either the Presbytery of New South Wales, or that of the Colonial Committee in Edinburgh prompted an extended discussion of the nature of the relationship between the colonies and

---

[61] D. MacFarlan, *Statement Relative to the Proceedings of the General Assembly's Colonial Committee, in Regard to Mr Robert Duff, Preacher of the Gospel* (n.p., 1841), p. 11.
[62] The Presbytery of Demerara was a particular concern.
[63] Baker's biography remains authoritative, though see also the reassessment of Lang by Bridges. D. W. A. Baker, *Preacher, Politician, Patriot: A Life of John Dunmore Lang* (Melbourne, 1998); B. Bridges, 'John Dunmore Lang: A Bicentennial Appreciation', *Church Heritage*, 11 (1999), pp. 70–81; B. Bridges, 'John Dunmore Lang's Crusade to Keep Australia Protestant, 1841–1849', *Church Heritage*, 11 (2000), pp. 146–54.

the General Assembly in Scotland. For the Colonial Committee, it was clear that they had no jurisdiction over the Presbyterian churches in the colonies. However, the Church did reserve the right to determine which synods and judicatories would be recognised as church courts in connection and communion with the Church in Scotland. By 29 June 1839, after lengthy deliberation, the Colonial Committee of the established Church determined that it had no connection with Dr Lang or his quarrels with other Presbyterians (and many other people) in New South Wales.[64] In a twenty-two-page memorandum, produced in response to a query from the Governor of New South Wales, they wearily attempted to resolve the mess Lang had created. The Committee acknowledged Lang's exertions and zeal, but regretted the violence, abuse and intemperance of his correspondence which, they said, had 'wrought much evil'.[65] As with other churches, the Church of Scotland's Colonial Committee was well aware that it had very limited capacity to effectively manage distant events, particularly where strong-minded individuals secured local power. Undeterred, Lang contrived to set up his own Australian Mission which made a direct appeal for funds from his supporters in Glasgow.[66]

More positive news flowed from North America where the synods were more united and prosperous and could therefore support a steady flow of subscriptions to pay for the passage and stipend of qualified ministers. While there were setbacks and disappointments, ten years after the Disruption it was evident that the established Church of Scotland was successfully continuing its expansion in the colonies. However, the schism with the Free Church remained an open wound.

Colonial Scheme of the Presbyterian Church in Ireland

Colonial aspirations were not confined to Presbyterians in Scotland. From the middle of the century, the General Assembly of the Presbyterian Church in Ireland, which was first established in 1840, also began to take a much more focused interest in Presbyterians overseas. Like the Church of Scotland, the Ulster synod embraced missions and church extension as a work of the whole church. Indeed, if anything,

---

[64] COS Acting CC Minutes, 29 June 1839, National Library of Scotland, Dep. 1298/226, pp. 36–77.

[65] COS Acting CC Minutes, 29 June 1839, National Library of Scotland, Dep. 1298/226, p. 37.

[66] J. D. Lang, *Australian Mission. To the Minister and Elders of the Secession and Relief Churches* (Edinburgh, 1847).

the Presbyterian Church in Ireland had an even more ambitious pro-gramme of missionary activity than the Church in Scotland. While, as is to be expected, it showed a particular concern with the specific task of taking the Reformation to fellow Europeans, especially Catholics in Ireland, there was also enthusiasm to fund missions to Jews, continental Europe and the colonies, all sustained by regular collections through-out the year.[67] Table 7.1 gives some idea of the comparable success of the different schemes of the Presbyterian Church in Ireland towards the end of the century. This shows that foreign missions (32.6 per cent) raised the largest collections in these years and the colonial and contin-ental mission collections trailed significantly behind those for the con-version of the Irish and soldiers. However, the commitment was there.

A mission to the colonies was first established through a com-mittee of the Irish General Assembly in 1848. It had two long-term secretaries, which helped its stability. Reverend William M'Clure of Londonderry conducted the committee's business for twenty-five years; the committee sent its first missionaries to North America and responded to calls for assistance from British colonies as resources permitted. There were also occasional visits from the colonies to plead their case directly. In 1860, the Reverend C. G. Glass, deputy from the Synod of the Presbyterian Church of New Brunswick, was deputed to come to the Irish General Assembly 'to communicate information as to their religious and educational wants'.[68] At the same meeting, Mr William Loughead, 'from Australia', 'gave cheering tidings of the present state of religion in that great continent'.[69] This was no doubt true. However, it should also be admitted that the proceedings of the General Assembly went for some twenty sessions of a day each, and colonial activities did not figure highly in the general flow of busi-ness. To try to sustain enthusiasm, in 1858, the General Assembly urged delegates to appoint a missionary agent in every Presbytery with responsibility for taking charge of the different collections. They were also to promote the circulation of the *Missionary Herald* to pub-licise mission work.[70]

Colonial work for Irish Presbyterians was also linked more explicitly to empire than was the case for the Church in Scotland. In the report

---

[67] *Minutes of the Proceedings of the General Assembly of the Presbyterian Church in Ireland*, vol. 2 (1851–60), p. 49.
[68] Minutes of the General Assembly of the Presbyterian Church in Ireland (Belfast, July 1860), p. 883.
[69] *Ibid.*, p. 884.
[70] Minutes of the General Assembly of the Presbyterian Church in Ireland (Belfast, July 1858), p. 675.

Table 7.1 *Summary of Congregational collections, Presbyterian Church of Ireland, 1890–2*

Year	Colonial Mission (£)	Continental Mission (£)	Irish Mission (£)	General Purposes (£)	Jewish Mission (£)	Soldiers etc. (£)	Foreign Mission (£)	Church Extension/ Temperance (£)	Total (£)
1890	1,748	NA	4,174	1,065	3,418	1,311	9,658	2,304	23,678
1891	2,588	NA	4,453	956	3,687	1,423	8,999	2,705	24,811
1892	1,856	2,086	4,266	4,266	961	3,778	9,384	2,165	28,762
1892 (%)	6.5	7.3	14.8	14.8	3.3	13.1	32.6	7.5	100

Source: Presbyterian Church in Ireland General Assembly, *Mission Reports and Accounts* (1890), p. 104; (1891), p. 101; (1892), p. 100.

to the General Assembly in Belfast in June 1891, the Reverend David Wilson of Limerick put this most starkly:

The Colonial Mission is based on the fact that as long as we are a colonizing people we require to be a colonizing Church; for the solemn charge given us by the Chief Shepherd is not simply to care for the ninety-and-nine within the fold, but to search out the one that may have gone into the wilderness. Its object is the maintenance and extension of the Kingdom of Christ all over the Colonies of the empire.[71]

Other than the SPG, few colonial missionary societies were so clear about the Christian objectives of colonial settlements.

Colonial Scheme of the Free Church of Scotland

In Scotland, the Disruption was seized by the Free Church as an opportunity to extend and entrench dissenting Presbyterianism, free of state control, in the colonies. Clearly, considerable planning preceded the final breach which occurred after evangelicals had secured a majority in the General Assembly.[72] Nevertheless, it is still astonishing that less than a fortnight after the Free Church schism at the General Assembly, a colonial committee for the new church was already up and running. The first meeting of the 'Committee of the Colonial Scheme of the Free Church of Scotland' was convened by David Welsh (1793–1845) in Edinburgh on 5 June 1843.[73] Even though he kept the position for only a few meetings until 10 July 1843, Welsh's leadership of the Colonial Committee is one measure of the importance of this committee to the Free Church. Welsh had been professor of church history at the University of Edinburgh and was a leading light of the Free Church movement. Indeed, as moderator of the Disruption Assembly of 1842,

---

[71] Presbyterian Church in Ireland General Assembly (1890–2), p. 44.

[72] Ewing, ed., *Annals of the Free Church of Scotland*, vol. 1, p. 2. According to Ewing (*ibid.*, vol. 1, p. 64), convenors of the Free Church Colonial Committee were: 1843, Reverend D. Welsh, DD, Reverend John Sym; 1844, Reverend John Sym; 1845, Reverend James Buchanan, DD, LLD; 1846, Reverend John Bonar, DD (in 1848 the Continental Committee was amalgamated with the Colonial Committee); 1864, Reverend Lewis H. Irving, Principal Lumsden (in 1868, the Colonial and Continental Committees were again separated); 1868, Reverend John Adam, DD; 1874, Reverend R. G. Balfour, DD; 1882, Reverend J. C. Burns, DD; 1889, Reverend R. Boog Watson, LLD; 1893, Reverend R. S. Duff, DD; and 1899, Reverend R. M'Intosh, DD. Secretaries were: 1843, James Balfour, Jr, WS [Writer to the Signet (a Scottish legal title)]; 1849, Reverend John Jaffray; 1853, James Balfour, WS; 1863, vacant; 1864, Reverend G. Divorty; 1870, Reverend Peter Hope; 1878, Reverend J. G. Mackintosh, interim; 1879, Reverend J. G. Mackintosh; and 1892, Reverend George Milne Rae, DD.

[73] Free Church of Scotland Colonial Committee (FCOS CC) Minutes, 5 June 1843, National Library of Scotland, Dep. 1298/260, p. 1.

it was Welsh who had led the 'exodus' which created the Free Church, something which he achieved at considerable personal cost since he was obliged to give up his chair at the University of Edinburgh.[74] He was also interested in colonial affairs and had taken over from MacFarlan following the latter's resignation from the General Assembly's Colonial Committee in 1841 on a point of principle. As convenor of the Colonial Scheme of the Free Church, Welsh was immediately given a leading role which carried with it considerable patrimony, something which would be vital for the hundreds of evangelical ministers who lost their positions in Scotland as a result of the Disruption.

At its first meeting, approval was given for a new committee to conduct the colonial scheme of the Free Church of Scotland. It consisted of thirty-four ministers, headed by the Reverend Dr MacKellar, and forty-three lay elders (laity), from the lawyer Henry Paul to James Blackadder. It would appear that about half of the ministers and elders who had belonged to the former colonial committee of the General Assembly had crossed the line to join the Free Church. High on the agenda of the first committee meeting was the issue of money: basically, there was none. Dr Welsh therefore called on all ministers who adhered to the Free Church to collect funds and take other measures in order to make it possible to extend the Free Church to the colonies, in order, as he put it, 'to accomplish the grand object which the Church has in view of supplying our countrymen in other lands with the means of grace'.

Almost immediately, this was translated into a major colonising venture in the Antipodes. The second meeting of the committee was devoted entirely to a presentation from Captain Cargill from the New Zealand Company who reported his intention to form a 'Scottish Colony in New Zealand', for which purpose they had set aside £25,000 for schools and churches, 'all in connection with the Free Church of Scotland'. What is more, Cargill requested the committee to appoint a minister and schoolmaster to accompany the emigrants.[75] The committee selected the Reverend Mr Burns of Monkton as minister for the settlement, still known as 'New Edinburgh, New Zealand', but required the New Zealand Company to guarantee that they would meet his salary, which should be at least £300, before confirming their support for the venture.[76] Captain Cargill undertook to work with the New Zealand

---

[74] On Welsh, see *Blackwell Dictionary of Evangelical Biography 1730–1860*, vol. II, ed. Donald M. Lewis, pp. 1168–9. See also Ewing, ed., *Annals of the Free Church of Scotland*, vol. 1, p. 59; W. Wilson, *Disruption Worthies*, ed. J. A. Wylie (Edinburgh, no date).

[75] FCOS CC Minutes, 7 June 1843, National Library of Scotland, Dep. 1298/260, p. 6.

[76] FCOS CC Minutes, 10 July 1843, National Library of Scotland, Dep. 1298/260, p. 12.

Company to this end. When arrangements were finally confirmed, the committee gave Burns a touching farewell in which regret at losing him was mingled with excitement for the 'vast importance of the projected settlement at Otago' and all it promised for the Free Church.[77] They also agreed to grant him £50 to purchase a library for the benefit of Otago settlers.[78]

Prospects for fund-raising on behalf of the Free Church's rapidly expanding colonial missions were significantly improved with the establishment of a Ladies' Colonial Association having for its general object 'the supply of the means of grace to Presbyterians in the colonies and dependencies of Great Britain, through the agency of missionaries, catechists, and teachers, under the sanction of the Colonial Committee of the General Assembly'.[79] The sorts of work supported by the ladies included aid for the Scottish and Irish Presbyterian soldiers in Gibraltar, Malta and serving with the Mediterranean fleet. The Ladies' Colonial Association received the correspondence from the missionaries sent out and responded to them. In this unique case, the 'Ladies' of the Free Church of Scotland were not just relegated to fund-raising but played an important role in seeking out and giving approval to ministers selected for particular colonial destinations. In July 1843, for example, the minutes noted that the Ladies' Colonial Association had 'unanimously resolved on recommending the Reverend Mr Wilson as a suitable teacher in connection with the Mission at Malta'.[80] While the qualifications of ministers were considered by the examination committee, women had an acknowledged position in the Free Church colonial committee, which was recognised from the earliest meetings of the new church, and was unprecedented. As letters from all over the British empire streamed into the committee, the various auxiliaries of the Ladies Committee expanded to meet particular needs. When Miss Mure of Warriston, Edinburgh, wrote to the committee about procuring a missionary for Australia, the convenor advised that the Ayrshire Ladies' Colonial Association should try to procure an 'efficient Missionary' themselves.[81] Seven years later, Miss Mure reported on the

[77] FCOS CC Minutes, 5 October 1847, National Library of Scotland, Dep. 1298/260, p. 302.
[78] FCOS CC Minutes, 8 November 1847, National Library of Scotland, Dep. 1298/260, p. 311.
[79] *Home and Foreign Missionary Record of the Free Church of Scotland*, vol. 2 (1845), p. 1811.
[80] FCOS CC Minutes, 17 July 1843, National Library of Scotland, Dep. 1298/260, p. 15.
[81] FCOS CC Minutes, 24 December 1843, National Library of Scotland, Dep. 1298/260, p. 178.

progress of their plans for supporting the Free Church in Geelong and Port Phillip in the Australian colony of Victoria.[82]

The work of the Free Church in the colonies, as reflected in their minute books, was full of excitement and friendly enthusiasm. They showed a remarkable flexibility in responding to letters from missionaries in the field, approving requests for a change of destination, or retirement on grounds of ill health, without creating difficulties. What could be done would be done. In general, the committee gave its approval to candidates after vetting by the examination committee, supplied passage money and outfit, and guaranteed their salary for one to three years until the colonial presbytery could manage this from their own resources. They also supplied books and bibles, provided grants to students studying for the ministry, and paid into the Widows Fund to provide for their families in the event of misfortune. As the imperial frontier expanded, so did the interests of the committee. However, all this enterprise came at a considerable cost.

The financial accounts and annual reports of the colonial missions of the Free Church of Scotland are contained in two large and regular published reports to the Free Church General Assembly.[83] Together with the Free Church Colonial Committee minutes, these volumes are the physical record of the heroic efforts taken to put the Free Church on a sound financial basis, thereby proving that the decision to break the chains of establishment had not been in vain, at who knows what personal cost to individuals and families. It is evident that, by 1845, the Free Church was already adapting well to the new, voluntary regime. The colonial scheme was an integral part of this expanding work. There is an almost obsessive focus on finances evident in the reports, with their constant exhortations to more vigorous fund-raising and long and elaborate financial statements of what had been achieved. In 1845, the General Assembly implored collectors to note 'how far her efforts and contributions have fallen short of what she owes to the cause of her blessed Redeemer', urging all to more strenuous efforts.[84] The key to

---

[82] *Ibid.*, p. 422.

[83] Free Church of Scotland, *The Home and Foreign Missionary Record for the Free Church of Scotland* (1843–62). See also David Preston, 'History of the Colonial Mission of the Church of Scotland' (1946?), Edinburgh University, New College Library, MSS BOX 29.1. According to the annotation of this item in Mundus, Gateway to missionary collections in the United Kingdom, www.mundus.ac.uk, the Reverend David Preston, BD, was the Minister-Emeritus of the Pollokshields-Tetwood Parish Church in Glasgow. Preston's book draws on the Free Church of Scotland Foreign Mission Board Archives, 1843–1934, held in the National Library of Scotland, Manuscripts Division. I have not seen this.

[84] *Home and Foreign Missionary Record of the Free Church of Scotland*, vol. 2 (1845), p. 105.

Table 7.2 *Receipts on the Schemes of the Free Church of Scotland, 1842–5*

Year	Home (£)	Colonial (£)	Indian/ Foreign (£)	Education (£)	Jews (£)	New College (£)	Total (£)
1843	5,029	4,160	4,577	5,684	5,839	NA	25,290
1844	5,337	4,268	6,909	4,858	4,474	NA	25,940
			Foreign			NA	
1845	4,005	3,313	4,128	3,102	4,269	3,257	22,074

Source: *Acts of the General Assembly of the Free Church of Scotland; Home and Foreign Missionary Record of the Free Church of Scotland, 1842–1845.*

all this giving was careful planning: annual collections were arranged for each of the five schemes of the Church, with the fourth Sabbath of June set aside for Colonial Churches, the fourth Sabbath of August for the Church Building Fund, the fourth Sabbath of October for the Home Mission, the fourth Sabbath of December for the Conversion of the Jews, and the fourth Sabbath of February for the Education Scheme. Perhaps the most striking feature of these figures is how little difference there is between the receipts for the various schemes, as indicated in Table 7.2.

After their initial bewilderment, the colonial presbyteries became key sites for the ongoing engagement on the issues that had led to the Disruption. There were Free Church deputations to the United States, Canada and Australia seeking support for the new church. These had mixed success. On Prince Edward Island, the Reverend John McMillan was encouraged by the response from two congregations, one consisting of Highlanders from the Isle of Skye and the other composed of North Highlanders and Lowland Scotch: 'It was gratifying to see these two congregations standing up to a man at the close of my addresses to them, respectively declaring their resolutions to take a minister from no Church but from the Church of their fathers – the Free Church of Scotland.'[85] Things were not so simple in Australia, where a request from one synod to be allowed to remain in connection with both the Free and the Established Church was rejected. John Dunmore Lang, as always, proved a thorn in everyone's side. Having set up his own Australia Synod and subsequently rebuffed the established church's colonial committee, Lang now informed the colonial committee of the

---

[85] *Home and Foreign Missionary Record of the Free Church of Scotland*, vol. 2 (1845), p. 1848. Not surprisingly, the established church also claimed to be the 'church of our fathers'.

Free Church of Scotland that he regarded them as 'a rival and antagonistic Presbyterian church'. He accordingly denounced the despatch of a deputation from the Free Church, calling it a 'personal insult to myself as the senior Presbyterian minister in the Australian colonies'.[86] While he could not prevent the arrival of the Free Church delegation, Lang now added 'Free Churchism' – along with Puseyism and Romanism – to the long list of enemy forces arrayed against him.[87] By July 1845, the schism had been successfully imposed on most of the colonial presbyteries and the Colonial Committee reported on moves to establish Free Church congregations with their own ministers in India, the West Indies, Australia, New Zealand, the Mediterranean and Madeira.[88]

With Burns' departure, the Reverend John Bonar of Renfield Street Free Church, Glasgow, convenor of the Colonial Committee of the Free Church of Scotland, became the leading advocate for the rapid colonial growth of dissenting Presbyterianism.[89] In 1849, Bonar reported proudly that teachers and ministers had been despatched throughout the year to Australia Felix (Gippsland, Victoria), Melbourne, the West Indies, New Zealand, Nova Scotia, Newfoundland and the Mediterranean.[90] There is real passion in Bonar's closing remarks that depicts Presbyterianism in the colonies as a refuge should a future persecution drive away true religion in the homeland: 'Let every Christian Church, improve the large and effectual door which God is now opening in the distant regions he

---

[86] Lang to the Colonial Committee of the Free Church of Scotland, 17 April 1847, in Lang, *Australian Mission*, pp. 9 and 12.

[87] *Ibid.*, p. 14. For diatribes by Lang against Puseyism and Romanism or 'Popedom', see J. D. Lang, *The Question of Questions! Or, Is This Colony to Be Transformed into a Province of Popedom?* (Sydney, 1841); J. D. Lang, *Popery in Australia and the Southern Hemisphere, and How to Check It Effectually: An Address to Evangelical and Influential Protestants of All Denominations in Great Britain and Ireland* (Edinburgh, 1847); J. D. Lang, *How the People of England Were Tricked out of Their Noble Inheritance in the Waste Lands of Australia* [*Extract from Lang's Historical and Statistical Account of New South Wales*] (London, n.d.).

[88] *Home and Foreign Missionary Record of the Free Church of Scotland*, vol. 2 (1845), p. 1159.

[89] There is a review of his sermon style not long after he took over the Renfield Street church by J. Smith, *Our Scottish Clergy: Fifty-Two Sketches, Biographical, Theological, and Critical, Including Clergymen of All Denominations*, Second Series (Edinburgh, 1849), p. 155. Smith states that Bonar was born in Cramond and was a cousin of the other Free Church Bonars, i.e. Andrew and Horatio, both also Free Church ministers. He was ordained in 1826, sent from there to Aberdeen, and from thence to Glasgow to take over from Dr Willis who had, like Burns, departed for Canada. Bonar was a fourth-generation clergyman of the Church of Scotland.

[90] Though he could not place ministers with every congregation which appealed to him. The Red River Settlement in remote Upper Canada waited three years for a reply to their letter requesting a minister; Bonar could only express regret that he had so far failed to find someone who had seen it 'their duty to accept'. See A. Ross, *The Red River Settlement; Its Rise, Progress, and Present State* (London, 1856), p. 352.

is peopling from the nations of the Old World!'[91] True to these convictions, Bonar was on hand to participate in the often emotional scenes
of departure, as, for example, when a party of Gaelic-speakers from
Skye, sponsored by the Highland and Island Emigration Society, left
Greenock on 13 July 1852.[92] Bonar was an enthusiast for the potential of colonial Presbyterianism, which he argued had something to
teach the home church. Canada, he suggested, was both beautiful and
vigorous; Australia was, if anything, an even more promising site for
the improvement of the British race. While he recognised that English
capital was one factor in both colonies' prosperity, Bonar pointed to
the spiritual resources which were the endowment of the free Scottish
church. 'Other bodies are strong in wealth derived from England and
in influence maintained from England; but the Presbyterian Church in
the colonies is a distinct Church.' He looked with pride on the separate
Synods of Victoria, New South Wales and the Presbyteries of South
Australia, Auckland and Otago as independent spiritual forces, which
underpinned the future greatness of the colonies.[93]

After more than a decade of strenuous exertion, the tide in favour
of colonial missions began to turn. In 1859, the total receipts submitted to the Assembly still showed a respectable increase to a total of
£31,641, but the schemes of work now show the pre-eminence of foreign missions (£19,418), chiefly in Kaffraria and India, as opposed to
Colonial (£4,487) and Jewish (£7,735) missions,[94] a difference which
was to become characteristic of Free Church collections. Colonial
work in Canada, Nova Scotia, New Brunswick, the West Indies, the
Mediterranean, Australasia and Natal, as well as the Highlands of
Scotland, had become self-supporting, and there were resources for
other fields. As Bonar prophesied, the Free Church had triumphed
in the colonies, helped by the transfer of a good many of the Free
Church ministry who had been forced to leave the established church
in Scotland. In New Zealand, for example, the 1858 census shows that
over twice as many of those polled identified with Presbyterian dissent
or the Free Church than with the 'auld kirk'.[95] Like Methodism, it was
a creed that suited the colonial climate.

[91] Free Church of Scotland, *Report of the Colonial Committee of the Free Church of Scotland, Presented to the General Assembly on Thursday, 31st May 1849 by the Reverend John Bonar* (Edinburgh, 1849), p. 12.
[92] M. D. Prentis, *The Scots in Australia* (Sydney, 2008), p. 35.
[93] *Ibid.*, p. 33.
[94] J. L. Aikman, *Cyclopædia of Christian Missions: Their Rise, Progress, and Present Position* (London and Glasgow, 1860), p. 200.
[95] Jackson, *Churches and People*, p. 21.

Colonial Scheme of the Established Church
of Scotland

The enthusiasm of Free Church agents for colonial Presbyterianism cannot be matched from the reports of the established Church of Scotland. The latter was hard hit by the Disruption, probably more so than the Free Church, and took longer to recover. In 1843, the report to the General Assembly made a brave show of a tepid demonstration of colonial loyalty: 'We have had the satisfaction of recording the testimony of not a few of the Colonial clergy in behalf of our venerable Church, and their firm adherence to her in her hour of trial.' But perhaps it would be more truthful to say that the colonists were generally appalled at the Disruption. The Canadian Synod prayed for an end to the division, and predicted 'fearful consequences' if it continued: 'Every preacher who comes from Scotland will carry with him the elements of contention.'[96] There is a rather sad letter written to the convenor of the Colonial Committee from the Reverend Alex McGillivray in Pictou, Nova Scotia, who had been abandoned by all his clerical colleagues:

Rev. Sir, You are of course aware that I am the only ordained clergyman in connection with the Church of Scotland now in this large and populous county. Before the late secession the presbytery of Pictou consisted of eight ministers. Of these six have gone home with the view of lending a hand in repairing the breaches made in our Zion in their native land; and one considered it his duty to join the Free Church.[97]

In New South Wales, the Presbyterian ministry decided to throw in their lot with the colony rather than return to Scotland. This involved negotiations with the redoutable J. D. Lang, the leading Presbyterian minister in the colony of New South Wales.[98] Lang had secured the passage of twelve ministers for the Australian colonies by applying directly to the colonial committee of the Church of Scotland. After the Disruption, ministers who found themselves in disagreement with Lang were presented with an invidious choice: they might continue in their chosen clerical profession by converting to the Church of England and submitting to episcopal ordination; they could make common cause with Free Churchers and face almost certain financial ruin, or they might join another Protestant church which lacked the social prestige and educational standards required of the Presbyterian ministry. Most chose the first option. Lang called those who bowed to the episcopate

---

[96] Church of Scotland, *The Home and Foreign [Missionary] Record of the Church of Scotland* (1842), vol. 2, p. 1243.
[97] *Ibid.*, p. 1243.   [98] Baker, *Preacher, Politician, Patriot.*

Table 7.3 *Receipts for the Colonial Scheme of the*
Church of Scotland, 1868–85

Year	Receipts for the Colonial Scheme (£)
1868	7,134
1873	9,579
1878	10,487
1879	9,013
1880	11,465
1881	7,454
1882	6,783
1883	7,470
1884	6,011
1885	5,437

Source: Reports to the General Assembly of the Church of
Scotland.

'Judases' who had abandoned the faith of their fathers in pursuit of
filthy lucre.[99]

In the colonies, the issue of state support for colonial Presbyterians
remained contentious. As the final decision was being made to secu-
larise the clergy reserves, the Colonial Committee made a last ditch
attempt to secure something by sending a deputation to London.
Despite this effort, the bill was passed leading to the practical disestablishment of both the Episcopal and Presbyterian Churches in Canada,
while leaving Catholic endowments in Lower Canada untouched.[100]
There was more progress to report on other fronts, such as the outfit
and passage money to six ministers for North America, two of whom
had knowledge of Gaelic. The report to the Assembly concludes opti-
mistically: 'A spirit of missionary enterprise has been awakened in
our land, and we are delighted to find that ministers and preachers
are more alive, than formerly, to the duty of carrying the glad tidings
of salvation to every corner of the globe; especially to our brethren
in the Colonies, so destitute of the means of grace.'[101] The colonial
churches were able to send funds for passage and outfit of ministers,
but it was alarming that receipts were falling and the total income of
the committee was only £3,535.

[99] Lang, *Popery in Australia*, pp. 41–2.
[100] D. MacFarlan and Thomas Clark, 'Report to the General Assembly by the Colonial
Committee, May 1853', *Home and Foreign Missionary Record for the Church of Scotland*
(1853), p. 148.
[101] *Ibid.*, p. 151.

By the 1860s, recovery in the established Church was well under-way – though there were no signs of reunification with the Free Church. In a tragic waste of resources, both churches continued to support rival schemes for India Missions, Home Missions, Colonial Missions and for the Conversion of the Jews. Along with these committees, the Colonial Committee submitted a full and careful report to each General Assembly.[102] Annual receipts to the Colonial Scheme of the established Church rose to a peak in 1880 and then slowly began to fall, as indicated in Table 7.3. This was not necessarily a bad sign, but an indication of the increasing independence of the colonial synods which no longer needed support from home to maintain their ministers and build their churches.

1880s: Britishness v. Scottishness

Whatever their differences, all the Scottish colonial missionary societies, whether voluntary or part of the Church structure, free or established, were practical organisations. Their effective organisations ensured that funds flowed. The evidence of their annual reports and sermons and committee meetings suggests that they felt no need to deviate from their central purpose: raising funds, choosing ministers, keeping the Presbyterian churches in the colonies in touch with the home trad-ition and encouraging self-sufficiency. This was all accomplished with a minimum of the promotional strategies which were a feature of the other colonial missionary societies. However, the ardour of Scottish patriotism simmered below the surface and occasionally came to the fore. In his brief survey of the Scottish colonial missionary movement, Williamson wrote approvingly of the links which the new Canadian churches continued to maintain with the land of their founders:

Wherever Scottish families settled, the ordinances of religion were established, and provision made for the education of youth. Innumerable names of stations planted by these colonists could be given – many of them bearing old familiar names of glens and hills and rivers, towns and farm-steadings 'at home' – all bearing evidence of the affection entertained by the exiles for that dear land from which they had gone forth.[103]

In 1878, Dr M'Gibbon wrote from New South Wales to plead for a continued flow of ministers from Scotland: 'I trust that there is hope of some of the *true* yet expected from you coming soon.'[104] This respect for

[102] *Reports on the Schemes of the Church of Scotland* (1868), p. 200.
[103] Williamson, *What Has the Church of Scotland Done for Our Colonies?*, p. 7.
[104] *Reports on the Schemes of the Church of Scotland* (1878), p. 235.

'the *true*', and for all that was familiar, also extended to the strict standards which were placed on the training required of ministers, standards
which the colonies frequently were unable to meet without recourse to
Scotland.

Yet the appeal to Scotland was also limited. By the turn of the century, the reports of the Colonial Scheme of the Church of Scotland
had shifted their focus from the successful independent settler societies which had occupied it in the 1860s. Its reports to the General
Assembly provide accounts of work among soldiers in India, or continental work such as provision of chaplaincy services at the Paris
World Exhibition (1889), or other equally remote, marginal and
challenging locations. In contrast with the Church of England, the
colonial churches achieved independence from the home church rapidly and without undue complications. Nevertheless, it was not until
1901 that the suggestion was made that the Presbyterian churches 'at
home' should send out delegates to the Assemblies of the Churches
in the Colonies.[105] It is final testimony to the conservatism of the
General Assembly and its administrators that it took more than a
hundred years before the Colonial Committee felt it had outlived
its usefulness. This did not happen until 1964, when the Colonial
and Continental Committee was incorporated into a single Overseas
Council which took over the activities of all the committees which
had formerly been engaged in foreign missions, the conversion of the
Jews and other schemes.[106] Adopting the motto 'The Mission is One',
the reluctance of the old committees to accept the new arrangement is
perhaps hinted at in the report of the former Colonial and Continental
Committee, which asserted: 'Within the Overseas Council the work
done so faithfully and effectively by the Colonial and Continental
Committee for well over a century has during the year been assidu-
ously continued.'[107]

While the Colonial Schemes of the Church of Scotland were always
practical rather than ideological in their outlook, its activities were
open to imperial interpretation in the right hands. No one was better
qualified for this task than John Buchan, the Scottish statesman and
novelist, who in 1934, while serving as Lord High Commissioner to the
General Assembly (1933–4), was invited to present a centenary address
on the Colonial Scheme of the Church of Scotland. For Buchan, the
Colonial Scheme was a 'great work', but one which was not strictly

[105] *Ibid.*, p. 335.
[106] Church of Scotland, 'Report of the Overseas Council for 1964', in *The Church of
Scotland Reports to the General Assembly* (Edinburgh, 1965), pp. 365–427.
[107] *Ibid.*, p. 392.

missionary since it was directed not at 'ignorance and savagery', but at 'our own people'.[108] Nevertheless, he argued that, because of its gospel-based simplicity, it was uniquely suited to becoming a church not just for Scotland but for the whole world: 'I believe that in a true sense Presbyterianism is fitted to be a universal Church.' It was, moreover, a church for the empire: 'Just as these islands of ours are a nation and also the centre of an Empire, so our Church, specifically the Church of Scotland has also its worldwide and Imperial aspect. For … it is at once evangelical and catholic, historic, liberal, and free.'[109] Such a speech would undoubtedly have pleased Buchan's strict Free Church mother; however, he also spoke for the Scottish diaspora who, despite the perennial conflict within their churches, held fast to the conviction of the cultural value of their home institutions.

Conclusion

The Scottish churches carried out effective colonial missions in the nineteenth century that ensured that Presbyterianism had a significant impact on most British settler colonies. In certain regions of Scottish settlement in British North America and New Zealand, Scottish Presbyterianism was established as the majority church, and this influenced all aspects of colonial society in these places, particularly education. Religious affiliation, as measured by the imperfect gauge of census returns, provides one way to measure the overall Scottish Presbyterian impact in the four largest colonies of British settlement.[110] In 1841, before depopulation began, the Scots made up 9.8 per cent of the population of Great Britain and Ireland. Reflecting high levels of Scottish imperial emigration throughout the nineteenth century, by 1901, Presbyterians made up more than 15 per cent of the settled population in Canada, 23 per cent in New Zealand, and 11 per cent in Australia. Only in Cape Colony, where the Dutch Reformed Church was congenial to many Scottish Calvinists, does the percentage of Presbyterians at the end of the century (1898) appear to be less than in Britain, namely, 4.26 per cent. Nevertheless, the achievement of the Scottish churches in the British empire was less distinguished than might have been expected from its status as one of only two established churches in the United Kingdom. In the 1830s, church leaders in Scotland aspired to establish Scottish Presbyterianism in the empire on a par with the Church of England. What happened to this aspiration?

[108] Buchan, *Scottish Church and the Empire*, p. 3.
[109] *Ibid.*   [110] See Tables 1.1–1.6.

The Colonial Committee of the General Assembly of the Church of Scotland was committed to this end. However, the colonial Presbyterian churches that were planted with such meticulous care and expense in the course of the next century differed in a number of critical ways from the Church of Scotland at home. The most important difference stemmed from the influence of evangelical Presbyterianism. While this colonial development may have happened anyway – evangelicalism was also an important strand of colonial Anglicanism – evangelicalism was given a significant boost by the Disruption. The schism in the Scottish church ensured that there was a pool of evangelical ministers keen to emigrate and pursue their vocation overseas just at the time when the whole Scottish population was seized with the fever for emigration. In the main, it was the Free Church movement – that is, those Presbyterians most closely allied with other evangelicals – who chose to emigrate and support the colonial mission cause. The Free Church accordingly left a strong imprint on colonial Presbyterianism and encouraged many to form close bonds with like-minded evangelicals.

Division at home, coupled with the economic success of Scottish emigrants, also hastened the independence of the colonial churches. Canadian federation, which began on 1 July 1867, was followed by Presbyterian federation in 1875, when four branches of Presbyterianism rejoined to form the Presbyterian Church in Canada. In British North America, there was a premium attached to Christian union which was not matched for some time by the home church which continued to be burdened with a complex constitutional legacy linking it to the state. In Scotland, the Free Church was not reunited with the Church of Scotland until 1929. However, following the secularisation of the Canadian clergy reserves in 1854, this impediment did not apply in the colonies where there was effectively no colonial church establishment from this date. This made links between the various British Protestant churches much less acrimonious. These links would eventually lead to successful unions of diverse groups of Presbyterians, Methodists and Congregationalists, first in Canada in 1925 and later in Australia in 1977. The tendency for all the churches involved in the ecumenical movement was to stress their evangelical inheritance, which they shared with the United States, and to pay less heed to their Scottish, British or other national origins. The wish to create an imperial Presbyterianism to rival Anglicanism seems to have evaporated at the time of the Disruption.

Thirdly, there is the possibility that emigration was itself a spur to detachment from traditional religion. In his discussion of religion and immigrants to Australia and New Zealand, Jackson notes that few emigrants had strong religious views, an informed opinion reinforced by Patrick O'Farrell in his study of Irish emigrants to Australia.[111] Instead, it was small groups of devotees, or clerical professionals, that were most likely to retain and demand high levels of religious conformity. Such groups included the strict Calvinists who emigrated to Waipu, north of Auckland in New Zealand, from Cape Breton, Nova Scotia, with Norman McLeod (1780–1866) in 1843.[112] Others had gone first to Nova Scotia attempting to find land that was suitable for the settlement of their entire community. However, having left their country to keep their people together and sustain their distinctive reformed religious traditions, the ultimate fate of the Scottish churches in most British colonies was to merge with other evangelical Protestants to form new national, united or 'uniting' churches. Presbyterian colonists, both women and men, had already voted with their feet when they left the United Kingdom; most were free churchers. Their new churches remained Scottish in aspiration and tradition, but had no formal association with the British state and the Scottish nation. They called themselves Presbyterians, not members of the Church of Scotland, which retained resonances of aristocratic and royal patronage, conflict with the state and theological controversy. In the colonies, the ecumenical and democratic churches which Scottish emigrants helped to create reflected the Christian consensus that I suggested in the first chapter made up the religious character of Greater Britain.

This section has now surveyed all the colonial missionary societies associated with the major churches of Great Britain in the nineteenth century. This movement required organisation, commitment and funds from all the home churches. But its key moveable component was what would later be called human capital – trained clergy with the capacity to reproduce the rituals, traditions and culture of their churches in new lands. So many were despatched that they came to form a special professional cadre – the colonial clergy. The next section of the book will examine the emigration and training of colonial clergy in colleges established for this purpose by the Anglicans and Catholics.

[111] Jackson, *Churches and People*, p. 18. For the tendency of emigration to weaken or at least transform the attachment to traditional religion, see also H. M. Carey, 'The Vanished Kingdoms of Patrick O'Farrell: Religion, Memory and Migration in Religious History', *Journal of Religious History*, 31 (2007), pp. 40–58. For O'Farrell's view of emigration as a kind of pilgrimage in reverse, away from rather than towards religion, see P. J. O'Farrell and B. Trainor, *Letters from Irish Australia, 1825–1929* (Sydney, 1984), p. 57.

[112] Jackson, *Churches and People*, p. 18.

Part III

Colonial clergy

8   Clergy

By the middle of the nineteenth century, thanks in part to the colonial missionary movement, the colonial churches were seen in a much more positive light than they had been in the eighteenth. Instead of a destination of last resort for those who could not find preferment at home, the colonies were appreciated as a particular calling which would benefit from specialised training and, for a small number, a positive career move. This chapter considers the response that was made to the need to train this new class of professional men. It concentrates on the Church of England and the legislative means that were devised to regulate the passage of clergy in and out of the United Kingdom. It also looks at the Colonial Missionary College movement, which grew out of the demand for more flexible, as well as more specialised, professional training for those going out to work overseas. A full study of the statistical profile of the clergy of all churches in Great Britain and Ireland and the settler colonies throughout the nineteenth century is not what is attempted (or achieved) here. Instead, the aim is to indicate some of the major questions which shaped the profession, as well as the factors which encouraged particular individuals to try their hand overseas. The two chapters which follow look at two special cohorts of colonial clergy, namely, the students of St Augustine's College, Canterbury, and the missionary college of All Hallows, Drumcondra, in Dublin.

Established clergy

The clergy of the established Church of England were originally the largest and most generic of the professions.[1] As many critics of the

[1] W. J. Reader, *Professional Men: The Rise of the Professional Classes in Nineteenth-Century England* (London, 1966), p. 194. The occupations discussed by Reader include teachers, surveyors, solicitors, priests, physicians and surgeons, musicians, ministers of religion, midwives, engineers (civil), dentists, commercial clerks, clergy (Church of England), barristers, authors, artists, architects, actors and accountants. See also A. Russell, *The Clerical Profession* (London, 1980).

system for the training of clergy in the United Church of England and Ireland complained in the first half of the nineteenth century, there was no special preparation for the ordained ministry. A prospective clergyman simply progressed from a shorter or longer spell at one of the established universities of England and Ireland before submitting to examination by a bishop and taking holy orders. If he could secure a competent living, he would then move on to enjoy a life-time sinecure with an independent income and responsibility for a parish. For those with a degree but no living, school teaching provided an alternative occupation to parish duties, though those with few alternatives might turn their hand to farming or even a trade to make ends meet. As we saw in Chapter 2, chaplaincy in the military or the colonies was another path to a professional career in the ministry for those of an adventurous disposition and the right connections.

Historians of the Anglican clergy have been divided on issues such as the extent to which the clergy were typical or differed from other Victorian professions, and whether their numbers, status and income kept pace with the rapid changes in British society.[2] Throughout the nineteenth century, there was a perennial concern at the quality and numbers of those coming forward as candidates for the Anglican ministry. However, much of the panic about the lack of clergy appears to have been exaggerated or, at least, based in part on the reluctance to admit men of less than middle-class standing for the appropriate training.[3] In the early decades of the nineteenth century, there was a problem with declining numbers, but this was addressed by ensuring that the payments made to stipendiary curates was not allowed to depend entirely on the whim of the absent rector. In fact, the number of ordinands to the Church of England appears to have risen steadily throughout the nineteenth century and more or less managed to keep pace with the rise in population, itself a remarkable achievement given high levels of emigration.[4] As estimated by Heeney and Haig, in England and Wales the overall number of clergy seems to have remained somewhere around

[2] For review, see F. Knight, *The Nineteenth-Century Church and English Society* (Cambridge, 1995), p. 13. For the variety of approaches, see A. G. Haig, *The Victorian Clergy* (London, 1984); B. Heeney, *A Different Kind of Gentleman: Parish Clergy as Professional Men in Early and Mid-Victorian England* (Hamden, CT, 1976); Reader, *Professional Men.*

[3] R. O'Day, 'The Clerical Renaissance in Victorian England and Wales', in *Religion in Victorian Britain: I Traditions*, ed. G. Parsons (Manchester, 1988), cited by D. Dowland, *Nineteenth-Century Anglican Theological Training: The Redbrick Challenge* (Oxford, 1997), p. 7.

[4] P. Virgin, *The Church in an Age of Negligence* (Cambridge, 1989), pp. 136 and 165. Figures cited by S. J. Brown, *The National Churches of England, Ireland, and Scotland 1801–1846* (Oxford, 2001), p. 91.

one clergyman for every thousand head of population judging by the census figures for the second half of the nineteenth century.[5]

The pattern differed slightly for the three major groups of religious professionals, which for convenience we will refer to as Anglican clergy, Nonconformist ministers and Catholic priests. In the census of 1911, at the end of the period considered by this book, there appear to have been at least 40,000 clergy, ministers and Catholic priests in England and Wales. Based on figures, where available, from the census, Reader suggests that the clergy of the established Church of England enjoyed a sharp rise in the 1840s when their numbers outpaced the general population growth, but that they failed to do more than keep pace after this and actually fell by 1 per cent in the first decade of the twentieth century. The number of Nonconformist ministers of religion in the United Kingdom some-times rose above the advance of the population and sometimes remained below it. However, they generally did rather better than the established Church. In contrast, the number of Catholic priests generally rose in excess of the population in England, though from an invisible base prior to the 1850s. Making use of Reader's data, it is also possible to suggest that clergy of all kinds experienced a strong period of growth between the 1841 and the 1881 census, but that their growth slowed markedly in later decades to about half that of the population. Although it is difficult to be sure what occupiers meant when they identified themselves as 'clergy' or a 'minister' or 'priest', the census also seems to suggest that the propor-tion of clergy to ministers rose markedly in the second half of the century, from 40 per cent in 1841 to 48 per cent in 1911.

In Ireland, the number of Catholic priests remained relatively low until the increase of the grant to Maynooth in 1845 made it possible for men of modest social backgrounds to train for the priesthood. By the 1861 census, which showed that the population was 77.7 per cent Catholic, 12 per cent Anglican and 9 per cent Presbyterian, the ratio between clergy and people in the Catholic church had been much improved, and all denominations were engaged in catering to emigrant communities. In Scotland, as we saw in Chapter 7, the Disruption created intense rivalry between different branches of the Church of Scotland and necessitated the founding of new clerical training insti-tutes outside the universities, notably New College in Edinburgh; this promoted the number and quality of candidates for the ministry.

How many of this vast clerical cohort left Britain in order to practise their profession in the colonies? That turns out to be quite a difficult question to answer, but the year books of the respective churches in the

---

[5] For discussion, see Dowland, *Nineteenth-Century Anglican Theological Training*, p. 6.

Table 8.1 *Number of clergy, ministers and priests in England and Wales for census years 1841, 1881 and 1911*

Occupation	1841	1881	1911
Clergy (Church of England)	14,527	21,663	24,859
Ministers (Dissenting)	5,923	9,734	11,984
Priests (Roman Catholic)	—	2,089	3,302
Total clergy (all denominations)	20,450	33,486	40,145
Increase (%)	—	64	20
Total population of England and Wales	15,914,000	25,974,000	36,070,000
Increase (%)	—	63	39

Source: Census returns for England and Wales, tabulated by Reader, *Professional Men* (1966), p. 209.

separate colonies and dominions suggest that, in Australia, Canada and New Zealand, though less so in southern Africa, the number of clergy rose steadily in line with emigration for all churches.[6] By the time of the great imperial census of 1901, the dominions could all boast that at about 0.3 per cent the number of clergy in proportion to their populations, especially in urban areas, was very close to that of England, Wales and Scotland, though still below that in Ireland where it was 0.4 per cent.[7] However, the inclusion of all the related occupations, for example mendicant holy men in India, makes the interpretation of these figures highly problematic.

Although the absolute numbers of clergy relative to the population at home may have remained relatively high, the same could not be said for clerical incomes. The most accessible figures are those for the Church of England. While at the upper levels of ecclesiastical preferment, salaries and endowments for bishops and archbishops were princely, most Anglican clergymen were not wealthy.[8] The income for a parish living

[6] More work is needed on the question of the size of the non-Anglican clergy in the UK and the colonies.

[7] Census of the British Empire, 1901, Report with summary and detailed tables for the several colonies, &c., area, houses and population; also population classified by ages, condition as to marriage, occupations, birthplaces, religions, *British Parliamentary Papers* (1905), vol. 102 (Cd 2660), p. xxxi.

[8] For a summary of data on clerical incomes, see Cook and Stevenson, *British Historical Facts 1760–1830*, pp. 166–7. In 1810, 1,500 resident incumbents had an income under £150, the usual salary offered to a colonial chaplain. 2,500 curacies paid £30–40 per annum. *Extraordinary Black Book or Corruption Unmasked* (1835) stated that, out of total Church revenues of £9,459,565, 2 archbishops had £26,465 each and 24 bishops had £10,174, while 4,305 incumbents, half of whom were resident in their parishes, had £764. Annual incomes for individuals would be much less, but the archbishop of Canterbury had £7,000 and Durham £6,000.

Table 8.2 *Relative percentage distribution of the clerical, legal, medical and teaching professions in the British empire, including subordinate occupations, 1901*

	Clerical	Legal	Medical		Teaching	
	Males	Males	Males	Females	Males	Females
England and Wales	0.3	0.4	0.2	0.4	0.4	1
Scotland	0.3	0.4	0.2	0.4	0.4	0.8
Ireland	0.4	0.2	0.2	0.1	0.3	0.6
Indian Empire	0.65	0.05	0.10	0.05	0.12	0.01
Ceylon	0.9	0.1	0.2	0.1	0.2	0.1
Cape of Good Hope	0.2	0.1	0.1	0.1	0.2	0.5
Orange River Colony	0.1	0.1	0.1	0.1	0.2	0.5
Australian Commonwealth	0.3	0.3	0.2	0.6	0.4	1
New Zealand	0.3	0.3	0.3	0.5	0.5	1

Source: Census of British empire, 1901.

generally came from rents that were controlled by gentry families who were able to bestow them on younger sons or others within their circle of patronage. Since stipends could be very low, especially in poor parts of the country such as rural Ireland, it was common for incumbents to hold more than one living. In this case, the rector would employ a curate to perform the essential services of the parish. As the mood for political and social reform swept the country in the 1820s and 1830s, some of the deficiencies in the administration of the Church were addressed by legislation that enforced payment of proper fees to curates and discouraged non-residence.[9] Still, curates could be very poor men indeed, and, for those at the bottom of the ladder of ecclesiastical pre-ferment, emigration to the colonies had many attractions.

Educational reform for the training of clergy was the next issue to be addressed in the course of church reform. Correspondents to the secular and religious press and sermon and pamphlet writers expressed concerns about the relaxed requirements for qualification to the ministry. 'A clergyman', in a published series of letters to the bishop of Llandaff, observed that there was very little in a university education

[9] The legislation is summarised by Russell, *Clerical Profession*, pp. 36–7. Acts passed in 1795 and 1813 enforced payment of curates in cases of non-residence; an Act of 1817 restricted clergy from engaging in farming and trade. Further Acts passed in 1826 controlled residence; the Clergy Resignation Bond Act of 1836 prevented the *de facto* award of livings to minors; the Pluralities Act of 1838 and the Clergy Discipline Act of 1836 further regulated the profession.

that prepared a graduate for the work of the ministry. Indeed, compared with other professions such as medicine or the law, the situation was parlous: 'A clergyman', he observed, 'is the only member of any of the learned professions, who has strictly no regular provision for an education, suited to the office, to which he aspires.'[10] The suggested remedy, a highly sensible one, was that, in addition to a degree, candidates for ordination should present a certificate that they had passed a year in the house of an experienced clergyman.[11] During this year, they might practise writing sermons, accompany him on pastoral visits, and learn the business of visitation to the poor and sick that forms the practical part of a minister's duties. In a second letter, the lack of supervision given to the clergyman is compared with that of other professional neophytes.[12] All of this was a good deal less than the minimum standard set for the education of Roman Catholic priests following the Council of Trent, let alone for the highly educated ministry of the Church of Scotland, which required a theological degree. Nevertheless, it was an improvement. In the middle of the century, there were strong moves to set up separate theological and missionary colleges to improve the training of clergy; there was also a small number of specialist colleges which provided training for colonial ministry, and these are discussed in Chapters 9 and 10.

For the colonial clergy, who until 1776 really meant those in America and the West Indies, matters were not so very different in terms of status, income and education. Since the number of overseas clergy was relatively small, the bishop of London was given responsibility for managing their affairs.[13] This included all the missionaries sent out by the Society for the Propagation of the Gospel who were required to wait upon the bishop of London, their diocesan, in order to receive 'Paternal Benediction and Instruction' before departing for the colonies.[14] From the beginning of the eighteenth century, the overseas matters that came under the eye of the bishop of London steadily increased until they became a pressing burden.[15] Bishop Henry Compton (1676–1713),

---

[10] Anon [A Clergyman], *On Clerical Education: A Letter Addressed to … Edward, Lord Bishop of Llandaff* (London, 1832), p. 7; F. W. B. Bullock, *A History of Training for the Ministry of the Church of England in England and Wales from 598–1799* (St Leonards-on-Sea, Sussex, 1969), p. 86.

[11] Anon [A Clergyman], *On Clerical Education*, p. 9.

[12] Anon [A Clergyman], *On the Office of Deacon: A Second Letter Addressed to … Edward, Lord Bishop of Llandaff* (London, 1832), p. 6.

[13] For the legal position, see Addleshaw, 'Law and Constitution'.

[14] Hawkins, *Historical Notices of the Missions of the Church of England*, p. 424.

[15] For correspondence relating to what was sometimes called 'the oversea episcopate', see the Fulham Papers, 'FP Compton 1' to 'FP Fisher 10', for successive bishops of London, in Lambeth Palace Library.

for example, considered matters relating to chaplaincies in Fort William, Bengal, in 1706 as well as problems with clergy in Jamaica and subscriptions for Protestant missions and schools in Tranquebar. Compton's successors as bishop of London were also kept busy with colonial clergy matters. For John Robinson (1713–23), there was correspondence from chaplains appointed to the British factory in Lisbon and about David Barry, army chaplain in Gibraltar. Edmund Gibson (1723–48) was consulted about baptisms and marriages overseas as well as salaries for chaplains on military bases such as Gibraltar in Europe as well as others in New England and the West Indies. Thomas Sherlock (1748–61) considered the procedure for the appointment of chaplains for the East India Company as well as appointments of chaplains for St Helena and Nova Scotia. Thomas Hayter (1761–2) and Richard Osbaldeston (1762–4) seem to have been untroubled by overseas matters, but Richard Terrick (1764–77) was worried about the rights of presentation to livings in the East Indies and appointments to English congregations in Holland, Kronstadt, the Scilly Isles, the Gold Coast in Africa and Fort Marlborough in Sumatra in 1770. Robert Lowth (1777–87) was consulted about resignations and licensing of chaplains from Constantinople to St Vincent in the West Indies.

The logical solution to the intractable problem of managing distant dioceses from London was that the colonies should train up their own clergy. However, colonial colleges of higher education were few and far between. According to denomination, these institutions were modelled on colleges in Oxford and Cambridge, or the dissenting academies in England, as well as the four Scottish universities.[16] For Catholic clergy, there was the Quebec Séminaire des Missions-Étrangères, which was re-established as Université Laval by royal charter in 1852. As noted by Thomas Clap, fifth rector of Yale College in 1754, most colonial colleges had been set up to supply clergy for the local churches: 'The original End and design of College was to Instruct, Educate, and Train up Persons for the work of the Ministry.'[17] For this reason they were ruled by governing bodies which were almost always confessional in character. The business about colonial clergy being, in a real sense, servants of the crown was dramatically proven at the time of the revolution when colonial clergy captured by British forces

[16] D. G. Reid, *Dictionary of Christianity in America* (Downers Grove, IL, 1990), pp. 378–80. The affiliations of these older institutions was: Harvard (Puritan/Congregational); William and Mary (Anglican); Yale (Congregational); Columbia (Anglican); Brown (Baptist); and Rutgers (Dutch Reformed).

[17] T. Clap, *The Religious Constitution of Colleges, Especially of Yale College in New-Haven in the Colony of Connecticut* (New-London, CT, 1754), p. 1.

might, like William Pierce, be banned from their clerical ministry.[18] The first American Episcopal bishop, Samuel Seabury, was not consecrated as bishop of Connecticut until 1784; until he began performing ordinations, American candidates were required to travel to Britain to receive holy orders.[19] Some of these difficulties were resolved by the passing of the Ordination for Colonies Act (1819) and later by the Colonial Clergy Act (1874). Suspicions about both the loyalty and theological orthodoxy of colonial clergy nevertheless remained as an irritant to those increasing number who needed, for many reasons, to travel throughout the British world.

Colonial Clergy Act (1874)

Despite these tensions, the Colonial Clergy Act provided an effective way to regulate clergy who had been ordained for the colonies and now wished to return, or who had been trained overseas and aspired to work for a church in Great Britain and Ireland. The Act required applicants to apply for a licence to officiate from either the archbishop of Canterbury or the archbishop of York, depending on where their prospective employment lay. An effective break on the number of applications was provided by the need for applicants already to have an offer of employment before applying to the relevant archbishop for a licence under the Act. Although there was some disgruntlement about the way in which this reflected on the standing of colonial orders, the system seems to have worked very smoothly.

In York, the records of applications date from 1884, though a more informal system may have been in place before then. Applicants had to fill in a standard form, which included the 'grounds for the application', the reasons for their absence from the colony or foreign country, letters of recommendation about their foreign service, including one from the bishop of the diocese where they had served, the proposed time of return, school education, degree and university, particulars of any time spent as a student in a theological college, details of their ordination to the diaconate and to the priesthood, the name of the ordaining bishop, whether their ordination examination included the Greek Testament and the Latin language, details of preferment and curacies since ordination, and the names and addresses of three clergymen or

---

[18] 'William Pierce', *Oxford Dictionary of National Biography*. Pierce suffered this after his capture at Charles Town in 1780.
[19] F. W. B. Bullock, *A History of Training for the Ministry of the Church of England in England and Wales from 598–1799* (St Leonards-on-Sea, Sussex, 1969), p. 128.

'laymen of position', who might be able to act as referees.[20] This was, in other words, by no means a matter of form. Candidates had to demonstrate exemplary character, references and education and usually have the support of a local bishop who had secured them a position before they would be allowed to officiate.

Candidates who had been trained and educated in Britain generally had a greater chance of being given a licence than those whose entire education had been undertaken in the colonies. There were also discrete arrangements in place to ensure that candidates did not, for example, try to apply to both Canterbury and York. If a bishop suspected that an unsuitable man was returning to Britain to try his luck, it was not uncommon for a letter suggesting that the candidate not be given a licence until the archbishop had written to him. There was a particular reluctance to allow candidates who had trained for a colonial or missionary posting to return to Britain instead. This created problems in the case of genuine illness. Tegid Aneurin Williams (34) of Tresaith in Wales, for example, was given permission to officiate for only two years.[21] He had been trained as a missionary at St Augustine's, Canterbury, before being sent to St John's, Kaffraria, where he was ordained deacon in 1884 and priest in 1886. Williams had been ill for a long time, and states that he was willing to return as soon as his health permitted it. There was less sympathy for Arthur Wellesley Chapman (41) of Berryfield, County Wicklow, Ireland. He had been ordained in London, Canada and Massachusetts and spent a period in the Episcopalian Theological College, Harvard. As a reason for the application, he states: 'It has ever been my intention to return to my native England.'[22] But this was not enough to be given a licence to officiate. He was refused. Thomas Greathind Harper was also refused. He wanted to 'attend to the education of my children'.[23] The challenging nature of the application, as well as the likelihood that it would not be supported, show the extent to which the Anglican churches in the colonies were starting to drift away from Canterbury in terms of their organisation, if not their theological views.

For clergy outside the Church of England, arrangements for their passage and return from metropole to colony were not complicated by the heavy burden of establishment. The movement of clerical personnel could therefore be managed centrally by the churches or by local congregations without the need to refer to colonial or imperial legislation.

---

[20] Applications for Licences under the Colonial Clergy Act, 1884–, Borthwick Institute, Col.C.1/1.
[21] *Ibid.*, p. 100.   [22] *Ibid.*, p. 101.   [23] *Ibid.*, p. 80.

Nevertheless, they were also closely controlled. Catholic secular priests were always subject to the local bishop (although they could make appeals to higher authority or to Rome); members of religious orders were under the direction of their provincial organisers though some, particularly in colonial dioceses, were also subject to the guiding hand of the local bishop. Methodists were governed by the relevant conference, and Presbyterians by the local synod which was subject in turn to the General Assembly. Nonconformists and Free Churchers were different because they emphasised the right of congregations to vote for their own choice of minister. This was the issue that split the established Church of Scotland at the time of the Disruption and was therefore taken extremely seriously.

While many clergy who made their way to the colonies were organised through the colonial missionary societies, which have been considered in detail in Chapters 3 to 7, a significant proportion (how many it is impossible to judge) made their own arrangements with bishops and churches. It was common for both Anglican and Catholic colonial bishops to make use of agents in Britain who could interview prospective candidates for them and arrange for their travel and outfit. While bishops and clergy from wealthy dioceses or those with an independent source of income were able to travel, for the majority of colonial clergy of small means, or those who took their vows of obedience seriously, the trip to the new world was a single, one-way journey. Only those who became ill or otherwise got into difficulties had the opportunity to renege on their decision to leave. A search of the relevant archival records of the churches would therefore uncover much fascinating detail about the arrivals and departures of the clergy of all churches who were coming and going between Britain and the colonies throughout the nineteenth century.

The Colonial College movement in Britain

The importance of the education provided for and by British missionaries has attracted increasing attention recently with historians recognising how profound the impact of such cultural institutions can be.[24] In their critique of the London Missionary Society in southern Africa, Jean and John Comaroff argued that the mission functioned as a 'pedagogic crusade' through which the missionaries were able to gain

---

[24] H. J. A. Bellenoit, *Missionary Education and Empire in Late Colonial India, 1860–1920* (London, 2007); J. A. Mangan, *'Benefits Bestowed?' Education and British Imperialism* (Manchester, 1988).

cultural control of the representation of the native people and facilitate the imperialising project of the British colonisers.[25] While other historians have focused their attention on the work of schools in the foreign and colonial mission fields,[26] there is also much to be learned from the education of missionaries themselves at the numerous colleges set up by the different churches in the second half of the nineteenth century. In their focus on training for the colonies, All Hallows and St Augustine's were not entirely unique: they had parallels with the East India College, commonly known as Haileybury, which was established in 1806 partly in response to a failed attempt to establish a college in India,[27] as well as secondary schools such as the Colonial College.[28] However, as the vehicles for the production of a professional cadre entrusted with the cultural production of a particular colonial ideology, they have few parallels. How effective were they as providers of clerical education in the great age of British emigration, and as cultural agents to the colonial world?

From the 1840s, while the call to foreign missions continued to have a romantic hold on readers of missionary periodicals, desperate calls for assistance continued to come from colonial churchmen. Typical of such pleas was that made by the bishop of Toronto who in 1844 claimed that the map of his diocese 'presents an appalling degree of spiritual destitution'. Many people in the diocese had never seen a clergyman other than the occasional itinerant missionary: 'We daily meet with settlers who tell us, in deep sorrow, that they have never heard divine service since they came to the country.'[29] No matter how hard his clergy struggled, they could do nothing without considerable reinforcements. In Canada, in the diocese of Toronto at least, it was anticipated that the clergy for the infant church would arise from training a local ministry,

[25] Comaroff, 'Images of Empire', vol. 1, p. 412.
[26] J. Scott, 'Penitential and Penitentiary: Native Canadians and Colonial Mission Education', in *Mixed Messages: Materiality, Textuality, Missions*, ed. J. S. Scott and G. Griffiths (Basingstoke, 2005), pp. 111–34.
[27] A. L. Lowell and H. M. Stephens, *Colonial Civil Service: The Selection and Training of Colonial Officials in England, Holland, and France* (New York, 1900), pp. 11–14. For the Colonial Service as a quasi-missionary calling, see unpublished paper by T. Barringer and C. Weber, '"A Kind of Missionary Service Too": British Colonial Service Reactions to Missionaries and Vice Versa' (paper presented at the Empires of Religion Conference, University College Dublin, May 2008).
[28] W. Stanner, 'Education, Emigration and Empire: The Colonial College, 1887–1905', in *'Benefits Bestowed'? Education and British Imperialism*, ed. J. A. Mangan (Manchester, 1988); Colonial College, *Colonia: The Colonial College Magazine*, vols. 1–7 (1889–1902).
[29] A. Cooper, '"Romanising" in Sydney', *Australasian Catholic Record* (2003); E. Hawkins, *Annals of the Diocese of Toronto* (London, 1848), p. 195.

inured to the hard conditions and poor remuneration. There does not seem to have been any very realistic expectation that men would make such sacrifices for the colonial call as the cry for more clergy continued. Responding to a report from the SPG, the *Colonial Church Chronicle* outlined the need: '[M]ore clergymen are required in all the Colonies, both for the ministrations of religion among British settlers, and for the instruction and conversion of the heathen. And while the deficiency in the means of grace is already so great, the stream of emigration flows on more rapidly than ever.'[30]

Like the East India Company, which struggled with similar problems in earlier days, the churches had two options to meet the demand for trained professional staff: set up colleges in the colonies, or, alternatively, create colonial missionary colleges in Britain. We consider first the campaign to provide training for the colonies in Britain.

From the end of the eighteenth century, there were occasional efforts to provide scholarships and bursaries for the training of clergy with a colonial missionary calling at the Universities of Oxford and Cambridge. Under the terms of the will of the Welsh jurist, Sir Leolyne Jenkins (1625–85), two fellowships were founded at Jesus College, Oxford, for clergy who would be ordained and go either to sea as naval chaplains or to the colonies. Unfortunately, it proved too easy to evade these obligations and it was not until 1850–2 that the first fellows, under pressure from the bishop of London, departed for duties in Canada and South Africa.[31] There was also a failed scheme to set up a missionary college on the Isle of Man, and a more successful one, Codrington College, established in Barbados.[32] In the meantime, Irish, Scottish and Welsh candidates continued to make up the bulk of the candidates presenting themselves for colonial service with the SPG.[33] Not until the 'hungry 1840s' and the consequent dramatic increase in emigration, was there a renewed sense of urgency for a college in England to train colonial clergy.

One of the most interesting proposals was that put forward by the Hebrew and Syriac scholar John Rustat Crowfoot (1817–75).[34] Crowfoot's plea for a 'Colonial and Missionary College at Cambridge'

[30] J. A. V., 'Four New Bishoprics in the Colonies', *Colonial Church Chronicle*, 1 (1847), p. 12.
[31] Pascoe, *Two Hundred Years of the SPG*, pp. 840–1.
[32] See Table 8.3, Anglican missionary colleges and training institutions supported by the SPG and number of students ordained, 1754–1900.
[33] Pascoe, *Two Hundred Years of the SPG*, p. 840.
[34] J. R. Crowfoot, *Plea for a Colonial and Missionary College at Cambridge* (London, 1854).

was addressed to the archbishop of Canterbury and was premised on the demand created by the enormous number of emigrants heading to Australia, America and other destinations. Crowfoot refers to the reports from the existing societies, the SPG and the CMS, concerning the dearth of men able to be sent out as evangelists. He was aware of the colleges of the two societies, St Augustine's at Canterbury (which he called the *de facto* College for the SPG) and the Islington Institution; both, he felt, were fatally weakened by their isolation and party identification; they also suffered by comparison with Propaganda College in Rome with its enrolment of 100 students a year, its rich library of costly books, its printing office in which all the books required by a missionary could be produced in all foreign languages, and its museum filled with fascinating objects: 'Praiseworthy and excellent as are the intentions of the supporters of these Colleges, it can hardly be expected that so great a task can be performed by them.'[35] Crowfoot also felt that the colleges established in the colonies were not ideal; what a Cambridge college would be able to provide was an institution for the 'sound education of emigrants who are to become the gentry of the colonies'.[36] Against the objection of cost, Crowfoot put forward some ready, if unconvincing, calculations under which budget a college might be established which would put a Cambridge education within the reach of all. He suggested that the minimum academic staff would comprise a master on £600 a year, professors of divinity, law and medicine, all on £300, with language, science and engineering, natural history, and history and moral science scraping by on £200. If funds permit, he states airily, more fellowships at £150 per year might be founded for 'celibate missionaries or colonists to expire at the end of twelve years'.[37] Such a college would provide an immediate boost to the cultural export of Cambridge-trained professionals, including ministers of religion, to the colonies.

Outside the universities, a more immediate and thrifty solution to the need for emigrant clergy was to be supplied by the theological colleges dominated by Evangelicals keen to maintain the isolation and party spirit denounced by Crowfoot. Theological colleges were established in Oxford and Cambridge in the 1870s and 1880s, sometimes with the assistance of retired colonial bishops. In addition, some public schools adapted their curricula in order to train boys to take up manly careers as gentleman emigrants and farmers in the colonies.[38]

---

[35] *Ibid.*, p. 22. [36] *Ibid.*, p. 23.   [37] *Ibid.*, p. 31.
[38] A. Hodge, 'The Training of Missionaries for Africa: The Church Missionary Society's Training College at Islington, 1900–1915', *Journal of Religion in Africa*, 4 (1971), p. 83; Stanner, 'Education, Emigration and Empire'.

Non-graduate theological colleges, including St David's, Lampeter, King's College, London and Highbury College (the Dissenting Academy which amalgamated with New College London in 1854), have been analysed by David Dowland.[39] Dowland speaks of the 'cold, suspicious, dispiriting reception' which many of the clergy trained by the non-graduate colleges received from the official church.[40] They were slow to make their mark, and, by the time of the report on the supply of candidates for ordination presented to the archbishop of Canterbury at the 1908 Lambeth Conference, the majority of ordinations (58 per cent) continued to be of university graduates with no formal theological training.[41]

While party politics may have had a salutary effect on the career prospects of ordinands in Britain, Evangelicals were often welcomed in colonial dioceses. The flow of candidates to staff the dioceses of Evangelical bishops such as Bishop Frederic Barker (1854–84) in Sydney was one of the factors that influenced the character of colonial Anglicanism. Of particular significance is the London College of Divinity, founded by the wealthy Bristol clergyman, Alfred Peache (1818–1900), which opened in 1863 and moved to Highbury in 1866, with Thomas Boultbee (1818–84) as the first principal.[42] By the end of the century, this college had produced several hundred alumni, including two colonial bishops, J. Taylor-Smith, bishop of Sierra Leone, and L. H. Gwynne, who, in 1920, became the first bishop of Egypt and the Sudan. While no one would ever appear to have believed that there was an excess of clerical graduates, the supply would seem to have increased by the middle of the century. Charlotte Brontë's novel, *Shirley* (1849), opens: 'Of late years, an abundant shower of curates has fallen upon the North of England; they lie thick upon the hills; every parish has one or more of them.'[43] Some at least of these men were to try their hand in the colonies.

Somewhere below the theological colleges in educational prestige, missionary training colleges were also a significant source of clergy for overseas postings. While it was initially hoped that piety and enthusiasm

[39] Dowland, *Nineteenth-Century Anglican Theological Training*.
[40] *Ibid.*, p. 8.
[41] Church of England, Committee Appointed to Consider the Question of the Supply and Training of Candidates for the Sacred Ministry, *The Supply and Training of Candidates for Holy Orders: Report ... Presented to the Archbishop of Canterbury* (Poole, 1908), cited by Dowland, *Nineteenth-Century Anglican Theological Training*, p. 215.
[42] Dowland, *Nineteenth-Century Anglican Theological Training*, pp. 70–106; A. F. Munden, 'Thomas Pownall Boultbee (1818–1884)', *Oxford Dictionary of National Biography*.
[43] Cited by F. W. B. Bullock, *A History of Training for the Ministry of the Church of England in England and Wales from 598–1799* (St Leonards-on-Sea, Sussex, 1969), p. 86.

in sufficient quantities were all that was required, the disastrous experiences of those despatched on the LMS missionary vessel, the *Duff*,
convinced nearly everyone that proper training was essential to the creation of effective missionaries.[44] The first dedicated missionary training school in Britain was David Bogue's Nonconformist Academy at
Gosport, which operated from 1800 to 1830, and was critical to the formation of the London Missionary Society. From its early days, it sent
more workers to the mission fields that it trained for work at home.[45]

The Church Missionary Society had established a missionary college
at Islington in 1820, and by 1886 Tucker reported that it had produced
between 400 and 500 missionary graduates.[46] Initially, it was a very
modest affair and operated out of the family home of the Evangelical
patriarch, Edward Bickersteth (1786–1850), whose son (1825–1906)
and grandson (1850–97), both also called Edward, became Anglican
bishop of Exeter and bishop of South Tokyo, respectively, creating three
generations of colonial and mission-minded churchmen. By 1825, the
college was located in a purpose-built building with accommodation
for students and a professional teaching staff.[47] A number of celebrated
bishops were trained at Islington, notably Samuel Ajayi Crowther
(c. 1807–91), bishop of the Niger Territories, who was ordained by the
bishop of London in 1843, and Samuel Gobat (1799–1879), who trained
first at the Basler Mission, then at Islington, prior to joining the CMS.
He was later consecrated as the bishop of Jerusalem by the archbishop
of Canterbury in July 1846 at Lambeth.[48] Although bishops were a mark
of the success of a college, it remained true that the vast majority of
the Anglican episcopate at home and overseas were trained in English
universities. While they were effective as training institutions, neither
Gosport nor Islington provided missionaries for the colonies.

Colonial theological and missionary colleges

The logical solution to the problem of obtaining clergy for colonial
work was the creation of theological colleges in the colonies themselves.
However, this took a surprisingly long time to happen, largely because
of the slow development of colonial bishoprics in the case of the Church

[44] Cox, *British Missionary Enterprise*, p. 102.
[45] R. Lovett, *The History of the London Missionary Society, 1795–1895*, 2 vols. (London, 1899), vol. I, p. 73.
[46] Tucker, *English Church in Other Lands*, p. 206.
[47] S. Piggin, *Making Evangelical Missionaries 1789–1858: The Social Background, Motives and Training of British Protestant Missionaries to India* (Abingdon, 1984), ch. 7.
[48] *Oxford Dictionary of National Biography*.

of England and the lack of funds available for this purpose to the other churches. George Berkeley (1685–1753), the Anglo-Irish philosopher and bishop of Cloyne, secured a charter in 1725 for St Paul's College, Bermuda, which had as its aims, first, that 'the youth of our English Plantations might be themselves fitted for ministry', and, secondly, that the 'children of savage Americans' might be trained as missionaries. However, this proposal lapsed for want of funding, even though it was generously supported by Berkeley himself.[49] There was more success with a proposal for a college in Barbados, which was endowed by Christopher Codrington, a soldier who bequeathed his slave plantations for this purpose to the SPG in 1710.[50] According to his will, Codrington wanted to establish a college 'for the use of the Mission in those parts of the British dominions, which should be a nursery for the propagation of the Gospel, providing a never-failing supply of labourers in the harvest of God'. However, it did not actually begin accepting candidates for ordination until 1829 when it received the support of William Hart Coleridge, first bishop of Barbados (1824–42). Although it was celebrated for its role in the education of the African slave people of the West Indies, Codrington was mostly a college for the education of white clergy for the Church of England, and, of the 390 students educated there from 1745 to 1900, only 39 were classed as 'Negroes' or 'Coloured'.[51] Nevertheless, in terms of its pool of candidates, who were mostly the sons of colonial settlers, it was relatively successful in training up candidates for the Anglican ministry. Of the 390 students who studied there, it ordained 168. While this number was exceeded by the large American colleges, including King's College (now Columbia University), Moore College in Sydney and St Augustine's in Canterbury, these numbers put Codrington well up the list of successful colonial training institutions for the Anglican ministry.[52]

Bishops were pivotal to the development of Anglican theological training colleges. Energetic bishops such as Selwyn in New Zealand, Gray in Cape Colony and Barker in Sydney tapped sources of private philanthropy (and sometimes their own wealth) and had the backing of the SPG, which could provide funds for colleges to train a colonial clergy.[53] However, these colonial ventures were slow to fire, particularly

---

[49] F. W. B. Bullock, *A History of the Training for the Ministry of the Church of England and Wales from 1800 to 1874* (St Leonards-on-Sea, Sussex, 1955).

[50] Pascoe, *Two Hundred Years of the SPG*, pp. 782–3.

[51] See Table 8.3.

[52] *Ibid.*

[53] Pascoe, *Two Hundred Years of the SPG*, pp. 774–97, provides a list of fifty-seven missionary colleges and training institutes supported by the Society: North America

when compared with the colleges in North America, which had rapidly achieved standing as the main theological training schools for their dioceses. Colleges in British North America, such as King's College, Windsor, in Nova Scotia and King's College, New Brunswick, benefited from the establishment of the Church of England and generous state grants. Both managed to survive the crisis of 1846 when all religious tests were abolished and government funding dried up. Elsewhere in the colonial world, colleges struggled, even though many were far from ambitious in their pretensions, such as the college founded by Aubrey John Spencer, first bishop of Newfoundland (1839–44), at St John's in 1842,[54] or St John's College at Waimate, founded by Bishop Selwyn of New Zealand.[55] Decent funding was critical – as was a source of vocations to the ministry, a perennial complaint of colonial bishops. The SPG committed £7,500 to Queen's College, Newfoundland. By 1900, it had educated 109 students, of whom 84 had been ordained, which was a respectable outcome for the investment. Elsewhere, the colonies were littered with failed collegial experiments such as St Cyprian's Theological College, Bloemfontein, founded in 1874 by friends of Bishop Webb and endowed by the SPG and SPCK with the object of training candidates for the ministry, including both native and colonial-born, which closed in 1883 for want of students.[56] Others limped on with the number of successful ordinands struggling to reach double figures. Colleges founded for the training of native clergy, which were often desperately poor, did no better. Those which attempted to mix European and native students invariably faced low enrolments: those which aimed at a more or less exclusively non-white clientele were generally highly successful in producing missionary agents but few ordained clergy.

The real difficulty for colonial seminaries was their lack of endowments along with a continued preference for ordinands who had received their training in Britain. It was also important not to attempt too much. In India, Thomas Fanshaw Middleton, first bishop of Calcutta (1814–22), raised over £50,000 for the college that opened in 1824.[57] This was probably the most ambitious ecclesiastical project ever attempted

(eight), West Indies and South America (three), Africa (seventeen), Australia, New Zealand and the Pacific (seven), Asia (twenty) and England (two). See Table 8.3 for a detailed summary.

[54] *Ibid.*, p. 781, credits Queen's College, St John's, Newfoundland to Bishop Feild.

[55] Davidson, *Selwyn's Legacy*.

[56] Pascoe, *Two Hundred Years of the SPG*, p. 786.

[57] Martin, *Statistics*, p. 304, notes that this was made up of £5,000 from the SPG, £5,000 from the SPCK, £5,000 from the Church Missionary Society and £5,000 from the British and Foreign Bible Society, together with collections from all the churches in England and Wales assisted by a 'King's Letter' urging generous donations.

in the British empire. It was intended to train both native Indians and 'other Christian youth' as preachers and schoolteachers, as well as provide Indian experience for English missionaries. Nevertheless, by 1874, it had been forced to close and its fine buildings were sold, though the native missionary college transferred with some success to Calcutta.[58] In contrast, the CMS colleges for native clergymen at Madras and Lahore were more long-lived. Altogether, Bullock names twenty-five theological colleges founded in British colonies for the training of European and indigenous clergy which were established before 1875.[59]

Money, patronage and the commitment of the bishop to train clergy locally were keys to the success of colonial theological colleges as the case of Moore Theological College in Sydney illustrates. Moore College is named for the colonial magistrate, Thomas Moore, who left £20,000 to the Church of England in his will when he died in 1840 specifying it should be used for a Protestant college.[60] Bishop Broughton had gone out to Sydney having poured a large part of his own fortune into the endowment for the see. In aid of a theological college he received additional assistance from Reverend Samuel Wilson Warneford, who gave the SPG £2,000 instructing that the interest be divided between the bishop of Nova Scotia for the benefit of King's College at Windsor, and the bishop of Australia, 'in aid of any Seminary or Institution'. From Edward Coleridge, his close friend, patron and correspondent, he also received £3,000 in aid of the college project that was directed through the SPG. Despite what looked like a propitious start, Broughton's college, St James Lyndhurst, opened in 1845 and seems to have closed after only a year or so of operation during which the press accused Broughton of using the college to nurture Tractarianism.[61] Two of the half-dozen students who enrolled departed for Rome, and the college did not survive the ensuing uproar. Among Sydney's Catholic clergy, the arrivals seem to have been viewed as curiosities. A graduate of All Hallows wrote in the alumni magazine of their arrival:

In March 1848, two parsons of the Episcopalian Establishment with their families, living in Sydney, embraced Catholicity. On yesterday morning, the Feast

[58] J. W. Burgon, *Lives of Twelve Good Men*, 2 vols. (London, 1888), p. 187; Pascoe, *Two Hundred Years of the SPG*, pp. 474–6 and 789–90.
[59] R. J. E. Boggis, *A History of St Augustine's College, Canterbury* (Canterbury, 1907), p. 30; F. W. B. Bullock, *A History of the Training for the Ministry of the Church of England and Wales from 1800 to 1874* (St Leonards-on-Sea, Sussex, 1955), p. 157.
[60] Boggis, *St Augustine's College*, p. 168; M. Loane, *A Centenary History of Moore Theological College* (Sydney, 1955), p. 7.
[61] Cooper, '"Romanising" in Sydney'. Although an old high churchman himself and anti-Catholic, Broughton had some sympathy for the Tractarian Movement.

of St John Baptist, I saw them both receiving Holy Communion at the hands of His Grace the Archbishop, and afterwards I saw one of them playing the organ in the cathedral at High Mass.[62]

Of the two converts, T. C. Makinson and R. K. Sconce, the former had been sent out by the SPG. The shame felt by the SPG in this event is mitigated by Pascoe's history who points out (with emphasis) that Makinson was in fact *the only case of this kind* in 150 years of the Society's history and also that there were dozens of cases of transfer to the Society from both Rome and Dissent.[63]

The real end for St James lay nevertheless with Sydney's incoming bishop who wished to create an Anglican Evangelical theological college which reflected his own churchmanship rather than resuscitate what Broughton had left behind. Frederic Barker, an Evangelical consecrated at Lambeth in 1854 for the diocese of Sydney, devised means to apply the Moore bequest to establish an independent theological college outside the newly established University of Sydney, fighting off the claims of St Paul's [Anglican] College for a share in the funds.[64] For his own diocese, Barker successfully built an independent Evangelical college resembling in many respects Highbury College in London.

Missionary training in Britain

The training of missionaries for the field was notoriously difficult because of the challenge of engaging individuals whose piety and desire for Christian adventure was matched by their learning. This was a particular problem for the Anglican and Presbyterian societies, which required missionaries to be ordained. This generally assumed a level of education equivalent to that of a university degree, though lay missionaries were also sent out after a shorter course of training with the expectation that they might be ordained in the field. A similar difficulty was faced by the continental Lutheran societies. This gap in education was bridged by the Missionary House of the Basel Society and the Church

---

[62] All Hallows Missionary College Drumcondra [Dublin], *Annual Report, 1850* (Dublin, 1850), p. 6.

[63] Pascoe, *Two Hundred Years of the SPG*, p. 393. There is also a 'Summary of the Missionary Roll' on p. 847 with columns showing 'Accessions to the Ranks of the Clergy a) from the Church of Rome: 2 from the American Colonies, 13 Newfoundland and Canada, 3 West Indies, 11 Africa, 2 Australasia, 17 Asia and b) from Dissent (98 – though probably higher)'. Reassuringly, there are only two secessions to the Church of Rome from the SPG.

[64] Boggis, *St Augustine's College*, p. 38; Loane, *Centenary History*, p. 24.

Missionary Society's Training College at Islington, which trained non-graduates for missionary service, and other theological colleges.[65] The CMS opened its Missionary Institution in 1825 in the tacit recognition that English candidates were unlikely to present themselves for the mission field in any other way.[66] The college magazine, *Islingtonia*, records details of their activities, and something about the background of candidates can be discerned from the archives which survived the Second World War.[67] Initially, the CMS was dominated by candidates from the continent. English candidates eventually enrolled in some numbers, and they came from a wide cross-section of society. The programme of study required students to acquire a good understanding of the bible, English language and history, and some elements of Latin and Greek. By 1893, there were also lectures on hygiene, elementary surgery and medicine, with technical training in carpentry and shoe-making. Not until the 1890s were there changes to the curriculum to allow the study of non-Western religions and cultures.[68] Although the demand for missionaries continued undiminished, the college closed in 1912 following a decline in numbers applying for courses, with the remaining students being transferred to nearby Highbury College.[69] By this date, the ideal of a separate training course for missionary clergy was declining as the new theological halls provided greater opportunities for candidates without the social and educational background required for admission to a university.

Despite its careful programme of study – and the achievement of a number of bishops from its ranks – the products of the Islington College were looked down upon. In Anthony Trollope's novel, *Rachel Ray* (1863), the heroine says that the Evangelical clergyman, Mr Prong, 'had been educated at Islington, and that he sometimes forgot his "h"s'.[70] This counted for a good deal, even though the narrator tells us that 'Mr Prong was an energetic, severe, hardworking, and, I fear, intolerant young man, who bestowed very much laudable care upon his sermons'.[71] Indeed, for Trollope and for other anti-Evangelical adherents of the Church of England, the strain created by the establishment of the theological colleges and the inevitable consequence that clergymen

[65] Hodge, 'Training of Missionaries', p. 84.
[66] Boggis, *St Augustine's College*, p. 57; Hodge, 'Training of Missionaries'.
[67] C. F. Childe, 'The Story of the College', *Islingtonian* (1899). Childe was a former principal of the College.
[68] Hodge, 'Training of Missionaries', p. 85.
[69] *Ibid.*
[70] A. Trollope, *Rachel Ray* [*1863*] (London, 1906), p. 70. I thank Professor Edward James for kindly bringing this reference to my attention.
[71] *Ibid.*, p. 68.

Table 8.3 *Anglican missionary colleges and training institutions supported by the SPG and number of students ordained, 1754–1900*

College	Date founded	Number educated to 1900	Number ordained or mission agents
North America			
King's College (now Columbia University), New York	1754–	About 17,000	—
King's College, Windsor, Nova Scotia	1789–	—	About 250
King's College, Fredericton, New Brunswick	1828	757	—
University of Trinity College, Toronto	1852	2,082	200
Bishop's College, Lennoxville, Quebec	1843	400	200
St John's College, Winnipeg	1866	—	100, including 29 of Indian descent
Emmanuel College, Prince Albert, Saskatchewan[a]	1879	40	12
Queen's College, Newfoundland	1842	109	84
West Indies and South America			
Codrington College, Barbados[a]	1745	390 including 13 Negroes, 26 Coloured	168
St Paul's College, Bermuda	1725		
Queen's College, British Guiana	1844 or 1845–1876	—	—
Jamaica Church Theological College[a]	1883	< 50	—
Africa			
St Mark's College, George, South Africa	1882	91	—
Diocesan College, Rondebosch[a]	1849	1,400 (300 European and 1,100 colonial-born)	9
Kafir College, Zonnebloem[b]	1858	336 (93 natives, 160 colonists, 83 mixed race)	Less than 16 mission agents

Table 8.3 (*cont.*)

College	Date founded	Number educated to 1900	Number ordained or mission agents
Kafir Institution, Grahamstown[b]	1860	380	11 ordained, 70 mission agents
Victoria Home, Keiskama Hoek[b]	1895	254	19 mission agents
St Alban's College, Maritzburg[b]	1883	96	3
St John's College, Umtata[b]	1877	Less than 422	
St Bede's College, Umtata[b]	1877	52	5 ordained, 38 other
McKenzie Memorial College, Isandhlwana[b]	1887	50	27 mission agents
St Cuthbert's College, Pretoria[b]	1898	12	—
St Mary's College, Thlotse Heights[b]	1877–83	—	
St Cyprian's College, Bloemfontein[a, b]	fl. 1897	—	
St Andrew's College, Bloemfontein	1878	150	18 ordained, 80 mission agents
St Paul's College, Madagascar[b]			
Indian Training Institution, Mauritius[b]	1892	20	1 ordained, 4 mission agents
Australia, New Zealand and Pacific Ocean			
Moore College, Sydney	1856	170	200
Christ's College, Tasmania	1846	—	—
St John's College, Armidale	1899	10	5
Selwyn College, Dunedin	1893	20	12
St John's College, Auckland	1842	340	70
St Barnabas College, Norfolk Island[b]	1851	—	Several
Asia			
Bishop's College, Calcutta[a]	1824	360	79
St Stephen's College, Delhi[a]	1859	550	1

St John's College, Rangoon[b]	1864	9,000	—
Kemmendine College, Rangoon[b]	1883	70	10
Karen Institution, Toungoo[b]	1884	50	40 mission agents
SPG Theological College, Madras[a]	1848	180	92
Sawyerpuram Seminary (SPG)[b]	1844	Less than 110	—
Nandyal Training College[b]	1884	326	—
Caldwell College, Tuticorin[b]	1885	1,546	65
Vediarpuram Seminary (SPG)[b]	1844	—	—
Theological Class, Ranchi[b]	1870	24	22
St Thomas's College, Colombo[b]	1848	3,000	10
St Paul's College, Hong Kong[b]	1849	—	—
Native Theological College, Tokyo[b]	1892	24	3
England			
St Augustine's College, Canterbury	1848	550	550
St Boniface's College, Warminster	1860	210	170

[a] Founded to train European and native ministry.
[b] Founded to train native ministry.

Source: C. F. Pascoe, Two Hundred Years of the SPG: An Historical Account of the Propagation of the Gospel in Foreign Parts, 1701–1900 (London, 1901), pp. 774a–797; F. W. B. Bullock, A History of the Training for the Ministry of the Church of England and Wales from 1800 to 1874 (St Leonards-on-Sea, Sussex, 1955), Appendix, pp. 149–58.

were trained who could not automatically be assumed to be gentlemen, was a source of endless debate and not a few novels.[72] Other missionary societies devised other strategies to ensure an adequate supply of candidates, including broadening the social qualifications of candidates.[73] In 1910, these were outlined by Commission V of the Edinburgh World Missionary Conference which reported on all aspects of missionary training in Britain.[74] Their report listed nineteen colleges that were involved in some degree of training missionaries, mostly for candidates, including women, who were unable to enter one of the universities or existing theological colleges. The Edinburgh Missionary College of the Free Church of Scotland, founded in 1887, trained women missionaries for India. Woodbrooke, founded in 1903, the first of the Selly Oak Colleges in Birmingham, was a Quaker initiative which aimed to provide training for Quaker leaders and missionary training for men and women of other denominations.

Of all these ventures, only two colleges in Great Britain and Ireland trained candidates specifically for the colonial mission: the missionary College of St Augustine, established by the high church party of the Church of England on the site of the ancient monastery at Canterbury in 1848, and the Roman Catholic Missionary College of All Hallows, Drumcondra, in Dublin, established in 1842. Although neither seems to have ever been conscious that they were serving a similar purpose, albeit for rival churches, their contrasting styles of education and training have much to tell us about the rival missions of the Church of England and the Catholic churches in the British world.

---

[72] On the status of the gentleman clergyman in Trollope, see J. F. Durey, *Trollope and the Church of England* (Basingstoke, 2002), pp. 83–106.

[73] P. Hinchliff, 'The Selection and Training of Missionaries in the Early Nineteenth Century', *Studies in Church History*, 6 (1970), pp. 131–5.

[74] World Missionary Conference, *Report of Commission V* (1910), pp. 236–7c; D. Harley, *Missionary Training: The History of All Nations Christian College and Its Predecessors (1911–1981)* (Zoetermeer, 2000), pp. 51–60.

The most visible sign of the revival of aspirations for the national Church in the colonies was the creation of the Colonial Bishoprics' Fund in 1841.[1] With the fund in place, it was possible for the Church to move almost immediately to the erection of a vastly expanded colonial episcopate and escape from its dependence on the missionary societies for personnel and policy. Cnattingius identifies the 1840s as an epoch-making period in what he calls 'the evolution of Anglicanism into a World Church. The heads of the Church of England had shown that, as builders of a spiritual empire, they were worthy to take their place beside the builders of the political empire.'[2] However, as the Evangelicals in the Colonial Missionary Society were fond of pointing out, there was little point in sending out bishops to colonial dioceses where there was no church for them to administer. It was exciting to create new bishops in unprecedented numbers for the Anglican world. The *Colonial Church Chronicle* exulted in reporting the elaborate service held in Westminster Abbey on 29 June 1847 for the consecration of William Tyrrell, bishop of Newcastle, New South Wales, Augustus Short, bishop of Adelaide, Charles Perry, bishop of Melbourne, and Robert Gray, bishop of Cape Town.[3] Bishops, however, if they are to be effective, must have clergy, and where were these to come from? The establishment of four new colonial bishoprics (and many more were to follow) immediately put considerable pressure on the available supply. It was anticipated that between sixteen and twenty clergy were to accompany the new bishops, who together would require £2,000 annually to support, and a further £3,000 for 'passage and outfit'.[4]

An immediate solution to the problem of increasing the supply of clergy for the colonial church was provided by the founding of the

---

[1] Cnattingius, *Bishops and Societies*, pp. 204–5; France, *Oversea Episcopate*; Strong, *Anglicanism and Empire*, pp. 198–221.
[2] Cnattingius, *Bishops and Societies*, p. 205.
[3] *Colonial Church Chronicle*, 1 (August 1847), p. 40.
[4] J. A. V., 'Four New Bishoprics', p. 13.

missionary College of St Augustine's. St Augustine's has been described as more of a 'spiritual romance' than a pragmatic assessment of the needs of the Anglican colonial mission.[5] Nevertheless, it was certainly seen as the answer to many prayers raised up by Anglican bishops in the colonies. St Augustine's was the logical outcome of the programme which had been set in train by the revival of the missionary movement within the Church of England. The establishment of St Augustine's was the achievement of the same enthusiasts who rallied to endow the Colonial Bishoprics' Fund. Although the SPG is sometimes given credit for its creation, it is important to stress that St Augustine's was created largely through private endowments and the high church Anglican network, not the SPG.[6] It was this private funding and its subsequent tarring with the brush of Anglo-Catholicism, which was to be both the strength and the weakness of the College.

The driving force behind the creation of St Augustine's was the Eton housemaster and classicist, Edward Coleridge (1800–83), largely it would seem out of his immediate friendship with two men: William Grant Broughton, his 'dear and revered friend', who became first bishop of Australia in 1836, and 'my most dear of all dear friends', George Augustus Selwyn, who set out five years after Broughton to the diocese of New Zealand.[7] Selwyn liked to give Broughton credit for being the first to suggest to the bishop of London that what was needed within the Church of England was what he called 'an institution for rearing up clergymen for the Colonies'.[8] However, at about the same time, the Reverend Charles Marriott was proposing that a missionary college for the colonies might be established at Oxford.[9] Marriott's suggestions were brought forward to the Heads of Houses, but he was unable to get a majority. At the time, Broughton declared that he was not surprised at its failure because of the cost of the venture. It was Coleridge who was subsequently able to get the funds together to finance an alternative project; he was eventually to raise £30,000 which was used to create

[5] A. J. Brown, 'The Founding of St Augustine's Missionary College: A Spiritual Romance' (Masters Thesis, University of London, 1970).
[6] Porter, *Religion Versus Empire?*, p. 159: '[T]he SPG was also instrumental in setting up St Augustine's College, Canterbury, in 1848, for the training of colonial clergy.' The first SPG missionary college would appear to be the Missionary College of the Ascension founded in connection with the Selly Oak Colleges in Birmingham. See Harley, *Missionary Training*, p. 60.
[7] L. J. Manners, *The Church of England in the Colonies: A Lecture Delivered before the Members of the Colchester Literary Institution, on Wednesday, January 22nd, 1851* (London, 1851), p. 32.
[8] Boggis, *St Augustine's College*, p. 30.
[9] Burgon, *Lives of Twelve Good Men*, p. 187, cited by Boggis, *St Augustine's College*, p. 30.

a fitting headquarters for the Anglican colonial missionary movement set in the grounds of the abbey named after the first missionary to the English people.

The Coleridge name was a powerful one for the Anglican establishment. It was Samuel Taylor Coleridge (1772–1834) who had given new prestige to the idea of a national church, an idea which was at the heart of conservative support for church projects throughout the nineteenth century. Other members of the extended family who were associated with St Augustine's was the college's first warden, William Hart Coleridge (1789–1849), who had been Secretary of the SPCK and first bishop of Barbados and the Leeward Islands (1824–42).[10] From Baroness Burdett Coutts, Coleridge was able to supply £2,000 for Bishop Selwyn's church buildings at Waimate and Auckland; Coutts later endowed an additional £35,000 towards the newly established sees of Adelaide and Auckland.[11] Coleridge continued to approach donors while Broughton did his bit by writing pleading letters which Coleridge might be able to use, calling for clergy to join him and share the missionary work of the diocese:

The extremity to which I am reduced through want of clergymen is truly heart-rending. The common ordinances of religion cannot be administered, and when the outward forms of Christianity disappear in a country like this, you may readily conceive that little of the inward spirit will be remaining … What gives more occasion to our adversaries and increases our dismay is that other denominations of Christians all find means of engaging men who, however deficient in certain respects, do nevertheless the work required of them.

Broughton's strongest card was the rivalry of other denominations: not just the clergy of the Roman Catholics, but dissenters and even the representative clergy of the established Church of Scotland, all of whom, he alleged, were better supplied with clergy than the Church of England:

The Roman Catholics are overflowing in the number of their priests, and many more are arriving. Last month we had an emigrant ship from Ireland; she brought two Presbyterians. Within these last four days has come an emigrant ship from England, but she brought no clergyman. Indeed we are altogether paralysed. I am willing to work, and do work, I believe, harder than any curate in the king's dominions, but without proper instruments it is impossible to do the work required.[12]

---

[10] Boggis, *St Augustine's College*, p. 168.
[11] *Ibid.*, p. 33; D. Orton, *Made of Gold: A Biography of Angela Burdett Coutts* (London, 1980).
[12] Boggis, *St Augustine's College*, p. 35.

In 1842, Coleridge responded to Broughton's letters by sending a letter to the headmasters of the grammar schools to see if they would support a missionary college and if they would supply candidates. He also sought clerical and lay support from bishop Denison of Salisbury, Gladstone, Keble, Dr Moberly, Dr Tait, Lord John Manners, Dr Pusey, the Reverend C. Marriott and Mr Beresford Hope – the entire inner circle of the high church party.[13] With their support, he moved to draw up a scheme for the college which from the beginning was intended to supply candidates not for foreign missions, but for 'the education and training of young men who may be willing to dedicate themselves to the ministry in some one of the British Colonies'.[14] At this stage, it was still hoped that the college would retain some connection with the University of Oxford. Bishop Wilberforce of Oxford gave the measure his support, noting: 'The advantages of training the missionaries in this country in preference to the Colonies are in my opinion decisive with respect to health, morals and efficient teaching.'[15] Coleridge continued to plan and seek funding for the College sending a long letter to possible sponsors among his Etonian connections, stressing that the project 'emanates in great measure from the suggestions of the bishops of Australia, New Zealand and Tasmania', and promising that bishop William Hart Coleridge, recently retired from Barbados, would take on the role of Honorary Principal.[16]

The proposal for St Augustine's hit a major squall when news of the plan reached the newspapers. It was condemned as 'a deep-laid Jesuitical scheme for Romanizing our Church',[17] presumably on the ground that it smacked too much of a Roman Catholic seminary. The major objection, and one that was never overcome, was that a missionary training school already existed run by the Church Missionary Society at Islington and any additional project was sure to draw off funds which might better be put at the disposal of the SPG.[18] The saving of the plan was the decision to tie the establishment of the College with the restoration of the ruins of St Augustine's Abbey. An article in the *English Churchman* had caught the attention of Alexander Beresford Hope (1820–87), who managed to purchase the site of the former Monastery of St Augustine for £2,020.[19] Hope was a politician and writer; as a high churchman he became swept up in the projects of the Anglican missionary revival. The College was the most ambitious project of the colonial mission movement and accounts

[13] One omission from Boggis' list is John Henry Newman. This may be deliberate.
[14] Boggis, *St Augustine's College*, p. 38.   [15] *Ibid.*, p. 40.
[16] *Ibid.*, p. 45.   [17] *Ibid.*, p. 57.
[18] Anon, 'St Augustine's, Canterbury', *Colonial Church Chronicle*, 1 (1847), p. 82.
[19] Boggis, *St Augustine's College*, p. 60.

of its much anticipated work were posted regularly in the *Colonial Church Chronicle*.[20] Hope secured the architect William Butterfield who embraced the project as an opportunity to rebuild the ancient monastery of St Augustine's. Much was anticipated of the site with all its associations and the wish that it would become 'the centre of the missionary operations of the country – the heart from which the life of the Gospel may flow forth to the ends of the world – on a spot hallowed by old and venerable recollections, in the very metropolitan city of Canterbury, and on the site of the old Priory of St Augustine'.[21] George Frederick MacLean (1833–1902), Warden of the College from 1880 until his death, gave lectures on missionary history which drew extensive parallels between the work of the medieval missionaries and that undertaken by the current students heading across the empire.[22]

From the beginning, however, the precise function of the College was uncertain. It seems apparent from the correspondence quoted by Boggis that the primary or at least major purpose of the college was to be that of training clergy for colonial dioceses. In this manner, it would be able to claim to complement, rather than compete with, the CMS's Training Institution at Islington. Nevertheless, it was the training of missionaries for work among the heathen that was a key factor in attracting students. This much seems clear from the article published in the *Colonial Church Chronicle* not long after its opening. St Augustine's should not be restricted, it was argued, to 'mere undistinguished preparation for the priestly office, such as is required to supplement the Church either at home or in our Colonies'. This, it was felt, 'seems to us to fall short of the calling reserved to such a College as this, and scarcely to come up to its elaborate construction and the influence of its name'. In addition, the colonial bishops argued 'with increasing unanimity' that they were better able to provide for themselves 'men fitted for their less prominent and important posts'. 'Among the children of the Colonists, and in their own Theological Seminaries, they can rear, under their own eyes, men competently instructed for their work, having the advantage too, of an acquaintance with the feelings and customs of the inhabitants.'[23] If the bishops did have reservations such as this, almost all of them appear to have been happy to accept graduates as they began to flow from Canterbury in the 1850s.

[20] Anon, 'St Augustine's, Canterbury'.
[21] *Ibid.*, p. 83; Ward, *Sequel to Catholic Emancipation*, pp. 244–51.
[22] *Oxford Dictionary of National Biography*. See MacLean's *Apostles of Medieval Europe* (1869).
[23] 'The Future of St Augustine's', *Colonial Church Chronicle and Missionary Journal*, 2 (1848), p. 44.

In fact, St Augustine's was never exclusively devoted to the colonial mission of the church. Young men from outside Britain, both colonials and native Christians, soon arrived who internationalised the environment of the college and made it less of a training school for the settler empire. Boggis provides accounts of a series of 'interesting foreigners' who studied at the College, beginning with Erasmus Augustine Kallihirua (c. 1832–5 to 1856),[24] who was brought to England by Captain (afterwards Sir Erasmus) Ommanney on his return from an expedition in search of Sir John Franklin and his vessels, the *Erebus* and the *Terror*. While on the Greenland coast, Kallihirua was taken on board to act as interpreter and never returned home. The Admiralty placed him in St Augustine's – largely it would seem because no one had any idea how else to care for him. Boggis found him exotic and teachable: 'it was marvellous how readily this poor savage, whose most delicate viands had been raw narwhals' flesh and seals' entrails and clotted blood, who knew not the use of soap and water, and who lived chiefly in a snow-hut, adapted himself … to European dress and to the customs and manners of civilization.'[25] In 1855, he travelled to Newfoundland with the intention of training at St John's College to work as a missionary to the natives of Labrador, but he died tragically of lung disease on 14 June 1856. Other exotics included a 'Hindu', Mark Pitamber, who went to Guinea as a catechist; Lambert McKenzie, a native African born in British Guiana to where he returned in 1855. McKenzie was ordained deacon by the bishop of Guiana in the presence of the Governor, and to the priesthood by Bishop Samuel Ajayi Crowther (c. 1807–91), the former slave who became bishop of the Niger Territories.[26]

There were also connections with other missionary colleges whose graduates, including native Christians, chose to extend their training in England. Perhaps the most remarkable example of these comes from Kafir College, Zonnebloem in Cape Town, which had been founded with the assistance of the Governor, Sir George Grey, in order to provide an education to the sons of native chiefs. In 1861, a new wing was constructed in order to provide space for four young men who were sent out to be educated in England after negotiations with the governor and the bishop of Cape Town. Unfortunately, the experiment, like that with Kallihirua, was cut short when Jeremiah Libupuoa Moshueshue, son of the Basuto chief Moshesh, went to an early grave and the three survivors, Arthur Waka Toise, Edward Dumisweni Kona and Maquoma

---

[24] Clive Holland, 'Kallihirua (modern spelling Qalasirssuaq), baptised Erasmus Augustine Kallihirua', *Dictionary of Canadian Biography Online*, vol. VIII (1851–60).
[25] Boggis, *St Augustine's College*, p. 190.
[26] For a sympathetic biography, see J. F. Ade Ajayi, *A Patriot to the Core* (Ibadan, 2002).

chose to return to Africa in July 1864. While Kona also died young, Toise is said to have continued working as a catechist in Africa. In another remarkable case, Anton Tien, an interpreter with the allied forces in the Crimea (1853–6), was a Lebanese Maronite who is said to have been personally persuaded by Gladstone to turn aside from his proposed studies at Propaganda Fide College in Rome to become an Anglican and study at St Augustine's. He was subsequently sent to Constantinople to conduct a mission to the Turks. Boggis concludes this international parade with the account of John Tsan Baw, 'famous in Canterbury for his prowess in cricket and football' and the first Burmese to be ordained.[27]

Letters from the colonial bishops were focused on the need and qualifications of missionaries. Broughton suggested that one solution was to look for younger and less qualified candidates who might find a colonial posting an adventure: 'There are hundreds every year doomed to inaction and obscurity, or to some unworthy use of their abilities, who, if they were systematically sought out and assisted very moderately, would supply exactly the description of persons that we should rejoice to have sent out to us to be trained as colonial clergymen.'[28] Here, clearly, Broughton seems to be indicating his preference to receive such budding youth unformed into his own hands – rather than the graduates of St Augustine's. In India, Bbishop Middleton of Calcutta also preferred that missionaries who anticipated working in India should spend time in his own Bishop's College. From Bishop Selwyn of New Zealand came the bracing demand for practical and determined men: 'We want a large supply of Oberlins and Felix Neffs, who having no sense of their own dignity, will think nothing below it.'[29] From Bishop Tyrrell of Newcastle, there was a more conservative wish to receive men who had already been trained in England. However, he did not want young men of 'inferior education and inferior station' who saw the colony as an easy pathway to the ministry. The usual supply must come from the colony, but he hoped to receive a small number who might leaven the mix: 'We must hope to receive from England, every now and then, an experienced clergyman of University education, who will devote himself to the work

---

[27] Boggis, *St Augustine's College*, p. 199. Tien wrote a phrasebook for English travellers in the Levant and prepared an edition of one of the works of the Muslim philosopher Al-Kindi.

[28] St Augustine's College, Canterbury, *The Calendar of the Missionary College of St Augustine, Canterbury* (Canterbury, 1851), p. 32.

[29] Johann Friedrich Oberlin (1740–1826) was pastor of a rural district on the borders of Alsace. Felix Neff (1788–1829) was a Swiss evangelist who used Oberlin's methods to improve the lives of his people through better education and agriculture as well as religious service.

with true Missionary spirit.'[30] Tyrrell also expressed the desire that such men who did come out should be in their late twenties, and have some university education and experience of ministry under their belts before tackling a bush parish. This sounds like a wise system – but it was not the one that St Augustine's was gearing up to provide. It is also well worth noting that Tyrrell was clearly planning personally to select every minister for his own diocese, rather than relying on the products of the missionary colleges or societies. From Melbourne, the bishop put in his request for men who need not necessarily be of deep learning so much as 'practical good sense and warm affections'. Of course, all these prelates were dreaming of ideal candidates, but perhaps the bishop of Cape Town more than most when he not only requested the usual zeal, earnestness, patience and love, but also noted that an aptitude for acquiring languages was essential, and that 'a knowledge of music, of medicine, and of mechanical arts' would also be handy.[31] Well, clearly, there was no harm in putting in an order for such a missionary paragon.

Endowments and scholarships are another indication of the organisation and individuals that fostered the closest links with St Augustine's and who were prepared to welcome its alumni. Donors of these included Mrs Shephard of Tunbridge Wells, sister of Reverend Martin Routh, President of Magdalen College, Oxford, and the SPCK. One of the College's most generous individual supporters was the Reverend Henry John Hutchesson (1782–1863).[32] Hutchesson, who was at one time headmaster of the King's School at Canterbury, had been Broughton's mathematical tutor. He was a keen supporter of the colonial church, and, when the chapel of St Augustine's was consecrated, he gave £1,000 for a scholarship for an Australian student. He later endowed another scholarship for students who had attended the Clergy Orphan School, Canterbury or 'any orphan son of any clergyman of the United Church of England and Ireland, of the Episcopal Church in Scotland, or of the Colonial Churches'.[33] Continuing the connection with the College initiated by Edward Coleridge, there was another scholarship donated by the members of Eton College. The Society for Advancing the Christian Faith in the British West India Islands provided assistance towards the maintenance of 'a young man of colour, a native of Berbice to be trained at St Augustine's for the ministry of the Church in British Guiana'.[34]

---

[30] St Augustine's College, Canterbury, *Calendar 1851*, pp. 35–6.
[31] *Ibid.*
[32] Obituary, *Gentleman's Magazine and Historical Review* (July 1863).
[33] *Ibid.*
[34] St Augustine's College, Canterbury, *Calendar* 1853.

St Augustine's had been set up to train students for work overseas. However, the course of study was substantially academic in content. There was a three-year programme. In the first year, students
studied Scripture History, the Gospels in Greek, Evidences of the
Christian Religion, Pearson on the Creed (over two years), as well as
Latin, Greek and elementary mathematics. In the second year, they
studied Jewell's *Apology* and Wordsworth's *Theophilus Anglicanus*, and
began the Thirty-Nine Articles, as well as commencing the Epistles in
Greek, Elementary Hebrew, a Greek Christian classical subject, a Latin
Christian classical subject, and the sciences including mathematics,
physical geography and Humboldt's Cosmos. The third year covered
the Book of Common Prayer, concluded the study of the Thirty-Nine
Articles, Butler's *Analogy*, Church and Missionary History, and further Christian and classical studies of Greek, Hebrew and Latin, and
Humboldt's Cosmos and Whewell's Bridgewater Treatise.[35] Overall,
there was a heavy emphasis on ancient languages, and the programme
differed very little from that which students received at one of the theological colleges springing up elsewhere in Britain. The only concession
to the missionary objectives of the college would appear to be that, for
those who intended to go to India or Borneo, students could also expect
to study Eastern languages. This field was taught by the distinguished
Orientalist, Reinhold Rost of the University of Jena. There was also
some practical studies of 'various branches of mechanical labour and
mechanical art' mingled in with the rest of the syllabus of study.[36]

The bishop of Cape Town would have been pleased that, by 1858,
final year students also received a medical course at the county hospital
run by the senior physician, Dr Lochée. An extract from the introductory lecture is reassuring: 'You are not expected to become learned
physicians, or expert surgeons, though it is to be hoped that you may
acquire a sufficient amount of knowledge to enable you to act under
the peculiar circumstances in which you will be placed, with safety and
advantage in either capacity.'[37] There was justification, too, for the considerable investment in supplying this kind of training: 'Missionaries
need to be equipped with all the appliances of European skill; and inas-
much as our superiority in the arts and sciences affords a very powerful
means for assisting that object, we should throw away an advantage
in not employing them.'[38] There follow the outlines of what appears
to be very thorough grounding in practical medicine over a course of

[35] St Augustine's College, Canterbury, *Calendar* 1858, p. 49.
[36] *Ibid.*, p. 50.   [37] *Ibid.*, p. 97.   [38] *Ibid.*, p. 98.

forty-nine lectures, beginning with basic anatomy, moving on to treatments including the use of mercury, the employment of bloodletting (two lectures), then purgatives, soporifics and sedatives; there are fifteen lectures on various kinds of fever and infectious diseases covering typhus, malaria, yellow fever, irritative, gastric, hectic and eruptive fevers, as well as scarlet fever, measles, the plague and cholera, with remarks on inoculation and vaccination. This was all very useful for those going out to tropical destinations, followed by another ten lectures on chemical treatments, almost all of which were utterly useless or dangerous, including the application of iodine, chlorine, sulphur, mercury and common chalk. At least there was opium to provide some real relief from pain, tobacco for pleasure and chloroform for oblivion.[39]

The alumni

The ordinands who were produced by St Augustine's can be counted among the best-travelled clergy in history. From the first graduating class in 1849, when they scattered to the dioceses of Cape Town, Newfoundland (two), Barbados (two), Nova Scotia, Newcastle (New South Wales) and Sydney, until 1904, 617 clergy were entered on its roll of graduates. They went wherever colonial dioceses could provide placements for them and so they followed the regions of British settlement and colonisation. As with the missionary appointments of the SPG, though not to the same degree, the ordinands were destined in the largest numbers for Canada and Newfoundland (147), but they went to Asia and India (126), Australia, New Zealand and the Pacific (98), Africa and the Middle East (76), the West Indies and Central and South America (23) and England and Gibraltar (10). Indeed, they crossed the globe, heading to 82 different dioceses from Adelaide (10) to Zululand (4). And, although 17 of them were not listed with their 'diocese of sailing', almost all seem to have left Canterbury for their new postings where many made distinguished colonial careers.

The Augustinians also achieved considerable ecclesiastical distinction, if we measure this in the number of those later appointed as bishops (five),[40] deans (three) and archdeacons (more than twenty), as well as one martyr, Sidney Malcolm Wellbye Brooks, who was murdered during the Boxer Rebellion in northern China in 1899. Two

---

[39] *Ibid.*
[40] John Millar Strachan (Rangoon), Bransby Louis Key (St John's, Kaffraria), William Chalmers (Goulburn), William Cyprian Inkham (Saskatchewan) and Geoffrey Durnford Iliff (Shantung).

Table 9.1 *St Augustine's College, Canterbury. summary table of graduate destinations*

Destination	Number of graduates
Africa and Middle East	76
Asia and India	126
Australia, New Zealand and Pacific	98
Canada and Newfoundland	147
West Indies and America	23
England and Gibraltar	10
Not Assigned	10
Total	490

Augustinians, J. W. Coe and W. L. Nanson, were principals of Bishop's College, Calcutta, and a half-dozen others had been decorated for service as military chaplains in the Crimean and Boer Wars.[41] They were a cohesive body – diligently returning letters to their alma mater with accounts of their journeys to their dioceses and adventures in travelling around remote and hostile locations, and of their achievements while on their postings. These were republished, in the way of missionary letters, in the college magazine.[42] As with other missionary writings, these include physical and spiritual adventures in equal measure: encounters with the elements and with adversity, with hostile Catholics and Dissenters, as well as indifference and anti-clericalism.

From the St Augustine's 'Occasional Papers', several themes present themselves: amusing events in frontier conditions; overcoming snakes, drought, ice, cold and snow (Canada), or heat and dust (Australia and Africa); and the small satisfactions of colonial work, as well as its challenges. Such anecdotes are part of the frontier clergyman's self-fashioning. But in some ways more heartfelt are the accounts of the long and lonely riding to provide religious services in remote locations. Reverend F. W. Samwell spoke of his work in South Australia:

My work during the past year has been very heavy, as our district is an extensive one covering over three thousand square miles. You may form some idea of it, when I tell you that every week during Lent I preached eight times; and I travelled two hundred miles every week during the same period. Most of our

[41] Boggis, *St Augustine's College*, pp. 228–9.
[42] St Augustine's College, Canterbury, 'Occasional Papers', No. 1 (May 1853) to No. 386 (December 1935) (microform) (Wick, Scotland, 1996); R. Withycombe, *Occasional Papers from St Augustine's College Canterbury, Published 1853–1941: Handlist of Materials Relating to Australia, New Zealand, South East Asia and the South Pacific* (Canberra, 1992).

travelling is done with horse and buggy, and I often have a drive of thirty miles home through bush tracks after evening service by myself.[43]

Augustinian graduates were also found in the thick of conflicts such as the Boer War in which they provided loyal and unquestioning support for British forces. Canon F. H. Fischer, rector of Pretoria, was chairman of a committee to provide relief for British refugees from the Transvaal in 1899. His colleague, Reverend A. Jeffery of Ceres (Cape Colony), spoke of the deaths of his own parishioners: 'I lost five of my best men whose homes were on the glebe. Two out of those five were ordered by those murderous rebels to dig their own graves, and then butchered in cold blood.'[44]

Tales of war were matched by tales of shipwreck, hailstorms, tempests and fire. Reverend J. Holland, while in charge of Kumara in the goldfields of New Zealand, awoke in Holy Week of 1882 to the smell of fire. In minutes the whole house was gutted and he lost all his possessions: 'My books are the greatest loss. I had over four hundred volumes, and it did not leave me with even a Bible.'[45] The Reverend M. A. Maggs of Herschel in the Cape Colony was dragged by his horse on his way home from Synod one moonlit night. In Sarawak, Reverend M. J. Bywater had the most varied encounters with the natural world. He claims to have seen a Dyak Christian taken by an alligator (which he shot), found a centipede down his back which bit him five times, killed a scorpion on his surplice, and killed snakes all over the house – 'in my bed-room, in the church, on the table, in a drawer' – and escaped the charge of a huge wild boar.[46] It is perhaps surprising that there were so few colonial clergy on the martyrs' roll. Such stories provided edifying and aspirational narratives for future Augustinians, and perhaps also justified the decisions that had taken them to remote, isolated, dangerous and impoverished parts of the empire.

Missionary motivation

We may assume that, besides a religious calling, the desire to better themselves or to pursue their chosen profession was a motivating factor which drew candidates to St Augustine's to train for the colonial church. In this respect, they mirror the career choices of other missionary

[43] Boggis, *St Augustine's College*, p. 279; J. MacDevitt, *Father Hand: Founder of All Hallows Catholic College for the Foreign Missions* (Dublin, 1885), p. 191, citing Occasional Paper, No. 241, p. 12.
[44] Boggis, *St Augustine's College*, p. 194, citing Occasional Paper, No. 224, p. 14.
[45] Boggis, *St Augustine's College*, p. 302, citing Occasional Paper, No. 234, p. 31.
[46] Boggis, *St Augustine's College*, p. 305, citing Occasional Paper, No. 239, p. 13.

clergy. In his analysis of the motivation of British Protestant missionaries who were sent to India, Piggin observes that there were sixteen
kinds of reason given by candidates who wished to undertake a mission
to the heathen: economic security, the desire for respectability, romantic or heroic aspirations; the honour of the missionary calling; heavenly
rewards; the cult of usefulness; educational and psychological aptitude;
imperialist impulse to civilise the heathen; pity; denominational competition; eschatological motives; the glory of God; duty; and, finally,
the love of Christ. Almost all of these can readily be attached to missions to the colonies. But, in addition, there was the aspiration of those
who wished to 'help our brothers and sisters' and to contribute to the
building up of the Empire – the kinds of values reflected in the anniversary sermons of the various colonial missionary societies, especially the
SPG and the CCCS.

The idea that the colonial mission was a special and particular calling
was reflected from the middle of the nineteenth century by a movement
to create colleges especially for this purpose. Nevertheless, it might also
be interpreted as part of the international flow of labour that was facilitated by the expansion of the empire. It was also conducted on a larger
scale than foreign missions. Piggin's study includes analysis of some
557 missionary candidates from ten societies (only a proportion of all
those who served). The field of inquiry for those seeking to study candidates for the colonial missions is much larger. The summary of the missionary roll of the SPG devised by Pascoe indicates that almost 4,000
missionaries served with the SPG, the majority of whom were engaged
in missions to colonists, including 1,597 to Newfoundland and Canada,
446 to the West Indies and South America, 505 to Africa, and 530 to
Australasia.[47]

Since there were about 500 candidates for the colonial ministry who
graduated from St Augustine's alone,[48] and, in the case of colonial mission societies, only the SPG has retained the papers relating to candidates' applications, it is evident that it will be difficult to match Piggin's
analysis of missionary motivation and social background. However, it
is likely that the motivation of men who considered taking up a missionary call to the heathen or to the colonies was very similar. In fact,
Piggin notes that Arthur Bell Nichols, the young curate who proposed

---

[47] Pascoe, *Two Hundred Years of the SPG*, p. 847. See Table 3.2, SPG: summary of the
missionary roll, 1701–1900. Pascoe does not distinguish missionaries sent to minister
to colonists from those sent to heathen missions but the majority of SPG missions (see
Chapter 3) were to settlers.

[48] See Tables 9.1 and 9.2. Pascoe gives the number of St Augustine's graduates as 550,
whereas Boggis only lists 480.

to the novelist Charlotte Brontë in December 1852 (echoing the enthusiasm of Brontë's fictional character, St John Rivers, who longed to be a missionary in India), offered himself to the SPG, asking to be sent to Sydney, Melbourne or Adelaide. He gave as his motive: 'I have for some time felt a strong inclination to assist in ministering to the thousands of our fellow Countrymen, who by Emigration have been in a great measure deprived of the means of grace.'[49] Nichols was a graduate of Trinity College, Dublin; he wanted to better himself (and to marry Charlotte). Although India was a more romantic aspiration, Australia was also a respectable missionary calling. This might seem endearing if it were not so likely to have been true for a good many young clerics. In 1849, the Reverend Henry Christmas published a memoir which gives an account of his own experiences when, after failing to obtain a living in England, he emigrated to Canada.[50] The second volume was written as an emigration manual for young clergymen. Nichols fits the profile outlined somewhat facetiously by Christmas of the impoverished curate who had been engaged ever since he was at college to his 'dear sweet cousin' but was afraid to 'commit matrimony' on his 'valuable preferment' of £80 per year.[51] All such men, Christmas advised, should head to the colonies where they could marry and live like gentlemen with their own land and carriage.

Assessment of St Augustine's

From the time of its foundation, St Augustine's attracted more than its fair share of adverse criticism, especially from low churchmen. Even the college historian appears to have had reservations. In his summary account, Bullock comments that the number of students who enrolled was always 'disappointingly small', and the project was not helped by the sudden death of bishop Coleridge in 1849. Like many others, Bullock seems to have disliked the captivity of the college by the high church party.[52]

To what extent did St Augustine's simply reinforce the colonial prejudices of the clergy it trained, delaying the development of colonial churches? To what extent did the 'missionary' standing of the college

---

[49] Piggin, *Making Evangelical Missionaries*, p. 125, citing A. B. Nicholls' answers to questions, 28 January 1853.
[50] H. Christmas, ed., *The Emigrant Churchman in Canada by a Pioneer in the Wilderness*, 2 vols. (London, 1849), p. 138.
[51] *Ibid.*, pp. 138–9.
[52] F. W. B. Bullock, *A History of the Training for the Ministry of the Church of England and Wales from 1800 to 1874* (St Leonards-on-Sea, Sussex, 1955), p. 88.

Table 9.2 *St Augustine's College, Canterbury. dioceses of sailing, 1849–1904*

Diocese	Number sailing	Diocese	Number sailing
Adelaide	10	Melbourne	4
Algoma	1	Montreal	5
Antigua	9	Nassau	9
Ballarat	19	Natal	4
Barbados	6	Nelson	1
Bathurst	3	New Westminster	2
Bloemfontein	8	Newcastle	7
Bombay	23	Newfoundland	37
Brisbane	11	Niagara	4
Calcutta	29	None	8
Calgary	1	North China	6
Cape Town	42	North Queensland	7
Central Africa	1	Nova Scotia	21
Christchurch	4	Ontario	25
Colombo	2	Orange River Free State	2
Columbia	5	Osaka	3
Corea	1	Persia	1
Dunedin	2	Perth	6
Egypt	1	Pretoria	9
England	7	Qu'Appelle	7
Falkland Islands	1	Quebec	13
Fredericton	19	Rangoon	14
Gibraltar	3	Riverina	1
Goulburn	1	Rockhampton	2
Grahamstown	27	Rupertsland	5
Guiana	25	Sarawak	7
Honduras	2	Saskatchewan	2
Honolulu	8	Shantung	2
Huron	1	St Helena	2
India	2	St John's, Kaffraria	13
Jamaica	8	Sydney	5
Jerusalem	1	Syria	1
Labuan	8	Tasmania	4
Lahore	2	Tinnevelly	1
Lebombo	1	Toronto	6
Lucknow	4	Trinidad	5
Madagascar	3	Waiapu	1
Madras	23	Wellington	5
Maritzburg	6	Windward Islands	1
Mashonaland	4	Zanzibar	14
Mauritius	3	Zululand	4
Melanesia	4	Total	617

Source: E. R. J. Boggis, *A History of St Augustine's College, Canterbury* (Canterbury, 1907).

act as a smokescreen for the other, less altruistic motives of those who decided to train for the colonial ministry? This is hard to determine. Certainly, the missionary vocation cultivated at St Augustine's with its high church patronage is something that is reflected in other imperial projects, including the Canterbury settlement in New Zealand, or the Melanesian mission. It was an institution of its time – the middle decades of the nineteenth century – which was also the most idealistic period for Christian colonisation with its own attendant ministry. Mission bursaries to St Augustine's did provide an avenue to train missionaries for places such as New Guinea. They also helped to bring a small number of exceptional 'native' Christians back to England to train at the missionary college. But the colonial foundation of the college continued for some time to leaden its prospects. The candidates had less prestige than those who completed their education at the universities and they were tainted by Anglo-Catholicism. Evangelical bishops preferred to obtain their clergy either from definitely Evangelical theological colleges or from their own diocesan colleges where they could oversee their training. Nevertheless, as a cohort of clergy who were inculcated with the value of the colonial mission at the same time as they received their training, the students of St Augustine's could hardly avoid being missionaries for both colonialism and Christianity.

The link with the SPG was not a part of the initial foundation, but, by the 1930s, the connection had become quite close. The connection is stressed by W. F. France, canon of Canterbury and a former Oversea Secretary of the SPG and warden of the college, who promoted the dignity of the overseas episcopate and the colonial mission in his writing.[53] But it was, by this time, an increasingly defensive posture. In 1942, the college chapel was badly damaged during the blitz and, in the absence of a new patron, it was not possible to repair it. The decision to discontinue the college as a missionary institution followed in 1947, and the buildings were eventually sold to King's School, Canterbury.[54] In the chapter which follows, we will compare the colonial achievements of St. Augustine's with its closest institutional equivalent, the Catholic missionary college of All Hallows, Drumcondra.

---

[53] All Hallows Missionary College Drumcondra [Dublin], *Annual Report, 1850*, p. 21; France, *Oversea Episcopate*; W. F. France, 'The Place of Missionary Societies within the Church', in *The Mission of the Anglican Communion*, ed. E. R. Morgan and R. Lloyd (London, 1948).

[54] H. Bailey, *Twenty Five Years at St Augustine's College: A Letter to Late Students* (Canterbury, 1873).

10 Missionary College of All Hallows, Drumcondra (Dublin)

Clerical training in Catholic Europe was reformed in the wake of the disastrous setbacks (or possibly 'opportunities') of the Protestant Reformation. The most important initiative flowed from the Council of Trent (1545–65) which provided directions aimed at professionalising the priesthood and providing uniform guidelines for seminaries for priestly training and formation. Under canon 18 of the twenty-third session of the Council, which met between 1562 and 1563, all bishops were required to create seminaries in their dioceses which would provide a course of study including grammar, humanistic studies, patristics and instructions in the liturgy and performance of the sacraments.[1] In reality, this was practically impossible, especially in countries such as France where there were numerous dioceses and it was simply too expensive to create colleges in all of them. These colleges were intended to provide both a general education and the special theological and liturgical training required for the priesthood. However, the most prestigious seminaries were those attached to the largest and wealthiest dioceses, above all that of Rome; others were extremely poor. Bishops retained considerable discretion on the length of training, the curriculum and the basis for the selection of applicants. This was retained until 1918 when the new Code of Canon Law specified the length and courses required for training for the priesthood and specified, for the first time, that all priests had to be trained in a seminary.[2]

In addition to these diocesan seminaries for the training of secular priests, Rome was the location for the Urban College, founded as a missionary seminary in the palace of the Sacred Congregation of Propaganda, and usually referred to as the College of Propaganda Fide. This was Paul Cullen's alma mater, from where he became doctor of theology in 1828, and it was one of Rome's most distinguished and

---

[1] C. H. Parker, *Faith on the Margins: Catholics and Catholicism in the Dutch Golden Age* (Cambridge, MA, 2008), pp. 74–5.
[2] Reid, *Dictionary of Christianity in America*, pp. 1070–2.

influential houses of learning. There were numerous other missionary seminaries, many in Rome, which were established by Catholic missionary orders and which served the same function.[3] These Roman colleges trained an elite cadre who might anticipate appointment in due course as bishops and heads of monastic houses either in their home countries or, increasingly, in the colonies. Under Cullen, who served as rector from 1832 to 1849, the Irish College in Rome became the powerhouse for the training of Irish bishops for the British empire.[4] This began under Cullen but continued after his death. In addition, Cullenite bishops went on to found seminaries modelled on the Irish College in their own dioceses, including Patrick Francis Moran's seminary in the Sydney suburb of Manly, and St Charles Borromeo Seminary in Wynnewood, Pennsylvania, and elsewhere, all of which extended his influence well into and beyond the generation after his death.

France also had a long tradition of providing college training for both foreign and poor French students for missionary and colonial work.[5] Prior to Catholic emancipation in Britain, there were colleges in various French dioceses for English, Scottish and Irish students – especially the latter.[6] While most trained priests for their home churches, they also provided a steady supply of priests who were devoted – or desperate – enough to take on religious duties in places where no French priest would agree to go. In Paris, the Séminaire des Missions-Etrangères trained priests for the French empire. However, the most important missionary seminary was that of the French Congrégation du Saint-Esprit, also known as the Spiritans or, in Ireland, the Holy Ghost Fathers.[7] The Order, founded in Paris in 1703, trained young men from poor backgrounds who had a vocation for the priesthood and who would accept hardship postings to rural frontiers, or as chaplains in hospitals, prisons and schools. Later, the order also conducted missions in North America, Africa and the Far East. Although suppressed during the Revolution, in 1802 the French government reopened the seminary specifically to train priests for missionary work in French colonies, including Acadie (Nova Scotia), places where they undertook the care of both Europeans and

---

[3] For a long list of these, see U. Benigni, 'Sacred Congregation of Propaganda', in *Catholic Encyclopedia* (New York, 1911).

[4] For Cullen's correspondence at the Irish College in Rome, which was largely responsible for this achievement, see the online Papers of Paul Cullen (1821–79), www.irishcollege.org/PDF/CullenCollectionLevel.pdf.

[5] J. McManners, *Church and Society in Eighteenth-Century France* (Oxford, 1998), p. 200.

[6] Walsh, *Irish Continental College Movement*.

[7] 'Religious Congregations of the Holy Ghost', *Catholic Encyclopedia* (New York, 1913). For an English history of the order, see H. J. Koren, *To the Ends of the Earth: A General History of the Congregation of the Holy Ghost* (Pittsburgh, 1983).

non-Europeans. This was a government enterprise, and colonial priests were effectively part of the colonial service, as colonial chaplains were in the British empire. The missionaries are said to have served the government well and gained for it the affections of the native people.[8] By the nineteenth century, training for missionaries to go out to the French-speaking colonies of the British empire was available from the Séminaire des Missions-Etrangères (Paris), the Séminaire de la Congrégation du Saint-Esprit (Paris) and some colonial diocesan seminaries, most notably that in Quebec. The Quebec Séminaire des Missions-Étrangères was established in 1663 as a daughter foundation of the Paris seminary of the same name.[9] During the English conquest (1759), it was used to garrison troops and the seminary was closed. However, in 1852, in a different building, it was re-established as Université Laval with a royal charter from Queen Victoria. By this late stage, Ireland had overtaken France in the production of Catholic missionary clergy for the British empire, and French colonial priests subsequently made little impact outside North America.

Until late in the eighteenth century, Catholic penal laws made it necessary for English, Irish and Scottish students who wished to study for the Catholic priesthood or join a religious order to study on the continent, and their numbers were relatively small.[10] When the French Revolution forced many of these colleges to close, there was a renewed push to provide for clerical training in Britain. A national seminary for Ireland was founded in 1795 at Maynooth in County Kildare, and within a short period many others were founded in dioceses across Ireland. As we have seen, in 1838, when the English mission was expanded, the Holy See proposed that a missionary college be established, either in England or in Ireland, in order to provide clergy for the English colonies.[11] When the English vicars apostolic proved unable to respond to this, it was inevitable that the papacy would give its backing to the creation of a suitable institution in Ireland. Following the well-established French model, this would be a seminary for young men of poor families who had the stamina for a regime of rigorous economy while training for the priesthood, followed by even greater privation in frontier dioceses upon their ordination. Passage money to the colonies, and a

---

[8] *Almanach du Clergé de France*, vol. 12 (Paris, 1835), p. 454.
[9] Hermann Giguère (Superior General of the Quebec Séminaire des Missions-Étrangères), 'Séminaire de Québec', www.geocities.com/hgig.geo/sme_history.htm.
[10] For a map of these, see R. D. Edwards, *An Atlas of Irish History*, 3rd edn (London, 2005), p. 103.
[11] 'Statuta Proposita', Appendix E, in Ward, *Sequel to Catholic Emancipation*. See also Chapter 4 above.

Table 10.1 *Irish missionary seminaries*

College	Date founded	Date of earliest mission
All Hallows College, Drumcondra	1841	1842
St Kieran's, Kilkenny	1782	1813
St Patrick's College, Carlow	1793	1842 Fund for Foreign Missions
St Patrick's College, Maynooth	1795	1838 India and Australia missions
St John's College, Waterford	1807	1830s Newfoundland
St Peter's College, Wexford	1819	Cape Colony, Eastern vicariate
St Patrick's College, Thurles	1838	1870s Renewed mission programme
St Mary's College, Youghal	1839–44	1839 'College for the Foreign Missions'

Source: Conlan, *Missionary College of All Hallows, 1842–91*, pp. 223–5.

guarantee of work, would be supplied by the colonial bishops, and they would never have to see Ireland again. Thousands of Irish aspirants to the priesthood were to find this offer irresistible.

Missionary College of All Hallows

All Hallows was founded to train men for Irish colonial missions in the British, which is to say the Irish spiritual, empire. However, compared with St Augustine's – let alone with Propaganda College in Rome – it had little to recommend it in terms of teaching, facilities or prestige. Its history is wracked with complaints about the excessive Irishness and ignorance of its priests and student-led revolts against its Spartan living conditions and arbitrary discipline.[12] Nevertheless, it was a spectacular success – because it was needed. From the time of its foundation in 1842 until 1892, when the College was put into the hands of the Vincentian Fathers, it produced over 2,000 priests for missions to the United States, Australia and New Zealand, and other settler colonies.[13] The scale of the All Hallows venture was beyond the capacity of the College itself to keep track of: in 1907, when contributing to the *Catholic Encyclopedia*,[14] the College claimed to have produced 1,500 priests in the previous sixty years: Condon and the researchers who contributed to his history of the

---

[12] K. Condon, *The Missionary College of All Hallows, 1842–1891* (Dublin, 1986).
[13] See Tables 10.2 and 10.4 for summaries of the dioceses to which All Hallows men were sent. For biographical entries on 2,013 individual priests, but unfortunately no summary or statistical analysis, see *ibid.*, pp. 290–364.
[14] Thomas O'Donnell, 'All Hallows College,' in *The Catholic Encyclopedia*, vol. 1 (New York, 1907), www.newadvent.org/cathen/01314b.htm.

Table 10.2 *All Hallows College, summary of destinations of matriculants, 1842–91*

Dioceses	Number	Percentage of known destinations
United States	961	41
Australia, New Zealand and the Pacific	618	26
England, Wales and Scotland	271	12
Canada and Newfoundland	104	4
West Indies, Central and South America	78	3
India, South Africa and Mauritius	106	5
Irish dioceses, communities and seminaries	101	4
Other seminaries	97	4
Total known	2336	
Total unknown	248	
Total	2,584	

Source: Conlan, *The Missionary College of All Hallows, 1842–91.*

College uncovered more than 500 additional names. It is important to recognise that All Hallows was designed to train the clerical proletariat and was relatively unsuccessful in contributing to the higher ecclesiastical ranks. Indeed, based on calculations by his students from Condon's matriculation records, Barr notes that less than 2 per cent went on to become bishops.[15] While one factor in this was the conspicuous preference of Paul Cullen and his Hiberno-Roman acolytes for candidates who had been trained in Rome, another was simply the poverty and poor prospects of most of its original pool of students.

All Hallows' matriculants went to dioceses all over the world where the Irish had established emigrant beachheads. Out of a total of 2,013 matriculants who emerged from All Hallows between 1842 and 1891, the largest number (638) went, as might be expected, to the United States. But, in proportion to its emigrant Irish population, All Hallows' men were a much more significant presence in Australia, New Zealand and the Pacific. A smaller number (104) went to Canada and Newfoundland, where they were important in dioceses in parts of Upper Canada, but French, German and American clergy were generally much more of a force than the Irishmen from All Hallows.

The migration programme of Catholic clergy to the colonies was not exhausted by the candidates of All Hallows, any more than Anglican clergy were by St Augustine's. Priests found their way to the colonies

---

[15] Barr, "'Imperium in Imperio'".

of the British empire from Ireland, France and elsewhere in Catholic Europe, by many paths. In addition to the parochial clergy trained at All Hallows, there were many thousands more men and women from the regular and some monastic orders who emigrated after their training in Ireland to serve as teachers, nurses and missionaries for the schools, hospitals and other Catholic institutions of the colonies.[16] Indeed, by the 1860s, not just All Hallows but most of the seminaries in Ireland were supplying priests for both colonial missions and for the expanding Catholic dioceses of England, Wales and Scotland. One of the most important, Carlow College, produced over 1,000 priests for dioceses in England, Scotland, Australia, Canada and other parts of the British empire, as well as the United States.[17] However, one institution was nothing short of a powerhouse for colonial clergy production: All Hallows, the most remarkable single institution in the complex pattern of the intersecting religious, commercial and emigrant imperatives that makes up the history of the colonial missions of Greater Britain.

The Missionary College of All Hallows was established in 1842 but it did not publish any account of its work, other than an annual list of subscriptions and donations received, until issuing its first annual report in 1849.[18] The College lands, leased from the Corporation of Dublin, had once belonged to the Priory of All Hallows, and this made an apt name for a missionary institution. The object of the College, it was stated, was

the education of Ecclesiastics for the FOREIGN MISSIONS. Millions of our fellow beings 'sit in darkness and in the shadow of death'; they have none to break to them the 'Bread of Life'; and this INSTITUTION would give activity to the zeal of numbers among the youth of Ireland, who are anxious to devote themselves to Religion in those countries where 'the harvest indeed is great, but the labourers are few'.[19]

It was a thrifty, spectacularly successful, venture launched on a winning formula: a subscription of £10 annually was sufficient to secure a free place for a student. This would secure not only the education of a candidate for the priesthood but also daily mass which was offered up for all the College's subscribers and benefactors. Any subscriber who

---

[16] For a very thorough (if rather bloodless) international survey, see Murphy, *History of Irish Emigrant and Missionary Education*. Also O. D. Edwards, 'The Irish Priest in North America', in *Studies in Church History* (1989), pp. 311–52; Fogarty, *Catholic Education in Australia*; and Hogan, *Irish Missionary Movement*.

[17] McEvoy, *Carlow College*. See Tables 10.1 and 10.3.

[18] All Hallows Missionary College Drumcondra [Dublin], *First Annual Report, 1849* (Dublin, 1849).

[19] *Ibid.*

Table 10.3 *Carlow College, destinations of alumni*

Destination	Number
Ireland	1,150
United States	1,043
England and Wales	381
Australia	303
Scotland	84
New Zealand	42
Canada	36
South Africa	11
Gibraltar	4
India	4
British Guiana	3
Trinidad	3
France	2
Mauritius	2
New Guinea	1

Source: McEvoy, Carlow College 1793–1993: The
Ordained Students and Teaching Staff of St Patrick's
College, Carlow (Carlow, 1993).

had contributed at least £1 to the College was included in the subscription list. In 1847, the largest donation of £312 was the allocation
from the Society of the Propagation of the Faith, while the President of
Maynooth College, Dr Renehan, had come up with £2.

All Hallows was therefore sustained by people of very small means
from all across Ireland and, in this form, it was the brainchild of John
Hand, a Dublin priest who was then living as St Vincent's School,
Castleknock.[20] Hand left Ireland in 1841 in order to visit colleges in
France and Italy which also served a missionary object, and succeeded
in obtaining a letter of approval from the Sacred Congregation of the
Propaganda to proceed with the establishment of a seminary. Given
French precedents, and the refusal of the English vicars apostolic to
take action, this decision by the Holy See is rather less surprising than it
might otherwise seem. The letter, signed by cardinal Fransoni stated: 'I
feel the greatest pleasure in having to inform you, that our Holy Father
Pope Gregory the Sixteenth has himself willingly and in strong terms
approved of your design of founding this college.'[21] Whether the pope
did give his individual stamp of approval is not certain, nor is it clear if
either Hand or the pope had consulted the archbishop of Dublin, who

[20] MacDevitt, *Father Hand*.
[21] All Hallows Missionary College Drumcondra [Dublin], *First Annual Report*, p. 3.

possibly for this reason never seems to have felt entirely warm about the missionary seminary. But it served a clear practical need and Murray was quick to add his approval to the project. The Dublin Committee for the Association for the Propagation of the Faith, the lay fund-raising organisation based in Lyons, also approved, which ensured that fund-raising could proceed through parishes for the College project.

Hand pushed hard and began renovating the Drumcondra site when he had collected a mere £800, trusting sufficient donations would follow. They did and the first intake of students was in November 1842. This included thirty-eight candidates destined for the missions of Vincennes and New York (United States), British Guiana, Trinidad, Scotland, Calcutta, Agra, Madras, the Cape of Good Hope and Sydney (Australia). From the beginning the College made no real distinction between work directed at the conversion of the heathen and that among Europeans already converted. Rather, the College provided missionaries who could be sent to all the British colonies and territories as well as the United States: everywhere the Irish diaspora had dispersed, lending their colonising backs and arms to the empire. The religious need was evident to the College: 'The spiritual destitution of these vast regions is extreme and most appalling. Truly, in these missions there are millions of the children of our Heavenly Father, "who cry out for bread, and there is no one to break it to them: the harvest is indeed great, but the labourers are few".'[22] This was the religious vocation to which All Hallows' men were called; however, it was also a way to earn a living in an honourable profession and to secure a passage to the colonies.

While the All Hallows' report recognised such service to 'our own poor exiled fellow-countrymen',[23] the kind of duty performed by All Hallows' men depended on the special needs of the territory. In India, the work was directed to Irish soldiers serving with the British army anywhere in the vast territories of the East India Company. There were also small numbers of converts – among both the European and the Indian population. Everywhere the number of Catholics without priests set an heroic challenge for the new arrivals. In Madras, for example, the vicar apostolic estimated there were 90,000 to 100,000 Catholics in a population of many millions. He put his pleas quietly: 'I have said enough to show you that I want more priests than you can send me. It is very easy for you to draw up supplications; but it is very difficult for me, with such destitution staring me in the face, to receive any advice, that would leave the people longer without the means of salvation.'[24] Large numbers of Irish soldiers

---

[22] *Ibid.*, p. 9.   [23] *Ibid.*, p. 16.
[24] Vicar Apostolic, Madras, 4 May 1846, quoted in *ibid.*, p. 12.

were serving in the city and territory of Lahore in the vicariate of Agra and where there was a pressing problem of the education of Catholic children, particularly for those orphaned by the brutal campaigns in the Punjab. The vicar apostolic wrote:

> I know that the Government has concocted a plan to suppress all the Regimental Schools of these provinces, and to send all the Catholic children of the soldiers to the Protestant Asylum. I am endeavouring with all my strength to oppose such an attempt against our holy religion, and especially to protect the poor orphans of the deceased soldiers of the army of the Sutledje; but I cannot do all that I wish; because I have not sufficient means, and I am greatly thwarted by Protestants.[25]

Across all of India there were only some twenty priests.

Mauritius had come into British hands only in 1814, having been subject to France prior to this; its population of British soldiers, slaves and planters was largely Catholic. Writing to the College, the vicar apostolic thought that the total conversion of the island to the one true faith was possible if he only had the clergy:

> I have every reason to believe that, if I had twenty priests, in addition to those whom I have at present, the whole island would in a few years be Catholic, excepting only the few English who come hither to make money. There is at present the greatest desire among the Blacks of the island to be instructed in the Catholic religion; and it is among these that Almighty God chiefly blesses our labours.[26]

The most promising and inviting field for Irish missionary clergy was Australia where, with some exaggeration it is true, the report stated that Catholics formed about one-third of the European population. Bishop Polding wrote of the qualities he was looking for in clergy for the mission: 'I shall rely upon your sympathy in our wants to procure for us priests such as God loves and man respects, not seeking filthy lucre, nor caring for ease; loving labour, and rejoicing to suffer, if such be the will of their Divine Master.' Decent missionary priests were essential to work with newly arriving convicts: 'Missionaries ought to be with the prisoners from the first; otherwise, the most horrible vices will become habitual, and hardness of heart will prevail.'[27]

The tiny budget of All Hallows was clearly an ongoing challenge, and there was understandable comparison with the much larger endowment for Protestant societies, whatever the latter's own expressions of need:

---

[25] Vicar Apostolic, Agra, 25 May 1846, quoted in *ibid*.
[26] Vicar Apostolic, Mauritius, 25 February 1847, quoted in *ibid*., p. 15.
[27] Bishop Bede Polding to Father Hand, 11 December 1844, quoted in *ibid*., pp. 16–17.

Vast sums are freely given every year by the United Missionary Societies of Great Britain and America, for the diffusion of error in the British colonies of India, Africa, America and Australia. These societies, which are the active and wealthy Propaganda of heresy, Ireland has to meet single-handed, by sending Catholic missionaries into these countries, and keeping up at the same time a large supply of priests to England and Scotland.[28]

From Agra, Nicholas Barry wrote to Bartholomew Woodlock, third rector of All Hallows and later bishop of Ardagh, of his duties. There were problems with the Protestants, but there was one great advantage: 'as long as *their* dominion in the north of India is stayed by an army, the two-thirds of which are Irish Catholic soldiers, a Catholic priest need not care much for their misguided zeal or their bigotry.'[29] He prepared candidates for confirmation, many from the west of Ireland 'whose education had been neglected. They often puzzled me, as they spoke nothing but Irish, so I had to get a catechist who understood the language.' On the day of the confirmation he signed them all up for the arch-confraternity of the Immaculate Heart of Mary for the Conversion of Sinners. 'They have still about them all the simplicity of the country people at home. They sometimes express their surprise at seeing a priest of their own so far away from their home.'[30]

By the time of its second report, All Hallows had developed an articulate message of imperial regeneration, but the language was that of exile and loss, not empire and dominion:[31] 'Whilst the exiled children of our poor country are spreading Catholicity to the utmost bounds of the hearth, she has herself in the midst of her poverty, raised up an Institution, whose Missionaries will go forth with the good tidings of salvation.'[32] The most attractive feature of these reports is not this sad rhetoric, but the letters from clergy back from the missionary dioceses. From Berrima in New South Wales, Father W. M'Ginty wrote to Reverend Dr Woodlock. He had arrived in Sydney and been sent almost immediately to a new district ('which is what they are called, and not parishes') but he managed to send off a letter when in Sydney on retreat, on 25 June 1849. His parish was in the small country town of Berrima, about eighty-six miles from Sydney. His parishioners numbered no more than 900 people, and most of them were Irish. He had a house in town, but no chapel other than a wooden hut, which did duty as a schoolhouse during the week. On Christmas Day and Easter Sunday up to 100 jammed in. There was no other priest, but still he

[28] MacDevitt, *Father Hand*, p. 191.
[29] All Hallows Missionary College Drumcondra [Dublin], *First Annual Report*, p. 46.
[30] *Ibid.*   [31] *Ibid.*
[32] All Hallows Missionary College Drumcondra [Dublin], *Annual Report, 1850*, p. 2.

would not exchange it for a mission in Ireland. The critical difference was the healthy climate:

> I would not exchange the ever clear and blue sky of Australia for the damp and cloudy atmosphere of Ireland. This place is most healthy. The last funeral I had was in the week before Christmas. Since I came to Berrima, in May, 1847, I have not had ten sick calls – I mean to ten different persons. It is now the middle of our winter, and I never saw such pleasant, beautiful weather in Ireland at any season. The weather is most temperate, neither too hot nor too cold. Do not think that this is the sole reason for my preferring this country to Ireland; there are many others, too numerous indeed to mention.[33]

This is a missionary recruiting letter, but the allure of a healthy climate where there were few funerals was hard to challenge. He then sends news of fellow All Hallows' men who were dispersed to places as far afield as Agra in India, Rhode Island in the United States, and Norfolk Island and Moreton Bay in Australia.

On 3 March 1849, there were more optimistic words from Denis Spellisy in Mauritius:

> You have no idea of the beauty of this island; it is lovely beyond conception. You can find here in the greatest abundance fruits of every description: it is, indeed, the garden of the world. [The black population] have the best dispositions possible ... Oh! it is a pleasure to labour among these people ... This is the wildest mission in the island: but I am as content to labour among my dear blacks as I would be to preach from the greatest pulpit in Europe.[34]

It was, however, essential to know French.

The news from the vicariate apostolic of Agra was less sanguine. There the continued wars ensured that the Catholic news could not be cheering: 'Religion cannot prosper when so much confusion reigns', wrote N. Barry from St Peter's College, on 23 August 1849.[35] Most of his work was with the Irish soldiers whose military duties interrupted their own devotions: 'In the regiment which is here at present, the Catholics of the band, who are the heads of our choir, are obliged to play to the Protestant church, and hence cannot be present at the commencement of Mass. We have complained of this grievance, but as yet we have not succeeded in getting it redressed.' The members of the regiment were active in the Confraternity of the Scapular: 'On weekdays they assemble at eight o'clock in the morning to say the Office of the Immaculate Conception, and on Sundays the office and litany are sung in the evening at six o'clock, before vespers.' There were also

[33] *Ibid.*, p. 6.
[34] All Hallows Missionary College Drumcondra [Dublin], *First Annual Report*, p. 32.
[35] *Ibid.*, p. 10.

conversions – whether native or European he does not say – but the number was not as high as last year.

In Madras, Nathaniel O'Donnell wrote that he had been able to meet up with two of his old class-fellows of All Hallows: 'One circumstance only would I mention, to show that Ireland, faithful Ireland, is still steadily fulfilling the high behest of enlightening those who sit in darkness and in the shadow of death; and this one circumstance is, that with the exception of one Portuguese and one native priest (this latter is now superannuated) all the priests in this vicariate are Irishmen.'[36] There is national pride in this statement as well as a challenge to other young men to come out and join him.

From New Zealand, Bishop J. B. F. Pompallier, bishop of Maronia and apostolic administrator of the diocese of Auckland, spoke of his experience in New Zealand thirteen years earlier when, by his account, the people of New Zealand were 'infidels and cannibals'.[37] As vicar apostolic, working with three priests and three catechists, he claimed to have achieved 50,000 native converts. The work was now shared among fourteen missionaries, almost all French. In 1840, New Zealand became a British colony to which many would certainly emigrate. 'Still our labours in New Zealand have met with great difficulties, not only from infidelity, but also from heresy. Protestantism is there so rich and active, that it sends the ministers of its various sects in every direction, and builds presbyteries, churches, and schools in all the principal places.'[38] But the great danger was the fate of the Catholics who had been earlier converted, many of the more remote tribes were going over to the Protestant missionaries. 'Alas! this is the cross of my crosses; this is what afflicts most deeply a pastoral heart.' Pompallier was in Europe seeking priests as well as religious from the Convent of Mercy, Carlow. He managed to get a group of three, headed by Cecilia Maher. The list of subscriptions and donations follows: again, all very tiny amounts, most no more than a pound. No less than Cape Colony, New Zealand was a hard mission for a Catholic priest.

Conclusion

By the end of the nineteenth century, the rush of clerical emigrants to the colonies had passed. From Ireland, the crest of the wave would appear to have been the 1890s, after which the many daughter institutions

---

[36] *Ibid.*, p. 13.
[37] All Hallows Missionary College Drumcondra [Dublin], *Annual Report, 1850*, p. 21.
[38] *Ibid.*, p. 22.

founded by Irish colonial missionaries were beginning to produce more of their own offspring and the absolute dependence on clergy production in Ireland had waned. The pattern was similar with the clergy provided to the colonies by the dissenting and established churches whose theological colleges were scattered elsewhere in Britain. And, while the two largest colonial missionary colleges, All Hallows and St Augustine's, both continued to provide clergy for the colonies after this period, the graduates were increasingly drawn to dioceses in India and majority black communities in Africa rather than to the white settler colonies.

It is almost impossible to estimate accurately how many clergy migrated from Britain to the colonies from all sources, though I have suggested in Chapter 8 that it is likely to be numbered in scores of thousands. Of this great outflowing, the 500 ordinands from St Augustine's, or even the 2,000 produced by All Hallows, were only a small proportion of all those who felt and responded to a colonial missionary calling. The creation of both institutions in the 1840s was at least partly a response to the terrible social conditions which underpinned the great emigration from the British islands over the following decades. Their motivation for leaving was similar in some respects to those of other educated, middle-class emigrants who left Britain at this time: the wish to pursue the profession for which they had been trained, the desire to better themselves economically and the attraction of colonial life with its promise of a more congenial lifestyle, a better climate (though not always) and engaging work. But, for emigrant clergy, there were other compelling, religious reasons which sustained their choice of career.

The two colleges pursued very different paths to idealise the predominately colonial calling which they were set up to supply. St Augustine's was a project which grew out of some of the most romantic aspirations of the high church party, aspirations which had already created the Colonial Bishoprics' Fund and the Christian colonisation of the province of Canterbury in New Zealand. All Hallows was a triumph of thrift and the enthusiasm of one man, John Hand, which could not afford to over-romanticise the colonial mission. It was set up to fulfil a need: the need of colonial bishops for clergy with few pretensions to serve in their dioceses, and the need for aspirational young men to secure a path out of Ireland. Both were smoothed on their way by a comforting ideology of colonial and spiritual usefulness.

What was the impact of these cohorts of trained clergy in the colonies? The ordinands of St Augustine's were inspired to follow the paths and seaways taken from England by medieval missionary saints such as Boniface and their latter day successors in the SPG and SPCK in the Americas, India and New Zealand. Their religious vocation was

Table 10.4 *All Hallows College, destination dioceses of matriculants, 1842–1900*

Australia		
New South Wales	Sydney	134
	Armidale	14
	Bathurst	21
	Grafton/Lismore	8
	Maitland	28
	Goulburn	26
Queensland	Brisbane	44
South Australia	Adelaide	27
Tasmania	Hobart	24
Victoria	Melbourne	160
	Ballarat	23
	Sale	6
	Sandhurst	23
Western Australia	Perth	34
	Geraldton	2
Total		574
New Zealand		
	Auckland	17
	Christchurch	2
	Dunedin	5
	Wellington	20
	Total	44
United States		
North	Albany, NY	32
	Syracuse, NY	2
	Buffalo, NY	6
	Brooklyn, NY	51
	New York, NY	11
	Hartford, CT	36
	Providence, RI	3
	Newark, NJ	32
	Trenton, NJ	8
	Boston, MA	43
	Springfield, MA	14
	Burlington, VT	16
	Manchester, NH	2
	Portland, ME	5
	Philadelphia, PA	7
	Pittsburgh, PA	25
South	Baltimore, MD	2
	Charleston, SC	7
	Richmond, VA	24
	Wheeling, WV	4
	Mobile, AL	9
	New Orleans, LA	2
	Nashville, TN	8
	Natchez, MS	10

Table 10.4 (*cont.*)

	Lewisville, KY	9
	Little Rock, AR	4
	Savannah, GA	16
	Galveston, TX	5
Mid-West and North	Chicago, IL	36
	Alton (Springfield), IL	40
	Belleville, IL	1
	Peoria, IL	10
	Cincinnati, OH	5
	Cleveland, OH	12
	Columbus, OH	1
	Vincennes, IN	7
	Fort Wayne, IN	6
	Dubuque, IA	70
	Davenport, IA	9
	Leavenworth, KS	13
	Concordia, KS	3
	St Louis, MO	11
	Kansas City–St Joseph, MO	19
	Omaha, NE	18
	Lincoln, NE	2
	St Paul, MN	38
	Duluth, MN	3
	Detroit, MI	8
	Green Bay, WI	2
	Milwaukee, WI	4
West	San Francisco, CA	120
	Marysville (Grass Valley, Sacramento), CA	76
	Monterey (and Los Angeles), CA	36
	Salt Lake City, UT	4
	Oregon City, OR	7
	Nesqualy, OR	3
Total		961
Canada and Newfoundland		
British Columbia	Vancouver's Island	4
New Brunswick	St John	6
Newfoundland	Harbour Grace	14
	St John's	21
Nova Scotia	Halifax	13
Ontario	Hamilton	2
	Kingston	11
	London	4
	Ottawa	6
	Peterborough	2
	Toronto	18
Quebec	Montreal	4
Not known		2
Total		104

Table 10.4 (*cont.*)

England and Wales

	Birmingham	9
	Beverley (Leeds)	25
	Hexham and Newcastle	15
	Liverpool	40
	Menevia (Wales)	20
	Middlesbrough	5
	Northampton	6
	Nottingham	10
	Plymouth	13
	Salford	28
	Shrewsbury	26
	Southwark	13
	Westminster	3
Total		213

Scotland

	Western District	45
	Eastern District	13
Total		58

Ireland

	Religious communities	52
	Dioceses	24
	Seminaries	25
Total		101

India, South Africa, Mauritius and others

	Agra	5
	Bombay	2
	Calcutta	15
	Ceylon	1
	Hyderabad	3
	Madras	28
	Cape Mission	24
	Cape Town	1
	Grahamstown (Eastern Cape)	11
	Mauritius	14
	Gibraltar	2
Total		106

West Indies, Central and South America

	British Guiana	3
	Jamaica	2
	Bermuda	1
	Trinidad	42
	Roseau, Dominica	13
	Buenos Aires	17
Total		78

Table 10.4 (*cont.*)

Seminaries		
	England	14
	United States	11
	Europe	71
	Australia	1
Total		97
Totals		
	Total known	2,336
	Unknown	248
	Total	2,584

Source: Conlan, *Missionary College of All Hallows.*

joined to a wider British patriotism which some at least demonstrated with their lives in late-nineteenth-century imperial conflicts.

The movement also had its wry side. The memorial raised over the body of Bishop Broughton of Australia in Canterbury cathedral was intended to be the focus of pious emulation for the students of St Augustine's. It was an apotheosis of sorts for the lame, former clerk of the East India Company. But, even if Broughton had had the charisma and energy of St Francis Xavier, whose restless body eventually came to rest in Goa,[39] or the prestige of St Thomas Becket, whose shrine in Canterbury cathedral was venerated by pilgrims until its destruction in the sixteenth century, there was little prospect that his body would attract the same kind of devotion. By the end of the nineteenth century, the Anglican colonial missionary movement was fragmented by competing church factions and it had few heroes. When Bishop Broughton was entombed in considerable state in Canterbury cathedral, a correspondent wrote to the archbishop of Canterbury and expressed his opinion that it was surprising that the Australians, with their immense goldfields, were not able to provide for his grave without assistance from home.[40] However, the fact was that Broughton's Evangelical successors had already moved on to provide for their own needs. Similarly, the pretensions of St Augustine's to be the seat of a great missionary movement to the colonies meant little to the Evangelicals, who saw it not as a powerhouse for the production of colonial clergy but as a dangerous nest of Anglo-Catholicism. Others were less hostile, but the practical need for the College, particularly once other theological colleges were

---

[39] Though not exclusively. One arm of the great Jesuit saint was preserved in Rome.
[40] Benjamin Harrison, archdeacon of Maidstone to William Howley, 8 November 1853, Lambeth Palace Library, Howley Papers, MS Lambeth 2203, fol. 278.

providing clergy for colonial dioceses with less party baggage, proved more limited than its founders had imagined.

In contrast, the supply of priests who streamed from All Hallows Missionary proved to be an addiction from which Catholic colonial bishops found it difficult to wean themselves. So long as the expansion of the emigrant population required trained priests to provide religious services, it was all too easy to rely on All Hallows to fill the need. The Irish cast that this gave to the colonial churches was not perceived as a problem so long as the bishops themselves, particularly those in Australia and New Zealand, shared their worldview. Such a perception only began to change with the rise of colonial nationalism and with bishops and archbishops with a wider, more international, vision for the Roman church in the British world.

Part IV

Promised lands

Introduction: emigrants and colonists

Throughout the nineteenth century, the attitude of the churches to emigration and colonisation remained ambivalent.[1] For those who saw emigration as inevitable, or even Providential, it was necessary for the Church to provide some guidance and protection to those who were leaving British shores. The Catholic and Presbyterian churches had the most pragmatic attitude towards this and had been supplying emigrant services for the Irish and Scottish diasporas since the outpourings of the 1830s.[2] However, even in Ireland, the clerical hierarchy was conflicted about the extent to which emigration was a boon or a hindrance to the church and nation. In response to a government inquiry on emigration, the bishop of Clonfert, when asked if he opposed emigration, responded 'I am, and I am not. I am opposed to emigration for the sake of the general welfare of the country ... But in another sense, for the individual himself, who leaves the country and takes his youth and strength to America, it may be a blessing.'[3] Most clergy were concerned that the duty of caring for emigrants and settlers should not impinge on the churches at home, which were already struggling to minister to the urban poor. Emigration was open to moral critique if it was seen to be motivated purely by the lure of material, rather than spiritual advancement. Balancing such fears was

---

[1] H. L. Malchow, 'The Church and Emigration in Late Victorian England', *Journal of Church and State*, 24 (1982), pp. 119–38.

[2] B. Aspinwall, 'Scots and Irish Clergy Ministering to Immigrants, 1830–1878', *Innes Review*, 47 (1996), pp. 45–68; M. Kells, 'Religion and the Irish Migrant', *Irish Studies Review*, 6 (1994), pp. 16–18; O. MacDonagh, 'The Irish Catholic Clergy and Emigration During the Great Famine', *Irish Historical Studies*, 5 (1947), pp. 287–302; W. Sloan, 'Religious Affiliation and the Immigrant Experience: Catholic Irish and Protestant Highlanders in Glasgow, 1830–1850', in *Irish Immigrants and Scottish Society in the Nineteenth and Twentieth Centuries*, ed. T. M. Devine (Edinburgh, 1991).

[3] Cited by D. Fitzpatrick, 'The Irish in Britain', in *A New History of Ireland*, vol. VI, *Ireland under the Union*, Part II, *1870–1921*, ed. W. E. Vaughan (Oxford, 1996), p. 629.

the abiding concern that the churches should not be outmanoeuvred in the colonies and that sufficient support should be provided to the colonial churches to keep up their end against rival sects. Colonisation was always dubious because, as the missionary societies made plain, the arrival of British settlers was invariably accompanied by the destruction of the original inhabitants. Only at the second half of the nineteenth century did the churches become fully engaged with the marketing and Christianisation of both emigration and colonisation. By 1900, it was possible to list more than thirty church agencies – from the Austrian Society to the Women's Christian Temperance Union – which provided a ministry to emigrants in the United States alone.[4] In contrast, the scale of church-led ministry for those heading to British settler colonies was never so extensive, and tended to arise in response to particular social needs.

In this section, we will examine the debate about the morality of colonisation in New Zealand, which was a great set-piece battle between the CMS and other missionary societies on the one hand, and Edward Gibbon Wakefield and the proponents of colonisation on the other. While Wakefield and the colonial reformers led the way, there were other groups within Victorian society who came to see the colonies as places for the renewal and reform of pressing problems in the home society. In Chapter 11, we look at the emergence of advocates for emigration as a social panacea, including Caroline Chisholm, the Highlands and Islands Emigration Society and General Booth of the Salvation Army. By century's end, from being reluctant colonists, some Christian leaders were advocating a general evacuation of Britain as the only solution to the ills of what General Booth of the Salvation Army liked to call 'Darkest England'.

The second chapter in this section looks at full-scale attempts to create church-based colonies, on the model of those that featured in the settlement of the colonies of North America. While to some degree Wakefield gave most of his schemes of systematic colonisation a moral or religious quality, the most notable imperial attempts at creating church-led settlements were the evangelical colony of Sierra Leone, the Free Church of Scotland settlement of Otago in New Zealand, the Anglican settlement of Canterbury in New Zealand and the Anglican Britannia Colony in Saskatchewan, Canada. In the

---

[4] For a list, see J. B. Clark, 'Emigrants and Immigrants, Mission Work Among', in *The New Schaff-Herzog Encyclopedia of Religious Knowledge*, ed. S. M. Jackson (New York and London, 1909), pp. 119–20.

course of these colonial ventures, we can see a complete reversal of earlier religious objections to colonisation – from one of outright condemnation, to wholesale endorsement. The churches, or at least some of their more enterprising adherents, were claiming these imperial lands as their own.

The most continuous form of religious service for emigrants was the simple text distributed by the religious publication societies.[5] The SPCK led the way here, mostly because it had the largest means at its disposal. In 1854, the Society reported that it had appropriated £3,000 on services for emigrants: clergymen, appointed by the Society, had visited emigrants in the ports of Liverpool, Plymouth and Southampton, and many had been given books, bibles, prayer books and religious tracts.[6] A good indication of the overall strategy of this tract-based mission can be obtained from a small volume entitled *The Emigrant's Friend*, which was intended, so we are told, as 'a companion for the voyage and a manual of instruction once he had arrived'.[7] Unfortunately, the collection is undated but it could have done useful work at any time throughout the emigration era of the second half of the nineteenth century. In the first tract, 'Address to an Emigrant', the emigrant is invited to ponder the significance of the step he is undertaking, the irrevocable decision to leave his home and everything that is familiar and comfortable. Nevertheless, he is comforted that there was a scriptural precedent for his decision to leave his country in God's injunction to Abraham, 'Get thee out of thy country, and from thy kindred, and from thy father's house, unto a land that I will shew thee' (Genesis 12: 1). The emigrant was then reassured that his decision to become a colonist was neither unlawful nor immoral but was, rather, 'one great means of peopling the earth, and causing the ground to yield its fruits for the sustenance of man and beast'. Having dismissed the kinds of ethical questions that had weighed so heavily in the colonisation of New Zealand, the emigrant was advised to beware of the major danger of emigration, the lure of material prosperity. Again there was reassurance: emigrants were motivated by many things in deciding to leave their native country including a love of adventure, the wish to get rich, the quest for freedom. But emigration could become a religious vocation if the Christian colonist was committed to building a more religious society in his new home: 'The first settlers in any land

---

[5] For the origins of the tract societies, see Chapter 2.

[6] 'Christian Knowledge Society: Report for 1853–54', *Missionary Register* (1854), p. 492.

[7] Religious Tract Society, *Emigrant's Friend*, p. 2.

lay the foundation of the social edifice and the building of after ages much accords with the foundation. 'And now, voyager, farewell!'[8] With that final admonition, the Christian emigrant could be sent on his way to colonise new British lands overseas.

[8] *Ibid.*, p. 7.

11   Christian colonisation and its critics

The province of Canterbury in New Zealand wears the history of its foundation as an Anglican colony of the British empire in a very public way. At the heart of the city of Christchurch, Cathedral Square is littered with monuments to the 'Canterbury pilgrims', including a fine statue of John Robert Godley (1814–61), the leader of the Canterbury Association. In the west porch of the cathedral, rocked but not damaged in the earthquake which struck the city on 4 Sept. 2010, the visitor is greeted by four plaques which commemorate the Christian founders of the settlement. In chronological order, these name the Reverend Samuel Hinds (1793–1872), later bishop of Norwich, who in 1832 'outlined and discussed the advantages of colonisation on a religious basis'; Edward Gibbon Wakefield, who in 1843 conceived the idea of a Church of England settlement in New Zealand; Godley, who in 1847 was chiefly responsible for realising the settlement of Canterbury and its seat of Christchurch; and Queen Victoria, who in 1856 issued letters patent appointing Henry John Chitty Harper as the first bishop of Christchurch. In the nave of the cathedral, there is a font designed for Arthur Penrhyn Stanley (1815–81), dean of Westminster, which he donated to Christchurch cathedral in honour of the memory of his brother, Captain Owen Stanley (1811–50).[1] This is inscribed with verses that celebrate Stanley's landing at Akaroa in 1840, allegedly beating the French to the prize of colonising the south island of New Zealand.

> Blest hour, in Akaroa Bay,
> When England's flag first won the way,
> On these bright shores for British youth
> To grow in Christian grace and truth
> O'er Church and Home, O'er Fell and Flood,
> The Fount and Origin of Good.[2]

---

[1] Font inscription from personal photograph, May 2008. For Dean Stanley and the font, see *Christchurch Cathedral New Zealand*, printed brochure, c.2008. Stanley's action pre-empted the arrival of a party of sixty-three French colonists, not an official attempt by the French government to colonise the South Island.

[2] Inscription on baptismal font in Christchurch cathedral, Canterbury, New Zealand, 1881.

These and other memorials date from the end of the nineteenth century. Together, they capture a particular Anglican reading of the history of New Zealand, one in which the colony was planned and shaped for a Christian purpose.

Samuel Hinds

Where did the idea of 'colonisation on a religious basis' come from? Was Hinds the first to promote such a scheme for the British empire? The short answer to the second question is, clearly, no. We have already seen that the SPG had been attempting to Christianise the colonies since early in the eighteenth century and that most of the larger churches participated in the colonial missionary movement by forming their own societies to do similar work from the first decades of the nineteenth. In addition, religion played a significant role in the settlement of the first thirteen American colonies and many settlers, including Quakers, Puritans, Presbyterians and Catholics, came to the New World in search of religious toleration.[3] Nevertheless, Hinds was one of the first Anglican clergymen to take up the ideas of Edward Gibbon Wakefield, and give systematic colonisation a religious twist. An account of his life provides important insight into the social milieu of those Christian leaders who came to see emigration as not just a solution to a social problem, but an opportunity to create Christian communities throughout the British world.[4]

Hinds was a liberal in theology and politics who had connections to the leading scholars, churchmen and politicians of the day through his intimate friendship with the logician, Richard Whately (1787–1863).[5] Hinds was born in Barbados to a prominent planter family; a namesake, Samuel Hinds, was President (i.e. administrator) of Barbados in 1821.[6] He was educated in Bristol and Oxford, and ordained before returning to the West Indies in 1822 as a missionary for the (Anglican) Society for the Conversion of Negroes.[7] William Howley (1766–1848), later

---

[3] Sites for religious settlements included: 1620, Plymouth, Massachusetts (Pilgrims); 1629, New England (Puritans); 1632, Maryland (Roman Catholics); and 1656, Pennsylvania (Quakers).
[4] B. H. Blacker, 'Samuel Hinds (1793–1872)', *Oxford Dictionary of National Biography*.
[5] For Hinds' intimacy with Whately, see E. J. Whately, *Life and Correspondence of Richard Whately, DD, Late Archbishop of Dublin*, 2 vols. (London, 1866), vol. 1, pp. 444–5; vol. 2, pp. 102, 143.
[6] R. H. Schomburgk, *The History of Barbados; Comprising a Geographical and Statistical Description of the Island; a Sketch of the Historical Events since the Settlement; and an Account of Its Geology and Natural Productions* (1848), pp. 686, 413.
[7] The Incorporated Society for the Conversion and Religious Instruction and Education of the Negro Slaves in the British West India Islands was under the presidency of the

archbishop of Canterbury (1828–48), recommended him as Principal of Codrington College in Barbados,[8] which had been established by the SPG from the income of two slave plantations bequeathed to it by Colonel Christopher Codrington in 1710.[9] Hinds returned to Oxford to work with Whately, and his career took off in 1831 when the latter was made Anglican archbishop of Dublin and invited Hinds to go with him as his examining chaplain. This was a testing time for the English episcopate when, led by Archbishop Howley, they mounted a stolid resistance in the House of Lords to the passage of the Reform Bill. Hinds and Whately had direct experience of the public antipathy to bishops this aroused when a mob surrounded their carriage in Birmingham, ready, according to Whately's daughter, 'for any violent act'.[10] In fact, Whately was one of the few bishops to support parliamentary reform; he also supported the abolition of convict transportation and the removal of all civic disabilities affecting Jews and Catholics – while reserving the right to criticise their beliefs.

Through Whately, Hinds was therefore in the vanguard of Anglican church reformers. He was part of the generation which had been swept up in the debates about the social and religious condition of Great Britain and which was radicalised by the economic and political crises of the 1840s. While retaining a deep affection for the Church of England, they were moderate liberals in their theology and politics and intrepid in embracing reform for the Church at home, and new opportunities for the Church in the colonies, with or without the benefit of establishment. Whately himself was later identified with the broad church group at the University of Oxford which included academics and intellectuals such as Benjamin Jowett, Master of Balliol College, Robert Baden Powell, founder of the Boy Scout movement, and Frederick Temple, educationist and later archbishop of Canterbury.[11] This was very different

bishop of London. In 1824, it was noted that the Report showed 'more promise than produce' in the effect of its purpose. *Report of the Incorporated Society for the Conversion and Religious Instruction and Education of the Negroe Slaves in the British West India Islands, July–December 1823* (London, 1824), p. 1.

[8] See the dedication to Howley in S. Hinds, *The History of the Rise and Early Progress of Christianity Comprising an Enquiry into Its True Character and Design* (London, 1828), p. vi.

[9] Schomburgk, *History of Barbados*, p. 313. The SPG thereby became implicated in the slave economy of the West Indies and used the income of slave labour to provide a college education for the sons of white planters.

[10] Whately, *Life and Correspondence of Richard Whately*, p. 114. In fact, Whately was one of the few bishops to have always voted for the Reform Bill.

[11] S. J. Brown, 'The Broad Church Movement, National Culture and Established Churches of the United Kingdom, c.1850–1914', in *Church and State in Old and New Worlds*, ed. H. M. Carey and J. Gascoigne (Leiden, in press).

to the social and intellectual milieu that had nourished the moral campaign to end the slave trade in the previous generation. While the early abolitionists had been Tory high churchmen and committed to the *status quo*, the anti-colonisation movement, discussed later in this chapter, was dominated by Evangelicals and Nonconformists. When Evangelicals moved to oppose colonisation in New Zealand, many in the high church who had earlier opposed slavery were unwavering in their support of the SPG and its colonial mission. On the issue of colonisation, Hinds joined the majority of Peelites (liberal Conservatives) who supported emigration as a solution to social problems, and high churchmen, who believed in the extension of the national Church in the colonies. It was these high churchmen who became most engaged in the scheme for the Canterbury colony.

Hinds' interest in what he dubbed 'Christian colonisation' began in the 1830s, when, as vicar of Yardley, he began to preach and publish on emigration and the colonisation of New Zealand.[12] In 1837, he was the sole clergyman on the Committee of the New Zealand Association.[13] According to Temple, it was Hinds who contributed the chapter on 'Religious Establishment' in the Association's major prospectus.[14] If Hinds is indeed the author of this chapter, it is striking that a future Anglican bishop should give such hearty endorsement to the principle, said to be characteristic of the Canadas, Australia and India, that no denomination should be given preferential treatment in British colonies. Instead, all denominations would be entitled to build churches, maintain a minister and take a share in religious establishment. The next suggestion – a brilliant counter to the (Evangelical) Church Missionary Society that was at the forefront of opposition to the New Zealand Association's plans – was to propose that an Anglican bishop be appointed for New Zealand. In

---

[12] S. Hinds and R. Bourke, *The Latest Official Documents Relating to New Zealand, with Introductory Observations* (London, 1838). I have not been able to verify that Hinds was writing on Christian colonisation as early as 1832, i.e. before he left Dublin for Yardley, as stated on the Christchurch cathedral plaque.

[13] See the preface to New Zealand Association, *The British Colonization of New Zealand; Being an Account of the Principles, Objects and Plans of the New Zealand Association* (London, 1837). The committee had seventeen members and was chaired by Francis Baring MP. Besides Baring, the committee included eleven other MPs (W. B. Baring, Walter F. Campbell, Charles Enderby, Robert Ferguson, Benjamin Hawes, Philip Howard, William Hutt, Thomas MacKenzie, Sir W. Molesworth, Sir George Sinclair and Henry George Ward), two members of the House of Lords (the Earl of Durham and Lord Petre), as well as Captain Sir William Symonds, W. Wolryche Whitmore and the Reverend Samuel Hinds, DD.

[14] P. Temple, *A Sort of Conscience: The Wakefields* (Auckland, 2002), p. 418. See New Zealand Association, *British Colonization of New Zealand*.

due course, this was to be George Augustus Selwyn, a school friend of Gladstone at Eton. According to the prospectus, while the missionaries were encouraged to continue their work of civilising the natives, it would be the task of the bishop to civilise and uplift the colonists.[15] While an Anglican bishop would only have authority over his own church, it was argued that the general civilising balm created by the presence of a bishop would benefit the whole colony, presumably by a kind of cultural osmosis.

Whether or not he actually wrote this piece (which has otherwise been attributed to Wakefield), Hinds was an early convert to the gospel of systematic colonisation. In 1838, while Wakefield and Durham were away in Canada, it fell to Hinds to represent the advantages of colonisation to the Select Committee of the House of Lords set up to report on New Zealand.[16] Against the views of the Church Missionary Society, he provided a justification for the conditions under which a modern state could impose its rule on what he called 'barbarous countries'. For Hinds, missionaries could only begin the process which must necessarily be completed by the establishment of a Christian state:

> A missionary station will spread Christianity immediately about; but when you come to contemplate the civilization of a whole country you must look for a stronger and more effective measure. What the savage wants is to have before his eyes the example of a civilized and Christian community.[17]

Setting aside the claims of the Maori, and more or less discarding the notion that they constituted in any way a sovereign people, Hinds also made an argument along Benthamite lines, suggesting that the full annexation of New Zealand was the policy solution which would lead to the greatest degree of happiness for the greatest number of people.[18] So many people of all classes in Great Britain wished to settle there, he argued, that it was essential that the government intervene to halt colonisation by default.

Hinds' original contribution to the colonisation debate may have been to unite ideas which came from commercial promoters of schemes of colonisation to the Anglican imperialism deployed by the SPG in support of its colonial mission to British settlers. Like Buchanan some

---

[15] New Zealand Association, *British Colonization of New Zealand*, p. 71.

[16] *Select Committee of the House of Lords Appointed to Inquire into the Present State of the Islands of New Zealand* (London, 1838).

[17] *Ibid.*, cited admiringly by Garnett, *Edward Gibbon Wakefield*, p. 138, who calls it 'a luminous address'.

[18] For a discussion of Hinds' comments to the Select Committee, see P. Moon, *Fatal Frontiers: A New History of New Zealand in the Decade before the Treaty* (Auckland, 2006), pp. 140–1.

decades earlier,[19] Hinds' high church missionary background made it seem right to him that British colonies should have their own bishops and church establishments and not be left to the interim arrangements provided by the Evangelical missionary societies. In 1840, Hinds delivered an anniversary sermon on behalf of the SPG and the SPCK in Hertford in which he gave his strong endorsement to the need for the Church of England to participate fully in the enterprise of systematic religious colonisation.[20]

> Thank God! a spirit has arisen in this country simultaneously almost with the spirit of emigration – a feeling that is daily gaining strength among Churchmen – a feeling in which I for one do most fervently participate – that wherever a new colony is planted, there we should at once, and with the settlement of the colony, plant the Church also; not, as heretofore, the Church imperfect and mutilated, but in all its integrity, with a Bishop as well as subordinate clergy.[21]

Hinds was here echoing the arguments which led the Colonial Bishoprics' Fund (1841), an initiative associated most closely with Bishop Blomfield of London, which had profound implications for the expansion of Anglicanism in the colonies.[22] But, more than this, Hinds was also capturing the spirit of the age in which emigrants, having been derided as those with no stake in the British nation, were to be lauded as the creators of a new, moral and Christian empire overseas.

Edward Gibbon Wakefield

While Hinds played his part, the man who deserves credit for incorporating what he called 'the moral factor' into emigration was not a cleric, but an unlikely, not particularly religious, former felon – Edward Gibbon Wakefield.[23] Wakefield was a man ever eager to promote his own importance and originality. Until the 1990s, the verdict of posterity has been to undercut the unique role he claimed for himself in inspiring the rebirth of colonisation on a religious – or any

---

[19] Buchanan, *Colonial Ecclesiastical Establishment*.

[20] S. Hinds, *Copy of a Speech of the Reverend Samuel Hinds, DD, Vicar of Yardley, Herts, Delivered at the Anniversary Meeting of the Hertford District Committee of the Two Societies for Promoting Christian Knowledge and for the Propagation of the Gospel in Foreign Parts, Held in the Shire Hall, Hertford, September 15, 1840* (1840).

[21] *Ibid.*, p. 7.

[22] For the long history of Anglican investment in the imperial ideal, see Strong, *Anglicanism and Empire*. For the Canterbury Colony, see Chapter 9.

[23] For the 'moral factor', see Wakefield, *Art of Colonization*, p. 156, cited by W. A. Carrothers, *Emigration from the British Isles with Special Reference to the Development of the Overseas Dominions* (London, 1929), p. 139.

other – foundation.[24] Temple sums up the consensus that Wakefield's religiosity was never more than a 'sort of conscience', pointing out that Wakefield was happy to leave the business of morality to the female members of his family, and religious institution building in the colonies to the churches.[25] Nevertheless, over the course of his life, Wakefield slowly moulded an argument for colonisation in which religion came to play a prominent role.

Wakefield began writing about colonisation while he was still enduring a sentence of imprisonment in Newgate gaol, between 1827 and 1830, for his role in abducting a minor and attempting to secure her fortune.[26] With the help of his friend and fellow theorist of colonisation, Robert Gouger (1802–46), Wakefield republished these studies as a book under the title, *A Letter from Sydney*.[27] This work contained most of the key ideas which Wakefield promoted throughout his life; indeed, they lived on after his death through his son's posthumous endorsement of his father's role as the founder of Canterbury and other schemes.[28] Wakefield's *Letter from Sydney* is presented in the voice of an imaginary free settler to Sydney (a place he never visited), and it provides a way to make everybody rich. According to Wakefield, the secret lay in the application of a simple economic formula: the colonies were poor in labour but rich in land and resources, while Britain was burdened by an excess of labour. Labouring emigrants should therefore be exported to fill the colonial need, ridding the home society of its burdensome population. In order, however, to prevent the creation of socially unbalanced societies, it was important that colonies be improved by supplying them with quality emigrants of all classes on the model of the Greek colonies of antiquity.[29] In later writing, he sometimes added a comparison with the religious settlements of the American colonies. Without this social and moral element, Wakefield's imaginary Sydney settler characterised the community of emancipated convicts as one that was forever poised on the brink of revolution: 'They are rebels, every one of them,

---

[24] For a reassessment of Wakefield on the bicentenary of his birth in 1997, see Friends of the Turnbull Library, *Edward Gibbon Wakefield and the Colonial Dream: A Reconsideration* (Wellington, 1997).

[25] Temple, *Sort of Conscience*, p. 419.

[26] *Sketch of a Proposal for Colonizing Australasia, Etc.* (pamphlet, London, June 1829); *Letter from Sydney* was published in the *Morning Chronicle* in instalments from August to October 1829.

[27] R. Gouger, ed., *A Letter from Sydney, the Principal Town of Australasia [by Edward Gibbon Wakefield]* (London, 1829).

[28] E. J. Wakefield, ed., *The Founders of Canterbury, with a New Introduction by Peter Burroughs* (Folkestone and London, 1973).

[29] Gouger, ed., *Letter from Sydney*, p. viii.

at heart.'[30] In order to suppress such uncivil habits, Wakefield proposed that colonies should be created which were effectively extensions of the old society; and the main means for doing this was to encourage the emigration of people of all stations in life, including clergy and other members of the professional middle classes.[31] Purified of the indigestible sources of social upheaval at home, including their civil, religious and economic constraints and inequalities, Wakefield argued that systematically colonised communities would inevitably generate wealth not only for the emigrants themselves but for the societies whose poverty they left behind in the old world.[32] All this would be achieved by the simple means of fixing the price of land at a level sufficient to secure colonial infrastructure with one-eighth of the revenue set aside to support educational and religious endowments such as churches, schools and clerical stipends.[33] Wakefield always claimed that it did not matter what creed colonists happened to profess; they could all be accommodated in one or other scheme of colonisation. Clergy are discussed in his early writing, including *A Letter from Sydney*, simply as one of many professional groups who might usefully be encouraged to form part of an ideal colony. It is also unclear if Wakefield was aware that his advocacy of commercial colonisation of new lands would open him up to conflict with missionaries who were, of course, already established in colonies and less than delighted with the prospect of new arrivals intent on personal gain.

South Australia was the first place where Wakefield and his National Colonization Society had the opportunity to test out their ideas.[34] Here, as in most other colonies where schemes of systematic colonisation were attempted, it is important to emphasise that Wakefield's direct input was relatively small: he was really what we would now call an ideas man. The colonists who eventually settled in South Australia, Western Australia or New Zealand mostly came there under their own steam, or with the benefit of government assistance, not thanks to him. What

---

[30] *Ibid.*, p. 61.   [31] *Ibid.*, p. 187.

[32] More fully expounded in Wakefield's elaborate commentary on A. Smith, E. G. Wakefield and D. Stewart, *An Inquiry into the Nature and Causes of the Wealth of Nations: With Notes from Ricardo, M'Culloch, Chalmers, and Other Eminent Political Economists*, new ed., 4 vols. (London, 1843).

[33] Gouger, ed., *Letter from Sydney*.

[34] E. G. Wakefield, 'Plan of a Company To Be Established for the Purpose of Founding a Colony in Southern Australia (1832)', in *The Collected Works of Edward Gibbon Wakefield*, ed. P. M. F. Lloyd (Auckland, 1969), p. 278. The first colonisation society was founded by Wakefield in 1831. It was renamed the National Colonization Society in 1833. Its members included John Stuart Mill, George Grote, Rintoul, Hobhouse, Sir Francis Burdett, Charles Buller and Sir William Molesworth. The Secretary was Robert Gouger, and it included no clerics.

the commercial colonisation companies provided was marketing, and this is where religion proved its usefulness. In the volume published by the South Australia Company, the Wesleyan journalist, John Stephens (1806–50),[35] promoted South Australia as 'The Land of Promise'[36] – a phrase which consciously invoked God's biblical promise of the land of Israel to Abraham.[37] The editor of the *South Australian Record* went further: the landing of the first colonists recalled for him the 'awful emigration' of Noah, the promise given to Moses,[38] the Tyrians of Carthage, of Aeneas and the founding settlement of Rome, or the 'stout-hearted Britons' who created the colonies in America.[39] It was to be a free colony, without convicts or established church, in which the 'voluntary principle' in relation to religion might be properly tested. In the chapter on religious provision, Stephens outlines how South Australia would give preference to no particular religion, but ample support for cultural provision of churches, schools and newspapers to all.[40] This was not really colonisation without religion, but simply without religious proscription, a different matter. Ultimately, while colonists were motivated primarily by commercial considerations in South Australia – as they were everywhere else – its Nonconformist character was underpinned through co-option of the Baptist businessman, George Fife Angas (1789–1879), by the South Australia Company.[41] Angas had earlier attempted to persuade the Colonial Office to support his own scheme for a colony without an established church or convict labour. He did more than anyone

---

[35] For Stephens, see *Australian Dictionary of Biography*, vol. 2, pp. 480–1. He was a founder of the Methodist *Christian Advocate* (1832), an important vehicle for the anti-slavery movement.

[36] J. Stephens, *The Land of Promise, Being an Authentic and Impartial History of the Rise and Progress of the New British Province of South Australia Etc. by One Who Is Going* (London, 1839).

[37] Genesis 12: 1: 'The LORD had said to Abraham, Leave your country, your people and your father's household and go to the land I will show you.' Also, Genesis 12: 7, 15: 7 etc.

[38] Exodus 6: 6–8. 'Therefore say to the children of Israel: "I *am* the Lord; I will bring you out from under the burdens of the Egyptians, I will rescue you from their bondage, and I will redeem you with an outstretched arm and with great judgments. I will take you as My people, and I will be your God. Then you shall know that I *am* the Lord your God who brings you out from under the burdens of the Egyptians. And I will bring you into the land which I swore to give to Abraham, Isaac, and Jacob; and I will give it to you *as* a heritage: I *am* the Lord."'

[39] Cited by Stephens, *Land of Promise*, p. 100.

[40] *Ibid.*, pp. 129–42. The chapter opens: 'South Australia is distinguished from all other British colonies, by the circumstances that no provision has been made by the state for the promotion of religion. The voluntary principle will, therefore, be fairly put to the test.'

[41] 'Angas, George Fife (1789–1879)', *Australian Dictionary of Biography*, vol. 1, pp. 15–18.

to earn the title of founder of the colony because he not only sustained it with his own capital but encouraged other Nonconformists to emigrate and invest there.[42]

When the settlement at South Australia showed signs of failing to live up to its promise, biblical or otherwise, Wakefield began turning his attention to the possibilities in Canada: he arrived there in 1838, not long after the 1837 rebellion had created a climate which was ripe for reform. Wakefield's views are reflected in an earlier comparative study of England and America.[43] This shows the extent to which he was developing his thinking about the nature of the middle class, whom in an evocative phrase he calls the 'middle or uneasy class' and who had not generally been incorporated into earlier schemes of emigration.[44] Among those distressed for employment in Britain, he included under-employed clergy 'eager to obtain a miserable curacy',[45] who would ben-efit professionally by emigration. Otherwise, he regarded the churches as lacking the initiative to contribute to effective colonial development. In Canada, he states, the politicised clergy of the established church had obtained title to great tracts of land which they were unable to use.[46] Wakefield saw the clergy reserves as a prime example of the mis-management of land by narrow-minded conservative forces.

Wakefield's studied indifference or, indeed, hostility to organised religion began to change in the late 1830s. At this time, he seems to have become convinced of the value of religion as a way to lend legit-imacy to the colonisation cause and undercut those who opposed it on moral grounds. New Zealand was the setting for this new struggle. The House of Lords Select Committee failed to decide one way or the other about the advisability of colonising New Zealand and in the meantime a New Zealand Association was formed as a successor to the failed New Zealand Company.[47] In Parliament, Lord Howick and Sir George Grey defeated an attempt to legislate in favour of systematic colonisation, but the Association could not be prevented from forming a joint-stock company, the New Zealand Colonization Company, which continued to promote the cause, now on a fully commercial basis independent of government. As a result of this protracted struggle, it was not until 1839

---

[42] Pike, *Paradise of Dissent*. Pike generally argues against the claims Wakefield makes for his role in the colonisation of South Australia. For an alternative view, see Prichard's introduction to M. F. L. Prichard, ed., *The Collected Works of Edward Gibbon Wakefield* (Auckland, 1969), p. 34.

[43] E. G. Wakefield, 'England and America: A Comparison of the Social and Political State of Both Nations (1833)', in *The Collected Works of Edward Gibbon Wakefield*, ed. P. M. F. Lloyd (Auckland, 1969).

[44] *Ibid.*, p. 355.   [45] *Ibid.*, p. 361.   [46] *Ibid.*, pp. 526–7.

[47] New Zealand Association, *British Colonization of New Zealand*.

that the company was able to begin practical plans for enlisting capital and colonists for settlements (discussed in the next chapter). By this time, Wakefield had also revised his earlier views about clergy, many of whom were quick to see the potential social benefits of emigration. No longer derided as starving curates who might be encouraged to hitch a ride on the colonisation bandwagon, clerics were invited to speak at meetings called by the National Colonization Society where they could give its promotion a new, religious spin.

Christian colonisation

A new term, 'Christian colonisation', starts to distinguish the talks and sermons of the promoters of what had been, up till now, the sternly commercial work of systematic colonisation. Hinds, of course, was one of the first, but members of all the churches found this idea appealing. In Scotland, the Reverend Dr Burns spoke on behalf of the Paisley–New Zealand Emigration Society in praise of emigration and Christian colonisation by means of which 'the industrious artisans and labourers of Scotland would carry abroad with them the arts, the literature and the religion of Scotland'.[48] In Ireland, a contributor to the *Dublin University Magazine* suggested that there was little likelihood that the native Maori of New Zealand could protect themselves, and so it was essential that the colonists, rather than the natives, be uplifted to prevent further bloodshed. 'Christian colonisation' would, in the writer's estimation, be a considerable improvement on the system of unregulated emigration by base Europeans, whom he calls 'devil's missionaries'.[49] There is a particularly eager note to the homily on Christian colonisation preached by the Baptist, Edward Bean Underhill, to the text: 'The earth is the Lord's, and the fulness thereof.'[50] And, in 1842, William John Conybeare (1815–57) addressed the theme of 'Christian colonisation' in a sermon preached in the Chapel Royal on behalf of the SPG. With copious use of capitals, he concluded that long after the collapse of 'British Law and Literature' the descendants of 'British Colonists' will look back in gratitude on the 'Mother of Empires': 'British Christianity shall bind them by the chains of reverential love, by the sympathies of

---

[48] *New Zealand Journal*, 15 August 1840, p. 191, cited by A. H. McLintock, *The History of Otago: The Origins and Growth of a Wakefield Class Settlement* (Dunedin, 1949), p. 157.

[49] 'New Zealand', *The Dublin University Magazine: A Literary and Political Journal* 4 (1839), p. 309.

[50] E. B. Underhill, 'Christian Colonization', in *The Baptist Record and Biblical Repository* (London, 1847).

common worship, by the fellowship of an unearthly communion, to the generations which have gone before.'[51] Clearly, there were attractions in this theme for clergy and adherents of all classes and creeds of British society, from the Baptist mechanic listening to Underhill, to the Queen herself following Conybeare's sermon in the Chapel Royal.

Following this new trend, the insertion of religious provisions into schemes of colonisation became *de rigueur*. Commercial emigration schemes would advertise that there were clergymen available to provide religious comforts to settlers. This was a marked contrast to the commercial priorities of the charter companies which had blazed the way on previous colonial frontiers. As we have seen, South Australia was the first settler colony to consider religious matters in its promotion. The Church of England was given priority in the plans of the Western Australian Company, which enlisted Wakefield as a director in 1838. According to its prospectus, the settlement of Australind in western Australia would have 'a high moral and religious tone'.[52] Like South Australia, it would be convict-free and the promoters aspired that the settlement be endowed with an Anglican bishopric;[53] there were equally grand plans for schools and churches. Western Australia was a poor colony, and none of this was realistic. No matter, Wakefield was determined that nowhere was too remote, poorly endowed with natural resources, or underpopulated to be uplifted by a properly managed scheme of emigration. When the schemes failed, he would blame this on the failure to implement his principles with sufficient rigour.

Anti-colonialism

Even as the colonial reformers were providing evidence to the Parliamentary Committee on Colonial Lands (1836), and facilitating the settlement of South Australia, Western Australia and townships in New Zealand, anti-colonial storm clouds were massing to rain on the parade of systematic colonisation.[54] As Edward Said was aware,

---

[51] 'Sermon XIV: Christian Colonization', in W. J. Conybeare, *Sermons Preached in the Chapel Royal at Whitehall, During the Years 1841, 1842, and 1843* (London, 1844), pp. 186–7. From 1842 to 1848, Conybeare was the first principal of the Liverpool Collegiate Institution, a public school for boys founded by the Edward Smith-Stanley (1799–1869), who was Secretary of State for War and the Colonies from 1841 to 1845.

[52] Western Australian Company, *Western Australia, Containing a Statement of the Condition and Prospects of That Colony … Compiled for the Use of Settlers* (London, 1843), p. 2.

[53] *Ibid.*, p. 137.

[54] For the humanitarians associated with the Select Committee on Aborigines, see E. Elbourne, *Blood Ground: Colonialism, Missions and the Contest for Christianity in the Cape*

there had been objections raised against colonies on both economic and moral grounds from well before the eighteenth century.[55] Now, humanitarians from across a wide range of churches launched a combined attack on British settler colonialism in the course of the hearings and subsequent published reports of the 1836 Select Committee of the House of Commons on Aborigines. Receiving testimony from British settlements in Canada, the Cape Colony, Australia and New Zealand, the Committee reached damning conclusions about the impact of colonisation on native people.[56] Against settler protests, the strongest voices against further British colonisation were those of the leaders of British missionary societies and colonial clergy. In evidence to the Select Committee, Dandeson Coates, the Lay Secretary of the Church Missionary Society, spoke specifically against the proposals to colonise New Zealand that he claimed would lead inevitably to the destruction of native society and a fatal interruption to the missionaries' successful work of Christian progress among the Maori people.[57]

After a slow beginning, the conversion of the Maori was hailed as one of the brightest success stories of the Evangelical missionary movement.[58] Christian conversion had been followed by several attempts to give recognition to the sovereignty of the Maori people, including the

Colony and Britain, 1799–1853 (Montreal and Kingston, 2002); E. Elbourne, 'The Sin of the Settler: The 1835–36 Select Committee on Aborigines and Debates over Virtue and Conquest in the Early Nineteenth-Century British White Settler Empire', *Journal of Colonialism and Colonial History*, 4 (2003). For economic objections to imperialism, see G. W. Martin, 'Anti-Imperialism in the Mid-Nineteenth Century and the Nature of the British Empire, 1820–70', in *Reappraisals in British Imperial History*, ed. G. W. Martin (London, Basingstoke and Toronto, 1975), pp. 88–120.

[55] Said, *Culture and Imperialism*, p. 240. Said sees Bartolomé de las Casas as the father of the anti-colonial movement. For the background in Australia, see H. Reynolds, *This Whispering in Our Hearts* (Sydney, 1998).

[56] Elbourne, *Blood Ground*; Elbourne, 'Sin of the Settler'; E. Elbourne and R. Ross, 'Combating Spiritual and Social Bondage: Early Missions in the Cape Colony', in *Christianity in South Africa*, ed. R. Elphick and R. Davenport (Cape Town, 1997), pp. 31–50. See also Elbourne's thesis, 'To Colonise the Mind: Evangelical Missionaries in Britain and the Eastern Cape, 1790–1837' (PhD Thesis, University of Oxford, 1991).

[57] Minutes of Evidence before Select Committee on the Islands of New Zealand, House of Lords, 1838, in W. D. McIntyre and W. J. Gardner, eds., *Speeches and Documents on New Zealand History* (Oxford, 1971), pp. 4–7.

[58] The first mission to the Maori was begun in 1814 under the auspices of the Church Missionary Society on the initiative of the Reverend Samuel Marsden. Wesleyan and Catholic missions followed in 1824 and 1838 respectively. By 1850, about 60 per cent of the Maori appear to have become affiliated with one or other missions in a conversion movement led by Maori evangelists. For general history of Christianity in New Zealand, including these early missions, see Breward, *Churches in Australasia*, pp. 83–7; and A. K. Davidson, *Christianity in Aotearoa: A History of Church and Society in New Zealand* (Wellington, 1991).

Declaration of Independence of New Zealand (1835) signed by thirty-five Maori chiefs on the initiative of James Busby, the first British Resident in New Zealand. As controversy about the progress of colonisation in New Zealand continued, missionaries helped to broker the Treaty of Waitangi (1840), eventually signed by 500 Maori, which was intended to create an equitable mechanism for the transfer of land between Europeans and the original inhabitants while preserving propitious conditions for the ongoing work of Christian conversion and uplift among the Maori. Among the Maori, its strongest supporters were those close to the CMS missionaries.[59] In reality, the signing of the Treaty settled nothing, least of all the material and religious sources of conflict between Maori and Pakeha. It also left unresolved the ongoing conflict between the mainly evangelical opponents of colonisation and those, especially from the high church party of the Church of England and the Free Church of Scotland, who not only failed to subscribe to the anti-colonial views of the CMS but were busy planning church-based colonies of their own. In his plan for the colonisation of New Zealand, which he called 'one of the finest countries in the world for colonisation, if not the finest, for British settlement', Wakefield told his brother-in-law, the Reverend Charles Torlesse, on 12 May 1837, that preparations for the colony were complete in all respects except one – there was no clergyman. Once that final piece of the jigsaw was put in its place, colonisation would proceed without further moral qualms: 'A main object will be to do all that can be done for inducing them to embrace the language, customs, religion and social ties of the superior race.'[60] Such views were at odds with the missionaries by then present in New Zealand, who claimed responsibility for Maori advances in religion, literacy and peace, and saw no need for a bishop to assume authority over them.[61] To their credit, missionaries in the field were also aware, as those who wrote pamphlets in Britain were not, that the Maori would negotiate their own terms under which they would choose to embrace Christianity.

There was therefore much at stake when Dandeson Coates, the lay secretary of the Church Missionary Society and the most articulate of the anti-colonialists, chose to direct all his eloquence at the overthrow of the planned colonisation of New Zealand. Coates laid down his objections in the form of a printed letter to Lord Glenelg, Secretary

---

[59] C. Orange, *The Treaty of Waitangi* (Wellington, 1987), pp. 32–59.

[60] Wakefield to Reverend Charles Torlesse, 12 May 1837, quoted by H. J. Rose, A. P. Newton, and E. A. Benians, eds., *The Cambridge History of the British Empire*, vol. VII, *New Zealand* (Cambridge, 1933), p. 67.

[61] For clashes between colonial bishops and Anglican missionaries, see Cnattingius, *Bishops and Societies*.

of State for War and the Colonies (1835–9).[62] For Coates, the colonisation of what he calls 'uncivilised countries' by Europeans was one of the most inglorious in the history of humanity: 'Like the Prophet's scroll, it is written within and without, with lamentations, and mourning, and woe.'[63] Whether examples were gathered from the Antilles, from North or South America, South Africa or New Holland, a single uniform pattern of desolation was evident: the aboriginal people were demoralised, diminished and, in some cases, extinguished altogether by colonisation.[64] The cruelties of the Spaniards denounced by Bartolomé de las Casas (1484–1566) in the New World, he insisted, were no less terrible than the effects of British colonisation in South Africa and New Holland revealed in the report of the Select Committee on Aborigines.[65]

The evocation of Las Casas is important here. For centuries, Anglo-Dutch and American propagandists had made polemical use of the 'Black Legend' of the cruel and fanatical Spanish colonisation of the Americas, which was traditionally reinforced with the testimony of Las Casas. Such stereotyping of Spanish Catholicism helped supply legitimating rhetoric to Protestant imperial expansion in Latin America.[66] However, a more careful reading of Las Casas would indicate that it was not casual contact, but the transformation of an evangelising and trading mission into the genocidal colonisation for commercial gain which aroused his passionate denunciation. For Las Casas, Christopher Columbus, the Christ-bearer (*Christum ferens*), had been ordained to bring Christ to the Indies, not those he called an 'uninterrupted series of Spanish plunderers who have done nothing but sail there, attack, murder and rob the people'.[67] For Coates, who *had* read Las Casas with care, the case of the Australian Aborigines nevertheless provided the proof, if any more were required, that European colonisation tended inexorably to destroy the indigenous people in any land unfortunate enough to receive them.[68] Coates argued that the 'crimes of Colonization'[69] were not only lamentable but also preventable in that they followed inevitably from the decision to settle colonists among native people. With withering contempt, he goes on to pour scorn on the idea of a superior, moral form of colonisation as proposed by the

---

[62] D. Coates, *The Principles, Objects and Plan of the New-Zealand Association* (London, 1837).

[63] *Ibid.*, p. 3.   [64] *Ibid.*   [65] *Ibid.*, p. 7.

[66] P. W. Powell, *Tree of Hate. Propaganda and Prejudices Affecting United States Relations with the Hispanic World* (New York, 1971), pp. 30–6.

[67] Bartolomé de las Casas, *A Short Account of the Destruction of the Indies* (Harmondsworth, 1992), p. 80.

[68] Coates, *Principles, Objects and Plan*, p. 8.   [69] *Ibid.*

New Zealand Association. He refused to accept that any good would come from the arrival of additional contingents of those he calls the 'immoral, vicious, and reckless British Subjects who are the pests of New Zealand'.[70] Deriding the misuse of the term 'Christian colonisation' for settlement by Europeans in any form, he concludes with a plea that the Maori should be preserved – at least for a time – from this great evil:

> Only let New Zealand be spared from Colonization, and the Mission have its free and unrestricted course for one half century more, and the great political and moral problem will be solved – of a people passing from a barbarous to a civilized state, through the agency of Europeans, with the complete preservation of the Aboriginal race, and of their national independence and sovereignty.[71]

Coates did not stand alone in his opposition to the colonial reformers. Some institutional support was provided by the Aborigines' Protection Society (1837–1909), which was set up in the wake of the 1836 Select Committee Report on Aborigines.[72] He also attracted individual supporters, particularly from the Nonconformist churches. While Coates can hardly be said to have pulled his punches, an even more radical critique of British imperialism and its impact on native people was published by the Quaker naturalist, writer and activist, William Howitt (1792–1879). Howitt's *Colonization and Christianity* appeared in 1838, and drew, like the publications of the Aborigines' Protection Society, on the 1836 Select Committee Report on Aborigines.[73] Howitt's purpose was polemical: he charges Europeans with crimes against humanity, equivalent in their barbarism and ferocity to the ravages of the Huns.[74] He attacks the pretension and delusion that European rule was either benevolent or anything other than a travesty of the Christianity they claimed to profess. From the discovery of the New World, European rule, he states, had been one long road of rapacity, plunder and bloodshed. If, he suggested, anyone entertained the delusion that the British were more suited to colonial rule than other Europeans, the history of their governance in India, revealed through the trial and impeachment

---

[70] *Ibid.*, p. 27.   [71] *Ibid.*, p. 41.

[72] The Society published the *Aborigines' Friend*, or *Colonial Intelligencer*, as well as an annual report, but was not successful in marshalling the moral coalition which came out in opposition to slavery.

[73] W. Howitt, *Colonization and Christianity: A Popular History of the Treatment of the Natives by the Europeans in All Their Colonies* (London, 1838). For Howitt, see Mary Howitt Walker, 'Howitt, William (1792–1879)', *Australian Dictionary of Biography*, vol. 4, pp. 435–6. Howitt published *Colonization and Christianity* while still living in England.

[74] There appears to be no one ready to stand up for the Huns.

of Warren Hastings, or the terrible history of the Atlantic slave trade, made a mockery of it. All Europeans were guilty of the same sins:

> We have now followed the Europeans to every region of the globe, and seen them planting colonies, and peopling new lands, and everywhere we have found them the same – a lawless and domineering race, seizing on the earth as if they were the first-born of creation, and having a presumptive right to murder and dispossess all other people.[75]

Howitt was appalled by the failure of Christianity that this litany of horror revealed: 'I look in vain for a single instance of a nation styling itself Christian and civilized, acting towards a nation which it is pleased to term barbarous with Christian honesty and common feeling.'[76] The only exceptions to this general rule which he allows are the work of the occasional Christian missionary or colonists of the exemplary piety of the Quaker settler of Pennsylvania, William Penn (1644–1718).[77] *Colonization and Christianity* was a fine, rousing polemic, somewhat mitigated by the knowledge that in 1852 Howitt and his two sons headed out to Victoria to try their luck on the goldfields. Howitt's son Richard went on to write a useful and popular book for intending emigrants.[78]

Despite the rhetoric of Coates and Howitt, the anti-colonialists appear to have been fighting a losing battle with both the government and public opinion. James Stephen (1789–1859), the Under Secretary of State for the Colonies from 1836 to 1847, recognised that the formal colonisation of New Zealand had become inevitable if only because New Zealand had effectively already been colonised by those he called 'British subjects of the worst possible character'. Hence, while not essentially disagreeing with Coates about the quality of the typical British colonist, he saw more merit in the idea that organised colonisation would lead to a better outcome for the Maori people than simply doing nothing to control the flow of undesirables. In 1839, he therefore gave his support to moves that would eventually establish a regular British colony in New Zealand.[79] Derided in a funny (if cruel) speech by Buller as 'Mr Mother Country' and the puppet of the Church Missionary Society, Stephen came to represent the impediments which the evangelical lobby placed in the way of colonising enterprise. However, in reality, he was a shrewd bureaucrat with a firm grasp of the limits

---

[75] Howitt, *Colonization and Christianity*, p. 499.
[76] *Ibid.*   [77] *Ibid.*, p. 507.
[78] R. Howitt, *Impressions of Australia Felix, During Four Years Residence in That Colony* (1845). William Howitt returned to England in 1854.
[79] Minute by James Stephen, 15 March 1839, Colonial Office 209/4, pp. 326–31, in McIntyre and Gardner, eds., *Speeches and Documents*, pp. 8–10.

of the possible in relation to aboriginal policy.[80] When New Zealand was finally annexed to the British crown as part of the colony of New South Wales, the instructions to the Consul of New Zealand, William Hobson, provided extensive instructions on his obligation to promote the 'Civilization of the New Zealanders', 'understanding by that term whatever relates to the religious, intellectual and social advancement of mankind'.[81] In January 1840, the British government went on to annex the whole of New Zealand to the British crown – an event which, as we have seen, was celebrated as a triumph for the British empire in Christchurch's Anglican cathedral. More to the point, under the guise of Christian colonisation, the colonial reformers had secured a major defeat for the Christian anti-colonial movement. Even Selwyn, who had arrived in 1842 and initially envisioned himself as a missionary bishop to the Maori and later the Melanesians, was soon largely engaged with the settler, rather than the missionary, church.[82]

Wakefield has long been suspected of cynical manipulation of the religion card in order to secure support for his schemes. However, this is not entirely just. Wakefield ascribed his conversion to the idea of the centrality of religion for colonial enterprises in the *Art of Colonization* (1849). He also noted that religion was not an original part of the precepts of the Colonial Society when it was formed in 1830, only later coming to embrace the colonising potential of religious movements.[83] The Canterbury colony (considered in the next chapter) was in some ways the culmination of his long-standing interest in the influence of religion on colonial settlements. Indeed, with typical braggadocio, Wakefield claimed that he was responsible for converting the archbishop of Canterbury to his view of colonisation and leading the way – presumably through the Colonial Bishoprics' Fund – to bishoprics not only in Canterbury, but also in Tasmania, South Australia, South Africa, 'Australia Felix' (Victoria) and elsewhere in the empire.[84] He also claimed to have encouraged religious provisions for colonists of all denominations, Catholics, Presbyterians, Dissenters and Jews. All were equally welcome to the embraces of the Canterbury Association.[85] In another moral twist, Wakefield also recommended that women should be encouraged to emigrate, for they gave virtue, politeness and stability

---

[80] Carrington, *British Overseas*, pp. 389–90.

[81] Instructions from the Secretary of State for War and Colonies, Lord Normanby, to Captain Hobson, 14 August 1839, Colonial Office 209/4, pp. 251–81.

[82] Breward, *Churches in Australasia*, p. 91.

[83] E. G. Wakefield, ed., *A View of the Art of Colonization, with Present Reference to the British Empire; in Letters between a Statesman and a Colonist* (London, 1849), pp. 53–4.

[84] *Ibid.*, p. 55.   [85] *Ibid.*, p. 56.

to colonial society.[86] Overall, it was essential to consider religion, if only to avoid giving offence to the most powerful group in society: 'If you had made no provisions for religion in your colony, and if people here only cared enough about you to find that out, your scheme would be vituperated by religious men, who are numerous; and by religious women, who are very numerous; and by the clergy of all denominations, who are immensely powerful.'[87]

Religion now lay at the heart of Wakefield's plans for new colonies, but for pragmatic rather than sectarian reasons. History, he believed, was on his side. All the most favoured colonial systems, from those of the ancient Greeks and Romans to the old colonisation of North America, incorporated a religious element. In America in particular, the English had created colonies which were so thoroughly imbued with religious character that they tended to be known by their religion more than anything else:[88] Virginia for the Church of England, Maryland for Roman Catholics, Pennsylvania for Quakers, New England for Puritans. But Wakefield was not interested in promoting one form of religion over another. Instead, he makes the astute comment that, although religious settlements were said to have been founded in order to enable the founders to enjoy liberty of conscience, the main reason for their success as colonies was that they allowed for the creation of exclusive settlements, with the Puritans pushing this to its most extreme forms: 'It was not persecution for its own sake that they loved; it was the power of making their religion the religion of their whole community.'[89] Wakefield goes on to state his fundamental view about the role to be played by religion in colonisation, which centred on its power to attract the 'best people' to colonise as it had done in America: 'All that colonisation was more or less a religious colonisation: the parts of it that prospered the most, were the most religious parts: the prosperity was chiefly occasioned by the respectability of the emigration: and the respectability of the emigration to each colony had a close relation to the force of the religious attraction.'[90] And Wakefield then argues that the time is right for Britain to once again plant religious colonies as had previously been done in America, and he looked encouragingly to the Church of England, the Church of Scotland, and the Wesleyan Methodists to bring this about.

---

[86] E. G. Wakefield, 'A View of the Art of Colonization with Present Reference to the British Empire: In Letters between a Statesman and a Colonist (1849)', in *The Collected Works of Edward Gibbon Wakefield*, ed. P. M. F. Lloyd (Auckland, 1969), p. 840. For the role of women in Wakefield's religious colonisation schemes, see Temple, *Sort of Conscience*, p. 419.
[87] Wakefield, 'A View of the Art of Colonization', p. 841.
[88] *Ibid.*   [89] *Ibid.*, p. 842.   [90] *Ibid.*

The humanitarian scruples of the anti-colonial movement and the needs of the New Zealand Maori or the Australian Aborigines seem to have caused him no qualms of any kind.

Emigration as a social panacea

While Wakefield's genius as a promoter of emigration may have been designed largely to benefit his own companies and reputation, the idea that colonisation was a way to secure a better life was not unique to him. Other colonisation societies directed at ameliorating the lot of many subject groups were formed at this time, some more successful than others. The earliest of these societies, such as the American Colonization Society (1816) or the African Colonization Society (1800–16), had as their object the resettlement of former slaves, either in America or by return to Africa. These were active both in the United States and in Britain. But, as early as the 1820s, the Protestant Colonization Society of Ireland was meeting in Dublin to discuss the opportunities for emigration to America, which they saw as a land of opportunity for poor Protestant families.[91] Philanthropists were increasingly attracted to the promised social benefits of emigration and began to demand that the government should make it possible for people of modest means to make their way to the colonies. Their printed letters addressed to successive Colonial Secretaries repeatedly recommended the benefits of colonisation as a solution to pauperism. Such recommendations – sometimes in the case of Ireland linked directly to the suggestion that colonisation was a convenient solution to social, political and economic difficulties which defied any other solution – created an odium which long attached to colonisation projects. In the shocking phrase of the reformer and politician, Charles Buller (1806–48), a founding member of the National Colonization Society and one of the Philosophical Radicals,[92] this was the equivalent to 'shovelling out of paupers' where their agony might not be observed by polite society.[93] This was the desperate unplanned emigration of the destitute which followed the famine years in Ireland and parts of Scotland; no one wished a repetition of that.

---

[91] Protestant Colonization Society of Ireland, *Report of Sub-Committee* (Dublin, 1829).

[92] Besides Charles Buller (1806–48), the group included transportation reformer William Molesworth (1810–55) and John Stuart Mill (1806–73).

[93] P. Gray, '"Shovelling out Your Paupers": The British State and Irish Famine Migration 1846–50', *Patterns of Prejudice*, 33 (1999), pp. 47–66; H. J. M. Johnston, *British Emigration Policy, 1815–30: 'Shovelling out Paupers'* (Oxford, 1972). Charles Buller: 'shovelling out your papers to where they might die, without shocking their betters with the sight *and* sound of their last agony', in Despatch of Governor FitzRoy to Earl Grey, 30 January 1847, *Papers Relative to Emigration*.

By the 1840s, however, the idea of systematic colonisation was being successfully promoted by Wakefield as a new kind of emigration which would enable men and women of all classes, not simply the desperate poor, to make their way to the colonies. By the time Buller rose to introduce the bill on systematic colonization (1843) in the House of Commons, he was able to speak of a great change which had occurred in the previous ten years. Emigration to Port Phillip, South Australia, and New Zealand was unprecedented in the extent to which men and women of every class were being attracted to try their luck in the new settlements: clergymen and schoolmasters, churches and schools, were providing the means to improve the colonists. This 'improvement' affected not just the emigrants but also the 'helpless native'.[94]

Surprisingly, some of Wakefield's most eloquent defenders came not from among his own liberal cronies but from the Tory party who saw systematic colonisation as a way to export the British class system and the established church throughout the empire. One of the highest of them all, the member for Oxford, Sir Robert Inglis, was one of many who argued that the old commercial way of running the empire was not good enough for creating British colonies: 'Nothing, in his opinion, could deserve the name of a colony of Great Britain, which did not represent all the interests, civil and religious, of the mother country, which was not, in fact, a miniature representation of England, complete in every part, according to its proportions.'[95] Joseph Hume (1777–1855), the Scottish radical and guardian of the public purse, was less impressed, and noted that there was one major difference between the classical mode of colonisation and those advocated in the present day: 'The hon. Baronet appeared to forget that New England was founded by men who had actually run away from bishops.' It was not the Church, let alone bishops, which allowed the colonies to prosper, but rather the economic and political power of England.[96] The Whig Leader, Lord John Russell, was particularly keen to knock on the head the idea that church establishments should be set up in the colonies. In New South Wales, the law made provision equally for all religious sects, he observed, and this was in his opinion the only way in which mixed communities of settlers could be governed effectively.[97] He endorsed a similar policy in Ireland.

---

[94] Systematic Colonization, House of Commons Debates, 6 April 1843, vol. 68, col. 522. The speech also circulated separately: *Systematic Colonization: Speech of Charles Buller* (London, 1843).
[95] Systematic Colonization, House of Commons Debates, 6 April 1843, vol. 68, col. 577.
[96] *Ibid.*, col. 579.   [97] *Ibid.*, col. 585.

Caroline Chisholm, Highlands and Islands

The 'hungry 1840s', which were preceded by a recession in trade, resistance to the harsh implementation of the 1834 Poor Law, and the rise of Chartism, and culminated in the failure of the potato crop and famine in Ireland and parts of Scotland from 1845–52, were the real watershed when it came to convincing British philanthropists of the moral value of colonisation. As a wave of disasters shook the nation, and revolutionary fires burned in Europe, debates about the 'condition of England' shook former conservatives into embracing reforms to traditional institutions that had formerly been sacrosanct. Emigration was presented as the solution for all kinds of troubled communities, from the impoverished and starving tenant farmers and fishers of Ireland to the Highlands and Islands of Scotland. Two or three of these reformers deserve special mention on account of their interest in church-based social reform connected to emigration.

Caroline Chisholm (1808–77) was born in England and began a life of colonial philanthropy when her soldier husband was posted to Madras in 1832. When the couple moved to Australia in 1838, she continued her earlier efforts to improve the conditions of female emigrants by creating accommodation and employment for them on their arrival in the colony. On her return to England in 1845, she turned her attention to the supply side of the emigration equation, advocating financial reforms which would open the benefits of emigration to those of modest means. She was the most articulate of those who argued that women and families made the best emigrants.[98] In 1850, she outlined her ideas in *The ABC of Colonization* which was addressed to the committee of the Family Colonization Loan Society, the organisation she helped to found in 1847.[99]

Chisholm directed her strongest protest against the Emigration Commissioners whom she derided as 'agents of the squatting interest, or men of capital in the Australian colonies' and their insistence that only young married couples without children were acceptable colonists. In her view, the ideal form of colonisation was one which provided appropriate protection for young women who wished to emigrate and

---

[98] For studies of female emigration and the role of Caroline Chisholm, see L. Chilton, *Agents of Empire: British Female Migration to Canada and Australia, 1860s–1930* (Toronto, 2007), p. 21; A. J. Hammerton, *Emigrant Gentlewomen: Genteel Poverty and Female Emigration, 1830–1914* (London, 1979); C. MacDonald, *A Woman of Good Character: Single Women as Immigrant Settlers in Nineteenth-Century New Zealand* (Wellington, 1990).

[99] C. Chisholm, *The ABC of Colonization in a Series of Letters* (London, 1850).

which encouraged families to emigrate as a group. Instead of colonisation for the few and the wealthy, she called for a national system of colonisation, an enterprise which would excite British patriotism and bring more women to the colonies. What men need in the bush was the domestic blessing of wives: 'Give them help-mates, and you make murmuring, discontented servants, loyal and happy subjects of the State.'[100] The addition of 100 couples in the bush would enable them to build a more religious and moral community, which would be able to support a clergyman without application to the State.[101] Such arguments were appealing enough to convince men of such different religious views as Lord Shaftesbury, an Evangelical, and Sydney Herbert, a Tractarian, of the benefits of her scheme. With their support, Chisholm founded the Family Colonization Loan Society which advanced small loans to emigrants. At a great meeting of the Society on 28 February 1852 in the British Institution in Tabernacle Row in London, some 2,500 people attended a great meeting chaired by the Earl of Shaftesbury which extolled the value of emigration under a banner which read 'Advance Australia' and 'God Speed the Plough'. By 1854, the Society had helped over 3,000 people migrate to the colonies and there was no more question of the morality and respectability of the colonisation enterprise. The manufacturer of a system of patented portable houses created an emigrants' hostel, with accommodation for seventy-nine people, to Chisholm's design, as well as an entire portable town including a church and parsonage, and churches constructed to the specifications of the bishops of Melbourne and Sydney.[102] It could truly be said that the export of migrants and providing for their religious needs was becoming an industrial operation.

The moral benefits of emigration were also seized on by the supporters of the Highland and Island Emigration Society, which had been established to provide a 'complete and final remedy' to the desperate conditions in the Island of Skye and surrounding Highland and Island districts. On 13 June 1852, Alexander Ewing, the Scottish Episcopal bishop of Argyle and the Isles (1847–73), preached a moving sermon on behalf of the Society which extolled the benefits of emigration to Australia using as his text Genesis 42: 1, 2: 'Now when Jacob saw that there was corn in Egypt, Jacob said unto his sons, Why do ye look one upon another? And he said, Behold, I have heard that there is corn in Egypt: get you down thither.' Ewing saw the work of Providence in the

---

[100] *Ibid.*, p. 30.   [101] *Ibid.*, p. 31.
[102] R. Carrick, *Hemming's Patent Improved Portable Houses* (London, 1853). The cover of this book reproduces a lithograph of the second church of Melbourne created by 'Hemmings Portable House Manufactury, Clift House, Bristol'.

consequences of dearth and rural poverty: 'Using the rod of famine, God is driving the Celtic races to people other lands. They are the first of the nations here: it is they who must go first.'[103] Yet, while driving them forth, the same Providence, Ewing argued, had also provided for a solution to the destitution of the Highlanders by providing them a new home in Australia.[104] As the strongest reason for inspiring generosity to the cause, Ewing spoke of the virtues of the Celts as the leaders of a new colonial race, a people of natural piety with a Providential destiny: 'They are the patriarchs of a Christian Israel now descending in distress to an abundant Egypt; the St Patricks and Columbas of a new-found world, conveying the blessings of Christianity there to generations yet unborn, as their fathers did to ours (for it is mainly to Celtic missionaries and bishops we trace the Christianity and apostolic succession of this country); their names may be looked back upon, ages hence in Australia, as we look upon their father's names in Britain.'[105] The generous subscription list – headed by the Queen, who had donated £300, and Prince Albert – included many of the titled aristocracy of Scotland; it listed £2,600 raised by subscription in Australia and another £200 from the Australian Agricultural Company. Under the rules of the scheme, entire families were, as much as possible, to be settled in British colonies under the administrations of the Colonial Land and Emigration Commissioners.

Scots were also targeted in the various emigration schemes of John Dunmore Lang. In his manual for prospective emigrants to 'Philipsland' (i.e. Victoria), Lang devoted a lengthy chapter to religion and education, noting his fears for the alleged 'Romanising' tendencies of all the Anglican bishops so far appointed to the Australasian colonies.[106] In order to head off these dangerous developments, Lang attempted to launch his own emigration company that would seek 'to give an impulse to emigration of a thoroughly Protestant character from England, Scotland, and the North of Ireland'.[107] For this purpose he travelled to England, Scotland and Ireland from 1847 to 1849, trying to get commercial backing for the scheme, often holding meetings in Protestant places of worship. What Lang was promoting was what he called 'schemes of Christian emigration' that would favour Scottish and

---

[103] A. Ewing, *Sermon on Emigration from the Highlands and Islands of Scotland to Australia by the Bishop of Argyle and the Isles* (London, 1852).
[104] *Ibid.*, pp. 5–6.   [105] *Ibid.*, pp. 18–19.
[106] J. D. Lang, *Cooksland in North-Eastern Australia: The Future Cotton-Field of Great Britain* (London, 1847), pp. 414–15.
[107] J. D. Lang, *Narrative of Proceedings in England, Scotland and Ireland During the Years 1847, 1848 and 1849, with a View to Originate an Extensive and Continuous Immigration of a Superior Character from the United Kingdom into This Territory* (Sydney, 1850), p. 26.

Irish Protestants in preference to the hordes of Roman Catholic labourers who, in his view, were arriving out of all proportion to their usefulness to the colony.[108] Meanwhile, Lang claimed to have done much to awaken public interest in emigration both through his weekly letters in the *British Banner* in favour of 'Australian emigration to be conducted on Christian principles' and his speaking tours throughout the country. For Lang it was a 'matter of life and death to the interests of our common Protestantism in Australia' that his scheme should prove successful. Lang also spoke of the other informal emigration networks that were springing up, not only in Australia but in Natal and elsewhere, in which bodies of emigrants together with ministers of religion were planning to head to the colonies.[109] It was just a short step from Lang's shoestring efforts to the launching of full-scale colonisation plans for Christian colonies, on the Wakefield model, which had the explicit backing of the home churches.

Other schemes of emigration came and went, sometimes with churchmen at their helm. The Queensland Immigration Society was devised by James Quinn, first Catholic bishop of Brisbane (1859–81).[110] The organisation had the blessing of the pope and allowed Quinn effectively to people his diocese direct from Ireland with the benefit of subsidised passage provided by the Queensland government. Before it was quashed, the Society secured the passage of 3,901 emigrants and £54,281 worth of orders for land in what was jokingly referred to as 'Quinnland'.[111] In terms of sheer numbers, it was one of the most successful of all emigration schemes under the patronage of clergy. However, apart from Quinn's involvement, this was not strictly a religious scheme. In recommending it to prospective colonists, Quinn's agent, the Reverend P. Dunne, bemoaned the conditions in Ireland which made it necessary for so many to leave; however, he added: 'I see no other hope at present for the poor down-trodden people of this country, but to fly to the most distant part of the world, where there is perfect equality, civil and religious liberty, no poorhouses to demoralize the people, and no landlords to exterminate them.'[112] By shipping out with vessels despatched under the auspices of the Queensland Immigration Society, Dunne gave pious emigrants his assurance that they would be accompanied by both a priest and a matron whose presence would serve to guarantee order and

---

[108] *Ibid.*, p. 9.   [109] *Ibid.*, p. 10.
[110] McLay, *James Quinn*, pp. 48–9.
[111] Henry Cleary, 'Archdiocese of Brisbane', *The Catholic Encyclopedia*, vol. 2 (New York, 1907).
[112] P. Dunne, *The Emigrant's Guide to Queensland and the Other Australian Colonies* (Dublin, 1863), p. 2.

morality on the journey out.[113] Others were less sanguine about the benefits of the Society, and Quinn was accused by both the anti-Catholic press and in complaints forwarded by bishop Polding to Propaganda of luring settlers to Queensland with false promises and then defrauding them of their land orders.[114]

The first major work on behalf of emigrants by the Church of England was the establishment of the Emigrants' Spiritual Aid Fund, which had been managed by the SPG since 1841.[115] From about 1870, however, there was renewed pressure on the national Church to be seen to be doing more for emigrants.[116] Now, with the support of the archbishop of Canterbury, Archibald Tait (1811–82), an emigration committee was established as a permanent committee of the SPCK. Clergy were also appointed to the National Association for the Promotion of State Colonization. In 1870, the National Emigration League was formed which crossed denominational lines and included seven bishops, nine Nonconformist clergy, and one Roman Catholic, Cardinal Manning, on its board.[117] In 1881, Tait published an Emigration Circular in *The Times*, which directed clergy to provide support to prospective emigrants and tried to encourage a positive attitude towards emigration.[118]

The largest Anglican organisation committed to the promotion of emigration as a cure for social ills was the Church Emigration Society, which was founded in 1886. The archbishop of Canterbury was sufficiently interested in their work to issue a number of letters which were included by the SPCK in its handbooks for colonists. He noted: 'It is no business of the Church to actually promote Emigration but it is our business to provide that they who emigrate shall do so under circumstances as religiously happy as we can ensure for them.'[119] The Society had its own journal, *The Emigrant*, and sufficient funds to assist between 300 and 600 emigrants per year. An early issue states that the object of the Church Emigration Society was: 'to assist persons duly approved by the Executive Committee to emigrate to British Colonies, where they may live and prosper under a British flag'.[120] Religion is not mentioned and the tone of editorials was bracingly patriotic. In 1891, *The Emigrant* asserted that the expansion of the empire made a call to the national and patriotic feelings of fellow countrymen, while stressing the appreciation

[113] *Ibid.*, p. 20.   [114] McLay, *James Quinn*, p. 72.
[115] For the Emigrants' Spiritual Aid Fund, see Pascoe, *Two Hundred Years of the SPG*, pp. 818–20.
[116] Malchow, 'Church and Emigration', pp. 121–6.
[117] *Ibid.*, pp. 130–1.   [118] *The Times*, 22 December 1881.
[119] Benson circular letter, June 1886, Lambeth Palace Library, Benson Papers, vol. 34 (1886), fol. 208.
[120] Church Emigration Society, *The Emigrant: The Quarterly Journal of the Church Emigration Society*, 1 (1891).

of close ties between 'the Mother Country and her Colonies'. Praise is given to the societies such as the Imperial Federation League and the Colonial Institute which fostered the common bond, while there was recognition of the team and electricity which provided the technology which made it possible. The Church Emigration Society also acted as an employment agency and attempted to assist British subjects to find homes and future employment in the colonies.[121] To this end, *The Emigrant* provided a medium for job advertisements, especially for female domestics and farm workers. There were also advertisements for passages on the different shipping companies, such as the Royal Mail Service between England and Australia, or the Dominion Line, Beaver Line and Allan Line to Canada and the United States, or the Union Line for the South African goldfields. The Church Emigration Society was clearly not so much a colonial missionary society as a colonial information service that made use of the imperial network of the Church of England to facilitate colonisation. About ten years later, the Society began producing a quarterly newsletter in a smaller, newsier format.[122] This continued to emphasise the Society's official 'Church' credentials, including the archbishop of Canterbury as president and the bishop of London as vice president. The objects are restated to be that of providing letters of introduction to colonial clergy in order to avert the danger of 'practical irreligion'. Subsequent issues covered articles on 'Emigration and Thrift' (January 1903), 'Farm Work in Ontario' (April 1904), 'Emigrant Children in Canada' and 'Are Educated Women Wanted in Canada?' (April 1910), and advertised schemes such as the 'Archbishop's Western Canada Fund and the CES' (April 1910). The work was surprisingly long-lived, and in 1916, it went on to promote settlement schemes for ex-servicemen in Canada after the war.[123]

Compared with the work of government agencies, the scale of assistance provided by church emigration societies was small; however, they were not insignificant. The largest of them, the Salvation Army Emigration Department, secured passages for close to 50,000 emigrants between 1908 and 1914.[124] In the same period, other church societies that sponsored emigrants included the Catholic Emigration Society (for children), the Church Army, the Church Emigration Society, the Jewish Board of Guardians, the Jews Emigration Society, St Andrew's Waterside Church Mission, and St Katherine's Mission Emigration

[121] *Ibid.*, p. 1.
[122] Church Emigration Society, *Quarterly Notes of the Church Emigration Society* (1902). I examined issues from No. 1 (January 1902) to No. 59 (August 1916).
[123] 'Land Settlement for Ex-Servicemen after the War', *Quarterly Notes of the Church Emigration and Commendation Society* (1916).
[124] Carrothers, *Emigration*, pp. 319–21.

Fund. The archbishop of Canterbury was also kept informed of the work of organisations such as the Female Middle Class Emigration Society, which was launched in 1862, and which aimed to find work for superfluous ladies in the colonies as 'superior governesses, trained lady nurses, nursery governesses, and lady helps'.[125] The Earl of Shaftesbury agreed to become the first president, and the bishop of Sydney was another patron. The society was managed by a ladies' committee including Miss Maria Susan Rye (1829–1903), who used the Society to help her to emigrate to New Zealand, Miss Bonham-Carter and Madame Bodichon (née Barbara Leigh-Smith). Like Caroline Chisholm, the Society provided loans to applicants seeking to better themselves in the colonies but who would otherwise be unable to afford the passage.

The churches were particularly active in emigration schemes for children, or 'rescue' as it was generally known.[126] A number of schemes for the support of emigration were launched in the 1880s and 1890s as an extension of mission programmes directed at the urban poor. These schemes sent children to many parts of the British world, but they had their focus on Canada, then at the height of its western expansion, as well as Australia. From her new home in New Zealand, Maria Susan Rye was one of the first to encourage schemes for child migration aimed at removing 'waifs and strays' from the streets of 'Darkest England' and securing them a new life abroad. Child rescue organisations used the language of missions to rhetorically reconfigure the tough streets of English cities as heathen territory from which children were waiting to be saved – washed clean and white from the dirt, heathendom and immorality of Britain by transfer to the 'Better Britain' of the Australian or Canadian colonies. The Catholic Church was just as active in child emigration as the Church of England.[127] In 1874, Cardinal Manning began the 'Crusade of Rescue' in the archdiocese of Westminster, which aimed to remove children from the social blight of London to healthier destinations in the colonies. Earlier, Father J. Nugent had sent children to Canada from Liverpool. Catholic child rescue organisations worked in partnership with religious congregations, such as the Sisters of Mercy, the Sisters of Nazareth and the Christian Brothers,

---

[125] Female Middle Class Emigration Society brochure, in Lambeth Palace Library, Benson Papers, vol. 3 (1883).

[126] M. Langfield, 'Voluntarism, Salvation, and Rescue: British Juvenile Migration to Australia and Canada, 1890–1939', *Journal of Imperial and Commonwealth History*, 32 (2004), pp. 86–114. S. Swain, '"Brighter Britain": Images of Empire in the International Child Rescue Movement', in *Empires of Religion*, ed. H. M. Carey (Basingstoke, 2008), pp. 161–76.

[127] For the examples which follow, see B. M. Coldrey, *Good British Stock: Child and Youth Migration to Australia* (Canberra, 1999), Appendix 3.

who operated orphanages and boarding schools, which could provide colonial placement for 'rescued' children.

Of all the churches, the Salvation Army, founded in London in 1865 by the Methodists, William Booth (1829–1912) and his wife Catherine (1829–90), became the most ardent proponent of church-led emigration for people of all classes.[128] In his hugely successful book, *Darkest England and the Way Out* (1890), Booth advocated the 'Colony over Sea' as a solution to poverty on a mass scale; the only problem he could foresee which might limit the success of the plan was that of homesickness. The solution to this was to ensure that as many people as possible emigrated together, including fathers, mothers and children who would meet together in what he envisioned as a communal utopia in the colonies. Once established there, families would work together in the fields and workshops, in between regular attendances at religious services: 'It will resemble nothing so much as the unmooring of a little piece of England, and towing it across the sea to find a safe anchorage in a sunnier clime.'[129] Booth was denounced for his escapist solution, which failed to address the structural basis of poverty or the related issue of working-class alienation from institutional religion.[130] However, the Salvation Army was the logical outcome of trends in the 'social gospel' that transformed a branch of his own Methodist tradition into one that was given over entirely to the single task of home and colonial mission work. By the 1880s, Booth had extended his army to many parts of the empire, including Australia, New Zealand, Canada, Jamaica and India. Booth personally visited many of these sites in his role as the 'General of Salvation'. However, whereas other religious travellers, such as John Clifford whom we encountered in the first chapter, were only tourists, Booth came as the founder of a new British imperial church.[131] The Salvation Army strived to fulfil the utopian vision of *Darkest England* as a world free of poverty; this was a colonial mission that would be the salvation of the English-speaking people.

Conclusion

Edward Gibbon Wakefield appears to have been a sincere Anglican, but there seems little doubt that his deepest spiritual feelings were all about

[128] M. Harper, 'Emigration and the Salvation Army, 1890–1930', *Bulletin of the Scottish Institute of Missionary Studies* (new series) 3–4 (1985), pp. 22–9.
[129] W. Booth, *In Darkest England and the Way Out* (London, 1890), p. 152.
[130] Considered in relation to Booth by H. McLeod, *Religion and Irreligion in Victorian England: How Secular Was the Working Class?* (1993), p. 17.
[131] For Booth and his travels, see the official biography by G. S. Railton, *General Booth*, 2nd edn (London, 1912).

systematic colonisation, not religion. Only in the last, New Zealand, phase of his colonising enterprises does he seem to have turned to the Church of England as his major supporter for what others had begun to call 'Christian colonisation'. Prior to this, he was fond of insisting that the adherents of all religious persuasions stood to profit from his ideas. For Wakefield, religion was useful chiefly as a means of galvanising support for schemes of colonisation. His repeated invocation of the example of the Pilgrim Fathers, like that of the Greek colonists of antiquity, was mostly part of the glib rhetoric of the colonisation salesman that he was. Convinced of the logic and merit of these principles of systematic colonisation, Wakefield was as unmoved by the strictures of Dandeson Coates and the anti-colonial movement, as he was by the sermons of the Society for the Propagation of the Gospel. If he had attended the anniversary sermons of the colonial missionary societies from the other major denominations, which are traversed in Part II of this book, he would undoubtedly have remained unmoved. The arguments from religion, patriotism and imperialism, which gave support to the colonial missionary movement, were not those that convinced him. Nevertheless, Wakefield had clearly started something. What he originally referred to as the 'moral element' in colonisation was taken up with enthusiasm and commitment by religious proponents of systematic colonisation as 'Christian colonisation'. In the 1840s, with the rural population of Great Britain facing famine and the desolation of economic reform, philanthropists were also prepared to leave aborigines to their fate. Coates pleaded that New Zealand might be left to the Maori for fifty years. Like Las Casas, he was to be ignored.

At the beginning of the nineteenth century, emigration and colonisation were both seen as solutions to social problems from pauperism to religious dissent. While Wakefield claims to have had the most influence, in fact all the churches took up the cause of emigration and colonisation. Those who supported emigration as a solution included those with a more or less transparent commercial motivation, such as Wakefield, but also included religious and social idealists with an unblemished reputation for altruism, including Caroline Chisholm, or General Booth. In at least four cases, churchmen were more directly engaged in the organisation of schemes of colonisation and attempts were made to create denominational settlements. These were the former slave colony of Sierra Leone, the high church Anglican settlement of Canterbury, and the Free Church of Scotland settlement of Otago, which were both in New Zealand, and the Anglican Barr (or Britannia) Colony of Saskatchewan. These will be our destinations in the next chapter.

12   Colonies

The previous chapter has examined the idea of Christian colonisation as promoted through the writing of colonial reformers including Edward Gibbon Wakefield and Samuel Hinds, and religious philanthropists including Caroline Chisholm and General Booth of the Salvation Army. As we have seen, the anti-colonial lobby who struggled to prevent the colonisation of New Zealand were defeated, which opened the way to systematic or planned colonisation of British colonial territory not only in New Zealand but also in Canada and parts of Africa. This chapter looks at the Christian colonies that were planned and imagined in the course of the nineteenth century and which were in some ways the culmination of the colonial missionary movement. The first Christian experiment in colonisation in the second British empire was that of Sierra Leone, a settlement intended to provide a home for liberated slaves. However, commercial schemes of colonisation were responsible for promoting many more, a number of which succeeded in some at least of their objectives. The two most ambitious Christian colonies in the later British empire were the Free Church of Scotland settlement of Otago and the Anglican settlement of Canterbury, both in the South Island of New Zealand. While historians, particularly those in New Zealand, have been right to question the strength of the religious element in systematic colonisation, Christian settlement has left a distinctive imprint on New Zealand society, which was so frequently imagined as not just a part of Greater Britain but a 'Better Britain'.[1] While it is important not to over-emphasise the significance of religion in Antipodean settlement – colonisation was overwhelmingly an economic rather than a spiritual enterprise – it is also true that the religious arguments: about missions to the native people, about

[1] Argued with flair by J. Belich, *Making Peoples: A History of the New Zealanders from Polynesian Settlement to the End of the Nineteenth Century* (Auckland, 1996), pp. 76–85. See also J. Belich, *Paradise Reforged: A History of the New Zealanders from the 1880s to the Year 2000* (Auckland, 2001).

Christian colonisation, were deeply influential in a way unmatched in any other British settler colonies.

Sierra Leone

As Deirdre Coleman has argued, the romantic discourse of escape to Elysium influenced a number of unlikely colonising ventures, including the convict settlement of Botany Bay and various attempts to resettle former slaves following the abolition of the trans-Atlantic slave trade.[2] But it was religion rather than romance which was the spur to the first attempt to plant a British colony in Africa. It was also the first attempt at a religiously based scheme of British colonisation since the distant days of the *Mayflower* and the English Pilgrims of the Plymouth plantation in the early seventeenth century.

By the end of the eighteenth century, America was no longer willing to accept British convicts or colonists, religious or any other kind. However, in the wake of the struggle with the American revolutionaries, there remained a debt of justice to be discharged in relation to former black slaves who had been promised freedom and land in return for offering military support to British forces in their confrontation with the American colonists. While they had been successful in earning their freedom, there was little will to secure land for the former slaves. Black refugees from the War of Independence were resettled in Nova Scotia, or they sometimes found their way back to Britain. It was in London that their plight and visibility drew them to the attention of Granville Sharp (1735–1813) and his friends in the Clapham Sect.[3] In 1786, Sharp succeeded in repatriating a group of 400 impoverished former slaves direct to Sierra Leone with the help of a parliamentary grant to ration the settlement until it could become self-sufficient. But the venture was blighted by disease and security problems: 84 died on route to East Africa, 100 died in the first year, and those who remained were dispersed in 1790 following an attack by local chiefs. It was this experience which inspired Sharp to attempt to revive the old instrument of a charter company with a licence from the crown to establish a colony, this time with a party of 1,196 black loyalist soldiers from Nova Scotia. In the imagination of the abolitionists, the settlement was to be not only a refuge from

---

[2] D. Coleman, *Romantic Colonization and British Anti-Slavery* (New York, 2004).
[3] The narrative which follows is taken from the centenary history of the settlement by the bishop of Sierra Leone, E. G. Ingham, *Sierra Leone after a Hundred Years* (London, 1894).

slavery and a life of poverty in London, but the spearhead for the Christian conversion of Africa.

The Sierra Leone Company, established in 1791 with letters patent but never really a fully commercial operation, enjoyed mixed fortunes in which the highest religious and romantic idealism clashed with the realities of colonial settlement in one of the most dangerous and disease-ridden places on earth. It was an empire-wide project that drew personnel from all over the world to participate in a great social, political and religious experiment. In 1792, Lieutenant John Clarkson (1764–1828) sailed to Nova Scotia with his party of former soldier colonists. The expedition included 100 whites: Clarkson was governor, and Zachary Macaulay (1768–1838) was the first superintendent. William Dawes (1762–1836), an astronomer and naval draftsman who had travelled with the First Fleet to the colony of Botany Bay in 1788, went to Sierra Leone in 1792 and served several terms as governor.[4]

Clarkson's diary recalls his misery at being unable to secure harmony in the colony. On Easter Day (8 April), he found himself trying to avert an attempt by the settlers to elect their own governor to replace him. He pleaded with them to remember the 'vast sums of money' which the Company had expended on them, as well as the Company's wish that they would be 'instruments to spread the blessings of Christianity through the wretched heathen nations of this vast continent'.[5] The second settlement was also attacked, and the colony thereafter drifted from crisis to crisis, subsisting on ever-increasing grants from parliament to sustain its existence. In 1807, by which time grants to the Sierra Leone Company had reached a total of £109,000, it was evident that it had failed as a commercial enterprise. It also failed in its religious objective to be a beachhead for the conversion of Africa to Christianity. One hundred years later, in 1894, the Anglican bishop of Sierra Leone was reluctant to describe the colony as Christian in any real sense, despite its origins as a Christian colony and the presence of numerous missionaries of all denominations ever since.[6] In parliament, Dent called for a refund and asked why parliament should continue to pay for 'the fanciful notions of any set of men'; Fuller called it a 'flagrant waste of the public money'.[7] In 1808, the Company was wound up and Sierra Leone was put in the hands of the Colonial Office which found it easier

[4] For Dawes, see Phyllis Mander-Jones, 'Dawes, William (1762–1836)', *Australian Dictionary of Biography*, vol. 1, pp. 297–8.
[5] Governor Clarkson's Diary, 8 April 1797, in Ingham, *Sierra Leone*, pp. 40–1.
[6] *Ibid.*, p. 319.
[7] Sierra Leone Company's Bill, House of Commons Debates, 29 July 1807, vol. 9, cols. 1002 and 1003.

to justify the support of a port in East Africa with a significant English-speaking population than a philanthropic settlement in the middle of nowhere.

The story of the Sierra Leone experiment has captured the imagination of a good many historians since the pioneering history of Christopher Fyfe.[8] While Fyfe saw the achievements of the Creole community of Sierra Leone as something worth celebrating,[9] many have emphasised the failure of evangelical expectations in light of the harsh economic realities of the colony. Catherine Hall has contrasted the sense of duty which took Zachary Macaulay to Sierra Leone with the evident distaste he felt for the fractious colonists he was required to administer.[10] While the Evangelicals who administered the colony endured the arduous conditions out of a combined sense of religious and imperial duty, the colonists generally proved unwilling to behave as dutiful Christians and demanded a say in their own governance. The limited success of the experiment ensured that parliament was not asked to give its approval to any other missionary gestures disguised as commercial schemes of colonisation. Instead, the Sierra Leone colony became incorporated into the wider plan that Evangelicals espoused for the conversion, rather than the colonisation, of the world. By the 1830s, foreign missions rather than colonies came to be seen as the highest good that could be promoted by sincere Christians. It is in the light of these global ambitions that we need to interpret the opposition of 'Exeter Hall' to commercial schemes for religious colonies in New Zealand.

New Zealand

Issues of church and state, as well as mission and settler churches, have central significance for the history of New Zealand.[11] However, the religious roots of New Zealand have also been seen as a burden which has been contested by historians writing the secular history of the nation in more recent times.[12] I will return to this historical problem at the

---

[8] C. Fyfe, *A History of Sierra Leone* (London, 1962); C. Pybus, *Epic Journeys of Freedom: Runaway Slaves of the American Revolution and Their Global Quest for Liberty* (Boston, 2006); S. Schama, *Rough Crossings: Britain, the Slaves and the American Revolution* (London, 2005).

[9] Fyfe, *History of Sierra Leone*, p. 378. uses the term 'Creole' to refer to all citizens of the colony.

[10] C. Hall, 'An Empire of God or of Man? The Macaulays, Father and Son', in *Empires of Religion*, ed. H. M. Carey (Basingstoke, 2008), p. 80.

[11] G. W. Wood, 'Church and State in New Zealand in the 1850s', *Journal of Religious History*, 8 (1975), pp. 255–70.

[12] J. Stenhouse, 'God's Own Silence: Secular Nationalism, Christianity and the Writing of New Zealand History', *New Zealand Journal of History*, 38 (2004), pp. 52–71.

end of this section; my purpose here is to give a fresh account of religious colonisation as much as possible from contemporary sources. The New Zealand Company and the like-minded affiliates, the Otago and Canterbury Associations, all of which were heavily infused with Wakefield's principles of systematic colonisation, were responsible for the seeding of five settlements in New Zealand in the 1840s: Wellington, Nelson and New Plymouth (1840–2) and Dunedin and Christchurch (1848 and 1850).[13] Clergy were included among the settlers and were sponsored by the different churches in cheerful insouciance of the proscriptions of the CMS. In the tumble of new settlements, there was little likelihood that any one church would emerge to dominate the others. George Augustus Selwyn, the first Anglican bishop of New Zealand, arrived in 1842, but attempts by his supporters to assert exclusive rights of establishment for the Church of England were met by effective Presbyterian and Nonconformist protests.[14] The following year, 'an ordinance for promoting the building of churches and providing for the maintenance of ministers of religion', without preference for the Church of England, was passed.[15] New Zealand was effectively up for grabs by parties of religious settlers. The first in line were members of the Free Church of Scotland.

Until the nineteenth century, Scottish colonial experiments had been limited in number and success. In 1698, an attempt by the Company of Scotland to establish a trading base on the Gulf of Darién (off the Caribbean coast of what is now Panama) was abandoned following devastating losses from disease and attacks by the Spaniards. The catastrophic financial strain of the scheme is said to have been instrumental in the decision to proceed with the 1707 Acts of Union, which brought an end to the separate Scottish parliament. Not surprisingly, this had a discouraging effect on Scottish schemes for plantations in the New World for some time to come. There were some exceptions: the Reverend Norman McLeod (1780–1866) was successful in leading parties of Scottish Highlanders to Nova Scotia and subsequently to New Zealand.[16] John Dunmore Lang brought many more to Australia. But, although these schemes involved Scottish Presbyterians and chaplains, none had a particularly religious character. Religion was more of an element in the emigration of Catholic Highlanders who sought to escape poverty, persecution and marginalisation in the eighteenth

---

[13] Belich, *Making Peoples*, p. 188.
[14] J. R. Elder, *The History of the Presbyterian Church of New Zealand, 1840–1940* (Christchurch, 1940), p. 31.
[15] *Ibid.*, p. 32.
[16] N. Robinson, *To the Ends of the Earth: Norman McLeod and the Highlanders' Migration to Nova Scotia and New Zealand* (Auckland, 1997).

century.[17] And, throughout the nineteenth century, Scots were enthusiastically engaged in the missionary movement and were articulate in the generation of schemes for the education, civilisation and organisation of the empire. Africa in particular, where the Scottish Congregationalist missionary David Livingstone (1813–73) made his reputation, could be represented as 'a kind of celestial Scotland', as Michael Fry has argued.[18] However, it was not until the Otago settlement that an explicitly religious scheme was attempted by Scottish colonisers.

Free Church of Scotland settlement of Otago, 1847

The Otago (or New Edinburgh) settlement was founded by the Scottish Free Church Lay Association as 'the first and only Free Church colony in the world'.[19] Scottish Presbyterian settlers had been part of the earlier settlements at New Plymouth and Nelson of the New Zealand Land Company (formed in 1833); however, the Otago project was the first to make them a central element of a colonisation scheme. The original plan was proposed by George Rennie (1801/2–60), a Scottish sculptor and politician who, as Liberal member for Ipswich (1841–7), had come under the spell of Edward Gibbon Wakefield. Enthused by the idea of systematic colonisation, in 1842 he put a proposal to the New Zealand Company for a Scottish settlement to be called New Edinburgh. Rennie's scheme included an investment in religious infrastructure, but only on a small scale. In 1843, however, the Disruption was greeted by Wakefield as an opportunity to attract high-quality, socially cohesive colonists for a class settlement. He therefore encouraged Rennie and his associate, William Cargill (1784–1860), a former British army officer and descendant of one of the Scottish Covenanters, to approach the Free Church.

As we saw in Chapter 7, the Colonial Committee of the Free Church was quick to embrace Rennie and Cargill's proposal. In May 1842, a lay association of the Free Church was formed, with paid officers in

---

[17] J. M. Bumstead, 'Highland Emigration to the Island of St John and the Scottish Catholic Church, 1769–1774', *Dalhousie Review*, 58 (1979), pp. 511–47.

[18] M. Fry, *The Scottish Empire* (Phantassie, East Lothian, 2001), Part 2, 'A Christian Empire'. See also Breitenbach, 'Religious Literature and Discourses of Empire'; J. MacKenzie, '"Making Black Scotsmen and Scotswomen?": Scottish Missionaries and the Eastern Cape Colony in the Nineteenth Century', in *Empires of Religion*, ed. H. M. Carey (Basingstoke, 2008), pp. 113–36.

[19] R. C. S. Ross, *The Story of the Otago Church and Settlement* (Dunedin, 1887), Preface. For a sympathetic portrayal of the settler church in Otago, see P. Matheson, 'The Settler Church, 1840–1870', in *Presbyterians in Aotearoa, 1840–1990*, ed. D. McEldowney (Wellington, 1990), pp. 15–42. For the history of Otago, see also E. Olssen, *A History of Otago* (Dunedin, 1984).

Edinburgh and Glasgow. The Edinburgh Secretary was Dr Andrew Aldcorn (1792–1877), who later emigrated to Australia in 1853 and served for a brief period (1858–9) as member of the New South Wales Legislative Assembly.[20] The Glasgow Secretary was John M'Glashan. As spiritual leader, the Free Church appointed the Reverend Thomas Burns (1796–1871), nephew of the Scottish national poet. It was Burns' insistence on an exclusive Free Church constituency for the venture which led to Rennie's departure in 1845. In a dignified letter of farewell, Rennie stated his view that the prosperity of the proposed colony was compromised by the decision to identify it with what he called 'an exclusive sectarian aspect'.[21]

For its part, the Free Church was anxious not to burden itself with the expense and possible controversy of a colonisation experiment. Nevertheless, after weighty deliberation, the General Assembly gave the following carefully expressed endorsement to the scheme:

Without expressing any opinion regarding the secular advantages or prospects of the proposed undertaking, the General Assembly highly approve of the principles on which the settlement is proposed to be conducted in so far as the religious and educational interests of the Colonists are concerned, and the Assembly desire to countenance and encourage the Association in those respects.[22]

This statement was reprinted in the *New Zealand Journal* and in the pamphlet published in 1845 to promote the Otago settlement as a 'Scheme of the Colony of the Free Church of Scotland'.[23] It was an essential lever in attracting investors and paying colonists to the scheme, but for Burns it was much more than this. Free Church endorsement was a way to vanquish the hated adversaries of the New Zealand Company in the Colonial Office whose ears were perpetually tuned to the rival missionary proposals of Anglican Evangelicals: 'Who can tell', wrote Burns, 'what new arrangements might be adopted by his Lordship in the plenitude of his despotic authority over these fine islands – and the Ch. Miss. Soc. and Ch. of England Puseyites pouring through Mr Jas Stephen their own favourite projects in his ear.'[24] In contrast, he suggested that the Otago colony would be a bastion for the Reformed faith,

[20] J. Barr, *The Old Identities* (Dunedin, 1879), p. 5.
[21] *The Colonial Gazette*, 1 November 1845, p. 692, cited by McLintock, *History of Otago*, p. 193.
[22] Sessions 13 and 19 of the General Assembly of the Free Church of Scotland, 29 May and 3 June 1845, cited by *ibid.*, p. 204.
[23] Free Church of Scotland, *Scheme of the Colony of the Free Church at Otago in New Zealand* (Glasgow, 1845).
[24] Burns to Cargill, 5 June 1845, cited by McLintock, *History of Otago*, p. 205.

holding back what he called 'the formidable energy with which Popery is now, and for years past has been wielding her gigantic resources and establishing her influence in every quarter of the world'.[25]

More practically, Cargill argued that the colony would give purpose to the unsystematic emigration under which an annual average of 4,000 souls was already 'oozing out of Scotland to the colonies'.[26] Like other schemes, the colony at Otago put forward enticements of material prosperity to potential settlers, but the distinctive feature of this scheme, in Cargill's view, was its attention to less tangible goals which included its commitment to religion and education, which was unprecedented in any British colony since the time of the Pilgrim Fathers.[27] Nevertheless, religion remains low key in the promotional literature of the Lay Association. Religious provisions, including arrangements for clergy, schools and teachers, and a college, were one of the inducements put forward to emigrants.[28] However, the pamphlet mostly sets out to provide information of a practical kind: the climate, the quality of the native grasses, and its potential to enrich any prospective emigrants. The pamphlet included two excellent colour maps. Religion, it might be concluded, was just one among many variables which emigrants were expected to weigh up when considering whether to head to New Zealand or some other destination. Even Burns stressed the physical attractions of the new settlement. In a letter dated 28 Jan. 1849 from the manse of Dunedin, he enthused about the conditions for agriculture: 'A richer soil, a better climate, does not, I believe, anywhere exist, even in New Zealand.'[29]

Perhaps it is not surprising that the settlers were so hard-headed about their decision to emigrate, or that commercial and spiritual matters were so thoroughly mixed in all its promotional literature. However, it does beg the question as to what the religious legacy of the founding settlement in Otago was for the later development of the province. At this point it is important to stress how small the original colonising party was and also how limited and short-lived its direct association with the Free Church of Scotland. Led by Cargill, the *John Wickliffe* sailed from Gravesend on 24 November 1847, with 97 passengers

[25] Burns to Cargill, 6 May 1845, cited by *ibid*., p. 204.
[26] Letter from Captain William Cargill to Dr Aldcorn of Oban, London 1847, in *Free Church Colony at Otago in New Zealand*, pp. 7–9, in McIntyre and Gardner, eds., *Speeches and Documents*, pp. 24–6.
[27] *Ibid.*
[28] Free Church of Scotland, *The Principles, Objects and Plan*, p. 11.
[29] Burns to the Secretary of the Otago Association, 28 January 1849, in Free Church of Scotland, [*Lay*] *Association for Promoting the Settlement of a Scotch Colony at Otago New Zealand* (London, 1850?), p. 3.

aboard. The *Philip Laing* sailed three days later from Greenock with 247 passengers. Burns and Cargill both came as settlers. Despite Cargill's dislike of 'the little enemy', as he liked to call members of the Church of England,[30] only two-thirds of the original Otago settlers were Free Church Presbyterians. A direct link to the Free Church of Scotland Assembly was also short-lived, and the Lay Association survived only until 1852 after which its affairs were wound up. As far as the religious character of the settlement was concerned, this came to depend a good deal on Burns. It was Burns who set his seal on the Free Church and religious ideals of the colony, identifying them in his own writings with the founding principles of Otago.[31] Other leaders in the association, including Cargill, M'Glashan and Aldcorn, as well as some at least of those who chose to emigrate, also forwarded the Free Church Gospel in their correspondence. On the other hand, many of the settlers who set out for Otago came from among the most hard-pressed classes of rural Scottish society and they had little energy to spare for religion. From his reading of the shipboard diaries of emigrants and the letters they published when they reached Otago, McLintock concludes:

They may have been ardent devotees of Wakefield's philosophy of colonization, though indeed this is most unlikely; they may have been zealous Free Churchmen, and this is in many cases probable; but it was primarily in an endeavour to ameliorate their lot, to build afresh in a new country which knew not the social evils of the old, that Otago's first emigrants set forth from their motherland late in 1847.[32]

This is no reason to suppose that the religious convictions of the Otago settlers were not heartfelt or locally significant. In his more recent history, Matheson stresses the warmth and practicality of settler religion in Otago, a faith which had few pretensions but also unexpected depths.[33]

The Scottish character of Otago was rather more evident than its religious ideals, although it is again true that this owed relatively little to the original settlers and much more to the nostalgia which set in later in Otago's settlement history. In the 1850s, immigration to Otago lagged and efforts to attract continuing settlement from Scotland were only

---

[30] Tom Brooking, 'Cargill, William 1784–1860', *Dictionary of New Zealand Biography*, updated 22 June 2007, www.dnzb.govt.nz.

[31] T. Burns, *A Discourse Delivered in the Church of Otago, Friday March 23, 1849* (Dunedin, 1849); T. Burns, *Address Delivered at the Inauguration of the Presbytery of Otago, June 27, 1854* (Dunedin, 1854); T. Burns, *A Brief Account of the Origin and History of the Presbyterian Church of Otago, February 16, 1865* (Dunedin, 1865).

[32] McLintock, *History of Otago*, p. 237.

[33] Matheson, 'Settler Church', p. 33.

partly successful. By the end of 1864, after the first gold rushes, little more than one-third of the population of Otago and Southland was Scottish-born. Nevertheless, some distinctive Scottish features of the colony were evident, notably its thriving educational institutions and majority Presbyterianism. By 1871, the province was distinguished by 100 public schools and its own university.[34] The creation of a university in Otago was perhaps the most significant outcome of the original Scottish settlement. Founded in 1869 and opened in 1871, it retained a reputation for social innovation. It was, for example, the first university in the British empire to grant degrees to women.[35]

Presbyterianism also left a physical imprint on Dunedin, represented most strikingly by the First Church of Otago (1874), the city's main Presbyterian church, which was designed in high Gothic style by Robert Arthur Lawson (1833–1902), a Scottish émigré architect. Lawson also designed Knox Church in the same city. Moreover, the distinctive Presbyterian communion season continued to be celebrated in Otago long after such public communal religious observations were in decline in the heart of the home church in Scotland.[36] Without doubt, this was less because of the original Presbyterian ethos of the Dunedin settlement but more a result of the continuing pull of the colony for later Presbyterian settlers who recognised it as a place that was hospitable to Scots and which valued their institutions. The churches in Scotland helped to perpetuate this, as Marjorie Harper has shown, by sponsoring emigration in the twentieth century.[37] On balance, the Otago settlement can probably be called a highly successful experiment in colonisation, but for reasons which have relatively little to do with the religious convictions of its founders. The same conclusion can be reached, *mutatis mutandis*, for the second major religious colony to be established in the south island of New Zealand.

John Robert Godley and the Canterbury Association (1849)

As we saw in the previous chapter, Wakefield's argument in favour of a moral or religious element in systematic colonisation struck a chord in

---

[34] Carrothers, *Emigration*, pp. 116–40.
[35] Elder, *History of the Presbyterian Church*; W. P. Morrell, *University of Otago: A Centennial History* (Dunedin, 1969).
[36] Clarke, 'Days of Heaven'.
[37] M. Harper, 'Making Christian Colonists: An Evaluation of the Emigration Policies and Practices of the Scottish Churches and Christian Organisations between the Wars', *Records of the Scottish Church History Society*, 28 (1998), pp. 173–216.

many Christian hearts. But his most eminent convert – and the man who secured him the kind of illustrious patrons he craved – was John Robert Godley, the man whose statue stands in front of Christchurch cathedral as the founder of Canterbury.[38] Born in Ireland and educated at Christ Church College Oxford, Godley was a likeable Tory who had many conservative friends in the high church party of the Church of England, including a number who later became avowed Tractarians. Godley first began publishing on social issues in 1842 after travelling to Europe and the United States. In his *Letters from America* (1842),[39] he argued that the answer to British problems lay in the regeneration of the traditional caring role of the governing aristocracy. He also gave his approval to a resurgent Church of England taking up its mission as the custodian of the national Church in the colonies. While Wakefield was clearly an influence on his thought, Godley needs to be ranked with other reformers who responded to the social and economic crisis of the 1840s including Richard Cobden, Thomas Carlyle, Robert Peel, F. D. Maurice and Prince Albert. Not just the challenge of famine, but the Europe-wide revolutions of 1848 excited old fears of popular insurrection and the need for social elites to defend their authority by demonstrating their utility to the sceptical masses.

By the time Godley began to show an interest in emigration as a solution to the social ills of British society, he was working as a lawyer and writer which allowed him to build connections with Peelites such as Gladstone, Palmer, Herbert and Lincoln.[40] Like Hinds, whom he may have known in Dublin, Godley was radicalised into more direct action by his experience of the Irish famine. In 1847, together with like-minded Tories who were then in opposition, he set up a joint stock company to be called 'The Irish Canada Company' which aimed to resettle up to 1.5 million destitute Irish Catholics, with the assistance of the Catholic clergy, in Canada.[41] Unlike the Sierra Leone Company, it is probably worth noting the commercial basis of this scheme which would be underwritten by the imperial government to the tune of £5 per emigrant.[42] As MacDonagh notes, this scheme was not supported

---

[38] M. Stocker, ed., *Remembering Godley: A Portrait of Canterbury's Founder* (Christchurch, 2001). On Godley, see also Carrington, *John Robert Godley*.

[39] J. R. Godley, *Letters from America*, 2 vols. (London, 1844).

[40] Carrington, *John Robert Godley*, p. 64.

[41] S. Grainer, 'Who Was Godley?', in *Remembering Godley: A Portrait of Canterbury's Founder*, ed. M. Stocker (Christchurch, 2001), p. 22.

[42] R. D. C. Black, *Economic Thought and the Irish Question 1817–1870* (Cambridge, 1960), p. 229.

by the Catholic hierarchy in Ireland, and to modern eyes has the lurid tinge of ethnic cleansing about it.[43]

While many agreed that large-scale emigration was the best solution to intractable social problems, Godley's distinctive contribution was in his commitment to the special role of the Church of England. When the Canterbury Association was founded on 21 March 1848, Godley was the driving force which secured patronage from social-reforming conservatives to the project. The 1848 prospectus included fifty names and it was probably Godley whose charm and powers of persuasion ensured the list included some of the most powerful and influential conservative leaders in English society. Tracking the connections and influence of what grew to become eighty-four members of the Canterbury Association has been the loving duty of local historians in Christchurch for generations and defies simple summary.[44] Perhaps the main point to stress is that the membership of the Association crossed political and church party boundaries. In the pamphlet advertising the first meeting of the Association in Ipswich on 13 November 1849, the meeting was chaired by Samuel Hinds, who had recently been appointed bishop of Norwich. John Bird Sumner, archbishop of Canterbury (1848–62), became president, and the list of members included seven bishops and senior clergy as well as the Secretary to the Society for the Propagation of the Gospel, Ernest Hawkins. Ties of family, friendship, politics and religion bound them all together in a dense interlocking network focused on an ideal project – the generation of an Anglican settlement in New Zealand, which would be the culmination of the Christian imperialism of a generation. The prosopographer Michael Blain, reflecting on the tangled skeins of school, college, family, the military, commerce, politics, influence and, of course, religion, that made up the membership of the Canterbury Association, likened its eighty-four members to a village, but, in the same sentence, emphasised that it was no village, but rather an oligarchy that stretched from England and Ireland across the empire. He suggested that motivations for joining the venture included political ambition, romantic fantasy, military and imperialistic power, commercial interests and a philosophical interest in the ideal of colonial settlements.[45]

---

[43] MacDonagh, 'Irish Catholic Clergy', pp. 287–302.
[44] A prosopographical dossier on eighty-four members of the Canterbury Association was prepared for the 150th anniversary of the establishment of the Canterbury colony in 1979 by Michael Blain and deposited in Christchurch Public Library: M. Blain, 'The Canterbury Association: A Study of Its Members' Connections: A Tribute on the 150th Anniversary of the Canterbury Settlement [Typescript]', (Christchurch, 2000).
[45] *Ibid.*, pp. 8–10.

Christian commitment was, nevertheless, the primary bond which linked the members of the Canterbury Association and, except for Thomas Jackson (who was a Wesleyan Methodist) they were all members of the Church of England. At a time of rising tensions between church parties, the churchmanship of the Association was nevertheless quite mixed and included Evangelicals, such as Sumner and Lord Ashley, high churchmen such as Samuel Wilberforce, the reforming bishop of Oxford, as well as Tractarians such as Richard Chenevix Trench and Robert Wilberforce (who later converted to Catholicism). In his profile of the Canterbury Association, Cookson lays stress on the social idealism of the project, which emerged in the wake of the debates about the 'condition of England', a range of issues which included industrial dislocation, the Chartist demand for greater access to the franchise by working men, the great famine that afflicted Ireland and parts of Scotland in the middle of the 1840s, and the fear sparked by the revolutions in Europe in 1848.[46] However, the members of the Canterbury Association, with the sole exception of Godley, were not colonists.

The actual story of the settlement was straightforward and is well understood;[47] in addition, the history of the Anglican diocese of Christchurch has a major literature, which reflects its importance in the expansion of the Anglican Communion.[48] After the creation of the Canterbury Association, land was purchased by Governor George Grey and this included land set aside for the Canterbury settlement. Hinds was on hand to send off the first four ships which left England in September 1850 and arrived in Port Lyttelton three months later. Eight additional Canterbury Association vessels arrived, together with seven which were privately chartered, ensuring that within a year there were over 1,000 settlers. Between 1850 and December 1852, a total of twenty-three ships arrived, bringing with them 3,500 people. While most came directly from England, a significant number arrived from elsewhere in New Zealand and Australia. As official resident, Godley arrived with his family in April 1850, but chose to return to England in 1852 a few months after the winding up of the Canterbury Association.

[46] J. E. Cookson, 'Canterbury Association (Act. 1848–1852)', in *Oxford Dictionary of National Biography*, online edition (Oxford, 2008).

[47] The chronology follows the Christchurch City library website, http://Christchurchcitylibraries.com/heritage/earlyChristchurch/earlyChristchurch.asp.

[48] C. Brown, M. Peters and F. J. Teal, eds., *Shaping a Colonial Church: Bishop Harper and the Anglican Diocese of Christchurch, 1856–1890* (Christchurch, 2006); S. Eldred-Grigg, *A New History of Canterbury* (Dunedin, 1982). For the background to the establishment of the colony, see M. Peters, 'Homeland and Colony', in *Shaping a Colonial Church: Bishop Harper and the Anglican Diocese of Christchurch, 1856–1890*, ed. C. Brown, M. Peters and J. Teal (Christchurch, 2006), pp. 19–34.

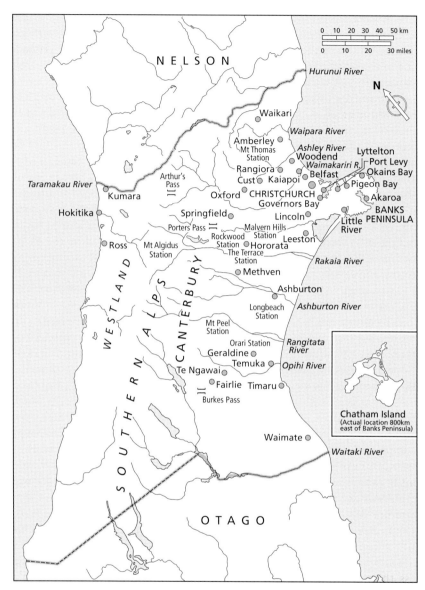

Map 12.1 Diocese of Christchurch, New Zealand, in the late
nineteenth century
Source: *Shaping a Colonial Church: Bishop Harper and the Anglican
Diocese of Christchurch, 1856–1890*, ed. Colin Brown, Marie Peters
and Jane Teal (Canterbury, New Zealand, 2006), p. 18.

The Australian gold rushes temporarily suspended the growth of the settlement but in time it prospered. Given the short duration of direct control by the Association, it is probably more reasonable to attribute this to the later economic development of the colony than any specific virtues of the settlement, religious or otherwise.

Assessments of the success or failure of the Canterbury settlement began almost immediately. Indeed, the whole venture took place in a blaze of publicity. The departures were minutely reported in *The Times*, and celebrated with illustrations and accounts of the formal departure ceremonies in the *Illustrated London News*. The most sympathetic view of the fortunes of the settlement was that of the *Colonial Church Chronicle and Missionary Journal*. This was published in the aftermath of the establishment of the Colonial Bishoprics' Fund 'by a few individuals at some risk of loss, but without the possibility of profit' with any potential profits going to endowment of new bishoprics in the colonies. It appeared monthly, with 2,000 copies being sold at home and in the colonies. It would appear to have become a commercial success, if we are to believe the editorial of the second volume. One key to this was the decision to embrace the issue of church-sponsored emigration with reviews of prospective projects, including those to South Australia and the Canterbury colony, correspondence advising how the Church might best be able to assist the needs of migrants, and occasional advertisements for clergy who might be interested in taking up work in any of the expanding colonies of the south.

For the editor of the *Colonial Church Chronicle*, there was a necessary connection between the two great fields of endeavour in the British empire, religion and colonisation, the subject of the first editorial article of the new volume. Colonisation, it argued, was closely connected with the propagation of the Gospel. And, because the 'means and opportunities' of the English are so much greater than other nations, it follows that they had much greater obligations to fulfil: 'We have commercial, and we ought to have religious, relations with every country in the world.'[49] A direct connection is then made between the call to convert the heathen, and the opportunities to plant colonies. Colonisation, especially in Australia and New Zealand, was nothing less than 'a champion able to cope with the Goliath of heathenism'. Indeed, with such aid, the conversion of the world would be appreciably advanced: 'If we could plant another England in the Antipodes, the task would be incalculably easier.'[50] This analysis is especially interesting

[49] 'Systematic Colonization', *Colonial Church Chronicle*, 2 (1848), pp. 2–6.
[50] *Ibid.*, p. 2.

because of the connections it seems prepared to make between the two fields of missionary endeavour, to the heathen and to colonists, which were increasingly seen as on opposing sides. It was clear that, for some mission-minded commentators, the best justiftelton for the creation of a colony that was both Christian and British in the Antipodes was its potential as a beachhead for an advance on the adjoining heathen mission fields of Melanesia and Asia.

Support for Church (i.e. Anglican) colonisation also came from other high church journals, such as the *Christian Remembrancer*.[51] Reviewing the *Canterbury Papers* (1850), a promotional volume produced by the Canterbury Association, and the pamphlet *Hints on Church Colonization* (1850) by the Reverend James Cecil Wynter (1807–77),[52] it makes a call on the English nation to take up its mission as 'the Christianizers and civilizers of the globe',[53] and for the Church to do its bit to prevent the continued barbarous neglect of colonisation, as opposed to mere emigration.

It is evident that the Canterbury Association came to mean different things according to the preconceptions of its members and supporters. At one extreme was Lord John Manners (1818–1906), a member of Disraeli's 'Young England' set who favoured all things medieval, chivalric and romantic, from the restoration of Don Carlos to the throne of Spain, to the foundation of Anglican sisterhoods and the Gothic revival in architecture. In 1841, in his 'Memorial of Other Lands' Manners had hinted at the potential allure of other Englands, both those in the past and those overseas: 'Let wealth and commerce, laws and learning die; but leave us still our old nobility.'[54] There is a certain mad romance about this, besides an unthinking Toryism which was slowly dying out in the wake of the 1832 Reform Bill. For Manners and his friends, the Canterbury Association represented an opportunity to make a grand chivalric gesture. He not only joined the Association but had been present on the East India docks to bid goodbye to the first pilgrims. In 1851, Manners gave a rousing address on the history of colonisation in the empire in which he described the Canterbury settlement as 'the great colonizing enterprise of the day'.[55] Manners supplied visionary enthusiasm to endorse the scheme which he imagined to be the answer to all the religious failures of the first British empire. After a lapse of some

[51] Edited by William Scott, Francis Garden and James Bowling Mozley.
[52] Blain, 'Canterbury Association', p. 93, notes that, on the strength of this pamphlet, Wynter was suggested for the proposed bishopric of Lyttelton.
[53] 'Art. VI', *The Christian Remembrancer: A Quarterly Review*, 9 (1850), p. 449.
[54] J. J. R. Manners, *England's Trust, and Other Poems* (London, 1841), Part 3, line 227.
[55] Manners, *Church of England in the Colonies*, p. 23.

centuries, he suggested, the New Zealand experiment would redress the lost opportunities squandered by England in the Americas. Quoting standard Wakefieldian authority, he argued that the key to creating loyal colonists was to ensure that there was a mixture of the classes, while ensuring that the ruling classes and the Church of England were part of the mix: 'With all the elements of English social life harmoniously blended together – with all the precautions which the united efforts of thoughtful and practical minds could suggest – with religion not only admitted as a feature of, but permeating the whole scheme – with a distinct government and legislative body – if the Canterbury settlement fails, its failure will be a clear proof that England has effectually lost the art of colonization.'[56] Religion was the key to this new, more successful experiment in colonisation.

At the other extreme were the assessments penned by the colonists themselves. They tend to be strong on the need for experienced mechanics and farmers and quiet on the sort of religion approved of by Manners. Samuel Hodgkinson (1817–1914), an English surgeon from a farming family, emigrated to Canterbury in 1851 and farmed there for three years. In 1856, after his temporary return to England, he published a guide for emigrants based on his experiences in the province. A second edition appeared in 1858; this was a cheaply produced pamphlet which carried an advertisement for assisted passages which were available on payment of £10 10s to the right sort of emigrant:

The Applicants preferred will be AGRICULTURAL LABOURERS, SHEPHERDS, COUNTRY MECHANICS, as Carpenters, Blacksmiths, Wheelwrights, Sawyers, Gardeners &ts; and Domestic Servants.[57]

Mirroring the views of farmer entrepreneurs such as himself, Hodgkinson stressed that what were needed were agricultural labourers and there was little or no call for professional men: 'Gentlemen without either a profession to practice, or capital to invest, are the most unsuitable of all.'[58] That being said, the Canterbury province was quickly more than a farming community and few emigrants faced the desperate conditions which confronted those seeking to make a living from the Canadian prairie, or the Gippsland mulga country which were both being opened up at much the same time.

[56] *Ibid.*, p. 24.
[57] S. Hodgkinson, *A Description of the Province of Canterbury, New Zealand, or, Zealandia: Founded on Experience Obtained During a Residence of Three Years as a Sheep-Farmer in the Colony*, 2nd edn (London, 1858).
[58] *Ibid.*, p. 12.

Table 12.1 *Race and religion in the Province of
Canterbury, New Zealand, 1857*

	Number	Percentage
Race		
English	4,256	77.3
Scottish	578	10.5
Irish	371	6.7
Welsh	40	0.7
French	86	1.6
German	82	1.5
Other	95	1.7
Religion		
Church of England	4,455	76.5
Presbyterian	573	9.8
Roman Catholic	232	4.0
Wesleyan	46	7.8
Baptist and Independent	78	0.1
Lutheran	36	0.6
Other	14	0.2

Source: New Zealand Census of 1857. Cited by
Hodgkinson, *Description of the Province of Canterbury*,
p. 13. Total enumerated 6,230.

As shown in Table 12.1, the Canterbury census of 1857 reflects both the English and the Anglican origins of the settlement. Out of a total enumerated population of 6,230, 4,256, or 77.3 per cent, were returned as English, and 4,455, or 76.5 per cent, as Church of England. It is difficult to make a direct comparison with the standing of Anglicanism in England, but, in the religious census of 1851, just 53 per cent of those who attended morning services went to an Anglican church, whereas almost 16 per cent went to a Wesleyan chapel.[59] This would seem to indicate the Church of England was doing rather better than might be expected against significant Wesleyan competition in the Canterbury province. At 4 per cent, the Catholic population was also smaller than might be expected, even with the reinforcements provided by the presence of some French colonists at Akaroa.

Hodgkinson has very little to say about religion except indirectly. The original plan of the colony, we are told, ensured 'a very superior class of settlers', but Hodgkinson is careful to point out that the

[59] Data on 1851 Census of Religious Worship from Cook and Keith, *British Historical Facts, 1830–1900*, p. 220.

Church of England was no longer in a privileged position but shared the same standing as other denominations. The colony, he noted, was neither exclusively Anglican, nor a 'hotbed of Tractarianism'.[60] This is particularly interesting in that it shows the extent to which the distinctive Anglican and, to some extent, high church character of the original Canterbury settlement was becoming something of a liability as it sought to sustain its existence as a viable commercial colony.

Lord Lyttelton (1867–8)

An even more sanguine view of the scheme was provided by the man after whom the principal port of the Canterbury settlement had been named, Lord Lyttelton. We last encountered him writing to Ernest Hawkins on the matter of the SPG and the colonial church.[61] Lyttelton delivered two lectures on the Canterbury colony after making a personal visit to New Zealand with his son and a companion from 1867 to 1868.[62] Lyttelton appears to have had the misfortune to have discovered that he suffered from chronic seasickness after he had embarked on a voyage of three-and-a-half months to New Zealand and back; possibly this contributed to his lack of enthusiasm for the project. At any event, he quotes Dr Johnson's well-known definition of a ship as 'a prison, with the chance of being drowned',[63] and gives a vivid account of the crowding, noise, discomfort, monotony, want of exercise and other discomforts of a long sea voyage. A pious man, he did not neglect his religious observances at sea, simply noting that it was no substitute for services at home.[64]

Lyttelton's account of New Zealand is a great curiosity. He clearly wrote it himself based on extracts from his diaries, and he tries hard to provide a balanced account of his experiences, neither exaggerating his claims to expertise nor acting as the agent for emigrants who might wish to visit the settlement. On the whole, he felt paternal about Canterbury, which he calls 'a cub of England'. He was intrigued, in turn, by the New Zealanders' assessment of himself:

What the people mostly thought of us three I never much learned, though I was very curious about it. Almost the only specific judgment I heard was that

---

[60] *Ibid.*, p. 15.
[61] See Chapter 3; and Lyttelton, *Letter to Hawkins*. At the same time, Lyttelton contributed articles on the Canterbury colony and the colonial church. See L. Lyttelton, 'Canterbury Colony', *Colonial Church Chronicle*, 2 (1849); L. Lyttelton, *The Colonial Empire of Great Britain Especially in Its Religious Aspect* (London, 1849).
[62] L. Lyttelton, *Two Lectures on a Visit to the Canterbury Colony in 1867–8: 1. The Voyage; 2. The Colony* (London, 1868).
[63] Croker's Boswell, iii.25, cited by *ibid.*, p. 4.   [64] *Ibid.*, p. 9.

of a worthy tradesman, a market gardener, and Mayor of Christ Church, who thought me a respectable person, but that I leaned against walls in a way unbefitting an English Peer.[65]

Lyttelton found the general appearance of Christchurch rather sad and slovenly, especially what had been grandly called Cathedral Square. This is the place I described at the beginning of Chapter 10, which is now scattered with public memorials to the Canterbury 'pilgrims' and its founding colonisers: 'It was the hope and intention of the people, some years ago, to set about building their Cathedral in this place; a large sum was subscribed, and solid foundations laid. But there, alas! the work stopped.'[66] There was more pleasure in driving out to Hagley Park where there was a cricket ground in which Lyttelton's son impressed the colonists by scoring more than 100 runs.[67]

Besides the length of his sea voyage, Lyttelton seems to have been chiefly repelled by the ethos of the Canterbury province which was attempting to make commercial capital out of its association with the Church of England. He was gratified that the original religious character of the settlement seemed to have given Anglican institutions an advantage over other churches. Overall, however, Lyttelton's lecture leaves the strong impression that he found the long expedition rather boring and far more trouble than he anticipated. His verdict on the prospects for the emigrant is relegated to a footnote: 'fair success is as nearly certain as anything human can be.'[68] This reflects a rather dismal realisation that, despite all its religious idealism, the Canterbury settlement had become simply another venture in colonial land speculation. This was a bitter pill to swallow.

Samuel Butler (1863)

Perhaps the most devastating critique, not only of the Canterbury settlement but of all attempts to undertake colonisation in the name of Christianity, was that of Samuel Butler (1835–1902), writer, artist and Canterbury sheep farmer. In the letters and journals which Butler sent home to his family during his first year in New Zealand, he was inclined to stress the education and gentle background of his fellow settlers: 'The men are all gentlemen and sons of gentlemen, and one of them is Cambridge man, who took a high second-class a year before my time.'[69] He speaks of encountering the occasional individual whose

---

[65] Ibid., p. 24.   [66] Ibid., p. 19.
[67] Ibid., p. 20.   [68] Ibid., p. 36.
[69] S. Butler, *A First Year in Canterbury Settlement* (London, 1863), p. 50.

reading ran to Tennyson's *Idylls of the King*, and an Oxonian perus-
ing Machiavelli on Livy, and the Church Fathers. But, he goes on to
state, these men were the rare exceptions. The chief work of all those in
the country was that of 'getting on': 'The fact is, people here are busy
making money.' Unlike Lyttelton, Butler shows more empathy for the
hard-headed attitude of men on the make, and he enjoyed their lack
of convention, formality and sentiment, as well as their indifference to
sectarian debates. However, his final advice to the prospective migrant
carries with it a certain sweeping cynicism, much like Lyttelton's dismissal of the materialism of most emigrants: 'If you have tolerably good
fortune, in a very short time you will be a rich man. Hoping that this
may be the case, there remains nothing for me but to wish you heartily
farewell.'[70]

On the surface, Butler's class and education would seem to have
fitted him for the role of supporter – rather than satirist – of the pretensions of the Canterbury settlement. Butler was the son of a clergyman and the grandson of a headmaster of Shrewsbury School, which he
attended before going to St John's College, Cambridge.[71] After taking
his degree, he began preparation for ordination but seems to have experienced something of a crisis of confidence in the Church of England
as much as a crisis of faith. At any event, his family supported his travel
to New Zealand where he succeeded in reversing his fortunes in the
Anglican settlement of Canterbury. From 1860 to 1864, he successfully
developed a sheep station, which he called Mesopotamia, in the high
country to the south of the province. He was also successful in contributing to the budding cultural development of Christchurch, writing
some of his most effective pieces for the Christchurch *Press*, as well as
the letters and journals which his family edited and published as *A First
Year in Canterbury Settlement* (1863). Although Butler sold his station
and returned to London, he continued to work on the fantasy satire,
Erewhon, which was ultimately published by Trübner in 1872.[72]

Erewhon provides a powerful anti-clerical satire directed chiefly
against the established Church of England in the style of Jonathan
Swift's *Gulliver's Travels* (1726). Erewhon is an imaginary country that
the traveller encounters beyond the high ranges of a country which

---

[70] *Ibid.*, p. 162.
[71] Biographical details from Elinor Shaffer, 'Butler, Samuel (1835–1902)', *Oxford
Dictionary of National Biography*. See also P. B. Maling, 'Samuel Butler', in *An
Encyclopaedia of New Zealand*, ed. A. H. McLintock (2007).
[72] Butler provides a detailed account of how *Erewhon* was written in the Preface to the
revised edition: S. Butler, *Erewhon, or Over the Range*, revised edn (London, 1920),
p. xiv.

bears a striking resemblance to Butler's own station in New Zealand. Indeed, the earliest descriptive account of the ranges was written while Butler was still in New Zealand, though by 1863 he was spending more time in the township of Christchurch than up in the country. The hero of the novel is characterised as a man of conventional, which is to say unthinking, piety who is inspired to continue his travels as much by the desire to work as a missionary as to seek his own fortune. Like Gulliver's Lilliput and Brobdingnag, Erewhon is inhabited not by exotic and intractable natives but by people who appear much like western Europeans in appearance. Yet, once he encounters the Erewhonians, he becomes convinced that they represent one of the lost tribes of Israel and he determines to either convert them if they are a lost tribe, or make money from them if they are not. And, while they seem at first to have no conception of religion and to object to the traveller's own attempts to observe the Sabbath,[73] he eventually discovers that their houses of worship were the Musical Banks. Just as Erewhonians were perverse in the way they regarded morality and health – rebuking and punishing individuals for being ill or ugly and sympathising and pro- viding therapy to those with moral failings – so it was with religion and commerce. The Musical Banks were housed in the most impressive part of the metropolis, yet were nearly empty most of the time. The cashiers or priests dealt in a kind of money which everyone realised to be worthless but nevertheless pretended to value, especially those who wished to demonstrate their respectability. The true religion of the country was not that of the Musical Banks, but rather the worship of the goddess Ydgrun (possibly an anagram for [Mrs] Grundy, the proverbial small-minded moralist of Victorian fiction). Here she repre- sents the spirit of commerce, 'a beneficent and useful deity' as Butler describes her.[74] When the traveller finally leaves Erewhon, the traveller remains convinced of his missionary purpose and he proposes to return there and seek to convert them. In order to pay for the expedition, he suggests using a gunboat to capture as many as possible and proceed from there to Queensland, 'or indeed … any other Christian colony', and enslave the population.[75] He would make sure that 'our emigrants' were placed in the households of religious sugar growers who would alternate their duties in the plantations with bouts of religious instruc- tion. We can assume from this that Butler was not one of those who promoted missionaries as the most suitable moral guardians of native

---

[73] *Ibid.*, p. 74. 'They appeared to have little or no religious feeling, and to have never so much as heard of the divine institution of the Sabbath, so they ascribed my observ- ance of it to a fit of sulkiness.'
[74] *Ibid.*, p. 175.   [75] *Ibid.*, pp. 320–1.

people. He would discount their claims to act in the best interests of the Maori, or other indigenous people, and preferred to allow commercial colonisation to take its course. Most subsequent historians of New Zealanders would appear to agree with him.

Since at least the 1950s, historians in New Zealand have led a systematic attack on the significance of Wakefield's schemes of systematic emigration, and of religion and missions, in the settlement of New Zealand.[76] In this debunking, not only is it pointed out that the Wakefield schemes were only a minor part of the overall pattern of emigration to New Zealand, but that, even in Canterbury and Otago, the 'systematic' and religious aspects of these schemes barely survived the voyage to New Zealand. Although the Company's promotional literature advocated the scrupulous selection of emigrants, there is no indication that this was effective. Religion was applied as the thinnest veneer, if at all, to schemes which were invariably commercial in nature. As Butler made plain, the real religion of settler New Zealand was the pursuit of wealth. On the other hand, McLintock and his followers may perhaps have gone too far. *The Oxford Illustrated History of New Zealand* (1990), for example, has a single index entry on 'religion and the church' in a chapter on railways, which states: 'European settlers in New Zealand came from a culture where religion was in decline. Even the settlements where religion was to be the basis of the new society – Otago, Canterbury, Albertland – rapidly lost their religious characters.'[77] Having stated so much, it is curious that the author then goes on to provide evidence for the strength of traditional religious culture and Protestant revivalism throughout New Zealand, with evidence of intense religious feeling in diaries and letters of both Europeans and Maori Christians. Jeanine Graham presents a more even-handed view, concluding: 'Christian faith and practice played a fundamental role in the shaping of colonial society.'[78] She notes that, while Anglicans dominated the census returns, with more than twice the number of Presbyterians, and four times the number of Catholics, there was no established church and sectarian conflict was relatively uncommon.[79] Nevertheless, in certain places, as Séan Brosnahan has discussed, sectarianism was intense, especially in

---

[76] A. H. McLintock, 'History, Myths in New Zealand', in *Te Ara – The Encyclopedia of New Zealand*, ed. A. H. McLintock (1966).

[77] R. Dalziel, 'Railways and Relief Centres (1870–1890)', in *The Oxford Illustrated History of New Zealand*, ed. K. Sinclair (Auckland, 1990), p. 120.

[78] J. Graham, 'Settler Society', in *The Oxford History of New Zealand*, ed. G. W. Rice (Auckland, 1992), p. 129.

[79] A. McCarthy, *Irish Migrants in New Zealand, 1840–1937: 'The Desired Haven'* (Woodbridge, Suffolk, 2005), p. 5.

both Canterbury and Otago where religion continued to play a stronger role in public life, education and welfare than elsewhere.[80]

The Prairie West, 1880s

After the settlement of New Zealand, and the Australian and New Zealand gold rushes which succeeded it, the next great pulse of imperial emigration occurred in the Canadian North-West.[81] Once again, the churches were swept up in the movement of people. In 1872, the Canadian government acquired land in western Canada from the Hudson's Bay Company. The passage of Canada's Dominion Land Act (1872), and the signing of a series of numbered treaties with the majority of the First Nations,[82] initiated a huge campaign of emigration and settlement. The construction of the Canadian Pacific Railway ensured that the pace of colonisation accelerated to fever pitch as parties of colonists arrived in the western prairies. In the 1880s, there were a large number of attempts to create intentional ethnic, religious and secular utopian settlements in these regions.[83] Nevertheless, few of these schemes actually succeeded in placing significant numbers of settlers on the soil who could manage the harsh farming conditions. As the failures drifted south to the United States, the effective work of farming the prairie was taken up by emigrants from central and northern Europe, particularly from Sweden and the Ukraine, who had previous agricultural experience in land with similar environmental conditions. The reality of successful commercial farming by Slavs and Swedes was seen as an affront to British and imperial aspirations for the rising dominion of Canada.

In Britain, therefore, settlement schemes proliferated which sought to profit from the speculation bonanza and ensure that Canada retained its British character in the face of a flood of new arrivals from all parts

---

[80] S. G. Brosnahan, '"The Battle of the Borough" and the "Saige O Timaru": Sectarian Riot in Colonial Canterbury', *New Zealand Journal of History*, 28 (1994), pp. 41–59.

[81] M. Harper, 'Rhetoric and Reality: British Migration to Canada, 1867–1967', in *Canada and the British Empire*, ed. P. A. Buckner (Oxford, 2008), pp. 160–80, provides background and also notes (p. 165) that the emigration continued to be offset by transfer of the new arrivals to the United States.

[82] According to Brock Pitawanakwat, 'Aboriginal Treaty Rights', *Encyclopedia of Saskatchewan* (Regina: University of Regina and Canadian Plains Research Center, 2007), the major historical treaties were signed between 1874 and 1907 with the Cree, Assiniboine and Saulteaux in the south, the Dene to the north, and Nakota and Dakota on the Plains.

[83] Not an exhaustive list. For review, see C. A. Dawson, *Group Settlement: Ethnic Communities in Western Canada* (Toronto, 1936).

of Europe and Asia. Promoters assured British professional emigrants, including teachers as well as clergy, that they were performing a patriotic service by heading to the prairies.[84] Compared with systematic colonisation schemes in Australia and New Zealand, a feature that distinguished these later imperial schemes was the extent to which they were directed at single men with capital. In many cases, the appeal to the hunter, the sportsman, the gentleman and (it was hinted) the ne'er-do-well whose family found it convenient to despatch him to the colonies, was tied to an improbable vision of securing an aristocratic lifestyle on a landed estate for those whose ambitions had been frustrated at home.

For gentlemen migrants, Canada was represented as a manly frontier, but one in which care was taken to plant and nurture British institutions, including the churches. The promotional brochure for the Edgeley Estate, Qu'Appelle Valley, on land purchased in May 1882 from the Canadian Pacific Railway, quotes from the report of Professor Henry Tanner, who had visited the valley in 1883. Tanner urged the advantages of immigration to the Canadian North-West for 'sons of gentlemen' who found their profession overstocked and thought to try their hand at ranching. These sentiments were directed at anxious parents, who might be persuaded to bankroll their offspring in a colonial adventure: 'I would far sooner see my son a farmer, active on horseback, making a little money and becoming independent before he was thirty years of age, than sitting still in a lawyer's office at home.'[85] With a view to attracting the sporting gentleman, Tanner goes on to praise the 'excellent sport' to be had around the land available for settlement, including prairie chickens, partridges, plover, snipe and hares, as well as lakes abounding in birds and fish. Beyond, there were hills with large game: wapiti, moose, antelope and other kinds of deer, mountain sheep, bear and buffalo. At the same time, the civilities of religion and culture had not been forgotten, and Tanner reports cheerfully on the churches springing up, complete with clergy and congregations ready to welcome the respectable English newcomer.[86] As in the Canterbury colony, religion was incorporated into the promotional literature of the land speculators, without any real intention to secure an established church, or secure an exclusively denominational cast to the settlement.

[84] For these themes, see M. Harper, 'Settling in Saskatchewan: English Pioneers on the Prairies, 1878–1914', *British Journal of Canadian Studies*, 16 (2003), pp. 88–101.
[85] Henry Tanner, *Successful Emigration to Canada* (London, 1885), cited by R. Sykes, *Guide to the Qu'Appelle Valley, Assiniboia, Canada* (Manchester, 1885), p. 23.
[86] Tanner, *Successful Emigration*, cited by *ibid.*, p. 22.

Barr (Britannia) Colony

This scheme for the Qu'Appelle Valley was only a precursor to a more comprehensive attempt to people the Canadian North-West with an Anglican settlement, which would attempt to reproduce in the Canadian prairie the most desirable features of English religious life. The scheme was initiated by the Isaac M. Barr (1847?–1937), Anglican curate of Tollington Park who, with less than becoming modesty, gave it his own name.[87] Barr's prospectus made a direct appeal to British sentiment, asserting with patriotic directness: 'Let our cry be "CANADA FOR THE BRITISH".'[88] About 2,684 colonists responded to the call and departed for Canada on the *SS Lake Manitoba* on 31 March 1903. Local reports encouragingly reported that a good proportion of the colonists were agriculturalists and, although the party included some sons of clergymen, they had all been 'hardened by cricket and football in the public schools for a life of outdoor labor'.[89]

The British theme was sustained when the Reverend George Exton Lloyd, later Anglican bishop of Saskatchewan (1922–31), displaced Barr as leader of the settlement, renaming it 'Britannia'.[90] As bishop, Lloyd would later stress the need to promote British emigration to Canada as a counterbalance to the 'alarming number of European undesirables' who were taking up land in the prairies. In a talk originally presented to the Orange Lodge, he contrasted the 'mongrel' character of the emerging Canadian population with the pure British character of colonies such as New Zealand.[91] Leading the call for a restrictive immigration policy with quotas on all races other than the British, he concludes: 'We want to be British in blood, language, laws, ideals, instincts and loyalties,

[87] I. M. Barr, *British Settlements in North Western Canada on Free Grant Lands* (London, 1902). For accounts of the colony, see L. Bowen, *Muddling Through: The Remarkable Story of the Barr Colonists* (Vancouver, 1992); J. H. MacCormick, *Lloydminster; or, 5,000 Miles with the Barr Colonists* (London, 1924); H. Pick, *Next Year. A Semi-Historical Account of the Exploits and Exploitations of the Far-Famed Barr Colonists* (Toronto, 1928); C. Wetton, *The Promised Land: The Story of the Barr Colonists* (Lloydminster, Saskatchewan, 1953).
[88] Cited by A. W. Rasporich, 'Utopian Ideals and Community Settlements in Western Canada, 1880–1914', in *The Prairie West*, ed. R. D. Francis and H. Palmer (Calgary, 2007), pp. 114–29.
[89] *Daily Phoenix*, 10 April 1902, p. 1. Transcribed at http://library2.usask.ca/sni/stories/beg9.html.
[90] Barr is usually said to have mismanaged the expedition. For the alternative view that Lloyd engineered Barr's resignation, see A. L. Hayes, *Anglicans in Canada: Controversies and Identity in Historical Perspective* (Chicago, 2004), p. 23.
[91] G. E. Lloyd, *The Building of the Nation: Natural Increase or Immigration: A Paper Read before the Grand Orange Lodge of British America at Edmonton, Alberta, July 26th, 1928* (Prince Albert, Saskatchewan, 1928), p. 7.

and to this end I bespeak the help of every true Orangeman. God Save the King.'[92] It is possibly significant that he omits to mention 'religion' in this list of aspirations. However, Lloyd had other ways to build the Anglican character of British Canada.

By linking their fortunes to the Church of England, the commercial speculators behind the Britannia Colony acquired powerful allies who shared their imperial vision of an Anglican utopia on the prairie. Henry Hutchinson Montgomery, the Secretary of the SPG, was touched by the challenge of rapid Canadian expansion and excited by the prospect it opened up. He visited Canada and wrote up his experiences in a book that promoted the Canadian North-West and its need for Anglican clergy and resources using the language of empire and the cultural mission of the British race. In the words of the bishop of Saskatchewan, who is quoted by Montgomery: 'The time past has been sufficient to have neglected Canada. Here in this new Empire of white men springing up upon the prairie we must haste to their aid.'[93] An additional factor focusing the mind of the Secretary of the SPG was rivalry with the Colonial and Continental Church Society. When Montgomery arrived in Canada, he found that the Secretary of the CCCS was already on the ground. They agreed that a mutual campaign, employing the resources of both colonial missionary societies, was called for.[94]

The Canadian Catechists' Mission to Saskatchewan, also known as the English Church Railway Mission, would be the last major project conducted by any colonial missionary society in a settler colony. According to Hayes, this would be the 'finest chapter in the Canadian history' of the CCCS.[95] A massive effort was made to raise the funds necessary to support the chosen catechists in the field and outfit them for a travelling mission that would follow the railway and plant preaching stations and churches along the route taken by the new settlers. The catechists' equipment included a buggy designed to roll along the corridor created for the coming railway while the young men slept in tents surrounded by their modest kit. The SPG and the CCCS appealed for at least £20,000, later raised to £30,000, to support training and outfit for catechists and funds to build churches. For personnel, Montgomery's main recruiting ground was the public schools where families were supportive of imperial ideals and had the funds to support one of their sons on a 'gap year', to use a modern term, before training for a profession.

[92] *Ibid.*, p. 29.

[93] H. H. Montgomery, *The Church on the Prairie* (London, 1908), p. 14. Presumably, this was Jervois Arthur Newnham, bishop of Saskatchewan, 1903–21. George Exton Lloyd succeeded Newnham from 1922 to 1931.

[94] *Ibid.*, p. 2.   [95] Hayes, *Anglicans in Canada*, p. 23.

On 18 April 1908, Montgomery presided over a service of dismissal in Lambeth parish church for the young men chosen to go out to Canada. The archbishop of Canterbury spoke at the conclusion of the service. Like Selwyn's lectures for young men thinking of a clerical career in the colonies, the Canadian catechists were inducted into the colonial mission of the imperial church, with its responsibilities and trials.[96]

As an exercise in the rapid deployment of a religious work force, the Catechists' Mission was a remarkable success. It was a military operation for the delivery of spiritual goods to which General Booth would have given his approval. However, it was also a temporary expedient which ultimately failed to secure more than a foothold for the Church of England in the prairie landscape. It also came at the cost, not acknowledged by Lloyd and his successors, of the CMS mission to the native people of Saskatchewan. It seems to have been Lloyd who attempted to evict the native catechists from 'Emmanuel College' and replace them with the newly arrived catechists supplied by the English church.[97] While settlers and their bishops averted their eyes, missionaries protested at the forced removal of their people under the direction of the Minister for the Interior and the Indian Department of Ottawa. In any event, the Anglican Britannia Colony and the Catechists' Mission would prove to be small gestures against the prevailing tide, which was running away from the Englishness of the episcopalian tradition and towards greater cultural diversity. When compared with the cultural impact of the Canterbury settlement in New Zealand, both the colony and the Catechists' Mission made little impact on the overall ethnic and religious profile of Saskatchewan, let alone that of Canada as a whole.

Conclusion

With the settlement of the Barr Colony, we come effectively to the final days of the colonial missionary movement. Although the work of the colonial missionary societies continued well into the twentieth century, the mass migration of the British people had achieved its original purpose, and both colonies and the colonial churches had become self-governing. Colonial missions continued, but only at the margins of the fully settled colonial empire, which was itself breaking apart into separate nations. The churches, like all other imperial institutions, were swept up in this movement. In the case of Sierra Leone, what began as

---

[96] See Chapter 3.   [97] Montgomery, *Church on the Prairie*, p. 50.

a humanitarian gesture, was also significant as an attempt to create a homeland for former slaves who had served the British empire loyally in the American revolutionary war.

The main difficulty in assessing the role of religious colonisation in New Zealand is that so much of our evidence comes from the highly problematic sources produced by missionaries or commercial proponents of settlement, and historians have quite rightly been highly sceptical about accepting any of it at face value. James Belich is just the most authoritative of the modern commentators who have stressed that it was not God alone who promoted the conversion of the Maori, but the combined forces of money, land and treaties.[98] By 1852, George Grey (whom Belich calls 'the wizard of Aotearoa'[99]) claimed that Maori and Europeans were united as 'one people', who followed the same economic and cultural activities, professed the same Christian faith, and followed the same laws.[100] The irony here is that, as settlers flooded into New Zealand, the Maori were soon to break out in the Taranaki War (1860–1). Physical violence between Maoris and settlers was matched by a war of words between bishop Selwyn and the Anglicans in the Church party who supported the Maori, and the settlers, especially Methodists and other Nonconformists, who derided their intervention in a secular cause. In these violent and divisive circumstances, the religious utopianism that had given birth to both the Dunedin and the Canterbury settlements seemed increasingly irrelevant to the contested realities of British colonisation.

Despite their undoubted idealism, the church colonies in New Zealand were not philanthropic or religious experiments but commercial ventures. In both the Free Church settlement of Otago and the Anglican settlement of Canterbury, it is evident that religion and commerce made for an unhappy mixture. Religious idealists, such as Lyttelton found the colony he had founded with such high hopes to be something of a disappointment. Harsher critics, such as Butler, found it a prime target for satire. New Zealand historians have been debating ever since about the significance of religion to the overall history of New Zealand settlement. In the Britannia Colony, the commercial element – and the inevitable spiritual discount on the ideals of its settlers – is even more marked. In the latter case, religion served not simply to promote a commercial scheme but was also deployed by Bishop Lloyd to argue for a racially and religiously exclusive settlement of Canada. With

---

[98] Belich, *Making Peoples*, p. 213.   [99] *Ibid.*, p. 190.
[100] Grey, cited by *ibid.*, pp. 212–13.

the possible exception of Sierra Leone, all cases of Christian colonisation in Greater Britain were achieved only with the eradication of the native population who had previously occupied British lands. While the Anglican and Presbyterian colonists did not engage directly in the displacement of the indigenous population, their presence ensured that it would be permanent.

Conclusion

With the planting of the Barr Colony, we come to the end of the colonial missionary movement, or as much of it as can reasonably be covered in a single book. Over the course of a century, the various churches and their colonial missionary societies sent out their pioneers, planted churches, squabbled with their rivals on the frontier and – finally – settled into the landscape. As national churches emerged in place of the colonial seedlings, the emigrant clergy who had spearheaded the movement began to do two things: they organised imperial congresses that would help to celebrate their achievements to the empire, and they wrote up their memoirs.

As the colonial churches were filled slowly with personnel, the bishops and higher clergy were constantly on the move between colony and metropole. Some journeys were professional requirements, such as that which compelled Catholic archbishops who functioned as metropolitan (leading bishop) of a province to return to Rome for consultation within a year of their consecration. From 1867, Anglican bishops returned to London for the Lambeth conferences. However, in the last decade of the nineteenth century – the heyday of imperialism – all the churches began to meet in great ecumenical gatherings that drew their representatives back to Britain from outposts and colonial cities around the world. For the British churches, these were effectively imperial meetings of the settler churches, since their membership was dominated by British, American and colonial delegates. The first Protestants to meet in this way were members of the World Evangelical Alliance, who gathered in Liverpool in 1845 and at irregular intervals in Europe and the United States thereafter. Churches came to Britain to discuss their institutional affairs for the same reason that other imperial organisations were drawn there: London, the wealthiest, most populous and imperious city in Europe, provided opportunities for pageantry, propaganda and celebration that were available nowhere else. Missionary conferences in the high Victorian age, as Cox points out,[1] were occasions on

---

[1] Cox, *British Missionary Enterprise*, p. 173.

which missionary elites could meet and compare notes. However, this ignores their other vital function, namely, to reinforce the connection of the colonial churches and societies to the imperial metropole, and to celebrate their emergence as world churches which had grown beyond their British and colonial roots.

Change was most evident for the Nonconformists. Baptists, Methodists and Congregationalists had expanded so vigorously in America that its British churches were beggars at the ecumenical table. Baptists were among the most proudly British of the colonial churches; however, they were transformed by their expansion in both America and the colonies, especially by the emergence of the Black Baptist churches which make a striking feature of the first Baptist World Congress, held in 1905. Although the Congress was overwhelmingly dominated by English-speaking delegates from England and America, it was noted, with naïve paternalism, that 'the picturesque element was supplied by the negro brethren, of whom about fifty were present, and who were cheered and seen everywhere'. John Clifford, whose aspirations for Anglo-Saxon union and God's Greater Britain we encountered in the first pages of this book, was a notable figure at the Baptist World Congress. Clearly, there was an even more glorious union to be hoped for which would include all races of men.

Methodist meetings were split equally between the American delegates and the British, and there was an interesting debate about where the Canadians should be placed. The first Oecumenical Methodist Conference was held in London in the newly restored City Road Chapel in September 1881.[2] It was a considerable gathering for its time: 400 delegates representing 4.8 million members and 28 Methodist churches met together over a single day, 7 September 1881. This was too brief a time for delegates, mostly senior leaders of their churches, to obtain more than a brief impression of each other; only those who felt comfortable speaking in English had much of a voice. Perhaps this was just as well, given the extensive divisions between black and white Methodists in the United States and in southern Africa, and between American and British Methodists on many issues.

By way of contrast with Nonconformists, Anglicans have remained intimately associated with the territorial expansion of Greater Britain, though only in New Zealand, Australia and South Africa did bishops and their flocks achieve in any measure the authority and numbers of the home church in England. Presbyterianism, another established

[2] Methodist, *Proceedings of the Oecumenical Methodist Conference, Held in City Road Chapel, London, September, 1881* (London, 1881).

church in Great Britain, also did rather better in Greater Britain than in America, especially in Canada and New Zealand; however, it also gained from its older links with northern European Protestantism. Finally, the expansion of Catholicism in the British empire reflects the dramatic widening of opportunities made possible by the liberal reforms of the mid-nineteenth century in Britain, as well as the success of the expansionist papacy of Pius IX and his successors. The internationalism of both Catholicism and Reformed Protestantism is reflected in the way they ran their congresses.

For the mission world, the 1890s was a decade of commemorations as first the Baptists, then the LMS and the CMS, celebrated centenaries; there were bicentenaries for the SPCK and the SPG. These older Anglican missionary conferences were held separately from the meetings of the other missionary bodies which had met for the first time in Liverpool in 1860. The Conference on World Missions had attracted 126 delegates, but it was dwarfed by the vast Centenary Conference on World Missions, which met in London in 1888 and attracted 1,600 delegates. The meeting which succeeded it, held in New York from 21 April to 1 May, was even grander: 200,000 attended the sessions which attracted 500 speakers.[3] The last decade of the nineteenth century was also a time for anniversaries and memorials in the colonies. In Australia, the sense of a turning point, of colonies and churches coming of age, was marked by a series of jubilees. The Melbourne diocese chose to recognise 1897 as a fiftieth jubilee of the consecration of bishop Perry, the first bishop of Victoria (1847), with the happy circumstance that this coincided with the Queen's Diamond Jubilee. These anniversaries were celebrated both in Britain and in her settler colonies where they became occasions to mark the advance of the colonial churches within the independent colonial democracies of Greater Britain.

The bicentenary of the SPG was celebrated in services that commenced on 16 June 1900, the 199th anniversary of the granting of the Society's charter by William III, and continued throughout the year. Pascoe notes that the final event of the Jubilee, a special service for children, was rather thinly attended. The main body of the Anglican communion participated with much more enthusiasm in what was arguably the largest and most important of all missionary conferences and church congresses of this era, the Pan-Anglican Congress of 1908.[4]

---

[3] W. R. Hogg, 'Conferences, World Missionary', in *Concise Dictionary of the Christian World Mission*, ed. S. Neill, G. H. Anderson and J. Goodwin (London, 1970).

[4] R. S. Bosher, 'The Pan-Anglican Congress of 1908', *Historical Magazine of the Protestant Episcopal Church* (June 1955), pp. 126–42.

Nevertheless, unlike the 100th anniversary of the World Missionary Congress held in Edinburgh in 1910 which was commemorated with considerable enthusiasm in 2010, the centenary of the Pan-Anglican Congress has come and gone with hardly an historical ripple. What this signifies is the extent to which the colonial missionary movement, of which it was arguably the high point, has withered away. The strength and cohesion of that movement, especially for the Church of England, has been the major theme of this book. However, the empire was not a totalitarian structure for the churches, but rather a vehicle that made their expansion possible in ways undreamt of by their founders. The proceedings of the world meetings of these very different bodies provides a fair indication of the extent to which most churches, from their British origins, succeeded in escaping their bonds to become something other than imperial dependencies. As the churches ceased to be English, Irish, Scottish or even 'British' in character and, instead, became nationalised and internationalised, their value as signifiers of imperial identity changed. This is remarkable enough since, as we have seen, almost all the colonial missionary societies made use of religious nationalism and the language of imperialism in order to raise funds and promote the colonial expansion of their separate churches. The disjunction between the means of achieving this expansion, and their contemporary standing detached from their imperial origins, may explain why the colonial missionary movement has not been remembered in the same way as the foreign missionary movement. In the twentieth century, all the British churches would become detached from both their national origins, and their transitory connection with the British World, and become part of world Christianities, putting aside their imperial past as rapidly as possible.[5]

Memoirs

With the congresses, also came the colonial clergy memoirs. Like the Pan-Anglican Congress of 1908, an event which has generally been seen to look back to imperial Anglicanism rather than forward to the ecumenical movement, many of these have become dated and lost their audience. There are probably thousands of book-length accounts of lives given in service to the colonial churches, and they arise in connection with every congregation. This account will concentrate on Australian clerical memoirs, many of which come from the unique collection

[5] For the many changes this involved, see H. McLeod, ed., *World Christianities c.1914–c.2000* (Cambridge, 2006).

donated to Mitchell Library in New South Wales by the bibliophile David Scott Mitchell (1836–1907).

Biographical writing was the mainstay of all the missionary journals and this heroic style formed a template for life-writing by retired missionary clergy, who continued the tradition of writing for the combined audience of potential contributors to missionary projects, and potential future missionaries. More recently, this writing has been recycled to meet the needs of the contemporary theological training schools. One account of colonial missionaries in Australia, written by the Deputy Principal of the Theological Hall in Melbourne, was prepared for the frankly stated purpose of providing models for current candidates for the ministry of pastoral work from the past.[6] A similar motivation seems to be behind the publication of Robert Withycombe's two collections of excerpts from the 'Occasional Papers' of St Augustine's College, Canterbury.[7] The need for compilations of this kind began quite early,[8] and led to some heroic work of amateur prosopography. The Catholic clergy were remembered in similar style through the researches of Southerwood.[9] The self-promotional quality of this literature explains why most were either self-published or distributed with a local, or internal church, audience in mind.

In biographies and memoirs, colonial clergy celebrated their lives and countered the slur that they were second-raters, without the education or cultivation of the home-grown product. Between hard covers they were reborn as apostles and martyrs, pioneers and church planters, founding fathers and bush parsons. The earliest published memoirs were as much emigration manuals as memoirs in the usual sense.[10] The SPCK published a collection of these under the title, *The Emigrant and the Heathen*.[11] This volume included the Reverend R. G. Boodle's account of his ministry in the Hunter Valley region of New South Wales, the Reverend R. J. Dundas on mission work in British Columbia, and shorter accounts of pastoral and mission work in New Zealand, Guiana, India and Burma, possibly with an eye to those who

---

[6] G. Griffin, *They Came to Care: Pastoral Ministry in Colonial Australia* (Melbourne, 1993).

[7] Withycombe, *Occasional Papers*; R. S. M. Withycombe, ed., *Anglican Ministry in Colonial Australia: Some Early Letters* (Canberra, 1993).

[8] For example, Christmas, ed., *Emigrant Churchman in Canada*. For a later collection, see *Illustrated Biographical Sketches, Memoirs Reprinted from the Catholic Home Annual and Directory of Australasia for 1892* (Sydney, 1892).

[9] W. T. Southerwood, *A Prayer-Calendar of Deceased Priests in Australia, 1788–1988* (Georgetown, Tasmania, 1988).

[10] See, for example, H. Hussey, *More Than Half a Century of Colonial Life and Christian Experience* (Adelaide, 1978).

[11] Halcombe, ed., *The Emigrant and the Heathen*.

were considering a range of possible destinations for their own missionary careers. Like all pioneers, Boodle stressed the virgin nature of
the territory he came to cultivate. Only twenty-seven years before the
arrival of Bishop Tyrrell, he wrote, the neighbourhood showed 'no sign
of civilisation': 'Not a human habitation had been built; not a spade, or
plough, or implement, however rough, had ever broken the surface of
the forest-covered ground. Not a herb, or tree, or seed, had ever been
grown, which did not spring of itself.'[12] Other memoirs described the
moral depravity of the conditions of early settlers, which their presence
helped to mollify. Colin Arrott Browning (1791–1858), a pious layman
and ship's surgeon, wrote of the dramatic conversions of convict passengers as a result of his religious instruction to them on a voyage to
Australia.[13] John Cowley Coles gives an account of his emigration to
Australia in 1843, and evangelisation among the Victorian gold dig-
gers for the Wesleyan Methodist Church in 1865.[14] The memoirs of
William Ullathorne, later Catholic archbishop of Birmingham, include
a trenchant denunciation of the convict system.[15]

Later, the lives of church-builders and pioneering chaplains were
remembered, especially those who were first in the field. John Medley
(1804–92), the Tractarian banished to the colonies as first bishop of
Fredericton, is honoured as the 'Apostle of the Wilderness' in a modern
biography.[16] While his memory was still fresh, the second colonial chaplain in New South Wales, Samuel Marsden, was hailed as the 'apostle
to the Maori'.[17] Charlotte M. Yonge, the high church Anglican novelist,
included a chapter on Marsden in her collection of missionary biographies: Marsden was the 'Australian Chaplain and Friend of the Maori',
and he enjoys elevated company along with John Eliot ('the Apostle
of the Red Indians'), David Brainerd ('the Enthusiast'), Christian
Friedrich Schwartz ('the Councillor of Tanjore'), Henry Martyn ('the
Scholar-Missionary'), John Williams ('the Martyr of Erromango'),
Allen Gardiner ('the Sailor Martyr') and Charles Frederick MacKenzie
('the Martyr of the Zambesi'). Later scholars have been less kind to

---

[12] R. G. Boodle, 'Recollections of Ministerial Work in New South Wales', in *The
Emigrant and the Heathen*, ed. J. J. Halcombe (London, 1874), p. 8.
[13] C. A. Browning, *The Convict Ship and England's Exiles*, 5th ed. (n.p., 1851).
[14] J. C. Coles, *The Life and Christian Experience of John Cowley Coles* (Melbourne,
1893).
[15] W. B. Ullathorne, *From Cabin-Boy to Archbishop: The Autobiography of Archbishop
Ullathorne* (London, 1941).
[16] B. L. Craig, *Apostle to the Wilderness: Bishop John Medley and the Evolution of the
Anglican Church* (2005).
[17] C. M. Yonge, *Pioneers and Founders or Recent Workers in the Mission Field* (London,
1884).

Marsden, deriding him as the 'flogging parson'.[18] William Cowper lived to a great age, and his memoirs were written only at the end of it; but they are an important source for the Evangelical foundations of the Church of England in New South Wales.[19]

Almost every colonial bishop was treated to a biography in heroic mode, so we can only take a representative sampling of the genre here. Bishops were especially admired for their role in touring the bounds of their dioceses, mapping out the territory of a new spiritual colony for the home church. Boodle, whose own memoirs have already been mentioned (they were originally serialised in the (Anglican) *Parish Magazine*),[20] wrote up the life of William Tyrrell, the first bishop of Newcastle in this style.[21] Like many a pioneering churchman, Tyrrell was defined by his riding: long, hard and often, 'an excellent horseman he became, however little he had ridden in England'.[22] In the absence of the railway, few men spent longer in the saddle than a colonial bishop. George Alfred St Clair Donaldson (1863–1935), Anglican bishop of Brisbane, extolled the pleasures of episcopal visitation to remote stations in the outback, declaring that '[t]he whole tour was to me one long picnic'.[23] The bush itself, with its endless isolation, he saw as a pastoral challenge and without romance.

There are isolated families; the boundary-riders; the rabbit-fence men; the swagmen. How can we reach them? What can we do to relieve the soul-destroying monotony and loneliness of their lives?[24]

By this stage, the bishop and his clergy were already making the transition from emigrants and pioneers to identification with the colonial church.

Anglican clergy might also be represented as British imperialists, whose religious calling was seen to be synonymous with that of the extension of the Anglo-Saxon race. For this last category of

---

[18] A. M. Grocott, *Convicts, Clergymen and Churches: Attitudes of Convicts and Ex-Convicts Towards the Churches and Clergy in New South Wales from 1788–1851* (Sydney, 1980), p. 233.

[19] Cowper, *The Autobiography and Reminiscences of William Macquarie Cowper, Dean of Sydney*.

[20] Boodle, 'Recollections'.

[21] R. G. Boodle, *The Life and Labours of the Right Reverend William Tyrrell, DD, First Bishop of Newcastle, New South Wales* (London, 1881); R. G. Boodle, 'Ministerial Recollections', *Parish Magazine* (1870).

[22] Boodle, *Life and Labours*, p. 47.

[23] St Clair Donaldson, in *Brisbane Church Chronicle*, cited by Batty in C. T. Dimont and F. de W. Batty, *St Clair Donaldson, Archbishop of Brisbane, 1904–1921; Bishop of Salisbury, 1921–1935* (London, 1939), p. 48.

[24] St Clair Donaldson, in *Brisbane Church Chronicle*, cited by Batty in *ibid.*, p. 49.

memorialist, the clergyman was a nation-builder as much as a builder of churches. Archdeacon F. B. Boyce wrote his memoirs late in life and in the aftermath of the First World War, but he represents an earlier age, one in which the work of the Church was seen as intimately involved in the development of the nation. In his first ecclesiastical appointment, he remembers riding in the dark towards the outback town of Bourke, failing to find a track that led to a homestead. 'I had constantly to stop and get off and strike a match down close to the road to see whether I was still upon it.'[25] From this experience, Boyce came eventually to be one of the major advocates of Empire Day in Australia. In more secular, anti-imperial literature, the bush parson formed part of an anti-clerical stereotype. The term was used by the Australian poet, Henry Lawson, for a character called 'Stiffner', proprietor of a New Zealand pub: 'He'd been a spieler, fighting man, bush parson, temperance preacher, and a policeman, and a commercial traveller, and everything else that was damnable.'[26] Nevertheless, for many others it was a term that was earned and worn with pride. The 'Bush Brothers' was the bold designation for the Anglican brotherhoods who took up service in remote parts of inland Australia in the last decades of the colonial missionary movement.[27] In 1899, the Methodist writer, G. Warren Payne, possibly in reaction to Lawson's denigration of the colonial parson, wrote a novel, *The Backblock's Parson*, which celebrates the 'wild free life of bush and plain' of the itinerant Methodist preacher.[28] Written under the pseudonym 'Tom Bluegum', this was a rollicking bush adventure, complete with hard riding, encounters with bushrangers and a parson hero who first rescues and then marries his lady love in the outback.

Clerical memoirs of all these kinds fulfilled a number of functions. They justified the life of the person who wrote them, and they provided an account of experiences which might be useful in attracting new recruits to the colonial frontier. They were also reminders to the imperial reading public that clergy, like other emigrants, were agents

---

[25] F. B. Boyce, *Fourscore Years and Seven: The Memoirs of Archdeacon Boyce, for over Sixty Years a Clergyman of the Church of England in New South Wales* (Sydney, 1934), pp. 30–1.

[26] Henry Lawson, 'Stiffner and Jim', in H. Lawson, *While the Billy Boils* (Sydney, 1896).

[27] Brotherhood of the Good Shepherd, *The Brotherhood of the Good Shepherd: A Church of England Mission in the Diocese of Bathurst* (Dubbo, New South Wales, 1913); C. H. S. Mathews, *A Parson in the Australian Bush* (London, 1908). For another 'bush parson', see J. W. Eisdell, *Back Country: Or the Cheerful Adventures of a Bush Parson in the Eighties* (London, 1936).

[28] T. Bluegum, *The Backblocks' Parson: A Story of Australian Life* (London, 1899), p. 10.

of empire and creators of new nations. To adapt a scriptural metaphor, they had helped to build God's empire; now, like Simeon (Luke 2: 30), having seen the light of salvation, they might depart in peace.

In the Victorian age, religious writers enjoyed deploying grand phrases to evoke sweeping visions of an empire united in Christ, generally under their own denominational direction. Yet, if this book has a single theme, it is about how Christian churches shook themselves free of the constitutional and cultural restrictions which had constrained their adherents in the United Kingdom; in the British world, God's empire was a house of many spiritual mansions, and was characterised by the variety and vigour of its competing religious forces. So I prefer not to end this book with an overly neat synthesis, which glosses over the complexity and difference which was characteristic of the colonial missionary movement and religious colonisation in the empire. However, I would like to suggest several themes that might profitably be pursued in future studies.

The first of these is the role of women in the colonial missionary movement. In this account, I have mentioned only one woman, Caroline Chisholm, in any detail, and I have referred briefly to the strategic importance of the women's auxiliary of the Colonial Committee of the Free Church of Scotland to the success of its colonial ventures. Yet, from other missionary studies, we know that women made up a significant proportion of those who worked as lay teachers and agents on foreign mission fields; they also dominated the auxiliaries that funded missionary work 'at home'. I suspect that the same was true for women and colonial missions. Hence, while I have had something to say about colonial missionary societies and the colonial ministry, including the training and despatch of Catholic and Anglican priests in England and Ireland, much more needs to be said about the role of women and men from the laity and the religious orders. By staffing schools, hospitals and other religious institutions across the empire, they made its explosive growth possible.

The second important work that needs to be done will involve a deeper study of archival records than has been possible within the constraints of this book. The candidates' records of the SPG, and – where they have survived – the papers and correspondence of colonial missionaries who applied to other societies, will repay full-length analysis. Another important body of archives which await future researchers are those of the colonial clergy who made applications to the archbishops of Canterbury and York for licences to work in English dioceses of the Church of England. Analysis of these records of individuals would help give a more human – and more spiritually idealistic – face to the colonial missionary movement than is reflected in official publications.

Thirdly, I am strongly aware that the story in this book has been told almost entirely from the point of view of the Christian churches in Britain, and has leaned heavily on their published proceedings and journals. However, for every letter sent from 'home', a recipient in the colonies was deeply engaged in its reception and execution. Local studies of the imperial connection, which should include the colonial church journals which reported, from a colonial point of view, on the development of the churches, would add new volumes to this initial study, filling the space between colonial missions and national churches.

Finally, there is much more that needs to be said about the impact of empire on the churches in the post-colonial age. The timeframe of this book covers the nineteenth century, somewhat extended to include the festival season of anniversaries, congresses and commemorations, which continued until the 1908 Pan-Anglican Congress – an event which requires a book of its own to do it justice – and the 1910 Edinburgh Missionary Congress. However, in many ways the imperial connection lingered on well into the twentieth century and, indeed, has not entirely faded, especially for Anglicans and Presbyterians, adherents of Britain's two formerly established national churches. Yet, the Christian churches of the settler empire were, eventually, both nationalised and internationalised. In the former colonies, they acquired organisations and religious characteristics that increasingly owed less to empire and more to the rising nations, with their independent legislatures and constitutions, into which they had been planted. In the process they looked to the world and not back to Britain for religious union. The collapse of the Nonconformist identity, which owed its existence to the constitutional relationship of some Protestant churches to the British state, and its evolution beyond the empire to the international evangelicalism of today, is one reflection of this. The Catholic Church, which in its British form was dominated by Ireland and an English elite, was internationalised in its turn by twentieth-century emigration in the former colonies. In all the settler churches, these processes led to the fading of the imperial religious connection that has been traced in *God's Empire*.

Bibliography

This bibliography covers archival and printed sources. For periodical literature, there is a comprehensive listing provided by the online Missionary Periodicals Database hosted by the Yale University Divinity School Library at http://divdl. library.yale.edu/missionperiodicals/.

ARCHIVAL COLLECTIONS

CAMBRIDGE, CAMBRIDGE UNIVERSITY LIBRARY

Royal Commonwealth Society Collection.
Society for Promoting Christian Knowledge Collection.

DUBLIN, CATHOLIC DIOCESAN ARCHIVES, DRUMCONDRA

Daniel Murray Papers.
Paul Cullen Papers.

EDINBURGH, NATIONAL ARCHIVES OF SCOTLAND

Church of Scotland, Colonial Committee.
Free Church of Scotland, Colonial Committee.
Society in Scotland for Propagating Christian Knowledge (SSPCK) Papers.

HOBART, ARCHIVES OFFICE OF TASMANIA

Bishop Montgomery Papers.

LONDON, GUILDHALL LIBRARY

Intercontinental Church Society [Colonial and Continental Church Society].

LONDON, LAMBETH PALACE

Davidson Papers.
Montgomery Papers.

LONDON, SCHOOL OF ORIENTAL AND AFRICAN STUDIES

Council for World Mission [Colonial Missionary Society].
Wesleyan Methodist Missionary Society.

OXFORD, BODLEIAN LIBRARY (RHODES HOUSE)

Society for the Propagation of the Gospel.

ROME, PONTIFICAL IRISH COLLEGE

Cullen Papers [online].

SYDNEY, STATE LIBRARY OF NEW SOUTH WALES

Mitchell Collection.
Methodist Church of Australasia.

AUSTRALIAN JOINT COPYING PROJECT MICROFILM

All Hallows College, Dublin.
Church of Scotland.
Commonwealth and Continental Church Society.
Free Church of Scotland.
Methodist Missionary Society.
United Society for the Propagation of the Gospel.

YORK, BORTHWICK INSTITUTE

Applications for Licences under the Colonial Clergy Act.

PRINTED SOURCES

Addleshaw, G. W. O., 'The Law and Constitution of the Church Overseas', in
    Morgan, E. R. and R. Lloyd, eds., *The Mission of the Anglican Communion*
    (London, 1948), pp. 74–98.
Aikman, J. L., *Cyclopædia of Christian Missions: Their Rise, Progress, and Present
    Position* (London and Glasgow, 1860).
All Hallows Missionary College Drumcondra [Dublin], *First Annual Report,
    1849* (Dublin, 1849). *Annual Report, 1850* (Dublin, 1850).
Allan, D., 'Protestantism, Presbyterianism and National Identity in
    Eighteenth-Century Scottish History', in Claydon, T. and I. I. McBride,
    eds., *Protestantism and National Identity: Britain and Ireland, c.1650–c.1850*
    (Cambridge, 1998), pp. 182–205.
Allen, R. B., *Slaves, Freedmen, and Indentured Laborers in Colonial Mauritius*
    (Cambridge, 1999).
Almanach du Clergé de France (Paris, 1835).

Anderson, B., *Imagined Communities: Reflections on the Origin and Spread of Nationalism* (London, 1991).

Anderson, G. H., *Biographical Dictionary of Christian Missions* (Grand Rapids, MI, 1999).

Anderson, J. S. M., *The History of the Church of England in the Colonies and Foreign Dependencies of the British Empire* (London, 1856).

Arnold, T., 'The Church and the State', in Stanley, A. P., ed., *The Miscellaneous Works of Thomas Arnold* (London, 1845), pp. 466–75.

'National Church Establishments', in Stanley, A. P., ed., *The Miscellaneous Works of Thomas Arnold* (London, 1845), pp. 486–92.

Aspinwall, B., 'Scots and Irish Clergy Ministering to Immigrants, 1830–1878', *Innes Review*, **47** (1996), pp. 45–68.

Aubert, R., *The Church in a Secularized Society*, vol. V (London, 1978).

Bailey, H., *Twenty Five Years at St Augustine's College: A Letter to Late Students* (Canterbury, 1873).

Baird, R., *The Christian Retrospect and Register: A Summary of the Scientific, Moral and Religious Progress of the First Half of the Nineteenth Century* (New York, 1851).

Baker, D. W. A., *Preacher, Politician, Patriot: A Life of John Dunmore Lang* (Melbourne, 1998).

Ballantyne, T., 'Religion, Difference and the Limits of British Imperial History', *Victorian Studies*, **47** (2005), pp. 427–55.

Ballhatchet, K., 'The East India Company and Roman Catholic Missionaries', *Journal of Ecclesiastical History*, **42** (1993), pp. 273–88.

Baptist, *The Baptist World Congress. London, July 11–19, 1905* (London, 1905).

Barclay, I. C., 'Chaplaincies, Military', in Cameron, N. M. D. S., ed., *Dictionary of Scottish Church History and Theology* (Edinburgh, 1993), pp. 162–3.

Barr, C., '"Imperium in Imperio": Irish Episcopal Imperialism in the Nineteenth Century', *English Historical Review*, **123** (2008), pp. 611–50.

Paul Cullen, John Henry Newman and the Catholic University of Ireland, 1845–65 (Leominster, 2003).

Barr, I. M., *British Settlements in North Western Canada on Free Grant Lands* (London, 1902).

Barr, J., *The Old Identities* (Dunedin, 1879).

Barry, A., 'The Function of the Colonial Churches in Our Missionary Expansion', *The East and the West: A Quarterly Review for the Study of Missions*, **1** (1903), pp. 182–94.

Bartolomé de las Casas, *A Short Account of the Destruction of the Indies* (Harmondsworth, 1992).

Bateman, F., 'Ireland's Spiritual Empire', in Carey, H. M., ed., *Empires of Religion* (Basingstoke, 2008), pp. 267–87.

Bayly, C. A., 'The Second British Empire', in Winks, R. W. and A. M. Low, eds., *The Oxford History of the British Empire*, vol. 5, *Historiography* (Oxford, 1999), pp. 54–72.

Bebbington, D., K. Dix and A. Ruston, eds., *Protestant Nonconformist Texts*, vol. 3, *The Nineteenth Century* (Aldershot, 2006).

Bebbington, D. W., *The Nonconformist Conscience: Chapel and Politics, 1870–1914* (London, 1982).

Evangelicalism in Modern Britain: A History from the 1730's to the 1980's (London, 1989).

Belich, J., *The New Zealand Wars and the Victorian Interpretation of Racial Conflict* (Auckland, 1986).

Making Peoples: A History of the New Zealanders from Polynesian Settlement to the End of the Nineteenth Century (Auckland, 1996).

Paradise Reforged: A History of the New Zealanders from the 1880s to the Year 2000 (Auckland, 2001).

Replenishing the Earth: The Settler Revolution and the Rise of the Anglo-World (Oxford, 2009).

Bell, D., *The Idea of Greater Britain: Empire, Nation, and the Future of Global Order, 1860–1900* (Princeton, NJ, 2007).

Bell, D. S. A., 'Unity and Difference: John Robert Seeley and the Political Theology of International Relations', *Review of International Studies*, **31** (2005), pp. 559–79.

Bellenger, A., 'The English Benedictines and the British Empire', in Gilley, S., ed., *Victorian Churches and Churchmen: Essays Presented to Vincent Alan McClelland* (Woodbridge, Suffolk, 2005), pp. 94–109.

Bellenoit, H. J. A., *Missionary Education and Empire in Late Colonial India, 1860–1920* (London, 2007).

Berkeley, G. F., *The Irish Battalion in the Papal Army of 1860* (Dublin, 1929).

Best, G., 'Libraries in the Parish', in Mandelbrote, G. and K. A. Manley, eds., *The Cambridge History of Libraries in Britain and Ireland*, vol. II, *1640–1850* (Cambridge, 2006), pp. 324–44.

Bickersteth, E., *The Duty of Communicating the Gospel: A Sermon Preached before the Colonial Church Society on Monday, May 13, 1839 at St John's Chapel, Bedford Row* (London, 1839).

Popery in the Colonies: A Lecture Delivered before the Islington Protestant Institute (London, 1847).

Binfield, C., 'Thomas Binney and Congregationalism's "Special Mission"', *Transactions of the Congregational Historical Society*, **21** (1971), pp. 1–10.

Binney, T., *Lights and Shadows of Church-Life in Australia* (London, 1860).

Black, J., 'Confessional State or Elect Nation?', in Claydon, T. and I. McBride, eds., *Protestantism and National Identity: Britain and Ireland, c.1650–c.1850* (Cambridge, 1998), pp. 53–74.

Black, R. D. C., *Economic Thought and the Irish Question 1817–1870* (Cambridge, 1960).

Blackstone, W., *Commentaries on the Laws of England [1765–1769]* (Chicago, 1979).

Blain, M., 'The Canterbury Association: A Study of Its Members' Connections: A Tribute on the 150th Anniversary of the Canterbury Settlement [Typescript]' (Christchurch, 2000).

Blake, P. C., *John Youl, the Forgotten Chaplain: A Biography of the Reverend John Youl (1773–1827) First Chaplain to Northern Tasmania* (Launceston, 1999).

Bliss, E. M., *The Encyclopaedia of Missions* (New York, 1891).

Bluegum, T. [G. Warren Payne], *The Backblocks' Parson: A Story of Australian Life* (London, 1899).

Blum, E. J., *Reforging the White Republic: Race, Religion, and American Nationalism, 1865–1898* (Baton Rouge, LA, 2005).

Boggis, R. J. E., *A History of St Augustine's College, Canterbury* (Canterbury, 1907).

Boodle, R. G., 'Ministerial Recollections', *Parish Magazine* (1870).

'Recollections of Ministerial Work in New South Wales', in Halcombe, J. J., ed., *The Emigrant and the Heathen* (London, 1874), pp. 1–184.

The Life and Labours of the Right Reverend William Tyrrell, DD, First Bishop of Newcastle, New South Wales (London, 1881).

Booth, W., *In Darkest England and the Way Out* (London, 1890).

Bosher, R. S. 'The Pan-Anglican Congress of 1908', *Historical Magazine of the Protestant Episcopal Church* (June 1955), pp. 126–42.

Bowen, D., *Paul Cardinal Cullen and the Shaping of Modern Irish Catholicism* (Dublin, 1983).

Bowen, L., *Muddling Through: The Remarkable Story of the Barr Colonists* (Vancouver, 1992).

Boyce, F. B., *Fourscore Years and Seven: The Memoirs of Archdeacon Boyce, for over Sixty Years a Clergyman of the Church of England in New South Wales* (Sydney, 1934).

Brackney, W. H., *Historical Dictionary of the Baptists* (Lanham, MD, and London, 1999).

Bradley, I., *The Call to Seriousness: The Evangelical Impact on the Victorians* (London, 1976).

Brain, J. B., 'The Irish Influence on the Roman Catholic Church', *Southern African–Irish Studies*, **2** (1992), pp. 121–31.

ed., *The Cape Diary of Bishop Raymond Griffith for the Years 1837 to 1839* (Mariannhill, South Africa, 1988).

Breitenbach, E., 'Religious Literature and Discourses of Empire: The Scottish Presbyterian Foreign Mission Movement', in Carey, H. M., ed., *Empires of Religion* (Basingstoke, 2008), pp. 84–112.

Empire and Scottish Society: The Impact of Foreign Missions at Home, c.1790 to c.1914 (Edinburgh, 2009).

Brendon, P., 'A Moral Audit of the British Empire', *History Today*, **57** (2007), pp. 44–7.

Breward, I., *A History of the Churches in Australasia* (Oxford, 2001).

Brewer, M. F., *Staging Whiteness* (Hanover, NH, 2005).

Bridenbaugh, C., *Mitre and Sceptre: Transatlantic Faiths, Ideas, Personalities and Politics* (New York, 1962).

Bridge, C. and K. Fedorowich, eds., *The British World: Diaspora, Culture and Identity* (London, 2003).

Bridges, B., 'John Dunmore Lang: A Bicentennial Appreciation', *Church Heritage*, **11** (1999), pp. 70–81.

'John Dunmore Lang's Crusade to Keep Australia Protestant, 1841–1849', *Church Heritage*, **11** (2000), pp. 146–54.

British and Foreign Anti-Slavery Society, 'Rebellion in Jamaica', *Anti-Slavery Reporter*, **5** (1833), pp. 242–48.

British Missions: Comprising the 34th Annual Report of the Home Missionary Society; the 39th Annual Report of the Irish Evangelical Society; and the 17th Annual Report of the Colonial Missionary Society (London, 1853).

Brosnahan, S. G., '"The Battle of the Borough" and the "Saige O Timaru": Sectarian Riot in Colonial Canterbury', *New Zealand Journal of History*, **28** (1994), pp. 41–59.

Brotherhood of the Good Shepherd, *The Brotherhood of the Good Shepherd: A Church of England Mission in the Diocese of Bathurst* (Dubbo, NSW, 1913).

Brown, A. J., 'The Founding of St Augustine's Missionary College: A Spiritual Romance' (Masters Thesis, University of London, 1970).

Brown, C., 'Hawkins, Ernest (1802–1868)', in *Oxford Dictionary of National Biography* (Oxford, 2004).

Brown, C., M. Peters and F. J. Teal, eds., *Shaping a Colonial Church: Bishop Harper and the Anglican Diocese of Christchurch, 1856–1890* (Christchurch, 2006).

Brown, F. K., *Fathers of the Victorians* (Cambridge, 1961).

Brown, J., *The Colonial Missions of Congregationalism: The Story of Seventy Years* (London, 1908).

Brown, R., *Church and State in Modern Britain 1700–1850* (London, 1991).

Brown, S. J., *Thomas Chalmers and the Godly Commonwealth in Scotland* (Oxford, 1982).

'Reform, Reconstruction, Reaction: The Social Vision of Scottish Presbyterianism, c.1830–1930', *Scottish Journal of Theology*, **44** (1991), pp. 489–517.

The National Churches of England, Ireland, and Scotland 1801–1846 (Oxford, 2001).

Providence and Empire: Religion, Politics and Society in the United Kingdom 1815–1914 (Edinburgh, 2008).

'The Broad Church Movement, National Culture and Established Churches of the United Kingdom, c.1850–1914', in Carey, H. M. and J. Gascoigne, eds., *Church and State in Old and New Worlds* (Leiden, 2010).

Brown, S. J. and M. Fry, eds., *Scotland in the Age of the Disruption* (Edinburgh, 1993).

Brown, W. E., *The Catholic Church in South Africa from Its Origins to the Present Day* (London, 1960).

Browning, C. A., *The Convict Ship and England's Exiles* (n.p., 1851).

Buchan, J., *The Scottish Church and the Empire: Centenary Address* (n.p., 1934).

Buchanan, C., *Colonial Ecclesiastical Establishment: Being a Brief View of the State of the Colonies of Great Britain, and of Her Asiatic Empire in Respect to Religious Instruction* (London, 1813).

Buckner, P. A., *Canada and the British Empire* (Oxford, 2008).

Buckner, P. A. and R. D. Francis, eds., *Rediscovering the British World* (Calgary, Alberta, 2005).

Bullock, F. W. B., *A History of the Training for the Ministry of the Church of England and Wales from 1800 to 1874* (St Leonards-on-Sea, Sussex, 1955).

A History of Training for the Ministry of the Church of England in England and Wales from 598–1799 (St Leonards-on-Sea, Sussex, 1969).

Bumstead, J. M., 'Highland Emigration to the Island of St John and the Scottish Catholic Church, 1769–1774', *Dalhousie Review*, **58** (1979), pp. 511–47.

Burgon, J. W., *Lives of Twelve Good Men* (London, 1888).

Burke, E., *The Works of the Right Honourable Edmund Burke*, vol. VIII, *Speeches on the Impeachment of Warren Hastings* (London, 1857).

Burns, R. F., *The Life and Times of the Reverend Robert Burns* (Toronto, 1872).

Burns, T., *A Discourse Delivered in the Church of Otago, Friday March 23, 1849* (Dunedin, 1849).

Address Delivered at the Inauguration of the Presbytery of Otago, June 27, 1854 (Dunedin, 1854).

A Brief Account of the Origin and History of the Presbyterian Church of Otago, February 16, 1865 (Dunedin, 1865).

Butler, S., *A First Year in Canterbury Settlement* (London, 1863).

Erewhon, or Over the Range (London, 1920).

Calloway, C. G., *White People, Indians, and Highlanders* (Oxford, 1997).

Campey, L. H., *With Axe and Bible: The Scottish Pioneers of New Brunswick, 1784–1874* (Toronto, 2007).

The Canada Year Book 1911 (Ottawa, 1912).

Carey, H. M., 'The Vanished Kingdoms of Patrick O'Farrell: Religion, Memory and Migration in Religious History', *Journal of Religious History*, **31** (2007), pp. 40–58.

ed., *Empires of Religion* (Basingstoke, 2008).

'Religion and the "Evil Empire"', *Journal of Religious History*, **32** (2008), pp. 179–92.

'Gladstone, the Colonial Church and Imperial State', in Carey, H. M. and J. Gascoigne, eds., *Church and State in Old and New Worlds* (Leiden, 2010).

Carrick, R., *Hemming's Patent Improved Portable Houses* (London, 1853).

Carrier, N. H. and J. R. Jeffery, *External Migration, a Study of the Available Statistics 1815–1950* (London, 1953).

Carrington, C. E., *John Robert Godley of Canterbury* (Christchurch, 1950).

The British Overseas: Exploits of a Nation of Shopkeepers (Cambridge, 1968).

Carrothers, W. A., *Emigration from the British Isles with Special Reference to the Development of the Overseas Dominions* (London, 1929).

Carruthers, J. E., *Lights in the Southern Sky: Pen Portraits of Australian Methodism with Some Sketches from Life of Humbler Workers* (Sydney, 1924).

Carson, P., 'The British Raj and the Awakening of the Evangelical Conscience: The Ambiguities of Religious Establishment and Toleration, 1698–1833', in Stanley, B., ed., *Christian Missions and the Enlightenment* (Grand Rapids, MI, 2001), pp. 45–70.

Catholic Directory, Almanac and Registry of Ireland, England and Scotland: Complete Ordo in English (1851–).

Census of the British Empire, 1901 (London, 1906).

Centennial History of Canadian Methodism (Toronto, 1891).

Chadwick, G. A. [Bishop of Derry and Raphoe], 'The Exiles', *The East and the West: A Quarterly Review for the Study of Missions*, **1** (1903), pp. 241–2.

Chadwick, O., *The Victorian Church, Part One, 1829–1859* (London, 1966).

Chalmers, T., *Discourses on the Christian Revelation Viewed in Connection with the Modern Astronomy Together with Six Sermons* (Andover, 1818).

Child, F. S., *The Colonial Parson of New England* (New York, 1896).

Childe, C. F., 'The Story of the College', *Islingtonian* (1899), pp. 24–7, 37–9.

Chilman, E., 'Bishops in the British Colonies: The Story of the Oversea Episcopate and the Colonial Bishoprics' Fund', *Crown Colonist*, **11** (1941), pp. 486–7.

Chilton, L., *Agents of Empire: British Female Migration to Canada and Australia, 1860s–1930* (Toronto, 2007).

Chisholm, C., *The ABC of Colonization in a Series of Letters* (London, 1850).

Christmas, H., ed., *The Emigrant Churchman in Canada by a Pioneer in the Wilderness* (London, 1849).

Church Emigration Society, *Quarterly Notes of the Church Emigration Society*, (1902).

'Church Establishment (Colonies). Return of the Number of Persons on the Establishment of the Church of England, and Other Religious Denominations, Maintained by Grant of Public Money, in Each of the Colonies', *House of Commons. British Parliamentary Papers*, **55** (1839).

Church of England, Committee Appointed to Consider the Question of the Supply and Training of Candidates for the Sacred Ministry, *The Supply and Training of Candidates for Holy Orders. Report … Presented to the Archbishop of Canterbury* (Poole, 1908).

Church of Scotland, 'Report of the Overseas Council for 1964', in *The Church of Scotland Reports to the General Assembly* (Edinburgh, 1965), pp. 365–427.

Clap, T., *The Religious Constitution of Colleges, Especially of Yale College in New-Haven in the Colony of Connecticut* (New-London, CT, 1754).

Clark, J. B., 'Emigrants and Immigrants, Mission Work Among', in Jackson, S. M., ed., *The New Schaff-Herzog Encyclopedia of Religious Knowledge* (New York and London, 1909), pp. 119–20.

'Home Missions', in Jackson, S. M., ed., *The New Schaff-Herzog Encyclopedia of Religious Knowledge* (New York and London, 1909), pp. 339–46.

Clark, J. C. D., *English Society, 1660–1832: Religion, Ideology and Politics During the Ancien Régime* (Cambridge, 2000).

Clark, S. D., *Church and Sect in Canada* (Toronto, 1948).

Clarke, A., 'Days of Heaven on Earth: Presbyterian Communion Seasons in 19th Century Otago', *Journal of Religious History*, **26** (2002), pp. 274–97.

Claydon, T. and I. McBride, eds., *Protestantism and National Identity: Britain and Ireland, c.1650–c.1850* (Cambridge, 1998).

Clear, C., *Nuns in Nineteenth Century Ireland* (Dublin, 1987).

Clifford, J., *God's Greater Britain: Letters and Addresses* (London, 1899).

Cnattingius, H., *Bishops and Societies: A Study of Anglican Colonial and Missionary Expansion, 1698–1850* (London, 1952).

Coates, D., *The Principles, Objects and Plan of the New-Zealand Association* (London, 1837).

Coghlan, T. A., *A Statistical Account of Australia and New Zealand 1902–3* (Sydney, 1904).

Coldrey, B. M., *Good British Stock: Child and Youth Migration to Australia* (Canberra, 1999).

Cole, K., *A History of the Church Missionary Society of Australia* (Melbourne, 1971).

Coleman, D., *Romantic Colonization and British Anti-Slavery* (New York, 2004).

Coleridge, S. T., *On the Idea of the Constitution of the Church and State, According to the Idea of Each* (London, 1830).

Coles, J. C., *The Life and Christian Experience of John Cowley Coles* (Melbourne, 1893).

Colley, L., *Britons: Forging the Nation, 1770–1837* (New Haven, CT, 1992).

Colonial and Continental Church Society, *Missions in Many Lands: The Work of the Colonial and Continental Church Society* (London, 1896).

Colonial College, *Colonia: The Colonial College Magazine*, vols. 1–7 (1889–1902).

Colonial Secretary's Office, *Statistical Register of the Cape of Good Hope, 1898* (Cape Town, 1899).

Colquhoun, J. C., *William Wilberforce: His Friends and His Times* (London, 1866).

Comaroff, J. L., 'Images of Empire, Contests of Conscience: Models of Colonial Domination in South Africa', in Cooper, F. and A. L. Stoler, eds., *Tensions of Empire: Colonial Cultures in a Bourgeois World* (Berkeley, CA, 1997).

Condon, K., *The Missionary College of All Hallows, 1842–1891* (Dublin, 1986).

Conybeare, W. J., *Sermons Preached in the Chapel Royal at Whitehall, During the Years 1841, 1842, and 1843* (London, 1844).

Cook, C. and B. Keith, *British Historical Facts, 1830–1900* (London, 1975).

Cook, C. and J. Stevenson, *British Historical Facts 1760–1830* (London, 1980).

Cook, S. B., 'The Irish Raj: Social Origins and Careers of Irishmen in the Indian Civil Service, 1855–1914', *Journal of Social History*, **20** (1987), pp. 506–29.

Cooper, A., ' "Romanising" in Sydney', *Australasian Catholic Record* 80 (2003), pp. 175–88.

Cowper, A. S., *SSPCK Schoolmasters, 1709–1872* (Edinburgh, 1997).

Cowper, W. M., *The Autobiography and Reminiscences of William Macquarie Cowper, Dean of Sydney* (Sydney, 1902).

Cox, J., *Imperial Fault Lines: Christianity and Colonial Power in India, 1818–1940* (Stanford, CA, 2002).

The British Missionary Enterprise since 1700 (New York, 2008).

'Were Victorian Nonconformists the Worst Imperialists of All?', *Victorian Studies*, **46** (2004), pp. 243–55.

Craig, B. L., *Apostle to the Wilderness: Bishop John Medley and the Evolution of the Anglican Church* (2005).

Crowfoot, J. R., *Plea for a Colonial and Missionary College at Cambridge* (London, 1854).

Cunich, P., 'Archbishop Vaughan and the Empires of Religion in Colonial New South Wales', in Carey, H. M., ed., *Empires of Religion* (Houndmills, 2008), pp. 137–60.

Daniel, A., 'Undermining British Australia: Irish Lawyers and the Transformation of English Law in Australia', *Studies*, **84** (1995), pp. 61–70.

Daughton, J. P., *An Empire Divided: Religion, Republicanism, and the Making of French Colonialism, 1880–1914* (Oxford, 2006).

Davidson, A., 'Colonial Christianity: The Contribution of the Society for the Propagation of the Gospel to the Anglican Church in New Zealand, 1840–80', *Journal of Religious History*, **16** (1990), pp. 173–84.

Davidson, A. K., *Christianity in Aotearoa: A History of Church and Society in New Zealand* (Wellington, 1991).

Selwyn's Legacy: The College of St John the Evangelist Te Waimate and Auckland 1843–1992 (Auckland, 1993).

Daw, E. D., 'Church and State in the Empire: The Conference of Australian Bishops 1850', *Journal of Imperial and Commonwealth History*, **5** (1976), pp. 251–69.

Dawson, C. A., *Group Settlement: Ethnic Communities in Western Canada* (Toronto, 1936).

Denis, P., *The Dominican Friars in Southern Africa: A Social History (1577–1990)* (Leiden, 1998).

Devine, T. M., *The Scottish Nation, 1700–2000* (London, 1999).

Dickey, B., 'Thomas Binney in South Australia, 1858–1859', *Lucas: An Evangelical History Review* (1991).

Dilke, C. W., *Greater Britain: A Record of Travel in English Speaking Countries During 1866 and 1867* (London, 1868).

Problems of Greater Britain (London, 1890).

Dimont, C. T. and F. de W. Batty, *St Clair Donaldson, Archbishop of Brisbane, 1904–1921; Bishop of Salisbury, 1921–1935* (London, 1939).

Doll, P. M., 'American High Churchmanship and the Establishment of the First Colonial Episcopate in the Church of England: Nova Scotia, 1787', *Journal of Ecclesiastical History*, **43** (1992), pp. 35–59.

Revolution, Religion and National Identity: Imperial Anglicanism in British North America (2000).

Donaldson, M., 'The Voluntary Principle in the Colonial Situation: Theory and Practice', in Sheils, W. J. and D. Wood, eds., *Studies in Church History* (Oxford, 1986), pp. 381–90.

Donaldson, S. A., 'Education in South Africa: Our Opportunity and Our Duty', *The East and the West: A Quarterly Review for the Study of Missions*, **1** (1903), pp. 390–401.

Dow, C. S., *Ministers to the Soldiers of Scotland: A History of the Military Chaplains of Scotland Prior to the War in the Crimea* (Edinburgh and London, 1962).

Dowd, C., *Rome in Australia: The Papacy and Conflict in the Australian Catholic Missions, 1834–1884* (Leiden, 2008).

Dowland, D., *Nineteenth-Century Anglican Theological Training: The Redbrick Challenge* (Oxford, 1997).

Duchaussois, P., *Mid Snow and Ice. The Apostles of the North-West* (London, 1923).

Dunne, P., *The Emigrant's Guide to Queensland and the Other Australian Colonies* (Dublin, 1863).

Durey, J. F., *Trollope and the Church of England* (Basingstoke, 2002).

Edwards, O. D., *Celtic Nationalism* (London, 1968).

'The Irish Priest in North America', in *Studies in Church History* (1989), pp. 311–52.

Edwards, R. D., *An Atlas of Irish History* (London, 2005).

Edwards, S. W., 'The Relation of Colonial to Foreign Missions', in *The British Missionary* (1913), pp. 107–11.

Eisdell, J. W., *Back Country: Or the Cheerful Adventures of a Bush Parson in the Eighties* (London, 1936).

Elbourne, E., 'To Colonise the Mind: Evangelical Missionaries in Britain and the Eastern Cape, 1790–1837' (PhD Thesis, Oxford University, 1991).

'The Foundation of the Church Missionary Society: The Anglican Missionary Impulse', in Walsh, J., ed., *The Church of England c.1689–c.1833* (Cambridge, 1993), pp. 247–64.

Blood Ground: Colonialism, Missions and the Contest for Christianity in the Cape Colony and Britain, 1799–1853 (Montreal and Kingston, 2002).

'The Sin of the Settler: The 1835–36 Select Committee on Aborigines and Debates over Virtue and Conquest in the Early Nineteenth-Century British White Settler Empire', *Journal of Colonialism and Colonial History*, 4 (2003).

'Religion in the British Empire', in *The British Empire: Themes and Perspectives*, ed. Sarah Stockwell (Oxford, 2008).

Elbourne, E. and R. Ross, 'Combating Spiritual and Social Bondage: Early Missions in the Cape Colony', in Elphick, R. and R. Davenport, eds., *Christianity in South Africa* (Cape Town 1997), pp. 31–50.

Elder, J. R., *The History of the Presbyterian Church of New Zealand, 1840–1940* (Christchurch, 1940).

Eldred-Grigg, S., *A New History of Canterbury* (Dunedin, 1982).

Eldridge, C. C., *England's Mission: The Imperial Idea in the Age of Gladstone and Disraeli 1868–1880* (London, 1973).

Elphick, R. and T. R. H. Davenport, *Christianity in South Africa: A Political, Social and Cultural History* (Oxford, 1997).

Erlank, N., '"Civilizing the African": The Scottish Mission to the Xhosa', in Stanley, B., ed., *Christian Missions and the Enlightenment* (Grand Rapids, MI, 2001), pp. 141–61.

Etherington, N., 'Missions and Empire', in Winks, R. W. and A. M. Low, eds., *The Oxford History of the British Empire*, vol. 5, *Historiography* (Oxford, 1999), pp. 303–14.

ed., *Missions and Empire* (Oxford, 2005).

Ewing, A., *Sermon on Emigration from the Highlands and Islands of Scotland to Australia by the Bishop of Argyle and the Isles* (London, 1852).

Ewing, W., ed., *Annals of the Free Church of Scotland 1843–1900* (Edinburgh, 1914).

Fanon, F., *The Wretched of the Earth* (London, 1967).

Black Skin, White Masks (London, 1986).

Fay, T. J., *A History of Canadian Catholics: Gallicanism, Romanism, and Canadianism* (Montreal, 2002).

Ferguson, N., *Empire: How Britain Made the Modern World* (London, 2004).

Fieldhouse, D. K., *Colonialism 1870–1945: An Introduction* (London, 1981).

Fitzpatrick, D., *Irish Emigration 1801–1921* (Dublin, 1984).

'The Irish in Britain', in Vaughan, W. E., ed., *A New History of Ireland*, vol. VI, *Ireland under the Union*, Part II, *1870–1921* (Oxford, 1996).

Fleming, P. and Y. Lamonde, eds., *History of the Book in Canada* (Toronto, 2004).

Fogarty, R., *Catholic Education in Australia, 1806–1950*, vol. 2, *Catholic Education under the Religious Orders* (Melbourne, 1959).

France, W. F., *The Oversea Episcopate: Centenary History of the Colonial Bishoprics' Fund, 1841–1941* (London, 1941).

'The Place of Missionary Societies within the Church', in Morgan, E. R. and R. Lloyd, eds., *The Mission of the Anglican Communion* (London, 1948), pp. 115–31.

Frappell, R., 'The Australian Bush Brotherhoods and Their English Origins', *Journal of Ecclesiastical History*, **47** (1996), pp. 82–97.

'Imperial Fervour and Anglican Loyalty 1901–1929', in Kaye, B., ed., *Anglicanism in Australia: A History* (Melbourne, 2002), pp. 76–99.

Fraser, M., *Report on the Results of a Census of the Dominion of New Zealand ... 2nd April, 1911* (Auckland, 1913).

Free Church of Scotland, *Scheme of the Colony of the Free Church at Otago in New Zealand* (Glasgow, 1845).

Report of the Colonial Committee of the Free Church of Scotland, Presented to the General Assembly on Thursday, 31st May 1849 by the Reverend John Bonar (Edinburgh, 1849).

Free Church of Scotland [*Lay*] *Association for Promoting the Settlement of a Scotch Colony at Otago, New Zealand* (London, 1850?).

Fréri, J., *The Society for the Propagation of the Faith and the Catholic Missions, 1822–1900* (Baltimore, 1902).

Friends of the Turnbull Library, *Edward Gibbon Wakefield and the Colonial Dream: A Reconsideration* (Wellington, 1997).

Fry, M., *The Scottish Empire* (Phantassie, East Lothian, 2001).

Frykenberg, R. E., *Christianity in India: From Beginnings to the Present* (Oxford, 2008).

Fulford, F., *Sermons, Addresses, and Statistics of the Diocese of Montreal* (Montreal, 1865).

Fyfe, C., *A History of Sierra Leone* (London, 1962).

Garnett, R., *Edward Gibbon Wakefield: The Colonization of South Australia and New Zealand, Etc.* (New York, 1898).

Gascoigne, J., 'Introduction: Religion and Empire, an Historiographical Perspective', *Journal of Religious History*, **32** (2008), pp. 159–78.

Giles, R. A., *The Constitutional History of the Australian Church* (London, 1929).

Gilley, S., 'The Roman Catholic Church and the Nineteenth Century Irish Diaspora', *Journal of Ecclesiastical History*, **35** (1984), pp. 188–207.

Gilley, S. and B. Stanley, eds., *World Christianities, c.1815–1914* (Cambridge, 2006).

Gladstone, W. E., *The State in Its Relations with the Church* (London, 1838).

The State in Its Relations with the Church (London, 1839).

Glasgow Colonial Society, *First Annual Report of the Glasgow Society (in Connection with the Established Church of Scotland) for Promoting the Religious Interests of the Scottish Settlers in North America* (Glasgow, 1826).

Godley, J. R., *Letters from America* (London, 1844).

Goodykoontz, C. B., *Home Missions on the American Frontier* (Caldwell, ID, 1939).

Gouger, R., ed., *A Letter from Sydney, the Principal Town of Australasia* [*by Edward Gibbon Wakefield*] (London, 1829).

Graham, J., 'Settler Society', in Rice, G. W., ed., *The Oxford History of New Zealand* (Auckland, 1992), pp. 112–40.

Grainer, S., 'Who Was Godley?', in Stocker, M., ed., *Remembering Godley: A Portrait of Canterbury's Founder* (Christchurch, 2001), pp. 19–27.

Gramsci, A., 'Notes on Italian History, 1934–5', in Hoare, Q. and G. Nowell-Smith, eds., *Selections from the Prison Notebooks of Antonio Gramsci* (London, 1971).

Grant, R., *Representations of British Emigration, Colonisation and Settlement: Imagining Empire, 1800–1860* (Basingstoke, 2005).

Gray, P., '"Shovelling out Your Paupers": The British State and Irish Famine Migration 1846–50', *Patterns of Prejudice*, **33** (1999), pp. 47–66.

Great Britain, Foreign Office, *Instructions to Her Majesty's Consuls Respecting Grants to British Church Establishments Abroad under the Act of Parliament 6 George IV, c.87* (Westminster, 1874).

Greene, J. P., *Between Damnation and Starvation: Priests and Merchants in Newfoundland* (Quebec City, 1999).

Griffin, G., *They Came to Care: Pastoral Ministry in Colonial Australia* (Melbourne, 1993).

Grocott, A. M., *Convicts, Clergymen and Churches: Attitudes of Convicts and Ex-Convicts Towards the Churches and Clergy in New South Wales from 1788– 1851* (Sydney, 1980).

Gwynn, S. and G. M. Tuckwell, *The Life of the Right Hon. Sir Charles W. Dilke* (London, 1917).

Haig, A. G., *The Victorian Clergy* (London, 1984).

Halcombe, J. J., ed., *The Emigrant and the Heathen, or, Sketches of Missionary Life* (London, 1870).

Hall, C., *Civilising Subjects: Metropole and Colony in the English Imagination, 1830–1867* (Oxford, 2002).

'An Empire of God or of Man? The Macaulays, Father and Son', in Carey, H. M., ed., *Empires of Religion* (Basingstoke, 2008), pp. 64–83.

Hall, C., K. McClelland and J. Rendall, *Defining the Victorian Nation: Class, Race, Gender and the British Reform Act of 1867* (Cambridge, 2000).

Hammerton, A. J., *Emigrant Gentlewomen: Genteel Poverty and Female Emigration, 1830–1914* (London, 1979).

Hanham, H. J., 'Religion and Nationality in the Mid-Victorian Army', in Foot, M. R., ed., *War and Society: Historical Essays in Honour and Memory of J. R. Wester, 1928–1971* (London, 1973), pp. 57–69.

Harley, C. D., *Missionary Training: The History of All Nations Christian College and Its Predecessors (1911–1981)* (Zoetermeer, 2000).

Harper, M., 'Emigration and the Salvation Army, 1890–1930', *Bulletin of the Scottish Institute of Missionary Studies* (new series) **3**–4 (1985), pp. 22–9.

'Glasgow Colonial Society', in Cameron, N. M. D. S., ed., *Dictionary of Scottish Church History and Theology* (Edinburgh, 1993), p. 365.

'Making Christian Colonists: An Evaluation of the Emigration Policies and Practices of the Scottish Churches and Christian Organisations between the Wars', *Records of the Scottish Church History Society*, **28** (1998), pp. 173–216.

'Settling in Saskatchewan: English Pioneers on the Prairies, 1878–1914', *British Journal of Canadian Studies*, **16** (2003), pp. 88–101.

'Rhetoric and Reality: British Migration to Canada, 1867–1967', in Buckner, P. A., ed., *Canada and the British Empire* (Oxford, 2008), p. 160.

Hastings, A., *The Construction of Nationhood: Ethnicity, Religion and Nationalism* (Cambridge, 1992).

The Church in Africa, 1450–1950 (Oxford, 1994).

Hawkins, E., *Documents Relative to the Erection and Endowment of Additional Bishoprics in the Colonies* (London, 1844).

The Colonial Church Atlas (London, 1845).

Historical Notices of the Missions of the Church of England in the North American Colonies, Previous to the Independence of the United States; Chiefly from the MS Documents of the Society for the Propagation of the Gospel in Foreign Parts (London, 1845).

Annals of the Diocese of Fredericton (London, 1847).

Annals of the Diocese of Toronto (London, 1848).

Annals of the Diocese of Quebec (London, 1849).

Hayes, A. L., *Anglicans in Canada: Controversies and Identity in Historical Perspective* (Chicago, 2004).

Heasman, K., *Evangelicals in the Church of England, 1734–1984* (London, 1962).

Heeney, B., *A Different Kind of Gentleman: Parish Clergy as Professional Men in Early and Mid-Victorian England* (Hamden, CT, 1976).

Helmstadter, R. J., 'Orthodox Nonconformity', in Paz, D. G., ed., *Nineteenth-Century English Religious Traditions: Retrospect and Prospect* (Westport, CT, 1995), pp. 57–84.

Herrick, F. H., 'Gladstone and the Concept of the "English-Speaking Peoples"', *Journal of British Studies*, **12** (1972), pp. 150–6.

Hilliard, D., *God's Gentlemen: A History of the Melanesian Mission, 1849–1942* (Brisbane, 1978).

Hinchliff, P., 'John William Colenso: A Fresh Appraisal', *Journal of Ecclesiastical History*, **13** (1962), pp. 203–16.

'The Selection and Training of Missionaries in the Early Nineteenth Century', *Studies in Church History*, **6** (1970), pp. 131–5.

'Whatever Happened to the Glasgow Missionary Society?', *Historiae Studia Ecclesiasticae* [*Church History Society of Southern Africa*], **18** (1992), pp. 104–20.

'Colonial Church Establishment in the Aftermath of the Colenso Controversy', in Aston, N., ed., *Religious Change in Europe, 1650–1914: Essays for John McManners* (Oxford, 1997), pp. 345–63.

Hinds, S., *The History of the Rise and Early Progress of Christianity Comprising an Enquiry into Its True Character and Design* (London, 1828).

Copy of a Speech of the Reverend Samuel Hinds, DD, Vicar of Yardley, Herts, Delivered at the Anniversary Meeting of the Hertford District Committee of the Two Societies for Promoting Christian Knowledge and for the Propagation of the

Gospel in Foreign Parts, Held in the Shire Hall, Hertford, September 15, 1840 (1840).

Hinds, S. and R. Bourke, *The Latest Official Documents Relating to New Zealand, with Introductory Observations* (London, 1838).

Hodge, A., 'The Training of Missionaries for Africa: The Church Missionary Society's Training College at Islington, 1900–1915', *Journal of Religion in Africa*, 4 (1971), pp. 81–96.

Hodgkinson, S., *A Description of the Province of Canterbury, New Zealand, or, Zealandia: Founded on Experience Obtained During a Residence of Three Years as a Sheep-Farmer in the Colony* (London, 1858).

Hogan, E. M., *The Irish Missionary Movement: A Historical Survey 1830–1980* (Dublin, 1990).

Hogg, W. R., 'Conferences, World Missionary', in Neill, S., G. H. Anderson and J. Goodwin, eds., *Concise Dictionary of the Christian World Mission* (London, 1970).

Holmes, R. F. G., *Thomas Chalmers and Ireland. Lecture Delivered at the Annual Meeting of the Presbyterian Historical Society of Ireland* (Belfast, 1979).

Hood, E. P., *The Lamps of the Temple: Shadows from the Lights of the Modern Pulpit* (1852).

Thomas Binney: His Mind, Life and Opinions (London, 1874).

Hopper, R. P., *Old-Time Primitive Methodism in Canada, 1829–1884* (Toronto, 1904).

Hosie, J., *Challenge: The Marists in Colonial Australia* (Sydney, 1987).

House of Commons, *Colonial Church Legislation. Part III, New South Wales* (London, 1852).

Howe, S., *Ireland and Empire: Colonial Legacies in Irish History and Culture* (Oxford, 2000).

Howitt, R., *Impressions of Australia Felix, During Four Years Residence in That Colony* (1845).

Howitt, W., *Colonization and Christianity: A Popular History of the Treatment of the Natives by the Europeans in All Their Colonies* (London, 1838).

Hunte, K., 'Christianity and Slavery in the British Caribbean', in Lampe, A., ed., *Christianity in the Caribbean: Essays on Church History* (Barbados, 2001), pp. 126–53.

Hussey, H., *More Than Half a Century of Colonial Life and Christian Experience* (Adelaide, 1978).

Ignatiev, N., *How the Irish Became White* (London, 1995).

Illustrated Biographical Sketches, Memoirs Reprinted from the Catholic Home Annual and Directory of Australasia for 1892 (Sydney, 1892).

Ingham, E. G., *Sierra Leone after a Hundred Years* (London, 1894).

Insh, G. P., *Scottish Colonial Schemes 1620–1686* (Glasgow, 1922).

Irwin, F. C., *The State and Position of Western Australia, Commonly Called the Swan-River Settlement* (London, 1835).

Jackson, H. R., *Churches and People in Australia and New Zealand 1860–1930* (Sydney, 1987).

Jeffery, K., *An Irish Empire?: Aspects of Ireland and the British Empire* (Manchester, 1996).

Johnston, A., *Missionary Writing and Empire, 1800–1860* (Cambridge, 2003).

Johnston, H. J. M., *British Emigration Policy, 1815–30: 'Shovelling out Paupers'* (Oxford, 1972).

Jones, W., *The Jubilee Memorial of the Religious Tract Society* (London, 1850).

Jose, A. W., *The Growth of the Empire: A Handbook to the History of Greater Britain* (London, 1909).

Jupp. J., *The Australian People: An Encyclopedia of the Nation, Its People and Their Origins* (Cambridge, 2001).

Kells, M., 'Religion and the Irish Migrant', *Irish Studies Review*, **6** (1994), pp. 16–18.

Kelly, H., 'Missionary Work in South Africa', *The East and the West: A Quarterly Review for the Study of Missions*, **1** (1903), pp. 156–70.

Kendall, H. B., *The Origin and History of the Primitive Methodist Church* (London, 1905).

Kendle, J. E., *Federal Britain: A History* (London, 1997).

King, J., *Ten Decades: The Australian Centenary Story of the London Missionary Society* (London, 1894).

Kirkpatrick, F. A., *Lectures on British Colonization and Empire* (London, 1906).

Knight, E. F., *With the Royal Tour* (London, 1902).

Knight, F., *The Nineteenth-Century Church and English Society* (Cambridge, 1995).

Knight, W., *The Missionary Secretariat of Henry Venn* (London, 1880).

Knights, B., *The Idea of the Clerisy in the Nineteenth Century* (Cambridge, 1978).

Koebner, R. and H. D. R. Schmidt, *Imperialism: The Story and Significance of a Political Word, 1840–1960* (Cambridge, 1964).

Koren, H. J., *To the Ends of the Earth: A General History of the Congregation of the Holy Ghost* (Pittsburgh, 1983).

Koss, S. E., 'Wesleyanism and Empire', *Historical Journal*, **18** (1975), pp. 105–18.

Kumar, K., *The Making of English National Identity* (Cambridge, 2003).

Lake, M. and H. Reynolds, *Drawing the Global Colour Line: White Men's Countries and the International Challenge of Racial Equality* (Cambridge, 2008).

Lambert, D. and P. Howell, 'John Pope Hennessy and the Translation of "Slavery" between Late Nineteenth-Century Barbados and Hong Kong', *History Workshop Journal*, **55** (2003), pp. 1–24.

Lang, J. D., *The Question of Questions! Or, Is This Colony To Be Transformed into a Province of Popedom?* (Sydney, 1841).

Australian Mission. To the Minister and Elders of the Secession and Relief Churches (Edinburgh, 1847).

Cooksland in North-Eastern Australia: The Future Cotton-Field of Great Britain (London, 1847).

Popery in Australia and the Southern Hemisphere, and How to Check It Effectually: An Address to Evangelical and Influential Protestants of All Denominations in Great Britain and Ireland (Edinburgh, 1847).

Narrative of Proceedings in England, Scotland and Ireland During the Years 1847, 1848 and 1849, with a View to Originate an Extensive and Continuous

Immigration of a Superior Character from the United Kingdom into This Territory (Sydney, 1850).

How the People of England Were Tricked out of Their Noble Inheritance in the Waste Lands of Australia [Extract from *Lang's Historical and Statistical Account of New South Wales*] (London, n.d.).

Langfield, M., 'Voluntarism, Salvation, and Rescue: British Juvenile Migration to Australia and Canada, 1890–1939', *Journal of Imperial and Commonwealth History*, **32** (2004), pp. 86–114.

Larkin, E., 'The Devotional Revolution in Ireland, 1850–75', *American Historical Review*, 77 (1972), pp. 625–52.

'Cullen, Paul (1803–1878)', in *Oxford Dictionary of National Biography* (Oxford, 2004).

Larkin, E. J., *The Pastoral Role of the Roman Catholic Church in Pre-Famine Ireland* (Dublin, 2006).

Latourette, K. S., *A History of the Expansion of Christianity* (London, 1938–45).

A History of the Expansion of Christianity, vol. IV, *The Great Century AD 1800–AD 1914: Europe and the United States of America* (London, 1941).

A History of the Expansion of Christianity, vol. V, *The Great Century in the Americas, Australasia, and Africa AD 1800–AD 1914* (London, 1943).

A History of the Expansion of Christianity, vol. VII, *Advance through Storm: AD 1914 and After* (London, 1945).

Lawson, H., *While the Billy Boils* (Sydney, 1896).

Leacy, F. H., ed., *Historical Statistics of Canada* (Ottawa, 1983).

Leneman, L., 'The SSPCK and the Question of Gaelic in Blair Atholl', *Scottish Studies*, **26** (1982), pp. 57–9.

Livingstone, F. V., *Bibliography of the Works of Rudyard Kipling* (New York, 1927).

Lloyd, G. E., *The Building of the Nation: Natural Increase or Immigration: A Paper Read before the Grand Orange Lodge of British America at Edmonton, Alberta, July 26th, 1928* (Prince Albert, Saskatchewan, 1928).

Loane, M., *A Centenary History of Moore Theological College* (Sydney, 1955).

Louis, W. R., ed., *The Oxford History of the British Empire* (Oxford, 1998–2000).

Lovegrove, D. W., *Established Church, Sectarian People: Itinerancy and the Transformation of English Dissent, 1780–1830* (Cambridge, 1988).

Lovett, R., *The History of the London Missionary Society, 1795–1895* (London, 1899).

Lowe, R. T., *Protest against the Ministration in Madeira of the Reverend T. K. Brown in Opposition to Episcopal Authority by the Reverend R. T. Lowe, the Chaplain Licensed by the Lord Bishop of London* (Funchal, 1848).

Lowell, A. L. and H. M. Stephens, *Colonial Civil Service: The Selection and Training of Colonial Officials in England, Holland, and France* (New York, 1900).

Lyttelton, L., *A Letter to the Reverend Ernest Hawkins: Secretary to the Society for the Propagation of the Gospel in Foreign Parts, on the Principles of the Operations of the Society* (London, 1849).

'Canterbury Colony', *The Colonial Church Chronicle*, **2** (1849), pp. 269–72.

The Colonial Empire of Great Britain Especially in Its Religious Aspect (London, 1849).

Two Lectures on a Visit to the Canterbury Colony in 1867–8: 1. The Voyage; 2. The Colony (London, 1868).

MacCormick, J. H., *Lloydminster; or, 5,000 Miles with the Barr Colonists* (London, 1924).

MacCulloch, T. and J. MacGregor, *A Memorial from the Committee of Missions of the Presbyterian Church of Nova Scotia, to the Glasgow Society for Promoting the Religious Interests of the Scottish Settlers in British North America; with Observations on the Constitution of That Society* (Edinburgh, 1826).

MacDevitt, J., *Father Hand: Founder of All Hallows Catholic College for the Foreign Missions* (Dublin, 1885).

MacDonagh, O., 'The Irish Catholic Clergy and Emigration During the Great Famine', *Irish Historical Studies*, 5 (1947), pp. 287–302.

MacDonald, C., *A Woman of Good Character: Single Women as Immigrant Settlers in Nineteenth-Century New Zealand* (Wellington, 1990).

MacFarlan, D., *Statement Relative to the Proceedings of the General Assembly's Colonial Committee, in Regard to Mr Robert Duff, Preacher of the Gospel* (n.p., 1841).

MacKenzie, J., '"Making Black Scotsmen and Scotswomen?": Scottish Missionaries and the Eastern Cape Colony in the Nineteenth Century', in Carey, H. M., ed., *Empires of Religion* (Basingstoke, 2008), pp. 113–36.

Mackeson, C., *The Year-Book of the Church: A Record of Work and Progress in the Church of England, Compiled from Official Sources* (London, 1882).

MacSuibhne, P., ed., *Paul Cullen and His Contemporaries with Their Letters from 1820–1902* (Naas, 1965).

Malchow, H. L., 'The Church and Emigration in Late Victorian England', *Journal of Church and State*, 24 (1982), pp. 119–38.

Maling, P. B., 'Samuel Butler', in McLintock, A. H., ed., *An Encyclopaedia of New Zealand* (2007).

Mandler, P., *The English National Character: The History of an Idea from Edmund Burke to Tony Blair* (New Haven, CT, 2006).

Mangan, J. A., *'Benefits Bestowed?' Education and British Imperialism* (Manchester, 1988).

Manners, J. J. R., *England's Trust, and Other Poems* (London, 1841).

Manners, L. J., *The Church of England in the Colonies: A Lecture Delivered before the Members of the Colchester Literary Institution, on Wednesday, January 22nd, 1851* (London, 1851).

Martin, G. W., 'Anti-Imperialism in the Mid-Nineteenth Century and the Nature of the British Empire, 1820–70', in Martin, G. W., ed., *Reappraisals in British Imperial History* (London, Basingstoke and Toronto, 1975), pp. 88–120.

Martin, R. M., *Statistics of the Colonies of the British Empire* (London, 1839).

Martin, T., *The Life of His Royal Highness the Prince Consort* (n.p., 1875).

Matheson, P., 'The Settler Church, 1840–1870', in McEldowney, D., ed., *Presbyterians in Aotearoa, 1840–1990* (Wellington, 1990), pp. 15–42.

Mathews, C. H. S., *A Parson in the Australian Bush* (London, 1908).

Mattelart, A., *The Invention of Communication* (Minneapolis, 1996).

Maughan, S. S., 'An Archbishop for Greater Britain: Bishop Montgomery, Missionary Imperialism and the SPG, 1897–1915', in O 'Connor, D., ed., *Three Centuries of Mission: The United Society for the Propagation of the Gospel 1701–2000* (London, 2000), pp. 358–70.

  'Imperial Christianity? Bishop Montgomery and the Foreign Missions of the Church of England, 1895–1915', in Porter, A., ed., *The Imperial Horizons of British Protestant Missions, 1880–1914* (Grand Rapids, MI, 2003), pp. 32–57.

McCann, P., 'The Newfoundland School Society 1823–55: Missionary Enterprise or Cultural Imperialism?', in Mangan, J. A., ed., *'Benefits Bestowed?' Education and British Imperialism* (Manchester, 1988), pp. 94–112.

McCarthy, A., *Irish Migrants in New Zealand, 1840–1937: 'The Desired Haven'* (Woodbridge, Suffolk, 2005).

McDougall, E. A. K. and J. S. Moir, eds., *Selected Correspondence of the Glasgow Colonial Society 1825–1840* (Toronto, 1994).

McDowell, R. B., *The Church of Ireland, 1869–1969* (London, 1975).

McEvoy, J., *Carlow College 1793–1993: The Ordained Students and Teaching Staff of St Patrick's College, Carlow* (Carlow, 1993).

McIntyre, W. D. and W. J. Gardner, eds., *Speeches and Documents on New Zealand History* (Oxford, 1971).

McLay, A., *James Quinn: First Catholic Bishop of Brisbane* (Toowoomba, Queensland, 1989).

McLeod, H., *Religion and the People of Western Europe, 1789–1970* (1981).

  Religion and Irreligion in Victorian England: How Secular Was the Working Class? (1993).

  Religion and Society in England, 1850–1914 (Basingstoke, 1996).

  'Protestantism and British National Identity, 1815–1945', in Van Der Veer, P., ed., *Religion and Nationalism in Europe and Asia* (Princeton, NJ, 1999), pp. 44–70.

  ed., *World Christianities c.1914–c.2000* (Cambridge, 2006).

McLintock, A. H., *The History of Otago: The Origins and Growth of a Wakefield Class Settlement* (Dunedin, 1949).

  'History, Myths in New Zealand', in McLintock, A. H., ed., *Te Ara – The Encyclopedia of New Zealand* (1966).

McManners, J., *Church and Society in Eighteenth-Century France* (Oxford, 1998).

McNamee, B., 'The "Second Reformation" In Ireland', *Irish Theological Quarterly*, **33** (1966), pp. 39–64.

McNeil, K., *Scotland, Britain, Empire: Writing the Highlands, 1760–1860* (Columbus, OH, 2007).

Methodist, *Proceedings of the Oecumenical Methodist Conference, Held in City Road Chapel, London, September, 1881* (London, 1881).

Methodist New Connexion, *Report of the Methodist New Connexion Missionary Society, for Ireland, Canada, Etc.* (Liverpool, 1847).

Mills, A., *Colonial Constitutions: An Outline of the Constitutional History and Existing Government of the British Dependencies* (London, 1856).

Mills, F. V., 'The Society in Scotland for Propagating Christian Knowledge in British North America, 1730–1775', *Church History*, **63** (1994), pp. 15–30.

The Missionary Register for the Year 1813(–55) Containing an Abstract of the Proceedings of the Principal Missionary and Bible Societies Throughout the World (London, 1813).

Mitchell, B. R., *British Historical Statistics* (Cambridge, 1988).

Moir, J., 'The Settlement of Clergy Reserves, 1840–1855', *Canadian Historical Review*, **37** (1956), pp. 46–62.

'Through Missionary Eyes: The Glasgow Colonial Society and the Immigrant Experience in British North America', in Kerrigan, C., ed., *The Immigrant Experience* (Guelph, Ontario, 1992), pp. 95–109.

Molony, J. N., *The Roman Mould of the Australian Catholic Church* (Melbourne, 1969).

Montgomery, H. H., *Handbook on Foreign Mission* (London, 1902).

The Church on the Prairie (London, 1908).

Service Abroad (New York, Bombay and Calcutta, 1910).

Montgomery, M., *Bishop Montgomery: A Memoir* (London, 1933).

Moody, M. E., 'Religion in the Life of Charles Middleton, First Baron Barham', in Cole, C. R. and M. E. Moody, eds., *The Dissenting Tradition: Essays for Leland H. Carlson* (Athens, OH, 1975), pp. 140–63.

Moon, P., *Fatal Frontiers: A New History of New Zealand in the Decade before the Treaty* (Auckland, 2006).

Moore, H. C., *Brave Sons of the Empire* (London, 1910).

Moore, T., *Dictionary of the English Church, Ancient and Modern* (London, 1881).

More, H., *Coelebs in Search of a Wife: Comprehending Observations on Domestic Habits and Manners, Religion and Morals* (London, 1809).

Morgan, H., 'An Unwelcome Heritage: Ireland's Role in British Empire Building', *History of European Ideas* **19** (1994), pp. 619–25.

Morrell, W. P., *University of Otago: A Centennial History* (Dunedin, 1969).

Mosley, O., *The Greater Britain* (London, 1932).

Mountain, G. J., *A Short Explanation of Circumstances Preventing Coalition with the Colonial Church and School Society* (Quebec, 1859).

Moyer, K. A., *My Saddle Was My Study: The Story of the Methodist Saddlebag Preachers of Upper Canada* (Elmira, Ontario, 1974).

Mullins, J. D., *Our Beginnings: Being a Short Sketch of the History of the Colonial and Continental Church Society* (London, 1923).

Murphy, D., *A History of Irish Emigrant and Missionary Education* (Dublin, 2000).

National Assembly of the Church of England, *The Official Year-Book of the Church of England* (London, 1883).

Neill, S., *A History of Christian Missions* (New York, 1964).

'Colonialism and Missions', in Neill, S., G. H. Anderson and J. Goodwin, eds., *Concise Dictionary of the Christian World Mission* (London, 1970), pp. 121–2.

New Zealand Association, *The British Colonization of New Zealand; Being an Account of the Principles, Objects and Plans of the New Zealand Association* (London, 1837).

Newcomb, H., ed., *A Cyclopedia of Missions: Containing a Comprehensive View of Missionary Operations Throughout the World* (New York, 1860).

Nockles, P. B., *The Oxford Movement in Context: Anglican High Churchmanship, 1760–1857* (Cambridge, 1997).

Noll, M. A., D. A. Bebbington and G. A. Rawlyk, eds., *Evangelicalism: Comparative Studies of Popular Christianity in North America, the British Isles, and Beyond, 1700–1990* (New York, 1994).

Norman, E. R., *Anti-Catholicism in Victorian England* (London, 1968).

Norris, R. W., *Annals of the Diocese of Adelaide* (London, 1852).

O'Brien, A. P., *God's Willing Workers: Women and Religion in Australia* (Sydney, 2005).

O'Brien, C. C., *God Land: Reflections on Religion and Nationalism* (Cambridge, MA, 1988).

O'Connor, D., ed., *Three Centuries of Mission: The United Society for the Propagation of the Gospel 1701–2000* (London, 2000).

O'Day, R., 'The Clerical Renaissance in Victorian England and Wales', in Parsons, G., ed., *Religion in Victorian Britain, vol. I, Traditions* (Manchester, 1988).

O'Farrell, P. J. and B. Trainor, *Letters from Irish Australia, 1825–1929* (Sydney, 1984).

Official Year Book of the Commonwealth of Australia, 1901–1912 (Melbourne, 1913).

Olssen, E., *A History of Otago* (Dunedin, 1984).

Orange, C., *The Treaty of Waitangi* (Wellington, 1987).

Orton, D., *Made of Gold: A Biography of Angela Burdett Coutts* (London, 1980).

Parker, C. H., *Faith on the Margins: Catholics and Catholicism in the Dutch Golden Age* (Cambridge, MA, 2008).

Parry, E., *Memoirs of Rear-Admiral Sir W. Edward Parry* (New York, 1857).

Pascoe, C. F., *Two Hundred Years of the SPG: An Historical Account of the Propagation of the Gospel in Foreign Parts, 1701–1900* (London, 1901).

Pascoe, C. F. and H. W. Tucker, eds., *Classified Digest of the Records of the Society for the Propagation of the Gospel in Foreign Parts, 1701–1892* (London, 1893).

Perry, W. S., *The Episcopate in America* (New York, 1895).

Pestana, C. G., *Protestant Empire: Religion and the Making of the British Atlantic World* (Philadelphia, 2009).

Peters, M., 'Homeland and Colony', in Brown, C., M. Peters and J. Teal, eds., *Shaping a Colonial Church: Bishop Harper and the Anglican Diocese of Christchurch, 1856–1890* (Christchurch, 2006), pp. 19–34.

Philips, P., ed., *The Diaries of Bishop William Poynter, VA (1815–1824)* (London, 2006).

Pick, H., *Next Year: A Semi-Historical Account of the Exploits and Exploitations of the Far-Famed Barr Colonists* (Toronto, 1928).

Piggin, S., *Making Evangelical Missionaries 1789–1858: The Social Background, Motives and Training of British Protestant Missionaries to India* (Abingdon, 1984).

Pike, D., *Paradise of Dissent: South Australia, 1829–1857* (Melbourne, 1967).

Pincus, S., '"To Protect English Liberties": The English Nationalist Revolution of 1688–1689', in Claydon, T. and I. McBride, eds., *Protestantism and National Identity: Britain and Ireland, c.1650–c.1850* (Cambridge, 1998), pp. 75–104.

Playter, G. F., *The History of Methodism in Canada* (Toronto, 1862).

Pope Gregory XVI, 'Encyclical Letter of Our Holy Father Pope Gregory XVI, to All Patriarchs, Primates, Archbishops and Bishops', *Annals*, **1** (1840), pp. 598–610.

Porter, A. N., '"Commerce and Christianity": The Rise and Fall of a Nineteenth-Century Missionary Slogan', *Historical Journal*, **28** (1985), pp. 597–621.

'"Cultural Imperialism" and Protestant Missionary Enterprise, 1780–1914', *Journal of Imperial and Commonwealth History*, **25** (1997), pp. 367–91.

Bibliography of Imperial, Colonial, and Commonwealth History since 1600 (Oxford, 2002).

Religion Versus Empire?: British Protestant Missionaries and Overseas Expansion, 1700–1914 (Manchester, 2004).

'Missions and Empire, c.1873–1914', in Gilley, S. and B. Stanley, eds., *World Christianities, c.1815–1914* (Cambridge, 2006), pp. 560–75.

'Evangelical Visions and Colonial Realities', *Journal of Imperial and Colonial History*, **38** (2010), pp. 145–55.

Powell, P. W., *Tree of Hate: Propaganda and Prejudices Affecting United States Relations with the Hispanic World* (New York, 1971).

Prakash, G., 'Subaltern Studies as Postcolonial Criticism', *American Historical Review*, **99** (1994), pp. 1475–90.

Prentis, M. D., *The Scots in Australia* (Sydney, 2008).

Prichard, M. F. L., ed., *The Collected Works of Edward Gibbon Wakefield* (Auckland, 1969).

Proceedings of the Society for Educating the Poor of Newfoundland. Third Year, 1825–26. Containing the Anniversary Sermon by Reverend Edward Cooper (London, 1826).

Protestant Colonization Society of Ireland, *Report of Sub-Committee* (Dublin, 1829).

Pybus, C., *Epic Journeys of Freedom: Runaway Slaves of the American Revolution and Their Global Quest for Liberty* (Boston, 2006).

Railton, G. S., *General Booth* (London, 1912).

Ralls, W., 'The Papal Aggression of 1850: A Study in Victorian Anti-Catholicism', *Church History*, **43** (1974), pp. 242–56.

Random Recollections of Exeter Hall, in 1834–1837. By One of the Protestant Party (London, 1838).

Rasporich, A. W., 'Utopian Ideals and Community Settlements in Western Canada, 1880–1914', in Francis, R. D. and H. Palmer, eds., *The Prairie West* (Calgary, 2007), pp. 114–29.

Read, C., *The Rising in Western Upper Canada, 1837–8: The Duncombe Revolt and After* (Toronto, 1982).

Reader, W. J., *Professional Men: The Rise of the Professional Classes in Nineteenth-Century England* (London, 1966).

Reid, D. G., *Dictionary of Christianity in America* (Downers Grove, IL, 1990).

Religious Tract Society, *The Emigrant's Friend: A Selection of Tracts, a Companion for the Voyage and a Manual of Instruction in His New Home* (London, n.d.).

Reynolds, H., *The Other Side of the Frontier: Aboriginal Resistance to the European Invasion of Australia* (Ringwood, 1982).

This Whispering in Our Hearts (Sydney, 1998).

Richards, E., *Britannia's Children: Emigration from England, Scotland, Wales and Ireland since 1600* (London, 2004).

Richards, H. C., 'The Imperial Claims of the SPG', *The East and the West: A Quarterly Review for the Study of Missions*, **1** (1903), pp. 60–4.

Robert, D. L., ed., *Converting Colonialism: Visions and Realities in Mission History, 1706–1914* (2008).

Roberts, D. A. and H. M. Carey, '"Beong! Beong! (More! More!)": John Harper and the Wesleyan Mission to the Australian Aborigines', *Journal of Colonialism and Colonial History*, **10** (2009).

Robinson, N., *To the Ends of the Earth: Norman McLeod and the Highlanders' Migration to Nova Scotia and New Zealand* (Auckland, 1997).

Robinson, R., 'Non-European Foundation of European Imperialism: Sketch for a Theory of Collaboration', in Owen, R. and B. Sutcliffe, eds., *Studies in the Theory of Imperialism* (London, 1972), pp. 117–42.

Rose, H. J., A. P. Newton and E. A. Benians, eds., *The Cambridge History of the British Empire, vol. VII, New Zealand* (Cambridge, 1933).

Ross, A., *The Red River Settlement: Its Rise, Progress, and Present State* (London, 1856).

Ross, R. C. S., *The Story of the Otago Church and Settlement* (Dunedin, 1887).

Roxborogh, J., *Thomas Chalmers, Enthusiast for Mission: The Christian Good of Scotland and the Rise of the Missionary Movement* (Carlisle, 1999).

Russell, A., *The Clerical Profession* (London, 1980).

Russell, W. T., *Maryland, the Land of Sanctuary: A History of Religious Toleration in Maryland from the First Settlement until the American Revolution* (Baltimore, 1908).

Ryan, V. W., *Christian Opportunity: A Sermon in Behalf of the Colonial Church and School Society* (London, 1855).

Said, E. W., *Yeats and Decolonization: Nationalism, Colonialism and Literature* (Derry, 1988).

Culture and Imperialism (New York, 1993).

Schama, S., *Rough Crossings: Britain, the Slaves and the American Revolution* (London, 2005).

Schenk, W. R., 'The Missionary and Politics: Henry Venn's Guidelines', *Journal of Church and State*, **24** (1982), pp. 525–34.

Schlenther, B. S., 'Religious Faith and Commercial Empire', in Marshall, P. J., ed., *Oxford History of the British Empire, vol. 2, The Eighteenth Century* (Oxford, 1998), pp. 128–50.

Schomburgk, R. H., *The History of Barbados; Comprising a Geographical and Statistical Description of the Island; a Sketch of the Historical Events since the Settlement; and an Account of Its Geology and Natural Productions* (1848).

Scott, J., 'Penitential and Penitentiary: Native Canadians and Colonial Mission Education', in Scott, J. S. and G. Griffiths, eds., *Mixed Messages: Materiality, Textuality, Missions* (Basingstoke, 2005), pp. 111–34.

Seeley, J. R., *The Expansion of England* (London, 1883).

'Ethics and Religion', *Fortnightly Review*, **45** (1889), pp. 501–14.

Natural Religion (London, 1891).

Sefton, H. R., 'The Scotch Society in the American Colonies in the Eighteenth Century', *Records of the Scottish Church History Society* (1971), pp. 169–84.

Select Committee of the House of Lords Appointed to Inquire into the Present State of the Islands of New Zealand (London, 1838).

Sellers, I., *Nineteenth-Century Nonconformity* (London, 1977).

Selwyn, G. A., *New Zealand, Part I, Letters from the Bishop to the Society for the Propagation of the Gospel, Together with Extracts from the Visitation Journal from July 1842 to January 1843* (London, 1844).

Selwyn, J. R., *Pastoral Work in the Colonies and the Mission Field* (London, 1902).

Shannon, R. T., 'John Robert Seeley and the Idea of a National Church', in R. Robson, ed., *Ideas and Institutions of Victorian Britain* (London, 1967), pp. 236–67.

Sheehy, D., 'Dublin Diocesan Archives – Pt 1 an Introduction; Pt 2 Murray Papers (7)', *Archivium Hibernicum: Irish Historical Records*, **40** (1987), pp. 39–48, 49–74.

Sloan, W., 'Religious Affiliation and the Immigrant Experience: Catholic Irish and Protestant Highlanders in Glasgow, 1830–1850', in Devine, T. M., ed., *Irish Immigrants and Scottish Society in the Nineteenth and Twentieth Centuries* (Edinburgh, 1991), pp. 67–90.

Smith, A., E. G. Wakefield and D. Stewart, *An Inquiry into the Nature and Causes of the Wealth of Nations: With Notes from Ricardo, M'Culloch, Chalmers, and Other Eminent Political Economists* (London, 1843).

Smith, J., *Our Scottish Clergy: Fifty-Two Sketches, Biographical, Theological, and Critical, Including Clergymen of All Denominations, Second Series* (Edinburgh, 1849).

Smith, W. E. L., *The Navy and Its Chaplains in the Days of Sail* (Toronto, 1961).

Smyth, J., *The Making of the United Kingdom, 1660–1800: State, Religion and Identity in Britain and Ireland* (London, 2001).

Snape, M. F., *The Redcoat and Religion: The Forgotten History of the British Soldier from the Age of Marlborough to the Eve of the First World War* (London, 2005).

The *Royal Army Chaplains' Department, 1796–1953: Clergy under Fire* (Woodbridge, Suffolk, 2007).

Society for Promoting Religious Knowledge Among the Poor, *An Account of the Society for Promoting Religious Knowledge among the Poor Begun 1750* (London, 1879).

Society for the Conversion and Religious Instruction and Education of the Negroe Slaves in the British West India Islands, *Report of the Incorporated Society for the Conversion and Religious Instruction and Education of the Negroe Slaves in the British West India Islands, July–December 1823* (London, 1824).

Society in Scotland for Propagating Christian Knowledge, *Short Account of the Object, Progress, and Exertions of the Society in Scotland for Propagating Christian Knowledge* (Edinburgh, 1825).

Southerwood, W. T., *A Prayer-Calendar of Deceased Priests in Australia, 1788–1988* (Georgetown, Tasmania, 1988).

Catholics in British Colonies: Planting a Faith Where No Sun Sets – Islands and Dependencies of Britain Till 1900 (London, 1998).

Spalding, J. L., *The Religious Mission of the Irish People and Catholic Colonization* (New York, 1978).

Spivak, G. C., 'Can the Subaltern Speak?', in Nelson, C. and L. Grossberg, eds., *Marxism and the Interpretation of Culture* (Urbana, IL, 1988), pp. 271–313.

St Augustine's College, Canterbury, *The Calendar of the Missionary College of St Augustine, Canterbury* (Canterbury, 1851–8).

'Occasional Papers', No. 1 (May 1853) to No. 386 (December 1935) (microform) (Wick, Scotland, 1996).

Stanley, B., 'Commerce and Christianity: Providence Theory, the Missionary Movement, and the Imperialism of Free Trade, 1842–1860', *The Historical Journal*, **26** (1983), pp. 71–94.

The History of the Baptist Missionary Society 1792–1992 (Edinburgh, 1992).

'Conversion to Christianity: The Colonization of the Mind?', *International Review of Mission*, **92** (2003), pp. 315–31.

Stanner, W., 'Education, Emigration and Empire: The Colonial College, 1887–1905', in Mangan, J. A., ed., *'Benefits Bestowed'? Education and British Imperialism* (Manchester, 1988), pp. 194–210.

Stenhouse, J., 'God's Own Silence: Secular Nationalism, Christianity and the Writing of New Zealand History', *New Zealand Journal of History*, **38** (2004), pp. 52–71.

Stephens, J., *The Land of Promise, Being an Authentic and Impartial History of the Rise and Progress of the New British Province of South Australia Etc. by One Who Is Going* (London, 1839).

Stephenson, F. C., *One Hundred Years of Canadian Methodist Missions, 1824–1924* (Toronto, 1925).

Stock, E., H. T. Andrews and A. J. Grieve, 'Missions', in *The Encyclopaedia Britannica* (Cambridge, 1910–11), pp. 583–99.

Stocker, M., ed., *Remembering Godley: A Portrait of Canterbury's Founder* (Christchurch, 2001).

Stormon, E. J., ed., *The Salvado Memoirs: Historical Memoirs of Australia and Particularly of the Benedictine Mission of New Norcia and of the Habits and Customs of the Australian Natives* (Nedlands, Western Australia, 1977).

Stoughton, J., *Religion in England from 1800 to 1850: A History, with a Postscript on Subsequent Events* (London, 1884).

Strong, R., 'A Vision of an Anglican Imperialism: The Annual Sermons of the Society for the Propagation of the Gospel in Foreign Parts 1701–1714', *Journal of Religious History*, **30** (2006), pp. 175–98.

Anglicanism and Empire (Oxford, 2007).

'The Church of England and the British Imperial State: Anglican Metropolitan Sermons of the 1850s', in Carey, H. M. and J. Gascoigne, eds., *Church and State in Old and New Worlds* (Leiden, 2010).

Swain, S., '"Brighter Britain": Images of Empire in the International Child Rescue Movement', in Carey, H. M., ed., *Empires of Religion* (Basingstoke, 2008), pp. 161–76.

Sykes, R., *Guide to the Qu'Appelle Valley, Assiniboia, Canada* (Manchester, 1885).

'Systematic Colonization', *Colonial Church Chronicle*, **2** (1848), pp. 2–6.

Szasz, M., *Scottish Highlanders and Native Americans: Indigenous Education in the Eighteenth-Century Atlantic World* (Norman, OK, 2007).

Tawse, J., *Report on the Present State of the Society in Scotland for Propagating Christian Knowledge* (Edinburgh?, 1833).

Taylor, G. C., *The Sea Chaplains: A History of the Chaplains of the Royal Navy* (Oxford, 1978).

Temple, P., *A Sort of Conscience: The Wakefields* (Auckland, 2002).

Thackeray, W. M., *The Virginians: A Tale of the Last Century* (New York, 1904).

Thomas, N., *Colonialism's Culture: Anthropology, Travel and Government* (Cambridge, 1994).

Thompson, H. P., *Into All Lands: The History of the Society for the Propagation of the Gospel in Foreign Parts, 1701–1950* (London, 1951).

Thompson, J., *Into All the World: A History of 150 Years of the Overseas Work of the Presbyterian Church in Ireland* (Belfast, 1990).

Thompson, P., *An Unquenchable Flame: The Story of Captain Allen Gardiner, Founder of the South American Missionary Society* (London, 1983).

Thorne, S., '"The Conversion of Englishmen and the Conversion of the World Inseparable": Missionary Imperialism and the Language of Class in Early Industrial Britain', in Cooper, F. and A. L. Stoler, eds., *Tensions of Empire: Colonial Cultures in a Bourgeois World* (Berkeley, CA, 1997), pp. 238–62.

Thornton, A. P., *The Imperial Idea and Its Enemies: A Study in British Power* (London, 1959).

Thwaite, B. H., *The Electoral Government of Greater Britain* (London, 1895).

Thwaites, R. G., ed., *The Jesuit Relations and Allied Documents: Travels and Explorations of the Jesuit Missionaries in New France, 1610–1791* (Cleveland, 1896–1900).

Tomlin, J. W. S., *The Story of the Bush Brotherhoods* (London, 1949).

Trisco, R. F., *The Holy See and the Nascent Church in the Middle Western United States, 1826–1850* (Rome, 1962).

Trollope, A., *Australia and New Zealand*, 2 vols. (London, 1873).

  Rachel Ray [1863] (London, 1906).

Tucker, H. W., *The English Church in Other Lands or the Spiritual Expansion of England* (London, 1886).

  The Spiritual Expansion of the Empire: A Sketch of Two Centuries of Work Done for the Church and Nation by the Society for the Propagation of the Gospel in Foreign Parts (London, 1900).

Tyerman, D. and G. Bennet, eds., *Journal of Voyages and Travels by the Reverend Daniel Tyerman and George Bennet Esq.* (London, 1831).

Ullathorne, W., *The Catholic Mission in Australasia* (London, 1838).

Ullathorne, W. B., *From Cabin-Boy to Archbishop: The Autobiography of Archbishop Ullathorne* (London, 1941).

Underhill, E. B., 'Christian Colonization', in *The Baptist Record and Biblical Repository* (London, 1847).

Underwood, B., *Faith at the Frontiers: Anglican Evangelicals and Their Countrymen Overseas (150 Years of the Commonwealth and Continental Church Society)* (London, 1974).

Faith without Frontiers (Cirencester, 1994).

Faith and New Frontiers: A Story of Planting and Nurturing Churches, 1823–2003 (Warwick, 2004).

Vaudry, R. W., 'Evangelical Anglicans and the Atlantic World: Politics, Ideology, and the British North American Connection', in Rawlyk, G. A., ed., *Aspects of the Canadian Evangelical Experience* (Montreal 1997), p. 154.

Anglicans and the Atlantic World: High Churchmen, Evangelicals, and the Quebec Connection (Toronto, 2003).

Vaughan, J., *Sermons Preaching in Christ Church, Brighton* (London, 1867).

Virgin, P., *The Church in an Age of Negligence* (Cambridge, 1989).

Wakefield, E. G., 'A View of the Art of Colonization with Present Reference to the British Empire: In Letters between a Statesman and a Colonist (1849)', in Lloyd, P. M. F., ed., *The Collected Works of Edward Gibbon Wakefield* (Auckland, 1969), pp. 753–992.

'England and America: A Comparison of the Social and Political State of Both Nations (1833)', in Lloyd, P. M. F., ed., *The Collected Works of Edward Gibbon Wakefield* (Auckland, 1969), pp. 314–636.

'Plan of a Company To Be Established for the Purpose of Founding a Colony in Southern Australia (1832)', in Lloyd, P. M. F., ed., *The Collected Works of Edward Gibbon Wakefield* (Auckland, 1969), pp. 269–310.

Wakefield, E. J., ed., *The Founders of Canterbury, with a New Introduction by Peter Burroughs* (Folkestone and London, 1973).

Waldersee, J., *A Grain of Mustard Seed: The Society for the Propagation of the Faith and Australia, 1837–1977* (Sydney, 1983).

Walker, G., *Our Sons Far Away: A Century of Colonial Missions* (London, 1936).

Walker, R. B., 'The Growth of Wesleyan Methodism in Victorian England and Wales', *Journal of Ecclesiastical History*, 24 (1973), pp. 267–84.

'Methodism in the "Paradise of Dissent", 1837–1900', *Journal of Religious History*, 5 (2007), pp. 331–47.

Walls, A. F., 'The Eighteenth-Century Protestant Missionary Awakening in Its European Context', in Stanley, B., ed., *Christian Missions and the Enlightenment* (Grand Rapids, MI, 2001), pp. 22–44.

Walsh, T. J., *The Irish Continental College Movement: The Colleges at Bordeaux, Toulouse, and Lille* (Dublin and Cork, 1973).

Ward, B., *The Sequel to Catholic Emancipation* (London, 1915).

Ward, S., *Australia and the British Embrace: The Demise of the Imperial Ideal* (Melbourne, 2001).

Ward, S. and D. Schreuder, eds., *Australia's Empire* (Oxford, 2007).

Webb, R. A. F., *Brothers in the Sun: A History of the Bush Brotherhood Movement in the Outback of Australia* (Sydney, 1978).

Western Australian Company, *Western Australia, Containing a Statement of the Condition and Prospects of That Colony … Compiled for the Use of Settlers* (London, 1843).

Wetton, C., *The Promised Land: The Story of the Barr Colonists* (Lloydminster, Saskatchewan, 1953).

Whately, E. J., *Life and Correspondence of Richard Whately, DD, Late Archbishop of Dublin* (London, 1866).

Whelan, I., *The Bible War in Ireland: The "Second Reformation" and the Polarization of Protestant-Catholic Relations, 1800–1840* (Dublin, 2005).

Whittington, F. T., *William Grant Broughton Bishop of Australia with Some Account of the Earliest Australian Clergy* (Sydney, 1936).

Williams, C., 'The United Kingdom', in Baycroft, T. and M. Hewitson, eds., *What Is a Nation?: Europe 1789–1914* (Oxford, 2006), pp. 272–92.

Williams, C. P., *The Ideal of the Self-Governing Church: A Study in Victorian Missionary Strategy* (Leiden, 1990).

Williamson, A., *What Has the Church of Scotland Done for Our Colonies?* (Edinburgh, 1889).

Wilson, A., 'The Clergy Reserves: "Economic Mischiefs" or Sectarian Issue', *Canadian Historical Review*, **42** (1961), pp. 281–99.

Wilson, K., 'The Island Race: Captain Cook, Protestant Evangelicalism and the Construction of English National Identity, 1760–1800', in Claydon, T. and I. McBride, eds., *Protestantism and National Identity: Britain and Ireland, c.1650–c.1850* (Cambridge, 1998), pp. 265–90.

Winslow, O., *The Lord's Prayer: Its Spirit and Its Teaching* (London, 1866).

Withers, C. W. J., 'Education and Anglicisation: The Policy of the SSPCK Towards the Education of the Highlander 1709–1825', *Scottish Studies*, **26** (1982), pp. 37–56.

Withycombe, R., *Occasional Papers from St Augustine's College Canterbury, Published 1853–1941: Handlist of Materials Relating to Australia, New Zealand, South East Asia and the South Pacific* (Canberra, 1992).

  ed., *Anglican Ministry in Colonial Australia: Some Early Letters* (Canberra, 1993).

  Montgomery of Tasmania: Henry and Maud Montgomery in Australasia (Brunswick East, Victoria, 2009).

Wolffe, J., 'Anti-Catholicism and Evangelical Identity in Britain and the United States, 1830–1860', in Noll, M. A., D. W. Bebbington and G. A. Rawlyk, eds., *Evangelicalism: Comparative Studies of Popular Christianity in North America, the British Isles, and Beyond, 1700–1990* (New York, 1994), pp. 179–97.

  God and Greater Britain: Religion and National Life in Britain and Ireland, 1843–1945 (London, 1994).

  ed., *Evangelical Faith and Public Zeal: Evangelicals and Society in Britain 1780–1980* (London, 1995).

  The Expansion of Evangelicalism: The Age of Wilberforce, More, Chalmers and Finney (Downers Grove, IL, 2007).

  'Anti-Catholicism and the British Empire, 1815–1914', in Carey, H. M., ed., *Empires of Religion* (Basingstoke, 2008), pp. 43–63.

Wood, G. W., 'Church and State in New Zealand in the 1850s', *Journal of Religious History*, **8** (1975), pp. 255–70.

Woodsworth, J., *Thirty Years in the Canadian North-West* (Toronto, 1917).

Woolverton, J. F., *Colonial Anglicanism in North America* (Detroit, 1984).

Wright, D. F., 'Chaplaincies, Colonial', in Cameron, N. M. D. S., ed., *Dictionary of Scottish Church History and Theology* (Edinburgh, 1993), p. 163.

Wright, P., ed., *Knibb 'the Notorious': Slaves' Missionary, 1803–1845* (London, 1973).

Wynne, G. R., *The Church in Greater Britain: The Donnellan Lectures Delivered before the University of Dublin, 1900–1901* (London, 1911).

Yarwood, A., 'The Making of a Colonial Chaplain: Samuel Marsden and the Elland Society, 1765–93', *Historical Studies*, **16** (1975), pp. 362–80.

Yeo, G., 'A Case without Parallel: The Bishops of London and the Anglican Church Overseas, 1660–1748', *Journal of Ecclesiastical History*, **44** (1993), pp. 450–75.

Yonge, C. M., *Pioneers and Founders or Recent Workers in the Mission Field* (London, 1884).

Index